COOK'S

ILLUSTRATED

~ 1997 ~

$29.95

Published by

Boston Common Press Limited Partnership

17 Station Street

Brookline, MA 02445

ISBN: 0-9640179-7-0

ISSN: 1068-2821

To get home delivery of future issues of *Cook's Illustrated*, call 800-526-8442 inside the U.S., or 515-247-7571 if calling from outside the U.S.

In addition to the Annual Hardbound Editions, *Cook's Illustrated* offers the following publications:

The *How to Cook* series of single topic cookbooks
Titles include *How to Make A Pie, How to Make An American Layer Cake, How to Stir-Fry, How to Make Ice Cream, How to Make Pizza, How to Make Holiday Desserts, How to Make Pasta Sauces, How to Make Salad, How to Grill, How to Make Simple Fruit Desserts, How to Make Cookie Jar Favorites, How to Cook Holiday Roasts & Birds, How to Make Stew, How to Cook Shrimp & Other Shellfish, How to Barbecue & Roast On The Grill,* and *How to Cook Garden Vegetables.* A boxed set of the first 11 titles in the series is available in an attractive, protective slip case. New releases are published every two months, so give us a call for our complete list of available titles.

Multi-Year Master Index
Quickly find every article and recipe *Cook's Illustrated* has published from the Charter Issue in 1992 through the most recent year-end issue. Recipe names, authors, article titles, subject matter, equipment testings, food tastings, cookbook reviews, wine tastings, and ingredients are all now instantly at your fingertips.

The Cook's Bible and ***The Yellow Farmhouse Cookbook***
Written by Christopher Kimball and published by Little, Brown and Company.

To order any of the books listed above, call 800-611-0759 inside the U.S., or 515-246-6911 if calling from outside the U.S.

You can order subscriptions, gift subscriptions, and any of our books by visiting our online store at
www.cooksillustrated.com

COOK'S ILLUSTRATED INDEX

⋝ C ⋜

⇒ D ⇐

COOK'S
ILLUSTRATED

Thick, Chewy Oatmeal Cookies
Crisp on the Outside, Chewy on the Inside

Whole Wheat Bread
Two Secret Ingredients Make All the Difference

Homemade Macaroni & Cheese
Rich, Creamy, and Fast

Curry Demystified
Discovering the Secrets of Spice Cookery

TESTING ROASTING RACKS

•

BIG, BEAUTIFUL MUFFINS

•

SUPERMARKET BRAND WINS
BAKING CHOCOLATE TASTING

•

ROASTING TURKEY BREAST

$4.00 U.S./$4.95 CANADA

Table of Contents

JANUARY/FEBRUARY 1997

"Winter Citrus"
See pages 16 and 17 for tips on dealing with citrus.

ILLUSTRATION BY
BRENT WATKINSON

"Cream-Filled Apricots"
adapted from *Taverna*
(Sunset, 1996)
by Joyce Goldstein

ILLUSTRATION BY
VINCENT McINDOE

COOK'S
ILLUSTRATED

Publisher and Editor CHRISTOPHER KIMBALL

Senior Editor JOHN WILLOUGHBY

Executive Editor PAM ANDERSON

Senior Writer JACK BISHOP

Associate Editor ADAM RIED

Consulting Editors MARK BITTMAN
STEPHANIE LYNESS

Editorial Assistant ELIZABETH CAMERON

Test Cooks MELISSA HAMILTON
EVA KATZ
DAWN YANAGIHARA

....

Art Director ANNE MURDOCK

Food Stylist MARIE PIRAINO

Special Projects Designer AMY KLEE

....

Managing Editor KEITH POWERS

Editorial Prod. Manager SHEILA DATZ

Copy Editor GARY PFITZER

....

Marketing Director ADRIENNE KIMBALL

Vice President Circulation CAROLYN ADAMS

Circulation Manager DAVID MACK

Newsstand Manager JONATHAN VENIER

Fulfillment Manager LARISA GREINER

....

Vice Pres. Prod. & Technology JAMES MCCORMACK

Advertising Prod. Manager PAMELA SLATTERY

Systems Administrator PAUL G. MULVANEY

Production Artist KEVIN MOELLER

Advertising Prod. Assistant DANIEL FREY

Editorial Prod. Assistant ROBERT PARSONS

....

Vice President JEFFREY FEINGOLD

Controller LISA A. CARULLO

Accounting Assistant MANDY SHITO

Office Manager TONYA ESTEY

Special Projects FERN BERMAN

Cook's Illustrated (ISSN 1068-2821) is published bimonthly by Boston Common Press Limited Partnership, 17 Station Street, P.O. Box 569, Brookline, MA 02147-0569. Copyright 1997 Boston Common Press Limited Partnership. Periodical postage paid at Boston, MA, and additional mailing offices, USPS #012487. For list rental information, please contact List Services Corporation, 6 Trowbridge Drive, P.O. Box 516, Bethel, CT 06801; (203) 743-2600, FAX (203) 743-0589. Editorial office: 17 Station Street, P.O. Box 569, Brookline, MA 02147-0569; (617) 232-1000, FAX (617) 232-1572. Editorial contributions should be sent to: Editor, *Cook's Illustrated.* We cannot assume responsibility for manuscripts submitted to us. Submissions will be returned only if accompanied by a large self-addressed stamped envelope. Subscription rates: $24.95 for one year; $45 for two years; $65 for three years. (Canada: add $6 per year; all other countries: add $12 per year.) Postmaster: Send all new orders, subscription inquiries, and change of address notices to *Cook's Illustrated,* P.O. Box 7444, Red Oak, IA 51591-0444. Single copies: $4 in U.S., $4.95 in Canada and other countries. Back issues available for $5 each. PRINTED IN THE U.S.A.

EDITORIAL

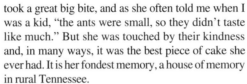

IN THE MEMORY HOUSE

In 1938 my mother spent a summer in a Quaker work camp near Dayton, Tennessee, an area that was still hard hit by the Depression. She became friendly with two local girls, who invited her back to their parents' home, a board shack with snakes under the front porch and holes in the floorboards. The father worked for the TVA, barely making a living, and his wife looked poorly, but they baked a cake for my mother, dressed up as best they could, and were proud to have her over. It was a white cake, and my mother still remembers the small red ants that covered the icing like jimmies on an ice cream cone. She smiled, took a great big bite, and as she often told me when I was a kid, "the ants were small, so they didn't taste like much." But she was touched by their kindness and, in many ways, it was the best piece of cake she ever had. It is her fondest memory, a house of memory in rural Tennessee.

CHRISTOPHER KIMBALL

For me, the memory house sits right up by the old dirt road in our town, heading up to an almost impassable track over the mountain, where the old-timers claim they could see "forty smokes" on a cold autumn morning. Today, there are just a few houses remaining, the rest surviving only as overgrown cellar holes. In that memory house lives a bachelor farmer. Like most old-time Vermont homes, you enter through a porch, filled with an old freezer and a cupboard. You wend your way back through the kitchen, down a short hallway, and then into a dark living room, where he sits in an old green armchair, surrounded by a calendar from the local lumber company, the obligatory mounted buck, a woodstove, and a large print of a red barn in the early morning with a pair of workhorses being groomed outside.

One afternoon last summer, I stopped by with my oldest daughter, Whitney, and we found ourselves in the back room of that farmhouse facing its owner, Charlie Bentley. As hunting season was coming up, we got to talking about deer, and he asked, "Do you remember the story about the Hayes brothers?" Well, I allowed as how I didn't, so he started in. One summer night, Chester and Claude Hayes went out to jack a deer. On the way home, as they drove past the old Hoyt farm in their horse-drawn cart, they propped the doe up between them to fool nearsighted Charlie Randall, who always peeked out the window to see who was passing. The next day, they ran into Charlie, who asked,

with a grin on his face (his eyesight was a whole lot better than he let on), "Who was that sittin' up in the cart last night?" Chester Hayes replied, "Just a local girl." Charlie shot back, "Well, kinda ugly, wasn't she?"

Well, once the conversation got started, we swapped stories about pigs getting out, the taste of Marie's baking powder biscuits, the time my father ditched both our cars in a snowbank after an ice storm, and my first day working for Charlie back in 1961, when I was asked to bring in a cow and her young newborn calf. I got chased under more barbed wire fences that day than I care to remember, the old cow taking after me like a bull in a ring. It is curious that as we grow older, we remember the ordinary more fondly than the extraordinary. A slice of cake, a story about jacking deer, pigs running down the town road. Vermont stories are hard to tell to strangers because they are, at their best, ordinary tales, warmed by a deep affection for daily life. The memory of a good biscuit makes more of an impression than winning first prize at the horse draw at the Washington County fair. Such memories remind us of the curious joy of existence, a celebration of the common rather than the uncommon.

As we started to leave, Charlie showed me a dusty black-and-white photo of Dixie, the high-strung collie that used to stand beside him in his old green Ford pickup. I instantly remembered summer evenings, Charlie and I driving back from the barn after milking, with Dixie, one leg on my thigh, nervously dripping saliva onto the dark green seat, the smell of manure on my boots, the baling twine, pliers, and a can of Bag Balm sitting up on the dashboard. I was ten years old again, Dixie's hot breath in my ear, sitting high up in the cab of an old pickup. It is this simple memory, the window rolled down, the day's work done, looking forward to supper, that will grow in time, like my mom's piece of cake in a board shack in 1938. And when I am sometimes disappointed with the world, I imagine our children when they are grown, stopping to take a bite of a just-baked biscuit and remembering a warm summer afternoon, work done, heading home to our supper table. Then I smile, hopeful that my wife and I have filled each of them with enough homemade biscuits to nourish them long after the two of us are just a young couple in an old photograph on the wall of their memory house. ∎

Notes from Readers

KITCHEN TIMER MEMORY

While I generally love your articles and find I agree with their findings, a line in the recent article "Multifeatured Electronic Timers Win Testing" (September/October 1996) surprised me. The authors write, "We were stumped as to why, but six out of the eight timers also had a 'memory' capability. . ." Stumped? Have the authors made batch after batch of cookies? Having the timer preset to nine minutes saves endless button pushing. I use timers for short-cooking foods that need to be timed accurately.

LEWELLYN DURNEY
Washington, D.C.

Thanks for pointing out the multiple batch of cookies example. You are absolutely right; the memory would be a real convenience in that instance. Another reader, Ken Hinckley of San Diego, California, writes to tell us that he uses the memory function on his timer while barbecuing to remind himself to turn vegetables or meat at regular intervals during their cooking time. Similarly, we might use the memory feature for a reminder to shake a pan of roasting vegetables a few times during cooking to ensure even caramelization or, as suggested by Bryan Logan of Washington, D.C., "for any recipe that says something like 'baste every fifteen minutes until done.' "

THE RIGHT SPEED TO KNEAD

The recipe for No-Knead Sandwich Bread in the May/June 1996 issue suggests using setting number 4 on a KitchenAid mixer to knead the dough for ten minutes, warning that the dough may cling to the hook at slower speeds. After five minutes at setting number 4, my new KitchenAid K5SS stopped and refused to run! Thankfully, the manufacturer is sending me a new machine.

MARY EDWARDS
Sauk Rapids, MN

In the "No-Knead Sandwich Bread" story, we suggested kneading the dough on speed 4 because we observed a tendency for this dough to creep up the dough hook at slower speeds. Because stopping to scrape the dough down is a nuisance, we wanted to avoid the creeping if possible. The higher speed seemed to take care of the problem.

Though we have successfully kneaded hundreds of batches of bread dough at speed 4 in our KitchenAid mixers, we called KitchenAid immediately upon hearing about your problem. Brian Maynard, KitchenAid's marketing communications manager, told us that the company recommends using speed 2, and no higher, to knead bread dough. KitchenAid's recommended kneading times depend on the type of dough hook that comes with your mixer. About five years ago, the company released a redesigned dough hook, which is somewhat higher and more rounded, and therefore more aggressive at kneading, than its predecessor. Suggested kneading time with the newer dough hook is three to four minutes; for the older dough hooks, you should double that time.

We tested kneading times using the newer dough hook on speed 2 with the whole wheat bread dough in this issue. We found the consistency of the bread kneaded for four minutes to be too cottony, preferring the more even crumb and lighter texture of the loaf kneaded for eight minutes. We got back on the phone with Maynard to discuss our results and received KitchenAid's blessing to recommend speed 2 for eight minutes, regardless of which dough hook you use. It turns out that the speed, more than the time, determines the load on the mixer's motor.

If you do own a KitchenAid with the older dough hook and are interested in purchasing the redesigned version, it costs $14.95 and is available by mail from the KitchenAid Customer Satisfaction Center (P.O. Box 218, St. Joseph, MI 49085; 800-541-6390). The new dough hook is compatible with most KitchenAid mixers manufactured after 1970. Call the Customer Satisfaction Center for details on models and years.

CLEANING A BURR COFFEE GRINDER, CAREFULLY

In the November/December 1995 Notes from Readers, Elaine Hofberg of Los Angeles, California, wrote to suggest using rice to clean burr-type coffee grinders. We tested her idea and found it to be successful for burr-type grinders, though it would not work nor would we ever recommend it for the more common blade-type grinders.

Recently, a Starbucks Coffee Company representative added a refinement. He'd heard of customers jamming their burr grinders with a grain or two of rice after dumping it all into the hopper at once and then switching on the motor. Instead, he suggested pouring the rice into the hopper in a slow, steady stream with the motor running. Hold the hopper cover at an angle over the front of the opening while you pour the rice into the back of the hopper opening with your other hand to prevent the rice from flying up and out. Also, make absolutely sure never to stick your finger into the hopper with the motor running.

Though we have never experienced jamming firsthand, we tested the steady stream method and found it to work just as well as the original process, so we'll go with the extra precaution from now on.

AND FOR DIRTY BLADE-TYPE COFFEE GRINDERS. . .

Lately our blade-type coffee grinder has gotten a real workout grinding spices to test the curry recipes on page 9. To clean it between uses, we tried Elaine Hofberg's rice method, and the results were great. Because this type of grinder will not run with the top even partially askew, simply place a scant one-quarter cup of long-grain rice in the grinder well, replace the top, and whir until the rice is ground fine. Pour out the rice powder, and with it goes any residual ground spices and their odors. With the utmost care wipe out any remaining rice powder with a paper towel. Though the blades in these grinders are nowhere near as sharp as those in food processors, they are still blades and must be treated with due respect.

PASTEURIZED EGG PRODUCTS

I am writing in reference to your article "The Ultimate Chocolate Mousse" in the July/August 1996 issue. First, I must say that Ms. Piraino did a nice job. On the second page, however, there was a sidebar article called "Healthy Mousses?" If there are any questions concerning the use of raw eggs in mousse, I suggest using pasteurized yolks. The home consumer surely can buy these yolks from a pastry shop or restaurant that makes its own pastries. Even some gourmet stores carry them or can get them for someone who would like them.

JEFFREY MARTOCCI
White Plains, NY

We understand pasteurized egg yolks, along with pasteurized whole eggs or just whites, to be strictly food service and manufacturing items not for sale at the retail level. Calls to many of our local supermarkets, bakeries, and gourmet stores confirmed this, as not one of them sold, or would even order, pasteurized eggs for retail customers. But that may not always be so. According to Candace Rivera, food service marketing coordinator for Papetti's Hygrade Egg Products in Elizabeth, New Jersey, the company is now developing a pasteurized whole egg product for retail sale. No release date has been set, but if the pasteurized whole egg sells well, pasteurized egg yolk and egg white products might follow.

By law, all egg products that are distributed in liquid, frozen, or dried form must be pasteurized. To accomplish this, the product is heated quickly to a minimum required temperature and held long enough at that temperature to eliminate unwanted microorganisms. The process is supposed to leave both texture and flavor uncompromised. Both Rivera and Nancy Bufano, of the Egg Products

Inspection Division of the USDA's Food Safety and Inspection Service, told us that the minimum temperature for pasteurizing liquid egg yolk is 142 degrees. The period for which the yolk is held at this temperature depends on whether other ingredients, most often salt or sugar, have been added and in what concentrations. The time required to pasteurize yolk alone, with no added ingredients, is three and one-half minutes. Both representatives stressed that pasteurization occurs in a controlled environment with highly specialized machinery and cannot be done at home.

We did manage to obtain pasteurized egg yolks and whites to try in our chocolate mousse recipe. The results were just fine; absolutely identical to the mousse made with fresh eggs in taste, texture, and aroma.

RAW BEEF AND FISH SAFETY

I would like to make steak tartare and sushi, but I want to avoid parasites. A doctor told me that freezing the meat or fish before using it will kill unwanted organisms. If this is true, can you give me more information?

NATALIE CAMPBELL
Pleasant Ridge, MI

We checked your information as it applies to beef with both C.J. Volenziano, director of public relations for the National Cattleman's Beef Association in Chicago, and Bessie Berrie, acting director of the USDA Meat and Poultry Hotline. Both authorities agreed that, regardless of the duration or temperature, freezing the beef is not an effective way to eliminate bacteria, specifically E. coli 0157:H7, in the meat. Public health associations advise that the application of heat, or cooking the meat, is the only reliable way to kill bacteria that may be present. According to the USDA, E. coli 0157:H7 bacteria, if they are present in beef, begin to die at an internal temperature of 145 degrees. Therefore, if the meat had been punctured by a contaminated knife during handling, minimal risk would still exist at 145 degrees. To eliminate one hundred percent of the risk, the USDA says that beef must be cooked to an internal temperature of 160 degrees.

The news is not much better for fish. Though Emily Holt, director of communications for the National Fisheries Institute, reports that freezing raw fish at a temperature range of 0 to -4 degrees for at least seventy-two hours will kill parasites if they are present, such temperatures are usually reached only in a commercial freezer. We tested many home freezers and found the temperatures to range consistently between 3 and 5 degrees, which is not cold enough to destroy parasites in fish.

CALIFORNIA-GROWN DATES

In the Sources and Resources section of a recent issue (May/June 1996), you mentioned

(May/June 1996)

WHAT IS IT?

This tool was purchased by my brother in Boston in the late 1970s or early '80s. Its original purpose is a mystery, as are its name and origin, but my mother makes tortellini with it. Both of the end wheels are sharp and turn, as does the center part. Can you tell me what it is, and perhaps more importantly, where to purchase another one?

ANNAMARIA BASILE
Takoma Park, MD

The tool is called a tagliapasta, and your mother has been right on target all these years. It is a handheld pasta cutter, used by rolling it over a thin sheet of pasta dough. The length of the pasta pieces is determined by the diameter of the wheels while the size of the shaft between the wheels dictates the width. Once cut, the pieces of pasta can be stuffed and folded into any number of shapes, such asagnolotti, ravioli, or tortellini or filled and layered with another piece of dough for ravioli. We found tagliapastas made by an Italian company, Pedrini; the Pedrini tools cut squares and circles in either 40- or 60-millimeter lengths or diameters, respectively.

Though the wheels and blade of your tagliapasta are made of metal, those appearing on current models are made of nonstick plastic. Handles are made of wood. The Pedrini tagliapastas can be special-ordered through Lamalle Kitchenware (36 West 25th Street, New York, NY 10010; 212-242-0750) for roughly $14, depending on the size and shape you choose.

Medjool dates grown in Israel. You stated that California does not grow many dates, but I have information to the contrary. I have toured the many date farms in the Palm Springs area where readers can purchase dates year-round.

JOY DESAI
Los Altos, CA

Though it remains true that the majority of the world's date crop grows in Middle Eastern and North African countries, we certainly did not intend to slight California's active date industry. The gigantic palm trees that produce dates require a desert climate with ample water and low humidity to thrive. These conditions exist in both the Coachella and the Bard valleys in California where, according to the California Date Administrative Committee, more than twenty-five varieties of dates are grown. Roughly 5,500 acres within the two valleys produce almost forty-six million pounds of dates a year, with the Deglet Noor and Medjool varieties leading the pack at forty million and four million pounds, respectively.

Among the many Coachella Valley date farms that sell their products by mail order are the Oasis Date Gardens (59-111 Highway 111, P.O. Box 757, Thermal, CA 92274; 800-827-8017) and Jensen's Date & Citrus Gardens (80-653 Highway 111, Indio, CA 92201; 619-347-3897). For additional information about date cultivation and a full list of mail-order outlets, contact the California Date Administrative Committee (P.O. Box 1736, Indio, CA 92202; 619-347-4510).

Incidentally, of all the oatmeal cookies we tested while developing the story on page 22, the variation that made every single taster swoon was made with dates.

the story on page 22

CLARIFYING BUTTER

Kindly explain how to clarify butter. How long can it be refrigerated or frozen?

PAT ALEXANDER
Chicago, IL

Clarifying butter separates the pure butterfat from the various nonfat components in butter such as water, salts, carbohydrates, and two major types of proteins known as casein and whey.

Our method is adapted from Madeleine Kamman's *The Making of a Cook* (Atheneum, 1985). Working in batches of one-half to one whole pound, we cut the butter into small chunks and melt it gently over very low heat, making certain that it doesn't boil. As it melts, some of the water content will evaporate, and the casein will coagulate and settle into a milky white residue at the bottom of the container. Once it is melted fully, we let the butter stand for thirty minutes, during which time the whey proteins form a foam at the surface of the butter that is easily removed with a spoon. Then we cool the butter in the refrigerator for at least one hour.

The yellow butterfat solidifies as it cools, trapping beneath it the milky casein residue. When the butter is completely solid, we loosen it by running the container under hot water and then remove the butter with a swift thwack of the container against the counter. The casein residue will pour out separately and should be wiped away. Clarified butter has both a higher smoke point than whole butter and will keep longer in the refrigerator (for three to four weeks) or the freezer (for four to six months) without picking up other flavors and odors. Honestly though, the only time we bother to clarify butter is for use with phyllo dough. Otherwise, we feel the hassle outweighs any benefit for everyday cooking. ∎

Quick Tips

REHYDRATING DRIED MUSHROOMS

While developing the recipes for the story on page 15, Jack Bishop discovered a couple of tips for rehydrating dried mushrooms.

1. When rehydrating dried mushrooms, lift the mushrooms from the soaking liquid with a fork so that the grit stays in the bowl.

2. The best way to remove the grit at the bottom of the bowl is to pour the soaking liquid through a small mesh strainer that has been lined with a single paper towel. The towel traps the dirt and absorbs a minimum of the precious liquid.

NEW USES FOR CHEESE SLICER

Phillippa Farrar of Santa Barbara, California, has discovered that the cheese slicer you probably have stuck in the back of a kitchen drawer is great for slicing garlic. (She also likes to run it across a stick of butter to form a thin, quick-melting ribbon.)

CITRUS AS CLEANER

Suzanne Semago of Bradenton, Florida, has found that rubbing an uncut orange, lemon, or lime over the residue from price stickers takes the gummy mess right off.

KEEPING BROCCOLI FRESH

Many of us know that to keep asparagus fresher longer you must trim the stems and refrigerate the spears with the cut stems in water. Barbara Juszezak of Trego, Wisconsin, has discovered that the same method works with broccoli.

1. Trim the broccoli stems and place each stalk in a crock or jar filled with several inches of water.

2. Cover the crock or jar with a plastic bag and refrigerate it. Change the water every 2 to 3 days.

HAND-PUREEING GARLIC

Follow these steps to puree garlic easily without a mortar and pestle.

1. Peel and roughly chop as many garlic cloves as you'll need.
2. Sprinkle the chopped garlic with a generous pinch of salt (table salt works fine, but the larger crystals of kosher salt work better).
3. Gently lay the flat side of your chef's knife, not quite halfway up the blade, on the salted garlic and push it away from you while applying light pressure. Repeat this process seven or eight times (or more) until the garlic is smooth and partially liquefied.

ILLUSTRATIONS BY WENDY WRAY

COATING GRILLED FOOD

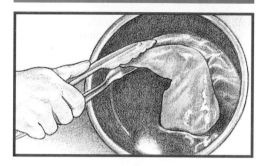

Rather than meticulously brush each piece of grilled meat on each side, Ann Cramer of Burt, Michigan, pours her sauce into a small saucepan (the handle makes it easy to maneuver). When the meat is ready for coating, she simply dips it into the sauce, shakes off the excess, and returns the meat to the grill rack for final cooking.

HOME-STYLE WINE COOLER

Leo and Olivia MacLeod of Portland, Oregon, have discovered that a chilled ice cream freezer canister makes an excellent cooler for keeping a bottle of wine chilled at the table.

AVOIDING SOGGY MUFFIN BOTTOMS

Susan Osborne of Saratoga, California, has solved the common problem of fruit muffins—soggy bottoms.

1. Before adding fruit to the batter, spoon a tablespoon or so of batter into each greased muffin cup.

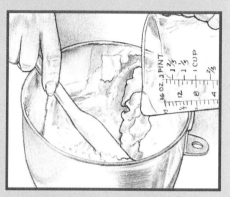

2. Stir the fruit into the remaining batter, then divide the batter among the muffin cups with an ice cream scoop.

KEEPING DOUGH FROM STICKING

Margaret Johanson of Greenwood, South Carolina, has discovered that spraying the dough hook of an electric mixer with vegetable cooking spray keeps especially wet bread dough from sticking.

PREPARING PEPPERS FOR STUFFING

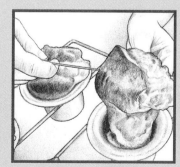

When making whole stuffed peppers, Carol Clark of Hampden, Maine, finds a melon baller great for scooping out the white, pithy membrane.

NEW USES FOR YOUR CAKE TESTER

Those small wire cake testers, useful enough for determining when your cake is ready to come out of the oven, also have many other kitchen uses. Here are a few from Dr. Martha Barclay of Mason City, Iowa:

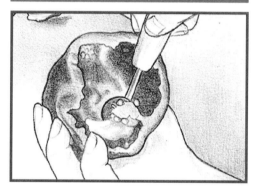

1. Testing vegetable doneness without breaking the food.

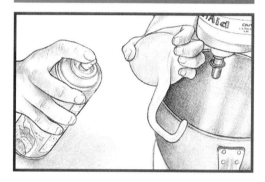

2. Poking popovers to let out the steam.

3. Unplugging the top of the saltcellar.

4. Retrieving pickles, olives, and so forth from the bottom of the jar.

Thanks to our readers for Quick Tips: The editors of *Cook's Illustrated* would like to thank all of the readers who have sent us their quick tips. We have enjoyed reading every one of them and have learned a lot. Keep them coming. We will provide a one-year complimentary subscription for each quick tip that we print. Send a description of your special technique to *Cook's Illustrated*, P.O. Box 569, Brookline Village, MA 02147-0569. Please write "Attention: Quick Tips" on the envelope and include your name, address, and daytime phone number. Unfortunately, we can only acknowledge receipt of tips that will be printed in the magazine. In case the same tip is received from two readers, the one postmarked first will be selected. Also, be sure to let us know what particular cooking problems you would like us to investigate in upcoming issues.

Curry Demystified

We discover the secret that unlocks the dreamy fragrance and clear, intense flavor of cardamom, cumin, cinnamon, coriander, and turmeric.

∼ BY STEPHANIE LYNESS ∼

Translating curry for a Western kitchen asks us to look beyond rules of French cooking technique to enter a culture defined by the evocative fragrance of spices.

Throughout my fifteen years of professional cooking up until now, I've never found my way to making Indian food at home. Each time I studied an Indian recipe for a recognizable structure that I might marry to my own cooking, I emerged disoriented by the dizzying number of ingredients and the seemingly unfathomable rules by which they were used. And many of my attempts to cook the wonderful-sounding curries in Indian cookbooks resulted in food with a heavy, murky taste.

So when I accepted this assignment to write about the dish we Americans (and even some native Indians) call curry, the work ahead of me was clear: I needed to translate the dish into a formula I could understand and in the process discover how to keep the flavors bright and clear.

My usual resources were of little help. Cookbooks couldn't give me hands-on experience, explain why an ingredient was used this way in one recipe, that way in the next. My training in French technique was worse than useless. Although I could pick out distinctly Indian cooking techniques, the food didn't seem to be inspired by technique in the way I was used to. While a French stew follows a series of commands—brown, deglaze, emulsify—an Indian curry seemed to waft on the whim of the cook from one ethereal fragrance to the next.

Ultimately, I found my way into the kitchens of two extraordinarily gifted cooks in New York City, one Indian and one Pakistani. Their food defined two key elements of curry making. One was a mysterious, complex, and highly personal dance of spice, flavor, and fragrance that is the soul of the cuisine. The other was a simple, accessible technique that provided a structure within which I could dance. The marriage of these two elements resulted in a quick, elegant formula for curry, the mood of which can be endlessly varied by substituting ingredients and adjusting the form and quantity of spice.

In Usha's Kitchen

To begin my quest, I studied a recipe for meat curry from one of my favorite Indian cookbooks. The dish was essentially a meat stew, flavored with onion, garlic, fresh ginger, ground coriander, cumin, turmeric, and cayenne and simmered in water with chopped tomato. It used techniques familiar enough to me from my French training, following the predictable route of browning the meat, browning the onions, adding the spices, then cooking for a couple of hours with the liquid.

But looking in other books, I found similar meat curries that used less familiar techniques: Spices were added and cooked at different points depending on whether they were dry or wet, whole or ground, and the meat was added to the mixture partway through the cooking process with no preliminary browning. Finding myself once again at a loss, I went to locate an Indian cook I could talk to.

I found Usha Cunningham, a Bombay-born home cook with no restaurant training. I laid out for her the two styles of curry I had found, and asked her to cook me a curry, in her own style, based on the ingredients in the meat curry recipe I had originally studied. Usha agreed but was a little hesitant about the recipe—it was such a plain dish, she said, like a plain roast chicken for an American; didn't I want her to show me something a bit more interesting? No, I assured her, I needed to start simple, to get my feet on the ground. Later, when I tasted her own cooking, I understood her reaction. Her food was astonishing and complex—bold, intense, and bright, each bite exploding in layers of distinct, individual tastes of sweet and sour, bitter, salty, and fragrant. When I had recovered sufficiently to ask her how she got this result, Usha shrugged and suggested that it might be in the way she used her spices, that is, with a heavy hand, as an Italian cook might use fresh herbs.

And so we began. She started work like a French chef, doing all her chopping and grinding first off; once we started cooking there would be no time for prep. And, as I pressed clove after clove of garlic through her press, it was clear that she did indeed flavor heavily: about one tablespoon each of ground coriander and cumin and pureed garlic and ginger per pound of meat, substantially more than the amounts used in the recipes I had found in cookbooks.

Then Usha hit the stove:

• First she heated a duet of whole spices—cinnamon and cloves—in hot oil until the cinnamon unfurled and the cloves popped. She explained that this step infused the oil with the fragrance of the spices, thus flavoring everything else that came in contact with the oil.

• Next she added sliced onion and cooked it until translucent, just to evaporate out the moisture and set the sweetness. It was sliced, rather than pureed or chopped, she said, because slicing was easier. She explained that as a general rule she cooked onions translucent for a lighter-tasting sauce, such as the one we were making that day with tomatoes, or to a rich brown color for heavier sauces, such as those based on yogurt or bound by ground nuts.

• The onions now cooked, she stirred in equal volumes of pureed garlic and ginger. Why pureed? Usha maintained that chopping was Western. While every Indian household would have a grinding stone to grind spices daily, she pureed the garlic and ginger with a little water in an electric minichopper until smooth (*see* "Tools That Will Change Your Life," page 7) or pressed the garlic through a press. This choice was in part based on speed and convenience. In addition, experience had shown her that puree, with no surfaces to burn, cooked more evenly than a mince and melted into the sauce for a smooth finish. And because a puree is wet where a mince is dry, this method gave her cushion against burning.

• Now Usha added bone-in lamb shoulder to the pan (what, no preliminary browning?) and cooked it for about ten minutes, stirring almost constantly, to evaporate all the moisture from the pan. As she stirred, she explained that the idea behind this traditional Indian technique was to release the flavors of the aromatic ingredients into the oil and cook them into the meat. If the meat were browned first, as in a French stew, the caramelized crust might inhibit the meat from absorbing the flavors.

The Key: Frying Spices

Now we were ready to add the ground spices. Usha explained that she ground the coriander and cumin herself from whole seed for better flavor but contented herself with preground turmeric (a rhizome like ginger) and cayenne.

• She mixed the ground dried spices with enough water to form a paste, then added the paste to the pan. Now she cooked, stirring, until enough moisture had been cooked out of the ingredients to allow the oil to separate out and pool around the clumps of meat, onion, and spice paste. This, Usha explained, was the secret to a well-made curry. The spices must fry in this hot oil, uninhibited by liquid, to release and develop their flavors. Once the final stewing liquid was added, the flavor of the spices would develop no further. (Spices may also be pan-roasted separately, ground, and then folded in at the end, but I will leave that option to another day.) Once the oil had separated, Usha turned the heat down and cooked everything for several more minutes.

• The spices cooked, Usha finished the curry with lots of chopped tomato (no water) and a handful of dried fenugreek leaves (she didn't con-

Cooking Spices: A Matter of Temperature

A conversation with cooking teacher Katherine Alford raised the question of why proper curry cooking requires spices to be fried in oil or pan-roasted while stewing leaves them tasting raw. Alford opined that it was the higher heat of the first two methods that must be responsible for the flavor transformation.

A phone call to food scientist Shirley Corriher confirmed this idea. According to Corriher, heat causes a madhouse of chemical reactions in foods, including spices. With high heat, the chemicals in spices break down and re-form into totally different compounds with new tastes and aromas. Simmering in a liquid, a spice can be heated to a maximum of 212 degrees only. Oil, however, will heat it a few hundred degrees higher, and depending on the metal, a dry skillet can get even hotter than that. — S.L.

Tools That Will Change Your Life

For about a minute, I considered grinding whole spices in my mortar and pestle. The truth is that, if you like this food, a coffee grinder devoted exclusively to grinding spices is a necessity. A mortar and pestle is useful for roughly crushing coriander seeds, garlic, and ginger. For garlic and ginger, cut both into small chunks and add a sprinkling of kosher salt to make the grinding easier.

I wasted substantially more time mincing and then pressing garlic and grating ginger until I gave in and bought a Cuisinart Mini-Mate Plus Chopper/Grinder. Although this machine would seem to be a luxury, it makes curries so much easier to prepare that it may make the difference, over time, between cooking them or not.

It's been the experience of my curry cooking guide Samia Ahad that spices stick more in stainless steel than in other materials. While that has not always been my experience, a nonstick pot makes sticking a moot point. I have found that Le Creuset enamelled cast-iron pans work well also. — S.L.

sider the seed to be right for this particular curry), thus introducing me to one of the more exotic Indian flavors. I'm a big fan of both the seed and the leaves. They don't taste the same, but their family resemblance is clear. Both are delicious with spinach, tomato, and sweet flavors.

We ate Usha's delicious curry with a pilaf of basmati rice, made with onion and whole spices. Usha showed me how to mash the curry and rice together with the tips of my fingers and then pop neat balls of the mixture into my mouth. (The less adventurous can mash with a fork as well.) The mashing opened up the flavors so effectively that the food had noticeably more flavor and fragrance than when eaten in the Western manner.

The Sensibility of Spices

As I smelled the spices cooking in Usha's kitchen, I noticed that their fragrance had quite an effect on me. Their smell pulled me into a dreamy, associative state different from the one I know from French cooking. The smells registered in a different part of my body than I was used to. Whereas I like French food because it smells tasty in an earthy, comforting, body-satisfying way, I was entranced by Indian food because it was heady and dreamy. Sour, bitter, and sweet flavors that wouldn't appeal to me in French food (bitter fenugreek, for example) were exquisitely satisfying in Indian food.

I reasoned that it was this particular dreamy, foreign sensibility that Usha navigated while she cooked. (She herself described her experience in the kitchen as a sort of a trance.) As I understood her, she improvised by associating to ingredients rather than building the dish within a formula so that she hardly knew at the beginning where she'd end up. Even the dishes I tasted from her refrigerator defied categorization. While her ethereal tomato-meat concoction was certainly a stew, such a term didn't begin to describe the experience of eating it. So even as we talked and cooked, I knew there was little hope of my walking out of her kitchen with a formula that could map out such an intuitive journey. I took good notes and went back to my own kitchen.

Finally, Curry Translated and Simplified

I spent the next week or so cooking curries with Usha's approach. I tested her method against the

technique used in the meat curry I had started out with and determined that Usha's method did infuse more flavor into the meat. What really sold me on it, however, was that I frankly enjoyed working with a new technique. It reminded me that this wasn't French food. And with no browning in batches, it was easy. I also worked to educate my nose and palate to the taste and smell of properly cooked spices, tasting and smelling raw spices and noting how their acrid fragrance and flavor transformed and mellowed with frying (see "Cooking Spices: A Matter of Temperature," left). I was getting very close; often my curries were delicious, but almost as often they came out heavy and muddy-tasting. I had no idea why.

As luck would have it, schedules and deadlines were such that Usha and I couldn't find another time to cook together. So I sought out another Indian cook, this time a Pakistani woman named Samia Ahad, who had cooked extensively in New York restaurant kitchens and was trained in French cooking.

Samia's food defined the other end of the spectrum. While Usha's genius lay in the ecstatic dance of her bright, bold, and complex flavors, Samia's lay in the elegant and understated simplicity of the food. She used spices sparingly, particularly the dry ones, to produce in her curries a light, clean, aromatic, but everyday mood. Although the ingredients were the same, her curries were quite different than Usha's.

With Samia I found the cultural bridge I was looking for. Presumably, because her own restaurant work had required her to shuttle regularly between the cooking of two cultures, Samia had managed to translate the heady sensibility that inspired Usha's cuisine into a simple, accessible formula that invited endless variation. And she'd vastly condensed traditional technique as well:

• Like Usha, Samia prepared all of her ingredients completely before cooking. Like Usha, she pureed garlic and ginger and sliced onion for convenience. She also ground her own cumin and coriander seed. However, she only used one-third of Usha's liberal quantity of aromatics: one teaspoon of pureed garlic and ginger and ground coriander and cumin per pound of meat.

• Like Usha, Samia started by frying sliced onion in oil until translucent. (And like Usha, she reserved browned onion for heavier sauces.)

• Then, to my surprise, Samia added most of the rest of her ingredients: all of the spices she had prepared as well as one pound of boneless cubed meat, salt, and one-half cup of chopped tomato. She cooked, stirring until the oil separated (about five minutes), and then cooked another thirty seconds to cook the spices completely. She explained, as had Usha, that this cooking of the spices was the heart of the dish.

• Then she added two cups of water and a halved chile pepper (she liked the flavor of the fresh chile better than that of cayenne) and simmered until tender, about forty minutes.

I asked Samia how she got away with condensing all the steps there at the end. She explained that, contrary to traditional technique, her experience was that as long as the oil separated so that the spices fried in the oil for about thirty seconds, there was no need for the long cooking. She further explained that her formula could be used as the base for many, many flavor combinations. I could fry whole spices before adding onion, as Usha had done. I could add any number of cubed vegetables. I could cook beef, lamb, chicken, fish, or shrimp this way. I could reduce the recipe to its bare roots—a very simple stew of protein, onion, garlic, ginger, turmeric (for some reason she always uses turmeric, she said), and water—or embellish it with more spice, vegetables, or legumes. That day, for example, she made a chicken variation using browned onion and one-half cup of yogurt (instead of the tomato) and flavored the curry with double the amount of coriander, but no cumin. The technique was exactly the same, but the richness of the yogurt and the browned onion produced a different result altogether.

A Marriage
When I got home, I cooked a number of curries to test out what these two women had taught me:

• First, I tested Usha's longer step-by-step cooking against Samia's condensed recipe and decided that, at least for this basic curry and for my taste buds, Samia's simplified method was as tasty, and far quicker. At the suggestion of a colleague, I also tried adding the tomato along with the water instead of reducing it with the spice; however, the reduced tomato in Samia's formula adds structure to the sauce, and I like the ease of adding everything at once.

• I then tested a curry made with sliced onion against one made with chopped and found that slicing was vastly quicker. I also preferred the texture of the sauce with sliced onion.

• I ran the same comparison between chopped and pureed ginger and garlic; not only was pureeing in a minichopper substantially easier than mincing, the wetness was an added cushion against burning, just as Usha had explained.

• Although up until now I had been cooking with bone-in lamb shoulder, I was sold on the ease of Samia's quicker-cooking boneless curries (forty minutes or less as against one and one-half to two hours) so I stuck to top sirloin, boneless leg of lamb, and chicken thigh. Shrimp also makes a delicious curry and cooks in a flash.

• I ran several experiments with spices: I compared a curry made only with ground spices against one using ground and whole spices. The comparison showed me that preground spices formed a kind of background wash; left whole, they came through as bright, individual flavors. (Thus, the cook can use the same spices to different effect.)

• Then I cooked three curries to determine how long the combined ground spices needed to cook to develop their flavor: I tried thirty seconds, five minutes, and ten minutes after the oil had separated. I found that thirty seconds was all it took. I also determined that the heavy, muddy taste of my early curries probably resulted from spices that had burned and turned bitter when they stuck to the bottom of the skillet. The spices were less likely to stick when cooked quickly, and the addition of yogurt or tomato, as in the master recipe on page 9, obviated the need to make a paste.

• Next I made a curry in which I added the stewing liquid before the oil had separated. Indeed, the curry tasted raw. Use your ear to help you recognize when the spices are frying in pure oil. The sound changes from the gentle sound of a simmer to the loud, staccato sound of frying.

• Finally, I played around with the amount of spice. It seems that the quantity was more a matter of personal preference than of rule, more spice resulting in heavier flavor. In the master recipe

Six Steps to Aromatic Curry

1. Cook the whole spices in the oil until the cinnamon sticks unfurl and the cloves pop, about 5 seconds.

2. Add the onion to the oil and sauté it until it is soft and translucent, until browned, or until fully caramelized, depending on the individual curry.

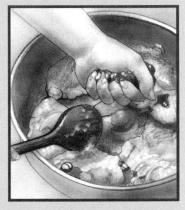

3. Add the spices, salt, tomatoes or yogurt, and the chicken, meat, or fish.

4. Cook until the oil separates, then continue to cook until the oil turns orange, about 5 minutes longer.

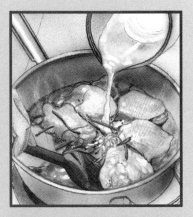

5. Add the water and cook until the meat is almost tender, about 20 to 30 minutes for the chicken or 30 to 40 minutes for the meat.

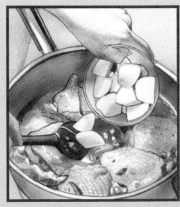

6. Add the vegetables and cook until both the meat and vegetables are fully tender, about 15 minutes longer.

ILLUSTRATIONS BY NENAD JAKESEVIC

that follows, I chose quantities that fell in between those given me by the two women who were my curry guides, simply because I liked that flavor. Precise quantities of wet spices are even less critical than of dry because their flavor is weaker, but I like equal quantities of garlic and ginger. In any event, the beauty of the formula is that it invites experimentation.

Cooking with the Master Recipe

The master recipe that follows is largely the same as the one Samia demonstrated for me. Like a standard French technique, it begins by heating the oil to provide a cooking medium. After that, however, it diverges completely from French style. Rather than browning the meat in the oil, I first saute the whole spices, then the onions. The wet spices (ginger and garlic) are then added, along with the meat, fowl, or seafood, and the moistening agent, either tomatoes or yogurt. All of these are cooked until the liquid evaporates, the oil separates, and the spices begin to fry and become fully aromatic. Greens in the form of either spinach or cilanto are then added, along with water and chile peppers, and the whole is cooked until the meat is tender, at which point the vegetables are added and cooked until tender.

The ingredients in the recipe are completely interchangeable, depending on what result you're looking for. The whole spice combination (cinnamon, cloves, cardamom, peppercorns, and bay leaf) can be abbreviated to cinnamon and cloves or to cinnamon, cloves, and cardamom, if you like. The cumin and the coriander may also be used crushed, as in the Beef Curry with Crushed Spices and Channa Dal variation. Let yourself be drawn into the trance of the spices and improvise combinations from there.

MASTER RECIPE FOR CURRY
Serves 4 to 6

Gather and prepare all of your ingredients before you begin. Garlic and ginger may be pureed by hand or in a minichop food processor. If pureeing by hand, follow the Quick Tip on page 4. If using a minichopper, process the garlic and ginger with one to two tablespoons of water until pureed. You may substitute a scant half teaspoon of cayenne pepper for the jalapeño, adding it to the skillet with the other ground dried spices. Feel free to increase the wet (garlic, ginger, jalapeños, and onions) or dry spice quantities. Serve the curry with basmati rice (page 10).

Whole Spice Blend (Optional)

- 1½   3-inch cinnamon sticks
- 4   cloves
- 4   green cardamom pods
- 8   peppercorns
- 1   bay leaf

- ¼   cup flavorless (vegetable or canola) oil
- 1   medium onion, sliced thin
- 4   large garlic cloves, pureed
- 1   chunk (1½ inches) fresh gingerroot, peeled and pureed
- 1½   pounds top sirloin or boneless leg of lamb, trimmed and cut into ¾-inch cubes, or 6 chicken thighs, skinned, or 1½ pounds shrimp, peeled and deveined
- 2   teaspoons ground cumin
- 2   teaspoons ground coriander
- 1   teaspoon ground turmeric
- ½   teaspoon salt, plus more to taste
- 3   whole plum tomatoes, chopped, plus 1 tablespoon juice, or ⅔ cup crushed tomato, or ½ cup plain low-fat yogurt
- 2   bunches (1½ pounds) spinach, stemmed, thoroughly washed, and chopped coarse (optional)
- 1   cup chopped fresh cilantro leaves (optional)
- 1   jalapeño pepper, stemmed and cut in half through the stem end
- ½   cup Indian split peas (channa dal), or 4 medium boiling potatoes, peeled and cut into ¾-inch cubes, or 4 medium zucchini, cut into ½-inch cubes, or 1 cup fresh or thawed frozen green peas
- 2–4   tablespoons chopped fresh cilantro leaves (use the lesser amount if you've already added the optional cilantro)

1. Heat oil in large deep skillet or soup kettle, preferably nonstick, over medium-high heat until hot, but not smoking. If using whole spice blend, add to oil and cook, stirring with wooden spoon until cinnamon stick unfurls and cloves pop, about 5 seconds. If omitting whole spice blend, simply add onion to skillet; sauté until softened, 3 to 4 minutes, or browned, 5 to 7 minutes.

2. Stir in garlic, ginger, selected meat (except shrimp), ground spices, ½ teaspoon of salt, and tomatoes or yogurt; cook, stirring almost constantly, until liquid evaporates, oil separates and turns orange, and spices begin to fry, 5 to 7 minutes, depending on skillet or kettle size. Continue to cook, stirring constantly, until spices smell cooked, about 30 seconds longer.

3. Stir in optional spinach and/or cilantro. Add 2 cups water and jalapeño and season with salt; bring to simmer. Reduce heat; cover and simmer until meat is tender, 20 to 30 minutes for chicken, 30 to 40 minutes for beef or lamb.

4. Add selected vegetable (except green peas); cook until tender, about 15 minutes. Stir in cilantro. Add shrimp and/or peas if using. Simmer 3 minutes longer and serve.

Until you get comfortable with the recipe, you may need help with meat and vegetable combinations. The following recipes are a few of my favorites.

CHICKEN CURRY WITH YOGURT, CILANTRO, AND ZUCCHINI

Follow Master Recipe for Curry, choosing optional whole spice blend, chicken, yogurt, optional 1 cup chopped cilantro, and zucchini and omitting optional spinach. Sauté onion until golden brown.

LAMB CURRY WITH WHOLE SPICES

Follow Master Recipe for Curry, choosing optional whole spice blend, lamb, tomatoes, and potatoes and omitting optional spinach and optional 1 cup chopped cilantro. Sauté onion until softened.

SHRIMP CURRY WITH YOGURT AND PEAS

Follow Master Recipe for Curry, choosing shrimp, yogurt, optional cilantro, peas, and omitting optional whole spice blend and optional spinach. Sauté onion until golden brown.

LAMB CURRY WITH FIGS AND FENUGREEK

Follow Master Recipe for Curry, choosing lamb and tomatoes and omitting optional whole spice blend and optional spinach and cilantro. Sauté onion until softened. Add ½ teaspoon fenugreek along with cumin and coriander and ¼ cup dried figs, chopped coarse, along with water. Omit the optional vegetable.

BEEF CURRY WITH CRUSHED SPICES AND CHANNA DAL

Channa dal is the name for yellow Indian split peas, available at Indian specialty food shops. Potatoes or regular green split peas may be substituted for the channa dal.

Follow Master Recipe for Curry, choosing beef, tomatoes, and channa dal and omitting optional spinach and cilantro. Rather than grind cumin and coriander, crush 1 teaspoon whole cumin seeds and 2 teaspoons whole coriander seeds in mortar and pestle, adding them to skillet in place of optional whole spice blend. Rather than puree garlic and ginger, simply crush them, along with pinch of kosher salt, in mortar and pestle. Add onion almost immediately to ensure cumin and coriander do not burn; sauté onion until softened.

CHICKEN CURRY WITH SPINACH AND FENUGREEK

Follow Master Recipe for Curry, choosing chicken, tomatoes, optional spinach, and potatoes and omitting optional whole spice blend and optional cilantro. Sauté onion until softened. Add ½ teaspoon fenugreek along with cumin and coriander. Once chicken parts are done, remove and keep warm. Continue to cook sauce over high heat until thickened, about 10 minutes. (The spinach becomes the sauce.) ∎

How to Cook Basmati Rice

Cook without soaking or rinsing, and use the pilaf method.

~ BY EVA KATZ ~

When I started testing basmati rice, the excitement began with the first pot I put on the stove. Every version I made was delicious, but I was looking for the ideal: a nutty, highly aromatic flavor and separate grains at once fluffy and firm to the bite.

Two major issues surfaced as I tested: Is it necessary to prepare the rice for cooking by soaking or rinsing it, and what is the best cooking method?

In the first series of tests, I examined the tradition of presoaking the rice, which is believed to maximize grain elongation and prevent the rice grains from breaking during and after cooking. I tested basmati rice prepared with a twenty-minute presoak in water as well as rice prepared with just a quick rinse and rice made with neither soaking nor rinsing. To make sure that my tests were not skewed because I had used more water overall with one method than with another, I weighed the rice before and after rinsing and soaking, then subtracted one ounce of water for each ounce of increased rice weight to compensate for absorbed water.

When I ran a taste test on these rice preparation methods, I was surprised. Presoaking resulted in overcooked rice and inconsistently sized grains, ranging from ten to fifteen centimeters, with a mushy texture due to water absorbed during soaking. Rice that was not soaked or rinsed was fluffy, and the grains were dry and separate with a firm,

toothy texture and a consistent grain size of eleven to twelve centimeters. This rice also had the nuttiest flavor.

Contrary to what I had expected from the research I did before I began testing, many of the presoaked rice grains broke. In contrast, the unsoaked grains remained intact.

The texture and flavor of the rinsed rice was in the same league as that of the soaked; definitely less aromatic and flavorsome than the unsoaked rice. Grains ranged in length from ten to fourteen centimeters. Despite the claim of some cookbooks that rinsing produces a less sticky product, my tests found the opposite to be true. All in all, I preferred the unsoaked rice with its slightly shorter grain and firmer texture.

The next series of tests focused on the cooking method. The three methods I tested were steeped, pilaf, and boiled and drained. In the steeping method, which is the standard way of making rice, water is brought to a boil, rice and salt are added, and the pot is stirred, returned to a simmer, then covered until all the water has been absorbed. In the pilaf method, the rice is first cooked in oil that has been infused with spice and onions, then steeped in water. In the boiled and drained method, the rice is cooked in a large quantity of boiling water and then drained, just as pasta is cooked.

The pilaf and steeped versions each had their merits. With the pilaf, an infusion of flavors resulted in a dish that can truly stand alone. My preference is for this method because of its dynamic flavors; it also produced somewhat more separate grains than the other methods. However, steeped basmati rice is a simpler method for everyday curries and produces a rice with an extremely fresh and nutty flavor. My least favorite is the boiled and drained version; the nutty flavor was washed out, and the rice ended up bland and waterlogged.

After determining the preferred cooking methods, I did some testing to make sure that the cooking times and quantities of water were correct. I tried various ratios of water to rice and found that one cup of rice to one and a half cups of water was ideal. The most consistent timing proved to be fif-

Some basmati rice is still harvested manually, and must be picked through for small sticks and stones.

teen to eighteen minutes from when the pot is sealed to the time the rice is done.

BASMATI RICE, PILAF-STYLE
Serves 4 as an accompaniment to curry

> 1 tablespoon canola, vegetable, or corn oil
> 1 3" cinnamon stick, halved
> 2 whole green cardamom pods
> ¼ cup thinly sliced onion
> 2 whole cloves
> 1 cup basmati rice
> 1 teaspoon salt
> 1½ cups of water

1. Heat oil in medium saucepan over high heat until almost smoking. Add whole spices and cook, stirring until they pop. Add onions and cook, stirring until translucent, about 2 minutes. Stir in rice and cook, stirring until fragrant, about 1 minute.

2. Add 1½ cups water and salt; bring to boil. Reduce heat, cover tightly, and simmer until all water has been absorbed, about 17 minutes. Let stand, covered, at least 10 minutes, fluff with fork, and serve. ∎

True Basmati is Best

Basmati rice has been grown in India and Pakistan for nearly nine thousand years. American versions of the aromatic rice can be found under the names of Texmati, Della, and Kasmati. After preparing a batch of each of these, I found that Texmati and Della do have a vague aromatic resemblance to Indian basmati rice, but the grains are bolder and wider and do not fully elongate. Instead, they tend to expand like standard long-grain rice, which grows in length by about 50 per cent when cooked, compared to true basmati rice, which doubles in length. Kasmati rice, on the other hand, is a close cousin to Indian basmati. It is not as fluffy as the authentic Indian variety and the grains are somewhat sticky, but the flavor holds its own. Imported basmati is available in well-stocked supermarkets, natural foods stores, and Indian grocery stores. I found it to be superior and more economical than the American varieties.—E.K.

The Best Hot Cocoa

Cook Dutch-process cocoa briefly with water before adding milk.

∾ BY ADAM RIED ∾

When was the last time you had a knock-out cup of cocoa? Made according to the ubiquitous "back-of-the-box" recipe, hot cocoa is weak and thin. Made in the European tradition of melting bittersweet chocolate in milk and heavy cream, it is "skip-two-meals" lush and fattening. My ideal hot cocoa lies somewhere between the two, with a serious chocolate flavor and a rich, satisfying consistency that doesn't require a day's fast afterward.

A Matter of Style

Looking at more than seventy recipes revealed that there are two distinct styles of hot, chocolate-flavored drinks. Most of them are referred to generally as "hot chocolate," but real hot chocolate derives from melting grated chocolate, usually bittersweet, in milk or cream. Hot cocoa, on the other hand, is flavored with unsweetened cocoa powder and sugar in milk or cream.

After testing hot chocolates made with varying amounts and types of chocolate (unsweetened mixed with sugar, bittersweet, and milk), my tasters and I agreed that these drinks fell short of the deep, complex flavor delivered by cocoa powder. Compared to hot cocoa, the hot chocolates tasted bland and one-dimensional, and in some cases even woody. Cocoa powder's flavor is stronger because it contains a higher concentration of cocoa solids and less of the fat and additional ingredients present in prepared chocolate. Cocoa powder also offers other advantages: It is designed to incorporate easily into liquids and other ingredients, it is a kitchen staple, and spooning cocoa powder from a canister is much neater than grating chocolate.

That said, though, there were still several key questions: What type and quantity of cocoa powder, sugar, and dairy taste best? Is the water used in many recipes really necessary? Should you cook the cocoa paste before adding the dairy?

The Cocoa Quotient

In the September/October 1995 Cook's Illustrated tasting of dutched and natural cocoa powders (see "Dutched vs. Natural Cocoas"), the panel preferred dutched (in which the natural acidity is reduced through treatment with an alkaline solution) in hot cocoa. I did too: In both flavor and color, Dutch-process won my tastings hands down.

The amount of cocoa powder and sugar to use per cup of liquid, however, was a thornier issue. My unabashed love for chocolate, which I've been told borders on obsessive, led me to start with three tablespoons of cocoa powder per cup of liquid. I thought this cocoa was great, but my tasters felt it was much too intense, losing the flavor of the dairy altogether. Fellow editor Pam Anderson brought me back down to earth by describing her perfect cup of cocoa as more intense than chocolate milk, but not liquid candy; as rich and mellow, but not so much as to ruin her appetite for dinner a couple of hours later.

With this ideal and the pleas of my tasters in mind, I scaled back and found that one and one-half tablespoons of cocoa powder, sweetened with one tablespoon of granulated sugar, made an indulgent, chocolaty, and well-balanced cup of cocoa.

Many recipes I consulted mixed the cocoa powder and sugar with a little water before adding the milk. I wondered if this was really necessary, so I first tried premixing the cocoa and sugar with a small portion of the milk in the recipe. My tasters and I immediately noticed that these hot cocoas were less flavorful than those made with some water. Because the milk fat in cream and milk has a very distinct flavor, dairy products can mask other flavors. They definitely had that effect on the cocoa powder, whereas mixing with a bit of water effectively releases the cocoa powder's fruit, chocolate, and coffee flavor nuances. Notably, I also found that allowing the cocoa powder-sugar-water mixture to cook gently for two minutes before adding the milk really deepened the flavor of the resulting drink, giving it a warm, roasted undertone. This occurs because the heat expands and swells the moistened cocoa powder molecules, thereby releasing and developing its many flavor compounds.

Add tiny amounts of salt and vanilla to round out the cocoa flavor.

The Dairy Dilemma

Another issue was the best type of milk to use. The flavor-masking qualities of the milk fat in half-and-half and heavy cream, along with my "no fasting afterward" goal, automatically eliminated them from the running. Milk was clearly the dairy product of choice here. Because the milk in my own refrigerator, and in those of virtually all my friends, is low-fat, I chose it as the base for my hot cocoa. Happily, the reduced fat content in 1 percent and 2 percent milk also allowed the greatest range of cocoa flavor. A small splash of half-and-half, about one tablespoon per cup, adds a pleasant richness without wreaking havoc on the cocoa flavor. Plain whole milk, without the addition of half-and-half, also tested well.

MASTER RECIPE FOR HOT COCOA
Serves 4 in small mugs

If you want to increase or decrease this recipe for hot cocoa, the key ratio to remember is one and one-half tablespoons of cocoa and one heaping tablespoon of sugar per cup of liquid. If you have whole milk on hand rather than low-fat, go ahead and use it, omitting the half-and-half.

- 6 tablespoons Dutch-process cocoa, measured by dip-and-sweep
- 4 heaping tablespoons sugar
  Small pinch salt
- 1 cup water
- 3 cups low-fat milk (1 or 2 percent)
- 1 teaspoon vanilla extract
- ¼ cup half-and-half

1. In heavy 2-quart saucepan, whisk together cocoa, sugar, salt, and water over low heat until smooth. Simmer, whisking continuously, for 2 minutes, making sure whisk gets into the edges of pan.

2. Add milk, increase heat to medium-low, and cook, stirring occasionally with whisk, until steam rises from surface and tiny bubbles form around edge, 12 to 15 minutes. Do not boil.

3. Add vanilla and half-and-half. For foamy cocoa, beat hot cocoa with hand mixer or transfer to blender and blend until foamy. Divide between four mugs, top with whipped cream or marshmallows if desired, and serve immediately.

HOT COCOA WITH ORANGE

Remove zest from 1 orange in strips about 1-inch wide. Follow Master Recipe for Hot Cocoa, adding zest along with milk. Remove zest strips with slotted spoon before beating or serving. ∎

Rediscovering Whole Wheat Bread

We set out to find the ideal compromise between heavy, dull-tasting rounds and soft, American-style breads with little flavor.

∼ BY CHRISTOPHER KIMBALL WITH EVA KATZ ∼

Our testing finally resulted in our ideal: a rich, nutty whole wheat loaf that is still light enough to be used for sandwiches.

If asked to describe the perfect loaf of whole wheat bread, you might say that it should be wheaty, but not grainy; chewy, but not tough; dense, but not heavy; and full-flavored, but balanced and not overpowering. In fact, you might come to the conclusion, as we did, that the perfect loaf of whole wheat bread is hard to define. There are literally hundreds of different types of loaves that use at least some whole wheat flour, but to earn the distinction of being a shining example of whole wheat bread is another matter entirely.

So we decided to make a few loaves from various cookbooks just to explore the range of possibilities. We started with the whole wheat variation of the American bread that ran in our May/June 1996 issue (*see* "No-Knead Sandwich Bread"). We found this to be very good but not sufficiently wheaty for our taste; we wanted something more substantial. So we tried recipes from five of our favorite bread books. A recipe for an Italian walnut bread was terrific but clearly a rustic European loaf, not the distinctly American whole wheat bread we were looking for. Other recipes were either bitter, had odd flavors, or had too many other grains or flours to qualify readily as a pure whole wheat experience. Still others were too dense, too salty, or not sweet enough, an important element for enhancing the rich flavor of the wheat flour.

We went back to the drawing board to create a master recipe that had the elements we liked best from each of the test breads. The recipe we started with contained one tablespoon of yeast, two and one-third cups of warm water, four cups of whole wheat flour, one and one-quarter cups of all-purpose flour, one-quarter cup of rye flour (to add complexity of flavor), one teaspoon of salt, and two tablespoons of honey.

The initial results from this recipe were good, but not great. The bread was too dense, and it needed a boost of both salt and honey for flavor. So we made a new loaf in which we doubled the amount of both yeast and honey and punched up the salt to two teaspoons. The taste test results were encouraging, and the loaf was even better when we tried making it again, using one-half tablespoon less yeast and adding one-quarter cup of melted butter for flavor. But there were still problems. The texture was still dense for our taste, and the flavor was a bit generic, reminiscent of what one might find at a diner, served with two individually wrapped pats of butter.

Having already tested a higher amount of yeast, we suspected that the texture might be improved by using a drier dough, which tends to produce a lighter bread, and therefore we increased the total amount of flour from five and one-half cups to six cups. We then varied the proportion of whole wheat flour to white to rye, testing the following combinations: three cups each of whole wheat and white flour, with no rye flour at all; three cups of whole wheat, two and three-quarters cups of white, and one-quarter cup of rye; and two and three-quarters cups of wheat, two and three-quarters cups of white, one-quarter cup of rye, and one-quarter cup of wheat flakes, a new addition. The first of these variations was bland and chewy, with a flat, uninteresting flavor. The last variation was dense with a slightly bitter aftertaste. The second loaf (a slightly higher amount of whole wheat than white flour, with rye flour but no wheat flakes) was the best of the lot, and actually quite good.

Now we were close, but the bread still lacked the proper texture and wheatiness that we expected from a whole wheat loaf. So I turned to one of my favorite bread books, *The Book of Bread* (HarperPerennial, 1982) by Evan and Judith Jones, and discovered that one of their whole wheat bread recipes contained wheat germ. As it turned out, this simple addition—a mere one-quarter cup of wheat germ—made a terrific difference in our loaf, producing a nutty flavor and slightly

What Is Whole Wheat Flour?

To understand the differences between the whole wheat products we tested in this article, I called the King Arthur Company. The experts there explained that a wheat berry contains three elements: the outer bran layer, the germ, and the heart of the berry, the endosperm. To make traditional whole wheat flour, the entire berry is ground. White flour, however, is made just from the endosperm, with the bran and germ removed. Graham flour, the winner in our taste test, also grinds all three elements, but the final product is more of a medium grind than the finely ground whole wheat flour. White whole wheat flour, sold by the King Arthur Company, is made from the whole white wheat berry, which lacks the phenolic acid that causes traditional whole wheat flour to be slightly bitter. Whole wheat flakes are simply the entire wheat berry put through a series of rollers to make flakes, a process similar to that used to make oats for oatmeal. Wheat germ is simply the germ of the wheat berry, separated from the rest of the berry through sifting. It is usually toasted by the manufacturer.— *C.K.*

more complex texture. We liked it so much that we tried a loaf with one-half cup of wheat germ, which turned out to be the ideal amount.

Testing Sweeteners, Fats—and Waters

Into our thirtieth loaf at this point, we decided to press on with the issue of sweeteners. I tend to use honey in bread doughs, but we also made loaves with a whole variety of sweeteners, including one-quarter cup of each of the following: white sugar, dark brown sugar, maple syrup, malt, and molasses. We also tested half quantities of malt and molasses paired with an equal amount of honey. Oddly, it was hard to differentiate among the different sweeteners. That said, though, the honey version was generally picked by our tasters as number one, with a nice, clean, sweet flavor and moist texture.

Having recently discovered the wonders of lard for frying chicken and doughnuts, we went on to try different fats. We sampled loaves made with vegetable oil (a noticeable lack of flavor); melted lard (a strong flavor but unwelcome in this recipe); the standard melted butter (by far the best: good texture, sweet flavor); cold butter kneaded into the dough (denser, not as moist); and the addition of a whole egg (grainy, gritty texture—almost cottony).

But the most shocking test was yet to come. Having read, admittedly with some skepticism, that the type of water is an important element in breadmaking, I proposed that we compare loaves made with tap water versus bottled water. To our great surprise, three out of four tasters immediately picked the bottled water loaf as substantially better, with a sweeter, fuller flavor. Of course, because this recipe uses more than two cups of water, it makes sense that the flavor and quality of the water should matter. So if someone tells you to use good, bottled water for breadmaking (or tap water if the local supply is of high quality), don't immediately assume that person is a culinary snob.

Kneading, Proofing, and Baking

Having found the dough recipe we wanted, we proceeded to test the variables of kneading, proofing, and baking.

One of the most interesting tests involved kneading times. Using a KitchenAid standing mixer, we kneaded for eight, twelve, and sixteen minutes, respectively, with no discernible difference in the finished loaves. This confirmed my suspicion, based on previous bread testing, that kneading is far from the exact science that some cookbooks would have you believe. As long as the ingredients are quite thoroughly mixed together and a reasonable amount of gluten is formed, it matters little whether the kneading is done by machine or by hand, for a short time or a long time. (For more information on hand kneading, *see* "No-Knead Sandwich Bread," May/June 1996.)

The master recipe calls for an initial proofing of just under one hour, a relatively short proofing time due to the relatively high amount of yeast. We tested a shorter proofing time of only thirty minutes, but the resulting loaf was dense and dry.

Basic Sandwich Style Loaf

Grease two 9-by-5-by-3-inch loaf pans. Divide the dough into two equal pieces. Gently press each piece into an oblong rectangle, about 1 inch thick and no wider than the length of the pan (illustration 1). With long side of the dough facing you, roll firmly into a cylinder, pressing down to make sure that the dough sticks to itself (illustration 2). Turn the dough seam side up and pinch it closed (illustration 3). Place each cylinder of dough into one of the prepared loaf pans (illustration 4) and press it gently so it touches all four sides of the pan.

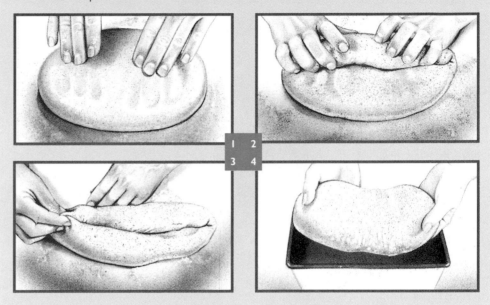

Dinner Rolls

Sprinkle fine cornmeal over two baking sheets. Cut the dough into sixteen 4-ounce pieces (illustration 1). Roll each portion of dough into a ball between your outstretched palm and the work surface (illustration 2). Loosely cover each baking sheet with plastic wrap. Let rise as in master recipe, about 20 minutes. Using scissors, make four to five cuts like the spokes of a wheel onto each of the fully risen dough balls (illustration 3).

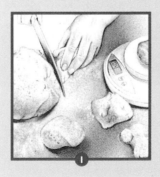 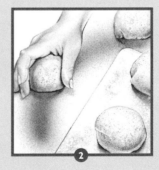 

Twisted Loaf
Baked in a Loaf Pan

Grease two 9-by-5-by-3-inch loaf pans. Turn the dough onto an unfloured work surface, gently deflate the dough, and divide it into four pieces. With your palms, roll each piece into a fat coil, 9 to 10 inches long. Place two pieces side by side and wrap one around the other to make a twist. Place in loaf pan and gently press down so that the dough is evenly distributed in the pan and is touching all sides. Repeat with the second loaf.

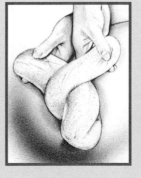 

For proofing the second rise, after the dough has been shaped, we found that twenty to thirty minutes was best. When left to rise for longer than this, the dough baked up into a light loaf with an unwelcome cottony texture and a crust that had separated from the rest of the loaf, causing a rippled effect.

We were also curious about proofing methods. In order to promote flavor, many bread recipes start with a sponge, which is nothing more than yeast, water, and flour, mixed together and allowed to stand for anywhere from one hour to overnight. As the yeast culture grows, it is thought that the depth of flavor is developed.

We tried four tests of the sponge method. A one-hour sponge produced a light bread, with a soft, cottony texture and mild flavor. A four-hour sponge had a nice rise but also evidenced no improvement in flavor. Finally, we tested a bread that rose three times (instead of the regulation two-rise system), and this loaf, with a slightly more developed flavor, edged out the basic master recipe (only two rises) for first place. However, the difference was very subtle and deemed not to be worth the extra time.

Although we were confident about oven temperatures and baking times, we did test them to be sure. As we had expected, the 375-degree oven worked best. A 350-degree oven turned out doughy bread while a 400-degree oven produced a loaf with a slightly burned bottom. To determine when a loaf is properly cooked, we used an instant-read thermometer inserted from one end into the middle of the loaf; for a free-form loaf, simply insert the thermometer into the bottom of the loaf. An internal temperature of 205 degrees proved ideal; at lower temperatures the bread was undercooked.

We also wondered if the introduction of steam into the oven would affect the crust. Although we liked the crust created without any steam, we tried adding boiling water to a pan in the oven and also spritzed water on the loaf as it baked, neither of which made any discernible difference.

It did occur to us that perhaps the brand of whole wheat flour might make a difference. We had performed all of our tests to this point with King Arthur flour, but we also tried Arrowhead Mills Stone Ground Whole Wheat. This flour produced a loaf with a nice wheat flavor, but it was lighter in both color and texture. Next we made a loaf using Hodgson Mill Whole Wheat Graham Flour, which produced a wonderful loaf with a terrific, nutty flavor. Graham flour is a bit coarser and perhaps flakier than regular whole wheat flour and, as we noted in our testing, provides a nuttier flavor. It is named after its inventor, Sylvester Graham. Although the King Arthur was also very good, we felt that the Hodgson flour was best suited for this recipe.

We also tested King Arthur White Whole Wheat Flour (see "What Is Whole Wheat Flour?" page 12), substituting it for the all-purpose white flour, and found that the bread was slightly sweeter and the texture was the same, but the taste seemed slightly flat. Finally, we tested Kretschmer's Original Toasted Wheat Germ

When Things Go Wrong

Here are a few troubleshooting tips:

BREAD IS DRY
You might have added too much flour to the dough. One way to avoid this is to slightly moisten your hands as a way to prevent sticking rather than sprinkling in more flour. You will also produce a slightly drier loaf if you substitute regular sugar for honey in a bread recipe without increasing the water.

DOUGH DOESN'T RISE DURING PROOFING
Check to make sure that the expiration date on your yeast has not passed. Another possibility is that the water was too hot and killed the yeast. Or you may have added too much flour or placed the bread in a cool, drafty spot to rise. To cure the latter situation, heat your oven for ten minutes at 200 degrees and turn it off; the oven can now be used as a proofing box. Thanks to one of our readers, we discovered that a microwave oven can also be used as a proofing box. To do so, fill a two-cup Pyrex measuring cup almost full with water, place it in the microwave, and bring the water to a boil. Now place the dough (which should be in a bowl covered with plastic wrap) into the oven with the measuring cup. The preheated water will keep the oven at the proper temperature for proofing.

BREAD IS RIPPLED WITH AIR POCKETS UNDERNEATH THE CRUST
The dough was allowed to rise too much after it was shaped. If you happen to leave your bread proofing too long, punch the dough down, shape it a second time, and let it rise properly.

DOUGH NEEDS TO BE RESHAPED
If you are shaping the dough and are not pleased with your efforts, simply let the dough rest for a few minutes, covered with a damp cloth. The dough will then be sufficiently rested to be shaped a second time. Otherwise, the dough can become elastic and difficult to manage.

DOUGH IS STICKY AND WET
This dough will, at first, seem very sticky as if it needs more flour. However, as it rises, the dough hydrates, that is, the water becomes more evenly distributed, and the texture will change to a very soft, smooth texture. Do not add additional flour.

against a health foods store wheat germ and could tell no difference in either taste or texture.

WHOLE WHEAT BREAD WITH WHEAT GERM AND RYE
Makes 2 loaves or 16 rolls

Because kneading this wet, sticky dough can cause damage to lower-horsepower mixers, it's best to use a heavy-duty mixer such as a KitchenAid. For those with less powerful mixers, be especially sure to use the low rather than the medium speed during kneading, or proceed instead with the instructions for hand kneading that follow this recipe.

- 2⅓ cups warm water, preferably bottled springwater
- 1½ tablespoons yeast
- ¼ cup honey
- 4 tablespoons unsalted butter, melted
- 2½ teaspoons salt
- ¼ cup rye flour
- ½ cup toasted wheat germ
- 3 cups whole wheat flour, preferably Hodgson Mill Whole Wheat Graham Flour
- 2¾ cups all-purpose flour
  Extra flour for work surface

1. In bowl of standing mixer, mix water, yeast, honey, butter, and salt with rubber spatula. Mix in rye flour, wheat germ, and 1 cup each of whole wheat and white flours.
2. Using dough hook attachment, mix in remaining flours on low speed (number 2 on a KitchenAid) until dough is smooth and elastic, about 8 minutes. Transfer dough to floured work surface. Knead just long enough to confirm dough is soft and smooth, about 30 seconds.
3. Place dough in lightly greased bowl; cover with plastic wrap or damp kitchen towel. Let rise in warm draft-free area until dough has doubled in volume, about 1 hour.
4. Heat oven to 375 degrees. Gently punch down dough, then follow one of the shaping instructions on page 13. Cover shaped dough; let rise until almost doubled in volume, 20 to 30 minutes.
5. For loaves, bake until instant-read thermometer inserted into loaf center reads 205 degrees, 35 to 45 minutes. For rolls, bake until golden brown, 15 to 20 minutes. Transfer bread immediately from baking pans to wire rack; cool to room temperature.

HAND-KNEADED WHOLE WHEAT BREAD
Follow recipe for Whole Wheat Bread with Wheat Germ and Rye, mixing water, yeast, honey, butter, salt, rye flour, and wheat germ in large mixing bowl. Mix 2¾ cup each of whole wheat and white flours in separate bowl, reserving ¼ cup whole wheat flour. Add 3½ cups of the flour mixture to wet ingredients; beat with wooden spoon 5 minutes. Beat in another 1½ cups of the flour mixture to make thick dough. Turn dough onto work surface that has been sprinkled with some of the served flour. Knead, adding as little of remaining flour as necessary, to form soft, elastic dough, about 5 minutes. Continue with step 3. ■

Porcini Mushroom Pasta Sauces

These robust, earthy sauces banish any notions of bland, watery mushrooms.

∼ BY JACK BISHOP ∼

For hearty, robust pasta sauces, I like to use porcini mushrooms. Available fresh in Italy, they are magnificent shaved over simple pasta. Unfortunately, fresh porcini are rarely sold in this country. Dried porcini re-create the flavor but require some preparation.

After a number of tests, I concluded that hot tap water extracts plenty of flavor from dried porcini without making them mushy. Boiling water works quickly but can result in listless texture, while lukewarm water does not soften the mushrooms quickly enough. Soaking times need not be precise. I found twenty minutes to be the minimum time necessary for proper softening in hot water, but another five or ten minutes does no harm. One cup of water per ounce of dried mushrooms is enough to cover them completely without diluting their flavor.

Perhaps more important than soaking technique is straining. Dried porcini are often packaged with foreign matter. Lifting the mushrooms from the soaking liquid with a fork helps keep the grit in the bowl (see "Quick Tips," page 4). A quick inspection, just to make sure that there are no twigs is all that is usually necessary.

The straining liquid should never be discarded, and the recipes below utilize this brown, fragrant liquid. It can also be added to stock for mushroom soup or risotto. The best way to remove the grit at the bottom of the bowl is to pour the soaking liquid through a small mesh strainer that has been lined with a single paper towel. The towel traps the dirt and absorbs a minimum of the precious liquid.

A final caveat: Proper handling can do nothing for inferior specimens. Although most dried porcini in markets are fine, some are nothing more than mushroom dust. If the porcini are sold loose, smell them; the aroma should be earthy, not musty or stale.

Poor-quality dried porcini (above) are thin and brittle with dust and crumbled pieces mixed in.

Look for dried porcini (above) that are large, thick, and tan or brown in color, rather than black.

HOW TO REHYDRATE DRIED PORCINI MUSHROOMS

Place 1 ounce dried porcini mushrooms in small bowl and cover with 1 cup hot water. Soak 20 minutes. Carefully lift mushrooms from liquid with fork and pick through to remove any foreign debris. Wash mushrooms under cold water if they feel gritty, then chop. Strain soaking liquid through sieve lined with paper towel. Reserve mushrooms and strained soaking liquid separately.

PORCINI MUSHROOM SAUCE WITH CREAM

Enough for 1 pound of pasta

Toss this intensely flavored sauce with one pound of dried (or one and one-quarter pound of fresh) fettuccine and one-half cup of Parmesan cheese. Pass extra cheese at the table.

- 3 tablespoons unsalted butter
- 1 medium onion, minced
- 2 ounces dried porcini mushrooms, rehydrated in 2 cups hot water, strained, and chopped coarse; soaking liquid reserved
- Salt and ground black pepper
- 6 tablespoons heavy cream
- 3 tablespoons minced fresh parsley leaves

1. Heat butter in large sauté pan over medium heat. Add onion; sauté until edges begin to brown, about 7 minutes. Add porcini and salt and pepper to taste; sauté to release flavors, 1 to 2 minutes.

2. Increase heat to medium-high. Add soaking liquid; simmer briskly until liquid has reduced by half, about 10 minutes.

3. Stir in cream; simmer until sauce just starts to thicken, about 2 minutes. Stir in parsley, adjust seasonings, and serve.

TOMATO SAUCE WITH PORCINI MUSHROOMS

Enough for 1 pound of pasta

Toss this sauce with spaghetti or fusilli and serve with grated Parmesan cheese.

- 3 tablespoons olive oil
- 1 medium onion, minced
- 1 celery rib, minced
- 1 small carrot, peeled and minced
- 1 ounce dried porcini mushrooms, rehydrated, strained, and chopped coarse; soaking liquid reserved
- 1 teaspoon salt
- 1 can (28 ounces) plum tomatoes packed in juice, drained, seeded, and chopped
- 3 tablespoons minced fresh parsley leaves

1. Heat oil in large sauté pan over medium heat. Add onion, celery, and carrot; sauté until vegetables soften, 8 to 10 minutes. Add porcini and salt; sauté to release flavors, 1 to 2 minutes.

2. Increase heat to medium-high; add tomatoes and soaking liquid. Bring sauce to boil, lower heat, then simmer until sauce thickens, about 15 minutes. Stir in parsley, adjust seasonings, and serve.

TWO MUSHROOM SAUCE WITH ROSEMARY

Enough for 1 pound of pasta

Button mushrooms get a tremendous boost from a handful of dried porcini. Serve with orecchiette or small shells. So that the pasta better absorbs the sauce, simmer the cooked pasta and one-third cup of grated Parmesan cheese with the sauce for a minute or two, then serve.

- 2 tablespoons unsalted butter
- 1 tablespoon olive oil
- 1 medium onion, minced
- 2 medium garlic cloves, minced
- 1 teaspoon minced fresh rosemary leaves
- 1 pound white button mushrooms, stems trimmed and sliced thin
- 1 ounce dried porcini mushrooms, rehydrated, strained, and chopped coarse; soaking liquid reserved
- Salt and ground black pepper
- 2 tablespoons minced fresh parsley leaves

1. Heat butter and oil over medium heat in large sauté pan. Add onion; sauté until translucent, about 5 minutes. Add garlic and rosemary; sauté until garlic is golden, about 1 minute.

2. Add button mushrooms; sauté until golden and liquid evaporates, about 8 minutes. Add chopped porcini; sauté to release flavors, 1 to 2 minutes. Season with salt and pepper to taste. Add soaking liquid; bring to simmer. Stir in parsley, adjust seasonings, and serve. ■

Citrus Secrets

~ BY ANNE TUOMEY ~

The tang of citrus is wonderful, but these fruits can sometimes be difficult to deal with. Follow the steps below for zesting, juicing, and creating easy-to-use wedges, pith-free sections, serving bowls, and candied zest.

Wedges

1. Cut the fruit in half lengthwise, from pole to pole.

2. Cut each half into quarters or eighths, again from pole to pole.

3. Slice off the center pith from each wedge. This not only removes the bitter pith but also makes it easier to squeeze out the juice.

Zest

There are a number of tools that can be used for zesting citrus. The one you use will be determined by the way you plan to use the zest.

Vegetable Peeler

A vegetable peeler produces citrus strips of roughly the same size, which makes them easy to stack and julienne.

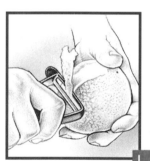
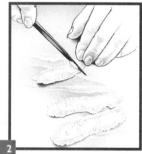

| 1 | 2 |
| 3 | 4 |

1. Hold the citrus so one full side is exposed. Grasping the peeler horizontally, use a downward motion to remove strips of citrus rind from the top of the fruit to the bottom.

2. If you have included much of the bitter white pith with the zest, you can remove it by scraping along the back of the zest with a paring knife.

3. Stack the rectangular pieces of peel on top of one another and slice them into very thin strips.

4. Finely mince the citrus strips for zest pieces that will be more noticeable in texture than those produced by a grater.

Zester

A zester can produce two types of zest.

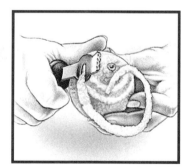

1. The small holes on the end of the zester produce soft, curly strings of zest, which are nice for decoration. To use the zester, hold the citrus firmly so that one side is exposed. Position the zester against the top of the fruit and gently pull down, avoiding the white pith.

2. The stripper tooth is best for producing long, medium-thick strips of zest. To make these strips, hold the citrus firmly with the top facing up and pull the zester gently around the circumference of the fruit, again avoiding the white pith.

Handheld Grater

This grater produces very thin, nearly transparent zest, almost like a puree, that will melt into whatever it is added to. To use the handheld grater, hold it down against the counter for support. Grate only the colored part of the skin; most of the zest should fall to the counter, but you can remove any that remains with a clean toothbrush or other small brush.

Decorative Slices

1. Using the stripper tooth of a zester, cut strips from pole to pole, leaving some distance in between. (The number of strips and their distance apart determines how decorative the slices will be.) Save the strips for another use.

2. Slice the fruit and arrange it around a platter or use it to garnish a tall glass of water or iced tea.

Juice

We tested several methods for increasing the amount of juice you can extract. Based on time and ease of use, we like rolling the fruit on a table or in our hands. Keeping the fruit at room temperature will also help juice extraction. We also tested several manual methods for juicing citrus fruits and found that a wooden reamer, a teardrop-shaped tool with a handle, works the best for extracting the most juice possible.

1. Place the fruit on a hard surface and firmly roll it back and forth several times with the palm of your hand.

2. Cut the fruit in half. Firmly grasp the fruit in one hand while using the pointed tip of the reamer to press in and around the pulp. Continue until all the juice is extracted. Note: If the fruit has seeds, place a mesh strainer over the bowl to catch them as you juice.

To extract a small amount of juice without cutting the fruit:

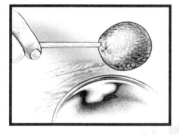

1. Insert a skewer into one end of the fruit, turning the skewer around several times to make a hole about ⅛ inch in diameter.

2. Squeeze out as much juice as you need, then refrigerate fruit for future use.

Sections

Many recipes call for sections of citrus that have been separated from the membrane that divides them. When you are sectioning, it is important to remove all remnants of white pith, which is rather bitter.

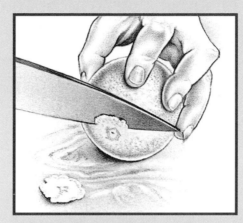

1. Slice a small section, about one-half inch thick, off the top and bottom ends of the fruit.

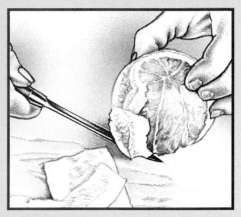

2. Using a very sharp paring knife, slice off the rind, including the white pith, by sliding the knife edge from top to bottom of the fruit. Try to follow the outline of the fruit as closely as possible.

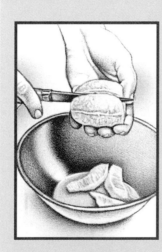

3. Slip the blade between the membrane and the section and slice to the center, separating one side of the section.

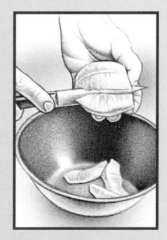

4. Turn the blade of the knife so that it is facing out and is lined up along the membrane on the opposite side of the section.

5. Slide the blade from the center out along the membrane to completely free the section. Continue until all sections are removed.

Citrus "Bowls"

A grapefruit knife works best for the final stage of this task. Because it is curved and serrated, it allows you to closely and cleanly follow the curves between the flesh and the pith.

1. Cut off a thin slice from each end of the fruit to create a steady base on each bowl.

2. Slice the fruit in half.

3. Use a grapefruit knife to loosen the flesh from the rind, being careful not to cut into the pith. The flesh should easily lift out. The bowls can now be filled with sorbet or ice cream, or you can cut up the flesh and return it to the bowl.

Big, Beautiful Muffins

Cream butter and sugar for a tender, delicate crumb; use butter and plain yogurt for flavor and texture; and make enough batter to fill up the cups for big, shapely muffins.

∽ BY PAM ANDERSON WITH KAREN TACK ∽

Have you ever tried to bake a batch of those jumbo muffins you see in bakeries and specialty coffee shops these days? If you follow most cookbook recipes, you won't get what you're looking for. I hadn't, and over the years I had tried scores of them. Some muffins came out flat-topped or misshapen. Other batches were either rich and leaden or dense and dry. The best were pleasant, but not outstanding.

My standards, admittedly, were high. I wasn't looking for a healthy muffin I could make part of my daily diet. I wanted a really great weekend muffin, one that would make brunch guests covet the recipe. This muffin had to have it all. It needed rich, full flavor with a thin, crisp crust protecting its fragile, tender crumb. What's more, this muffin had to be a real looker, too. I would settle for nothing less than a perfectly round, mushroom-like cap with a pronounced, crisp overhang.

Mix It Up

Working with a conservative six-muffin recipe, we decided to start our tests with mixing techniques. Our review of recipes pointed to three possible methods. The most common technique calls for measuring wet and dry ingredients separately, pouring wet into dry, then mixing them together as quickly as possible. Batters for pancakes, popovers, and most quick breads rely on this approach. A second method, more common to cake batters, starts with creaming the butter and sugar, adding eggs and flavorings, then alternately mixing the dry and liquid ingredients into the creamed fat. A final possibility comes from the biscuit and pie dough–mixing tradition, in which the fat is cut into the dry ingredients. When the mix is cornmeal-textured with pea-size flecks, liquid is added and quickly mixed in.

To create large, rounded tops we increased the batter recipe by one-third but made the same number of muffins.

Although the recipe we were working with at this point was way too lean (the muffins were small, dry, tough, and unappetizing), we still favored the creaming method. The creamed-batter muffins were more tender-crumbed than the competitors (see "Choosing Your Mixing Method," page 19, for the final outcome).

With the mixing method semidecided, we moved on to testing individual ingredients. Because our original formula was too dry and savory, we increased the butter and sugar, then moved on to testing the primary ingredient: flour. We made muffins with cake flour, unbleached flour, bleached flour, and an equal mix of cake flour and bleached all-purpose.

Similar to our experience with pancakes (see "Perfect Pancakes," January/February 1996), the batter made with cake flour was incredibly loose compared to the other batters, resulting in muffins that were squat, wet, and greasy. They also lacked a distinct, crisp outer crust. Muffins baked with half cake and half all-purpose were a step up from the cake flour muffins. Their texture was a tad wet and greasy, and they lacked the beautiful shape of those made with all-purpose. Although the formula still needed work, both all-purpose muffins were shapely and fairly tender, with a nice contrast between crust and crumb. After our flour tests, we decided that the formula still needed more sugar, so we increased the sugar, once again, by another tablespoon.

Plain Yogurt Offers Flavor and Texture

By now our formula was beginning to take shape, and we were ready to test liquids. We made muffins using low-fat milk, whole milk, half-and-half, cream, powdered milk plus water (common in commercial baking), buttermilk, yogurt, and sour cream. Leavening adjustments were made (reducing the amount of baking powder and including baking soda) for all the buttermilk, yogurt, and sour cream muffins.

The thin liquids—low-fat milk, whole milk, powdered milk,

and half-and-half—naturally produced thin batters that baked into smooth-topped muffins. They looked more like cupcakes. Low-fat milk muffins were soufflé-shaped with straight sides and flat tops.

The thicker liquids—cream, buttermilk, low-fat yogurt, and sour cream—delivered thicker batters and muffins with rounded, textured tops. The higher-fat muffins, particularly those made with sour cream and cream, were squatty, dense, heavy, and wet. The buttermilk muffins were good, but the yogurt-enriched were even better, giving us a rough-textured rounded top, a sweet-tangy flavor, and a light, tender crumb.

Now that we had a working base, we started adding fruits and flavorings. Three additional adjustments to the recipe came during this part of the testing. Although the sugar level seemed right in the plain muffin, the addition of tart fruit and other ingredients made the muffins seem not sweet enough. We found that increasing the sugar again helped immensely both in the plain and fruit variations. We also found that one more tablespoon of butter gave us additional tenderness without weighting down the muffin. Increasing the batter by one-third—from a two-cup flour to a three-cup flour recipe—gave us not only a beautifully rounded top but a nice big lip. This base worked with all of the following variations, so you should feel free to plug in your own favorites.

MASTER RECIPE FOR BASIC MUFFINS
Makes 1 dozen large muffins
Remember, if you're short on time, you can melt the butter, mix it with the eggs, and stir it into the

Choosing Your Mixing Method

Practically every pancake and quick bread recipe cautions not to overmix the batter once wet and dry ingredients have been combined. Better, most authors reason, to leave streaks of flour in the batter than to overdevelop the flour's gluten, resulting in smaller, denser, and tougher muffins.

Because we found the standard creaming method (creaming butter and sugar, then alternately beating in dry and wet ingredients) to deliver a lighter, more tender muffin than the gingerly mixed quick-bread method, we were puzzled. In the creaming method, the flour was beaten by machine up to two minutes, depending on the recipe. If overbeating caused gluten development and tough muffins, why were these muffins tender?

For an explanation, we turned to food scientist Shirley Corriher, who quickly pointed out the differences. In the creaming process butter is aerated with sugar, then fat- and moisture-rich eggs are beaten into the mix. Dry ingredients are added, alternately with the wet ingredients.

Corriher observes that flour is added to the creamed butter mixture before the wet ingredients and notes that a high proportion of the flour should be added at this point. That way, the fat from the butter and egg coats most of the flour, protecting it from any gluten forma-

tion. The remaining flour and wet ingredients are added alternately at this point, stimulating only a part of the flour's gluten. Certainly, she adds, some of the flour's gluten must be activated; otherwise the muffin would have no structure at all. (Maggie Glazer, Atlanta-based baking expert, confirms Corriher's speculation that fat inhibits gluten development.)

In the quick-bread method, all wet ingredients and fats are added at once, denying the flour an opportunity to be coated with fat. We naturally questioned why the quick-bread method couldn't approximate the creaming method of coating the flour with fat first. So we made a batch of muffins, mixing the dry ingredients, then adding melted butter and the eggs to disperse the fat. When the flour was sufficiently coated, we stirred in the yogurt.

The results proved Corriher's observation correct. The muffins were just as tender as those made using the creamed method. But because the batter had not been aerated by the mixer, they lacked the height of the mixer muffins. So when you're short on time, you can achieve more tender muffins by simply mixing the butter and eggs into the dry ingredients. The muffins will not rise high enough to develop a lip, but their texture and flavor will be fine. When perfection counts, however, get out the mixer.—P.A.

---

butter and sugar and folding 1½ cups finely diced dried apricots into finished batter. Sprinkle each top with portion of ½ cup sliced almonds.

RASPBERRY ALMOND MUFFINS

Follow Master Recipe for Basic Muffins, creaming 1 ounce (3 tablespoons) almond paste with butter and sugar. Spoon one-half portion of batter into each muffin cup. With small spoon, make well in center of each cup of dough. Spoon 1 to 1½ teaspoons raspberry (or any flavored) jam into each well. Fill with remaining batter.

CRANBERRY-WALNUT-ORANGE MUFFINS

Follow Master Recipe for Basic Muffins, adding 1 teaspoon grated orange zest to butter-sugar mixture and folding 1½ cups coarsely chopped fresh or frozen cranberries and ¾ cup coarsely chopped walnuts into finished batter.

LEMON BLUEBERRY MUFFINS

Follow Master Recipe for Basic Muffins, adding 1 teaspoon grated lemon zest to butter-sugar mixture and folding 1½ cups blueberries that have been tossed in 1 tablespoon flour into finished batter. (Top with Cinnamon Sugar Topping, if desired.)

BANANA WALNUT MUFFINS

Follow Master Recipe for Basic Muffins, adding ½ teaspoon grated nutmeg to dry ingredients, substituting 1 cup packed light brown sugar for granulated sugar, and folding 1½ cups finely diced bananas (about 3 small) and ¾ cup chopped walnuts into finished batter.

LEMON POPPY SEED MUFFINS

Follow Master Recipe for Basic Muffins, adding 3 tablespoons poppy seed to dry ingredients and 1 tablespoon grated lemon zest to butter-sugar mixture. While muffins are baking, heat ¼ cup granulated sugar and ¼ cup lemon juice in small saucepan until sugar dissolves and mixture forms light syrup, 3 to 4 minutes. Brush warm syrup over warm muffins and serve. ∎

---

dry ingredients. When thoroughly mixed, beat in the yogurt and proceed with the recipe. To cinnamon-coat muffin tops, dip warm muffins in melted butter, then in mixture of one-half cup granulated sugar and two teaspoons cinnamon.

- 3 cups all-purpose flour
- 1 tablespoon baking powder
- ½ teaspoon baking soda
- ½ teaspoon salt
- 10 tablespoons unsalted butter, softened
- 1 cup minus 1 tablespoon granulated sugar
- 2 large eggs
- 1½ cups plain low-fat yogurt
  Vegetable cooking spray or additional unsalted butter for muffin tins

1. Adjust oven rack to lower middle position and heat oven to 375 degrees. Mix flour, baking powder, baking soda, and salt in medium bowl; set aside.

2. Beat butter and sugar with electric mixer on medium-high speed until light and fluffy, about 2 minutes. Add eggs, one at a time, beating well after each addition. Beat in one-half of dry ingredients. Beat in one-third of yogurt. Beat in remaining dry ingredients in two batches, alternating with yogurt, until incorporated.

3. Spray twelve-cup muffin tin with vegetable cooking spray or coat lightly with butter. Use large ice cream scoop to divide batter evenly

among cups. Bake until muffins are golden brown, 25 to 30 minutes. Set on wire rack to cool slightly, about 5 minutes. Remove muffins from tin and serve warm.

MOCHA CHIP MUFFINS

Follow Master Recipe for Basic Muffins, dissolving 3 tablespoons instant espresso powder in yogurt and folding 1 cup chocolate chips into finished batter.

APRICOT ALMOND MUFFINS

Follow Master Recipe for Basic Muffins, creaming 1 ounce (3 tablespoons) almond paste with

---

Do Muffin Papers Help?

A few recipes advised against muffin papers, warning that muffins would not rise as high. We also saw a couple of recipes that instructed one to grease the bottom, but not the sides, of the muffin cups. So we tested three batches of muffins—one baked in papers, one baked in greased cups, and a final batch baked in cups in which only the bottoms were greased.

We observed shape, more than height, differences among the three. The muffins baked in papers were, indeed, shorter than those baked right in the cup, but they had a more rounded, filled-out look than the other two muffins. But we still disliked muffin papers for other reasons. When peeling off the papers, we lost a good portion of the muffin. Muffin papers also keep the muffins sides from browning as well as those baked right in the cup. We observed no difference between those baked in greased cups compared to those baked in cups with greased bottoms only.—P.A.

Reinventing Macaroni and Cheese

In about the time that it takes to prepare a boxed macaroni and cheese dinner, you can make the real McCoy.

~ BY PAM ANDERSON WITH KAREN TACK ~

Macaroni and cheese has always been on our "must-explore" list. It's just eaten too often in this country for us to ignore it. Kids in particular say yes to macaroni and cheese when they turn up their noses to everything else. Unfortunately, it's the boxed version, complete with orange cheese powder, that's made most often. My eleven-year-old daughter loves to watch me cringe as she reminds me that her standard nursery school lunch was boxed macaroni and cheese and celery sticks.

As I looked over recipes for homemade macaroni and cheese, I saw two distinct styles. The more common variety is béchamel-based, in which macaroni is blanketed with a cheese-flavored white sauce, usually topped with crumbs, and

Crunchy topping and a silky smooth sauce that oozes from every tube— part of our definition of great macaroni and cheese.

baked. The other variety, the kind my mother always made, is custard-based. In this style, a mixture of egg and milk is poured over layers of grated cheese and noodles. As the dish bakes, the eggs, milk, and cheese set into a custard. This macaroni and cheese is also bread crumb–topped and baked, although my mom always sprinkled crushed saltine crackers over hers.

Even though macaroni and cheese is a wonderful, satisfying dish, many of the recipes we looked at seemed tired, leaden, and uninspired. Others attempted to perk up the dish with canned green chiles, scallions, or olives. And, of course, there were those who tried to lighten it. No one seemed to really love the dish.

After compiling the usual tests from the stack of utility recipes, I began to wonder if I really did still love this simple dish. Then I read the chapter on macaroni and cheese in John Thorne's *Simple Cooking* (Penguin, 1989). "As it happens," he begins, "I'm very fond of macaroni and cheese, and keep a special spot in my heart for cooks who genuinely love it: they are not that many." After reading his four-page essay, we suspected that his recipe for macaroni and cheese was the real one, the others mere shadows.

No Comparison

Making the dish confirmed what we suspected to be true. John Thorne's macaroni and cheese was the best. We could do our usual in-depth testing, but we knew up front we wouldn't come up with anything better.

Thorne's recipe starts with macaroni cooked just shy of al dente. The hot, drained macaroni is then tossed with butter in a heatproof pan or bowl. Evaporated milk, hot red pepper sauce, dry mustard, eggs, and a large quantity of cheese are stirred into the noodles. The combination is baked for twenty minutes, with cheese and milk additions and a thorough stir, every five minutes. Frequent stirrings allow the eggs to thicken without setting, which results in an incredibly silky sauce. During cooking, the sauce settles into the tubular openings, offering a burst of cheese with each new bite. We were delighted. Never had we gotten a dish right on the first try. For once, someone else had done our homework.

But just to confirm our beliefs, we baked the two styles of macaroni and cheese defined earlier: one with a cheese-flavored béchamel sauce, the other thickened with eggs, milk, and cheese. Neither compared to Thorne's dish. The béchamel-based version was grainy and tasted exactly as Thorne predicted: not like macaroni and cheese, but "macaroni with cheese sauce." In clothing terms, Thorne's macaroni and cheese was smooth silk while the béchamel dish was thick velvet.

Of the two baked macaroni and cheeses, we preferred the cheesier-flavored custard version. Because this custard-based macaroni and cheese was simply a baked version of Thorne's recipe, we thought we might offer it as an alternative to stirring. A side-by-side tasting proved the two macaroni and cheese dishes to be very different, however, and the stirred version remained superior in our minds. Compared to the luxuriously silky cheese sauce of the stirred macaroni, the baked egg, milk, and cheese formed a dry custard that set around the noodles. When asked if we would ever make the baked version over the stirred one, our answer was no.

Putting It to the Test

The competition ruled out, we moved forward to study Thorne's recipe a little more closely. We wondered if the dish really required evaporated milk or if this was an idiosyncrasy of the late '30s when the recipe was first published in *The Home Comfort Cook Book* (Wrought Iron Range Company, 1937). Wouldn't regular milk or half-and-half work equally well? What other cheeses, besides sharp cheddar, would taste good?

Though the recipe was virtually perfect, we had thought of a few possible refinements. First, we found that at the end of the twenty minutes of baking, the dish was hot, but hardly piping. By the time a person had consumed his or her portion, the cheese sauce had cooled and set a bit. We also missed the contrasting textures of crunchy bread crumbs and soft noodles and sauce offered by the baked versions. Thorne's advice to sprinkle the macaroni and cheese with crumbled common crackers (*see* "Sources and Resources," page 32) was one possibility, but we were looking for something a little more finished. Although we liked the rich, full cheese flavor Thorne achieved with a whole pound of cheese, we found ourselves full after only a few bites. We wanted to find out if the dish was just as good with less cheese.

After testing the recipe with whole and low-fat milks and half-and-half, we realized that evaporated milk was not an ingredient thoughtlessly left in. All the macaroni and cheese dishes made with fresh milk curdled a bit, resulting in a chalky, grainy texture. The one made with evaporated milk remained silky smooth. The evaporation and sterilization process stabilizes the milk, which in turn, stabilizes the macaroni and cheese.

After making the dish with Vermont, New York, and Wisconsin cheddars, we preferred the less sharp Wisconsin variety. Because the recipe calls for such a large quantity, a slightly milder cheese is preferable. Further testing confirmed this point. Macaroni and cheese made with Gruyère was so strong we couldn't even eat it. To our surprise, highly processed cheeses like American performed quite well in this dish. Much like evaporated milk, the more processing, the more stable the cheese and the more creamy the dish. For flavor, use cheddar; for texture, buy American. We also found the dish did not suffer with only twelve ounces of cheese compared to the one pound called for in the original recipe.

We found that you could not remedy the dish's lukewarm temperature problem by leaving it in the oven much longer than the suggested twenty minutes. If you do, you run the risk of curdling the eggs, and the dish starts to develop a subtle grainy texture. So we tried two solutions, both of which worked. To avoid pouring hot macaroni into a cold dish, we stuck our pan in the preheating oven. By the time the macaroni was ready to drain, the pan emerged from the oven pot holder hot. Warming the milk a bit before mixing it with the pasta also gave the dish a warm head start.

As suggested by Thorne, crisp common crackers sprinkled over the macaroni and cheese offer a much needed foil to the rich, unctuous sauce. For a further refinement, we toasted buttered bread crumbs alongside the heating casserole.

After I shared this recipe with friend and cooking colleague Stephen Schmidt, he reported back his finding that if one used a heavy-bottomed pot and cooked it over low heat, it was possible to make the macaroni and cheese on top of the stove in less than five minutes. We tried his suggestion and found the stovetop macaroni and cheese to be as good as the stirred one. By following his method, it was possible to complete this dish in virtually the same amount of time it would take to make the boxed stuff.

Béchamel-based macaroni and cheese will always be the more popular dish, Thorne maintains. "It's cheap to make and pretty to look at." The real recipe, similar to the one printed below, he continues, "lives a life of exile in its own country . . . biding its time in the few homes willing to grant it sanctuary, awaiting the counterrevolution." Thorne can take on the béchamel lovers. Anybody who's willing to make macaroni and cheese from scratch is an easy sell once they try this recipe. Our target is the boxed macaroni and cheese crowd. The same preparation time and a few dollars more buy you the difference between an institutional experience and the real *Mac*Coy.

STOVETOP MACARONI AND CHEESE
*Serves 4 as a main course or 6 to 8
as a side dish*
If you're in a hurry or prefer to sprinkle the dish with crumbled common crackers (saltines aren't bad either), you can skip the bread crumb step.
Toasted Bread Crumbs
    1   cup fresh bread crumbs from French
          or Italian bread

Tasting the Past—and Hating It

Many of us remember with great fondness the macaroni and cheese we had as kids even though it was either boxed or frozen. After tasting Pam Anderson's delectable version of this childhood favorite, we decided to resurrect the past by holding a tasting of the packaged versions.

The test kitchen prepared eleven boxed and frozen brands. Boxed mixes included Kraft, Annie's, Land O' Lakes, Sun Glory, Prince, and Fantastic Foods; the frozen ones were Amy's, Stouffer's Lean Cuisine, Stouffer's regular, Howard Johnson's, and Michelina's.

We found that our warm and fuzzy memories were definitely a case of selective memory. Not a single one of the packaged macaroni and cheeses was appraised with any great regard. As one taster commented, "I never quite realized before just how bad these premade mac and cheeses are." Eagerly lined up to taste, with fork in hand, he was quickly enlightened by the lackluster texture and artificial flavor of this "all-American" packaged food. All six of our tasters shared his disillusionment. Comments ran along the lines of "too processed tasting," "cheese is flavorless," "too oily," "totally fake," and "pasty, doughy noodles."

That said, the frozen versions generally scored higher than the boxed. Although testers said they were hard-pressed to pick their favorites, Stouffer's regular frozen came in first by a small margin. So if you must buy a packaged mix, that is probably your best option. Far better, however, to spend a few extra minutes in the store and over the stove and make your own from scratch. — *Eva Katz and John Willoughby*

      Pinch salt
1½ tablespoons melted unsalted butter

Creamy Macaroni and Cheese
  2 large eggs
  1 can (12 ounces) evaporated milk
 ¼ teaspoon hot red pepper sauce
  2 teaspoons salt
 ¼ teaspoon ground black pepper
  1 teaspoon dry mustard, dissolved in
       1 teaspoon water
 ½ pound elbow macaroni
  4 tablespoons unsalted butter
12 ounces sharp Wisconsin cheddar,
      American, or Monterey
      Jack cheese, grated
      (about 3 cups)

1. Heat oven to 350 degrees. Mix bread crumb ingredients together in small baking pan. Bake until golden brown and crisp, 15 to 20 minutes; set aside.

2. Meanwhile, mix eggs, 1 cup of the evaporated milk, pepper sauce, ½ teaspoon of the salt, pepper, and mustard mixture in small bowl; set aside.

3. Meanwhile, heat 2 quarts water to boil in large heavy-bottomed saucepan or Dutch oven. Add 1½ teaspoons of the salt and macaroni; cook until almost tender, but still a little firm to the bite. Drain and return to pan over low heat. Add butter; toss to melt.

4. Pour egg mixture over buttered noodles along with three-quarters of the cheese; stir until

thoroughly combined and cheese starts to melt. Gradually add remaining milk and cheese, stirring constantly, until mixture is hot and creamy, about 5 minutes. Serve immediately topped with toasted bread crumbs.

"BAKED" MACARONI AND CHEESE
Developed from the stovetop recipe by Stephen Schmidt, this dish is his answer to those who prefer their macaroni and cheese topped with crumbs and served out of a baking dish. Smooth and creamy like the stovetop version, this one is broiled just long enough to brown the crumb topping. The macaroni and cheese can be made up to eight hours ahead, but it must be reheated over very low heat, adding extra milk to moisten it, if necessary, before pouring into the baking dish.

1. Heat 2 tablespoons butter in large skillet over medium heat until foam subsides. Add 1 cup lightly packed soft fresh bread crumbs; cook, tossing to coat with butter, until crumbs just begin to color. Season to taste with salt; set aside.

2. Adjust oven rack 6 inches from heating element; heat broiler. Follow recipe for Stovetop Macaroni and Cheese, mixing ¼ cup of the grated cheese in with the bread crumbs.

3. Pour cooked macaroni and cheese into 9-inch pan (or another heatproof pan of similar surface area). Spread crumbs evenly over top. Broil until crumb turns deep brown, 1 to 2 minutes. Let stand to set a bit, about 5 minutes, and serve. ■

The Problem with Oatmeal Cookies

Why did it take six months to develop the right recipe for a chewy, thick, buttery oatmeal cookie? Well, it all started and ended with the back of the Quaker Oats box....

~ BY CHRISTOPHER KIMBALL WITH EVA KATZ ~

I admit that, for years, I have used the oatmeal cookie recipe printed on the back of the Quaker Oats box. Although I have not yet succumbed to feasting on recipes from the packaging for Perdue chickens, Corn Flakes, or Rice Krispies, I have found that the folks at Quaker Oats have done a rather good job of recipe development. And the oatmeal cookie recipe should be good. When I called Quaker Oats, I found that this recipe has gone through hundreds of variations since the first version, The Famous Oatmeal Cookie, which used shortening instead of butter for crispness.

However , I was never entirely happy with the back-of-the-box cookies. They were not chewy enough, not quite moist enough, and I wanted a major league cookie, not some diminutive cookie jar offering. I also couldn't taste the oats for the cinnamon, a problem I later found repeated with most oatmeal cookie recipes. These aren't supposed to be spice cookies; one ought to be able to taste the oats, which, unfortunately, are subtle enough to be knocked out of the ballpark by a heavy hand in the spice drawer.

So, we hunted through our library of cookbooks and called our staff for favorite recipes, selecting those that were most different in proportions or technique. With nine contenders assembled, we went to work and baked up a blind tasting.

Only two received more than a cursory bite from the testers. But the recipe submitted by Jack Bishop, one of our editors, was quite good: It puffed a bit, had a hint of chew, and was simple enough in concept that the flavor of the oats came through nicely. The Quaker Oats recipe, although it needed work, was also highly rated. What was exceedingly apparent, however, was that each of these cookies was quite different; small differences in proportions and ingredients created cookies with little or no family resemblance.

To get a better handle on what made a great oatmeal cookie, we compared the two blind tasting winners. One striking difference was that Quaker Oats calls for baking soda while Jack's recipe uses both baking powder and baking soda. We then turned to the ratio of butter to flour and found an interesting correlation. Both of these recipes used about two parts of butter to three parts of flour whereas all of the other recipes except one (the very greasy version, in which the butter-to-flour ratio was 1:1) used a higher ratio of butter to flour.

We also reviewed the ratio of oats to flour and found that the less oaty cookies had oats-to-flour ratios of 1:1, whereas Quaker Oats, perhaps in a bid to promote use of its product, used a full 2:1. Jack's recipe also had a high proportion of oats to flour, so we determined that a high proportion was best. So, lots of butter and a high ratio of oats to flour were clearly desirable for both texture and flavor.

It was now time to construct our own master recipe. Starting with the Quaker Oats recipe because we liked the high proportion of oats, eggs, and butter, we changed the baking soda in that recipe to baking powder for lift (*see* "Soda or Powder? The Lift Question," page 23, for details on the chemistry). This did provide more rise, which made the cookies less dense and a bit chewier.

As a second change, we dumped the cinnamon, which we felt overpowered the flavor of the oats.

Finally, we decided to make much larger cookies, dropping two-inch balls of dough onto the cookie sheet instead of the meager "rounded" tablespoons called for by the Quaker Oats test kitchen. We did this because of our feeling that bigger cookies tend to be moister and chewier whereas small cookies tend to be cakier and more uniform. To be sure we were correct, we baked two batches of Quaker Oats cookies, one large and the other small. The larger cookies were substantially better, that is, they were moister and chewier. We also tested our final recipe in a diminutive size, and they were considerably drier and more cakelike.

Now, after literally months of testing, we had come out very close to the Quaker Oats recipe with which I had started, but the three simple little changes that we had made (baking powder instead of baking soda, no cinnamon, and larger cookies) had made a significant difference in the end result.

Local Baker Lends a Hand

We had a good cookie but were still looking for the perfect texture: crisp on the outside, yet chewy on the inside. Then one evening, my wife and I stopped by a local Boston eatery, the Claremont Café, and ordered a cup of tea and two oatmeal cookies. Sprawled across a dessert plate, easily covering the full diameter, were thick, chewy, moist, crunchy-on-the-outside, big league cookies, packed with real oat flavor. I begged for the recipe, and we made a batch the next day in our test kitchen. These cookies were big winners.

But the shock set in when we compared the Claremont recipe to our revised Quaker Oats cookie. They were almost the same! The only major difference was an extra half cup of white granulated sugar. But, boy, what a difference. This sugar added loads of extra moisture and rich texture to the cookie. The reason for this is simple: Sugar makes baked goods both more tender and moister because it helps the cake or cookie retain water during the baking process. In addition, sugar encourages exterior browning, which promotes crispness. We did try the middle ground, using three-quarters cup of sugar, less than the Claremont recipe but still an increase of one-quarter cup over our revised Quaker Oats recipe. But the resulting cookies lacked the crispy exterior that the full cup of white sugar provided; hence the full amount was deemed necessary.

The Claremont Café recipe was also a bit overspiced for us, calling for ginger and cinnamon as well as one-eighth teaspoon of nutmeg. After many taste tests, we discovered that nutmeg and oats, both of which have clean, subtle flavors, make a good pair whereas cinnamon is overpowering and unwelcome in a basic oatmeal cookie. So, as a final adjustment, we upped the amount of freshly grated nutmeg to one-quarter teaspoon but got rid of the other spices. We made a final test batch and reached our version of the perfect oatmeal cookie.

For us, the ideal oatmeal cookie is a big, moist, chewy cookie with plenty of real oat flavor.

Soda or Powder? The Lift Question

As has been pointed out many times in this publication, baking powder is nothing more than baking soda (about one-quarter to one-third of the total makeup) mixed with an acid and double-dried cornstarch. The acid produces carbon dioxide when it comes into contact with the baking soda, while the cornstarch keeps the two elements apart during storage, preventing the premature production of the gas.

Many cooks believe that since only one-third of baking powder is baking soda—the actual leavening agent—then full-strength baking soda must be a more powerful leavening agent in all situations. Although it seems logical, this is incorrect. Baking soda is only fully effective if there is an acid component in the batter for it to react with and create carbon dioxide. In an alkaline (low acid) batter, a teaspoon of baking powder is a more effective leavening because the baking soda in the powder will combine with the leavening acid, also contained in the powder itself, to produce a more complete chemical reaction. This is the reason why recipes that contain acidic ingredients such as buttermilk usually call just for baking soda. That being said, even in the absence of an acid, baking soda will decompose during baking and throw off some carbon dioxide gas, but far less than baking powder. Generally, however, the choice of whether to use baking soda or baking powder depends on the acidity of the batter, rather than on the issue of leavening horsepower.

One other major difference exists between these two leavenings. Most baking powders are double-acting, which means that two different chemical leavening acids are used in the mixture: One works at room temperature, and the other works best at oven temperatures. In a cake, for example, it is important to have an early release of carbon dioxide during the batter preparation so that small bubbles will be created to form the foundation of the cell structure. These cells expand during baking because of additional carbon dioxide production caused by the action of the second leavening acid, and the dough firms up into the final cake structure. In a stiff cookie batter, however, especially one that has a good deal of structure from butter and eggs, the double-acting issue is less critical.

But the question still remained, In this particular recipe should we use baking soda, baking powder, or both? And how much of the leavening(s) should we use? To get the answer, we made six new batches of the master recipe, using one-quarter teaspoon, one-half teaspoon, and one full teaspoon each of baking powder and then baking soda.

The cookies baked with one-quarter teaspoon of leavening were too flat, regardless of whether they used baking powder or baking soda. Curiously, the cookies made with a full teaspoon of baking soda were also flat while those made with a full teaspoon of baking powder rose nicely. After some research, we discovered that this was because a full teaspoon of baking soda was too much leavening; the bubbles of carbon dioxide got too big, ran into each other, floated to the top of the mixture, and then popped, causing the cookie to deflate.

We also noticed that the baking soda cookies were all slightly darker and the outer crust crisper, particularly those baked with the larger amounts of the leavening. This, we discovered, is because baking soda, being alkaline, increases the pH of dough more than baking powder. The reaction causes browning as well as a crispier exterior. This is why professional bakers add baking soda—about one-quarter teaspoon per cup of flour—to cookie dough; it encourages browning. However, in our tests, we found that the baking soda cookies had an unpleasant, quite bitter flavor as opposed to the clean, pure taste of the baking powder cookies.

Finally, we found little difference in either lift or flavor between cookies made with a full teaspoon of baking powder versus a half teaspoon, so we voted for the lesser amount.

So, the answer to this complicated problem turned out be rather simple: Use a half teaspoon of baking powder because it provides substantially better flavor. But because we also wondered why some recipes call for both powder and soda, we decided to try a combination. Perhaps, we reasoned, using a half teaspoon of baking powder along with just one-quarter teaspoon of baking soda would give us browning as well as good flavor. The resulting cookie was very crispy and nicely browned around the edges, but it was also relatively flat, with a slightly bitter aftertaste. Clearly, there was an excess of leavening in this recipe; the additional one-quarter teaspoon of baking soda created too much leftover sodium carbonate in the finished cookie, resulting in a slight collapse of the cookie as well as the aftertaste. So that left us with our original recommendation: Because flavor was our top priority, we decided to go with baking powder.—*C.K.*

BIG CHEWY OATMEAL-RAISIN COOKIES
Makes 16 to 20 large cookies

If you prefer a less sweet cookie, you can reduce the white sugar by one-quarter cup, but you will lose some crispness. Do not overbake these cookies. The edges should be brown but the rest of the cookie should still be very light in color. Parchment makes for easy cookie removal and cleanup, but it's not a necessity. If you don't use parchment, let the cookies cool directly on the baking sheet for two minutes before transferring them to a cooling rack.

- 2 sticks (½ pound) unsalted butter, softened but still firm
- 1 cup light brown sugar
- 1 cup granulated sugar
- 2 eggs
- 1½ cups all-purpose flour
- ½ teaspoon salt
- ½ teaspoon baking powder
- ¼ teaspoon freshly grated nutmeg
- 3 cups rolled oats
- 1½ cups raisins (optional)

1. Adjust oven racks to low and middle positions; heat oven to 350 degrees. In bowl of electric mixer or by hand, beat butter until creamy. Add sugars; beat until fluffy, about 3 minutes. Beat in eggs one at a time.

2. Mix flour, salt, baking powder, and nutmeg together, then stir them into butter-sugar mixture with wooden spoon or large rubber spatula. Stir in oats and optional raisins.

3. Form dough into sixteen to twenty 2-inch balls, placing each dough round onto one of two parchment paper–covered, large cookie sheets. Bake until cookie edges turn golden brown, 22 to 25 minutes. (Halfway during baking, turn cookie sheets from front to back and also switch them from top to bottom.) Slide cookies on parchment onto cooling rack. Let cool at least 30 minutes before serving.

Date Oatmeal Cookies: Substitute 1½ cups chopped dates for the raisins.

Ginger Oatmeal Cookies: Omit raisins and add ¾ teaspoon ground ginger.

Chocolate Chip Oatmeal Cookies: Substitute 1½ cups semisweet chocolate chips for the raisins.

Nut Oatmeal Cookies: Omit raisins, decrease flour to 1⅓ cups, and add ¼ cup ground almonds and 1 cup walnut pieces along with oats. Almonds can be ground in food processor or blender.

Orange and Almond Oatmeal Cookies: Omit raisins and add 2 tablespoons minced orange zest (remove zest with peeler, being careful to leave behind any white pith) and 1 cup toasted chopped almonds (toast almonds in 350-degree oven for 5 minutes) along with oats. ∎

How to Roast a Whole Turkey Breast

For flavorful, juicy meat and rich, crisp skin, brine the breast, loosen its skin, and roast it on high, then moderately low heat.

⤙ BY MELISSA HAMILTON ⤚

My paternal grandfather's favorite meal was a roasted whole turkey. After he died, though, our whole family boycotted the dreadful dry bird at all holidays, including Thanksgiving. But recently I became interested in turkey again. As a freelance catering chef with roasted turkey a popular menu item, I found myself lusting after the smell, only to be disappointed again by the cottony, dry white meat. Is it possible, I wondered, for roast turkey breast to be full-flavored, tender, and moist, with crisp, golden skin, so that it actually tastes as good as it smells?

My preliminary research revealed scores of recipes for roasting a whole turkey. Yet, with turkey parts a relatively new phenomenon, few recipes existed for simply roasting a whole breast. I was pretty much on my own.

As a starting point, I roasted one fresh and one frozen six-pound, whole turkey breast at 325 degrees on a wire rack set in a roasting pan to an internal temperature of 170 degrees. Neither breast was seasoned beforehand or basted while roasting.

Both cooked turkey breasts had a flat, dusty flavor with anemic, rubbery skin. The frozen breast was also stringy, tough, dry, and chewy while the fresh breast held the advantage with moister, more tender flesh. At this point, I decided to abandon frozen in favor of fresh turkey breast. I now set out to produce a breast with flavor I could truly relish.

Searching for Flavor

I am a proponent of brining (soaking in salted water) when it comes to poultry. This process firms up the meat and flavors it internally, producing delicately seasoned, tender, juicy meat. This clearly would be my next move. Familiar with both salt-only and salt-sugar brines, I decided to experiment with each.

I began with two solutions: one with two cups of kosher salt to one and one-half gallons of water and another with two cups each of kosher salt and granulated sugar to one and one-half gallons of water. I soaked one turkey breast in each solution for eight hours in a cool spot. When roasted, both were indeed more tender and juicy than the nonbrined breast, but both were a little too salty. I needed to adjust the brine strength.

I continued with these brining experiments, decreasing strengths and times, ultimately realizing that I preferred the turkeys brined with salt and sugar to the salt-only ones. I finally developed

two solutions. The method I liked best was to brine the breast for five hours in a solution of one and one-half cups each of kosher salt and granulated sugar to one and one-half gallons of water. For cooks who are in a rush, I found that brining for two hours in a double-strength solution was also acceptable. The five-hour brine offered a slightly gentler flavor than the two-hour version, but in each case the meat had a delicately seasoned turkey flavor with room for additional salting at the table and was considerably moister and juicier. Now that good flavor had been established, I began roasting in earnest.

Incidentally, many turkey breasts have already been injected with saline solution. Read the packaging before you make a purchase; better to buy one that has not been injected. If you do, however, skip the brining step and simply follow the roasting instructions in the recipe on page 25.

Internal Temperature, Oven Temperature

From previous experience, I thought the common advice to roast the turkey breast to an internal temperature of 170 degrees was suspect. I was right. Brining had significantly improved both flavor and juiciness, but the meat still had a dry, lean mouth feel. I hoped to remedy this situation by reducing the internal temperature.

I roasted three more turkey breasts in a 325-degree oven, testing internal temperatures of 165

degrees, 160 degrees, and 155 degrees. I initially thought the breast roasted to 155 degrees was ideal, as it was exceedingly moist and juicy and all traces of lean and dry were gone. But as I neared the bone, the meat, although not pink, was too tender, verging on mushy, and the flavor was mildly metallic. I found an internal temperature of 160 degrees perfect to my taste. The meat retained the good qualities of the breast roasted to 155 degrees, was tender with a trace of chew, and was now cooked through.

But I still had a problem. Slow roasting at a constant 325 degrees to an internal temperature of 160 degrees ensured an evenly cooked, tender interior yet did nothing to remedy the pale, rubbery skin. A moderately high oven temperature would most likely deliver a crispier skin but would risk drying out the exterior meat. Achieving both would entail a compromise.

There are many schools of thought when it comes to roasting. Some advocate a constant high heat of 500 degrees throughout the entire roasting period while at the other end of the spectrum are those who believe firmly in slow roasting at 200 degrees. Keeping an open mind, I tried many combinations of high, medium, and low oven temperatures.

The best method turned out to be roasting at an initial 450 degrees for thirty minutes, then reducing the oven temperature to 325 degrees for

But What Kind of Turkey Breast?

When buying a turkey breast, you will often find that you have two different options, which depend on what exactly is included with the breast.

"Regular," or "true cut," is the most readily available style of turkey breast, either fresh or frozen. It is a whole turkey breast, bone-in, with skin and usually with ribs, a portion of wing meat, and a portion of back and neck skin. The best ones are USDA (United States Department of Agriculture) Grade A and are minimally processed. Try to avoid buying those that have been injected with a saline solution, often called "self-basters," as the solution masks the natural flavor of the turkey. Also best avoided are those sold with a "pop-up" timer; it won't pop up at the temperature you want, but it will break the skin and allow juices to escape. If you have no choice, leave the timer in place until the turkey breast is fully roasted and then remove it. This will minimize the skin rupture.

Although this style is excellent carved at the table, it lacks the wings, neck, and giblets that are practically essential for making a good gravy (although these parts can always be bought separately). This style, therefore, is particularly good when gravy isn't called for.

A bit harder to locate, "hotel" or "country-style" turkey breasts usually can be found only fresh, not frozen. Expect to pay a little more (unless they are on sale), given that these turkeys come with the wings, neck, and giblets. It may be a way for the store to make a little more profit on parts they would normally sell for less, but this style presents well at the table, especially with a giblet gravy or pan sauce on the side.—M.H.

Preparing a Turkey Breast for Roasting

1. Cut out the remaining portion of the neck and reserve it for another use.

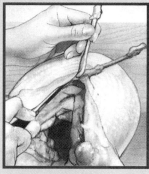

2. Remove the wishbone to facilitate carving.

3. Cut off the extra flap of skin at the neck end, leaving a 1-inch overhang. Cut the flap in half and set it aside.

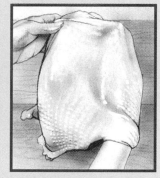

4. Being careful not to tear the delicate membrane around the perimeter of the breast, release the skin on either side of the breastbone to form two pockets.

5. Shove a piece of reserved skin flap under the released skin on either side of the breastbone point.

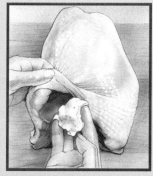

6. Rub seasoned butter under the released skin; brush the breast skin with the remaining melted butter.

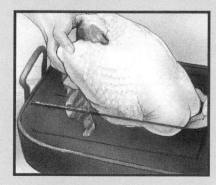

7. Place the prepared turkey, skin side up, on a lightly oiled oven rack set in a roasting pan. Position the breast so that the narrow pointed end sits lower on the rack than the larger neck end.

---

the remaining roasting time. The interior remained tender and moist, and the skin cooked more gently than at 500 degrees, making it less susceptible to burning and easier to control how dark I wanted the skin before lowering the temperature for the final roasting period.

Unfortunately, though, the skin was not browning enough, and it wasn't doing it evenly. I needed to introduce butter.

A Crisping Discovery

I brushed some melted butter on the turkey breast before it went into the 450-degree oven, basted it every fifteen minutes throughout the roasting period, and finished with golden yet limp skin. I tried again, this time brushing the skin with melted butter just once—before it went into the 450-degree oven. Now the skin was evenly golden and slightly crispy. It was at this point that I made an important discovery.

The crispiest part of the skin was where the skin touched no meat, a small section that stretches across the two halves of the breast, where the extra flap of skin from the neck rests. I wondered, if all the skin were released from the meat, might it become even crispier? And what if cold or room temperature butter was rubbed under the "released" skin to give it a little lift and flavor? And while I was at it, how about seasoning the butter with some freshly ground pepper?

Most turkey breasts I purchased came with an excessive flap of skin from the neck that dangled uselessly and remained rubbery and inedible with each roasting. I removed all but one inch of it (*see* illustration 3, left). After carefully lifting up the skin all over the surface of the breast without breaking the thin membrane attached to the meat (illustration 4), I realized the fatty neck skin I had initially removed was perfectly suited for elevating the skin while larding the meat. So I divided it in two and tucked each piece under the released skin all the way toward the front, the narrowest and most exposed part of the breast (illustration 5). I seasoned three tablespoons of butter with black pepper and smoothed it out under the rest of the skin. Hoping to achieve the crispiest skin yet with the most tender interior, I then brushed the skin with one tablespoon of melted butter and proceeded to roast with my preferred method.

Ninety minutes later, I had achieved my goal. The meat trickled juice when sliced, while the texture was firm, yet tender; the flavor was that of delicately seasoned turkey meat while the skin

was both tender and crispy, browned a deep bronze and packed with flavor. At long last, a turkey breast that tasted as good as it smelled.

ROAST BRINED TURKEY BREAST WITH CRISP SKIN
Serves 6 to 8

If you are unable to purchase a turkey breast without a pop-up timer, leave it in place and ignore it. If removed, the timer will leave a gaping hole for juices to escape during roasting. If making an accompanying pan gravy, you may want to throw some carrots, celery, onions, and garlic in the roasting pan and refer to "Make-Ahead Pan Gravy" in our November/December 1996 issue.

- 1½ cups kosher salt
- 1½ cups sugar
- 1 6- to 8-pound fresh, whole, bone-in, skin-on turkey breast, rinsed and prepared according to illustrations 1 and 2, left
- 4 tablespoons unsalted butter, 3 tablespoons at room temperature, 1 tablespoon melted
- ¼ teaspoon ground black pepper
- ½ cup white wine or chicken stock (optional)

1. Mix salt and sugar in 1½ gallons cool water in large clean bucket or stockpot until completely dissolved. Set turkey breast in brine, making sure it is submerged. Cover and refrigerate 5 hours.

2. Twenty minutes before roasting, adjust oven rack to middle position and heat oven to 450 degrees. Mix room-temperature butter with pepper in small bowl. Set aside.

3. Remove turkey breast from brine and pat dry. Following illustrations 3 through 7, left, prepare breast for roasting.

4. Place turkey breast in oven, wide neck end toward oven rear. Pour ½ cup water or optional white wine or stock over pan bottom to prevent drippings from burning. Roast 15 minutes, then rotate roasting pan. Roast until skin turns golden, 15 minutes longer. Reduce oven temperature to 325 degrees; continue to roast breast, rotating pan once, about halfway through cooking until internal temperature in deepest part of breast registers 160 to 165 degrees (depending on preference), 30 to 45 minutes longer.

5. Remove turkey breast from oven. Let stand 20 minutes. Carve and serve. ■

Supermarket Baking Chocolate Takes Top Honors

Nestlé is the clear favorite among unsweetened brands, as experts and nonexperts alike focus on strong, clear chocolate flavor.

~ BY JACK BISHOP ~

Back in 1994, this magazine tested bittersweet and semisweet chocolates to see if there was any relation between price and quality (see "Are Expensive Chocolates Worth the Money?" November/December 1994). We found that specialty brands were clearly better than most supermarket options. The one exception was Nestlé's semisweet, a decent product that held its own against much more expensive brands.

Bittersweet and semisweet chocolates are generally used to make European desserts such as flourless chocolate cakes, truffles, or mousses. However, many American desserts have traditionally been made with unsweetened chocolate. Brownies, frostings, and fudge, for example, start with baking chocolate, also called unsweetened chocolate or chocolate liquor.

Chocolate liquor is simply cocoa beans that have been fermented, roasted, shelled, and then ground into a molten paste and cooled in forms to make bars or squares. Nothing else is added—no sugar or milk. By law, the cocoa butter content can vary from 50 percent to 58 percent. However, the differences between brands are fairly slight.

We Taste Frosting and Brownies

Because it's very difficult to taste baking chocolate as is, we decided to make two different preparations with each brand. We made a simple blender frosting (sugar, boiling water, butter, and chocolate) that chocolate expert Alice Medrich designed especially for our tasting. We also made the basic brownie (no nuts or other additions) that appeared in our March/April 1994 issue (see "Basic Brownies Are Best").

We assembled a group of thirteen bakers, chefs, teachers, and candy makers who work with chocolate daily. The results were astounding. Nestlé took top honors in the brownie tasting (by a wide margin) and finished second among the frostings. It was the clear favorite.

Guittard, Merckens, Ghirardelli, Van Leer, and Baker's finished fairly close together. The surprise here was that Baker's, which had done poorly in the semisweet and bittersweet chocolate tasting, placed relatively well.

Hershey's and Callebaut showed quite poorly. The low ranking of Hershey's may not be much of a surprise, but our panel was shocked at the last-place finish of Callebaut, an expensive Belgian chocolate that many of our professional tasters use at work.

Analyzing the Results

After reading our panelists' comments about each chocolate, I saw several factors that might explain these results. First, as compared to sweetened chocolates, unsweetened brands are actually quite similar in composition. All contain roughly the same amount of cocoa butter. This factor may explain why the range of scores was not terribly wide.

However, our panel did detect some real style differences, especially between the chocolates at the top and bottom of the list. Industry experts tell me that sourcing as well as blending and roasting can affect the final flavor of chocolate liquor. Some companies obviously want a spicier flavor while others are aiming for a more neutral or middle-of-the-road approach.

Our panel of professional tasters favored samples with a strong, clean chocolate flavor. With a high proportion of chocolate and no cooking involved, distinct character traits were easy to detect in the frostings. Chocolates with unusual flavors (especially coconut, cherry, and cinnamon tones) showed poorly in the frosting tasting.

However, when it came time to taste brownies, some of these oddities faded. Such was the case with Baker's, which zoomed from last place among the frostings to fourth among the brownies. Flour, eggs, sugar, and the effects of baking masked many individual peculiarities in chocolate samples. Brownies also require less chocolate than frosting.

Familiarity may also be a factor affecting the results. So many Americans grew up eating brownies made with Baker's that this assertive chocolate in some sense defines brownies. In contrast, several premium chocolates, especially Callebaut, were considered too mild in the brownies.

From my discussions with industry experts, it's clear that many premium manufacturers source and treat their unsweetened chocolate (either by conching, dutching, or water processing) to remove harsh or aggressive notes.

However, our tasters did not like this milder style of chocolate in an all-American brownie. ■

Similar Results from Experts and Lay Testers

For some time we have wondered how our results (based on scores awarded by a panel of food professionals) might stack up against the preferences of the average person on the street. Would the subtle differences that our expert panel deemed so important go undetected by lay tasters?

To answer these questions, we decided to make the same frosting and brownies with the same chocolates and see how nonprofessionals might react. Our standard evaluation forms ask experts to supply their own descriptions of each sample. Because nonexperts have a less developed food vocabulary, we turned to David Fishken, president of Sensory Resources, a consumer-oriented product development firm. His evaluation forms ask a series of questions about sweetness, texture, and aroma, and tasters respond by awarding numerical scores. For tasters, we borrowed twenty staff members from our sister publication Natural Health. Although fairly young, they otherwise represent a good mix of men and women, people who are passionate about chocolate and those who are not. None works with food.

There were some similarities in the results from this second tasting and some surprises. Expert and lay panels both came to the same conclusion about two of the supermarket brands: They both liked Nestlé and disliked Hershey's. There was no consensus on Baker's. It was deemed fine, especially for brownies, by the experts and severely downgraded by the nonexperts in both frosting and brownies. As for the premium brands, the nonexpert panel tended to give them higher ratings.

When looking over the scores awarded by the nonexpert panelists, I found it interesting that they, too, focused on the strength of the chocolate flavor as a key factor. Aroma, texture, and color were not especially important considerations. However, chocolates, like Baker's, that had strong nonchocolate components (e.g., coconuts, cherries, and bitterness) or weak chocolate flavor were downgraded. — J.B.

PHOTOGRAPHS BY DAVE HENDERSON

Eight unsweetened baking chocolates were tasted in a simple frosting as well as a plain brownie by two separate panels, one with food professionals, the other with nonexperts. Our expert panel included Rebecca Alssid, director of the culinary program at Boston University; Ellen Bartlett, owner of Cakes to Remember, a specialty cake business in Brookline, Massachusetts; Michael Ehlenfeldt, chef at Hamersley's Bistro in Boston; David Fishken, president of Sensory Resources, a consumer-oriented product development firm in Newton, Massachusetts; Stephanie Hersh, baker and assistant to Julia Child; Susan Logozzo, pastry instructor at Cambridge School of Culinary Arts in Cambridge, Massachusetts; Judy Rosenberg, cookbook author and owner of Rosie's Bakery, a chain in the Boston area; Lisë Stern, chocolate aficionado and author of The *Boston Food Lover* (Addison Wesley, 1996); Ben Strohecker, owner of Harbor Sweets in Salem; and four members of the *Cook's Illustrated* editorial staff.

The chocolates are listed in order of preference based on their combined score in the frosting and brownie tastings from both our expert and nonexpert panels. Comments come from our expert panelists. Chocolates that scored at the top of both the frosting and brownie tastings are highly recommended, those scoring well in one preparation are recommended, and those landing at the bottom of both tastings are not recommended. The place of origin refers to the location of the corporate headquarters and/or manufacturing plant. Prices are based on supermarket purchases in Boston or on mail-order sources where indicated.

HIGHLY RECOMMENDED CHOCOLATE

Nestlé Unsweetened Baking Chocolate Bars (Glendale, California), four 2-ounce bars in one box for $1.99. This supermarket chocolate was the clear favorite in the brownie tasting and took second place among the frostings. Panelists  thought the frosting made with this chocolate was "less sweet" than the others, with a "very good chocolate flavor." The frosting was especially creamy and "rich-tasting on the tongue." The brownies were "very brownielike" and "especially moist" and "fudgy." Available in supermarkets nationwide.

RECOMMENDED CHOCOLATES

 **Guittard Unsweetened Chocolate** (Burlingame, California), small disks sold for $4 per pound. This specialty chocolate finished fourth among the frostings and second in the brownie tasting. The frosting made with this chocolate was "very mild" or "too light" in flavor and "one-dimensional." Brownies were better received with comments like "very fudgy," "creamy mouth feel," and "familiar." Available by mail from Paradigm Foodworks (5775 S.W. Jean Road, 106A, Lake Oswego, OR 97035; 800-234-0250).

 **Merckens Robin Liquor Chips** (Mansfield, Massachusetts), roughly chopped small chunks sold for $3.75 per pound. This chocolate finished fifth among the frostings and third in the brownie tasting. The texture of the frosting seemed "off" to many tasters, who also objected to the "overpowering" vanilla notes. Other panelists detected fruity flavors (cherry, coconut, and so forth) as well as "an unpleasant aftertaste." In the brownie, many of these characteristics faded. "Very moist," "good chocolate hit," and "tastes like a brownie should" sum up the tasters' reactions. Available by mail from Country Kitchen (3225 Wells Street, Fort Wayne, IN 46808; 219-482-4835).

 **Ghirardelli Unsweetened Chocolate for Baking** (San Leandro, California), 4-ounce bar for $2.39. This "premium" supermarket brand took third place in the frosting tasting but fell to sixth in the brownie tasting. Panelists described the frosting as "very complex" with "full," "ripe," "fruity," or "floral" flavors. "A mature chocolate" that's "not as one-dimensional" as the others. Many of these qualities faded in the brownies. Although the brownies had a few supporters ("moist" and "very nice"), most tasters felt the chocolate flavor was "shallow" or "muted." Available in many supermarkets and gourmet stores and by mail from Paradigm Foodworks.

 **Van Leer CRS Liquor Ribbon** (Jersey City, New Jersey), small chips sold for $5 per pound. Although this chocolate took top honors in the frosting tasting, it finished a disappointing seventh among the brownies. The frosting was described as having "classic chocolate flavor" with "good depth" or as being "more complex than others." The brownie elicited more pointed comments, including "not very chocolaty," "simplistic flavor," and "not fudgy enough." Generally, the brownies were deemed not bad but were not especially noteworthy either. Available by mail from New York Cake (34 West 22nd Street, New York, NY 10010; 212-675-2253).

 **Baker's Unsweetened Baking Chocolate Squares** (White Plains, New York), eight 1-ounce squares in one box for $2.29. This chocolate was the surprise of the tasting. It finished last among the frostings but generated enough support to finish in fourth place in the brownie tasting. The frosting was deemed "artificial-tasting" or "like cough syrup." Others found it "very coffee-ish" and "acrid." Although uniformly disliked in the frosting, this chocolate made a brownie that most deemed good. A few tasters picked up "odd, chemical notes," but most thought the brownies tasted "rich," "full-bodied," "earthy," or "nutty." The same qualities everyone hated in the frosting, most tasters liked (or could not taste) in the brownie. Available in supermarkets nationwide.

CHOCOLATES NOT RECOMMENDED

 **Hershey's All-Natural Unsweetened Baking Chocolate** (Hershey, Pennsylvania), eight 1-ounce squares in one box for $2.29. This popular brand took seventh place in the frosting tasting and fifth among the brownies. The frosting was described as "bitter" and "very cinnamon-y." Most panelists detected something "odd" or "artificial" here. The mouth feel was also off. As for the brownies, panelists thought them "dry" with an odd flavor that "tastes more like cinnamon than chocolate." Available in supermarkets nationwide.

Callebaut Unsweetened Chocolate (Belgium), rough chunks sold for $5.99 per pound. This pricey import is a favorite among professionals but showed poorly, taking sixth place in the frosting tasting and last place among the brownies. The frosting seemed "very sweet" to many tasters, who generally liked the "richer mouth feel" and "more buttery consistency" but complained about "an off aftertaste." The brownies were deemed "too light," "unremarkable," and "not chocolaty enough." Available in gourmet stores and by mail from Sutton Place Gourmet (10323 Old Georgetown Road, Bethesda, MD 20814; 800-346-8763).

Testing Roasting Racks for Poultry

We tried racks that are raked, curved, flat, and tall and found that the basket rack one-upped our previous standard.

∽ BY ADAM RIED WITH EVA KATZ ∽

Perhaps kindness, but more likely hunger, moved a noncooking friend to give me her untouched vertical poultry roaster as a gift just after college. Without even a second thought, I've used that roaster to prepare our weekly Sunday night chickens for years.

Yet in his January/February 1996 *Cook's Illustrated* article "Roasting Chicken 14 Ways," Chris Kimball tested a vertical roaster and found that he preferred his old adjustable V-rack. My results with the vertical roaster had always been adequate, though never carefully scrutinized. Was the V-rack really that much better, I wondered? Was having an adjustable roaster crucial, or could I use a fixed V-rack to good avail? Perhaps we were both barking up the wrong tree, and an entirely different type of rack would improve my roast chicken. Because Chris hadn't tested any racks beyond the vertical and the V, I thought I'd pick up where he left off.

What We Tested, and How

A quick survey of local stores and mail-order catalogs turned up five distinct types of roasting racks, so we tested each kind. They included the following: a flat rack made of stainless steel wire; a stainless steel wire adjustable V-rack; a heavy steel wire, nonstick-coated, nonadjustable V-rack; a U-shaped basket rack (that none of the *Cook's Illustrated* editors had ever seen before) made of nonstick-coated, perforated stainless steel; and a nonstick-coated, medium-gauge, tempered steel wire vertical roaster. We chose this particular vertical roaster, by HealthWorks Products, based on extensive kitchen tests of eight different models (*see* "We're Not High on Vertical Roasters," page 29), including two unusual examples, one made from stoneware and the other from glass. Though the verticals taken as a group left us cold, the HealthWorks, with its own drip pan, eked out the distinction of being the best of the bunch. Last, we considered testing a clay roaster but decided against it because the method differs from the other racks, given that the covered pot shields the food from direct heat.

We tested the various racks by using each to roast three-and-one-half- to four-and-one-half-pound chickens, a very common size in most supermarkets, at an oven temperature of 375 degrees. This kept the playing field even, since all the racks but the vertical can be used for other types of meat as well. In keeping with Chris Kimball's recommendations, we preheated the pan, which he found to be crucial for even roasting, rubbed the skin of

each chicken with two tablespoons of butter and, on all but the vertical rack, rotated the chicken so that each wing side, as well as the breast, faced up during a stage of the cooking. We aimed to cook the breast meat to an internal temperature of 160 degrees and the thigh to between 165 degrees and 170 degrees.

Judging Criteria and Performance

The general challenge in roasting a chicken is to achieve simultaneously tender, moist white breast meat and fully cooked dark thigh and leg meat. This combination is difficult because the breast is exposed directly to the oven heat while the dark meat of the inner thigh, hunkered down into the structure of the bird, is not. Therefore, the outer layers of the breast meat can easily overcook before the inner layers of thigh meat are done.

Whether they do it horizontally or vertically, roasting racks are meant to help this problem by elevating the bird slightly from the floor of the

roasting pan. The air space created between the bird and the pan floor should help even cooking in two ways. First, the space allows hot air to circulate under the chicken, helping to cook it from beneath. Second, heat from the pan itself can radiate up through that air space to hit the bottom of the bird.

Our first and most important testing criterion was whether the white and dark meat were both cooked properly when the bird came out of the oven. In this arena, all of the racks did a fine job. Dark meat is, by nature, a little moister and richer than white and therefore more forgiving in roasting. As long as the meat is cooked all the way to the bone, flavor and texture will almost always be fine. Textural differences in the more delicate white meat cooked on each rack were also very subtle. We did notice a tendency for the outer layers of the flat rack–cooked white meat to be slightly chewier than the others, but not to an unacceptable degree.

BEST ROASTER:

Basket Rack: This rack proved stable and solid; it browned and crisped the skin more thoroughly than the others, and its U-shape cradled the chickens snug, keeping wings and legs in good position and making them easy to turn. Finished chickens had a neat and compact appearance overall, better than any in the testing. This rack's small size, however, was a limitation. It just barely accommodated a big seven-pound roasting chicken, but it won't fit anything larger, such as geese or small turkeys. See Sources and Resources, page 32, for availability.

Nonadjustable V-Rack: A solid rack that stayed put when we moved the chicken. Like its adjustable counterpart, the chicken wings and legs had a tendency to slip through the wires, which could then leave them dangling and make it difficult to turn the bird.

Adjustable V-Rack: Made from thin wire; seemed flimsy overall. The wings and legs of the chicken could slip through the wires and stick, which made it difficult to turn the bird and even risked collapsing the lightweight rack altogether. It did, however, adjust to seven different positions, giving you more choice and control in roasting small and large poultry. And it's cheap.

Flat Rack: Tended to overcook the outer layers of breast meat. Rotating proved difficult because the bird sits on its wing sides without support, so it could roll over easily if not propped up with balls of foil or vegetables. The finished bird could look misshapen.

Vertical Poultry Roaster with Drip Pan: Less versatile than the others because it is limited to poultry only. On the plus side, though, the chicken tended to cook approximately ten minutes faster than it did on the other racks, and this rack was a breeze to use. The chicken meat was fine, the skin uneven.

We're Not High on Vertical Roasters

The original concept for this story was to evaluate vertical roasters exclusively, but we had to scrap that notion after full testing of eight different models. Though we did determine that both the HealthWorks (bottom right), included in the larger rack testing, and the similarly designed Spanek roaster (second from top right in photo below) slightly outperformed the others, none of the verticals, including these two, truly impressed us. Certainly not enough to recommend them to our readers.

Most of the verticals did an OK job of cooking the meat evenly. The skin, however, was a different story. Consistently, the skin of vertically roasted chickens was dark brown and crisp on the top, but yellow and rubbery on the bottom. Because vertical roaster design and construction varies widely, we found that the primary reason for this failing was that most of the verticals were either too short (less than seven inches tall) or too flimsy to elevate the birds fully off the floor of the roasting pan. Birds on these roasters sat so far down that they bunched up on the pan, which defeats the purpose of vertical roasting because the juices and fat accumulate between the skin and the meat at the bottom of the chicken, rather than draining off. Certainly the meat surrounded by those juices stays moist, but this accomplishes very little by way of rendering the fat from the bird, a popular packaging claim.

At roughly eight inches in height, the HealthWorks and the Spanek both performed slightly better than the rest of the vertical pack because they were tall and wide enough to keep the chicken off the pan.— A.R. & E.K.

Now, I have to admit to being a skin freak. It may not be tremendously healthy, but a crisp, browned skin looks great and packs a lot of flavor. So criterion number two became skin cooked well and evenly over the entire bird. The only rack that really disappointed in this area was the vertical, which produced skin that was pleasingly crisp and brown on top of the bird, but unfailingly yellow and rubbery on the bottom. By comparison, the skin of chickens roasted in a horizontal position was much crisper, darker, and more evenly colored.

It was the basket rack, though, that really excelled in this arena, producing the best skin of all. To help explain why, our food science consultant Shirley Corriher simplified oven cooking into three basic dynamics of heat transfer: convection, which is the movement of hot air itself; radiation, which is the heat energy carried through the air; and conduction, which is when a hot surface transfers heat to the adjacent surface. The basket rack is especially successful at conduction because it has more surface area than the wire racks. This rack is made out of a stainless steel sheet from which drainage holes have been punched. The metal sheet absorbs the oven heat (with the help of its black, nonstick coating), which it conducts onto the skin of the chicken wherever it touches the metal. Because there is greater contact between the metal sheet and the chicken skin than there is with the wires of the other horizontal racks—not to mention the vertical rack, on which the chicken skin has no contact with any metal—the basket roaster conducts heat better. The downside of the basket rack's design is that it does not allow as much drainage of rendered fat as the wire racks. In our minds, though, the superior skin more than compensates for this flaw. We should mention that to obtain reasonably even skin coloration using any of the racks but the vertical, you must open the oven and turn the chicken twice.

Whether it was easy to change the chicken's position on the rack as it cooked was another important evaluation point for all but the vertical roaster. Turning on the basket roaster was a breeze because the chicken could simply slide around without any lifting. On both V-racks, the wings and legs had a tendency to fall between the wires and catch when you lift the bird. The nonadjustable V-rack was heavy enough to stay put during the turning of the bird, but the lighter adjustable V-rack would lift right off the roasting pan, sometimes losing its adjustment in the process. On the flat rack, chickens had a tendency to topple over when the rack was pushed back into the oven to shut the door.

In addition to our official evaluation criteria, we watched carefully to see if one rack made more of a mess in the oven from splattering fat than another. The reality is that hot chicken fat will splatter somewhat, especially as it drips onto a hot, essentially dry pan. With all the racks, the liquid fat and juices in the pan were such that splattering could not be prevented altogether. We did find that adding about a one-quarter-inch layer of water to the roasting pan limited splattering. But the tradeoff was the crisp, brown skin. The water vaporized in the hot oven, creating a moist-heat environment that hindered skin crispness, leaving it yellow and rubbery. The water was also bad news if you wanted caramelized drippings in the roasting pan to make a quick pan sauce. ■

Tasting Burgundies

Reasonably priced, good-quality Burgundies turn out to be less rare than we thought.

~ BY MARK BITTMAN ~

Not surprisingly, I have not had many great Burgundies, but I have searched for decent, inexpensive ones. Like many wine drinkers with some experience, I find the pinot noir grape (the only one used in a top red Burgundy) to be enormously appealing, indeed, like the smell of great cooking. Buying relatively inexpensive Burgundies, however, has always been a tiresome task, filled with disappointments.

So I was hardly shocked when we set out to find a flock of under-$20 Burgundies and immediately ran into a stone wall. We were looking not just for pinot noir wines, which are made all over the world and are quite plentiful, but for true Burgundies, wines that offered more than good fruit, but some distinction as well—the *goût de terroir* ("taste of the earth") for which Burgundy is famous.

There are plenty of such wines as it turns out. But the very nature of Burgundy means that the production of these inexpensive wines is almost as limited as that of top wines. Burgundy is dotted with tiny vineyards, and most of these are still owned by farmers, rather than by producers or, as in Bordeaux, by châteaus. Go to Burgundy, and you might well find dozens of relatively inexpensive wines, but none in any large quantity.

Here, there's a typical scenario in the States: You find a splendid $15 Burgundy, but the store owner can't sell you a case—he just doesn't have it. The distributor, who had maybe six cases to begin with, is sold out. One state over, no one may have seen the wine at all. This is all because "small" Burgundies are shipped to the United States in lots of a couple of hundred cases, an amount that means that distribution is not only limited, but allocated.

Fortunately, there are some nationally distributed, widely available Burgundies (their numbers are small compared to those of other wines, but at least you can find them). For the most part, these are the blended wines of well-known producers—and our list was dominated by them—with a few smallish wines thrown in. Happily, the wines showed well. Even more happily, the two top wines, which showed brilliantly, are widely available.

There are a couple of reasons these wines were good: One, the 1993 vintage, which dominated the tasting (we substituted only when a wine we felt must be included could not be found in the '93 vintage), was a good one. Some critics have written that the wines were too acidic, but there was little evidence of that here.

In addition, it's clear that real Burgundies, even lesser ones, have real character. Although some wines showed much better than others, there was not a single wine that did not have its adherents. At worst they were short in fruit, but this is not uncommon even in well-made Burgundies. Burgundy is, after all, the world's northernmost district for great red wines, and the fruit almost never achieves perfect ripeness. (This is one of the great mysteries of winemaking; the best wines are produced where the vines are stressed almost to their limit.) Even those wines, however, had more character than your run-of-the-mill $15 merlot.

It's worth singling out two wines in addition to the winners. Neither of the least expensive wines—the Drouhin ("Laforet") and Rodet Bourgogne—were aged in wood at all. These are crowd-pleasing wines made for quick consumption. Surprisingly, however, both did very well, and not just with our amateur tasters; one of our professionals chose the Drouhin as his first-place wine.

Pinot noir is difficult to grow, and Burgundy is difficult to make. But this tasting demonstrated that, with a little guidance, it is not as difficult to buy as I once thought. ∎

RATING THE WINES

The wines in our tasting, held at Mt. Carmel Wine and Spirits, in Hamden, Connecticut, were judged by a panel made up of both wine professionals and amateur wine lovers. Comments below reflect the respective opinions of these two groups. In the judging, seven points were awarded for each first-place vote, six for second, five for third, and so on. The wines were all purchased in the Northeast; prices will vary considerably throughout the country.

Within each category, wines are listed based on the number of points scored. In this tasting, Highly Recommended wines received what amounted to rave reviews. Recommended wines had predominantly positive comments. The wines in the Recommended with Reservations category had low quantitative scores but were still enjoyed by several tasters.

HIGHLY RECOMMENDED

1993 Latour Savigny-les-Beaune, $16. Savigny-les-Beaune has long been a favorite of bargain hunters (and rightly so), and Latour is a great producer. The combination is a wine that was ranked in the top five by all tasters. Amateur: "Delicious, smooth, and very fruity." Pro: "Just a bit lean, but almost great"—real praise for a $16 Burgundy.

1993 Drouhin Ladoix, $19. Ladoix, until recently sold as Côte-de-Beaune-Villages, is a new appellation, and one to look for. Amateur: "Soft, easy to drink, but somehow 'significant.'" Pro: "Complex, loads of round, ripe fruit, great balance."

RECOMMENDED

1993 Arnoux Bourgogne, $18. A serious, but perhaps slightly disappointing wine from a great producer. Amateur: "Really nice, balanced, and rich." Pro: "A serious wine, more weight and class than most, but still short on finish."

1994 Drouhin Bourgogne "Laforet," $11. Ranked first by two—one amateur, one pro—each of whom found it "well made, nicely balanced, a wine with a future." But others, both amateurs and pros, found it a "lightweight." At this price, definitely worth a shot.

1993 Rodet Château de Chamirey Mercurey, $17. The pro who loved it: "Intense, great balance." The pro who didn't: "Not wine enough for this tasting." The general amateur opinion: "Very dry and quite thin."

RECOMMENDED WITH RESERVATIONS

1993 Drouhin Côte-de-Beaune-Villages, $17. Some saw all tannins here; some found fruit. Amateur: "All tannins, no fruit." Pro who liked it: "Intense tannins, acid, and fruit." Pro who didn't: "Thin and unattractive."

1992 Clerget Volnay, $20. The nose, described variously as "greasy," "inky," and "soapy," put off many tasters, but the flavor overcame that for one or two tasters, both pros: "Odd nose, but quite pleasant, with good fruit and finish."

1994 Rodet Bourgogne, $10. Generally considered "light" and "one-dimensional," this was ranked third by one pro: "Rich, full-flavored, and nice, peppery quality." A wine that is not aged in wood.

1993 Faiveley Mercurey "La Framboisière," $20. Decent wine that is probably better than its showing indicated. Amateur: "Thin and acidic." Pro: "Light wine, but at least in balance."

1993 Angerville Bourgogne, $18. Most found this wine "neutral," but one pro saw "intense, tight fruit" and a good future for it.

1990 Leroy Bourgogne, $18. Amateur: "Coarse." Pro: "Might be a good food wine."

1993 Bouchard Côte-de-Beaune-Villages, $13. "Very light," but "lots of life."

1993 Latour Côte-de-Beaune-Villages, $12. "Not much here," but "decent balance."

1993 Jadot Côte-de-Beaune-Villages, $19. "Short on the finish," but "pretty fruit."

Book Reviews

Sunset Series: Casual Cuisines of the World
Various authors
Sunset Publishing, $19.95 each

This series of "casual cuisine" books intrigued us with its premise. This is a kind of culinary Cliff Notes, a quick hit-and-run approach for cooks who do not wish to work their way through the classic cookbooks on a particular national cuisine. Like a whirlwind packaged tour, one expects to experience a great deal in a short amount of time. The question is, Are we truly plumbing the essence of the food, or are we, like tourists, catching a quick glimpse of say, the Amalfi coast, as our tour bus negotiates the next curve?

After weeks of testing, we found that the results were uneven. *Taverna* (Mediterranean cooking), by Joyce Goldstein, was a big hit. All but one of the recipes we tested were excellent. To start with the downside, a recipe for Braised Pork with Quinces was good, but not stellar and required a whopping five hours in the kitchen. The Garlic Shrimp, on the other hand, was easy and fabulous, Sautéed Mushrooms with Garlic was quick and delicious, and the Grilled Eggplant Salad is now the standard by which one of our editors will judge other such recipes.

Cantina, by Susan Feniger and Mary Sue Milliken, was similarly well received. Every recipe tested, from Jicama and Blood Orange Salad to Grilled Shrimp with Mango Salsa to Pork Stew with Green Chilies, was simple to prepare and delivered the clear, strong flavors of good Mexican cooking.

Joyce Jue's *Far East Cafe*, on the other hand, while still pleasing, was less successful. A Red Curry Mussels over Noodles was a winner as was a Grilled Beef, Tomato, and Mint Salad. Mangoes with Sticky Rice, on the other hand, produced very dry rice, and the cooking time was off; a Crispy Vegetable-Stuffed Crêpe, was labor-intensive and not for beginners, a fault in a book designated as "The Best of Casual Asian Cooking"; and Sour Fish Soup was too bland for our tester, lacking heat, acidity, and salt.

Trattoria (Italian cooking) by Mary Beth Clark, was also a mixed bag. To the book's credit, the food is authentic, not watered down for culinary tourists. However, much of it was not all that well suited to home cooking. The appetizers were mostly enjoyable, for example, but were neither quick nor easy, while five of the eight pasta dishes required making pasta from scratch. A roast lamb dish was a disaster in terms of cooking time; the author calls for cooking it an hour and a half, yet after only forty minutes, the lamb was already overcooked.

Oven-Roasted Potatoes with Rosemary and Garlic on the other hand, introduced us to a new culinary trick and was a big hit, and Almond Biscotti was delicious.

The two remaining volumes, Diane Rossen Worthington's *Diner* (American cooking) and *Bistro* (French cooking) by Gerald Hirigoyen, were both competent in execution, but somewhat unexciting, perhaps because they include many recipes that are already familiar to almost every American cook. *Diner*'s Fudge Brownies, Baked Beans, and Seafood Louis were good, and the Fried Chicken excellent. The Mile-High Chocolate Layer Cake was on the dry side, however, saved only by the moist frosting. *Bistro* offered a roast chicken that was supposed to be stuffed with a whole cut-up baguette, a process akin to trying to park a stretch limo in a small, one-car garage. The Sautéed Shrimp with Fried Garlic and Baked Tomato was delicious, though, and the steak, with red wine shallot butter, was fine.

After our testing, we felt a bit like travel-weary tourists back home, feet up, comparing notes on the trip. The food was generally good, the recipes authentic, the execution mixed (every tour bus has at least one flat tire), and we missed staying in one place long enough to really get a deep sense of place and culture. But if you are inclined to take such a tour, these folks do a good job of introducing you to the unfamiliar. Pick your destination carefully, though, be prepared for recipes requiring varying degrees of culinary skill, and take the occasional traffic jam or breakdown in stride.

The Dean & DeLuca Cookbook
David Rosengarten with Joel Dean
  and Giorgio DeLuca
Random House, $24

To claim that the retail operation Dean & Deluca has been an important part of the culinary revolution in America over the last twenty years is certainly fair. It has helped transform the retailing of victuals in this country from the dark days of frozen foods and shrink-wrapped vegetables to the present, in which the quality of foodstuffs, even in small-town America, has been dramatically improved. We owe both founders a debt of gratitude for standing at the barricades, helping to prod and incite this American culinary transformation along its tasteful way. But the introduction to *The Dean & Deluca Cookbook* ups the ante considerably, rhetorically asking, "Is anyone in a better position to document the food that Americans have come to love over the last twenty years?" The leap of faith is clear. Because they were indubitably instrumental in the development of fine food retailing, D & D now lay claim to authorship of the one book that best captures for the home cook the tastes and textures of the last twenty years of culinary eclecticism. Is this a fair claim, we wondered, or should it bring to mind Michael Jordan, baseball glove in hand, setting out to conquer new worlds?

After testing over a dozen recipes, we came to the conclusion that these folks are better retailers than cookbook writers. This is not to say that one cannot find some top-notch, quick and easy recipes in their book. I made a Fresh Tomato with Fresh Ginger Sauce for pasta that was outstanding. A Pugliese Beet Salad with Fresh Mint was also terrific as was Brined Pork Chops. Three other recipes—Cuban Black Bean Soup with Sherried Onions, Fagioli al Fiasco (seasoned white beans), and Spinach-Stuffed Chicken Breasts with Cognac and Tarragon—produced very good results with only minor quibbles about recipe directions.

Other recipes tested, however, suffered from a variety of problems, the most common of which was underseasoning. A Couscous Tabouli with Raisins didn't even include salt and used only one small clove of garlic for three cups of couscous, while Steamed Fish Fillets with Delicate Vegetables had little flavor. Other recipes called for steps that were truly unnecessary, such as an elaborate peeling and slicing process for eggplant, followed by simmering and then grilling. We would have been happy to just cut it up and throw it on the grill. I finished my testing with a Mexican Rice Salad with Mussels that was bland and a bit contrived, a shortfall shared by quite a few of the recipes tested.

The best cookbooks are written by individuals with lots of hands-on experience, a lifelong commitment to a style of cooking, and a strong, informed point of view. One thinks of Marcella Hazan, Jacques Pépin, Julia Child, James Beard, Richard Olney or, more recently, Paula Wolfert, Barbara Tropp, Richard Sax, Alice Waters, or Marion Cunningham. I may disagree with some of their methods, ingredients, or even techniques, but these are pros, people who draw you into their world with a depth of knowledge and experience that makes a style of cooking accessible to the home cook while breathing life into the simple preparation of foodstuffs. *The Dean & Deluca Cookbook* feels, by contrast, more like a corporate report than an offering from an inspired cook. This book has its successes, but unlike Michael Jordan, its uneven performance lacks the pathos of an individual's struggle for excellence. Even in defeat, Jordan inspired us with his effort. Here, we don't know who we are rooting for, and when the recipes fall short, the voice of the author is not there to see us through. ■

—*Christopher Kimball*

Sources and Resources

Most of the ingredients and materials necessary for the recipes in this issue are available at your local supermarket, gourmet store, or kitchen supply shop. The following are mail-order sources for particular items. Prices listed below were current at press time and do not include shipping or handling unless otherwise indicated. We suggest that you contact companies directly to confirm up-to-date prices and availability.

BASKET ROASTING RACK

A piece of equipment new to all of the *Cook's Illustrated* editors, the basket rack that won our testing of poultry roasting racks on page 28 is manufactured by Amco Houseworks exclusively for Williams-Sonoma. The rack is currently available for $19.00 through the Williams-Sonoma Catalog (800-541-2233) only, and not in the Williams-Sonoma stores.

CURRY SPICES AND INGREDIENTS

Carefully prepared spices and herbs are the soul of the curry recipes on page 9. These spices should be easy to find locally, but it may be convenient to mail-order the whole lot, including cinnamon stick, whole peppercorns, whole cloves, bay leaves, ground cumin, ground coriander, and ground turmeric, from Adriana's Caravan (409 Vanderbilt Street, Brooklyn, NY 11218; 800-316-0820 or 718-436-8565). Adriana's can also provide less common ingredients such as green cardamom pods ($6.50 for two ounces) and fenugreek seed ($2 for two ounces) and leaves ($3 for two ounces), the Indian split peas known as channa dal ($1.95 per pound), and dried figs ($4.95 to $6.95 per pound depending on the variety in stock, with a one-pound minimum order) for several of the curry variations. Also available is high-quality basmati rice ($3.25 per pound), the traditional fragrant accompaniment for curry (*see* page 10).

MINICHOPPER

Like author Stephanie Lyness, you can considerably ease your groundwork for making curry by using a minichopper to produce the wet spice puree of garlic and ginger. She chose the Cuisinart Mini-Mate Plus Chopper/Grinder, Model MM-2M, which features a nine-ounce bowl, a reversible blade, and two speeds. The suggested retail price for the Mini-Mate is $40, but through the end of February 1997, A Cook's Wares (211 37th Street, Beaver Falls, PA 15010-2103; 412-846-9490) will carry it at a sale price of $24.90.

COMMON CRACKERS

Crumbled common crackers make an ideal topping for the Stovetop Macaroni and Cheese recipe on page 21. Generally attributed to the State of Vermont, common crackers are small, plain, puffed biscuits that were traditionally eaten split open, buttered, and broiled until crisp. These crackers are available by mail order in both plain and cheddar cheese flavors, as well as salt-free, from The Vermont Country Store (Mail Order Office, P.O. Box 3000, Manchester Center, VT 05255-3000; 802-362-2400). The crackers are packed in either sixteen-ounce decorative tins ($9.95 for the plain and $10.95 for the cheese-flavored) or refill bags ($3.90 for the plain and $5.25 for the cheese-flavored).

WHOLE WHEAT GRAHAM FLOUR

We went wild for the flavor and texture of Hodgson Mill Whole Wheat Graham Flour in our recipe for Whole Wheat Bread with Wheat Germ and Rye on page 14. Though this flour benefits from excellent national distribution, we learned that its availability may be limited in several western states. Not to worry, though, because Hodgson Mill has a mail-order program for all of its products, including the graham flour, which costs $3 per five-pound bag or $16 for a case of six five-pound bags. For more information or to order, contact Hodgson Mill, Inc. (1901 South 4th Street, Suite 26, Effingham, IL 62401; 800-525-0177 or 217-347-0105).

MUSHROOMS: DRIED AND FRESH

You learned in the story on page 15 that good dried porcini have a deep, earthy aroma and come in large pieces. Aux Delices Des Bois (14 Leonard Street, New York, NY 10013; 800-666-1232 or 212-334-1230), a New York City shop that specializes in both dried and fresh mushrooms, offers some of the best dried porcini we have encountered, at a cost of $4 per ounce. Among the other varieties of dried mushrooms that are available are cèpes, morels, chanterelles, black trumpets, and mousserons. There are also more than a dozen types of fresh mushrooms, of which some come only during their season (May through June and October through December for fresh porcini), while others (shiitake, portobello, and white trumpet) are available all year. Call Aux Delices Des Bois for a catalog and information on pricing and specific product availability.

SORGHUM

We've had calls from a number of readers inquiring about the sorghum called for in the Sorghum-Glazed Baked Country Ham recipe from the November/December 1996 issue. While the sorghum plant itself is a cereal grass with broad leaves and tall stalks topped by large grain clusters, the product to which we refer in our recipe is the juice that has been extracted from the stalk and boiled down to a thick, syrupy consistency. Also called sorghum molasses or sorghum syrup, sorghum is produced generally in the southeastern states in early autumn. The quantity made and the rate at which it is sold vary from producer to producer, so we cannot guarantee its availability throughout the winter. Nonetheless, a good source is Townsend's Sorghum Mill (11620 Main Street, Jeffersonville, KY 40337; 606-498-4142). Townsend's sells sorghum in containers of one-half pint for $3, one pint for $4, one quart for $6, and one and one-half quarts for $9, all plus shipping. ∎

UNITED STATES POSTAL SERVICE — Statement of Ownership, Management, and Circulation (Required by 39 U.S.C.)

Publication Title: Cooks Illustrated
Publication No.: 012-487
Filing Date: 10/10/96
Issue Frequency: bi-monthly
No. of Issues Published Annually: 6
Annual Subscription Price: $24.95

Complete Mailing Address of Known Office of Publication: 17 Station St., Brookline Village, MA 02147

Complete Mailing Address of Headquarters or General Business Office of Publisher: same as above

Full Names and Complete Mailing Addresses of Publisher, Editor, and Managing Editor:
Publisher: Christopher P. Kimball, 17 Station St., Brookline Village, MA 02147
Editor: Christopher P. Kimball, 17 Station St., Brookline Village, MA 02147
Managing Editor: Keith Powers, 17 Station St., Brookline Village, MA 02147

Owner: Boston Common Press Limited Partnership, 500 Boylston St., #1880 Boston, MA 02116
(Christopher P. Kimball)

Known Bondholders, Mortgagees, and Other Security Holders: None

Publication Name: Cooks Illustrated
Issue Date for Circulation Data Below: Nov/Dec '96

Extent and Nature of Circulation	Average No. Copies Each Issue During Preceding 12 Months	Actual No. Copies of Single Issue Published Nearest to Filing
a. Total No. Copies (Net Press Run)	310,918	354,928
b. Paid and/or Requested Circulation		
(1) Sales Through Dealers and Carriers, Street Vendors, and Counter Sales	42,702	48,630
(2) Paid or Requested Mail Subscriptions	192,425	213,253
c. Total Paid and/or Requested Circulation	235,127	261,883
d. Free Distribution by Mail (Samples, Complimentary, and Other Free)	3,220	3,220
e. Free Distribution Outside the Mail (Carriers or Other Means)	160	175
f. Total Free Distribution	3,380	3,395
g. Total Distribution	238,507	265,278
h. Copies Not Distributed (1) Office Use, Leftovers, Spoiled	39,095	52,300
(2) Return from News Agents	33,317	37,350
i. Total	310,918	354,928
Percent Paid and/or Requested Circulation	98.6%	98.7%

This Statement of Ownership will be printed in the February '97 issue of this publication.

Signature and Title of Editor, Publisher, Business Manager, or Owner [signature] President — Date 10/5/96

RECIPE INDEX

ASSORTED MUFFINS
page 19

STOVETOP MACARONI AND CHEESE
page 21

SHRIMP CURRY WITH YOGURT AND PEAS
page 9

PORCINI MUSHROOM SAUCE WITH CREAM
page 15

ROAST BRINED TURKEY BREAST WITH CRISP SKIN
page 25

DATE OATMEAL COOKIES
page 23

PHOTOGRAPHS BY DAVE HENDERSON; TURKEY BREAST PHOTOGRAPH BY ALISON MIKSCH; STYLING BY MELISSA HAMILTON

CREAM-FILLED APRICOTS

Rehydrate ½ pound (1¼ cups) dried whole apricots in water to cover, about 4 hours or overnight; drain. Simmer 1½ cups sugar and 2 cups water until thickened slightly, about 10 minutes. Add apricots; simmer until tender, about 20 minutes. Stir in 2 teaspoons lemon juice; simmer 1 minute longer. Remove apricots with slotted spoon; cool to room temperature.

Continue to simmer liquid to syrup consistency, 5 to 10 minutes. Pipe or spoon portion of 8 ounces softened cream cheese or mascarpone cheese into the opening of each apricot. Arrange on serving platter, drizzle with 2 to 3 tablespoons of the syrup, and refrigerate until syrup sets, about 30 minutes. Sprinkle with ½ cup chopped unsalted pistachios and serve. *Serves 10 to 12*

COOK'S
ILLUSTRATED

Rating Electric Knife Sharpeners

Do They Really Work? We
Test Six Models to Find Out

Key Lime Pie Made Easy

Three Simple Ingredients
Yield Intense Lime Flavor

All-New Chicken and Dumplings

Classic Flavor, Updated
Technique

Tasting Canned Crushed Tomatoes

Italian Brands Finish
Dead Last

BUTTERMILK DOUGHNUTS

CREPE COOKING LESSON

TENDER SPINACH SALADS

NEW ENGLAND BOILED DINNER

IRISH SODA BREAD

$4.00 U.S./$4.95 CANADA

Contents

MARCH/APRIL 1997

NUMBER TWENTY-FIVE

About *Cook's Illustrated*

Cook's Illustrated *is published every other month (6 issues per year) and accepts no advertising. A one year subscription is $24.95, two years is $45, and three years is $65. Add $6 per year for Canadian subscriptions and $12 per year for all other countries. Gift subscriptions may be ordered for $19.95 each. You will receive a* Cook's Illustrated *gift card for each subscription which can be used to announce your gifts. The editors of Cook's Illustrated also publish an annual hardbound edition of the magazine which includes an annual index. These are available for $21.95 each plus shipping and handling. Discounts are available if more than one year is ordered at a time.*

Cook's Illustrated *also publishes two single topic books,* How To Make A Pie *and* How To Make An American Layer Cake. *Both are available for $14.95 each. The* Cook's Bible, *authored by our editor and published by Little Brown, is also available for $24.95. Back issues are available for $5 each. We also accept submissions for both Quick Tips and Notes From Readers. See page 5 for more information.*

All queries about subscriptions or change of address notices should be addressed to Cook's Illustrated, P.O. Box 7445, Red Oak, IA 51591-0445. *A free trial issue of our sister publication,* Handcraft Illustrated, *may be requested by calling 800-526-8447.*

To order either subscriptions or books use the cards bound into this issue or, for faster service, call 800-526-8442 for subscriptions and 800-611-0759 for books and annuals.

"Spring Greens"
Illustration by
Brent Watkinson

"Pickled Grape Relish with Ginger and Chiles,"
adapted from *Salsas, Sambals, Chutneys, and Chowchows* (Morrow, 1993) by Chris Schlesinger and John Willoughby
Illustration by Rene Milot

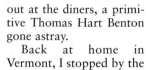

Publisher and Editor	Christopher Kimball
Executive Editor	Pam Anderson
Senior Editor	John Willoughby
Senior Writer	Jack Bishop
Associate Editor	Adam Ried
Contributing Editors	Mark Bittman Stephanie Lyness
Test Kitchen Director	Eva Katz
Test Cook	Dawn Yanagihara
Assistant Editor	Maryellen Driscoll
Editorial Assistant	Elizabeth Cameron
Art Director	Cathy Copeland
Food Stylist	Marie Piraino
Special Projects Manager	Amy Klee
Assistant to the Publisher	Jennifer Salomon
Managing Editor	Keith Powers
Editorial Prod. Manager	Sheila Datz
Copy Editor	Gary Pfitzer
Marketing Director	Adrienne Kimball
Circulation Manager	David Mack
Fulfillment Manager	Larisa Greiner
Newsstand Manager	Jonathan Venier
Marketing Assistant	Connie Forbes
Vice President Production and Technology	James McCormack
Systems Administrator	Paul Mulvaney
Production Artist	Kevin Moeller
Editorial Production Assistants	Robert Parsons Daniel Frey
Controller	Lisa A. Carullo
Accounting Assistant	Mandy Shito
Office Manager	Tonya Estey
Special Projects	Fern Berman

Cook's Illustrated (ISSN 1068-2821) is published bimonthly by Boston Common Press Limited Partnership, 17 Station Street, P.O. Box 569, Brookline, MA 02147-0569. Copyright 1997 Boston Common Press Limited Partnership. Periodical postage paid at Boston, MA, and additional mailing offices. USPS #012487. For list rental information, please contact List Services Corporation, 6 Trowbridge Drive, P.O. Box 516, Bethel, CT 06801; (203) 743-2600, FAX (203) 743-0589. Editorial office: 17 Station Street, P.O. Box 569, Brookline, MA 02147-0569; (617) 232-1000, FAX (617) 232-1572. Editorial contributions should be sent to: Editor, Cook's Illustrated. We cannot assume responsibility for manuscripts submitted to us. Submissions will be returned only if accompanied by a large self-addressed stamped envelope. Subscription rates: $24.95 for one year; $45 for two years; $65 for three years. (Canada add $6 per year; all other countries: add $12 per year.) Postmaster: Send all new orders, subscription inquiries, and change of address notices to Cook's Illustrated, P.O. Box 7446, Red Oak, IA 51591-0446. Single copies: $4 in U.S., $4.95 in Canada and other countries. Back issues available for $5 each. PRINTED IN THE U.S.A.

EDITORIAL

Fast Food

Christopher Kimball

On a recent visit to Cleveland, I found myself at Ruthie & Moe's, a diner out at 40th and Prospect. In fact, it was two diners: one a Mahoney '38, built in 1939 by the Jerry O. Mahoney Company, and the other a '56 Kuhlman that the owners found in West Chester, Pennsylvania. The Mahoney was out front, a shiny aluminum railway car with black Formica tabletops and black vinyl seating. The Kuhlman, stuck on the back, was a temple of green plastic, the roadhouse equivalent of an indoor patio at a fancy Manhattan restaurant.

I sat at the counter, spread out the Cleveland Plain Dealer, and ordered up the special: meat loaf with mashed potatoes, gravy, and a side of applesauce. While I was waiting, I noticed a few eccentric touches: an Atomic Café postcard, a sign that read "Try Our FABULOUS Shakes," and a '50s-style illustration of a cheese sandwich, a chocolate milk shake, and a pickle. But any concerns that this was merely an exercise in soulless nostalgia quickly faded when I tucked into the two thick slices of perfectly cooked, bacon-wrapped meat loaf. This was followed by a homemade dish of peach-apple cobbler topped with pie crust, a rich, juicy plate of intense fruit and flavor. I then struck up a conversation with a middle-aged, ponytailed waiter who soon revealed that he was indeed Moe and that his wife Ruthie did the cooking. We were soon off on a personal guided tour of his city, windows rolled down on his old pickup, Moe the quintessential tour leader, enthusiastic and knowledgeable.

Soon after my visit to Cleveland, I found myself in Kansas City, at Gates' Barbecue. When I walked in, the girl behind the cash register shouted out enthusiastically like a drill sergeant, "May I help you, sir?"—a startling wake-up call that this wasn't any old fast-food joint. I ordered the combo platter, a Fred Flintstone plate of ham, brisket, and short ribs served with a stack of white bread and plenty of homemade fries, plus a tall glass of strawberry soda, a shocking cooler of tangerine-colored high-test. The brisket was moist and tender, even better than Texas chopped brisket, and the sauce was perfect: not too sweet with a hint of spice. But the clincher was the full-length wall mural in the dining room, a despondent cow and pig looking mournfully

out at the diners, a primitive Thomas Hart Benton gone astray.

Back at home in Vermont, I stopped by the State Line Diner for Sunday lunch with my oldest daughter Whitney. It's not much of an establishment, just a double-wide set near the state line with a large Pepsi sign out front and old-fashioned sleigh bells on the front door. The plastic-sheathed menu was peppered with small ads for Day's Small Engine Repair, Downey's Rubbish Removal, Ushak's Supermarket, and Peabody & Bates, Inc., the last offering screened and bankrun gravel. The waitress, in her best Vermont deadpan, gave us "two minutes to decide what to order and one minute to eat it." It was a gray November day and the food no more than one might expect, but the company was good, from the farmers at the lunch counter to the teenagers ordering up a mess of breakfast past noon.

My daughter and I hopped in the old orange Ford pickup and drove home by the back road. As we climbed slowly through the small mountain valley, I realized that it was no coincidence that the American diner is built like a railway car. It is filled with transients, people on the move to somewhere else, yet it also embodies the essence of American road food: a streamlined, mass market version of mom's suppers, potluck dinners, and church socials. It's home for anyone who walks in the door that day—a surprisingly intimate gathering of neighbors and perfect strangers.

As we turned into our driveway, I had a vision of Whitney in the booth a few minutes before: quiet, beautiful, eyes wide open, and self-assured. Little kids live in the moment, but as they mature, they start living in the future, no longer content to sit at a Formica tabletop, engrossed by the food and the attention of a parent. They look through you, toward what they might become, planning a path of their own choosing. That day, my daughter was watching the great flow of people, aware of the possibilities and becoming eager to grab hold of the train of humanity as it passed by. And when the day comes that she finally buys a ticket and hops aboard, I will give Moe a call and ask him to watch over her and reserve the best seat at the counter. I know that she will be in good hands.

Bread Machine Yeast

I have seen yeast for bread machines in the grocery stores. Is this really different from other yeast? What would you recommend for my machine?

Eleanor Weisman
Clearfield, KY

Representatives from the King Arthur Flour Baker's Hotline and both the Bake Lab and Consumer Products Divisions of the Fleischmann's Yeast Company explained that the term "bread machine yeast" (as well as "rapid-rise" and "quick-rise," for that matter) fall under the general category of instant yeast. That said, there are important differences between instant yeast (in all of its guises) and the old standby, active dry yeast.

To package yeast cells (which are living organisms), manufacturers must deactivate them by drying. This procedure kills some of the cells and slows down the activity of those left living, in effect making them dormant. The dormancy not only prevents the cells from reacting until activated by the other ingredients in bread dough, but makes them shelf-stable as well.

All yeasts are dried through heating, but instant and active dry yeast products are heated to different temperature ranges. Instant yeast is heated to a far lower temperature, leaving roughly 95 percent of the cells alive and active. This makes instant yeast especially fast-acting and vigorous when it hits flour and water. By comparison, most active dry yeasts are heated to the point where between 45 and 65 percent of the cells remain alive and active, so they take a little longer to work.

We also asked our sources which type of yeast they suggest using with bread machines, and opinions varied. Both King Arthur and Fleischmann's recommended yeast from the instant category, whereas a representative of the customer assistance hotline for Regal bread machines advised using active dry. All of our bread machine testing, which was completed at the end of 1993 for the May/June 1994 issue (*see* "Are Bread Machines Worth the Dough?"), was conducted using active dry yeast; after further testing of yeast types, we can still say that we prefer the active dry. In side-by-side tests using the three-hour-and-fifty-minute cycle on our Regal Automatic BreadMaker, Model K6770, we found a marked difference in the rising performance and appearance (although not the flavor) of loaves made with the different yeasts. Active dry yeast produced a shorter, denser loaf with a tight crumb. In comparison, the loaf made with bread machine yeast rose one and one-half inches taller and had a soft, open structure that tore like cotton candy. Without a doubt, this loaf had a higher rise and was more impressive looking, but overall we like the more substantial texture of the active dry yeast loaf for sandwiches and toast.

Bread Blowout

Lately, whenever I bake bread, I find that it invariably splits and tears along the top of one side. It doesn't seem to matter how I form the loaf, nor does this defect seem to correspond to any other variable I can think of. The bread rises each time and in general is turning out well, except for this tear that makes for less beautiful slices and causes little bits to fall off each piece. So, what gives?

Steve Klein
West Springfield, NH

Information gleaned from the King Arthur Flour Baker's Hotline and Nancy Silverton's very well-written book, *Breads from the La Brea Bakery* (Villard Books, 1996), as well as from our own kitchen testing, indicates that the culprit most likely responsible for the tears in your loaves is underproofing of the dough. In the simplest terms, dough develops flavor, texture, and rise through a fermentation process that occurs as a by-product of yeast activity. The carbon dioxide gas given off during that fermentation gets trapped in the gluten network formed by the protein in the flour, and the accumulation of trapped gases causes the dough to rise.

Proofing is the dough's final rise, after it has been shaped into the loaf, but before it is loaded into the oven. In dough that is risen and proofed properly, there will be just enough energy left in the yeast to provide one final burst of activity, and therefore rise, when it hits the high heat of the oven. This last gasp is called "oven spring." Underproofing leaves the yeast with too much energy when the loaf is loaded into the oven, so the bread will develop too much oven spring. The abundance of gas produced, along with the steam created by the moisture in the dough, has to escape from the loaf somehow, and the pressure it causes as it builds up can result in bulges or, as you have experienced, blowouts in the side of the loaf. Lopsided loaves are another peril of underproofing. In our test kitchen we purposely underproofed a couple of loaves of simple, lean white bread dough to see what would happen when the dough was baked, and, sure enough, we got both blowouts and misshapen loaves. A common safeguard against blowouts is to make two or three one-half-inch-deep slashes in the top of the loaf before loading it into the oven. The slashes provide an escape route for the gas and steam developed within the loaf as it bakes, and they help bakers identify different types of bread.

Yeast activity, and therefore rising and proofing, is temperature-sensitive. To coax the best performance from yeast, dough should rise and proof at high humidity and a warm room temperature, between 70 and 80 degrees. If the weather outside is extremely hot, we try to find a cool (but not frigid, such as with air conditioning) spot, like a

Notes *from..*

basement, for dough to rise. Likewise, if it's cold out, we seek a warm spot such as an oven preheated to 200 degrees for ten minutes, with the heat then shut off. If you do use the oven in this way, make sure to put a tea towel between the metal rack and the pan, lest the rack overheat the pan and the dough.

The huge variety of doughs and breads makes it impossible to generalize about a correct degree of proofing applicable to them all. That said, there are a couple of visual and tactile cues we use to determine the degree of proof in most breads we bake here. First, a loaf should almost double in size. Second, a loaf that is proofed sufficiently will be full and fluffy, with a pillow-like look and feel. Many sources suggest pressing the dough with your fingertips and gauging the degree to which it springs back, but we found this method unreliable.

Bean Nutrition

I read with interest the column in the October 1996 issue dealing with techniques to render dried beans more digestible (see "Stop the Music?" page 15). One of our favorite recipes is for "French Market Soup" using ten different types of beans. My question is: After all the boiling and soaking of these beans, are there any nutrients left in them?

Claire Blumenstein
Medford, NJ

We have good news: Beans remain rich in protein, complex carbohydrates, starches, complex sugars, dietary fiber, B vitamins, calcium, iron, zinc, and potassium even after boiling and soaking overnight.

Citing kidney beans as an example, Dr. Nancy L. Cohen, a registered dietitian and an associate professor in the Nutrition Department at the University of Massachusetts at Amherst, said that more than 70 percent of bean nutrients are retained during cooking, including 86 percent of the protein, 83 percent of the iron, 96 percent of the zinc, 66 percent of the niacin, and 70 percent of the thiamine. About 53 percent of the calcium content, however, is lost. These numbers take into account that nutrient concentration diminishes during cooking because the beans take on moisture. For instance, one cup of dry kidney beans containing 44 grams of protein expands during soaking and cooking to two and one-half cups containing 38 grams of protein.

Several other considerations come into play as well. While 14 percent of kidney beans'

.........Readers

protein is lost through cooking, the heating process is necessary to activate trypsin, an enzyme in the bean that releases protein into the digestive system. In addition, we learned from Dr. Donald Schlimme, a professor in the Nutrition and Food Science Department at the University of Maryland, that cooking also activates in beans an enzyme called phytase, which breaks down phytic acid. This is important because phytic acid, which is found in the outer coating of beans, can tie up minerals such as calcium, iron, or zinc and prevent their absorption by the body.

Soaking dried beans is necessary for hydration, which accelerates the cooking process. While both slow and quick bean-soaking techniques exist, the heated water used with the quicker methods increases the solubility of water-soluble nutrients, such as calcium, magnesium, thiamine, riboflavin, and niacin. Also, the heat of boiling water breaks down cell membranes within the beans, which speeds the release of water-soluble nutrients. For these reasons, quick soaking tends to leach somewhat more of the nutrients out of the beans than do slow soaking methods.

Flavoring Bean Soups

I have an incredibly easy way to improve white bean soup. After grating a piece of hard Italian cheese, such as Parmesan or Romano, save the rind and add it to a pot of any white bean soup, allowing it to simmer until the soup is done. This adds a richness and creaminess that I believe makes bean soup a whole new experience.

Phyllis Baker
Wilmington, DE

Several of our editors use this tip in their home kitchens. We collect rinds in a zipper-lock bag stored in the freezer because we've found that those kept in the refrigerator sometimes develop mold. For any soup or stew that you would consider serving with grated cheese, add a two- to three-inch piece of frozen rind to the pot at the beginning of the simmering time and fish it out at the end, when it is softened and has released its flavor.

Blue Garlic

As part of my Thanksgiving meal last year, I made the Pickled Green Beans with Dill from your September/October 1994 issue (see "Quick Pickle Recipes," page 19). I used all the seasonings you recommended except for the mustard seed; the pickling liquid was made with rice vinegar of 4.5 percent acidity and white wine vinegar (which, according to its label, contains sulfites "to preserve color") of 5 percent acidity. The beans were delicious, but the garlic cloves turned bright robin's-egg blue! What happened?

Zoë Johansson
Cambridge, MA

Though somewhat jarring to behold, your blue garlic should have tasted fine and was safe to consume. The color change was due, for the most part, to a reaction between the acid in the vinegars and the pigments that normally give garlic cloves their creamy white appearance.

Dr. Susan Brewer, Associate Professor of Food Chemistry at the University of Illinois, told us that the molecular structure of the pigments that color most fruits and vegetables changes when different enzymes are activated. Acidity is one of the catalysts that sets the enzymes to work. Another cause, in Dr. Brewer's opinion, was the age of the garlic.

If you used older garlic (which is likely if, as is common, it was harvested in the summer and stored until the fall), natural enzymes in the garlic may already have begun to change the molecular structure of the pigment molecules. In other words, the rearrangement of the chemical bonds between individual atoms changed the behavior of the pigment molecules and with it the absorption and refraction of light that dictates the colors seen by the eye.

In the case of the pickles, this change was intensified by the acid. In garlic, which is alkaline, acid accelerates the enzymatic action that shifts the molecular bonds within the pigment, which ended up absorbing most of the colors in the light spectrum, but reflecting the blue back to your eye.

Brewer mentioned that this odd color change happens to garlic more often than we might expect. To avoid it in the future, she suggested using garlic that has been stored for less time so that the pigments have not become so susceptible to change. The freshest garlic is available in the summer. She added that a sixty-second steam-blanch of the garlic can help because the heat deactivates the enzymes that cause the pigments to change.

Shapely Biscotti

Thanks for your biscotti article in the January/February 1994 issue. My grandmother passed the following biscotti-making tip on to me. Turn the dough into a greased, metal ice cube tray, without the cube insert, and bake it right in the tray. This method helps prevent overhandling of the dough, which comes out in a neat, easy-to-slice loaf. After slicing the loaf, toast the biscotti on a cookie sheet.

Nancy Desiderio
Albuquerque, NM

Your idea worked well for us. The biscotti's texture benefited from a minimum of handling, forming the loaves in the pan was a breeze, and the final cookies were uniformly sized and attractive.

What Is It?

I bought this implement at a secondhand store as part of a set of old kitchen utensils. The rest of the items are basic, but I have no idea what this one is for. Some of the rings are solid, and others are grooved. Also, some of the rings are loose and move around. It is about twelve inches long and made of hardwood. What is this for?

Jill Drown
Salt Lake City, UT

You have come across a Mexican hand beater designed expressly for whipping hot cocoa (the beverage) into a froth. Called a molinillo, which translates to "little mill," it is a common implement found in most Mexican home kitchens. The end with the rings is inserted into a tall kettle of hot cocoa while the handle is held between the palms of your hands. Rapidly rubbing your hands back and forth sets the loose rings twirling against the fixed ones, which agitates the liquid, incorporates air, and causes the drink to become light and foamy. Most molinillos are wooden, and different designs exist in other Latin American countries. Yours is the particularly decorative Mexican variety, which is usually about twelve inches long and sometimes features simple carved designs on some of the rings. Look for molinillos in Latin American markets, or mail-order one from Don Alfonso Foods (P.O. Box 201988, Austin, TX 78720-1988; 800-456-6100). The cost is approximately $5, plus shipping. We tried a molinillo in the test kitchen and found that it works best with a full recipe of hot cocoa, as opposed to only one or two cups, in the tallest, narrowest pot you can find so that the rings will be submerged fully in the liquid.

Stacking Small Bakeware Tins

Lisa Yockelson of Washington, D.C., finds that every time she stacks individual brioche tins, they stick together. To solve this problem, she uses the following technique.
1. Drop a lightweight rubber band, slightly askew, into the bottom of each tin.
2. Stack the tins one on top of the other. The rubber band prevents the tins from bonding.

Quick

Thanks to our readers for Quick Tips: The editors of *Cook's Illustrated* would like to thank all of the readers who have sent us their quick tips. We have enjoyed reading every one of them and have learned a lot. Keep them coming. We will provide a one-year complimentary subscription for each quick tip that we print. Send a description of your special technique to *Cook's Illustrated*, P.O. Box 569, Brookline Village, MA 02147-0569.

Decorating Cookies

In addition to those listed in our November/December 1996 issue (see "Freestyle Cookie Decorating"), another gadget that works well for decorating sugar cookies is an empty plastic thread spool. To use it, Paula S. Bahr of Forest Park, Illinois, simply presses the thread spool firmly into the cookie dough, imprinting the dough with a delightful flower design.

Quick Muffin Topping

For a quick, low-fat, crunchy topping for muffins, Joan Hartman of Brighton, Colorado, recommends sprinkling the tops with Grape-Nuts cereal before baking.

Keeping a Cookbook Flat

To keep the open pages of a cookbook or magazine flat, readable, and clean while cooking, Joyce Kolokousis of Walnut Creek, California, puts a clear glass (Pyrex) baking dish over them.

Lifting Hot Pot Lids

In response to our tip about using corks to lift hot pot lids (see Quick Tips, November/December 1996), Laura M. Langdon of Durango, Colorado, recommends using a wooden cooking spoon for the same purpose, first making sure that the bowl of the spoon is larger than the space between the handle and lid.

Cleaning Out a Meat Grinder

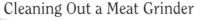

It is important to clean out a grinder after grinding meat in it, but it can also be a frustrating and time-consuming task. Eva Katz came up with this effective method of cleaning the grinder.
1. Run the meat through the grinder as thoroughly as possible.
2. To push out the last of the meat, run through a piece of stale bread, then rinse out the grinder.

Working with Phyllo

When using phyllo dough, test kitchen director Eva Katz finds that spraying the sheets with olive oil or melted butter from a spritzer bottle is a fast, easy way to apply the fat in a very thin layer.

ILLUSTRATIONS BY HARRY DAVIS

Tips

Spice Funnel

Cooks often need a small funnel to replace excess dry ingredients, such as salt, spices, or a premade spice rub mixture, into a small bottle. Susan Dunham of Plattsburgh, New York, has come up with this solution.
1. Roll up a large Post-it Note into a cone shape, keeping the glue strip on the outside.
2. Use the cone to replace the ingredients, then throw it away.

Packed Brown Sugar

When a recipe calls for some quantity of packed brown sugar, Beth Bromfield of San Francisco, California, fills the correct size of dry measuring cup with the sugar and then uses the next smaller cup to pack the brown sugar into its cup.

Achieving Low Flame

If you cannot adjust the flame on your gas stove low enough to maintain a slow simmer, try this handy tip from test kitchen director Eva Katz.
1. Place two burner grates one on top of another. By elevating the pan above the flame, this technique gives you the equivalent of a very low flame, perfect for simmering.

Rolling Out Sticky Dough

Teri Calicchia of Albuquerque, New Mexico, has found a way to minimize the frustration of rolling out a very sticky dough: She slips a clean, knee-high nylon over her rolling pin. Dusted with a little flour, the nylon helps prevent the dough from sticking.

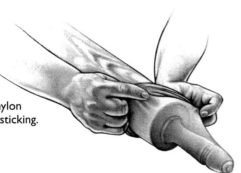

Holding Recipe Cards

To keep recipe cards and notes at eye level while cooking, Sonny Cohen of Dallas, Texas, clips them in a magnetized paper clamp attached to the range hood.

Well-Seasoned Pita Chips

Whenever he made seasoned pita chips, Scott Whitehead of Fishers, Indiana, found that the seasonings would fall right off the chips. He has now found this ingenious way to make the seasonings adhere.
1. Before baking, spray the pita triangles with water from a spritzer bottle.
2. Sprinkle seasonings on the dampened triangles before baking. The baked chips will remain coated with the seasoning.

Drying Cooked Greens

When preparing a dish for which the removal of excess moisture from cooked spinach or other greens is important, Mildred Langer of Las Vegas, Nevada, makes it easy by putting the greens in a collapsible basket steamer and folding the sections shut to squeeze out the water, which escapes through the holes.

Chicken and Dumplings

An oven roaster delivers a flavorful broth and generous chunks of chicken, while dumplings made with hot milk and no eggs are tender, yet substantial.

by Pam Anderson with Melissa Hamilton

❦

Despite America's ongoing love affair with comfort food, chicken and dumplings hasn't made a comeback like its baked cousin, chicken pot pie. After making several dozen batches of dumplings, I think I know why.

As tricky as pie pastry and biscuits are for pot pie, dumplings are far more temperamental. With pot pie, dry oven heat and rich sauce camouflage minor biscuit and pastry flaws, whereas moist, steamy heat highlights gummy or leaden dumplings.

With its meat, vegetables, bread, and sauce, chicken pot pie is a perfect complete meal. But chicken and dumplings is, well, chicken and dumplings. A few hearty vegetables would make it a complete meal—just the selling point to attract today's busy cook.

Our mission was twofold. First, we wanted to develop a chicken and dumplings recipe as foolproof and complete as chicken pot pie. Second, we wanted to develop a dumpling that was light yet substantial, tender yet durable. But which style of dumpling to explore?

I grew up in the South and lived in the Midwest, where dumplings are either rolled thin and cut into strips or rolled thick and stamped out like biscuits. Melissa, on the other hand, has lived all her life near Pennsylvania Dutch country, where dumplings are round and dropped. Could these three styles come from the same dough, or would we need to develop separate doughs to accommodate each style?

First, the Dumpling

Most flour-based dumplings are made of flour, salt, and one or more of the following ingredients: butter, eggs, milk, and baking powder. Depending on the ingredients list, dumplings are usually mixed in one of three ways.

The most common mixing method is a biscuit or pastry style in which cold butter is cut into the dry ingredients, then cold milk and/or eggs are stirred in until just mixed. Other dumplings are made by simply mixing wet into dry ingredients. Also, many of the eggier dumplings are made pâte à choux–style, adding flour to hot water and butter, then whisking in eggs, one at a time.

We spent a full day making batch after batch of dumplings in some combination of the above ingredients and following one of the three mixing methods. (We even made a yeast-based dumpling that, when cooked, tasted like soggy bread!)

By the end of the day, we hadn't made a single dumpling that we really liked. In short, we found dumplings made with eggs tended to be tough and chewy while dumplings made without eggs tended to be fragile, often disintegrating into the cooking liquid. Dumplings made without enough liquid tended to be leaden while those made with too much liquid were particularly prone to disintegrate.

We finally made progress after looking at a recipe in *Master Recipes* (Ballantine, 1987), in which author Stephen Schmidt cuts butter into flour, baking powder, and salt. Instead of the usual cold liquid into the dry ingredients, he adds hot liquid to the flour-butter mixture. Dumplings made according to this method were light and fluffy, yet they held up beautifully during cooking. These were the firm yet tender dumplings we were looking for. According to science expert Shirley Corriher, this type of dumpling is a success because hot liquids, unlike cold ones, expand and set the starch in the flour, keeping it from absorbing too much of the cooking liquid.

Now that we had the technique down, it was time to test the formula. Would a dumpling made with cake flour be more tender than one made with all-purpose? Was butter the best dumpling fat, or would ones made with shortening or chicken fat taste better? Which liquid offered the best flavor and texture: milk, buttermilk, chicken stock, or water?

We thought that cake flour dumplings would be even lighter-textured than those made with all-purpose. In fact, just the opposite was true. They were

When made with hot liquid, dumplings absorb less of the cooking liquid, so they stay light.

tight, spongy little dumplings with a metallic, acidic aftertaste. Attributing this odd flavor somehow to the baking powder, I called Corriher for further explanation. According to Corriher, the problem lies with the cake flour, not the baking powder. The process by which cake flour is chlorinated leaves it acidic. One of the benefits of acidic flour is that it sets eggs faster in baking, resulting in a smoother, finer-textured cake. This acidic flavor, less distractive in a batter rich with butter, sugar, and eggs, really comes through in a simple dumpling dough.

Although we were pretty sure the dumplings made with vegetable shortening wouldn't taste as good as those made with butter, we had high hopes for the ones made with chicken fat. After a side-by-side test of dumplings made with butter, shortening, and chicken fat, we selected those made with butter. The shortening dumpling tasted flat, like cooked flour and chicken stock, while the one made with chicken fat tasted like flour and stronger-flavored chicken stock. The butter gave the dumpling that extra flavor dimension it needed.

Liquids were simple. Dumplings made with chicken stock, much like those made with chicken fat, tasted too similar to the broth. Those made with water were pretty dull. Because buttermilk tends to separate and even curdle when heated, buttermilk dumplings felt a little wrong. Whole milk dumplings were tender with a pleasant biscuity flavor and were our first choice.

Up to this point, we had made all of our dumplings by cutting the fat into the dry ingredients, then adding hot liquid. Because we were adding hot milk, we questioned why it was necessary to cut in the cold butter. Why couldn't we simply heat the milk and butter together and dump it into the dry ingredients? A side-by-side tasting of dumplings made from the two different mixing techniques made us realize that cutting the butter into the flour was indeed an unnecessary step. The simpler route of adding the hot milk and melted butter to the dry ingredients actually yielded more substantial, better-textured dumplings.

Having decided on dumplings made with all-purpose flour, butter, milk, baking powder, and salt, we tested the formula by shaping them into balls, cutting them into biscuit shapes, and rolling them thin and cutting them into strips. Regardless of shape, we got the same consistent results: tender, sturdy dumplings.

The Rest of the Dish

After refining the dumpling, we turned our energies to updating the chicken part of the dish. Our first few attempts were disastrous. To make the dish clean and sleek, we left the chicken pieces on the bone, cut the vegetables into long, thin strips, and thickened the broth ever so slightly. As we ate the finished product, we realized that we needed a knife (to cut the chicken off the bone), a fork (to eat the vegetables, dumplings, and meat), and a spoon (for the broth). Although we wanted the dish to look beautiful, it had to be eater-friendly. In order for the dish to work, the chicken had to come off the bone, the vegetables needed to be cut a little smaller, and the broth quantity required reducing and thickening. As the dish evolved, we worked toward making it not only a one-dish, but a one-utensil meal.

Even though chicken and dumplings and chicken pot pie share common ingredients and similar techniques, each dish has a different feel. Chicken pot pie is more casserole-like, while chicken and dumplings is more stewlike. So even though we thought boneless, skinless chicken breasts were a wonderful timesaving substitute for a whole chicken in chicken pot pie (*see* "One-Pot Chicken Pot Pie," May/June 1996), the breasts just didn't seem right for this dish. We wanted large, uneven chunks of light and dark meat. For us, only a whole chicken would work.

Because we wanted this dish to serve six to eight and because we preferred bigger chunks of meat, we chose the larger oven roasters over the small fryer hens. We also preferred oven roasters over the stewing hens called for in many recipes. Although we loved the flavor of the hen's broth, she had to simmer for two hours before becoming tender. And once tender, the meat was dry.

Because we had already developed a method for rich, flavorful chicken stock and perfectly poached chicken parts (*see* "Quick Homemade Chicken Soup," March/April 1996), we simply adapted the technique to this recipe. For those who did not read the article, I will review the method (developed by Karen Tack and me) that allows the richest broth with the most flavorful meat.

We remove and cut the back, the wings, and the giblets (excluding liver) of a roasting hen into two-inch pieces. The remaining parts—legs, thighs, and breasts—are set aside for poaching. We sauté the chicken pieces with onion until they loose their raw color. The heat is turned down, the pot is covered, and the pieces cook until all their liquid is released, in just twenty minutes.

Once the chicken pieces have "sweated," the chicken parts and water are added. This step allows the cook to finish the stock and poach the chicken at the same time, the rich poaching liquid infusing the chicken and the chicken parts, further enriching the broth. In twenty minutes, the parts are perfectly cooked, and the stock is incredibly potent. Once this step is complete, the dish can be made in less than a half hour. If you are short on time, you can poach the chicken parts in low-sodium canned chicken broth. I'm partial to making the broth because every ounce of the chicken can be used to make the dish.

How to Cut Up a Chicken

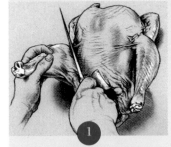

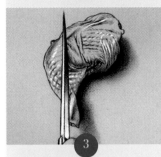

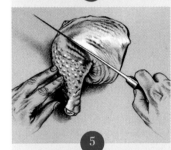

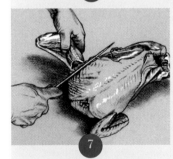

1. Using a sharp chef's knife (see "Rating Electric Knife Sharpeners," page 29), cut through the skin around the leg where it attaches to the body.

2. Pop each leg out of its socket and then use your chef's knife to cut through the flesh and skin to detach each leg from the body.

3. To separate the drumstick from the thigh, first place your chef's knife along the length of the drumstick so that it follows the bone from top to bottom.

4. Turn the handle of the knife 60 degrees to the right.

5. Move the knife 1/8 inch toward the thigh. You should now be exactly above the joint separating the thigh and drumstick.

6. Push the knife straight down with some force, separating the thigh and drumstick.

7. To remove the wing, start by cutting into the side of the breast. For this recipe, the wings are only going to be used for stock so as little meat as possible should be removed from the breast.

8. Bend the wing out from the breast and cut to remove the wing.

9. Using poultry shears, cut down the ribs between the back and the breast, first on one side of the bird and then on the other.

10. The back and breast should be neatly separated.

11. Split the breast down the breastbone, cutting right through the bone with your chef's knife. Set the two breasts aside, along with the legs and thighs. Before cooking, you will need to remove the skin from all of these.

12. Use poultry shears, as shown, or a chef's knife to hack the back, neck, and wings into 1- to 2-inch pieces.

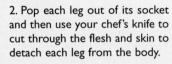

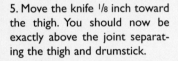

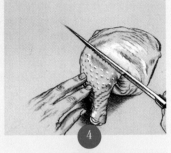

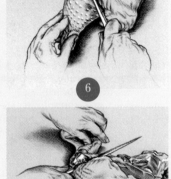

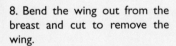

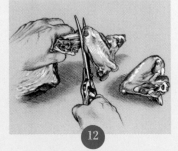

When to Cook the Vegetables?

Our updated chicken and dumplings needed vegetables, but where and how to cook them? In an attempt to streamline the process, we tried cooking the vegetables along with the poaching chicken parts. After fishing out hot, slightly overcooked vegetables from among the chicken parts and pieces, we decided this little shortcut wasn't worth it. So we simply washed the pot, returned it to the stove, and steamed the vegetables for ten minutes while removing the meat from the bone, straining the stock, and making the dumpling dough. Because the vegetables would cook again for a short time in the sauce, we wanted them slightly undercooked at this point. Steaming them separately gave us more control.

With our meat poached and off the bone, our stock degreased and strained, and our veg-

Dumplings

For flat noodle-like dumplings, roll dough to 1/8-inch and cut them into about 2-by-1/2-inch strips.

For biscuit-like dumplings, roll dough to 1/2-inch thick. Use a 2-inch biscuit cutter or a round drinking glass top to cut dough rounds.

For round puffy dumplings, divide dough into 18 pieces. Roll each piece of dough into a rough round.

etables steamed to perfection, we were ready to complete the dish, like someone ready to stir-fry. We chose thickening at the beginning of this final phase, rather than at the end, because once our chicken, vegetables, and dumplings were added to the pot, thickening became virtually impossible.

To a roux of flour and chicken fat (once again, using every bit of the chicken to make the dish), we added our homemade stock and stirred until thickened. Although we needed six cups of stock to poach the chicken parts, we found this quantity of liquid made the dish much too saucy, more like chicken and dumpling soup. Pulling off and reserving two cups of stock solved the problem.

To the thickened liquid, we added our shaped dough for steaming. But when it came time to add the meat and vegetables to the pot, we found it difficult to stir them in among all those fragile little dumplings. With the major meat and vegetable additions, the dish cooled down dramatically and required additional cooking. So we switched the order, adding chicken and vegetables to the thickened sauce, then steaming the dumplings. Not only did the dumplings remain undisturbed, the chicken and vegetables had an opportunity to marry and mingle with one another and the sauce.

A few peas and a little parsley made the dish beautiful, and a little dry sherry or vermouth, as we found with chicken pot pie, heightened the flavor. A touch of cream enriches and beautifies, but the dish is equally good without it for weeknight dining.

Not only was our final dish eye-catching and palate-pleasing, it was simple to make. Best of all, we could eat it with a fork.

CHICKEN AND DUMPLINGS WITH AROMATIC VEGETABLES
Serves 6 to 8

A touch of heavy cream gives the dish a more refined look and rich flavor, but for a weeknight dinner, you may want to omit it. If you are in a hurry, you may poach boneless chicken breasts in low-sodium canned stock, then pull the breast into large pieces, and skip step 1 below.

Poached Chicken with Creamed Gravy and Aromatic Vegetables

1	large roasting chicken, 6 to 7 pounds, butchered according to illustrations 1-12, page 7
1	large onion, cut into large chunks (not necessary to peel)
2	bay leaves
	Salt
3	celery stalks, trimmed and cut into 1-by-1/2-inch pieces
4	carrots, peeled and cut into 1-by-1/2-inch pieces
6	boiling onions, peeled and halved
4	tablespoons softened butter or chicken fat from the cooked chicken
6	tablespoons all-purpose flour
1	teaspoon dried thyme leaves
2	tablespoons dry sherry or vermouth
1/4	cup heavy cream (optional)

3/4	cup frozen peas, thawed
1/4	cup minced fresh parsley leaves
	Ground black or white pepper

Baking Powder Dumplings

2	cups all-purpose flour
1	tablespoon baking powder
3/4	teaspoon salt
3	tablespoons butter
1	cup milk

1. *For the chicken*: Heat deep 11- or 12-inch skillet or Dutch oven over medium-high heat. Add hacked-up chicken pieces (back, neck, and wings; *see* illustration 12, page 7) and onion chunks; sauté until onion softens and chicken loses its raw color, about 5 minutes. Reduce heat to low, cover, and continue to cook until chicken pieces give up most of their liquid, about 20 minutes. Increase heat to medium-high, add 6 cups hot water, chicken parts (legs, thighs, and breasts), bay leaves, and 3/4 teaspoon salt, then bring to simmer. Reduce heat; continue to simmer, partially covered, until broth is flavorful and chicken parts are just cooked through, about 20 minutes longer. Remove chicken parts and set aside. When cool enough to handle, remove meat from bones in 2- to 3-inch chunks. Strain broth, discarding chicken pieces. Skim and reserve fat from broth and set aside 4 cups of broth, reserving extra for another use.

2. Meanwhile, bring 1/2-inch water to simmer in cleaned skillet fitted with steamer basket. Add vegetables; cover and steam until just tender, about 10 minutes. Remove and set aside.

3. *For the dumplings*: Mix flour, baking powder, and salt in medium bowl. Heat butter and milk to simmer and add to dry ingredients. Mix with a fork or knead by hand two to three times until mixture just comes together. Following illustrations at left, form dough into desired shape; set aside.

4. Heat butter or reserved chicken fat in cleaned skillet over medium-high heat. Whisk in flour and thyme; cook, whisking constantly, until flour turns golden, 1 to 2 minutes. Continuing to whisk constantly, gradually add sherry or vermouth, then reserved 4 cups chicken stock; simmer until gravy thickens slightly, 2 to 3 minutes. Stir in optional cream and chicken and vegetables; return to simmer.

5. Lay formed dumplings on surface of chicken mixture; cover and simmer until dumplings are cooked through, about 10 minutes for strip dumplings and 15 minutes for balls and biscuit rounds. Gently stir in peas and parsley. Adjust seasonings, including generous amounts of salt and pepper. Ladle portion of meat, sauce, vegetables, and dumplings into soup plates and serve immediately.

CHICKEN AND HERBED DUMPLINGS WITH AROMATIC VEGETABLES
Follow recipe for Chicken and Dumplings with Aromatic Vegetables, adding 1/4 cup minced soft fresh herb leaves such as parsley, chives (or scallion greens), dill, and tarragon to dumpling mixture along with dry ingredients. If other herbs are unavailable, all parsley may be used.

Tender Spinach Salads

Flat-leaf spinach is more tender and flavorful than dry, curly varieties and makes better salads. Look for it in bundles, not packages.

by Jack Bishop

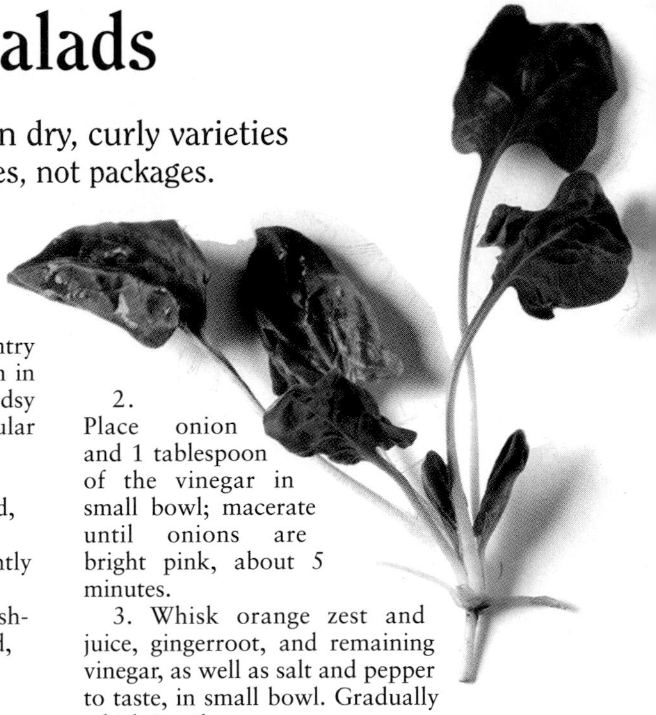

When choosing spinach for salads, I find it especially important to select a flavorful, tender variety. The dried-out curly leaves packaged in cellophane are fine for pasta fillings or side dishes. However, when used raw, they often make a tough, tasteless salad.

A better option is the flat-leaf spinach sold in bundles at most supermarkets. The spade-shaped leaves tend to have thin, less fibrous stems, which are often edible. The leaves themselves are not as stringy as curly spinach leaves, and their flavor is far superior, sweeter and with more mineral and earthy notes. And, most important in terms of salads, flat-leaf spinach is not as dry or chewy. The leaves are tender and moist, more like lettuce.

One drawback is perishability. Unlike curly spinach, flat-leaf varieties will wilt and become slimy very quickly. In tests, I found that wrapping the root ends in damp paper towels and keeping the spinach in an open plastic bag can prolong freshness an extra day or two in the refrigerator.

When you're ready to use the spinach, pinch off and discard the stems as needed, based on their thickness and toughness. In my tests I found that the portion of the stem near the leaf is usually quite tender and just a little crunchy. In really fresh bundles that come with the pink rootlets attached, the entire branch—leaves, stems, and pink crowns—may be eaten.

As you trim the stems, drop the leaves into a bowl, sink, or salad spinner full of cold water. Swish the leaves around and continue washing in several changes of water until there is no grit on the bottom of the container you are using. Spinach that will be wilted or sautéed can be left damp. For salads, however, spinach should be spun-dry in a salad spinner and then laid out over paper towels to blot off any remaining water. Spinach leaves can be prepped to this point and then refrigerated in zipper-lock plastic bags for several hours.

In addition to flat-leaf spinach sold in bundles, many supermarkets now sell baby spinach in bulk. Look for it near the mesclun. These tender leaves have no stems and are usually fairly clean. One wash and a thorough drying are all that is required.

The substantial salads that follow are designed to serve four as a lunch entrée or light dinner. They will also feed six as a first course.

SPINACH SALAD WITH MUSHROOMS, CROUTONS, AND WARM LEMON DRESSING
Serves 4

Homemade croutons are better than any you can buy and are a good use for stale bread. Cut a hunk of leftover baguette or country white bread into small cubes and fry them in olive oil until crisp. I prefer slightly woodsy cremini mushrooms in this salad, but regular white mushrooms are fine.

1½	pounds flat-leaf spinach, stemmed, washed, dried, and torn into large pieces (about 9 cups, tightly packed)
½	pound fresh cremini or white mushrooms, cleaned, stems trimmed, sliced thin
½	cup extra-virgin olive oil
3	cups stale French or Italian-style bread, cut into ¾-inch cubes
2	medium garlic cloves, minced
¼	cup juice from 2 medium lemons
	Salt and ground black pepper

1. Place spinach and mushrooms in large bowl; set aside.

2. Heat oil in large skillet over medium-high heat until shimmering. Add bread; fry, turning several times with slotted spoon, until crisp and golden, about 3 minutes. Transfer to paper towel–lined plate. Off heat, let remaining oil cool slightly, about 1 minute. Add garlic; cook until lightly colored, about 2 minutes. Whisk in lemon juice and salt and pepper to taste. Pour warm dressing over salad; toss. Add croutons; toss again. Serve immediately.

SPINACH SALAD WITH SHRIMP, MANGO, AND RED ONION
Serves 4

To save time, buy shrimp that has been peeled and cooked. If you want to boil the shrimp yourself, buy slightly more than one pound with the shells on.

1½	pounds flat-leaf spinach, stemmed, washed, dried, and torn into large pieces (about 9 cups, tightly packed)
1	pound cooked medium shrimp
1	large ripe mango, peeled, pitted, and cut into thin strips
½	small red onion, sliced thin
2	tablespoons rice wine vinegar
1	teaspoon grated zest and 2 tablespoons juice from 1 orange
1	tablespoon minced fresh gingerroot
¼	cup canola or other mild vegetable oil
1	tablespoon Asian sesame oil
	Salt and ground black pepper

1. Place spinach, shrimp, and mango in large bowl. Set aside.

2. Place onion and 1 tablespoon of the vinegar in small bowl; macerate until onions are bright pink, about 5 minutes.

3. Whisk orange zest and juice, gingerroot, and remaining vinegar, as well as salt and pepper to taste, in small bowl. Gradually whisk in oils.

4. Add onion to salad bowl. Pour dressing over salad; toss and serve immediately.

SPINACH AND AVOCADO SALAD WITH CHILI-FLAVORED CHICKEN
Serves 4

A creamy yogurt dressing spiked with lemon and garlic is a good match for the strong flavors in this salad.

2	teaspoons chili powder
1	teaspoon ground cumin
	Salt
1	pound boneless, skinless chicken breasts, trimmed
2	teaspoons vegetable oil
1½	pounds flat-leaf spinach, stemmed, washed, dried, and torn into large pieces (about 9 cups, tightly packed)
4	ripe plum tomatoes (about ¾ pound), cored and cut into wedges
1	Hass avocado, halved, pitted, peeled, and cut into thin strips
3	tablespoons juice from 1 large lemon
¾	cup plain yogurt
2	tablespoons extra-virgin olive oil
1	large garlic clove, minced

1. Heat broiler or light grill. Mix chili powder, cumin, and ½ teaspoon salt in small bowl. Rub oil then spice mixture into both sides of each chicken breast. Broil or grill, turning once, until cooked through, about 10 minutes. Set aside.

2. Place spinach and tomatoes in large bowl. Sprinkle avocado with 1 tablespoon of the lemon juice; add to salad bowl.

3. Whisk yogurt, oil, garlic, and remaining lemon juice, and salt to taste, in small bowl.

4. Slice chicken crosswise into ¾-inch-wide strips and add to salad bowl. Pour dressing over salad; toss and serve immediately.

Rediscovering Corned Beef and Cabbage

Supermarket corned beef borders on inedible. But a simple method for home curing yields rich, meltingly tender corned beef that transforms this workhorse recipe into something special.

by Adam Ried with Eva Katz

A bumper sticker I saw recently read "Minds function better when open." Working on this piece about corned beef and cabbage, the venerable one-pot meal composed of boiled corned beef, cabbage, and other winter vegetables (also known in this part of the country as New England boiled dinner), reminded me that the same lesson applies to palates as well.

My tastes run most often to bright, bold, and complex flavors. By that standard, corned beef and cabbage had always struck me less as a dish with big flavor and genuine dinner table appeal than as a symbol of the stalwart Yankee ethics of hard work and thrift. That misconception, however, was the first of several to be busted during our testing. In the course of tasting umpteen corned beef and cabbages, I came to realize that this dish needn't be mushy, overwhelmingly salty, and one-dimensional, as it had always seemed. Instead, it can be a full-flavored medley of meaty, tender, well-seasoned beef, subtle spice, and sweet, earthy vegetables, each distinct in flavor and texture.

I was also wrong about where our testing would focus. Because boiled vegetables can easily overcook into mush, I expected that most of our tests would be devoted to their correct preparation and cooking time, rather than to the meat itself. In fact, we found vast differences among the various styles of corned beef available, from commercial to home-cured, and it was here that we concentrated our efforts, finally making a major flavor breakthrough.

Go for the Gray?

We commenced our research and testing with the usual spate of recipes, most of which were based on a four- to six-pound piece of corned beef. The term "corned" refers to the curing of meat with salt, often used as a method of preservation before refrigeration became widespread. Legend

has it that the salt grains were roughly the same size as corn kernels, hence the name "corned beef." The cut of beef most commonly corned is boneless brisket, which is a trimmed, twelve- or thirteen-pound piece taken from the front part of the cow's breast. For retail sale, the whole brisket is usually split into two parts, called the first, or flat, cut and second, or point, cut. Of the two, the point cut is thicker, fattier, and, to our tastes, both more flavorful and more tender than the flat cut. Both of these cuts can be trimmed further into smaller pieces of meat, and both are available as commercially corned beef.

At the supermarket, we found more commercial corned beef options than we had anticipated from reading our research recipes. In addition to "low-sodium" corned beef, there were regular and "gray," each in both flat and point cuts in sizes ranging from three to six pounds. We were told by a representative from Mosey's, a national producer of corned beef, that the gray style is popular only in, and therefore limited to, New England. The difference between these types is made clear on the package. The brine for gray corned beef contains only water and salt whereas the "regular" corned beef brine also contains sodium nitrite. According to Hal McGee in *On Food and Cooking* (Macmillan, 1984), nitrite chemicals help the meat retain its red color by reacting with purple color pigments and turning them to pink and red.

We brought home an example of each type and took to the stove. Cooking directions on the packages and in our research recipes really did not vary much. Generally, instructions were to cover the meat by one to three inches of water and simmer until tender, anywhere from two and one-half to three and one-half hours, depending on the size of the brisket.

To our surprise, the regular corned beef choices disappointed us across the board. Though they remained an appealing pink even when cooked, our tasters described the flavor of both the full- and low-salt versions as "sharp and somewhat chemical," most likely from the nitrite. In addition, the texture was deemed to be grainy, with a noticeably chalky mouth feel. By comparison, the gray corned beef looked, well, gray, because it lacked the color boost given to regular brisket by the nitrite. The flavor, however, was superior, and for that, we'll gladly trade the pink color. Whereas the chemical qualities we noted in the regular versions obscured

the flavor of the beef, the gray corned beef tasted cleaner and beefier. The salt had a stronger presence than we preferred, and the spice we look for in ideal corned beef was non-existent, but we knew we wanted to stick with the gray for further testing.

Corning Our Own

But because the gray corned beef we preferred is a product limited to a small region of the country, we decided to try corning our own brisket. We figured that this would also make it easier to control the saltiness. Our research turned up two methods, the wet and the dry cures, of corning your own beef. Both methods do require close to a week, but they are also mindlessly easy: All you need to do is prepare the meat and its cure. Beyond that, there is no work whatsoever. Of course, we tested each method, using five-pound fresh briskets in both flat and point cut.

Because meat preservative is readily available in drugstores in the form of the potassium nitrate called saltpeter, we still had the option of producing regular and gray corned beef. Even in our home-corned beef, though, the preservative added a harshness to the flavor that competed with the taste of the beef. Because the color of the meat was less important to us than the flavor, we dropped the saltpeter from further testing.

This decision made, we went on to test the wet method first, tasting briskets cured in a brine of two cups of salt and three quarts of water for fourteen, twelve, ten, seven, and five days. Among all of them, we liked best the brisket soaked for five days, noting a pleasing saltiness alongside the distinctive flavor of beef. We also determined a strong preference for the fattier point cut of brisket. Fat carries flavor in all cuts of meat, and beef brisket is no different. The flat cut is especially lean and therefore less flavorful and moist than the point cut.

The Dry Cure

At this point, we also gave the dry-cure method a go. Adapting a recipe from Julia Child's *The Way to Cook* (Alfred A. Knopf, 1989), we rubbed our six-pound, point cut brisket with one-half cup of salt and a few crushed herbs and spices, placed it in a huge, two-gallon zipper-lock bag, weighted the meat with a brick, and let it sit for five days in the fridge. Lo and behold, the result was the best corned beef of them all, even better than the five-day wet-cured corned beef, with a concentrated beef flavor, assertive yet not overpowering salt, and a pleasant spiciness. Curing the brisket for two extra days, seven in total, brought out the flavor of the spices a little more, without affecting the saltiness. The difference was subtle, and we liked it slightly better than the five-day version.

We also tasted the brisket after ten, twelve, and fourteen days but felt the flavor difference to be so slight that it just wasn't worth the extra time. In addition, we tinkered with the salt quantity in the dry-cure mixture, trying one-quarter cup less and more, but neither improved the flavor.

Julia Child's recipe suggested desalting the dry-cured meat by soaking it in several changes of water for at least twenty-four hours or up to three days, depending on the size of the brisket. To be honest, we initially overlooked this step; we simply rinsed the surface of the meat to remove shards of crumbled bay leaf and cracked peppercorns and went ahead with the cooking. When we finally did try the full desalting, we found that the meat tasted slightly richer because of the diminished salt presence, but not so much better that it justified a twenty-four-hour soak versus a quick rinse.

Despite the fact that brisket is the cut usually associated with corned beef, we tried our dry-curing method on a couple of other cuts. After seven days in the salt, a four-pound top round roast was much like the flat cut of brisket, that is, too lean for our tastes. The texture was dry and reminiscent of sawdust chipboard. A three-and-three-quarter-pound chuck blade roast, a fattier cut, tasted quite good and had a melting, buttery texture, but it lacked a certain degree of chew and elasticity we look for in the best corned beef brisket.

Cooking Refinements

With the corned beef tasting just the way we wanted, we turned our attention first to the cooking method, then to the vegetables. Though most recipes call for cooking corned beef and cabbage on the stove, we did try a couple of tests in the oven. Our advice is to stick to the stove, on which the meat cooked faster and was easier to monitor. Also, we found that adding the vegetables and adjusting the heat to compensate was easier with the pot on the stove, rather than in the oven.

On the stove, we noticed that the meat emerged from the pot tender and flaky if cooked at a lively simmer, as opposed to tight and tough when cooked at a full boil. We also preferred to cook the meat covered to prevent water evaporation and a resulting overconcentration of salt in the broth. We experimented with different quantities of water in the pot, covering the corned beef by one-half inch to three inches, and found that it makes no difference in terms of the meat or vegetables. The amount of water does matter to the broth, though. The broth produced from covering the meat by one-half to one inch (8-10 cups fo a 4½ pound brisket in our 8-quart pot) and cooking it with the pot lid on was nicely seasoned and suitable to use on its own or in another soup.

The last, though not insignificant, variable was the vegetables. We tested a wide variety of vegetables from the appropriate to the exotic and settled on the traditional green cabbage, with the added interest of carrots, parsnips, potatoes, turnips, rutabagas, onions, and brussels sprouts all borrowed from New England boiled dinner, as our favorites. We tried cooking the vegetables along with the meat, but there were two distinct disadvantages to this approach. First, it made it too difficult to judge when the vegetables were

properly done. Second, it would require a pot larger than any that we had in the test kitchen or in our own homes.

The best method turned out to be removing the meat from the broth when done, then cooking the vegetables in the broth. This not only benefited the vegetables, giving them a full, round flavor from the salt and rendered fat in the broth, but it also allowed us time to let the meat rest before cutting. For vegetable preparation and cooking times, see the chart.

HOME-CORNED BEEF BRISKET

If you prefer a leaner piece of meat, feel free to use the flat cut. In fact, we found more flat cut than point cut briskets in supermarket meat cases, so you'll probably have to ask the meat department attendant or butcher to bring you a point cut. Leave a bit of fat attached for better texture and flavor.

½ cup kosher salt
1 tablespoon black peppercorns, cracked
¾ tablespoon ground allspice
1 tablespoon dried thyme
½ tablespoon paprika
2 bay leaves, crumbled
1 fresh beef brisket (4 to 6 pounds), preferably point cut, trimmed of excess fat, rinsed and patted dry

1. Mix salt and seasonings in small bowl.
2. Spear brisket about thirty times per side with meat fork or metal skewer. Rub each side evenly with salt mixture; place in 2-gallon-size zipper-lock bag, forcing out as much air as possible. Place in pan large enough to hold it (a jelly roll pan works well), cover with sec-

ond, similar-size pan, and weight with two bricks or heavy cans of similar weight. Refrigerate 5 to 7 days, turning once a day.

HOME-CORNED BEEF AND CABBAGE, NEW ENGLAND STYLE
Serves 8 with leftovers

The meat is cooked fully when it is tender, the muscle fibers have loosened visibly, and a skewer slides in with minimal resistance. Serve this dish with horseradish, either plain or mixed with whipped or sour cream, or with grainy mustard.

1 Home-Corned Beef Brisket (*see* recipe), rinsed and patted dry
7–8 pounds prepared vegetables of your choice (*see* chart)

1. Bring brisket to boil with water to cover by ½ to 1 inch in large soup kettle or stockpot (at least 8 quarts), skimming any scum that rises to surface. Cover and simmer until skewer inserted in thickest part of brisket slides out with ease, 2 to 3 hours.
2. Heat oven to 200 degrees. Transfer meat to large platter, ladling about 1 cup cooking liquid over it to keep it moist. Cover with foil and set in oven.
3. Add vegetables from category 1 to kettle and bring to boil; cover and simmer until vegetables begin to soften, about 10 minutes. Add vegetables from category 2 and bring to boil; cover and simmer until all vegetables are tender, 10 to 15 minutes longer.
4. Meanwhile, remove meat from oven and cut across the grain into ¼-inch slices.
5. Transfer vegetables to meat platter, moisten with additional broth, and serve.

Vegetables for Corned Beef and Cabbage, New England Style

The vegetables listed below are some of our favorites. However, if you love potatoes but cannot abide parsnips, choose vegetables to suit your tastes. To make sure that the vegetables are evenly cooked, we trim them all to sizes appropriate for their density and cooking characteristics and add them to the pot in two batches.

Category 1
Once the meat has been removed from the pot, add the desired selection and quantity of vegetables from this category. Return the liquid to a boil and simmer for ten minutes before adding vegetables from category 2.

VEGETABLE	PREPARATION
Carrots	Peeled and halved crosswise; thin end halved lengthwise, thick end quartered lengthwise.
Rutabagas (small)	Peeled and halved crosswise; each half cut into six chunks.
White turnips (medium)	Peeled and quartered.
New potatoes (small)	Scrubbed and left whole.
Boiling onions	Peeled and left whole.

Category 2
At the ten-minute mark, add selected vegetables from this category, return cooking liquid to boil, then continue to simmer until all vegetables are just tender, ten to fifteen minutes longer.

Green cabbage, uncored	Blemished leaves removed (small head) cut into six to eight wedges.
Parsnips	Peeled and halved crosswise; thin end halved lengthwise, thick end quartered lengthwise.
Brussels sprouts	Blemished leaves removed and left whole.

Irish Soda Bread

For bread with a moist, flavorful crumb and a crisp, tender crust,
use both cake flour and all-purpose flour, and go light on the buttermilk.

by Marie Piraino

Until a few years ago, my knowledge of Irish soda bread was limited to a popular American version filled with raisins and caraway seed. It was delicious, but its uses were limited.

This all changed after I moved to a predominantly Irish neighborhood in Boston. I quickly became a fan of the soda bread available in the many neighborhood bakeries within a few blocks of my new home. The white and brown loaves baked daily were very different from the rich, sweet Irish soda bread to which I was accustomed. These versions were unpretentious loaves with a velvety crumb and rough-textured, crunchy crust that were versatile enough to be served with butter and jam at breakfast, for sandwiches at lunch, or alongside the evening meal. My initial attempts to duplicate this simple loaf were disappointing, but the curious baker in me was determined.

As I looked over a multitude of recipes for soda bread, I found that they fell into two categories: American style and traditional Irish. The American versions contained eggs, butter, and sugar in varying amounts along with caraway seed, raisins, and a multitude of other flavorings. But most Irish cookbooks combined only four ingredients: flour (white and/or whole wheat), baking or "bread" soda, salt, and buttermilk.

I was intrigued by the prospect that only four basic ingredients could produce the bread I had recently come to love. But an initial test of a basic recipe (four cups of flour, one teaspoon of baking soda, one tea-

Ancient lore dictates that a cross cut into the top of unbaked soda bread is necessary to let the demons out; in modern baking reality, the cuts ensure even heat distribution and allow the loaf to expand without any unattractive cracks.

spoon of salt, and enough buttermilk to make a moist but firm dough) did not deliver the bread I wanted. Instead of a loaf with a tender, dense interior and crunchy crust, I ended up with a doughy, heavy bread with a thick, tough crust. I was now on a mission. After more tests and almost as many inedible loaves of bread, my tasters started asking, why bother? But the hope of finding a simple recipe that required no special ingredients, equipment, or technique and that could be completed in little more than an hour kept me going.

Testing Ingredients
Flour, being the predominant ingredient, seemed like a good place to start in my investigative baking. Because of Ireland's climate conditions, the wheat grown there is a "soft," or low-protein, variety. While not suitable for strong European-style yeast breads, this flour is perfect for chemically leavened breads. This is basically because flour with a lower protein content produces a finer crumb and more tender product, key for breads that don't have the light texture provided by using yeast as a leavener. (For more information, see "The Art of Biscuit-Making," May/June 1993.)

So after suffering through several tough, heavy loaves made with unbleached all-purpose flour, I started exploring different proportions of cake flour—a low-protein flour—and bleached all-purpose flour. And, in fact, the bread did become more tender and a little lighter with the addition of some cake flour. As the ratio of cake to all-purpose exceeded 1:1, however, the bread became much more compact and heavy with an undesirable mouth feel—one cup of cake flour to three cups of bleached all-purpose flour proved best.

Because the liquid-to-dry ratio is important in determining dough texture and bread moistness, I decided to make buttermilk my next ingredient to explore. (I also knew that the amount of this acidic liquid would have a direct effect on the amount of baking soda I would be able to use. Baking soda reacts with acids such as those in buttermilk to provide leavening; however, if there is too much soda, some remains intact in the bread, giving it a slightly metallic taste. For more information about this and other properties of chemical leaveners, see "Soda or Powder? The Lift Question" on page 23 of the January/February 1997 issue.) As it turned out, bread made with one and three-quarters or one and two-thirds cups of buttermilk gave me soft dough, which I liked, but produced bread that was doughy, almost gummy, which I definitely did not

like. With one and one-half cups, the dough was firmer, yet still moist—and the resulting bread was no longer doughy. If you don't have buttermilk on hand, by the way, yogurt can be substituted for an equally delicious bread with a slightly rougher crust and lighter texture.

With the amount of buttermilk decided upon, I was now ready to explore the amount and type of leavening used. After trying various combinations of baking soda, baking powder, and cream of tartar, I found that one and one-half teaspoons of soda, combined with an equal amount of cream of tartar, provided just the right amount of lift for a bread that was light, but not airy.

Unfortunately, the flavor of these basic loaves was mediocre at best, lacking depth and dimension, and they were also a bit tough. Traditionally, very small amounts of sugar and/or butter are sometimes added to soda bread, so starting with sugar, I baked loaves with one and two tablespoons. Two tablespoons of sugar added just the flavor balance that was needed without making the bread sweet. It was only with the introduction of butter, though, that the loaves began to lose their toughness and become outstanding. I really wanted to maintain the integrity of this basic bread and avoid making it too rich. After trying tests with from one to four tablespoons of unsalted butter, two tablespoons proved a clear winner. This bread was tender, but not crumbly; compact, but not heavy. More than two tablespoons of butter began to shift the flavor balance of the bread and add unnecessary richness.

Bake It, Cool It, Serve It
I was getting very close, but the crust was still too hard, thick, and crumbly. I wanted crunch, but crispness and tenderness as well.

In my research, various techniques were suggested for modifying the crust. Some dealt with the way the bread was baked while others concentrated on how the bread was treated after baking. Trying to inhibit the formation of a thick crust by covering the bread with a bowl during the first thirty minutes of baking did help some, but the resulting bread took longer to bake and was paler and uneven in color. Using a large flowerpot and clay dish to simulate a cloche (a covered earthenware dish specifically designed for baking bread) again gave me a bread that didn't color well, even with both preheating the tray and buttering the dough.

But the next test, which, not coincidentally, closely simulated historical cooking methods for Irish soda bread, was a breakthrough. Baking the loaf in a well-buttered Dutch oven or cast-iron pot (covered for the first thirty minutes) produced a well-risen loaf with an even, golden crust that was thin and crisp, but with a bit of chew.

I realized, however, that not everyone has a cast-iron pot available, so I explored ways of softening the crust after baking. Wrapping the bread in a clean tea towel as soon as it emerged from the oven helped soften the crust, while a slightly damp tea towel softened it even more. The best technique though, was to brush the warm loaf with some melted butter. This gave the loaf an attractive sheen as well as a delicious, buttery crust with just enough crunch. Although I liked the crust of the bread baked in the Dutch oven a little better, the ease of baking the bread on a baking sheet made the loaf brushed with butter an attractive alternative as well.

Finally, make sure that you cool the bread for at least thirty to forty minutes before serving. If cut too hot, the bread will be dense and slightly doughy.

CLASSIC IRISH SODA BREAD
Yields 1 loaf

Fresh out of the oven, this bread is a great accompaniment to soups or stews, and leftovers make fine toast. The variations following this recipe, with their flavorful grains and additions, can stand alone.

3	cups bleached all-purpose flour, plus more for work surface
1	cup cake flour
2	tablespoons sugar
1½	teaspoons baking soda
1½	teaspoons cream of tartar
1½	teaspoons salt
2	tablespoons unsalted butter, softened, plus 1 tablespoon melted butter
1½	cups buttermilk

1. Adjust oven rack to upper-middle position and heat oven to 400 degrees. Whisk flours, sugar, baking soda, cream of tartar, and salt in large bowl. Work softened butter into dry ingredients with fork or fingertips until texture resembles coarse crumbs.

2. Add buttermilk and stir with a fork just until dough begins to come together. Turn out onto flour-coated work surface; knead until dough just becomes cohesive and bumpy, 12 to 14 turns. (Do not knead until dough is smooth, or bread will be tough.)

3. Pat dough into a round about 6 inches in diameter and 2 inches high; place on greased or parchment-lined baking sheet or in cast-iron pot, if using. Score dough as in illustration 4, right.

4. Bake until golden brown and a skewer inserted into center of loaf comes out clean or internal temperature reaches 180 degrees, 40 to 45 minutes. Remove from oven and brush with melted butter; cool to room temperature, 30 to 40 minutes.

IRISH BROWN SODA BREAD
Yields 1 loaf

Unlike the Classic Irish Soda Bread dough, which is dry, this dough is extremely sticky.

Follow recipe for Classic Irish Soda Bread, making following changes: Decrease all-purpose flour to 1¾ cups and cake flour to ½ cup, adding 1¼ cups stone-ground whole wheat flour and ½ cup toasted wheat germ. Substitute 3 tablespoons brown sugar for granulated sugar. Bake bread to internal temperature of 190 degrees, 45 to 55 minutes.

OATMEAL-WALNUT SODA BREAD
Yields 1 loaf

Follow recipe for Classic Irish Soda Bread, making the following changes: Increase buttermilk to 1¾ cups. Soak 2 cups old-fashioned rolled oats in buttermilk for 1 hour. Decrease all-purpose flour to 2 cups and cake flour to ½ cup, compensating with ½ cup stone-ground whole wheat flour and ½ cup additional oats. Substitute ¼ cup brown sugar for granulated sugar and add 1 cup toasted walnuts (toasted in a pan over medium heat, stirring, until just fragrant, 4 to 5 minutes), along with buttermilk-soaked oats, to dough. Bake bread to internal temperature of 190 degrees, 45 to 55 minutes.

AMERICAN-STYLE SODA BREAD WITH RAISINS AND CARAWAY
Yields 1 loaf

Follow recipe for Classic Irish Soda Bread, making the following changes: Increase sugar to ¼ cup and softened butter to 4 tablespoons. Substitute 1 lightly beaten egg for ¼ cup buttermilk and add 1 cup raisins and 1 tablespoon caraway seeds (optional) along with buttermilk. Bake to internal temperature of 170 degrees, 40 to 45 minutes, covering bread with aluminum foil if it is browning too much.

Proper Handling for a Proper Irish Bread

1. Mix the dough with a fork until it just comes together.

2. Turn the dough out onto a work surface and knead just until loose flour gets incorporated; do not overknead.

3. Shape the dough into a six-inch round.

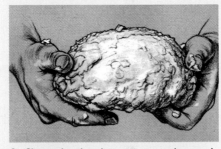

4. Place the loaf on a cookie sheet and cut a cross shape into the top.

4a. For a golden crust that's thin and crisp, with a bit of a chew, bake in a cast-iron pan.

A Light Hand

While testing the various ingredients, I discovered that the way the dough is handled while you are mixing it is as crucial as the amount and type of leavening used. Because baking soda begins reacting immediately with the acidic buttermilk, without the big second rise provided when you use double-acting baking powder, it is important to mix the dough quickly and not too vigorously. If you mix too slowly or too enthusiastically, too much carbon dioxide will be formed and dissipate during the mixing process, and therefore not enough will be produced during baking to provide the proper rise. Extended kneading also overdevelops the gluten in the flour, toughening the bread. It's no wonder that in Ireland a baker who produces a superior loaf of soda bread is traditionally said to have "a light hand," a great compliment.—M.P.

Food Processor Crepes

We find that mixing the batter in a food processor or blender and giving the batter only a short rest results in tender crepes that can be filled with easy, no-cook fillings.

By Lou Seibert Pappas with Eva Katz and Dawn Yanagihara

It's not a big surprise that crepes have been out of fashion on this side of the Atlantic for several years. Crepes, as most of us remember them, demand the creation of multistep sauces and fillings in addition to the work of putting together and cooking the batter—and in a special French pan, no less.

But I think we may be missing the point. We love wrappers, after all, when they're Asian or south of the border. Crepes are nothing more than that: Tasty, delicate, surprisingly practical wrappers that, once made, can turn everyday ingredients (including leftovers) into brunch food, dessert, spur-of-the-moment appetizers, or Sunday supper—and they take no more time than a burrito.

I thus set out to rethink crepes so they'd make sense for our American tastes. First, I did some kitchen testing to make sure I had the best-tasting and most practical recipe for the crepes themselves. I wanted them to be tasty enough to eat right out of the pan, with a texture that was tender rather than rubbery. They also needed to be thin (a thick crepe is unpleasantly heavy and stodgy) and flexible enough to fold in a number of different ways (see "Folding Crepes Step-by-Step," page 16). I then tested pans to find out whether I could forgo a special pan (see "Do I Need a Real Crepe Pan?" page 15). Finally, I developed recipes that made sense for quick everyday American meals.

Ultimate Crepe Batter, in a Flash

As I played around with a number of crepe recipes, I found that a batter slightly thicker than heavy cream worked best, coating the pan easily and thinly and yielding thin, delicate crepes. Thinner batters bubbled when they hit the pan, making holes, while a thicker batter produced heavy, rubbery crepes.

The ideal batter coats the pan easily and thinly, producing thin, delicate crepes.

While working to achieve just the right consistency, I ran several other tests designed to produce crepes with the best possible taste and texture. I found homogenized 4 percent (whole) milk preferable to both low-fat milk (not as rich and full of flavor) and beer (crepes ended up splattered with small holes). I also found that bleached all-purpose flour made a more tender crepe than unbleached all-purpose and that reducing the eggs from three to two made the crepes less rubbery and less eggy-tasting. An additional two tablespoons of water made up for the third egg. Finally, I tested crepes made with from one to four tablespoons of melted butter and discovered that while the texture of the crepes made with one tablespoon of butter was absolutely fine, the flavor was better with more. Four made a greasy batter, but three was perfect.

Having settled on a formula, I was ready to look at the mixing process. I found that hand-mixed batter needed sieving to get rid of an excessive amount of lumps. I also found that the batter didn't coat the pan as easily and the finished crepe wasn't as attractive; in addition, the texture was spongy and less tender. I figured a blender or food processor would prevent these problems, eliminate the sieving step, and be quicker and easier than a whisk. I was right; both machines made the batter effortless to put together. I chose the processor over the blender because the latter left unblended lumps around the blade and made more foam than the food processor.

A Short Rest, a Tender Crepe

Traditional recipes call for allowing the batter to rest for a minimum of two hours to let the gluten relax, ensuring tender crepes. In addition, the resting time determines, in part, the consistency of the batter: As the batter rests, the flour absorbs the liquid, causing the batter to thicken. Foam subsides during resting as well.

I tested resting times at thirty-minute intervals—from thirty minutes to two hours—to find the shortest possible resting time needed to settle the foam, bring the batter to the proper thickness, and thus ensure tender crepes. The finished crepes were noticeably more tender with the passing of each thirty-minute interval up to the two-hour mark; after that, there was no difference. Nor could I find any appreciable difference in the finished crepes when the batter sat, covered and refrigerated, for up to forty-eight hours. Occasionally, after two hours of resting, the batter got to be slightly thicker than optimal; a teaspoon or so of water will remedy this situation.

Beyond Béchamel

Now that I had a crepe I loved, I turned my attention to stuffing and saucing it. Much as I like béchamel-based fillings and sauces, I wanted something quicker. Remembering blintzes and fillings for stuffed pastas, I hit on ricotta cheese as an excellent updated base for fillings; cooks are likely to have it on hand, it makes a moist filling, and it can be flavored for both sweet and savory fillings.

As I experimented, however, it became clear that I didn't even need that formal a filling: A slice of ham and grated cheese worked as well, as did a sprinkle of sugar and lemon rind or ice cream or fruit.

As for the sauce, I knew that even though flavor was no longer a pressing issue, sauces also keep filled crepes moist while they heat in the oven. Could I get away without one? I found that if I covered the baking dish with aluminum foil during oven heating, the crepes stayed moist. If you like a richer finish, savory crepes can be buttered and sprinkled with grated cheese, sweet crepes buttered and sprinkled with sugar.

Freezing and Thawing Crepes

Crepes freeze well—as long as you defrost them correctly. To freeze, place the crepes in stacks of eight, then wrap them first in plastic and then in foil. When it comes time to thaw the crepes, remove them from the freezer and place them directly into the refrigerator to thaw. This process takes about three hours but is the best method for maintaining the quality and texture.

SAVORY CREPES

Makes sixteen to twenty 6- to 7-inch crepes or twelve to sixteen 9- to 10-inch crepes

To make the batter by hand, sift the flour and salt together in a medium mixing bowl. In a separate bowl, combine the milk, eggs, water, and melted butter and whisk them gradually into the flour. Pass the batter through a fine strainer or sieve. It takes a few crepes to get the heat of the pan right; your first two or three will almost inevitably be unusable.

2	large eggs
1	cup whole milk
6	tablespoons water
1	cup bleached all-purpose flour
1/2	teaspoon salt
3	tablespoons unsalted butter, melted, plus extra for brushing pan

1. Mix all ingredients (except extra melted butter) in food processor or blender (or by hand as noted above) until smooth batter is

formed, 3 to 4 seconds. Transfer batter to covered container; refrigerate at least 2 hours or, if desired, up to 2 days.

2. Gently stir batter if ingredients have separated. Heat 7- to 8-inch crepe pan or heavy skillet over medium-high heat. Using natural bristle brush, brush pan bottom and sides very lightly with butter, which should sizzle when it hits pan. When butter stops sizzling, pour 2½ tablespoons (use ¼-cup measure just over half full) batter into pan, following illustrations below. Cook until mottled brown on bottom, loosening crepe from pan side with table knife or metal icing spatula to check doneness, 30 seconds to 1 minute. Flip loosened crepe quickly with fingertips or spatula; cook until spotty brown on other side, about 30 seconds longer.

3. Place cooked crepe on plate and repeat cooking process with remaining batter, brushing pan as necessary, every two to three crepes. For 9- to 10-inch skillet, follow same cooking process using full ¼ cup of batter for each crepe. (Crepes can be double-wrapped in plastic and refrigerated up to 3 days or frozen up to 2 months.)

SWEET CREPES
Follow recipe for Savory Crepes, reducing salt to ¼ teaspoon and adding 2 tablespoons sugar and 1 teaspoon vanilla.

CREPES WITH RICOTTA, HAM, AND SPINACH FILLING
Fills sixteen 6- to 7-inch crepes, serving 6 to 8
If you have the time, make these crepes with one bunch of fresh spinach (about 1 pound), stemmed, steamed 3 to 4 minutes to wilt it, then refreshed, squeezed dry, and chopped. As a variation, substitute smoked turkey for the ham, blue cheese for the Gruyère, and add ⅓ cup chopped walnuts.

2   tablespoons olive oil
1   small onion, chopped coarse
2   small garlic cloves, minced
1   package (10 ounces) frozen chopped spinach, thawed and squeezed dry
10   ounces whole milk ricotta (1¼ cups)
6   ounces Gruyère cheese, grated (3 cups)
   Pinch ground nutmeg
   Salt and ground black pepper

16   slices thin-sliced baked deli ham (preferably in 6- to 7-inch rounds)
1   recipe 6- to 7-inch Savory Crepes

1. Heat oil in medium skillet over medium-high heat. Add onion and garlic; sauté until softened, 2 to 3 minutes. Transfer mixture to medium bowl; add spinach, ricotta, 2 cups Gruyère, and nutmeg as well as salt and pepper to taste; set aside.

2. Adjust oven rack to upper-middle position and heat oven to 425 degrees. Grease two 13-by-9-inch baking pans. Working one at a time, place one ham slice on a crepe; spoon 3 tablespoons filling over ham, then fold as desired (following illustrations for technique of choice, pages 16 and 17). Place in prepared baking pan; top with remaining cheese; cover with foil. Bake until heated through, about 15 minutes. Serve immediately.

CREPES WITH RICOTTA, LEMON, AND RAISIN FILLING
Fills sixteen 6- to 7-inch crepes, serving 8 to 10
2   cups ricotta cheese
4   ounces cream cheese, at room temperature (½ cup)
1   large egg
½   cup sugar, 2 tablespoons reserved
2   tablespoons grated zest from 3 lemons
1   teaspoon vanilla extract
½   teaspoon salt
⅓   cup raisins
3   tablespoons unsalted butter, melted
1   recipe 6- to 7-inch Sweet Crepes

1. Mix all ingredients except reserved sugar, melted butter, and crepes in medium bowl.

2. Adjust oven rack to upper-middle position and heat oven to 475 degrees. Grease two 13-by-9-inch baking pans. Working one at a time, spoon 3 tablespoons filling onto crepe; fold as desired (following illustrations for technique of choice, pages 16 through 17) and place on prepared baking pan.

3. Brush tops lightly with melted butter; sprinkle evenly with reserved sugar; cover with foil. Bake until heated through, about 14 minutes. Serve immediately.

Lou Seibert Pappas is a food writer and cookbook author living in Palo Alto, California.

Do I Need a Real Crepe Pan?

Since crepes are French in origin, it's no surprise that we found the classic French crepe pan (top) to be ideal for crepe making. Its sharply angled, flared sides help form perfectly round crepes, its shallow depth allows for easy flipping, and its proportionately long handle makes for easy "twirling."

These pans come in various sizes, all of which need to be seasoned before use. To do so, rub vegetable oil into the pan using a paper towel that has been folded several times. Place the pan over medium heat and continue to rub with additional oil every ten minutes for about an hour.

The second echelon of pans included the classic cast-iron frying pan as well as the All-Clad nonstick and a standard Calphalon anodized aluminum omelet pan. None was ideal, yet all were capable of producing good crepes. The cast-iron pan, like the French steel pan, has sharply angled sides that help form round crepes. However, the sides are also higher and slightly less flared than those of the crepe pan, so it is awkward to get in there with a spatula and flip the crepe. Both of the omelet pans have rounded sides, which makes it difficult to form perfectly round crepes; gentler twirling and a little practice minimize this problem. In addition, the All-Clad pan requires an additional thirty seconds of cooking time for each crepe. Caution should be taken when using a metal spatula, as it could damage the nonstick coating.

The real losers in the test were inexpensive, lightweight pans and two convex contraptions. The Revereware and Wearever pans we tested heated poorly, causing uneven browning and difficult temperature control. The Nordicware French Crepe Pan (below) and Maxim Electric Crepe Maker both use a rather unusual method. The pans are heated up, then dipped upside down into the batter and turned upright to cook on one side only. Both produce an inferior, papery crepe.—*Eva Katz*

1. Tilt the buttered and heated crepe pan just slightly to the left and begin pouring in the batter.

2. As you continue to pour the batter in a slow, steady stream, twirl the pan slowly counterclockwise until the crepe is formed.

3. To flip the crepe, loosen edge with a spatula and, with fingertips on top side, slide it toward you until you can grab edge and flip.

Blintz/Egg Roll

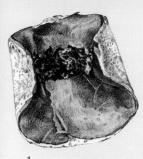
1

1. Place a portion of filling in the center, and fold both sides over about 1 inch.
2-3. Roll from the bottom of the crepe, forming a neat cylindrical shape. The finished shape will resemble an egg roll.

Recommended Fillings: Ricotta, Ham, and Spinach Filling or Ricotta, Lemon, and Raisin Filling (see page 15).

2

3

Folding Crepes

By following the steps below, you can easily form crepes into a variety of shapes, suitable for appetizers, main dishes, or desserts. In addition to the fillings on page 15, we have included here instructions for quick and easy fillings. Although we have recommended particular fillings for each shape, these are simply suggestions; feel free to mix and match as you choose. Each recommended filling

Quesadilla

1. Spread one crepe with a portion of filling, then place a second crepe over the top.
2-3. Cut the filled and baked crepe into six or eight wedges, like a pizza. The finished "quesadillas" are just right for appetizers.

Recommended Fillings: Ricotta, Ham, and Spinach Filling (see page 15), or try Smoked Salmon and Cream Cheese (see Cornucopia).

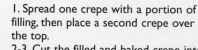

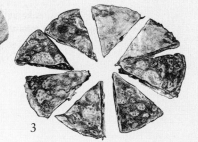
2
3

Cornucopia

1. Spread each crepe with a portion of filling and cut it into quarters.
2-3. Roll up each quarter into a cone shape. The rolled-up quarters will resemble small cornucopias.

Recommended Fillings: Smoked Salmon and Cream Cheese: Mix 8 ounces whipped cream cheese, 2 teaspoons finely grated lemon zest, 2 tablespoons lemon juice, and 2 tablespoons minced fresh dill as well as black pepper to taste. Spread 1 heaping tablespoon cream cheese mixture over crepe; lay 1/2 ounce sliced smoked salmon over cream cheese (8 ounces needed whole recipe). Or try Caviar and Crème Fraîche (see Purse).

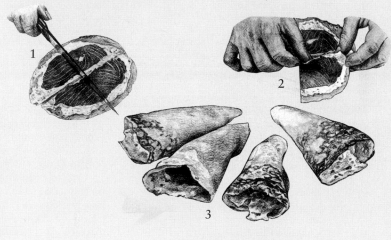
1
2
3

Half-Moon and Triangle

1-2. Spread one side of each crepe with a portion of filling; fold the crepe in half.
3. For a triangle shape, fold the crepe in half again.

Recommended Fillings: Chocolate Filling: Bring 1 2/3 cups heavy cream to simmer in large saucepan. Adjust heat to lowest setting; add 12 ounces chopped bittersweet chocolate, then stir until melted. Bake filled crepes in 425-degree oven until crisp at edges, 8 to 10 minutes. Or try Ham and Cheese Filling (see Cigarette/Roulade). Half-Moon may also be filled with Fresh Fruit Filling (see Roll/Foldover), or Sautéed Apple Filling (see Cup).

1
2
3

Roll/Foldover

1. Spoon a portion of filling along the center of the crepe. Fold one side over, almost covering the filling.
2. Fold the opposite side over, making a neat packet. The filling should show at each end of the finished crepe.

Recommended Fillings: Fresh Fruit Filling: Mix 8 cups sliced soft fruit (peaches, pears, kiwi, plums) or berries (or a mix) with 1/4 cup sugar (or to taste) and optional 2 tablespoons fruit liqueur.

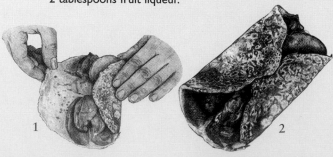
1
2

ILLUSTRATIONS BY ANATOLY

Step-by-Step

makes enough to fill about sixteen crepes. If you have made your crepes in advance and refrigerated them, heat them in the microwave, wrapped in plastic, for one minute, or in a 350-degree oven, covered with foil, for fifteen minutes, before filling and folding. When filling the crepes, make sure to place them best-looking side down.

Cigarette/Roulade

1. Spread a portion of the filling over the surface, leaving a $1/2$-inch border.
2. Roll up the crepe, forming a small cylinder.
3. Slice the crepe cylinder into thirds diagonally for appetizer-sized pieces if desired.

Recommended Fillings: Ham and Cheese Filling: Spread each crepe with 1 teaspoon Dijon mustard; top with 1 thin slice each baked ham and Swiss cheese. Bake on upper-middle rack of preheated 350-degree oven until heated through, 10 to 15 minutes. Or Ricotta, Ham, and Spinach Filling (see page 15); or Smoked Salmon and Cream Cheese, (see Cornucopia).

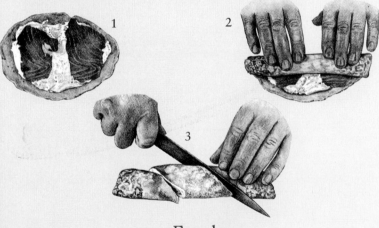

Envelope

1. Spoon a portion of filling in the center, and fold both sides over to meet in the center.
2. Fold the top half of the crepe down.
3. Fold the bottom half of the crepe up over both sides.
4. The finished crepe will resemble an envelope.

Recommended Fillings: Fresh Fruit Filling (see Roll/Foldover), Ricotta, Ham, and Spinach Filling or Ricotta, Lemon, and Raisin Filling (see page 15).

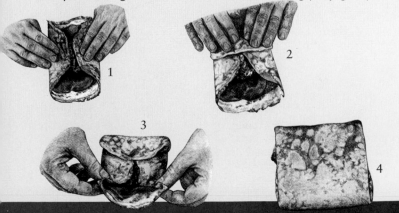

Purse

1. Place each crepe in a small ramekin and spoon in a portion of the filling.
2. Bring up the sides, forming pleats on the top, and tie them with a blanched green onion top or chive.
3. The finished crepe will resemble a purse.

Recommended Fillings: Caviar and Crème Fraîche: Fill each crepe with $1/2$ tablespoon crème fraîche or sour cream ($1/2$ cup needed for full recipe) and generous $1/2$ teaspoon caviar of choice (2 ounces needed for full recipe). Or try Smoked Salmon and Cream Cheese (see Cornucopia).

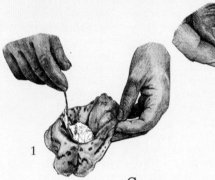

Cup

1. Place each crepe in a greased muffin cup or custard cup, carefully arranging the top in flutes.
2. You may fill the crepes before or after baking. If baking the crepes unfilled, place a small wad of foil in the pan to keep the sides up, as shown with the crepe at the front, below. Bake at 350 degrees for ten minutes unfilled, fifteen minutes filled.
3. The finished cups may be used for dessert or appetizers.

Recommended Fillings: For baked filled cups, try Ricotta, Ham, and Spinach Filling or Ricotta, Lemon, and Raisin Filling (see page 15). For baked crepe shell, fill with $1/4$ cup ice cream or frozen yogurt. Or try Fresh Fruit Filling (see Roll/Foldover).

How to Cook Shoulder Lamb Chops

These cheap, funny-looking chops deliver good flavor, are less exacting to cook
than more expensive loin or rib chops, and make for a speedy braise for weeknight dinners.

by Stephanie Lyness

❧

Like most of us when buying lamb chops, I've tended to pass over those inexpensive, weirdly shaped shoulder chops and pay more for premium rib and loin. I've always assumed that the connective tissue in shoulder should make it too tough for quick cooking methods like grilling. But, I wondered, what are these peculiar-looking chops good for? I set myself the task of figuring this out and discovered that shoulder is a much more versatile cut than I'd imagined.

Grilling and Broiling Make the Grade
As luck would have it, my first package of shoulder chops ended up on the grill because I didn't have time to braise them that night as planned. It seemed a good idea anyway to confirm my assumption that grilling could only produce tough chops. Using a fire hot enough to sear (see "How to Grill a Steak," May/June 1996), I grilled three chops: one to rare, one to medium/medium-rare, and one to well-done.

I was more than a little startled by the results. With the exception of the rare chop (which stopped short of the deliciously melting texture of the other two), the meat was tender, meaty, and juicy with excellent flavor. It seems that grilling is, in fact, an exceptional way to cook these chops; the hot fire melts the fat that runs through the meat while searing to a dark, brittle crust on the outside. As with any grilled food, the chops had enough flavor on their own to do without a sauce; a half hour in a flavorful marinade, however, made them even better.

On this first test I also discovered a clear advantage that these chops have over the more expensive rib and loin chops: Your timing needn't be so precise. While a rib chop cooked just a hair past medium-rare begins to dry out, even a well-done shoulder chop is moist. (For more information, see "Comparing Shoulder, Rib, and Loin Lamb Chops," at right.)

As a rule, I steer clear of broiling. I've never met a broiler that could brown meat as well as a grill. But because I was looking for year-round cooking methods, I took a shot at it in my electric broiler, placing the chops about two inches beneath the element. The broiler gave a very serviceable, if not brilliant, result and offers the advantage of the juices that collect on the broiling pan. Pour them over the meat as a simple sauce.

Spurred on by my successes, I tried panfrying next and was underwhelmed. There was nothing particularly wrong with this method except that the meat often curled at the edges and so didn't cook as evenly as I would have liked. But because the great delight of panfrying is the promise of the deglaze, I went on to see if I could find a way to incorporate the deglaze into a braise.

Working Out a Quick Braise
My first test in this arena was a simple stove-top braise using a minimal amount of liquid that could be quickly reduced and thickened for a sauce. I browned the chops with sliced onion in a deep sauté pan large enough to hold the chops in a single layer. Then I deglazed with white wine, herbs, a little tomato, and water to barely cover the chops and simmered the whole thing, covered, for an hour and a half until the meat was tender. I was surprised at how long the relatively thin chops took to cook, and the results were disappointing. The lamb had a sticky, gummy quality that I attribute to the scant quantity of liquid; a survey of recipes confirmed that I was using much less than the recommended amount per weight of meat.

Next I tried boning and defatting the meat, cutting it into rough cubes, and cooking it as a stew modeled on Pam Anderson's beef stew in our January/February 1996 issue. The meat cooked fine, but the boning was time consuming and the scraggly, thin pieces looked awful.

Undaunted, I tried whole chops again, this time not only switching to red wine (and more of it), but also braising the chops just to medium. I decided to try this experiment after it occurred to me that if the grilled chops were tender, I needn't actually stew the meat at all—just cook it through. The red wine improved the flavor, and cooking the meat to a lesser degree of doneness vastly shortened the cooking time. Using chops about 3/4 inch thick, I found that I now had a delicious stovetop braise that cooked in just fifteen to twenty minutes—a true weeknight supper dish for the winter months, with grilling in reserve for the summer.

BRAISED LAMB SHOULDER CHOPS WITH TOMATOES AND RED WINE
Serves 4
Because they are generally leaner, round bone chops, also called arm chops, are preferable for this braise (see "Which Chop's the Best?"). If available, however, lean blade chops also braise nicely.

4	shoulder lamb chops, about 3/4 inch thick, trimmed of external fat
	Salt and fresh ground pepper
2	tablespoons olive oil
1	small onion, chopped fine
2	small garlic cloves, minced
1/3	cup dry red wine

1	cup canned tomatoes packed in puree, chopped
2	tablespoons minced fresh parsley leaves

1. Sprinkle chops with salt and pepper to taste.

2. Heat 1 tablespoon of the oil in 12-inch heavy-bottomed nonreactive skillet over medium-high heat. Cooking in batches if necessary to avoid overcrowding, add chops; sauté until brown on both sides, 4 to 5 minutes. Remove from pan; set aside.

3. Pour fat from pan; return pan to medium heat, adding remaining tablespoon of oil. Add onion; sauté until softened, about 4 minutes. Add garlic; cook until fragrant, about 1 minute longer. Add wine; simmer until reduced by half, scraping browned bits from pan bottom with wooden spoon, 2 to 3 minutes. Stir in tomatoes, then return chops to pan. Reduce heat to low; cover and simmer until chops are cooked through but tender, 15 to 20 minutes.

4. Transfer chops to each of four plates. Stir parsley into braising liquid; simmer until sauce thickens, 2 to 3 minutes. Adjust seasonings, spoon portion of sauce over each chop, and serve.

BRAISED LAMB SHOULDER CHOPS WITH TOMATOES, ROSEMARY, AND OLIVES

Follow recipe for Braised Lamb Shoulder Chops with Tomatoes and Red Wine, adding 1 tablespoon minced fresh rosemary along with garlic and stirring in ⅓ cup pitted and sliced Kalamata olives along with tomatoes.

BRAISED LAMB SHOULDER CHOPS WITH CAPERS, BALSAMIC VINEGAR, AND RED PEPPERS

Follow recipe for Braised Lamb Shoulder Chops with Tomatoes and Red Wine, adding 1 red pepper, seeded and diced, along with onion and stirring in 2 tablespoons drained capers and 2 tablespoons balsamic vinegar along with parsley.

BRAISED SHOULDER LAMB CHOPS WITH FIGS AND NORTH AFRICAN SPICES

Soak ⅓ cup stemmed dried figs in ⅓ cup warm water for 30 minutes. Drain and reserve the water. Cut the figs into quarters. Follow recipe for Braised Lamb Shoulder Chops with Tomatoes and Red Wine, adding 1 teaspoon ground coriander, ½ teaspoon each ground cumin and cinnamon, and ⅛ teaspoon cayenne pepper to the pan with the onion and garlic mixture during the last minute of cooking. Omit red wine and replace with the ⅓ cup water from soaking the figs. Add 2 tablespoons honey with the tomatoes. Stir in the quartered figs at the end with the chopped parsley.

GRILLED SHOULDER LAMB CHOPS WITH GARLIC-ROSEMARY MARINADE

These chops can be grilled on a gas grill as well as over charcoal. To test the grill heat, hold your hand five inches over the cooking grate. When you can hold it in place for no more than two seconds, the fire is ready. Half-inch-thick chops, which you often find at the grocery store meat counter, need less cooking time—about thirty seconds less per side.

Garlic-Rosemary Marinade

2   large garlic cloves, pureed (about 1 tablespoon)
1   tablespoon minced fresh rosemary
     Pinch cayenne
2   tablespoons olive oil
4   shoulder lamb chops (blade or round bone), about ¾ inch thick
     Salt and ground black pepper

1. Mix marinade ingredients in small bowl. Rub both sides of each chop with the paste; let stand at least 30 minutes. (Can be refrigerated overnight.)

2. Heat enough coals to cover surface area large enough for four chops. Once coals are covered with gray ash, spread them, set grill rack in place, and cover grill with lid in order to heat rack, about 5 minutes. Or heat oven broiler.

3. Sprinkle both sides of each chop with salt and pepper to taste.

4. Position chops over hot coals. Grill until bottom of each chop is well browned, about 2 minutes. (If chops start to flame, pull off heat for a moment or extinguish flames with squirt bottle.) Turn each chop and cook about 2 more minutes for medium-rare or 2½ minutes for medium. If broiling, position chops 2 to 3 inches from heating element and cook about 3 minutes each side for medium-rare and 3½ minutes each side for medium.

GRILLED SHOULDER LAMB CHOPS WITH SOY-SHALLOT MARINADE

This variation is adapted from a recipe taught at Peter Kump's New York Cooking School. Follow recipe for Grilled Shoulder Lamb Chops with Garlic-Rosemary Marinade, substituting the following soy-shallot marinade: ¼ cup minced shallot or scallion, 2 tablespoons each of minced fresh thyme and parsley leaves, 3 tablespoons juice from small lemon, 2 tablespoons olive oil, and 2 tablespoons soy sauce. Marinate chops for at least 20 minutes or up to 1 hour.

Which Chop's the Best?

Lamb shoulder is sliced into two different cuts, blade and round bone chops. You'll find them sold in a range of thicknesses (from about one-half inch to over one inch thick) depending on who's doing the butchering. (In my experience, supermarkets tend to cut them thinner while independent butchers cut them thicker.) Blade chops (see illustration 1) are roughly rectangular in shape, and some are thickly striated with fat. Each blade chop includes a piece of the chine bone (the backbone of the animal) and a thin piece of the blade bone (the shoulder blade of the animal), which intrudes into the meat.

Arm chops (illustration 2) are more oval in shape and as a rule are substantially leaner than blade chops. Each contains a round cross-section of the arm bone so that the chop looks a bit like a mini ham steak. In addition to the arm bone, there's also a tiny line of riblets on the side of each chop.

As to which chop is better, I didn't find any difference in taste or texture between the two types except that the blade chops generally have more fat. I grill both blade and round bone chops: I like the way the fat in the blade chop melts on the grill, flavoring and moistening the meat, and I love the grilled riblets from the round bone chop. For braising, though, I always prefer round bone chops because they add less fat to the sauce. (That said, blade chops vary quite a bit in fat content; those with little intermuscular fat will work fine if well trimmed.) For a very quick braise, search out half-inch-thick chops.—S.L.

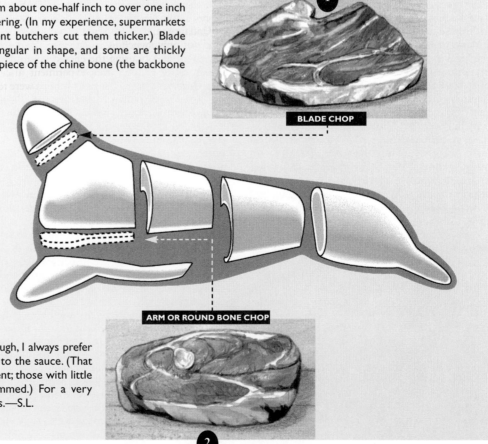

1 BLADE CHOP

2 ARM OR ROUND BONE CHOP

The Best Buttermilk Doughnuts

In just forty-five minutes, you can fry up two dozen robust country doughnuts with great crunch and flavor. The secrets to success are the right dough and the right frying medium.

by Christopher Kimball with Eva Katz

❦

Marie Briggs always wore sensible black, square-heeled shoes, hair pulled back tight in a bun, and thick, black-frame glasses. She was the town baker in our little village in the Green Mountains of Vermont, and on rainy days, when we weren't mowing, tedding, raking, or baling hay, I would spend a few hours at the small yellow farmhouse that served as her bakery. Of all the items that she baked and bagged for sale at the Wayside Country Store, the farmhands were keenest on her doughnuts, substantial rounds of nutmeg-spiced dough, fried in lard so the outside was crisp and rich in flavor. The dough was rolled out on a red-checkered, plastic tablecloth set up in the middle of the small room that served as the town center, where people checked in and out as they crossed the town line. The water came from a hand pump in the sink, and the cooking, including the frying of the dough, was done on an old soot-black woodstove, which the high-strung collie, Dixie, and the more bovine mongrel, Bonnie, sidled up to in the winter months. Years later, those of us who spent time in that tiny farmhouse remember the doughnuts best, for their toothsome chew, their hint of crunch on the first bite, and their long-lasting sturdiness.

For the past couple of years, I have made my version of these doughnuts for coffee hour at the local Methodist church. Those who remember Marie's cooking offer suggestions through the time-honored Vermont technique of asking questions. Instead of saying, "These doughnuts don't have enough nutmeg," they'll ask, "Well, do you think that Marie used a little more nutmeg in her doughnuts?" Through trial and error and the polite but earnest comments of my neighbors, I finally came up with a good approximation of Marie's original recipe. So when I offered to write a piece on doughnuts, I thought that my work was pretty much complete. As usual, I still had a lot to learn.

Defining the Goal

Before beginning our kitchen research, we had to define what sort of doughnut we were seeking. We quickly eliminated yeast doughnuts because the dough needs to rise, which makes them less practical for a quick breakfast. We also decided that fried doughnuts were the method of choice because when we tested baked doughnuts, they turned out with dull, smooth exteriors. These may be fine for delicate doughnuts, but not for the crunchy, fried rounds we were after.

Having set the parameters, we proceeded to test half a dozen different recipes for nonyeast fried doughnuts, choosing methods that seemed as different as possible so that we could judge a wide range of outcomes. And this is exactly what we got: everything from flat, greasy rounds of dough to high-rise cakey rings. After a fair amount of discussion, we agreed that the ideal doughnut would be crispy on the outside and tender on the inside, which meant we would steer clear of recipes that were extra crunchy and therefore extra greasy. (Although many factors affect greasiness in fried foods, we discovered that the deeper the oil penetrated into the doughnut, the crispier the exterior. In general, the wetter doughs allowed more oil penetration and were therefore crispier.) Our final recipe, therefore, needed to give us a doughnut with good crunch and a minimum of grease, a true country doughnut, rather than an airy Dunkin' Donuts confection.

Developing a Master Recipe

As a starting point, we cobbled together a master recipe using buttermilk, eggs, flour, sugar, baking powder, baking soda, melted butter, salt, and ground nutmeg. We made up a batch of dough and fried it in generic vegetable oil. The resulting doughnuts were good but needed improvement. So we set out to test each ingredient, starting with the buttermilk.

As is often the case with baking, buttermilk provided a superior product to regular milk; the doughnuts made with the latter were denser, firmer, and less crisp. We also tried skim buttermilk, and because we found no noticeable differences in flavor or texture, we recommend that you simply take your choice.

Our master recipe used both baking powder and baking soda for lift, so in an attempt to simplify things, we tested leaving out the baking pow-

der altogether, increasing the baking soda to a full teaspoon. The doughnuts made with this formula were far too dense. We also tried decreasing the amounts of both leavenings but found that the master recipe had a slightly better chew.

Next we tried increasing the amount of butter in the recipe, but it did not improve the flavor. Likewise, bumping the sugar up one-quarter cup (from one cup to one and one-quarter cup) simply made the doughnuts brown up more readily, which was not necessarily an improvement. Besides, they were sweet enough already. At first we thought we liked the addition of vanilla, but after a few tastings it became clear that this extra flavor overpowered the delicate taste of nutmeg, our spice of choice. When bread flour was substituted for all-purpose, the dough was firmer and drier; this resulted in a doughnut that was less crisp on the outside, not what we were looking for. Bleached flour made no noticeable difference.

So far none of our testing had yielded improvements in the master recipe, but we had some luck when we added one extra egg yolk. This made a moister dough, and the extra fat also created a more tender doughnut. Additionally, we tried boosting the flour by one-quarter cup and determined that this drier dough does make a less crispy, but also less greasy, product. It is a bit firmer too and more chewy inside, but the lack of crackle on the outside placed this variation in second place.

Testing the Frying Oil

With the recipe set, we were ready to begin our most important set of tests, the frying oil. First, though, we had to settle on the proper pot for frying. We found the best implement by far to be a cast-iron kettle; it retains heat extremely well, so the oil stays at the right temperature even when the doughnuts go in. This is crucial in getting nongreasy doughnuts. We found that the twelve-inch-diameter model was superior to the ten-inch because it maintains a nice, steady heat, keeping the oil at the proper temperature without our having to adjust the burner. We also tested anodized aluminum pots, but they were a disappointment because they really do not retain heat well. An enameled cast-iron pan worked fine, but is much more expensive, retailing for about $130 versus $45 or so for a simple cast-iron kettle.

The first fats we tried were soybean oil, corn oil, and canola oil, all of which were given

When rolling out the dough, make sure that it is no more or less than one-half inch thick, about the width of the last joint of your little finger. Thinner doughs make doughnuts that are squat, with insufficient height to provide contrast between the exterior and interior. Dough that is rolled out to five-eighths inch or more will produce a bloated orb that is undercooked on the inside because of its excessive corpulence.

mediocre grades by the tasters. However, we went on to test peanut oil and safflower oil, both of which were well liked. We then did a head-to-head taste-off between the two favorites, and peanut oil came in first, producing doughnuts with rich flavor as well as good texture.

The doughnuts were still on the greasy side, though, so I called on an old friend of mine, Drew, who runs Mrs. Murphy's Doughnuts in Manchester, Vermont. He suggested that we try a commercial shortening used by doughnut makers called Super Fry. We ordered the minimum quantity (a whopping fifty pounds!), and in a blind taste test, it won hands down. Even the doughnuts fried in peanut oil were greasy by comparison. We then tested Crisco, a hydrogenated vegetable oil. To our surprise, this was a close second to the Super Fry, absorbing much less oil than the peanut oil, our previous reigning favorite. We also found that doughnuts fried in the vegetable shortenings (Super Fry and Crisco) held up better than those fried in oil. We did note, though, that Crisco has a slightly off flavor; one taster noted that the doughnuts tasted a bit like circus food. However, the lack of greasiness more than made up for the slight imperfection in flavor.

What About Lard?
Marie Briggs swore by lard for her doughnuts, and over the years I have found that a combination of lard and oil works very well for most fried foods. But I also knew that lard has changed over the years. In the old days, the lard used in cooking was "leaf" lard, the fat around the kidneys. This superior lard has no strong flavor. Today, lard consists simply of pork fat, which may come from any portion of a pig. Generally speaking, it is much stronger and of lower quality than the lard Marie was probably using on the farm.

Even knowing this, though, we pressed on with our tests. We started off by using all lard, but it was much too meaty-tasting. We then cut back and used five ounces of lard to five cups of Crisco. This was good, very similar to the Vermont country doughnuts I grew up with, but little different from doughnuts fried in Crisco alone. We then increased the lard to two ounces per cup of shortening. This resulted in a nice boost of flavor. However, because many people want to avoid lard for health reasons and because doughnuts made without lard are very satisfactory, this is purely an optional ingredient.

Cooking Temperatures and Times
In terms of cooking temperature, we found that with the oil at 350 degrees the dough absorbs too much oil; at 385 degrees the outside starts to burn before the inside can cook through. A temperature of 360 seemed the ideal. We discovered, though, that it works best to start out with the oil at 375 degrees because the temperature will fall back to between 360 and 365 as soon as the doughnuts are put in. Also be sure to bring the shortening back up to temperature between batches.

We also wanted to find out if the shortening was reusable. Although we had been successful when reusing peanut oil, Crisco just didn't hold well; a batch of doughnuts made the next day using the same shortening suffered a good deal in terms of flavor.

Many recipes call for cooking doughnuts for one and one-half minutes per side, a time that we found to be much too long. Once the doughnuts had been placed in the hot shortening and flipped, we tested forty seconds, fifty seconds, sixty seconds, and seventy seconds and found that fifty seconds was ideal. The center was just cooked, and the doughnut did not take on that dry, catch-in-your-throat texture. The big surprise, however, was that doughnuts cooked longer were also greasier. The shorter the frying time, the less chance the shortening had to penetrate the dough.

BUTTERMILK DOUGHNUTS
Makes 15 to 17 doughnuts
There are two variations on this recipe. For a bit more flavor, add two ounces of lard to every cup of shortening. You can also add one-quarter cup of flour to the recipe, which will produce a chewier doughnut with a less crispy exterior. Regardless, these doughnuts are best eaten very warm, as soon out of the pot as possible. The dough can be made by hand, using a large bowl with a wooden spoon, or in a mixer as directed. Like cookies, doughnuts rolled from scraps will be a little drier and less crisp than those cut from the first roll.

3½	cups all-purpose flour, plus extra for surfaces
1	cup sugar
½	teaspoon baking soda
2	teaspoons baking powder
1	teaspoon salt
1½	teaspoons freshly grated nutmeg
¾	cup buttermilk
4	tablespoons unsalted butter, melted
2	large eggs, plus 1 yolk
6	cups vegetable shortening for frying

1. Mix 1 cup flour, sugar, baking soda, baking powder, salt, and nutmeg in bowl of standing mixer fitted with paddle attachment.

2. Mix buttermilk, butter, and eggs in 2-cup Pyrex measuring cup. Add wet ingredients to the dry; beat on medium speed (number 4 setting on a KitchenAid) until smooth, about 30 seconds. Decrease speed to low (number 2 setting on a KitchenAid); add remaining flour and mix until just combined, about 30 seconds. Stir batter once or twice with wooden spoon or rubber spatula to ensure that all liquid is incorporated. (The dough will be moist and tacky, a cross between cake batter and cookie dough.)

3. Fit candy thermometer to side of cast-iron kettle or large, heavy-bottomed soup kettle; gradually heat shortening over medium-high heat to 375 degrees. Meanwhile, turn dough onto floured work surface. Roll with heavily floured rolling pin to ½-inch thick. Stamp out dough rings with heavily floured doughnut cutter, reflouring between cuts. Transfer dough rounds to jelly roll pan or large wire rack. Gather scraps and gently press into disk; repeat rolling and stamping process until all dough is used. (Cut doughnuts can be covered with plastic wrap and stored at room temperature up to 2 hours.)

4. Carefully drop dough rings into hot fat four or five at a time, depending on kettle size. Turn doughnuts as they rise to surface with tongs, a Chinese skimmer, or a slotted spoon. Fry doughnuts until golden brown, about 50 seconds per side. Drain on paper towel–lined jelly roll pan or wire rack. Repeat frying, returning fat to temperature between each batch.

SUGARED BUTTERMILK DOUGHNUTS
Regular confectioners' sugar breaks down into a gummy glaze on the doughnuts, but Snow White Non-Melting Sugar (*see* Sources and Resources, page 32) makes a long-lasting coating. If you do not have it, try the Cinnamon-Sugared Buttermilk Doughnuts below.

Follow recipe for Buttermilk Doughnuts, tossing doughnuts in nonmelting sugar to coat (about 1 cup) after cooling for 1 minute.

CINNAMON-SUGARED BUTTERMILK DOUGHNUTS
Follow recipe for Buttermilk Doughnuts. Mix 1 cup sugar with 1½ tablespoons cinnamon in small bowl. Cool doughnuts about 1 minute and toss with cinnamon sugar to coat.

Doughnut Tips

1. Roll dough out on a heavily floured surface, then stamp out rounds as close together as possible. Gather the scraps, press into a disk, and repeat rolling and stamping.

2. As the doughnuts rise to the surface of the hot oil, flip them over with a Chinese skimmer, slotted spoon, or tongs.

Key Lime Pie in Minutes

With only three ingredients (including regular limes), in just over 30 minutes you can produce a four-star dessert.

by Stephen Schmidt

I will start with a confession. Until I embarked on this article, I had never made a classic key lime pie. By "classic" I mean the kind of key lime pie with a filling that consists solely of four simple ingredients: sweetened condensed milk, egg yolks, and lime juice and zest. These ingredients, when simply mixed together and poured into a pie shell, magically thicken into a filling that sets up stiff enough to slice within a couple of hours. No baking is required (though, as I will tell, I found baking an improvement). While the "magic" of the filling is easily explained (see "Thickening Without Cooking," at right), this does not gainsay the ease, convenience, and sheer fun of the recipe.

Why, then, had I never made a condensed milk key lime pie? Because the versions that I had sampled in restaurants had tasted harsh and artificial to me. I had assumed that this unpleasant flavor had something to do with the condensed milk, but once I made a classic key lime pie myself, I understood the true source. Restaurant key lime pies are prepared with bottled, reconstituted lime juice, which tastes terrible.

If, like me, you have judged, and condemned, condensed milk key lime pies on the basis of commercial offerings, I urge you to make one yourself using fresh squeezed juice. You will find the pie an entirely different experience: pungent and refreshing, yet also cool and creamy, a very satisfying dessert indeed.

The standard recipe for condensed milk key lime pie is incredibly short and simple: Beat four egg yolks, add a fourteen-ounce can of sweetened condensed milk, and then stir in one-half cup of lime juice and a tablespoon of grated lime zest. Pour it all into a graham cracker crust and chill it until firm, about two hours. Top the pie with sweetened whipped cream and serve.

It would be lovely if this recipe worked, but I found that it doesn't, at least not to my total satisfaction. Although the filling does set firm enough to yield clean-cut slices, it has a loose, "slurpy" consistency that I do not like. I tried to fix the consistency by beating the yolks until thick, as some recipes direct, but this did not help. Nor did it help to dribble in the lime juice, rather than adding it all at once, as other recipes suggest. I also made the filling with only two yolks and with no yolks at all (such "eggless" versions of the recipe do exist) but this yielded even thinner fillings.

Still, I am glad that I spent a day mixing key lime pie fillings in various ways. While in the heat of experimenting, I inadvertently threw the lime zest into a bowl in which I had already placed the egg yolks. When I whisked up the yolks, they turned green, and the whole filling ended up tinted a lovely shade of pale lime. What a great way to dispense with food coloring!

Having found the mix-and-chill method wanting, I decided to try baking the pie, as many recipes suggest. I used the same ingredients as I had before and simply baked the pie until the filling stiffened slightly, about fifteen minutes in a moderate oven. The difference between the baked pie (which was really a custard) and the unbaked pie (which had merely been a clabber) was remarkable. The baked filling was thick, creamy, and unctuous, reminiscent of cream pie. It also tasted more pungent and complex

Thickening Without Cooking

The extraordinarily high acid content of limes and the unique properties of sweetened condensed milk are responsible for the fact that key lime pie filling thickens without cooking.

The acid in the lime juice does its work by causing the proteins in both the egg yolks and the condensed milk to coil up and bond together. This effect is similar to that of heat. The same process can be observed in the Latin American dish ceviche, in which raw fish is "cooked" simply by being pickled in lime juice.

But this process does not work well with just any kind of milk; it requires both the sweetness and the thickness of sweetened condensed milk. This canned product is made by boiling the moisture out of fresh milk and then adding sugar. Because the milk has been evaporated, or condensed, it is thick enough to stiffen into a sliceable filling when clabbered by the lime juice. The sugar, meanwhile, plays the crucial role of separating, or "greasing," the protein strands so that they do not bond too tightly. If they did, the result would be a grainy or curdled filling rather than a smooth and creamy one. Of course, a liquidy, curdly filling is exactly what one would get if one tried to use fresh milk instead of canned, because fresh milk lacks the crucial added sugar and is also much thinner. Cream, as I discovered, is not a viable substitute for sweetened condensed milk either. It does not curdle the way milk does because its fat, like the sugar in condensed milk, acts as a buffer to the lime juice. However, cream is roughly 50 percent liquid, and thus it will only thicken, not stiffen, when clabbered.—S.S.

than my raw fillings had, perhaps because the heat of the oven released the flavorful oils in the lime zest.

I had discovered that condensed milk key lime pie, when prepared according to the standard recipe and baked, was a delicious dessert. However, before I settled on the standard recipe, curiosity impelled me to try a

Is a Lower Fat Pie Really Worth It?

I tested my master recipe for key lime pie with low-fat and fat-free condensed milk and found that both worked quite well, though I did detect a slight grittiness in the fat-free filling. But before you rush out to buy these products (which I had some difficulty finding in New York supermarkets), you should consider the following.

Regular sweetened condensed milk, which is 23 percent fat, derives most of its calories from sugar, not fat. One serving of key lime pie prepared with regular sweetened condensed milk derives 163 of its calories from the milk, but only 38 of those calories come from the fat in the milk, which amounts to roughly one teaspoon. Switching to low-fat milk yields only a very small savings: There are approximately 150 calories from the milk and 19 of them from the fat in the milk in each slice. Fat-free milk is not much more exciting. A slice of key lime pie made with fat-free milk still derives 138 calories from the milk, which is only 25 calories fewer than the total milk calories in a pie prepared with the regular product. For this small difference, my advice is to go for the fuller flavor of the standard product.—S.S.

couple of other recipes that I had come across in cookbooks. I had two recipes on hand that called for folding stiffly beaten egg whites into the filling: One called for three whites and the other for just one. The three-white pie surprised me. The filling was light and fluffy, as I had expected, but also slightly curdish and rich, reminiscent of cheesecake. However, I do not think that these whites-only versions are key lime pie as most people understand it; they are what might be called "fluffy key lime pies."

I also tried a recipe with heavy cream but found that the filling did not stiffen on mixing, which to my mind disqualified it.

I was ready to declare the standard recipe—lightly baked—a winner, but before I could call it quits, I needed to test the recipe with a meringue topping. In her article on lemon meringue pie in the November/December 1994 issue of this magazine (see "No-Weep Lemon Meringue Pie"), Pam Anderson gave us all the last word on weep-proof meringues. I have used Pam's recipe for meringue ever since, with a few minor touches of my own, and I used it, of course, on my experimental key lime pie. The pie looked fine when it came out of the oven, but to my horror, the meringue began to pull away from the sides of the crust within an hour. I had been careful to touch the meringue to the rim of the crust all around, so I couldn't at first imagine what had gone wrong. But when I cut the pie, I discovered the problem. The crust was too crumbly; it had given way as the meringue shrank back, as all meringues do when they cool.

How interesting, I thought. I often find crumb crusts a bit too hard, even difficult to cut, and over the years, I have deduced that an excess of butter, which is the glue that holds the crumbs together, is the culprit. With this in mind, I had deliberately prepared the crust of my experimental key lime pie with slightly less butter than I usually use. Evidently, though, I had gone too far: A certain minimum amount of butter was essential.

I did some cookbook sleuthing and noticed something I had never noticed before. There was a surprising consistency in recipes for crumb crusts. To one package of cracker rectangles, crushed, most cookbook recipes call

for either five tablespoons or five and one-third tablespoons of butter. I experimented. I couldn't really tell the difference between crusts made with these two amounts of butter, but four tablespoons, the amount I had used in my experiment, was definitely too little while six tablespoons was definitely too much, making a tough, chewy, almost candy-like crust. There are, of course, other variables to be considered in the making of crumb crusts—underbaking, for example, causes the crusts to soak through—but I now feel that I understand the most important point in the making of this indispensable American dessert component and that I could make a crust to which meringue would adhere with no problem.

KEY LIME PIE
Serves 8

If you prefer a meringue topping, follow the instructions in "No-Weep Lemon Meringue Pie" in the November/December 1994 issue. Bake pie only 7 minutes, then apply meringue gently, first spreading a ring around the outer edge, then filling in the center. Return to oven and bake 20 minutes more.

Lime Filling
4	teaspoons grated zest plus 1/2 cup strained juice from 3 to 4 limes
4	large egg yolks
1	14-ounce can sweetened condensed milk

Graham Cracker Crust
11	full graham crackers, processed to fine crumbs (1 1/4 cups)
3	tablespoons granulated sugar
5	tablespoons unsalted butter, melted

Whipped Cream Topping
3/4	cup heavy cream
1/4	cup confectioners' sugar
1/2	lime, sliced paper thin and dipped in sugar (optional)

1. *For the filling*: Whisk zest and yolks in medium bowl until tinted light green, about 2 minutes. Beat in milk, then juice; set aside at room temperature to thicken.

2. *For the crust*: Adjust oven rack to center position and heat oven to 325 degrees. Mix crumbs and sugar in medium bowl. Add butter; stir with fork until well blended. Pour mixture into 9-inch pie pan; press crumbs over bottom and up sides of pan to form even crust. Bake until lightly browned and fragrant, about 15 minutes. Transfer pan to wire rack; cool to room temperature, about 20 minutes.

3. Pour lime filling into crust; bake until center is set, yet wiggly when jiggled, 15 to 17 minutes. Return pie to wire rack; cool to room temperature. Refrigerate until well chilled, at least 3 hours. (Can be covered with lightly oiled or oil-sprayed plastic wrap laid directly on filling and refrigerated up to 1 day.)

4. *For the whipped cream*: Up to 2 hours before serving, whip cream in medium bowl to very soft peaks. Adding confectioners' sugar 1 tablespoon at a time, continue whipping to just-stiff peaks. Decoratively pipe whipped cream over filling or spread evenly with rubber spatula. Garnish with optional sugared lime slices and serve.

Stephen Schmidt is a cooking teacher, regular contributor to Cook's Illustrated, *and author of the forthcoming* Dessert America *(Scribner).*

True Key Limes vs. Supermarket (Persian) Limes

True key limes (above right), or *Citrus aurantifolia*, have not been a significant commercial crop in this country since storms destroyed the Florida groves early in this century. However, a few growers have recently begun to revive the crop, and key limes occasionally show up in supermarkets. Most food writers seem to like key lime juice much better than Persian lime juice, but they give wildly divergent reasons for their preference. One book that I have on hand describes key limes as "sourer and more complex" than their supermarket cousins. But another writer holds that key limes differ from Persian limes (above left) in being more "mild" and "delicate."

I could not find key limes at the market when I was working on this article, but I have used them twice in the past in preparing lime curd. I'd love to be able to say that key lime juice made all the difference in the world, but it didn't. To my palate at least, it tasted pretty much the same as the juice of supermarket limes. I also feel duty-bound to add that key limes are a nuisance to zest and squeeze for they are thin-skinned, full of seeds, and generally little bigger than walnuts. You need only three or four Persian limes to make a key lime pie, but you will need up to a dozen key limes. So despite the name of the pie, I actually find the juice of Persian limes preferable as an ingredient.—S.S.

1. To make sure the graham crackers form a firm, coherent crust on the bottom of the pie pan, press them down firmly with a cup or glass. Be careful not to cover the pan's lip with crumbs, however.

2. If the finished pie sticks to the pie pan when you're ready to cut, simply dip the pan into a bowl of warm water to loosen the pie.

Braised Celery

Braise on top of the stove with a bit of butter, celery seed, and a dash of vermouth.

by Katherine Alford

In today's world of fashionable vegetables, celery is about as hip as a bingo night. But as a celery fan, I wanted to find a way to transform the crunch of this underrated vegetable into a tasty, tender, cooked side dish. I decided to focus on braising, a method with lots of variations.

When buying celery, I had three choices: loose heads topped with bushy leaves, plastic-bagged celery heads with clipped leaves, and packages labeled "celery hearts" containing two or three dwarfed and cropped heads. I preferred the loose celery; these heads tended to be fuller and fresher without brownish edges and yellowing leaves. Also, the stalks were glossier and had fewer external ridges, indicating a less fibrous stalk. The outer stalks' color is a sign of taste and freshness; I found that bleached-out stalks tended to be more pithy and dark green ones edged on the acrid. The bagged celery hearts had paltry, bitter outer stems and shabby brown edges. Celery stored in a perforated plastic bag in the vegetable bin of my refrigerator lasted for about a week; after that the flavor faded and the celery became rather flabby.

Find the Right Braising Liquid

Braising—cooking something partially immersed in a liquid while covered—is an easy cooking technique with the added benefit of producing a wonderfully flavored broth. I started cooking the celery in water; not surprisingly, it was pretty lackluster. The braising liquid was perfumed by the celery, but the stalks' well-deserved reputation as diet food needed something to enrich them. Next I braised the celery in chicken stock, a usual medium for this vegetable, but found that I lost the distinctive celery taste in the broth. Braising the celery in cream was unappealingly rich.

I returned the celery to the water but with bits of butter. I found that a moderate amount of butter added a pleasing finish. I tried braising with olive oil but found that the flavor didn't suit the celery as well as that of butter.

Unfortunately, as the celery cooked, its flavor faded. I tried adding celery leaves, which boosted the taste, but the whole leaves were stringy. Chopping the leaves helped, but the real solution became one of sprinkling celery seed into the liquid, which added the right aromatic punch to both broth and stalks. For another dimension I tried adding a bit of vermouth or white wine to the braising liquid. The vermouth was the better partner with the celery, contributing a needed touch of herbal sweetness and acidity.

Peeling and Cutting

As I tested various braising liquids, I also tested cutting the celery stalks in different ways: curved thin slices, whole and split heads, cut stalks, and peeled and unpeeled. Peeling really improved both the texture and color of the dish. The unpeeled celery, especially the large outer stems, were like a mouth full of string, even after extended cooking. Peeling also stripped away the surface green color, which tended to go drab when cooked, and the resulting hue of the cooked celery was a pretty sea-washed bottle green. Although attracted to the idea of cooking whole heads of celery, I found them awkward to peel as well as difficult to fit into a pan. And because of celery stalks' unique bowed shape, the curved thin pieces didn't lie flat when cooking. This in turn increased the amount of water I needed, an undesirable aspect given the fact that the celery itself released liquid during cooking. By splitting the stalks lengthwise, however, and then slicing them into two-inch-long pieces, I got ample pieces that cooked evenly and were adaptable to numerous variations.

I found that the best cooking procedure was to bring the liquid, flavorings, and celery to a boil in a medium sauté pan, cover everything with parchment paper (*see* illustration), and then simmer the celery for about fifteen minutes, until tender, but not mushy. The parchment held moisture at the surface of the liquid, helping to cook any pieces that were not submerged. Of course, the pan can also be covered with a lid, but when I tried this the celery didn't cook as evenly and needed to be stirred during braising. Braising in the oven took twice as long to get tender, and the celery acquired a drab green color.

Depending on how you want to serve the celery, several choices exist for finishing the dish. If you want a very loose broth, the celery can be served at this point or transformed into a gratin. For glazed celery, a personal favorite, remove the parchment and simmer the broth for five to seven minutes until the pieces are coated with a light sauce. Glazed celery's pure flavor is a wonderful complement to sautéed fish. If you continue to boil the liquid until it evaporates, the celery can be browned in the residual butter, giving it a nutty edge.

Covering with parchment paper helps cook any pieces not submerged, with no stirring needed.

BRAISED CELERY WITH VERMOUTH-BUTTER GLAZE
Serves 4

- ½ cup dry vermouth
- 3 tablespoons unsalted butter, cut into small pieces
- ¼ teaspoon salt
- ¼ teaspoon celery seed
- ⅛ teaspoon ground black pepper
- 1 head celery (1½ pounds), leaves trimmed and reserved; stalks separated, rinsed, and outer fibers removed with a vegetable peeler; each stalk halved lengthwise and cut on an angle into 2-inch lengths
- 2 tablespoons minced celery leaves
- 2 tablespoons minced fresh parsley leaves (optional)

Bring 1 cup water and vermouth, butter, salt, celery seed, pepper, and celery to boil in medium sauté pan, covering surface of celery with parchment or waxed paper circle. (Liquid should come about ¾ of the way up the celery pieces.) Reduce heat to simmer; cook until celery is tender, but not mushy, 15 to 20 minutes. Remove paper; stir in celery leaves. Continue to simmer until broth reduces to light glaze, 5 to 7 minutes. Sprinkle with optional parsley, adjust seasonings, and serve.

GLAZED CELERY WITH PARMESAN CHEESE

Follow recipe for Braised Celery with Vermouth-Butter Glaze, adjusting oven rack to upper middle position and heating broiler. Transfer glazed celery to ovenproof dish, sprinkle with ¼ cup grated Parmesan cheese, and broil until cheese browns, 1 to 3 minutes, depending on broiler.

CELERY-ROQUEFORT GRATIN

Follow recipe for Braised Celery with Vermouth-Butter Glaze, heating oven to 400 degrees. Braise celery until just tender, about 15 minutes. As celery braises, cream 4 teaspoons flour and 3 ounces Roquefort cheese together with spoon. Remove parchment or waxed paper circle and transfer celery pieces with slotted spoon into 4-cup (10-inch round) gratin dish. Whisk cheese mixture into reserved broth. Bring to boil; simmer until thickened, about 1 minute. Pour cheese sauce over celery, shaking pan to distribute sauce evenly. Sprinkle top with ¼ cup chopped walnuts. Bake until sauce is bubbly and nuts are lightly browned, 25 to 30 minutes. Remove from oven, cool 5 minutes, and serve.

Katherine Alford is a cooking teacher and food writer living in New York.

ILLUSTRATION BY HARRY DAVIS

All Canned Crushed Tomatoes Are Not the Same

Panelists unerringly pick brands with a higher proportion of tomatoes than puree. Surprisingly, the two Italian brands come in dead last.

by Jack Bishop

❧

If you think all brands of crushed tomatoes are basically the same, think again. I have been running tastings for this magazine for many years. Rarely has a group of products shown such a wide range of quality and styles. Despite the diversity, however, our panel of thirty tasters had no trouble deciding on their favorites. And those brands at the bottom of the list? So bad, they "wouldn't feed them to the dog," as one opinionated panelist quipped.

Starting with this tasting, we are adding a new dimension to our evaluations of food products. In the past, we have relied on expert panels of ten or twelve tasters to judge products. This time, we expanded the field to include twenty nonprofessionals as well. All tasters, both experts and nonprofessionals, filled out the same form developed by David Fishken, president of Sensory Resources, a consumer-oriented product development firm in Newton, Massachusetts. On the form, panelists rated how much they liked each brand overall as well as assessing various sensory characteristics.

Because we wanted to see how samples would perform in the kitchen, we tasted each brand both raw and cooked into a simple sauce. Panelists rated every sample on appearance, color, visible skin, number of seeds, smoothness, chunkiness, wateriness, thickness, tomato flavor, sweetness, saltiness, acidity, bitterness, and metallic taste. When we compared each of these characteristics with the "overall liking" ratings for each brand, it became clear that some characteristics were positive influences, some negative, and others made no difference at all.

We found that the perception of "overall flavor" was the single most important factor affecting how much people liked the individual brand. The second greatest predictor of the overall score was the strength of the tomato flavor. A thick (as opposed to thin or watery) consistency was the third most important factor, followed by the appearance (panelists liked brands with some seeds, a possible indication that these samples were perceived as being more "natural" than brands without seeds), chunkiness, and color.

Likewise, our research found that several attributes had a strong negative correlation with overall scores. Brands with low scores were likely to be metallic-tasting, bitter, or overly acidic.

Defining the Ideal

So how did our panel describe the ideal can of crushed tomatoes? First of all, they were looking for knockout tomato flavor that was slightly sweet, with a light acidic component. They wanted the tomatoes to be thick and chunky, with a healthy dose of seeds and a bright red color.

Progresso and Muir Glen scored well in all the areas our tasters found important. Both brands were found to have an excellent tomato flavor, with a good balance of sweetness and acidity. Muir Glen is a tad thicker and much chunkier than Progresso. In fact, the pieces are so big in the Muir Glen cans that some tasters wondered what kind of machine was used to "crush" these tomatoes.

Redpack and Contadina are a step down in quality, according to our panel. Contadina is considerably thinner than the top brands, and both were judged to have less tomato flavor.

Tuttorosso, an American brand with an odd, saucelike consistency, too much basil, and not enough tomato flavor, came in fifth. The smooth texture was less of a problem when the tomatoes were made into sauce, but the odd flavor issues remained. At the bottom of the rankings are two imports from Italy, Rienzi and Pomi. As indicated by the chart below, these brands rated quite far behind the leaders. Our tasters found the Rienzi tomatoes too sour while Pomi, which is a strained product, was as smooth as baby food, another characteristic that our panel did not appreciate.

Interestingly, our tasters ranked raw and cooked samples the same, even though they did not know which samples went together. For instance, when scores for raw and cooked samples were separated (not combined as they are in the chart below), the sauce made with Progresso tomatoes came in first, followed by Progresso raw tomatoes, Muir Glen made into sauce, Muir Glen raw tomatoes, Redpack made into sauce, Redpack raw tomatoes, and so on down the line. So go ahead and open a can of crushed tomatoes and stick in a spoon; if you like what you taste straight from the can, you will be happy with the sauce these tomatoes make. Incidentally, we were also interested to find that the scores given by our expert tasters and our nonprofessionals were identical.

Two Types of Tomatoes

To figure out if there was any unifying characteristic among the top-rated tomatoes, we did some research into the way tomatoes are canned. We spoke with Peter Mueller of Tri-Valley Growers, the California company that manufactures Redpack and Tuttorosso as well as other regional brands like Libby's and S & W. (In a pre-tasting, we found the latter two brands to be quite similar to Redpack. Libby's and S & W are popular in the Midwest and West.)

According to Mueller, tomatoes are sorted into two groups when they reach a canning facility. The first group is called paste tomatoes. These tomatoes (which may be any one of many tomato varieties) have a high solid content and are difficult to peel. They must be cooked to loosen their peels and are used to make tomato paste and puree.

The skins on the second group, called solid-packed tomatoes, are easily removed. Because minimal heat is needed to peel these tomatoes, they are used in whole and crushed tomatoes, for which fresh tomato flavor (as opposed to cooked flavor) is paramount. Because consumers expect a brilliant red color in crushed tomatoes, Mueller says the brightest and ripest specimens are saved for this use.

Before crushing, solid-packed tomatoes can be peeled by one of two processes: steaming or treatment with lye. Lye maintains better color and does less damage to the layer of flesh under the skin. Steaming, however, has its advocates, especially among natural foods enthusiasts. Other than Muir Glen (which never uses lye), most manufacturers select one or the other of these two processes

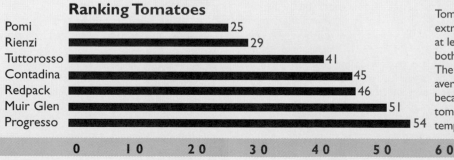

Ranking Tomatoes

Brand	Score
Pomi	25
Rienzi	29
Tuttorosso	41
Contadina	45
Redpack	46
Muir Glen	51
Progresso	54

0 10 20 30 40 50 60 70 80 90 100

Tomatoes were ranked from 0 to 100, with 0 indicating extreme dislike and 100 indicating extreme like. The scores at left are an average between the two tastings of tomatoes, both raw and cooked in a simple sauce with olive oil and salt. The scores for the two tastings were similar and not much averaging was needed. The numbers are somewhat low because of the unappetizing but straightforward way the tomatoes were tasted: straight from the can and in a room temperature sauce that was served as is and not over pasta.

depending on the variety and the ripeness of the particular tomatoes.

At this point, the crushed tomato solids and liquid are usually reinforced with tomato puree to give the product some body and viscosity. While this is standard procedure, the amount of puree that is added turned out to be the crucial factor in our tasting. When we analyzed the results, it became clear that adding too much puree (which, after all, is a cooked product) diminishes the fresh tomato flavor and has a negative impact on overall quality.

Our top brands both list tomatoes first on their labels, then tomato puree. Redpack and Contadina contain more puree than tomatoes while the primary ingredient in Tuttorosso is tomato concentrate (water and tomato paste). This brand does not contain any fresh tomatoes, which explains why tasters thought it seemed more like sauce than crushed tomatoes. The labels on the Italian products are less precise, as is often the case with imported products.

We decided to run our own physical analysis of each brand to see how much tomato was actually in a standard twenty-eight-ounce can, which holds a total of three cups of solids and liquid. We wanted to see if there was any correlation between tomato solids and the tasting results. We also wanted to clear up the confusion regarding the labels on the Italian products.

We poured one can of each brand into a strainer set over a measuring cup and allowed the liquid to drain off for thirty minutes. We then used a wooden spatula to press out the remaining liquid, and measured the solids. We found that the three top-rated brands—Progresso, Muir Glen, and Redpack—contain the most tomato solids, at least one and one-half cups per can. The bottom-rated Italian brands, Rienzi and Pomi, contain the least amount of tomato solids, barely one cup per twenty-eight ounces.

A note on some of the other ingredients you may see on labels. Salt is added for flavor and citric acid helps to fix the color and keep it bright while calcium chloride prevents softening and helps maintain the shape of the tomato solids.

CRUSHED CANNED TOMATOES EVALUATED

We assembled a panel of thirty food experts and nonprofessionals to taste canned crushed tomatoes in two preparations. Several cans of each brand were mixed together (so everyone would taste the same sample and not from different cans) and then ladled into small plastic cups. We also made a batch of sauce with several cans of each brand. The sauce contained tomatoes, olive oil, and salt. The sauce was served at room temperature in plastic cups. Tasters had access to bread and water. The entries below indicate the site of the manufacturing plant or company headquarters, the price for a twenty-eight-ounce can unless otherwise noted, and the ingredients as listed on the label.

HIGHLY RECOMMENDED

These brands were the clear favorites of the our panel. Muir Glen is much chunkier than Progresso, which may influence your choice.

Progresso Recipe Ready Crushed Tomatoes with Added Puree (Missouri), $1.29.
This sample had the overall best tomato flavor and was judged to be fairly chunky, second only to Muir Glen. As one expert taster wrote, "the type of product I prefer: a bit sweet, a slight acidic finish, and good texture." Another panelist wrote, "the best," and most tasters agreed. Label reads "tomatoes, tomato puree, salt, and citric acid."

Muir Glen Organic Premium Ground Peeled Tomatoes (California), $2.19.
These tomatoes were much chunkier than the other samples. They also were the thickest. Although most tasters liked "the fresh, clean tomato flavor" and chunky texture, a few wished the tomatoes had been more finely crushed. Label reads "organically grown and processed tomatoes and tomato puree, sea salt, and naturally derived citric acid."

RECOMMENDED

These brands showed respectably in the tasting. Panelists thought the tomato flavor was a bit more muted than in top brands.

Redpack Unpeeled Crushed Tomatoes with Thick Tomato Puree (California), $1.19
These tomatoes were deemed to have the most appealing color. However, they were less sweet than top brands, with a higher bitterness quotient. One expert panelist wrote, "good tomato flavor almost masks the strong acidic component but needs more sweetness to work." Label reads "tomato puree, tomatoes, salt, and citric acid."

Contadina Crushed Tomatoes in Tomato Puree (California), $1.39.
This brand was almost identical in scoring to Redpack. It was judged to be the brightest in color and the sample with the toughest skin and most seeds. Considerably thinner and saltier than the top choices. Tasters did not seem to mind the seeds but complained about "tiny bits of tough skin which stick in the back of throat like rolled-up paper." Flavor was judged to be "quite good" though. Label reads "tomato puree, crushed unpeeled tomatoes, salt, calcium chloride, citric acid."

NOT RECOMMENDED

These brands showed poorly in the tasting. Note that both Italian products are in this group.

Tuttorosso New World Style Crushed Tomatoes (California), $.99.
This very smooth sample was both sweet and salty with not enough tomato flavor. The addition of dried basil was problematic for many panelists. "I want crushed tomatoes that are plain, not overwhelmed by herbs." Another taster wrote, "tastes like sauce and not like fresh ripe tomatoes." When made into sauce, this brand scored slightly better. Label reads "tomato concentrate (water, tomato paste), salt, citric acid, dehydrated basil."

Rienzi Crushed Peeled Tomatoes Puree (Italy), $1.09.
The texture of these tomatoes was deemed too smooth and watery. The flavor, however, was the real problem. It was judged the least sweet and most sour and bitter sample in the group. "Too acidic and bitter. Not a good product," wrote one taster. A few dissenters liked the "strong tomato jolt," but they were in the minority. Label reads "selected Italian tomatoes in puree with basil."

Pomi Strained Tomatoes (Italy), $1.69 for thirty-five-ounce aseptic carton.
This sample received the lowest scores in the tasting for appearance and tomato flavor. The complete absence of seeds and skins disturbed most panelists, as did the absolutely smooth texture. "Like sauce already" or "looks like ketchup," wrote our tasters. "Bland" or "missing" tomato flavor did not help either. Label reads "tomatoes, salt."

Do Electric Knife Sharpeners Really Work?

If you don't have an electric knife sharpener, chances are you have dull knives.
But to improve the situation, you must choose carefully.

by Mark Zanger

It's true that a well-sharpened knife can't make food taste better, but it certainly can make routine kitchen tasks suddenly pleasurable. Vegetables cut cleanly and without hesitation, herbs mince rapidly, and sandwiches can be halved with one satisfying thwack.

Until fairly recently, there were two ways to restore a sharp edge to a dull knife: either take the knife to a professional sharpener or figure out how to use a sharpening stone and do it yourself. Sharpening stones require tremendous patience and a real commitment of time, more than most cooks are willing to make. The problem with relying on a professional (if you can find one) is that even the most conscientious cook will wait months between sharpenings before taking their knives to the sharpener.

So I decided to investigate the third option, electric sharpeners. These tools for the home cook promise to deliver great edges without the need to set up complicated machine tools and calculate sharpening angles. Ideally, they should be quick and easy to use, allow frequent sharpening, and therefore ensure that the knives in your home are consistently sharp. I set out to discover whether any of the home electric sharpeners presently on the market meet these criteria.

Living on the Edge

First I needed to understand the geometry of a knife edge and what electric sharpeners do to the blade to restore its sharpness.

Most electric sharpeners have several slots, each of which cuts the knife edge at a different angle. In the first stage of grinding, sometimes called presharpening, the knife is placed in a slot that removes the dull edge and creates the first bevel, or angle, of the two that together make up the knife's edge. This first angle (called the relief angle) is typically around fifteen

degrees to the face of the blade. The knife is then moved to a different slot, which makes a slightly more steeply sloped bevel (the sharpening angle) that comes to the point of the edge. The result is a double-beveled edge (*see* illustration 1) with plenty of metal behind it to resist dulling. Some sharpeners, including our winner, cut a third bevel for an even stronger edge.

There is a clear and convincing reason for this dual-angled edge. Although single grinding at a lower angle (as possible on a stone) creates an edge that is actually sharper, such edges are more vulnerable to nicks and wearing down because there is not as much metal supporting the edge (illustration 2). Unless you're cutting sushi, it is definitely worth sacrificing ultimate sharpness for durability.

Along the edge of the knife, the blade material is pushed out into a thin, irregular burr. If this burr is kept short and straight, it makes a fine ribbon of metal that leads to a razor-sharp slice. If the burr is bent to one side, however (illustration 3), the knife will cut as though it were duller than it really is. Reducing the burr and keeping it straight is the traditional task of steeling: sliding the knife across a steel rod. But because steeling at the wrong angle can bend the burr even more and result in an even duller knife, most contemporary knife experts actually advise against using a steel. (Most people steel too vigorously and do not keep their wrists locked.) Manufacturers of electric sharpeners suggest a few quick passes through the "stage two" slots at the end of sharpening to remove and align the burr.

Once the burr has broken the surface of whatever food is being cut, sharpness depends upon the smoothness and consistency of the sharpening angle and the relief angle to push the material apart. The weight and balance of the knife also affect cutting power regardless of the edge.

The Tests

To test the various electric sharpeners on the market, I decided that it made sense to obtain a number of identical chef's knives. I then assigned one knife to each sharpener and proceeded to perform a number of tests. Since I would be sharpening the knife as many times during a two-week period as the average home cook would in a year or more, the effect each sharpener would have on a knife over the course of repeated sharpenings would quickly become evident.

I chose to test the eight-inch chef's knife because it is the one tool that can do it all, from carving and slicing to chopping, mincing, and cutting up chicken parts. I obtained a supply of the Forschner Fibrox eight-inch chef's knife that was picked as the best buy in our testing of chef's knives back in the March/April 1994 issue. One reason this stamped knife outdid some of the more expensive forged knives was because of its superb factory edge. This sharp initial edge set a high standard against which we could judge the sharpeners.

I used both culinary and nonculinary cutting tests and examined blades and sharpeners with a magnifier and a low-power microscope, then resharpened the blades and did it again, for a total of more than twenty tests of each edge.

To measure each blade's slicing ability, I used them to cut paper in two ways—cutting paper that I was holding in the air and cutting the paper as it floated down in the air. These were good tests of the sharpness of both the tip and the full length of each blade, translating into the ability to take one-sixteenth-inch slices of ripe tomato and to dice plum tomatoes without hesitation on the skins. I also tested whether each knife could make clean

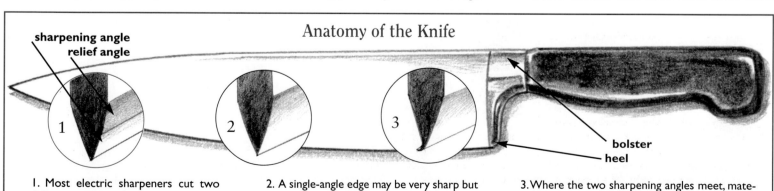

Anatomy of the Knife

sharpening angle
relief angle

1

2

3

bolster
heel

1. Most electric sharpeners cut two different angles (one in each slot) to create a double-beveled edge with plenty of metal behind it.

2. A single-angle edge may be very sharp but tends to dull quickly because there is less metal behind it.

3. Where the two sharpening angles meet, material is pushed out into a thin, irregular burr. If this metal is bent to one side, as shown, the knife becomes dull.

ILLUSTRATIONS BY TONY DELUZ

slices of raw corn kernels off the cob as well as clean slices of computer foam packing.

I chose cutting apart chicken wings to test the sharpness near the tip of the knives, and cutting parsley stems tested the smoothness near the heel. I noted the ease of slicing corncobs with the front half of the knives and mincing the slices with the back half. While there isn't a lot of call for sliced or minced corncobs in modern cuisine, the tests are extreme examples that translate to performance on slicing and chopping any fibrous vegetable or fruit.

Finally, I filed a notch about as large in diameter as a paper clip in the knives to see how many sharpenings (and how much time) it would take to regrind the entire edge. I set up this test to judge what kind of toll the sharpeners would exact on knives over time. I wanted to know if it is feasible to do a knife repair this extreme at home, relatively how much material the sharpeners remove from the knife blades, and how the knives might look after a year's sharpening (*see* "Will Electric Sharpeners Reduce the Life of Your Knives?").

The Results

When I finished all the tests, Chef's Choice had emerged as the clear leader. They produce sharp edges with a minimum of lost metal. The Chef's Choice 110 has six slots (three for each side of the knife) and yields the best edge. With four slots, the Chef's Choice 310 is similar but lacks the two presharpening slots found on the 110, making it impossible to regrind neglected knives. You can save $30 by buying the 310 but will need to send gouged or damaged knives out for professional sharpening.

I also liked the Chef's Choice Commercial 2000 but felt that the extra speed was not worth an extra $300. As for the edge, when I followed the literature that came with the sharpener, I was not able to get a truly sharp knife. This was especially apparent when slicing tomatoes. I talked to a representative at the company, and I was given some suggestions for a "bitier" edge. I got a better edge, but the average home user won't.

With just two slots, the Sabatier was very easy to use, but the edge was not quite as sharp or durable as with the top models.

For most of the tests, I used the manufacturer's printed instructions. After little success with the Presto and Oster, I tried using the loose slots on these machines to get faceted edges by leaning toward the center of the slots in the first stage of sharpening, then leaning the knives against the outside of the slots for a higher sharpening angle. This unorthodox technique worked remarkably well with the four-slot Presto and somewhat well with the single-slot Oster, neither of which sharpen as well if one tries to keep the knife upright as directed.

However, the Presto has a high-rpm motor and small abrasive wheels that remove a lot of material during sharpening and emit lots of sparks with carbon steel knives. Because the sparks indicate heat, and too much heat can actually soften a blade by undoing the effects of tempering steel, I still don't recommend the Presto. And because I was unable to get a really good edge from the Oster, with or without the manufacturer's instructions, I can't recommend this unit either.

Mark Zanger is a freelance writer living in Boston, MA.

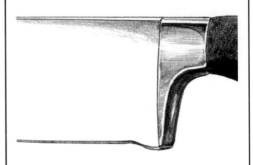
Sharpening by Hand

In the old days, every culinary school student had to demonstrate his or her ability to sharpen knives on a stone. Many famous chefs still complain about the arduous nature of this task. For home cooks, sharpening stones and other manual systems are even more daunting. However, many serious knife hobbyists believe that manual sharpening systems remove less material than electric sharpeners (prolonging the life of your knives) and also produce smoother, sharper edges.

I wanted to see if I could figure out how to use these stones, whether some models were better than others, and if it was worth the bother: Would I get sharper edges with less metal removed?

The good news is that with much practice and patience, it is possible to use a stone with excellent results. You can get knives that are actually sharper than you need.

Of the five different hand-sharpening systems I tested, the cream of the crop is the Edge Pro Apex. The arm-mounted abrasives adjust for sharpening angles from 10 to 35 degrees. Thus I was able to make an ultrathin, 10-degree blade that actually outperformed the Forschner factory edge on slicing tasks. Of course, the blade was so thin that there were visible nicks left on it after I used this knife to chop chicken wings, so this is no

edge for a chef's knife, but if you own a long slicing knife, this is the sharpener of choice.

Although it took me about an hour to really get the hang of the Edge Pro, the manual is excellent and the company also has a useful video, which can be returned for purchase credit. The two drawbacks of the Edge Pro Apex are price ($125) and speed. With the medium and fine abrasive stones provided, it takes about fifteen minutes to turn a sharp Forschner knife into a sharper one. The supersharp blade was a thirty-minute grind. Order an additional stone with your Edge Pro if you plan on major rehabilitation jobs.—M.Z.

The best, and most expensive, hand-sharpening system is the Edge Pro Apex at $125, but it takes up to 30 minutes to sharpen a knife.

Rating Electric Knife Sharpeners

Six electric sharpeners were evaluated according to the following criteria and are listed below in order of preference. Each sharpener was assigned the same eight-inch chef's knife throughout the testing, and the knives were numbered below the handle so the edge tests could be graded before the tester knew which knife and sharpener were being tested.

Price: Retail prices from New York and Boston kitchen stores and from mail-order catalogs (*see* Sources and Resources, page 32, for mail-order information).

Ease of Use: Highest ratings went to manuals that clearly defined how rapidly and how many times to pull the knife through the sharpener and how to check for the development of a burr.

Edge Sharpness: More than twenty tests were performed with each knife, from slicing tomatoes to mincing corncobs. The blades were also checked with a magnifier and a low-power microscope after each sharpening. The ability of each model to sharpen an edge using the printed manufacturer's directions is listed.

Heavy Grinding: To see which sharpeners remove the most material (which over the long run may be damaging to your knives), I filed a $3/64$ -inch nick, big enough for a number-one paper clip, in each knife. The chart shows the time required to restore a smooth edge, followed by the equivalent number of sharpenings. Models that took more time removed less material from the edge during each individual

sharpening and therefore received higher ratings because this showed they would not cut short the life of the knife. The Chef's Choice 310 is not rated because it was judged to remove too little material to use in this way.

Bolster Distance: I measured how close to the heel of a forged knife each sharpener can grind. The figures below reflect the average distance from the bolster to where sharpening actually began on ten-inch forged chef's knives from Henckels and Sabatier. The smaller the distance, the better the sharpener's design. The three lower-rated sharpeners also left visible indentations next to the handles of the stamped Forschner knives after the heavy grinding test, which simulates a year's regular sharpening.

| Best | Fair | Poor |

Name	Price	Ease of Use	Edge Sharpness	Heavy Grinding	Bolster Distance
Chef's Choice Professional 110: Easy and reliable sharpening of even the dullest knives. Diamond abrasives are gentle on knives.	$85			70 minutes/ 103 sharpenings	$1/16$"
Chef's Choice 310: Smaller and handier than the 110, but no presharpening wheel means it's too slow to work on neglected knives.	$55			N/A	$1/16$"
Chef's Choice Commercial 2000: Very high price mostly buys high speed. Also, edge does not quite measure up with top models.	$360			15 minutes/ 50 sharpenings	None
Sabatier Cuisine France: Easiest machine to use gives a decent but unfaceted edge.	$50			23 minutes/ 45 sharpenings	$5/16$"
Presto Eversharp: Loose slots are hard to use, and this model tends to remove too much metal. Also, sparks on carbon steel.	$20			15 minutes/ 20 sharpenings	$3/16$"
Oster Cutting Edge: The single loose slot can't sharpen a whole chef's knife. Not recommended.	$20			38 minutes/ 43 sharpenings	$7/8$"

Tasting Non-Chardonnay White Wines

We ran a tasting for those tired of chardonnay and came up with a striking and little-known alternative.

by Mark Bittman

Although it is generally agreed that the chardonnay grape produces the best dry white wines, there has been something of a backlash against it in the United States in recent years. There are several reasons for this.

First, it isn't clear that California provides the best climate and/or soil for growing the grape. There are good California chardonnays, but there have been very few great ones. Second, California chardonnays routinely have been over-oaked, which deprives them of some of their individual character. Finally, other regions, such as the Northwest and the Northeast, began production of the grape later and therefore have not yet reached their potential.

The result has been a plethora of ABC (Anything But Chardonnay) wines in recent years as consumers begin to look elsewhere and farmers and producers have realized that many vineyards are better suited to other white wine grapes. The trend began with a surge in the growth of sauvignon blanc and has continued to the point where even relatively obscure grapes such as viognier and pinot gris are now grown up and down the West Coast.

This tasting was our attempt to sort out the alternatives among American white wines. It was successful in several ways. It identified one varietal, pinot blanc, as the clear preference of our panel. It identified another, viognier, as having potential in reaching a wider audience. And it succeeded in reestablishing the conviction—held by all of the panel's veteran tasters—that at least in the United States, sauvignon blanc is not a grape that shows especially well when it is left unblended.

In alphabetical order, these are the grapes represented in the wines we tasted:

Chenin Blanc: The grape of Vouvray, probably better suited to soft, semisweet wines than to the drier style of wine most American wine drinkers buy most of the time. Did not show well here, but probably more due to stylistic differences than to poor winemaking.

Pinot Blanc: Widely grown in Alsace, but also in Burgundy, Italy (where it is called *pinot bianco*), and central Europe. Known for its ability to produce wines with good body and flavor, but little aroma, characteristics that make it deceptive because many good wines are first recognized by the nose. Pinot blanc wines finished first and second in our tasting, and most tasters wished there had been more of them included.

Pinot Grigio/Gris: Grown in Italy and France, a grape capable of producing light, crisp, high-acid, and sometimes nutty wines. Neither of the wines representing this grape did well in the tasting.

Riesling: The great white wine grape of Germany has had mixed success here.

Sauvignon Blanc: A widely grown grape, made into splendid unblended wine in the Sancerre and Pouilly Fumé regions of France and blended with Sémillon in Bordeaux. Many U.S. winemakers have made it into grassy, herbaceous wines, but these have fallen into disfavor of late, and there is a tendency to begin blending it here. Note that the Beringer wine, in which sauvignon blanc is blended with sémillon, was the only wine containing this grape to make it into the Recommended category.

Sémillon: *See* previous entry, above. Sémillon's most important roles are in the production of the great sweet wines of Sauternes and neighboring regions and in blending with Sauvignon Blanc in Bordeaux. Not usually a solo player; the lone entry in this tasting finished, undistinguished, in the middle of the pack.

Viognier: The white wine grape of the northern Rhone, powerful at its best, and one that shows great promise in California, where other grapes indigenous to southern France have developed nicely. Good, if not great, showing here; but this is not an easy grape to grow, and that is reflected in a relatively high price.

Rating the Wines

The wines in our tasting—held at Mt. Carmel Wine and Spirits in Hamden, Connecticut—were judged by a panel made up of both wine professionals and amateur wine lovers. In the judging, seven points were awarded for each first-place vote, six for second, five for third, and so on. The wines were all purchased in the Northeast; prices will vary considerably throughout the country.

Highly Recommended

1995 Lockwood Monterey Pinot Blanc, $13. Super wine, well made and generally agreed to be the class act of the tasting. Ranked in the top five by all but two tasters. Amateur: "Rich and fruity." Pro: "Full-flavored and spicy, with a long finish."

Recommended

1995 Mirassou Monterey Pinot Blanc, $8.99. Strong but distant second-place finisher must be considered a best buy. Very flavorful, especially for a light wine. Amateur: "Light, spicy, and fruity." Pro: "Subtle," but "well made and well balanced."

1995 McDowell Mendocino Viognier, $18. Nearly tied for second, this wine showed why viognier is an up-and-coming varietal. Amateur: "Buttery, with an attractive aroma." Pro: "Nice aperitif, and maybe even more serious."

1994 Beringer Knights Valley Meritage (Sauvignon Blanc and Sémillon), $12. The most chardonnay-like nonchardonnay of the tasting; oaky and full. Amateur: "Coconut-vanilla nose, reminiscent of chardonnay." Pro: "Serious nose that follows through."

Recommended with Reservations

1994 Chateau Ste. Michelle Columbia Valley (Washington) Sauvignon Blanc, $8. Decent enough wine, but excited no one.

1995 Preston Dry Creek Valley Viognier, $20. The biggest reservation here turns out to be price. For a "fragrant but light" wine (pro), it was generally considered "nondescript" (amateur). In all fairness, would probably show better in a tasting of lighter wines; unquestionably well made and without major flaws.

1993 Dry Creek Vineyard Sonoma Fumé Blanc, $11. Most of our professional tasters liked this wine as did some of our amateurs. But three amateur tasters found it objectionable, with a "nasty bite." Worth a try.

1995 King Estate Oregon Pinot Gris, $12. "Soft, light" wine (amateur) with "few defects" and "nice floral character and complexity" (pro). But some found it "too sweet."

1994 Columbia Crest Columbia Valley (Washington) Sémillon, $7. Sole sémillon was not appreciated: "Seaweed" (pro), "chemical" (amateur). Two lovers of white Bordeaux liked its "subtle" nature and "crispness."

1995 Fetzer California Fumé Blanc, Echo Ridge, $7. "Good flavor" (amateur) and "well made" (pro), but "lacks depth and finish."

1995 Pine Ridge Napa Valley Chenin Blanc, Yountville Cuvée, $9. "Lively wine" with a "bit of spritz," but one that was found "too sweet" by many. Again, in fairness, this would have done considerably better in a tasting of semisweet wines (in fact, the 1992 Pine Ridge finished second in our tasting of chenin blanc wines close to three years ago).

1994 Glen Ellen California Sauvignon Blanc, $6. Two admirers ("fruity" and "enjoyable") and exceptionally low price make this wine from a large producer worth a shot. But beware: Most tasters found it "bland."

Not Recommended

N.V. Chappellet Old Vine Cuvée, $12.
1993 Bonny Doon California Riesling, $9.
1995 Martin Brothers Central Coast Pinot Grigio, $13.

Book Reviews

by Mark Zanger

I like to cook, so I collect cookbooks. But I also enjoy using my home computer. Hoping to combine two enthusiasms, I recently reviewed sixteen of the multimedia cooking CD-ROMs to see, hear, and mouse-click the newest medium for cooking lessons and recipes.

Based on the one cooking CD-ROM I truly enjoyed, and the better aspects of the fifteen others I reviewed, software has more potential in the area of cooking lessons, rather than individual recipes. It's true that computers can index and recalculate recipes in an instant and then print out the results, but these little conveniences don't yet outweigh the familiarity and superior content of really first-rate cookbooks.

But computer software already has cookbooks beat on one crucial point, and that is in the video illustration of cooking techniques. No one has yet been able to render in prose or printed photos a completely effective explanation of kneading dough, beating egg whites to hard peaks, folding egg whites into a batter, carving a turkey, opening oysters, sharpening a knife, or cutting up a whole chicken. It's just more helpful to see these things done. You can see techniques demonstrated on cooking TV shows and videotapes, but the computer CDs are much more useful because you can quickly find the technique you need at the time you need it. The digital images make for easier replays and clearer freeze-frames, and the technique video can be just a mouse-click away from the recipe.

Any CD-ROM needs some great video to get a second look. And it needs serious, original content to get a third look. But it has to be easy to use and *fun to play with* even to get the first look. Part of the fun, for me, is having an engaging, entertaining personality as my instructor.

I suppose, therefore, that it should not have come as too much of a surprise that eighty-something Julia Child would turn out to be my top choice for bringing the fun of cooking to yet another medium. *Julia Child: Home Cooking with Master Chefs* (Microsoft Home, $30, Windows only) is the one CD that was amusing to browse, the one that tempted me to try some new dishes, and the one that demonstrated the tricky cooking techniques better than a cookbook. This does not mean the CD was perfect, though. Only twenty-five recipes get the full video treatment. This would be no disadvantage if the sixteen guest chefs were more interested in everyday home cooking so the techniques would be generic rather than recipe-specific. But while the dishes presented are certain to impress any dinner party guests, there are few generally useful principles.

After Julia, the pickings become increasingly slim. In fact, looking for a general cookbook on CD-ROM quickly reveals how immature the medium is, as none of the producers but Microsoft can get more than one of the basic elements working at a time. If there is a large video library, the videos aren't good enough, or the program doesn't function well, or the recipes are silly, or the fun has gone out of it.

A near miss is the new *Williams-Sonoma Guide to Good Cooking* (Bröderbund, $40, Windows 95 and Power Mac) with 126 videos tied in pretty well to one thousand recipes taken from the Williams-Sonoma Kitchen Library series. The technique videos artfully blend slide shows (sequences of still photographs) and full-motion video, and cover some of the basics, as with a very good video of folding in egg whites and a stimulating selection of pie decoration ideas. Doing kneading as a slide show is ineffective, however. And the recipes, developed by various authors for a series of specialized books, don't add up to a basic cooking course or a coherent style. Unfortunately, Chuck Williams never appears, nor does anyone else—just the impersonal hands of studio test cooks. The programming is sophisticated: This and Microsoft's Julia Child have the only menu-scaling programs that know enough to go from six portions up to eight without demanding 2 1/3 eggs or a cake pan of nonexistent size. Warning: This disk only runs on computers sold within the last two years, as the program demands high-color video and 16 megabytes of RAM, and runs slowly even when it gets all that. On the plus side, it is the only cooking CD-ROM that comes with an old-fashioned print manual.

Better Homes and Gardens Healthy Cooking Deluxe (Multicom, $40, Windows/Macintosh) has about 150 videos of techniques, including a fair survey of the basics, and one thousand recipes. But the recipes have a dumbed-down quality that doesn't stop with using canned vegetables and margarine. I actually preferred the smaller,

older version of the same program, *Better Homes and Gardens Healthy Cooking*, which had a simpler, quicker navigation system.

Unlike many other CD-ROMs, *John Ash's Wine Country Cuisine* (Pinpoint, $30, Windows only) actually has a live human being, who appears in 128 videos and lots of audio clips from Ash's Bay Area radio program. Alas, radio chef-ing was not great training for the videos, in which Ash talks and points, but seldom cooks. On the whole, the same material was more fun to use in the form of Ash's award-winning cookbook *From the Earth to the Table*. Score one for the printed word.

The bonus with this disk, though, is the underlying database program, Micro Cookbook, which not only performs all kinds of nutritional calculations and ingredient searches, but also incorporates recipes from ten other file formats, lets you add your own recipes, lets you edit John Ash's recipes (most CDs just let you attach notes), and lets you export the Ash recipes into some other database programs.

For just a lot of recipes, I rather enjoyed *Elle Cooking* (Grolier Interactive, $30, Windows and Mac), with two thousand recipes and two thousand color pictures of those recipes from the French women's magazine *Elle*, whose detachable recipe cards have been traded by French home cooks for decades. The program is rudimentary, but has a hint of Gallic charm, and the pictures are tempting. The twenty-six videos are no real help, though, and I would bet the French keep buying those paperback collections of the recipe cards.

You might think that specialized cooking areas would be easier for producers to approach, but that wasn't the case with *Vegetarian Delights* (Arôme, $40, Windows or Mac), which had novel recipes like a giant sushi loaf made in a terrine, but confusingly short videos. Or with *World Cuisine Chinese* by Madeleine Greey (Oasis Blue, $16, Windows or Mac), which was simple and solid, but boring. Or with *4 Paws of Crab* (Live Oak Multimedia, $32, Windows or Mac), which may be an intriguing look at Thai cooking but barely ran without constantly crashing the computer.

After many hours in front of my computer screen, I have to conclude that while there are definite advantages to CD-ROMs, it's going to be awhile before they outdistance cookbooks in either usefulness or pleasure. For the time being, these will remain separate enthusiasms.

Sources and Resources

Most of the ingredients and materials necessary for the recipes in this issue are available at your local supermarket, gourmet store, or kitchen supply shop. The following are mail-order sources for particular items. Prices listed below were current at press time and do not include shipping or handling unless otherwise indicated. We suggest that you contact companies directly to confirm up-to-date prices and availability.

Knife Sharpeners

Among the four different brands of electric knife sharpeners tested in the story on page 24, top ratings were garnered by two Chef's Choice models. The Williams-Sonoma Catalog (800-541-2233) carries the Model 110 for $85 and the Model 310 for $55. If you have an urge to indulge the artisan lurking deep within, you may want to try a manual sharpener. Of the five manual sharpeners we used, Edge Pro Apex was the best. The Apex, which comes with two stones, one fine and one medium, and a carrying case, is available directly from the small Oregon company that makes it, Edge Pro (P.O. Box 95, Hood River, OR 97031; 541-387-2222—call between 11:00 A.M. and 2:00 P.M., Pacific time), for $125. With average home use, the stones should last well over a year, and additional stones can be ordered for $12 apiece.

Cast-Iron Pot

Testing showed that several of the recipes in this issue, namely the buttermilk doughnuts on page 20 and the soda bread recipes on page 13, turn out particularly well when made in cast-iron cookware. The advantages of cast iron include fantastic heat retention, heft, unbeatable durability, and price, which is often half the cost of comparable, well-made cookware. Our favorite vessel for frying the doughnuts was the seven-quart, twelve-inch-diameter Dutch Oven, which is a size 10 in the parlance of the maker, Lodge Manufacturing Company. The full line of Lodge cast-iron pots and pans is available by mail from the Lehman's Non-Electric Catalog (One Lehman Circle, P.O. Box 41, Kidron, OH 44636; 330-857-5757). The size 10 Dutch Oven, with lid, costs $45.

Doughnut Cutter

Having tried several different types of doughnut cutters while developing the doughnut article on page 20, we realized that some cutters were much easier to use than others. First, the center hole should be held in place with spot welds so it will not dislodge as you remove your dough round. Second, the top of the cutter should be open so you can push down on the sticky dough round with your fingers to help release it from the cutter. The closed-top, assemble-it-yourself cutters we purchased in supermarkets disappointed us, but not so the tinned steel doughnut cutters we purchased at a local cookware store called Kitchen Arts (161 Newbury Street, Boston, MA 02116; 617-266-8701). These comparatively sturdy cutters, which sell for $1.25 apiece, measure roughly three inches in overall diameter with a three-quarter-inch-diameter doughnut hole. Slightly larger doughnuts cutters, with a four-inch overall diameter and a fluted edge, are also available for $1.95, but we did not experiment with these. Kitchen Arts accepts phone orders from any U.S. or Canadian location, though there is a $5 handling fee, above the normal shipping costs, to ship to Canada.

Nonmelting Sugar

The regular supermarket confectioners' sugar we were using to dress up the buttermilk doughnuts from the recipe on page 28 kept melting on us, or rather, on the doughnuts, to make a gooey, unpleasant glaze. The solution to our problem was Snow White Non-Melting Sugar sold for $3.75 per pound in the King Arthur Flour Baker's Catalogue (P.O. Box 876, Norwich, VT 05055; 800-827-6836). Each grain of the Snow White Non-Melting Sugar is encapsulated in a microthin layer of lecithin, which prevents it from melting in all but the greatest heat. The lecithin changes the flavor of the sugar only slightly so it is not as intensely sweet as regular confectioners'. Rest assured, though, it's still plenty sweet.

Crepe Pan

After testing a wide range of pans for crepe making in the article on page 14, we decided that our very favorite among them was the classic French design. La Cuisine Kitchenware (323 Cameron Street, Alexandria, VA 22314; 800-521-1176) offers imported French crepe pans, made of carbon steel, in several sizes. The centimeter measurements given for these pans refer to the diameter across the top rim. The base of each pan, and therefore the size of the crepe it will produce, is just over one inch smaller. We prefer the pan with the eighteen-centimeter (about seven-inch) top diameter and roughly six-inch base for $9. Other sizes are also available: a smaller pan with a sixteen-centimeter (about six-inch) top diameter and a five-inch base for $7, and larger sizes, including a twenty-centimeter (almost eight-inch) top diameter with a seven-inch base for $11, a twenty-two-centimeter (roughly eight-and-three-quarter-inch) top diameter with a seven-and-one-half-inch base for $13, a twenty-four-centimeter (about nine-and-one-half-inch) top diameter with an eight-and-one-half-inch base for $15, and finally a twenty-six-centimeter (about ten-and-one-quarter-inch) top diameter with a nine-and-one-quarter-inch base for $17.

Potatoes to Grow and Eat

The letter about Yukon Gold potatoes in the September/October 1996 issue's Notes from Readers section inspired Bernard Krainis, a reader from Great Barrington, Massachusetts, to send us the catalog from his favorite mail-order source for all things potato, Ronniger's Seed Potatoes (Star Route 40, Moyie Springs, ID 83854). Ronniger's is geared toward home gardeners and farmers who want to grow their own potatoes. The catalog itself tells you almost everything you need to know to plant, grow, and harvest potatoes and lists more than fifty seed potato varieties for sale, along with books, some equipment and fertilizers, and roughly ten types of organically grown eating potatoes, including Yukon Gold. The eating potatoes are sold, subject to availability, both full size for $19.50 per ten-pound bag and as smaller fingerlings for $16.50 per five-pound bag. Generally, the potatoes are harvested in September and shipped through the first frost in November. Shipping suspends during December and January and resumes, weather permitting, in February through May. Ronniger's is a small, farm-run business that prefers customers to write, rather than call, for a free catalog and information.

Appliance Replacement Parts

If you're as tough on small kitchen appliances as our editors and test kitchen are, you've undoubtedly broken a handle, loosened a knob, or cracked a cover here and there. Too often, such minor accidents have meant having to retire the damaged appliance forever. But there is a much more sensible alternative. A huge variety of replacement parts and accessories, including many for older or discontinued models, is available by mail-order from a California business called Culinary Parts Unlimited (80 Berry Drive, Pacheco, CA 94553; 800-543-7549). By special arrangements with the producers, Culinary Parts Unlimited is able to carry parts for appliances made by thirty-five manufacturers, from Bodum, Braun, Brita, and Bunn right through to Zojirushi.

Meat Loaf Pan Update

A number of readers wrote and called to let us know that the Chicago Metallic brand of perforated meat loaf pan listed in September/October 1996 Sources and Resources is no longer available from The Chef's Catalog. An alternate source for that pan, albeit one-half inch longer for a total of nine inches, is A Cook's Wares (211 37th Street, Beaver Falls, PA 15010-2103; 412-846-9490), where it sells for $9.90. Other than the overall length, all features, including the nonstick coating and perforated inner pan with outer drip pan, are the same.

Corned Beef and Cabbage, pg. 10
with Oatmeal Walnut Soda Bread, pg. 12

Recipe Index

PHOTOGRAPHS BY DAVE HENDERSON

Braised Lamb Shoulder Chops with Tomatoes,
Rosemary, and Olives, pg. 18

Crepes with Ricotta, Ham, and Spinach, pg. 17

Spinach Salad with Shrimp, Mango, and
Red Onion, pg. 9

Buttermilk Doughnuts, pg. 28

Key Lime Pie, pg. 22

Pickled Grape Relish
with Ginger and Chiles

In large saucepan over medium heat, bring to boil 1½ cups distilled white vinegar, ½ cup light brown sugar, ¼ cup granulated sugar, 2 tablespoons coriander seeds that have been crushed, 2 cinnamon sticks (or 1 tablespoon ground cinnamon), 3 whole cloves, and 1 teaspoon salt. Remove from heat; mix in one 2-inch piece peeled fresh gingerroot, sliced very thin; 2 red or green unseeded jalapeno peppers, sliced thin; 3 cups rinsed, mixed red and green seedless grapes. Soak grapes 1 hour or longer and serve with roasted or grilled poultry or pork. Makes about 1 quart.

Number Twenty-Six

June 1997

COOK'S
ILLUSTRATED

20-Minute Tomato Sauce
The Best Pantry Pasta Sauce

Rating Two-Quart Saucepans
Nonstick Pans
Take Top Honors

How to Cook Lobster
Most Lobster Lore Is More
Fiction Than Fact

Best Strawberry Shortcake
More Than a Biscuit,
Better Than a Cake

AUTHENTIC HOMEMADE
FOCACCIA

ORANGE JUICE TASTE TEST

SECRETS OF PANFRYING STEAKS

FRENCH TOAST TWO WAYS

PERFECT POACHED EGGS

$4.00 U.S./$4.95 CANADA

Contents

About *Cook's Illustrated*

Cook's Illustrated *is published every other month (6 issues per year) and accepts no advertising. A one-year subscription is $24.95, two years is $45, and three years is $65. Add $6 per year for Canadian subscriptions and $12 per year for all other countries. Gift subscriptions may be ordered for $19.95 each. You will receive a* Cook's Illustrated *gift card for each subscription, which can be used to announce your gifts. The editors of* Cook's Illustrated *also publish an annual hardbound edition of the magazine, which includes an annual index. These are available for $21.95 each plus shipping and handling. Discounts are available if more than one year is ordered at a time.*

Cook's Illustrated *also publishes two single topic books,* How to Make a Pie *and* How to Make an American Layer Cake. *Both are available for $14.95 each. The* Cook's Bible, *authored by our editor and published by Little Brown, is also available for $24.95. Back issues are available for $5 each. We also accept submissions for both Quick Tips and Notes from Readers. See page 4 for more information.*

All queries about subscriptions or change of address notices should be addressed to Cook's Illustrated, *P.O. Box 7446, Red Oak, IA 51591-0446. A free trial issue of our sister publication,* Handcraft Illustrated, *may be requested by calling 800-526-8447.*

To order either subscriptions or books use the cards bound into this issue or, for faster service, call 800-526-8442 for subscriptions and 800-611-0759 for books and annuals.

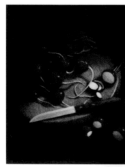

"Radishes"
Illustration by
Brent Watkinson

"Watercress, Endive, and Radicchio with Smoked Salmon"
Illustration by
Rene Milot

COOK'S
ILLUSTRATED

Publisher and Editor	Christopher Kimball
Executive Editor	Pam Anderson
Senior Editor	John Willoughby
Senior Writer	Jack Bishop
Associate Editor	Adam Ried
Contributing Editors	Mark Bittman Stephanie Lyness
Test Kitchen Director	Eva Katz
Test Cook	Dawn Yanagihara
Assistant Editor	Maryellen Driscoll

Art Director	Cathy Copeland
Special Projects Manager	Amy Klee

Managing Editor	Keith Powers
Editorial Prod. Manager	Sheila Datz
Copy Editor	Gary Pfitzer

Marketing Director	Adrienne Kimball
Circulation Manager	David Mack
Fulfillment Manager	Larisa Greiner
Newsstand Manager	Jonathan Venier
Marketing Assistant	Connie Forbes

Vice President Production and Technology	James McCormack
Systems Administrator	Paul Mulvaney
Production Artist	Kevin Moeller
Editorial Production Assistants	Robert Parsons Daniel Frey

Controller	Lisa A. Carullo
Accounting Assistant	Mandy Shito
Office Manager	Tonya Estey
Special Projects	Fern Berman

Cook's Illustrated (ISSN 1068-2821) is published bimonthly by Boston Common Press Limited Partnership, 17 Station Street, Brookline, MA 02146. Copyright 1997 Boston Common Press Limited Partnership. Periodical postage paid at Boston, MA, and additional mailing offices, USPS #012487. For list rental information, please contact List Services Corporation, 6 Trowbridge Drive, P.O. Box 516, Bethel, CT 06801; (203) 743-2600, FAX (203) 743-0589. Editorial office: 17 Station Street, P.O. Box 470589, Brookline, MA 02146; (617) 232-1000, FAX (617) 232-1572. Editorial contributions should be sent to: Editor, *Cook's Illustrated*. We cannot assume responsibility for manuscripts submitted to us. Submissions will be returned only if accompanied by a large self-addressed stamped envelope. Subscription rates: $24.95 for one year; $45 for two years; $65 for three years. (Canada: add $6 per year; all other countries: add $12 per year.) Postmaster: Send all new orders, subscription inquiries, and change of address notices to *Cook's Illustrated*, P.O. Box 7446, Red Oak, IA 51591-0446. Single copies: $4 in U.S., $4.95 in Canada and other countries. Back issues available for $5 each. PRINTED IN THE U.S.A.

EDITORIAL

Sweet and Sour

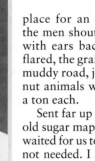

Christopher Kimball

I once attended a cooking conference at which the speakers described the difference in tasting abilities from person to person. They explained that some of us have more taste buds than others and are therefore more sensitive to overly sweet frostings or the sharp, sour taste of rhubarb.

As with most people, flavor memories are as strong and complex for me as scents; to this day, the slightly sour mouth-filling sweetness of apple butter brings back a kitchen full of faces long gone: Floyd and Herbie, Obie and Marie, Bernie and Wally, suddenly alive again, all busy telling stories and then, without warning, sitting in complete silence, as only country people know how to do.

As we were developing the recipe in this issue for tomato sauce, I rediscovered the complexity of taste. We found that with just the right sort of canned tomatoes, prepared in just the right manner, a rich, sweet tomato flavor would burst on the tongue, followed by a kick of acidity, a hint of garlic, an underlying layer of salt, a tongue-coating burst of olive oil, and the fresh scent of basil to finish. In cooking, we aspire to complexity, avoiding the consolidation of tastes and textures to achieve unexpected but rewarding marriages. It is this maturity of taste, a recognition perhaps that life is infinitely diverse and unpredictable, that defines a great cook.

I am fortunate, as a parent of three children, to spend much time in the small Vermont town of my youth, the kids exploring the same logging roads and playing in the same barns as I did growing up. But last summer, I decided that my oldest daughter should learn a bit about hard work by helping out a local farmer. Her first job was to help us corral a few Belgian draft horses from the upper pasture above the old Lomberg farm so they would be ready for our horse-drawn Fourth of July parade. These were working animals, about sixteen hands high, and they didn't much like the look of our rope halters. We funneled three of them into a small spot by the gate, trees on one side and a steep bank on the other, but it was dangerous work, one of them spinning up on his hind legs, muscled forequarters up over the back of a second horse taking flight through the woods. It was no

place for an eight-year-old, the men shouting, the horses with ears back and nostrils flared, the grain spilled on the muddy road, jostled by chestnut animals weighing almost a ton each.

Sent far up the bank, by an old sugar maple, my daughter waited for us to finish, left out, not needed. I looked up, saw the tears just starting down her cheeks, and had a sharp memory of times on the farm when I was young, rebuked for running a tractor downhill out of gear, pulling a fully loaded hay wagon; or standing helplessly by while the old-timers hooked up the teams to the old-fashioned mechanical mowers, snapping the ancient wooden hames around the collars, sorting out the tugs and traces, pole straps and lazy straps, whippletrees and eveners, britchens and back pads. It was a lonely time in those moments. I felt unwanted and painfully aware that I was just a kid.

After the horses were safely in the barn, our family jumped into the pickup and went up to the swimming hole just past the Methodist church. It's not really a hole, but a series of pools and chutes, used by generations of town kids. It was late afternoon, the sun lighting up the crystal pools, turning the water a radiant green. I dove in, an icy baptism, came up to the surface, and saw the dappled leaves, the rush of water, a hint of trout and moss-covered schist in the stream's moist, fresh scent, the sour taste of the heat of the day gone in an instant. And then all three kids followed, my oldest daughter jumping into my arms, exhilarated, happy, immersed in the rush of the stream and the wildness of the moment, as if we had all been together forever, and would live on forever, suspended in time by the swirl of water, the sparkle of sun through the waving birches.

It was a day of contradictions, of disappointment and pure joy, but, as it seemed later, the two events were intertwined, one needing the other. My daughter had tasted first of sour, then of sweet, the latter enhanced and made more joyous by the former. I remember that we all slept well that night, but I like to think that she slept best, having tasted the full measure of life on a day that ended with a full moon rising over the hollow, the sweet smell of fern in her hair, and a father who lay awake for just a moment, thinking of other summer days long ago.

Notes *from* Readers

A Different Take on Vertical Roasters

Having read your last two articles on roasting chicken [see "Roasting Chicken 14 Ways," January/February 1996 and "Testing Roasting Racks for Poultry," January/February 1997], I would like to suggest a technique to help your vertical roaster deliver better results.

Used as directed, I have found that the vertical roaster can dry out the sensitive breast meat while leaving the dark meat around the thigh pink and underdone. My solution is to invert the chicken on the roaster so the neck is at the bottom and the legs and thighs at the top. This seems to accomplish several things—for one, cooking the more forgiving dark meat in the upper half of the oven where the temperature is hotter so that the dark meat cooks completely in a time frame that does not dry out the breast. Second, having the dark meat positioned above the breast automatically bastes it with the juices that run down from the dark meat. Fringe benefits include the tighter fit of the narrow neck opening around the roaster, which prevents the bird from bunching up at the bottom of the pan, and the effect of gravity, which pulls the legs away from the body, better exposing the inner thigh to the heat for more even cooking.

ED INFURNA
DARIEN, CT

We tested your idea several times and found everything you say to be true. Yet we are still not vertical roasting fans. Here's why: Our disappointment with the vertical roasters was due primarily to their inability to brown and crisp the skin of the bird. This held true even for the chickens we roasted upside down, on which only the skin on the legs, which were at the top, got crisp and brown. The skin at the front of the breast and the neck remained, by comparison, flabby, yellow, and chewy.

The meat was a totally different story. Though we felt all along that the better vertical roasters do a reasonably good job of cooking the white and dark meat evenly, the results from your upside-down method were remarkable. Compared to the chicken roasted right side up, the breast meat of the upside-down-roasted chicken was dramatically juicier and more tender. Not only was the breast meat kept moist by the descending juices of the dark meat on the upside-down bird, but also the thigh registered 175 degrees and the breast registered 160 degrees (perfectly done, to our taste) at the same time. On the right-side-up chicken, the breast registered 170 degrees, which to our taste is overdone, by the time the thigh reached 175 degrees.

The upside-down chicken does rest high on the roaster, but it's also a little more difficult to fit onto the roaster because of the narrow neck opening. And you're right that the legs pull away from the body, making for a slightly unruly presentation. But these are minor points. If crisp skin and a tidy presentation are low on your priority list, inverting the chicken is a good way to use a vertical roaster.

Cutting Whole Canned Tomatoes

To cut up whole canned tomatoes without squirting, I dump them in a bowl and go over them a few times with my pastry cutter. It works perfectly, and the mess is minimal. Plus, it's another way to utilize a seldom-used piece of equipment.

REBECCA CLEMMER
RIDLEY PARK, PA

Your idea was particularly timely, as we tried it over and over while developing the tomato sauce article on page 10. Just as you say, the pastry cutter makes fast and easy work of dicing the canned tomatoes, and it minimizes the squirting of juice.

Thickening Our Macaroni and Cheese

I tried your Stovetop Macaroni and Cheese recipe from the January/February 1997 issue, and it came out like soup. There was way too much liquid in relationship to the pasta.

EDWARD D. GING
PITTSBURGH, PA

Several readers had similar experiences with this recipe, and we must admit that it even happened to us one time when we retested it based on readers' comments. Fortunately, we figured out why, so we can make two suggestions to help ensure a thick, creamy dish the next time around. First, the size and shape of the pot in which the mac and cheese cooks really matters. The recipe specifies a large, heavy-bottomed saucepan or Dutch oven because they offer greater surface area than smaller pots. With increased surface area comes quicker cooking and, therefore, superior thickening. Our most successful and consistent results came from using a seven-quart Dutch oven. If no Dutch oven is available, use the widest saucepan you have, perhaps one with slightly flared sides.

Second, if you're stuck with a pan that's a little too small and the mac and cheese has not thickened sufficiently after five minutes, increase the heat slightly to medium-low or medium and continue cooking for a few more minutes. Burners and pans all differ slightly, so the egg in the cheese sauce may need a little extra heat or time to reach the temperature at which it coagulates, thus thickening the sauce.

On their own, both egg white and yolk start to coagulate at roughly 145 degrees. However, the presence of the evaporated milk and grated cheese will raise that temperature. In several test batches, we have found that between 160 and 165 degrees is ideal to thicken the sauce properly, to about the same consistency as a loose pudding. At 150 degrees, the sauce was still too runny, but by the time 170 degrees was reached, the sauce was gummy and had taken on a grainy texture because the egg had been cooked too much and solidified into tiny bits. Also, we noted that the sauce continues to thicken as it cools, which means that by the time your mac and cheese is dished onto serving plates and set on the table, it will be thicker than it was when it was removed from the stove.

Making Crab Cakes

I have often had problems keeping crab cakes and salmon cakes together when I cook them. I solved the problem by making molds from plain biscuit cutters, about three-quarters of an inch deep, from which I removed the handles.

Holding the cutter in one hand, pack the mixture into the cutter and allow the extra liquid to run out. Unmold the cakes directly onto the bread crumbs before cooking. The resulting uniform, compact cakes do not fall apart when handled and cooked.

FORBES MANER
WASHINGTON, D.C.

We gave your method a try in our test kitchen, and it worked beautifully. In our July/August 1995 article on crab cakes (see "How to Make Crab Cakes"), we found that chilling the formed cakes for at least thirty minutes before frying allowed them to firm up enough to keep their shape in the pan. Though the cakes lose a little of the rough, handmade appearance that appeals to us, no refrigeration time is required with your biscuit cutter method, which thus speeds the overall preparation time. For information on ordering biscuit cutters, *see* Sources and Resources, page 32.

Sheet Gelatin

I want to try out the Raspberry Orange Bavarian on the back cover of your Charter Issue. The recipe instructions make it clear that you're calling for powdered unflavored gelatin, but I have some gelatin sheets hanging around in my cupboard. Can I use these in place of the powder?

BRIGITTE FRIELUND
ELYRIA, OH

Yes, you can use the sheets, also known as leaf gelatin. A representative from the consumer hotline for Knox Gelatin recommended substituting five 2$^{7}/_{8}$-inch-by-8$^{1}/_{2}$-inch gelatin sheets for each quarter-ounce envelope (one tablespoon by volume). We tested this ratio by making two batches of raspberry mousse and found that the mousse made with five sheets of gelatin was significantly stiffer than the powdered gelatin version. In fact, it was much too stiff and gelatinous for our taste. After further experimentation, we settled on a ratio of three and one-half sheets per envelope of gelatin. With this ratio, the sheet gelatin mousse set well, yet softly, and was indistinguishable in consistency from the powdered gelatin mousse. Just as with powdered gelatin, the sheets must be softened for five to ten minutes in cold liquid. Once the excess water has been wrung out of them, they will look and feel like wet plastic wrap. At that point, they can be added directly to hot ingredients without further warming to dissolve them, as is necessary with powder. Some authorities claim that sheet gelatin has a less noticeable flavor than powder, though our tasters noted no disagreeable flavor from either type. For availability of sheet gelatin, *see* Sources and Resources, page 32.

Wilting Cabbage Leaves for Stuffing

A couple of days before you plan to make stuffed cabbage, place the head in a plastic bag and freeze it. The night before you want to prepare the cabbage rolls, remove the cabbage from the freezer and defrost it. The leaves will be wilted, pliable, and easy to handle.

ZIPPORAH HYMAN
HEWLETT, NY

Because many readers have made this same suggestion over time, we decided to try it out. Freezing softens the leaves because most of the water present in the plant cells crystallizes. As this happens, the sharp frozen water crystals puncture the walls and membranes that separate the cells, thereby damaging the entire cellular structure. The torn cell walls and membranes allow the water within the cells to leak out, a process that thawing accelerates. Because the plant can no longer hold water effectively, it loses some of the crispness it had when fresh, in effect, wilting and becoming limp.

After cooking and tasting the stuffed cabbage, however, we found that we prefer the traditional method of blanching the whole head, and then the separated leaves, to soften them. Overall, we felt that both the color (*see* "Keeping the Green," below) and texture of the blanched leaves were more appealing than that of the frozen and thawed leaves. Also, freezing the cabbage a couple days in advance, and thawing it the day of the meal, requires forethought—sometimes more than we are able to devote. Blanching, on the other hand, adds a few extra minutes of preparation time, but it allows us to make stuffed cabbage on a whim.

Keeping the Green

After reading your article on pesto in the July/August 1996 issue, I'd like to share my method for preventing the basil from darkening. Before blanching the garlic cloves in the boiling water, toss the basil in, dip it out instantly with a Chinese skimmer, place it in ice water, and spin-dry in a salad spinner. Blanching and "shocking" sets the color.

BILL MORAN
SAN DIEGO, TX

During testing and development of the pesto article (*see* "Pesto at Its Best"), we tried blanching the basil to help preserve its green color. The method does work, but with several important caveats. As you say, "instantly" is the key word here. To make this work, you need a lightening quick hand. Second, the water must be at a vigorous, rolling boil. On the continuum of green-leaved herbs and vegetables, basil leaves are particularly delicate. Thus, they cannot stand more than a split second in the boiling water before they begin to discolor and become slimy. Also, we had better luck placing the leaves in the mesh bowl of a small, handled strainer. This helped avoid the inevitable fishing for stray leaves in the water, even with a large Chinese skimmer, because they stay together in the strainer, which can be dipped and removed in a flash. Last, the ice water dip and the spin-dry must also be completed as quickly as possible. Thus, we did not recommend this process in the article because of its rushed and risky feel.

Dr. Susan Brewer, Associate Professor of Food Chemistry at the University of Illinois, suggests an alternative method of blanching the basil by steaming it in a basket or colander over one quart of rapidly boiling water, without submerging the leaves, followed by the usual "shock" in ice water. This process worked very well when we tried it and was easier than the traditional submersion.

Basil notwithstanding, blanching and shocking in ice water has been common kitchen practice to set the color of sturdier green vegetables for generations. So what happens with the application of heat? Several things. A very short, strong heat treatment causes an abrupt expansion and escape of gases trapped between the cells of the plant. Normally, these pockets of gases and air refract, and therefore dim, the color of the chloroplasts, which are the structures within the cells that contain the chlorophyll, the plant's green pigment. With the collapse of these air pockets, the pigment becomes more visible. Simultaneously, explained Dr. Brewer, the heat activates chlorophyllase, a natural enzyme in plants that converts chlorophyll, normally a grassy green, into chlorophyllin, which is even brighter green. All of this occurs in just seconds.

The dousing of the vegetable in ice water immediately after its brief submersion in the boiling water, called "shocking," simply halts further heating, which causes color degradation.

What Is It?

Years ago, a distant uncle of mine had a small bakery in New York City that specialized in cheesecake. At a family reunion last fall, my cousin, knowing of my interest in cooking, gave me an old box filled with kitchen tools. Most of them turned out to be from my uncle's shop. I recognized everything in the box but this. What is it?

JEFFREY REIS
LAKE OSWEGO, OR

It makes sense that this item came from a professional setting. You have a pie marker, which is much more a trapping of the food service industry than a home kitchen. Good for marking round cakes as well as pies, this tool is used to lightly imprint the top crusts of pies prior to baking, or the top of a finished cake, with equally spaced lines along which the server cuts. This way, even if the pie or cake is cut slice by slice rather than all at once, it will yield a set number of uniformly sized pieces. Knowing for sure how many slices each pie or cake will produce is crucial to small and large businesses alike in terms of food cost, portion control, and presentation.

Pie markers are made in different diameters (some reach all the way to the outer edge of the pie or cake while others do not) and numbers of slices. The huge, Seattle-based kitchenware supplier Sur La Table (410 Terry Avenue North, Seattle, WA 98109; 800-243-0852) sells a twelve-slice marker for $10.95, an eight-slice marker for $9.95, and seven- and six-slice markers for $8.95 by mail order, even though they are not pictured in its catalog.

STEAMING A SINGLE TORTILLA

To quickly and easily steam individual tortillas, Ken Mitchell of Fullerton, California, recommends that you roll up the tortilla in a paper towel that has been wet and then squeezed to remove excess water. After 25 seconds in the microwave on high power, unroll the towel for a hot steamed tortilla.

TESTING PASTA DONENESS

Isabelle Wolters of Scituate, Massachusetts, has discovered that a serrated knife blade, held upward, is perfect for retrieving long strands of cooking pasta from boiling water to test for doneness. The notches in the blade prevent the strands from slipping back into the pot.

MAKING A LOW-TECH MILKSHAKE

Irene Ventura of San Francisco, California, who owns neither a regular jar-type nor an immersion-type blender, has devised a way to make milkshakes using her handheld electric mixer. She places the milk, ice cream, and syrup in a pint-size glass, then grasps the glass firmly at the bottom and gently lowers in her handheld mixer, fitted with only one of its beaters, to blend the shake.

OVEN REMINDER

Ever left the oven on after you've removed whatever you're cooking? To avoid this, Joan Grace of Bath, Maine, suggests tying a fire-resistant ribbon onto the oven door handle whenever the oven is in use, removing it only when you have turned off the oven.

Quick

The editors of *Cook's Illustrated* would like to thank all of our readers who have sent us their quick tips. We have enjoyed reading every one of them and have learned a lot. Keep them coming. We will provide a one-year complimentary subscription for each quick tip that we print. Send a description of your special technique to *Cook's Illustrated*, P.O. Box 470589, Brookline Village, MA 02146. Please write

FREEZING GROUND BEEF

Sandra Barry of Ramsey, New Jersey, has found a convenient way to freeze and use ground beef.

1. Place about 1 pound of fresh ground beef in a zipper-lock freezer bag and flatten the meat with a rolling pin.

2. When you're ready to use it, the thin slab of beef can easily be cut into chunks for browning in a skillet.

KEEPING THE CAKE PLATE CLEAN

Claire Jones of Sparks, Maryland, suggests this method for keeping your cake plate neat while frosting the cake.

1. Gently slide a 6-inch strip of waxed paper under each side of the cake (four in total), leaving an overhang. Frost at will.

2. Once the cake is fully frosted and the frosting has had a chance to set slightly, pull the strips away leaving a perfectly clean plate.

STORING POACHED EGGS

While researching the article on page 24, Elaine Corn found that poached eggs can be made ahead and stored for up to three days. Simply drop the finished eggs into a bowl with enough ice water to submerge them, then refrigerate the bowl. Before serving, gently transfer each egg on a slotted spoon into a skillet full of boiling water, turn off the heat, cover, and leave them there for twenty to thirty seconds.

Tips

"Attention: Quick Tips" on the envelope and include your name, address, and day-time phone number. Unfortunately, we can only acknowledge receipt of tips that will be printed in the magazine. In case the same tip is received from two readers, the one postmarked first will be selected. Also, be sure to let us know what particular cooking problems you would like us to investigate in upcoming issues.

GETTING PIZZA INTO THE OVEN

Having never really mastered the quick hand maneuver necessary to slide a prepared pizza from the peel onto the preheated stone in the oven without losing much of the toppings and ruining the round shape of the dough, Paul Kanciruk of Kingston, Tennessee, came up with this easier method.

Lay a large piece of parchment paper, bigger than the pizza on all sides, on the peel or upside-down baking sheet. Construct the pizza on the parchment. Place the peel right next to the preheated stone, then pull the parchment paper by its edge (and the pizza along with it) onto the stone.

FILLING A PASTRY BAG

In response to a tip we ran in our September/October 1996 issue about steadying a pastry bag in a Pilsner beer glass, Jonathan Bloom of Richmond, New Hampshire, writes to suggest using a blender jar for the same purpose.

1. Set the pastry bag, fitted with a tip and cuffed at the top, into the blender jar. Fold the cuff over the top of the jar.

2. Fill the pastry bag.

MAKING CANNED BROTH FAT-FREE

Kenneth Danko of San Francisco, California, has found an easy way to separate fat from canned stock as you pour it out of the can.

1. Using a manual can opener, punch a small hole in the top of the can without turning. Rotate the can 180 degrees and make an opening of about $1/2$ to 1 inch.

2. Pour the stock through the larger slit. The liquid will pass through, while the more viscous fat will remain trapped in the can.

REMOVING CAPERS FROM THE JAR

To remove capers from their tall, narrow jars, Jorden Bennett of Carrollton, Texas, tilts the jar slightly and inserts an old-style vegetable peeler. The capers line up in the trough of the peeler without rolling out, and the liquid drains back into the jar.

GRABBING THE RIGHT TOOL

Often, when hurriedly reaching into a partially opened drawer to grab a kitchen tool, you get the wrong one because all the handles look and feel so similar. Polly Tarpley of Seattle, Washington, makes it easier to distinguish among the tools by placing them in the drawers with the handles toward the back.

PAPER TOWEL HOLDER

Sandy Moertel of Conneautville, Pennsylvania, finds that the heavy meat pounder with the tall handle that she keeps on her counter makes an ideal base for a roll of paper towels. The weight of the pounder stabilizes the towels so they can be ripped off easily.

Foolproof Focaccia

*Potatoes add softness, height, and moisture to the dough
while a quick sponge creates air pockets and chewiness.*

by Jack Bishop

I was living in Florence when I first got hooked on focaccia. The bakery on my block turned out marvelous sheets of rosemary focaccia glistening with olive oil and coarse sea salt. Every afternoon as the heady aroma of rosemary, yeast, and olives wafted down the street toward the local high school, students would gather around the bakery counter, handing over 500 lire for a square of warm bread. The heavenly scent attracted a crowd, but the bread itself, at once chewy and soft, ensured repeat business.

This focaccia was designed to be a snack, served in a sheet of waxed paper and eaten by hand. Many of the focaccia recipes I have tried since then produced a crusty, crisp bread that was only slightly thicker than pizza. These dense, hard breads were often loaded down with toppings. They were more a meal than a snack or accompaniment to Sunday dinner.

I wanted something quite different. I was after that same soft, chewy texture and high rise I remember from my Florentine bakery. The crumb in those breads was filled with small to medium-size air pockets, which helped give the bread a good rise and create an overall impression of lightness and chewiness. Despite many attempts over the years, I had never been able to reproduce this bread at home. This time, I was determined to succeed.

Looking for High-Rise Breads

I began my investigations with a composite recipe of yeast, warm water, olive oil, flour, and salt. After more than a dozen initial tests, I was not much closer to a solution. I tried reducing the salt because it can inhibit the action of the yeast and ended up with a better rise but bland bread. I tried bread flour, all-purpose flour, whole wheat flour, and all possible combinations of these three. Bread flour makes focaccia chewy but also dry and tough. Whole wheat flour is at cross-purposes with my stated goal of a soft texture and high rise. Unbleached all-purpose flour turned out to be the right choice, but I still needed to do much more work.

I tried milk instead of water and got better browning and a softer dough, but the bread was kind of flat. Increasing the yeast produced a high focaccia, but the flavor of the yeast was too dominant. I tried letting the dough ferment in the refrigerator for a day. This lightened

the texture and gave me larger holes in the dough but seemed like a lot of work for a relatively small improvement. I wanted to be able to make and enjoy my focaccia on the same day.

In my research I ran across two recipes from southern Italy that added riced potatoes to the dough. When I tried a recipe from Carol Field's *The Italian Baker* (Harper & Row, 1985), I liked the moistness, high rise, and soft texture of this bread. However, the crumb was fairly dense and compact like a cake. This bread had several appealing traits but was not quite what I wanted.

I knew that sponges (relatively thin mixtures of yeast, water, and flour that are allowed to ferment briefly) are often used to lend flavor and create airholes in breads. I was not terribly concerned about flavor. With olive oil, salt, and herbs, I was sure that any flavor boost from a sponge would be hard to detect. But I did want those airholes, so I tried a quick sponge.

I stirred the yeast, half the water, and a small portion of the flour together in a small bowl, covered the bowl with plastic wrap, and let the sponge rest for thirty minutes before adding the remaining water, flour, oil, and salt. The difference was quite remarkable.

The extra half hour of fermentation produced wonderfully large bubbles. The result was a bread that rose very high but still had a nice, light texture. I tried longer sponges and found that thirty minutes was enough time for the yeast to work its magic.

With the sponge having been successful in my basic composite recipe, I now tried it with Carol Field's potato focaccia that I liked so much. The result was perfect. The sponge transformed the crumb from dense and cake-like to chewy and airy. The bread rose higher than the version made with just flour, and the crumb was softer and more moist. As a final adjustment, I tried rapid-rise yeast to see if I could cut the rising times. This yeast works fine in this recipe and shaves off more than an hour from the process.

Shaping Techniques

A couple of notes about working with this dough. The moisture from the potatoes helps keep the crumb soft but also makes the dough very sticky. Adding extra flour makes the dough easier to handle, but the results are not as good because the wet dough helps produce bread with air pockets and chewiness.

Sticky doughs are best kneaded in a standing mixer or a food processor. You can make the dough by hand, but you will probably end up incorporating slightly more flour.

When it comes time to shape the dough, moisten your hands with a little water. This will prevent the dough from sticking to your fingers. If trying to stretch the dough into a rectangular pan, you may need to let it rest before completing the final shaping. The dough is quite elastic and will put up a good fight without this rest.

An easier method is to divide the dough in half and shape it into two eight-inch disks on a large, oiled baking sheet. These free-form disks rise and bake on the same pan, thus avoiding the tricky task of transferring such a sticky dough. You may also form disks on wooden peels that have been liberally coated with cornmeal, then slide them onto a pizza stone. The bottom crust is especially thick and chewy when cooked on a stone.

The problem with using a peel is that the dough often sticks, even when the peel is well dusted with cornmeal. When I was able to get the dough onto the stone without incident, however, the re-

Just before sliding it into the oven, press your finger into the risen dough at regular intervals to give the focaccia its characteristic look of hills and valleys. The dimples should be large enough to hold small pools of olive oil.

PHOTOGRAPH BY CARL TREMBLAY

sults were excellent. For the sake of simplicity, I opted to rise and bake the dough on an oiled metal pan as described in the recipe below.

An oven temperature of 425 degrees bakes the focaccia quickly without any burning. Lower temperatures produce an inferior crust, and high temperatures can cause the bottom to burn. Keep the focaccia away from the bottom of the oven to prevent the crust from scorching. Once the bread is golden brown, immediately transfer it to a cooling rack to keep the bottom crust from becoming soggy. Focaccia tastes best warm, so wait about twenty minutes and then serve.

MASTER RECIPE FOR ROSEMARY FOCACCIA

Makes one 15 1/2-by-10 1/2-inch rectangle or two 8-inch rounds

Rapid-rise yeast reduces the preparation time by more than an hour. If you use an equal amount of regular active dry yeast instead, let the sponge in step 2 develop for thirty minutes rather than twenty, and increase the first and second rises to one and one-half hours each.

Dough

1   medium baking potato (about 9 ounces), peeled and quartered
1 1/2   teaspoons rapid-rise yeast
3 1/2   cups unbleached all-purpose flour
1   cup warm water (105 to 115 degrees)
2   tablespoons extra-virgin olive oil, plus more for oiling bowl and pan
1 1 1/4   teaspoons salt

Topping

2   tablespoons extra-virgin olive oil
2   tablespoons fresh rosemary leaves
3/4   teaspoon coarse sea salt (or 1 1/4 teaspoons kosher salt)

For the dough

1. Boil 1 quart water in small saucepan; add potato and simmer until tender, about 25 minutes. Drain potato well; cool until it can be handled comfortably and put through fine disk on ricer or grate through large holes on box grater. Reserve 1 1/3 cups lightly packed potato.

2. Meanwhile, in large bowl of electric mixer or workbowl of food processor fitted with steel blade, mix or pulse yeast, 1/2 cup flour, and 1/2 cup warm water until combined. Cover tightly with plastic wrap (or put workbowl lid on) and set aside until bubbly, about 20 minutes. Add remaining dough ingredients, including reserved potato. If using mixer, fit with paddle attachment and mix on low speed (number 2 on KitchenAid) until dough comes together. Switch to dough hook attachment and increase speed to medium (number 4 on KitchenAid); continue kneading until dough is smooth and elastic, about 5 minutes. For food processor, process until dough is smooth and elastic, about 40 seconds.

3. Transfer dough to lightly oiled bowl, turn to coat with oil, and cover tightly with plastic wrap. Let rise in warm, draft-free area until dough is puffy and doubled in volume, about 1 hour.

4. With wet hands (to prevent sticking), press dough flat into generously oiled 15 1/2-by-10 1/2-inch jelly roll pan (*see* illustration 1). Or, halve and flatten each piece of dough into 8-inch round on large (at least 18 inches long), generously oiled baking sheet (illustration 2). Cover dough with lightly greased or oil-sprayed plastic wrap; let rise in warm, draft-free area until dough is puffy and doubled in volume, 45 minutes to 1 hour.

5. Meanwhile, adjust oven rack to lower-middle position and heat oven to 425 degrees. With two wet fingers, dimple risen dough (illustration 3) at regular intervals.

For the topping

6. Drizzle dough with oil and sprinkle evenly with rosemary and coarse salt, landing some in pools of oil.

7. Bake until focaccia bottom(s) are golden brown and crisp, 23 to 25 minutes. Transfer to wire rack to cool slightly. Cut rectangular focaccia into squares or round focaccia into wedges; serve warm. (Focaccia can be kept on counter for several hours and reheated just before serving. Or, wrap cooled focaccia in plastic and then foil and freeze for up to 1 month; unwrap and defrost in 325-degree oven until soft, about 15 minutes.)

HAND-KNEADED FOCACCIA

Follow Master Recipe for Rosemary Focaccia, through step 1. In step 2, mix starter ingredients with wooden spoon in large bowl; cover and let stand 20 minutes. Add 1 1/2 cups flour to starter, then beat with wooden spoon for 5 minutes. Add 1 1/4 cups flour along with remaining dough ingredients; continue beating until dough comes together. Turn dough onto floured surface; knead in remaining 1/4 cup flour until dough is elastic and sticky, 4 to 5 minutes. Transfer dough to oiled bowl as in step 3 and follow remaining instructions.

SAGE FOCACCIA

Follow Master Recipe for Rosemary Focaccia, adding 1 tablespoon chopped fresh sage leaves with other dough ingredients in step 2 and substituting 24 whole fresh sage leaves (one per oil-filled dimple) for rosemary.

PARMESAN FOCACCIA

Follow Master Recipe for Rosemary Focaccia, substituting 2/3 cup grated Parmesan cheese for rosemary and coarse sea salt.

FOCACCIA WITH BLACK OLIVES AND THYME

Follow Master Recipe for Rosemary Focaccia, substituting 1 teaspoon fresh thyme leaves and 24 pitted large black olives (one per oil-filled dimple) for rosemary.

SHAPING FOCACCIA DOUGH

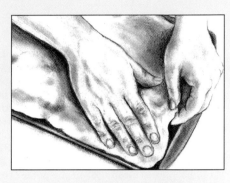

1. Press the dough into an oiled jelly roll pan, stretching it so that the dough reaches all sides of the pan and fills all four corners. If the dough resists going into the corners (and it probably will), cover it with a damp cloth and let it relax for 15 minutes. You should then be able to push the dough into the corners.

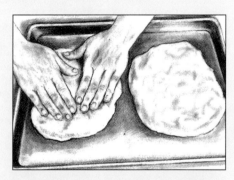

2. If you prefer, divide the dough in half and lightly press each piece with your palms into an 8-inch round on a large, oiled baking sheet.

3. After the dough has risen for the second time, wet two fingers and use them to make indentations at regular intervals. The dimples should be deep enough to hold small pieces of topping, herbs, and/or pools of olive oil. There should be about two dozen dimples.

The Secrets of Panfrying Steaks

Buy strip, rib eye, or sirloin steaks for the best flavor.
A cast-iron pan is not only economical, but works as well as the pricier competition.

by Stephanie Lyness

Last year when I explored the best way to grill steaks (*see* "How to Grill a Steak," May/June 1996), I discovered that what I really liked in a grilled steak was an allover caramelized crust. I figured that, when the weather did not make grilling practical, I could get that same result from panfrying.

When I tried this approach, however, it turned out to be not as simple as I had thought. Sometimes I did get the great crust I was looking for, but sometimes I didn't. It seemed like my cast-iron pan worked particularly well, but I had never tested it against pans made from other materials. So I set to work to establish a foolproof technique for panfrying steak. Along with the technique, I figured I also needed to discover which steaks and which pans were best suited for the job.

Which Steaks?

My first thought was to focus on large, relatively inexpensive, boneless London broil–type steaks. Because these thick steaks are served sliced thin, I reasoned that I'd be able to comfortably fit a steak large enough to serve four in a large (but not unwieldy) frying pan. I also chose these steaks because they're so much cheaper than premium cuts such as rib eye or strip. And because several of us at the magazine have become fans of beef shoulder, I was eager to see how it would fare as a panfried steak.

For a perfect sear, heat a cast-iron pan for ten minutes before starting to cook.

So I went to the meat shelf at my local supermarket and bought all the large, thick boneless steaks I could find, eliminating rib eye, strip, sirloin, and fillet. I ended up with quite a selection: top round, bottom round, flank, chuck underblade, chuck shoulder, and something called round top steak, cap-off. All of these cuts were lean with very little intramuscular fat (marbling).

When I fried all the steaks, regardless of what pan or technique I tried, the results were uniformly unsatisfying. All the steaks browned spottily. The cooked steaks varied in texture, the shoulder cuts tougher but moister than the rounds, and the rounds softer but drier. When it came to flavor, I couldn't taste much difference among the cuts, and I didn't much like any. They all tasted like a generic and somewhat bland piece of beef to me. Not like steak.

It occurred to me that maybe it was me; perhaps I was just tired of the taste of steak. So I tested strip, rib eye, and sirloin steaks for comparison. Not only did these steaks brown much better than the first batch (and essentially in their own fat), but they tasted the way I expected a steak to taste: round, interesting, and rich-flavored rather than just beefy. London broil–type steaks clearly benefit from the flavor added by marinating and grilling. I decided to stick with boneless strip, sirloin, and rib eye steaks.

Does the Pan Make a Difference?

It was obvious to me from the beginning that the key to browning the steaks was going to be preheating the pan so that when the steaks hit the pan, the surface would already be hot enough to sear the steak before it overcooked. (I've also found out the hard way that the steak may stick if the pan isn't well heated, leaving the delicious seared flavor in the pan, not on the steak.) In this regard, I had two questions: Do different types of pans heat and cook differently? And does it make more sense to brown quickly over a high heat and then finish over a low heat, or cook the steaks over a constant high heat?

I started all my testing with both a ten-and-one-half-inch and a twelve-inch cast-iron pan, figuring that, at $10 to $15 a pop (as opposed to $100-plus for many sauté pans), these were the pans most folks were likely to own or want to own. I used one-inch- to one-and-one-quarter-inch-thick boneless strip steaks to begin, but ultimately found that there was no difference in technique between cooking strip, sirloin, and rib steaks.

I tried preheating the pan for various lengths of time at different temperatures on my electric stove. After several tests, I found that my favorite method was to preheat the pan at a medium temperature for about ten minutes before cooking the steak. (Testers at the *Cook's Illustrated* test kitchen were happy with ten minutes on a home gas range as well. If you're using a powerful professional gas range, however, cut the time to five minutes.) This method allowed me to cook the steak all the way through, turning once, without having to adjust the heat. When I started with a higher heat, lowering it once the steak had browned, the process not only required more attention for no better result, but the splattering, a problem to be reckoned with even on medium heat, was much worse.

In fact, a splatter screen—a round mesh screen with attached handle that is set over

---

Can You Deglaze a Cast-Iron Pan?

I'd always heard that if you deglaze a cast-iron pan with an acidic liquid such as wine, the sauce will taste funny. Given that information, I questioned whether even the mustard in the sauce in this article might cause a reaction. Some cooks had told me, however, that they regularly make tomato sauces in cast-iron to no ill effect. What was the deal here?

To find out, I tested both the mustard recipe and a red wine pan sauce in my seasoned cast-iron pan. The mustard sauce, as I had thought, collected some tiny black flecks from the pan, but because the mustard was in the pan for only seconds, the taste was fine. I'd certainly make this sauce in cast-iron. The red wine sauce, however, tasted distinctly "off": not metallic, surprisingly, but unpleasantly sour. Finally, I tested a quick tomato sauce (roughly chopped canned tomatoes, garlic, basil, olive oil, and salt, cooked ten minutes to thicken). It tasted perfect.

Confused by the results, I called food scientist Shirley Corriher to find out why I should have had better luck with a tomato sauce than with a red wine sauce, when both cooked for approximately the same length of time and both were high in acid. Corriher explained that while iron reacts quite easily with acid to cause a metallic taste, ten minutes wasn't long enough to produce this reaction. The sour taste in the red wine sauce was due to the reaction of the tannins in the wine to the iron. Therefore, don't deglaze with red wine or red wine vinegar, but feel free to do quick pan sauces based on stock, water, and even tomato.—*S.L.*

the pan like a lid to keep grease inside without causing the meat to steam as it would if covered with a lid—is a *must* for panfrying, even on the lower heat (*see* Sources and Resources, page 32).

I then went on to try this same technique with an All-Clad stainless steel pan with an aluminum core, a Calphalon pan, an All-Clad nonstick pan, and a thin, inexpensive stainless steel pan of the type many of us have sitting in a back drawer somewhere. The All-Clad stainless and the cast-iron pans held the heat and browned the steaks better than the other two. To test the nonstick pan, I cooked two steaks, each coated with one teaspoon of oil, in the nonstick and the cast-iron pans; the steak browned better in the cast-iron (although not as well as with more oil) and didn't stick in either, so I see no advantage to the nonstick.

Using my two favorite pans, I tested for the optimal amount and type of fat. I fried steaks in two tablespoons, one tablespoon, two teaspoons, and one teaspoon of oil. As these cuts of steaks give off some fat as they cook, two tablespoons made more mess and didn't brown better than one. One teaspoon browned spottily; two teaspoons and one tablespoon browned equally well without outrageous splattering. I decided to stick with one tablespoon because it's simpler to measure; at any rate, the goal is to lightly coat the pan with oil.

Then I tested one tablespoon each of peanut, corn, canola, and half-and-half butter and canola oil. As I expected, the butter burned immediately, even with the oil. The other three oils browned equally well.

As a final test, I tried a technique described to me by two *Cook's Illustrated* editors in which the pan is coated with a light film of oil (one editor uses a vegetable spray) and then a layer of kosher salt before the steak (itself unsalted) is added to the pan. The idea is that the salt will keep the meat from sticking and will season it at the same time. I tried this a couple of times in my cast-iron pan (I ended up with an unpleasantly salty steak on the first go-round) before I hit on the right amount of salt. The proper technique turns out to be sprinkling the salt into the pan as you would onto the steak. This technique did season the steak beautifully, but with only the light film of oil, the meat didn't brown as well as I wished. The steak stuck no more or less than without the salt. Adherents to this technique are crazy about it, but I must confess that I don't get it.

In my research on grilled steaks, I had determined that five minutes of resting gave the meat even color; the same held true for panfrying. Any longer than that, and the steak gets cold. Chances are that it will be about that long before you actually cut into the steak at the table anyway.

MASTER RECIPE FOR PANFRIED STEAKS
Serves 2
Covering the skillet with a splatter screen will reduce the mess that panfrying inevitably makes. Serve the steaks as is or with one of the sauces or condiments that follow.

2   boneless strip or rib eye steaks, or 1 sirloin, 1 to 1¼ inches thick (8 to 10 ounces each)

Salt and ground black pepper
1   tablespoon vegetable oil

1. Heat 11- to 12-inch skillet (preferably cast-iron or stainless steel with an aluminum core) for 10 minutes over medium heat (on either gas or electric stove). Generously sprinkle each side of each steak with salt and pepper.

2. Add oil to pan; swirl to coat bottom. Add steaks, cover pan with splatter screen, and cook until well browned on one side, 5 minutes. Turn steaks; cook 3 more minutes for rare, 4 minutes for medium-rare, or 5 minutes for medium. Remove steaks from pan; let rest 5 minutes or while making pan sauce or condiment, then serve immediately.

ROQUEFORT BUTTER
Mash together 1 tablespoon room temperature butter, ½ ounce crumbled Roquefort cheese, and ¼ teaspoon brandy. Season with salt and pepper to taste. Top each cooked steak with portion of flavored butter and serve immediately.

HORSERADISH CREAM
Stir together 2 tablespoons each sour cream and prepared horseradish. Season with salt and pepper to taste and serve alongside each cooked steak.

MUSTARD SAUCE
Wipe fat from skillet; add ¾ cup chicken stock, then boil until reduced by one-half. Stir in 1½ tablespoons Dijon mustard and 1 tablespoon butter as well as salt and pepper to taste; spoon portion of sauce over each cooked steak.

How to Season a Cast-Iron Pan

Nothing causes so much confusion about cast-iron pans as the question of how, and how often, to season them. To find the best method, I spoke to Billie Hill, customer service manager at Lodge Manufacturing Company, a major manufacturer of cast-iron cookware, and to food scientist Shirley Corriher.

Because the main component of cast iron is iron, which combines more easily with oxygen than other metals, cast iron rusts quickly. One object of seasoning, therefore, is to penetrate the pores of the iron with fat to protect the metal from the water and food that will rust it. Another lesser-known reason, however, is to create a temporary nonstick surface: When fat is heated at a certain temperature for a particular length of time, it polymerizes. In other words, the fat breaks down into units that like to hook up with other units to create very stable chains; these chains make a fairly durable coating on the pan that acts much like Teflon. Heating the pan while seasoning, therefore, is necessary for two reasons: First, as explained above, heat is needed for the creation of polymers. Heating also expands the metal and seals in the fat.

Armed with this knowledge, I proceeded to test two seasoning methods, one from Lodge and one recommended by Barbara Tropp in *The Modern Art of Chinese Cooking* (Morrow, 1982) for seasoning a wok. Instructions attached to Lodge's pans recommend coating the pan with solid vegetable shortening (liquid oils go rancid, according to Hill) and baking upside down (upside down so that the fat doesn't collect as sticky gunk on the bottom of the pan) on an oven rack (over a baking sheet to collect drips) for an hour at 350 degrees. Tropp's directions call for heating the pan over high heat on top of the stove until a bead of water evaporates immediately upon hitting the pan, then wiping the inside of the pan with a wad of paper towels dipped in liquid oil, wiping out the excess and repeating as needed. A new pan will need several rounds of this.

I tried both methods, and there was no contest: Lodge's was lengthy and still left gunk in the pan while Tropp's was brilliantly simple and quick and left the pan smooth and glossy. Nor did I find over several weeks of testing that liquid oil caused any rancid flavor in food cooked in the pan.

So here is the way to season: Heat the pan over high heat until a drop of water sizzles immediately upon contact. Dunk a wad of paper towels in cooking oil and wipe the entire inside of the pan with the oil (see illustration). Then use another wad of toweling to rub the oil into the metal and wipe out any excess. Use another clean wad if needed. Repeat three to four times for a new pan until it blackens. If your pan has rusted from misuse, scrub off the rust with soap and an abrasive pad, and then season.—*S.L.*

20-Minute Tomato Sauce

*We test the best method for making a quick, simple pasta sauce using
only canned tomatoes, garlic, salt, olive oil, a dash of sugar, and basil.*

by Christopher Kimball with Eva Katz

❧

Trying to define the "best" quick tomato sauce is almost as silly as trying to settle on the best type of corn. I am still partial to the old standby, Silver Queen, but others swear by the new supersweets: Kandy Korn, Kiss and Tell, or Peaches and Cream. And calling good Italian cooks such as Julia della Croce or Marcella Hazan and asking them to choose the best all-purpose tomato sauce is akin to asking them which of their children they prefer. On the face of it, it seems like an exercise in culinary hairsplitting.

After some thought, however, we managed to define a style of sauce that would be particularly useful to an American home cook: a quick year-round sauce that would be best served over fresh-boiled pasta. In narrowing our definition, we decided that canned tomatoes were in and the fresh variety was out, given that good, fresh tomatoes are a rare commodity most of the year. We wanted to use the fewest ingredients possible, so we selected the key players—tomatoes, oil, garlic, and salt—and eliminated nonessentials such as carrots, meat, wine, and so forth. This immediately eliminated a whole category of longer-cooked, full-bodied Italian sauces. The sauce we were looking for had to be quick to make, twenty minutes or less from pantry to table. Finally, it had to taste first and foremost of tomatoes, with a nice hint of acidity and a light, fresh flavor.

With this fairly limited mission statement, a number of fundamental issues came to mind. What sort of canned tomatoes are best: whole, chopped, or crushed, packed in puree or juice? How do you get a nice hint of garlic without overpowering the sauce? How does cooking time affect flavor? Do you need sugar to boost tomato flavor? And what about tomato paste?

To get a better sense of the possibilities, we went into the kitchen and cooked a batch of different sauces from our favorite Italian cooks. To our surprise, there was considerable agreement among the staff as to what worked and what didn't. Butter tended to dull the bright, slightly acidic flavor of the tomatoes. Nobody was enthusiastic about the rather one-dimensional flavor of tomato paste. More than two cloves of garlic and three tablespoons of olive oil for one twenty-eight-ounce can of tomatoes was too much. In general, shorter cooking times of ten to fifteen minutes produced a fresher, brighter tomato flavor. A large sauté pan was preferred to a saucepan because it hurried up the cooking.

We also came to some conclusions about overall flavor. The sauces we preferred tasted predominantly like tomatoes, not garlic, basil, or any other ingredient. The better recipes also had a nice balance between sweetness and acidity to give the sauce some depth. This layering of flavors in fact became the Holy Grail of this story. The proper balances between sweet and tart, smoothness and bite, tomato and garlic, basil and olive oil, were crucial to achieving an exciting, multidimensional sauce.

With these decisions made, we compiled a master recipe using one teaspoon of minced garlic, three tablespoons of olive oil, one can of diced tomatoes, eight chopped basil leaves, one-quarter teaspoon of sugar, and salt to taste. This was to make enough to sauce one pound of pasta.

The first test was aimed at finding the best method of preparing the garlic. Early on we discovered that recipes that browned the garlic often resulted in a bitter sauce. In a recent story (*see* "Curry Demystified," January/February 1997), we had discovered that using a garlic puree that was diluted with water and sautéed briefly in olive oil provided a mild, even garlic flavor while greatly reducing the possibility of overcooking the garlic. When we tried this method, it turned out to be superior to any of the following ones: mincing and sautéing, simply crushing the cloves, using slices, adding minced garlic just before serving without cooking it, or cooking minced garlic along with the tomatoes without sautéing it. The puree method resulted in a sweeter, less bitter garlic flavor, which helped the sauce achieve a nice balance between sweet and tart.

Next we tried making sauces with no sweetener, with one-quarter teaspoon of sugar, and with carrots instead of sugar. (Although we had initially decided to forego additional ingredients such as carrots, we thought they were worth testing as a sweetener.) The results were as follows: The no-sugar sauce had a reduced tomato flavor, the quarter teaspoon was judged to be just right (we ended up testing higher and lower amounts as well), and the carrot method added too much cooking time.

The quantity of olive oil was also evaluated and judged to be ideal at three tablespoons. We also tested whether all of the olive oil should be added at the beginning of cooking or some withheld and added at the end to provide a nice burst of fresh flavor. As we suspected, it was best to use two tablespoons of olive oil for cooking and a third tablespoon at the end to finish the sauce. Not surprisingly, we preferred a high-quality, extra-virgin oil because it delivered a pleasant hint of fresh olives.

Which Canned Tomatoes?

As we continued testing variant after variant of our simple sauce, a key issue began to emerge: What is the best type of tomato to use? We had already established in a testing conducted for our March/April 1997 issue (*see* "All Canned Crushed Tomatoes Are Not the Same," page 10) that among canned crushed tomatoes, we preferred Progresso, Muir Glen, and Redpack, in that order.

For our current testing, we started with crushed tomatoes but were disappointed with the lackluster flavor they showed in this particular recipe. We then moved on to whole tomatoes, with mixed results. Fortunately, we then stumbled onto what was to be our clear favorite, Muir Glen Diced Tomatoes. To begin with, they were very convenient because the entire contents of the can could be used; with whole tomatoes, using all of the packing liquid resulted in substantially thinner sauce. Even better, the flavor was fresh and bright with a good balance of sweet and acid. (Incidentally, Muir Glen also sells ground tomatoes, which we did not like as much given that they had a flatter, duller flavor. This supported our finding that overly processed sauces tend to have less flavor.)

However, because Muir Glen Diced Tomatoes may not be available in your supermar-

Ground canned tomatoes (left) produced a disappointing sauce; whole ones (center) were a definite improvement; diced (right) were our favorite.

ket, we retested crushed versus whole tomatoes and decided that the latter was the clear winner. Our favorite brands were Muir Glen once again, followed closely by Progresso. The thick puree used in the Redpack brand we found unappealing for this particular recipe although the tomatoes themselves are high quality. While we were at it, we tested the claim of many cooks that seeding the tomatoes is important to remove bitterness, and found that seedless sauce tasted no different than the version with seeds.

We also decided that, when using whole tomatoes, it is important to drain the tomatoes first, reserving the liquid, in order to prevent the tendency of the quick-cooked sauce to be too thin.

Introducing Pasta

Now we were ready to taste the sauce on pasta. Much to our surprise, we found that it did not properly cling to the pasta, and the flavor was unexpectedly bland. Our complex, well-balanced sauce, it turned out, was too delicate for the texture and flavor of the pasta. Our first fix was to add back a quarter cup of pasta cooking water to the drained pasta once it had been returned to its original pot. This dramatically improved the consistency of the sauce and, to our great surprise, also improved the flavor.

We also noted that, in the tradition of most Italian cooks, we were using two cups of sauce for one pound of pasta. We all agreed that this was insufficient for our quick, fresh-tasting sauce. By reducing the amount of pasta to three-quarters of a pound, the balance between sauce and pasta was clearly improved. Now we had finally arrived at our goal: a quick, fresh-tasting, all-season tomato sauce that can be made in under twenty minutes and that also makes a terrific base for many variations, three of which follow the master recipe.

As a final note, we found that adding the tomato sauce, stirring to coat the pasta, and then heating everything for one minute was the most effective saucing method, giving the sauce better distribution and overall consistency.

MASTER RECIPE FOR PASTA AND SIMPLE TOMATO SAUCE
Dresses 3/4 pound pasta: Serves 3

If you use whole canned tomatoes, avoid those packed in sauce or puree, which results in a dull, relatively flavorless sauce without the interplay of sweetness and acidity. If you choose Muir Glen Diced Tomatoes instead, use the can's entire contents, without discarding any liquid. The pasta and sauce quantities can be doubled, but you will have to simmer the sauce for an extra five or six minutes to thicken it. If you do not have a garlic press, mince the garlic very fine and sauté it for one minute rather than two. Note that the salt in this recipe is added in two batches; if you are using the sauce for something other

than pasta, simply salt to taste rather than adding the second quantity of salt. Although three-quarters of a pound of pasta may seem an odd quantity, a full pound of pasta will dilute the sauce, resulting in a lack of flavor. You can, however, stretch the sauce to cover one pound of pasta if you make one of the more flavorful variations.

1	28-ounce can diced or whole tomatoes (*not* packed in puree or sauce)
2	medium garlic cloves, peeled
3	tablespoons extra-virgin olive oil
2	tablespoons coarsely chopped fresh basil leaves (about 8 leaves)
1/4	teaspoon sugar
11/2	teaspoons salt
3/4	pound pasta

1. If using diced tomatoes, go to step 2. If using whole tomatoes, drain and reserve liquid. Dice tomatoes either by hand or in workbowl of food processor fitted with metal blade (three or four 1/2-second pulses). Tomatoes should be coarse, with 1/4-inch pieces visible. If necessary, add enough reserved liquid to tomatoes to total 2 cups.

2. Process garlic through garlic press into small bowl; stir in 1 teaspoon water (*see* note, above). Heat 2 tablespoons oil and garlic in 10-inch sauté pan over medium heat until fragrant but not brown, about 2 minutes. Stir in tomatoes; simmer until thickened slightly, about 10 minutes. Stir in basil, sugar, and 1/2 teaspoon salt.

3. Meanwhile, cook pasta until al dente in large pot of boiling, salted water. Reserve 1/4 cup cooking water; drain pasta, and transfer it back to cooking pot. Mix in reserved cooking water, sauce, and remaining oil and salt; cook together over medium heat for 1 minute, stirring constantly, and serve immediately.

PASTA AND TOMATO SAUCE WITH BACON AND PARSLEY
Dresses 3/4 pound pasta: Serves 3

In 10-inch skillet, fry 4 ounces sliced bacon, cut into 1/2-inch pieces, over medium-high heat until crisp and brown, about 5 minutes. Transfer with slotted spoon to paper towel–lined plate; pour off all but 2 tablespoons fat from pan. Follow Master Recipe for Pasta and Simple Tomato Sauce, omitting olive oil from sauce and heating garlic and 1/2 teaspoon dried red pepper flakes in bacon fat until fragrant but not brown, about 2 minutes. Continue with master recipe, substituting 2 tablespoons chopped fresh parsley leaves for basil and adding reserved bacon, crumbled, along with parsley.

PASTA AND TOMATO SAUCE WITH ANCHOVIES AND OLIVES
Dresses 3/4 pound pasta: Serves 3

Follow Master Recipe for Pasta and Simple Tomato Sauce, increasing garlic to 3 cloves and adding 1/2 teaspoon dried red pepper

flakes and 3 minced anchovy fillets along with garlic puree and oil. Substitute 1/4 cup minced fresh parsley leaves for basil. Add 1/4 cup pitted, sliced Kalamata olives and 2 tablespoons drained capers along with remaining seasonings.

PASTA AND TOMATO SAUCE WITH VODKA AND CREAM
Dresses 1 pound pasta; Serves 4

Follow Master Recipe for Pasta and Simple Tomato Sauce, adding 1/4 teaspoon dried red pepper flakes along with garlic. Halfway through the 10-minute simmering time, add 1/2 cup vodka. Continue with master recipe, adding 1 cup heavy cream and ground black pepper to taste along with remaining seasonings. Transfer sauce to workbowl of food processor fitted with a steel blade; pulse to a coarse puree. Return sauce to pan; simmer over medium heat to thicken, 2 to 3 minutes.

The Happy Marriage of Sweet and Tart

The surprising, almost shocking, subtext to this story is the delicate but crucial balance between sweet and tart. Some sauces tasted flat and dull while others sparkled with an underlying tang of acidity, fresh tomato flavor, and a nice up-front boost of sweetness. We first noticed this disparity in outcomes when using tomatoes packed in puree. In this simple tomato sauce, they were simply lackluster. I made a few calls to discover why and quickly found one answer: The puree (referred to as a "topping medium" in the industry) must be cooked longer than simple canned whole tomatoes because cooking is necessary to produce a thicker product. Of course, during cooking, the fresh, bright flavor of tomatoes diminishes, losing acidity and bite. Perhaps this is why we preferred quick-cooking sauces in the initial tastings done for this article.

Caroline Coughlin of Muir Glen Company also suggested that if a sauce is totally homogenized, without small pieces of tomatoes left intact, the tongue does not experience flashes of both sweet and tart in the same manner. Although this is more conjecture than science, we did find that the texture of the sauce was crucial; totally pureed sauces consistently received low marks in our informal taste tests.

We also ended up adding a bit of sugar to the sauce. This not only boosted flavor but made the overall taste of the sauce more complex, perhaps from the improved balance of acidity and sweetness. Although strictly anecdotal evidence, Paul Prudhomme often demonstrated this relationship by cooking chopped chiles in a cream sauce, which, when sampled by his students, was unbearably hot. He then simmered the chiles slowly with a sweet ingredient, and the resulting sauce was transformed into a complex and exceedingly palatable result—a burst of sweetness followed by acidity, followed by a subtle interplay of both.—*C.K.*

How to Cook Sugar Snap Peas

Blanching followed by an immediate shock in ice water yields tender peas that hold their shape.

by Diana Shaw

Foods with a long cultural heritage can be daunting, coming to the kitchen loaded with the cumulative expectation created by everyone from Brillat-Savarin and Catherine de Médicis to your own great-great-grandmother.

So it's liberating to have a food that comes unencumbered by tradition and memory. One thing I love about sugar snap peas is we don't have to concern ourselves with all of that because the modern sugar snap pea was not born until the 1970s.

A sweet, crispy cross between the snow pea and the green garden pea, the sugar snap is completely edible, pod and all. While peas with edible pods have been around for centuries, it took an American horticulturist to perfect their breeding and turn them into a mass-market item.

Good sugar snaps look like compact fresh garden peas, in the shell. They are firm and lustrous with barely discernible bumps along the pods. Expect to find robust fresh peas from late spring through summer.

Cooking Tests

Because raw sugar snaps taste chalky and flat, the peas should be eaten cooked, but just barely. They taste best when they are still quite crisp, which takes some liquid, a little time, and heat.

I tested various cooking methods, including steaming, microwaving, sautéing, and blanching. Sautéing was problematic from the start. The peas did not soften quickly enough. By the time they were tender enough to eat, they had lost their bright green color and turned into an unappealing mush. Clearly, moist heat was needed.

I found that microwaving did not cook the peas evenly. Opening the microwave and stirring helped, but I soon abandoned this method. Steaming yielded tender peas, but they tasted flat. I found that sugar snaps greatly benefit from the addition of some salt as they cook, something that can only be done if the peas are blanched.

Although blanching yielded peas with excellent taste and texture, I found that the blanched peas tended to shrivel or pucker a bit as they cooled. I solved this problem by plunging the cooked peas into ice water as soon as they were drained. This also helped set their bright color and prevent further softening from residual heat.

BLANCHED SUGAR SNAP PEAS

Have a bowl of ice water ready to "shock" the drained peas and prevent further softening and shriveling.

1 teaspoon salt
4 cups loosely packed sugar snap peas (about 1 pound), stems snipped off and strings removed if needed

1. Bring 6 cups water to brisk boil in 3- or 4-quart saucepan. Add salt and peas and cook until crisp-tender, 1½ to 2 minutes depending on size of peas.

2. Drain peas, shock in ice water, drain again, and pat dry. (Peas can be set aside for up to 1 hour. *See* recipes below for seasoning ideas.)

SUGAR SNAP PEAS WITH HAZELNUT BUTTER AND SAGE
Serves 6

Because you must judge the color of the butter as it cooks, avoid dark-colored pans like unlined anodized aluminum or nonstick for this recipe.

2 tablespoons chopped hazelnuts
2 tablespoons unsalted butter
1 recipe Blanched Sugar Snap Peas
2 tablespoons chopped fresh sage leaves
½ teaspoon salt
Ground black pepper

1. Toast hazelnuts over medium heat in small skillet, shaking pan often to promote even cooking, until just fragrant, 3 to 4 minutes.

2. Heat butter over medium heat in medium sauté pan until it browns to color of brown sugar and smells nutty, about 5 minutes. Take care not to burn. Add peas, sage, and nuts; toss to combine. Cook until just heated through, 1 to 1½ minutes. Season with salt and pepper to taste; serve immediately.

SUGAR SNAP PEAS WITH HAM AND MINT
Serves 6

Do not use sliced ham for this recipe. Rather, buy a small hunk of country or smoked ham and cut it into a quarter-inch dice.

1 tablespoon unsalted butter
½ cup country or smoked ham, diced to ¼ inch
1 recipe Blanched Sugar Snap Peas
2 tablespoons chopped fresh mint leaves
½ teaspoon salt
Ground black pepper

Melt butter over medium heat in medium sauté pan. Add ham; sauté 1 minute. Add peas and mint; toss to combine. Cook until just heated through, 1 to 1½ minutes. Season with salt and pepper to taste; serve immediately.

SUGAR SNAP PEAS WITH LEMON, GARLIC, AND BASIL
Serves 6

2 tablespoons olive oil
Zest of 1 medium lemon, sliced very fine, plus 1 tablespoon juice
1 medium garlic clove, minced
1 recipe Blanched Sugar Snap Peas
6–8 fresh basil leaves, chopped fine
½ teaspoon salt
Ground black pepper

Heat oil over medium heat in medium sauté pan. Add zest and garlic; sauté until garlic is soft but not browned, about 2 minutes. Add peas, lemon juice, and basil; toss to combine. Cook until just heated through, 1 to 1½ minutes. Season with salt and pepper to taste; serve immediately.

SUGAR SNAP PEAS WITH ASIAN DRESSING
Serves 6

To mingle the flavors, you can let the peas and dressing stand for up to ten minutes. More than that and the peas start to lose their bright green color.

2 teaspoons sesame seeds
2 tablespoons orange juice
2 tablespoons rice wine vinegar
1 teaspoon honey
½ teaspoon soy sauce
1 scallion (white and green parts), sliced thin
½ teaspoon peeled and grated fresh gingerroot
2 tablespoons peanut oil
1 teaspoon Asian sesame oil
Salt and ground black pepper
1 recipe Blanched Sugar Snap Peas

1. Toast sesame seeds over medium heat in small skillet, shaking pan often to promote even cooking, until light brown and fragrant, 4 to 5 minutes.

2. Meanwhile, combine juice, vinegar, honey, soy sauce, scallion, and ginger in small bowl. Whisk in oils. Season to taste with salt and pepper. Stir in sesame seeds. (Dressing can be set aside for several hours.)

3. Toss dressing with peas and serve.

Diana Shaw's most recent cookbook is *The Essential Vegetarian Cookbook* (Clarkson Potter, 1997).

How to Buy, Cook, and Serve a Lobster

Should lobsters be steamed, boiled, microwaved, or roasted? Are hard-shells better than soft-shells?
Can lobsters be hypnotized? Are older, larger lobsters better? Here's what works.

by Pam Anderson with Karen Tack

Ever notice how tough some lobster tails are? Perhaps we eat them so infrequently it doesn't register. Or perhaps we're so awed by this high-priced crustacean we don't question its texture. But after tasting tails from more than three dozen lobsters in just two short days last summer, we began to notice. Regardless of how we cooked them—roasted, broiled, steamed, or boiled—most of the tails were at least slightly rubbery and chewy.

During those two days of initial tests, we confirmed our preference for steamed lobster, not because it tasted better than boiled, but because the process was simpler, neater, and the finished product was less waterlogged. But as I sat down to write the story, I couldn't ignore my notes. I kept coming across the same adjectives: Tough. Rubbery. Chewy.

This was a problem I was confident I could solve by some adjustment in the cooking method. I reasoned that if tough cuts like pork shoulder and beef brisket could be made tender by long, slow heat, so could lobster. If that didn't work, I ventured that if scallops and shrimp could be saved from toughness by quick, high heat, so could lobster. I thought, "A few phone calls, and I'll have this lobster thing in the trap."

Down a Lobster Trail

I thought wrong. What started as a mild curiosity turned into an obsessive six-month search. After talking to U.S. and Canadian research scientists, renowned food authorities, chefs of all varieties, fishmongers, restaurateurs, industry types, seafood experts, university professors, lobstermen, cookbook authors, caterers that specialize in lobster bakes, and a couple of Maine home cooks, I had scores of lobster-cooking "secrets," which ranged from the obscure to the bizarre (*see* "Lobster Lore," page 15). But after testing every one, we still didn't have a cooking method that consistently delivered a tender lobster tail.

After our initial fruitless experiments in pursuit of tenderness, I interviewed Dr. Curtis Melton, head of food science and technology at the University of Tennessee. Although his specialty is beef, he made this comparative observation. Unlike cattle, which are slaughtered, bled, then set aside to pass through rigor mortis, lobsters are cooked live. Because beef is inedibly tough if butchered pre-rigor-mortis, I thought there might be a connection.

I knew of a study that suggested the superiority of post-rigor-mortis catfish. In this experiment, Washington State seafood expert John Rowley found that three-day-old catfish fillets had better texture and flavor than fillets from a freshly killed fish.

Might this be true, I wondered, for lobster as well? Would killing the lobster and then letting it rest on ice before cooking ensure a tender tail?

Because no one seemed to know if lobsters actually go through rigor mortis, we weren't sure how long to let them sit. (We also knew it couldn't be too long; bottom-feeding lobsters carry plenty of bacteria.) To play it safe, we killed six lobsters, refrigerated them, and cooked one every hour after their death, comparing each to one that was steamed live.

The results were varied, but generally the dead lobster meat looked dull compared to the bright, fresh-looking tail meat of the live-cooked ones. Many of the dead lobsters tasted "off," and most of them were mushy textured. We subsequently learned that at death, lobsters release gastric enzymes from the stomach sac that cause the meat to deteriorate. Although the meat was less tough, the attendant mushy texture was undesirable.

We were stymied, but undaunted. If the stomach sac releases destructive gastric enzymes, we decided to see what would happen if we took it out. Although the procedure may

Tenderness comes at a price—summer lobsters are cheap and plentiful, but the more expensive hard-shell lobsters of spring are of premier quality.

sound a bit excessive, the stomach sac is routinely removed when the lobster is split before broiling or baking. Located right behind the eyes, the sac is easily removed from a chilled lobster with kitchen shears. Removing the stomach sac also meant we were removing the brain, an organ many scientists (for humane reasons) thought should come out before cooking. This little operation, we reasoned, might save the tail meat from destructive gastric juices and guarantee the lobster would feel no pain.

Some scientists also suggested there might be gastric juices in the tomalley as well, so we prepared three different lobsters. We killed one lobster, then severed the tail from its body, thus ensuring that the tail was completely isolated from the stomach sac and the tomalley. For lobster two, we removed the stomach sac and brain, making sure the bulk of gastric enzymes could not deteriorate the tail. Lobster three was wrapped in wet newspaper and kept alive while the two dead lobsters rested on ice overnight. To our surprise the following day, each cooked lobster was equally delicious and tender. The results of this test finally made us suspect that the secret to tender lobster was not so much in the preparation and cooking as in the selection.

Susan Waddy, research scientist and lobster-molting expert at the Department of Fisheries and Oceans in New Brunswick, Canada, confirmed our hunch by explaining the lobster's yearly cycle.

A Year in the Life of a Lobster

Before working on this story, the terms hard-shell and soft-shell lobster meant little to me. Unlike crabs, there's certainly no distinction between the two at the retail level. Ever seen a sign on the lobster tank advertising soft-shell lobsters?

I knew, of course, that some lobster claws rip open as easily as an aluminum flip-top can, while others require shop tools to crack. I had certainly noticed the wimpy, limp claw meat of some lobsters and the full, packed meat of others. (At the time, I attributed the shrunken claw to starvation in the tank.) And I had surely noticed that some lobsters were more watery than others. What I didn't know was that all of these variations were the result of the particular stage of molting that the lobster was in at the time I bought and ate it.

As it turns out, most of the lobsters we eat during the summer and fall are in some phase of molting. During late

PHOTOGRAPH BY CARL TREMBLAY

spring, the waters begin to warm, and the lobsters start to form the new shell tissue underneath their shells. According to Waddy, lobsters start to molt as early as June off the shores of New Jersey, and July or August in the colder Maine and Canadian waters.

Because the most difficult task in molting is pulling the claw muscle through the old shell, the lobster dehydrates its claw (hence the smaller, wimpier claw meat).

Once the lobster molts, or casts off its old shell, it emerges with nothing but a wrinkled, soft covering. Within fifteen minutes, the lobster inflates itself with water, increasing its length by 15 percent and its weight by 50 percent. This extra water expands the wrinkled, soft covering, allowing the lobster room to grow long after the shell starts to harden. The newly molted lobster immediately eats its old shell, digesting the crucial shell-hardening calcium.

Understanding the molt phase clarifies the deficiencies of the soft-shell summer lobster.

If You Buy a Soft-Shell...

Some people won't eat soft-shell lobsters, others buy them for chowder or lobster rolls, and still others can't get enough of them. In the summer, they're usually cheap and plentiful, and if you buy them, here's what you need to know.

First, they are much more perishable than hard-shells. Wrapped in wet newspaper, frisky hard-shell lobsters are usually just as feisty the following day. Soft-shells, on the other hand, slow way down after a night in the refrigerator, and I'm never surprised to find one dead.

For claw meat fans, soft-shells will surely disappoint. Their claws are small, underdeveloped, and spongy textured (see illustration below).

Also, because the newly molted lobster is full of water and not fully developed, you are getting the meat equivalent of a smaller-size lobster. The meat from a one-and-one-half-pound soft-shell lobster, we found, was equal to that of a one- to one-and-one-quarter-pound hard-shell. If serving soft-shell lobsters, you may consider buying larger ones (one-and-one-half- to one-and-three-quarter-pounders for each person), or if the price is really good, two small ones per person.

Soft-shell lobsters are much easier to eat than hard-shells because they don't require special equipment. The claws readily snap open by hand, and because the tail meat is not filled out, it easily slips out of its shell.—P.A.

It explains why it is so waterlogged, why its claw meat is so shriveled and scrawny, and why its tail meat is so underdeveloped.

For the next three or four months, according to Waddy, the lobster continues its calcium-rich diet and its shell continues to harden. Lobsters caught and impounded during this postmolt phase, she adds, are slow to develop hardened shells. Because the lobsters are fed very little in the pounds and not at all in the tanks, they don't get the calcium they need for shell development. Perhaps this explains why as late as early January we were still buying lobsters with soft shells.

Lobsters are prime when their shells are fully hardened—unfortunately this only starts to happen in fall and early winter. If you can find hard-shells this time of year, enjoy them. Before buying them, however, squeeze their bodies for shell hardness (see illustration at top of page 17).

As winter sets in, weather conditions keep the lobster fishers from checking their traps as often, and cold water slows the lobster's metabolism so that it loses interest in food. Short winter supplies drive up the price. I paid $3.99 per pound for one- to one-and-one-quarter-pounders on Labor Day weekend, but in January the same size lobster cost me $8 a pound.

Late-spring lobsters are among the best. Because they have been developing meat since the previous year's molting, spring hard-shell lobsters are packed with meat. In addition, because they are more plentiful (warmer water stimulates the lobster's appetite, and better weather makes it possible for the lobster fishers to bait and check their traps), the price is right. As a rule of thumb, hard-shell lobsters are reasonably priced from Mother's Day through the Fourth of July.

Full Circle

After my interview with Waddy, I checked our original notes from the summer. For flavor and taste comparison, we had special-ordered a few pricey hard-shells along with a larger quantity of the more reasonably priced seasonal soft-shells. Our notes suggested that most of the hard-shell lobster tails were not rubbery and chewy, but we didn't test enough of them to see a pattern, and because the focus had been on preparation and cooking technique, we didn't make the connection.

For the rest of the summer and fall, we tested with whatever happened to be swimming in the tank. In retrospect, I know most of them were postmolt lobsters because they didn't require special equipment to crack the claws until the final three we cooked in late January.

It's spring now, and I cook up a lobster every few weeks to test my theory. Occasionally I find a hard-shell lobster with a tough tail, but for the most part I find their tails meaty and firm, not chewy like those I experienced in the summer. Tails aside, spring lobsters are feisty and full of meat. Go ahead

---

and enjoy lobsters in the summer when they're plentiful and cheap and their meat is sweet (see "If You Buy a Soft-Shell...," left), but from now on, make sure you savor at least a couple in late spring and early summer before they start the cycle all over again.

How to Cook the Lobster

Once we determined that lobster quality was mostly dependent on its molt cycle, figuring out how to cook it was anticlimactic. Except for the larger water puddle on the plate, we couldn't tell much difference between boiled and steamed lobsters. Steaming was more efficient and less messy, though, so we opted for that method. Steaming the lobster on a rack or steamer basket kept it from becoming waterlogged (if you happen to be near the ocean, seaweed makes a natural rack). Neither beer nor wine in the pot improved the lobster's flavor.

As for dry heat cooking methods, we found the steady, even heat of the oven preferable to broiling. To keep the tail from curling during roasting, run a skewer through it (see illustration 8, page 16).

STEAMED WHOLE LOBSTERS
Serves 4

Because hard-shell lobsters are more packed with meat than soft-shell ones, you may want to buy one-and-one-half- to one-and-three-quarter-pounders if serving soft-shells.

  4 lobsters
  8 tablespoons butter, melted until hot
      (optional)
      Lemon wedges

Bring about 1 inch water to boil over high heat in large soup kettle set up with wire rack, pasta insert, or seaweed bed. Add lobster,

---

APPROXIMATE STEAMING TIMES AND MEAT YIELDS

Lobster Size	Cooking Time: Minutes	Meat Yield: Ounces
1 lb		
soft-shell:	8 to 9	about 3
hard-shell:	10 to 11	4 to 4½
1¼ lbs		
soft-shell:	11 to 12	3½ to 4
hard-shell:	13 to 14	5½ to 6
1½ lbs		
soft-shell:	13 to 14	5½ to 6
hard-shell:	15 to 16	7½ to 8
1¾ - 2 lbs		
soft-shell:	17 to 18	6¼ to 6½
hard-shell:	about 19	8½ to 9

ILLUSTRATIONS BY WENDY WRAY

cover, and return water to boil. Reduce heat to medium-high; steam until lobsters are done (*see* chart, page 14, for approximate cooking times). Serve immediately with warm butter and lemon wedges.

OVEN-ROASTED LOBSTER WITH HERBED BREAD CRUMBS
Serves 4

4   tablespoons butter
½   cup dried bread crumbs
2   tablespoons minced fresh parsley
      leaves, or 1 tablespoon minced
      fresh tarragon leaves or snipped
      chives
4   lobsters, prepared according to
      illustrations 1 through 8, page 16
      Salt and ground white pepper
      Lemon wedges

1. Adjust oven rack to middle-high position and heat oven to 450 degrees. Heat 1 tablespoon of the butter in small skillet over medium heat. When foaming subsides, add bread crumbs and cook, stirring constantly, until toasted and golden brown, 3 to 4 minutes. Stir in herbs and set aside.

2. Arrange lobsters crosswise on two 17-by-11-inch foil-lined jelly roll pans, alternating tail and claw ends. Melt remaining butter and brush over body and tail of each lobster; season with salt and pepper to taste. Sprinkle portion of bread crumb mixture evenly over body and tail meat.

3. Roast lobsters until tail meat is opaque and bread crumbs are crisp, 12 to 15 minutes. Serve immediately with lemon wedges.

To Kill a Lobster

For those who eat meat, I think it's fair to have to kill what we eat once in a while. I don't like killing anything, lobsters included, but the occasional act reminds me of what someone spares me every time I eat a boneless, skinless chicken breast or a piece of filleted salmon.

Lobsters are particularly troublesome. Like slaughtered chickens, they continue to move long after everyone assures you they are dead. I once observed the swimmerets on a lobster tail moving eighteen hours after I had severed body from tail.

There is much debate over how much or how little pain a lobster feels once it hits the lobster pot. Some experts say a lobster cannot survive in temperatures over 80 degrees, so death is instant in a pot of steaming or boiling water (scratching on the pot by the lobster notwithstanding). Others say the lobster should be frozen and its brain removed before cooking. Yet others argue that freezing is painful.

But judging from experience, I prefer freezing the lobster before cooking it. After ten minutes in the freezer, the lobster is numbed. At that point, you can steam it, or split it for roasting.—P.A.

 **LOBSTER LORE**

Ever wonder why some lobster tails are tougher than others? The following are some of the suggestions I got when writing this story. Interestingly, a couple of people suggested that soft-shell lobsters might be more tender, but no one suggested the opposite. In fact, none of these tips proved correct, but they provide a sure sign that the problem of tough tails has inspired many creative, if wrongheaded, solutions.

Choose the Right Gender. While females often contain the treasured roe, their tails are no more tender than those of their male counterparts.

Select Soft-Shells over Hard-Shells. The tail meat of a soft-shell lobster might be sweeter, but compared to a hard-shell of the same size, it's smaller and tougher. The claw meat is also wimpy, watery, and limp.

Microwave It. Of all the methods we tried, the microwave seemed the cruelest way to cook a lobster. Without going into detail, the microwave appeared to electrocute the creature.

Avoid Chicken Lobsters. Some speculate that the small one-pound lobsters swim more, thus developing a tougher tail muscle. We found chicken lobsters that were tough, but also some that were tender.

Avoid Large, Older Lobsters. Some say that after years of exercising its tail, older lobsters are tougher. Again, we found both tough and tender old geezer lobsters.

Freeze the Lobster. Based on the theory that an adrenaline rush at death causes the tail to toughen, a few suggested freezing the lobster ten minutes before cooking. Though freezing numbs the lobster, preventing it from moving around so much, it doesn't prevent toughness.

Pet the Lobster. Working on the same adrenaline rush theory, some stroke the lobster's body to hypnotize it. Before the lobster wakes up, they speculate, it is cooked. While the lobster may enjoy this premortem massage, it doesn't guarantee a tender, succulent tail.

Don't Overcook the Lobster. Many suggest cooking the lobster until the thickest part of the tail is barely opaque. Some of the toughest tails we encountered were cooked to this doneness.

Don't Undercook the Lobster. Mainers in particular laugh at recipes that recommend eight minutes per pound. Many of them steam their one-and-one-quarter-pounders at least fifteen to twenty minutes. It didn't take too many lobsters to convince me that overcooking wasn't a good idea either.

Let the Lobster Rest. A California chef told me that after cooking sixty lobsters, he discovered that a five-minute rest after cooking delivered a more tender tail. After testing, we let this idea rest in peace.

Start the Lobster in Cold Water...Then Gradually Bring It to Simmer. Some believe this method also kills the lobster humanely. Our notes read to the contrary: "The lobster cooked this way was tough. It was still moving even when the eyes had turned white from the heat. Perhaps his slow death might have contributed to his toughness. Hardly lulled to sleep."

Use a Chopstick to Kill the Lobster. One person was certain the secret lay with the Chinese. A chopstick run up the tail and through the body guaranteed instant death and a tender tail. (A scene from the movie *Eat, Drink, Man, Woman* made me think he might be right.) After performing this method on a lobster, we decided we couldn't ask anyone to kill a lobster this way. Next to microwaving, this execution method seemed most cruel and unusual. The tail may have been slightly more tender, but it looked torn and mutilated.

Steam the Lobster over Very Low Heat. Because the lobster tail is all muscle, I thought long, low heat might work. This method did not work, and the slow low heat caused the lobster to retain its body liquids. Thus, the tomalley, which many people enjoy, turned from a soft liverlike texture to soup.

Stretch the Tail During Cooking. When combined with low-heat steaming, it seemed to me that this method was promising. The low heat did allow me to put my hand in the pot and stretch out the lobster tail during steaming. Although the lobster tail was straight, not curled, when it came out of the pot, its tail meat was really no more tender.—P.A.

Lobster Techniques

by Pam Anderson

Because lobsters are often special occasion food, most of us don't work with them enough to get comfortable handling them. The result is that for many people, preparing a lobster can be overwhelming and eating it can be intimidating. The following step-by-step illustrations are meant to put the cook and diner at ease.

To Prepare a Lobster for Roasting

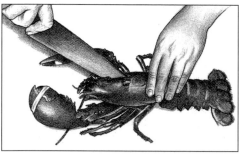

1. With the blade of a chef's knife facing the head, kill the lobster by plunging the knife into the body at the point where the shell forms a "T." Move the blade down until it touches the head.

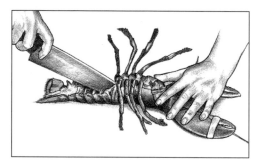

2. Turn the lobster over, then, holding the upper body with one hand and positioning the knife blade so it faces the tail end, cut through the body toward the tail, making sure not to cut all the way through the shell.

3. Move your hand down to the lower body and continue cutting through the tail.

4. Holding half of the tail in each hand, crack, but do not break, the back shell to butterfly the lobster.

5. Use a spoon to remove and discard the stomach sac.

6. Remove and discard the intestinal tract.

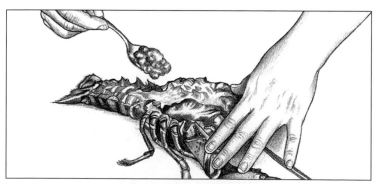

7. Remove and discard the green tomalley if you wish.

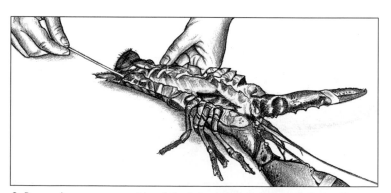

8. Run a skewer up one side of the lobster tail to keep it from curling during cooking.

Hard-shell lobsters are much meatier than soft-shell (see "How to Buy, Cook, and Serve a Lobster," page 14). To determine whether a lobster is hard-shell or soft-shell, squeeze the side of the lobster's body; a soft-shell lobster will yield to pressure while a hard-shell will be hard, brittle, and tightly packed.

— How to Eat a Lobster (or Remove Cooked Meat) —

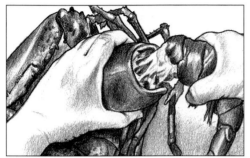

1. Twist the tail to separate it from the body.

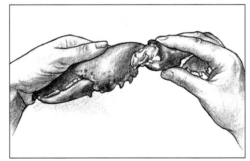

2. Twist off the tail flippers.

3. Use a fork or your finger to push the tail meat up and out through the wide end of the tail. Pull the tail meat out the other end.

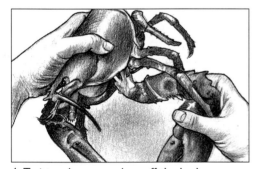

4. Twist a claw appendage off the body.

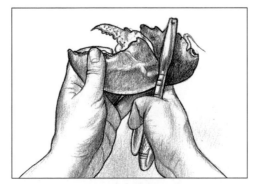

5. Twist the claw from the connecting joint.

6. Remove the pincher portion of the claw. If you use a gentle motion, the meat will often stay attached to the rest of the claw; otherwise, you'll need a cocktail fork to pick out the meat from the shell.

7. If the lobster is a soft-shell, use your hands to break open the claw and remove the meat.

8. If the lobster is a hard-shell, use lobster crackers to break open the claw and remove the meat.

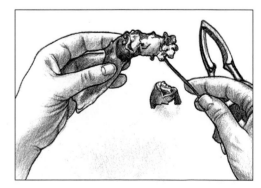

9. Crack open the connecting joint and remove the meat with a cocktail fork. Repeat steps 5 through 9 with the remaining claw.

Real Strawberry Shortcake

*For a light, rich, cakelike biscuit, add an egg and
use just enough rich milk to bind the dough.*

by Pam Anderson with Karen Tack

It's curious that I grew up in the heart of biscuit country, yet I didn't eat a biscuit-based strawberry shortcake until I was in my twenties and living in Chicago. Just about everybody I knew down South spooned strawberries over pound cake or angel food cake. Why, I don't know.

But having since enjoyed strawberries over all sorts of pastries and cakes, these days I'm definitely a biscuit fan. Cakes and other pastries just don't offer the contrast of cool strawberries sandwiched between warm, tender-crisp biscuit halves and chilled whipped cream.

In search of this ideal, we baked four very different sweetened biscuits: baking powder biscuits (a standard biscuit where fat is cut into flour, baking powder, salt, and sugar and moistened with milk), buttermilk biscuits (buttermilk takes the place of milk and baking soda is substituted for part of the baking powder), cream biscuits (cream stands in for the fat and liquid), and egg-enriched biscuits (egg takes the place of part of the milk).

After sampling each, we felt that the egg-enriched biscuit had the advantage. Even with the added sugar, the baking powder and buttermilk biscuits seemed more at home in a bread basket than on a dessert plate. The cream biscuits were good-looking, but gummy inside. But the egg and light cream–enriched shortcakes, although still very much a biscuit, were finer-textured and more cakelike.

A Few Refinements

As a result of this tasting, we decided to start with a simple egg-enriched shortcake recipe adapted from *The Fannie Farmer Baking Book* (Knopf, 1984) and see if we could add any recipe refinements.

We began our testing by making three batches of biscuits, one with all-purpose bleached flour, another with a mix of all-purpose and cake flour, and a final with all cake flour. Because biscuits are supposed to be tender, we placed our bet on cake flour delivering the best biscuit. Defying the odds, the cake flour biscuit came in last, with a meltingly tender, yet powdery dry texture, much like shortbread. This low-gluten flour didn't seem strong enough to support the fat.

In previous quick bread tests ("Big, Beautiful Muffins," January/February 1997 and "Perfect Pancakes," January/February 1996) we've never found a mix of all-purpose and cake flour superior to straight bleached all-purpose. These biscuits were no exception. Shortcakes made with bleached all-purpose were our favorites—tender, moist, and somewhat cakelike.

With the flour issue resolved, we moved on to test the liquids (in addition to the egg we decided upon earlier). We made biscuits using milk, buttermilk (substituting baking soda for part of the baking powder), half-and-half, and heavy cream. Buttermilk, my usual favorite in quick breads, felt a little out of place in this recipe. Though they smelled great, the distinct tang of the buttermilk seemed to place the cakes solidly in the savory category rather than promote them as dessert. The cakes made with cream were squatty and dense textured. The half-and-half and the milk biscuits were tall and light textured. Though both were good, those made with milk were comparatively flat-tasting for our dessert biscuit. Because of their good looks and rich flavor, the half-and-half biscuits were our favorite.

Biscuits made with four teaspoons of baking powder tasted slightly metallic. By reducing the baking powder to one tablespoon, we lost the off flavor, but not the height.

Less butter gave us taller biscuits, but they were comparatively dry and tough, as were biscuits made with cream cheese.

Pat a Cake

Just because we had worked our way through the ingredients list didn't mean we had a great shortcake yet. There were still unresolved issues with mixing, cutting, brushing, and baking the cakes.

Each mixing method—pastry cutter, food processor, fingertips—has its assets and liabilities. The pastry cutter works well, but cutting the butter into small cubes beforehand can be a problem. If the butter is soft enough to cut easily, then it's too soft for the pastry and must be refrigerated or frozen (plus it tends to stick to the knife). If the butter is hard enough for the pastry, then it's difficult to cut. I like the food processor for big jobs, but I like it less for quick jobs like cutting butter into flour for six shortcakes. As for using your fingers, some cooks have got cold fingertips, perfect for cutting butter into flour, but apparently my circulation is too good; I usually soften the butter too much in the process of getting it pea-sized.

We eventually settled on a method suggested by a *Cook's Illustrated* reader. We grated a frozen stick of butter on the large holes of a box grater right into the flour mixture, then finished the job with the pastry cutter. The hardened butter is the perfect texture for grating. A few cuts with the pastry cutter and the butter is fully incorporated and pea-sized.

We made an interesting discovery when testing dough shaping. Although hand-formed biscuits look attractive and rustic, we found they were fairly easy to overwork, and a pair of warm hands can cause the dough's surface

STRAWBERRY SHORTCAKE TRICKS

1. For best taste and appearance, crush one-third of the berries.

2. Grating frozen butter into the flour makes for easy mixing.

3. Split biscuits by hand before adding strawberries.

ILLUSTRATIONS BY TONY DELUZ

butter to melt. Using a biscuit cutter requires less handling, and dough rounds cut with a biscuit cutter develop a natural crack around the circumference during baking, making them easy to hand-split. We also realized we didn't need a rolling pin. Patting the dough to three-quarters inch thick on a floured work surface was fast and simple.

Split Apart

Some people butter the split biscuits before topping them with strawberries. I'm not sure if this is done to keep strawberry juices from making the biscuit soggy or to enrich the dessert. Regardless, we found the butter unnecessary. It didn't keep the juice from penetrating the biscuit, and it took away from the freshness of the berries and gave them a greasy mouth feel.

I don't like just quartered or sliced strawberries on my strawberry shortcake. They slip and slide around and remain separate little pieces of fruit that must be individually forked. On the other hand, I don't like the look of a crushed berry shortcake either. So we found a happy compromise by quartering a majority of the berries, then crushing the remainder to unify the quartered fruit.

RICH AND TENDER SHORTCAKES WITH STRAWBERRIES AND WHIPPED CREAM
Serves 6

After cutting six perfect rounds of dough, you can reknead the scraps and repeat the cutting process to get one or two more rounds. These shortcakes will be a little tougher and less attractive than those from the first cutting.

If you prefer to make the shortcake dough in the food processor, pulse the dry ingredients to combine them, then add cold butter that has been cut into half-inch pieces and continue to pulse until the mixture looks like coarse cornmeal flecked with pea-sized bits of butter. Pour the mixture into a bowl; stir in the egg and half-and-half with a rubber spatula until the mixture comes together. Continue with step 4 of the recipe instructions.

Topping
3   pints strawberries, hulled; 1 pint crushed with potato masher or fork (*see* illustration 1, page 18), 2 pints quartered
6   tablespoons sugar

Shortcakes
2   cups all-purpose bleached flour, plus more for work surface and biscuit cutter
$^1/_2$ teaspoon salt
1   tablespoon baking powder
3   tablespoons sugar, plus 2 tablespoons for sprinkling
1   stick (8 tablespoons) unsalted butter, frozen
1   egg, beaten
$^1/_2$ cup plus 1 tablespoon half-and-half
1   egg white, lightly beaten

BEST CREAM, BEST SUGAR, BEST WHIPPED CREAM

Supermarkets offer several creams for whipping, from pasteurized organic heavy cream to ultrapasteurized heavy whipping cream. After we tested them all side by side, pasteurized organic heavy cream emerged as our favorite. It delivers the sweetest cream flavor, and although it pours the thinnest, its whipped volume is equal to that of regular pasteurized heavy cream, a full two cups per cup of liquid. Regular pasteurized heavy cream is expectedly thicker than its organic cousin and has a richer mouth feel—the result of various additives put in for just these reasons. However, it is not as creamy sweet as the organic version. Ultrapasteurized heavy cream is the thickest of the three but gives the smallest yield when whipped (only one and one-half cups) because the high temperature required for ultrapasteurization destroys some of the protein and enzymes that promote whipping. This higher heat also leaves the cream with a slightly cooked taste, eliminating the more complex, fresh taste of pasteurized cream.

Unfortunately, it is becoming increasingly difficult to find heavy cream other than ultrapasteurized. But seeking out pasteurized cream will give you better volume and flavor every time.

Of the two sweeteners we tested, granulated sugar was our favorite because of its unmuddled sweetness. Adding the granulated sugar to the cream at the beginning allows enough time for the granules to dissolve by the time the cream is whipped. By contrast, it took twice as much confectioners' sugar to equal the sweetness of granulated sugar, while leaving a faint chalky aftertaste. Although many think that confectioners' sugar–sweetened whipped cream holds better than granulated sugar whipped cream, we found that when stored in a strainer in the refrigerator, both creams held equally well for up to eight hours.—*Sharon Kebschull Barrett with Melissa Hamilton*

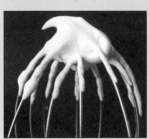
Soft peaks of whipped cream should look like this.

Stiff peaks stand straight rather than flopping over.

Cream beaten too long becomes granular and separated.

PERFECT WHIPPED CREAM
Makes about 2 cups

If using pasteurized cream, safeguard against overwhipping by slightly underwhipping with the handheld mixer, then hand-whipping with a whisk for a few strokes to finish. Whipping times will be longer for ultrapasteurized cream.

1   cup ($^1/_2$ pint) chilled heavy cream, preferably pasteurized or pasteurized organic
1   tablespoon granulated sugar
1   teaspoon vanilla extract

1. Chill nonreactive, deep, 1- to $1^1/_2$-quart bowl and beaters for a handheld mixer in freezer for at least 20 minutes.

2. Add cream, sugar, and vanilla to chilled bowl; beat on low speed until small bubbles form, about 30 seconds. Increase speed to medium; continue beating until beaters leave a trail, about 30 seconds more. Increase speed to high; continue beating until cream is smooth, thick, and nearly doubled in volume, about 20 seconds for soft peaks or about 30 seconds for stiff peaks. If necessary, finish beating by hand to adjust consistency. Serve. (Can be transferred to fine sieve or strainer set over measuring cup and refrigerated up to 8 hours.)

1. Mix crushed and quartered berries with sugar in medium bowl; set aside while preparing biscuits (or up to 2 hours).

2. Adjust oven rack to lower middle position; heat oven to 425 degrees. Mix flour, salt, baking powder, and 3 tablespoons sugar in medium bowl. Using large holes of box grater, grate butter into dry ingredients (*see* illustration 2, page 18). Toss butter with flour to coat. Use pastry cutter to finish cutting butter into flour. Or scoop up coated butter with both hands, then quickly rub butter into dry ingredients with fingertips until most of butter pieces are size of split peas.

3. Mix beaten egg with half-and-half; pour into flour mixture. Toss with fork until large clumps form. Turn mixture onto floured work surface and lightly knead until it comes together.

4. Pat dough into 9- by 6-inch rectangle, $^3/_4$ inch thick. Flour $2^3/_4$-inch biscuit cutter; cut 6 dough rounds. Place 1 inch apart on small baking sheet; brush dough tops with egg white and sprinkle with remaining sugar. (Can be covered and refrigerated up to 2 hours before baking.) Bake until golden brown, 12 to 14 minutes. Place baking sheet on wire rack; cool cakes until warm, about 10 minutes.

5. Split each cake crosswise (*see* illustration 3, page 18); spoon a portion of berries and then a dollop of whipped cream over each cake bottom. Cap with cake top; serve immediately.

Lace Cookies

We find that the right sweeteners and the proper ratio of flour to butter create gossamer-thin, lacy wafers; three tips make them easy to get off the baking sheet.

by Anne Tuomey and Ann Flanigan

❧

When we were growing up, lace cookies were "special occasion" fare. Made from a dropped batter that spreads and separates as it bakes into lacy, brittle, see-through wafers, these fancy-looking cookies crunch when you bite them and immediately melt in your mouth with the rich taste of butter and brown sugar. They look and taste so complicated, in fact, that you assume they took hours to make.

After making countless batches, we are happy to report that these cookies are actually easy to make, using ingredients that you probably have in your cupboard right now. Because there is no rolling or cutting of dough, they are also fast.

But despite their simplicity, we found a number of issues to resolve when making lace cookies. Getting the texture of the batter just right was important for controlling the spread of the cookies during baking, and thus the shape of the finished cookie. We also wanted to temper the sweetness a bit in order to bring out the flavor of the nuts or oats included as an ingredient. In addition, because the thirty recipes we tested included different sweeteners, we needed to settle on which sweetener tasted best and how it would affect the texture of the batter. Finally, we needed to resolve the most widely recognized difficulty with these cookies (and the actual reason why our mothers made them so rarely): their tendency to stick to the pan, bunching and tearing when you remove them.

The Recipe

Because we were looking for a gossamer-thin cookie with a brittle texture, we quickly eliminated all recipes that included eggs and chemical leavening. These additions produced flat but vaguely puffy cookies.

We then moved on to consider sweeteners. After toying with every combination we could think of—from all white or all brown sugar to mixtures that included molasses and light or dark corn syrup—we ended up being happiest with one-half cup of light corn syrup mixed with three-quarters cup of dark brown sugar. The brown sugar contributed not only an appealing deep brown color but also a wonderful praline flavor; the corn syrup added a more subtle sweetness and also gave the cookies a less crumbly consistency. Our science adviser, Shirley Corriher, explained that this is because corn syrup inhibits crystallization, keeping the cookie soft and supple compared to a crystallized confection, which would be hard and easily broken.

The flour-to-butter ratio was the second key to the texture of the batter and therefore to its spreading behavior. In our research, we had found recipes with ratios ranging from one and one-half tablespoons to two cups of flour per stick of butter. We tested them all and had the most success with six tablespoons of flour per stick of butter. More butter made greasy cookies that flowed right off the pan; less butter destroyed the lacy quality we wanted, giving us a compact cookie. Had corn syrup not been part of our formula, we could have gotten away with as little as four tablespoons of flour. But in our recipe, we needed the extra two tablespoons to compensate for the moisture in the corn syrup.

Finally, we tested the effects of heavy cream and milk. It turned out that adding a tablespoon of heavy cream to the batter made the baked cookies easier to shape because the added fat and emulsifiers in the batter helped keep the cookie soft for a little extra time just out of the oven. And because the cream imparted richness to the flavor as well, we decided to include it in our master recipe.

A Sticky Issue

The sticking problem turned out to have a three-part, yet very straightforward, solution.

First, it serendipitously turned out that eliminating eggs from the batter helped reduce sticking because the liquid protein in eggs can get into even the most minute holes in the surface of a cookie sheet, even a nonstick one, and make the cookies stick like crazy.

Second, we found that using a nonstick baking sheet liner made a tremendous difference in how well the cookies came off the sheets. The performance differences between various types of liners were subtle (*see* "Rating Nonstick Baking Sheet Liners," below), but whichever you choose, we definitely recommend using one.

Careful timing once the cookies emerged from the oven was the final part of the solution. After cooling on the baking sheet for one to two minutes, the cookies were just starting to firm up, and we could handle them comfortably. If you are going to shape the cookies, you must work within this limited time frame, for even one extra minute renders them too firm to work with.

MASTER RECIPE FOR LACE COOKIES
Makes about 6 dozen
Using a nonstick bakeware liner prevents the cookies from sticking. Parchment paper, though a little less effective, can also be used. Our recipe contains nuts for flavor, but oats are traditional as well. Humidity is the archenemy of lace cookies, so try to make them on a dry day. Otherwise, they will absorb too much moisture and be chewy instead of caramelized and brittle.

 8   tablespoons unsalted butter
 3/4 cup dark brown sugar

Rating Nonstick Baking Sheet Liners

Nonstick baking sheet liners proved the optimum baking surface for delicate lace cookies. While there were subtle distinctions among the four brands of nonstick liners we tested, all proved more effective than unlined cookie sheets, parchment paper, or waxed paper.

Our favorite was the Silpat nonstick pan liner. Made from woven glass fabric coated with silicone, this flesh-colored, flexible liner rendered the thinnest, roundest cookie. And because silicone is a chemically inert, nonporous material, there was nothing for the cookies to cling to. We also liked the fact that the liner did not shift around and was light enough in color to allow us to see the cookies baking. A Silpat sheet costs $16, is made to last for about two thousand bakes, and can be used in the oven, freezer, or microwave, according to its manufacturer.

A silicone-coated nonstick liner from King Arthur ($11.95) also proved to be an excellent surface from which to remove the cookies. We found it shifted slightly on the baking sheet, and its tan color made visibility only fair. Not as sturdy as the Silpat, it is still guaranteed for two hundred bakes.

We also tested DuPont's Teflon nonstick liner. While the cookies spread well with lots of "lacy" holes and released readily, they were harder to see on this charcoal-colored liner. This liner can be used hundreds of times before replacing it, according to DuPont, and at $4.99 is definitely the best bargain.

If using one of these nonstick liners is not an option, we found that the recipe works adequately with parchment paper or a heavy nonstick cookie sheet. Lighter, supermarket-bought nonstick cookie sheets and aluminum sheet pans did not conduct heat well enough, burned the cookies, and were unreliable for removing the cookies—warm or cool. We found waxed paper to be the most disastrous surface of all, producing a gooey cookie that crumbled before it released from the paper.—*Maryellen Driscoll*

SHAPING LACE COOKIES

Until you get the hang of shaping these cookies, we recommend baking only two or three at a time. After making each of the shapes below, gently hold the cookie in place until it is set, about ten seconds, then cool on a wire rack. If the cookies cool on the cookie sheet too long and become too brittle to shape, place the entire sheet back in the oven for a minute or two until soft again. If any of the cookies shatter after you have shaped them, save the crumbles to sprinkle on ice cream sundaes.—A.T.

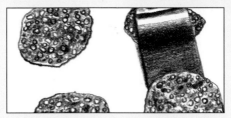  

1. After cooling, slide a spatula under one cookie. If it does not bunch or tear, cookies are ready to move.

2. To make "cigarettes" place the cookie against the handle of a wooden spoon and roll the cookie over itself as quickly as possible.

3. To form a tuile, lay the cookie over a rolling pin or a wine bottle set on its side so that the cookie forms a gentle curve.

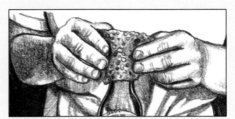  

4. To form a tricornered hat, mold the cookie over the opening of a wine bottle or other bottle of similar shape, then flute the edges to form a tricornered hat shape. Hold until set.

5. Cones are easiest shaped by hand. Holding both sides of the cookie, wrap one side over the other, overlapping about an inch or so.

6. To form a bowl, lay the cookie over the bottom of a small bowl turned upside down and gently mold the cookie to follow the contour of the bowl.

DECORATING WITH CHOCOLATE

You can melt about six ounces of semisweet chocolate over simmering water or use any glaze of your choice. Lay cookies on waxed paper to set.

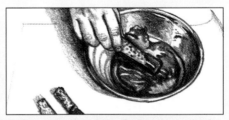  

1. Cigarette shapes or flat cookies may be dipped halfway into the glaze.

2. Flat cookies may be painted with a pastry brush or spoon, or you may dip the bottom into the glaze.

3. Another option for flat cookies is to place them on a sheet of waxed paper, and then drizzle chocolate with a pastry bag.

½ cup light corn syrup
1 teaspoon vanilla extract
¼ teaspoon salt
6 tablespoons all-purpose flour, sifted
1 cup pecans or almonds, chopped fine
1 tablespoon heavy cream

1. Adjust oven rack to center position and heat oven to 350 degrees. Bring butter, brown sugar, and corn syrup just to boil in medium saucepan over medium heat, 5 to 6 minutes, stirring frequently. Off heat, beat in vanilla, salt, flour, nuts, and cream until smooth.

2. Drop rounded teaspoonsful of batter at 3-inch intervals onto cookie sheet lined with baking sheet liner or parchment, estimating six cookies per sheet. For larger cookies, substitute 1 tablespoon for the teaspoon and estimate five cookies per sheet. Bake cookies until spread thin, deep golden brown, and bubbling has subsided, 6 to 7 minutes, or 7 to 8 minutes for larger cookies.

3. Let cookies cool and firm up slightly on sheet, 1 to 2 minutes. Following instructions in "Shaping Lace Cookies," above, transfer to wire rack with thin spatula or shape as desired. If desired, follow instructions in "Decorating with Chocolate" to decorate cookies. Cookies can be stored in airtight container up to 1 month.

ORANGE-OATMEAL LACE COOKIES
Follow Master Recipe for Lace Cookies, substituting 1 cup quick-cooking oats for nuts and adding 1 tablespoon finely grated zest from 1 large orange with vanilla.

SPICED WALNUT LACE COOKIES
Follow Master Recipe for Lace Cookies, substituting 1 cup finely chopped walnuts for pecans or almonds and adding ½ teaspoon each nutmeg and cinnamon and ¼ teaspoon each allspice, ground cloves, and ground ginger with vanilla.

Two French Toasts

For toast that's consistently crisp on the outside but custardlike on the inside, the secret is to match the batter to the bread.

by Sharon Kebschull Barrett

❧

Good cooks know they can often "taste" a recipe just by reading it. When I started on my quest for fabulous French toast, I experienced the reverse: I could taste what I wanted in my head, but I couldn't find a recipe for it that came close. In fact, my *Cook's Illustrated* editor and I agreed that we couldn't remember ever having had truly great French toast. After dozens of tests, it wasn't hard to see why this was so.

French toast (or *pain perdu*, "lost bread") started out as a simple way to use up old bread by dipping it in a beaten egg and frying it. Many current recipes deviate little from that, calling for a couple of eggs and a touch of milk. Those recipes, though, produce a toast that tastes mostly of fried egg and that, depending on the amount of liquid, is either overly soggy or still dry in the middle.

I wanted something quite different: bread that was crisp and buttery on the outside, soft and custardlike inside. I wanted to taste a balance of flavors, rather than just eating egg. I wanted it sweet enough to eat with only a sprinkling of confectioners' sugar, but not so sweet that I couldn't top it with syrup or macerated fruit if I chose to.

Breaking Bread

I started testing with a simple formula: two eggs beaten with one-half cup of milk to soak four slices of three-quarter-inch-thick, day-old French bread. From this starting point, I wanted to settle first on which bread works best for French toast, but that proved to be the hardest part of my testing. At first, it seemed simple. A variation of one-inch-thick bread of any sort was too thick; it either soaked up too much liquid and didn't cook through, or it stayed dry in the middle with shorter soaking. So I stuck with three-quarter-inch bread and started trying various baguettes, supermarket breads, challah and brioche, and a dense white bread.

At the end of these tests, I thought I had the answer. Challah was clearly best, adding a lot of flavor and richness, staying generally crisp outside and somewhat moist inside—not perfect, but likely to improve with changes in the liquid component. Baguette slices and slices of a high-quality Italian bread, so long as they weren't more than a day old, came in second. Hard-to-find brioche was only acceptable. Brioche can vary widely, and my open-textured version failed to take up the liquid evenly. Dense white bread simply tasted like fried bread, so it rated near the bottom. Presliced sandwich bread was acceptable in a pinch, although just barely. Worst, though, was the supermarket bakery version of French or Italian bread. Spongy and flabby, this bread simply fell apart when I took it out of the liquid. For the moment, the bread issue seemed resolved. So, using challah for testing, I moved on to the liquids.

Less Egg, More Flavor

Because I didn't want it too eggy, I first tried dropping one egg from my test recipe. That showed an immediate improvement, yielding a finished product that was crispier outside but still soft inside. To be sure fewer eggs were better, I tried going the opposite way, using three eggs to my one-half cup of milk. That confirmed it: More egg seems to create a barrier on the outside of the bread, so that the interior stays dry while the outside ends up tasting like fried egg.

Finally, I tried a variation I'd seen that called for beating the whites separately and folding them in. When cooked, though, this bread ended up with a froth of egg white around the edge that cooked first. The outside didn't crisp, and the inside didn't cook through.

The next logical step seemed to be to increase the milk, given that a higher proportion of milk to egg had worked so far. A jump to one cup of milk made the bread too wet inside, but it was better than one-half cup. Dropping to three-quarters cup of milk proved ideal, as the toast stayed custardlike inside and fairly crisp outside.

When I tried half-and-half instead, I could not taste enough difference to warrant the fat grams. Cream was certainly good, but after I added other flavorings to the basic recipe, I returned to milk, as the cream became too rich. A test with buttermilk, which I love, was awful, with a sharp, almost metallic edge. Throughout the egg and milk test-ings, the basic recipe had tasted flat, and I had been looking forward to the final tests, when I would add lesser ingredients. I first tried salt, and that gave the recipe a big boost: Adding one-quarter teaspoon of salt made a toast that finally had some taste. I added sugar next, which also made a great difference. At this point, one tablespoon seemed like a good amount for toast that would be covered with syrup; after the recipe adjustments described below, though, two tablespoons proved the best amount.

At last, I added vanilla. Few recipes call for it, but two teaspoons pull everything together, balancing the flavors.

At that point, though, I needed some variations from all the French toast I was consuming. So instead of vanilla, I tried cinnamon, almond extract, and various liqueurs. The cinnamon and almond were nice alternatives, but the liqueurs were wholly unsuccessful. Save them to add to sauces.

Final Adjustments

After all this, I had a French toast that was better than any I could remember, but still not my ideal. It was fairly crisp, but not the texture I

Oven-Baked French Toast: Just Say No

Even more than pancakes, French toast must be eaten immediately after cooking. That can make cooking for a crowd a challenge. So after I had a recipe I liked for French toast, I tried to adapt it to oven baking as a second choice.

To say I had no luck would be putting it mildly. I couldn't get toast that crisped, didn't stick, and didn't get tough. Keeping it from sticking wasn't impossible: Heating butter and oil together in a jelly roll pan before adding the soaked bread helped, but it spattered badly and seemed dangerous. Keeping the toast from getting tough, though, was almost impossible. By the time both sides were even vaguely browned, at high or moderate temperatures, the bread had baked too long and turned chewy. I tried broiling, in the hope that would keep it crisp, but all I got were irregular burned spots.

The closest I came was to heat one tablespoon of butter and one tablespoon of oil in a 375-degree oven just as I started soaking the bread, so that the butter was barely melted and not spattering. I baked the slices for ten minutes, flipped them, and went ten minutes more. It wasn't awful. But even in desperation, I think I'd leave my oven off.—S.K.B.

PHOTOGRAPH BY CARL TREMBLAY

wanted: an almost deep-fried crispness. I knew the sugar helped, but there had to be something else. More butter in the skillet (until now I'd been using one and one-half tablespoons to four pieces of bread) only made the challah greasier, and heat higher than medium to medium-high simply burned it. When executive editor Pam Anderson mentioned a French toast version she'd had once in which the bread was dipped in pancake batter, plus a recipe that called for a pinch of flour, it got me thinking about what flour could do. Ultimately, what it did was solve the puzzle.

At first, I liked one tablespoon of flour to help get the exterior extra crisp and not greasy, but in later testings I noted that this made the breads somewhat soggy inside; yet when I went up to two tablespoons, my bread became tough. So I started trying more flour—but with butter added to keep the bread from toughening. And after a few more tests, I finally had fabulous French toast: A batter with one-third cup of flour balanced by two tablespoons of melted butter gets the outside of the challah evenly crisped and brown and lets just enough moisture through to the interior to keep it custardlike but not heavy.

A few other tests answered some final questions: I tried cooking in all my skillets and ended up liking my cast-iron best, with a regular (not nonstick) skillet a close second. Using medium heat with one tablespoon of butter worked well with these skillets; nonstick skillets made the bread too greasy, even with less butter and other heat settings.

So Many Breads, So Little Consistency
Unfortunately, my perfect French toast recipe worked wonders with challah but failed with chewy French or Italian breads. While I strongly recommend using challah if you can, I know it's less likely to be the day-old bread people have on hand. So I worked out a separate recipe for French and Italian breads, but with a caveat.

From tests done by *Cook's Illustrated* editorial staff in other parts of the country, it became clear that differences in bread and dryness would make it hard to declare definitively how long your bread should soak or how old it should be, or even, in some cases, which recipe you should use. I tried several national brands of heat-and-serve French and Italian breads, some of which, even after heating, were practically as soft as challah. (Of these, I most liked the Earthgrains International Hearth Basket French bread, which baked up crisp and was a good width at four inches across; skinny baguettes may be more crust than many people like.) So if you have a soft French bread or sliced white sandwich bread, go with the challah recipe.

With the chewier French or Italian loaf, though, the high amount of flour in the batter used for challah now kept needed moisture from soaking into the bread. Also, the exterior had a harder time crisping because the rougher surface of this somewhat open-textured bread

didn't make good contact with the pan. To get the interior moist, I tried dropping some of the flour; to get the exterior crisped, I tried again with a two-egg recipe. Neither trick worked. In the end, more tests showed that the recipe needed even more milk for a custardlike interior and just one tablespoon of flour to aid in crisping; with this little flour, the batter needed no butter.

FRENCH TOAST I (FOR CHALLAH OR SANDWICH BREAD)
Makes 4 to 5 slices from challah or 6 to 8 slices from sandwich bread
Though thick-sliced challah is best for French toast, you can substitute high-quality, presliced sandwich bread. Flipping challah is easiest with tongs, but a spatula works best with sandwich bread. To speed the cooking of large quantities, heat two or more skillets to brown a few batches at once. To vary the flavor of the batter, add three-quarters of a teaspoon of ground cinnamon or one-half teaspoon of ground nutmeg with the dry ingredients, or substitute almond extract for the vanilla.

1 large egg
2 tablespoons unsalted butter, melted, plus extra for frying
3/4 cup milk
2 teaspoons vanilla extract
2 tablespoons sugar
1/3 cup all-purpose flour
1/4 teaspoon salt
4–5 3/4-inch-thick slices day-old challah bread or 6 to 8 slices day-old sandwich bread

1. Heat 10- to 12-inch skillet (preferably cast-iron) over medium heat for 5 minutes. Meanwhile, beat egg lightly in shallow pan or pie plate; whisk in butter, then milk and vanilla, and finally sugar, flour, and salt, continuing to whisk until smooth. Soak bread without oversaturating, about 40 seconds per side for challah or 30 seconds per side for sandwich bread. Pick up bread and allow excess batter to drip off; repeat with remaining slices.

2. Swirl 1 tablespoon butter in hot skillet. Transfer prepared bread to skillet; cook until golden brown, about 1 minute 45 seconds on first side and 1 minute on the second. Serve immediately. Continue, adding 1 tablespoon butter to skillet for each new batch.

FRENCH TOAST II (FOR FIRM EUROPEAN-STYLE BREAD)
Makes 4 to 8 slices, depending on the loaf
Less flour in this recipe allows the batter to penetrate more easily into the denser bread.

1 large egg
1 cup milk
2 teaspoons vanilla extract
2 tablespoons sugar
1 tablespoon all-purpose flour
1/4 teaspoon salt
4–8 3/4-inch-thick slices day-old firm

European-style bread such as French or Italian
Unsalted butter to grease skillet (about 1 tablespoon per batch)

Follow recipe instructions for French Toast I, omitting melted butter in batter, soaking each bread slice about 30 seconds per side, and cooking bread about 2 minutes on the first side and 1 minute 15 seconds on the second.

Sharon Kebschull Barrett is a food writer and owner of Dessert First, a catering company in Chapel Hill, North Carolina.

Griddle Riddle

You just can't make a lot of French toast at the same time in a skillet, so we decided to test griddles, which have a much larger surface area, to see if any could do the trick.

First we checked out four nonstick electric griddles, including the Vitantonio Gourmet Griddle ($88), the Toastmaster Cool-Edge Grill ($40), the Bethany Heritage Grill ($95), and the Presto Electric Griddle ($30). We preheated each to 400 degrees, gave it a coating of butter, and placed on it as many batter-dipped bread slices as would comfortably fit. We then looked for even browning and a crispy crust.

All four electric griddles accommodated between seven and nine slices of challah French toast, versus only two in the cast-iron skillet, but none was able to produce the crustiness we were after. Some browned a little more evenly than others, but even the best of them had cool spots around the edges or corners, perhaps because a single heating coil runs beneath the cooking surface.

The best of these griddles was the Vitantonio Gourmet Griddle. With its solid construction, nonskid feet, grease drain tray, and four stay-cool edges, this model had cool spots only in the extreme corners of the cooking surface. All this, however, comes at a rather high price. The other three griddles performed more or less equally, but among them, only the Toastmaster has a grease drain tray and three stay-cool edges.

We next tested a stovetop cast-iron griddle (about $30) that spans two burners, ideally of equal size. We heated it up over medium heat, coated the surface with butter, and placed six slices of bread on top to cook. As we expected, the slices that rested on the center surface of the griddle, with no burner underneath, failed to brown at all. Hence, we were able to successfully make only four slices of French toast. These four slices, however, did have the crispy crust that we were looking for.

After all this testing, though, we concluded that our hands-down preference for making French toast was still the cast-iron skillet, even if it means making slices continuously as people eat them.—*Dawn Yanagihara*

How to Poach an Egg

*For perfectly cooked eggs with no feathering of whites,
poach in shallow, not-quite-simmering water.*

by Elaine Corn

❧

Poaching is the nicest way to treat an egg, provided you know the nicest way to poach. Eggs don't respond well to random acts of culinary violence. Cast them about like a raft at sea in water that's too hot and too rough, and they will get revenge by tightening, toughening, getting stringy, and falling apart.

A poached egg should be something quite different than that: a lovely, tender white pouch cooked evenly all the way through. The top of the egg yolk should look a little pink, and when cut, the yolk should run just a little. The whites that surround it should glisten and jiggle a little like baked custard, and the cooking liquid should be left with no stray strands of egg white.

By trial and error, I have found a foolproof method that consistently produces poached eggs that live up to these expectations every time.

My first fix was to ditch the standard saucepot. In its place, I now own an eight-inch-diameter nonstick skillet, with flared sides two inches high, that I reserve just for poaching eggs.

When poaching eggs, I first fill the skillet nearly to the rim with water. The first advantage of the skillet quickly becomes clear: The shallower water comes to a boil more quickly, making poached eggs a speedy proposition. Second, an egg meets the bottom of a skillet sooner than it does the bottom of a pot just a few inches taller. This gives the egg an early floor on which to land gently, before velocity builds. The sooner the egg is on solid ground, the quicker the whites hold. Hence an egg will not stick to this shallow skillet.

The highest heat possible upon impact sets egg whites most quickly. Because water is the cooking medium, that means 212 degrees Fahrenheit. This high heat also gooses the yolks to hurry up and cook. I also perform a corrective measure to prevent those feathering whites; I add vinegar to lower the pH of the water. This lowers the temperature at which the whites and yolks set, which means that after the initial dunk into boiling water, the egg can cook in water that's slightly cooler and, hence, calmer.

It is here that I depart completely from any concept of water held at a "poach." Yes, my poaching liquid is at a boil when the eggs go in. But for the actual cooking time, I've concluded that absolutely still water, as long as it's very hot, will poach an egg just the same.

So I turn off the heat and cover the skillet. During the three and one-half to four minutes that it takes the captured heat to cook the eggs, the temperature of the covered water drops only about twenty degrees. This means that poaching eggs in residual heat eliminates the need to simmer, which can create rough waters that cause the egg to partially disintegrate. It also outwits home stoves that run "hot" and can't hold a simmer.

Now that my eggs have safe haven, how will they taste? Heavily salted water, I found, makes the eggs taste more mellow than lightly salted water. I use at least one full teaspoon in the filled skillet; otherwise the eggs are bland.

The next question is how to get the eggs into the boiling water without breaking them apart. Cracking the egg onto a saucer is often mentioned in old recipes, but you lose a lot of control as the slithery egg and gravity derail your aim. Cracked into a small cup, the egg stays in one piece through its entire descent into purgatory. *Each* egg is cracked into its *own* cup before the water boils. Working two-handed and using cups with handles for easy grasping, I can dump four eggs into the water in two motions. Refilling the same little cup with a freshly cracked egg just so I don't have to wash four of them throws off the timing. If the eggs aren't in the water within seconds of each other, I lose track of which egg went in when, making it impossible to time them separately.

When time's up, I use an oval-bowled slotted spoon to get the eggs out of the poaching liquid. The spoon mimics the shape of the egg so it can nestle comfortably. A skimmer picks the egg up nicely, but I find the shape too flat to pick up something that's fragile and, uh, egg-shaped, so that it rolls about.

I let the egg "drip-dry" by holding it aloft briefly over the skillet. For really dry eggs a paper towel blots to the last drop. I actually like a little of the cooking water to come with my poached eggs, the better to taste the vinegar. Pass the salt and pepper and give me a bottle of Tabasco, and I'm ready to eat poached eggs.

MASTER RECIPE FOR POACHED EGGS
Serves 2, two eggs each

Poached eggs take well to any number of accompaniments. Try serving them on a bed of grated mild cheddar or Monterey Jack cheese or creamed spinach; in a pool of salsa; on a thick slice of tomato topped with a slice of Bermuda onion; on a potato pancake; or simply with plain buttered toast.

4   large eggs, each cracked into a
      small handled cup

1   teaspoon salt, plus more to taste
2   tablespoons distilled white vinegar
      Ground black pepper

1. Fill 8- to 10-inch nonstick skillet nearly to rim with water, add 1 teaspoon salt and the vinegar, and bring mixture to boil over high heat.

2. Lower the lips of each cup just into water at once; tip eggs into boiling water, cover, and remove from heat. Poach until yolks are medium-firm, exactly 4 minutes. For firmer yolks (or for extra large or jumbo eggs), poach 4½ minutes; for looser yolks (or for medium eggs), poach 3 minutes.

3. With slotted spoon, carefully lift and drain each egg over skillet. (Can be dropped into ice water and refrigerated up to 3 days; *see* "Storing Poached Eggs," page 4.) Season to taste with salt and pepper and serve immediately.

ESCAROLE SALAD WITH BACON AND POACHED EGG
Serves 4

Creamy Vinaigrette
2   teaspoons Dijon mustard
1   tablespoon juice from 1 small lemon
1   tablespoon white wine vinegar
      Salt (about ¼ teaspoon) and
      ground black pepper, to taste
2   tablespoons sour cream, crème
      fraîche, buttermilk, or yogurt
¼   cup olive oil

For the salad
1   head escarole, cleaned, dried, and
      torn into pieces (about 8 cups)
4   poached eggs, following Master
      Recipe for Poached Eggs
4   strips bacon, cooked, drained, and
      crumbled
12   cherry tomatoes, halved
2   ounces Roquefort cheese, crumbled
2   tablespoons minced fresh chervil or
      parsley leaves

1. Measure vinaigrette ingredients in covered jar; shake well.

2. Toss greens and vinaigrette in large bowl. Divide greens among four salad plates. Top each with poached egg and portion of bacon, tomato, Roquefort, and chervil or parsley. Serve immediately.

Elaine Corn's most recent book is *365 Ways to Cook Eggs* (HarperCollins, 1996).

Choosing the Right Saucepan

Nonstick saucepans are our favorites, especially when cleaning up, although we also find good conventional pans. In either case, a worthwhile two-quart saucepan can be had for under $60.

by Jack Bishop

A two-quart saucepan is an essential piece of cookware, supremely useful for a wide variety of tasks. I use my two-quart saucepan to boil carrots for my young daughter, make oatmeal or one cup of rice, heat milk for hot cocoa, or to whisk up a small batch of pastry cream.

After years of wondering about it myself and getting questions from friends and relatives who think I might have inside knowledge about cookware, I was determined to find the ideal saucepan. So I designed a series of tests to assess the crucial qualities of a range of saucepans. I wanted to know which one conducted and retained heat best, cooked most evenly without burning, cleaned up most easily, and handled best.

To check the sauté speed, I sautéed one-quarter cup of minced onion for six minutes, then checked whether the onion was properly done or under- or overcooked. I then tested the pans' ability to cook evenly by cooking one cup of long-grain rice according to the recipe that ran in our May/June 1996 issue (*see* "The Best Way to Cook Long-Grain White Rice"). To assess which pans could cook without the burning or scorching caused by poor materials or hot spots, I scalded milk in each saucepan and then cooked pastry cream over medium heat until it registered 180 degrees on an instant-read thermometer.

While running these tests of the various pans' performance, I also carefully noted which were easiest to work with and which had handles that stayed cool rather than heating up during cooking.

Surprise Conversion
It was only at the last minute that I decided to include several nonstick pans in this testing. I understand the value of a nonstick skillet for scrambling eggs and the like. But a nonstick saucepan? I didn't own one. I have always thought nonstick cookware sets, which often include everything from a nonstick saucepan to a soup kettle, were stupid. I still have my doubts about a nonstick soup kettle, but don't ask me to give back my nonstick saucepan.

Many of the jobs suited for a small saucepan involve ingredients that stick and leave a mess in a pan. Scalding milk or making hot chocolate can require hours of soaking and minutes of scrubbing to get a pan clean. Likewise, oatmeal, rice, and pastry cream are all prone to sticking, and that's if the recipe comes out right. Leave a pot of rice unattended or burn some pastry cream, and you may have to soak the pot for hours and then put in a lot of elbow grease to get it back

in shape. I once burned milk onto a saucepan so badly I threw the pot out.

After weeks in the kitchen working with saucepans, my advice is to buy nonstick. The main disadvantages of a nonstick surface (it doesn't brown as well, and the pan can't go into a hot oven for any length of time because the coating can be harmed) don't apply to a small saucepan.

Of course, if you are the kind of person who only boils vegetables in a saucepan (so sticking and cleanup aren't really issues) or if you are rough on your pots and won't remember to use wooden or plastic implements with nonstick surfaces, then you may be better off with a conventional saucepan. But once I realized I could clean burned-on milk from the bottom of a nonstick saucepan with a paper towel (no scrubbing, no soaking), I was a convert.

Once you have decided whether you want a nonstick or conventional saucepan, turn to the chart on page 27 for specific recommendations. The All-Clad pans are my favorites. I performed a dozen or so tests, and these pans always came out at or near the top. At $108 for the pan with the nonstick surface and $75 for the conventional option, All-Clad is not cheap. However, I was able to locate some reasonably priced pans that performed almost as well.

The Tramontina is made of stainless steel like the All-Clad but has a conductive layer of aluminum only on the bottom and not on the sides. It sautés a little faster than the All-Clad and does not come in a two-quart size, but at $48 for a two-and-three-quarters-quart pan (it really holds three quarts), this Brazilian cookware represents an excellent value.

Among nonstick saucepans, the Look pan from Iceland ($57) performs nearly as well as the top-rated All-Clad, although the design is uninspired. I liked this pan just as well as the Calphalon nonstick, the other expensive entry in this category. The Berndes pan ($60) also makes a decent midpriced alternative to the All-Clad.

Three Key Tests
Among the dozen tests performed on each pan, I found three tests to be especially important. Sauté speed was perhaps the most influential factor in determining the overall ratings. The Wearever and Cuisinart pans invariably burned butter and onions when set over medium heat. Other pans, especially the Mauviel, Paderno, and T-Fal, cooked fast. It was possible to get nicely golden onions, but walk away to answer the phone or leave the

burner setting a tad too high and the onions and butter would burn. The All-Clad, Tramontina, Berndes, and Le Creuset pans had the perfect sauté speed. Although the Calphalon pans never burned onions, they were quite slow to get going.

In addition to sauté speed, my testing demonstrated that the weight of the pan is

---

Different Pans for Different Stoves?

The testing for this article was done on a gas stove, but I was curious if the pans would perform differently on an electric range. Electric stoves require direct contact between the pan bottom and the heating element. If the bottom is not perfectly flat, some parts of the pan may be resting right on the burner and others may be slightly off the burner. Theoretically, this could cause hot spots and scorching.

I examined the underside of each pan by laying the thin metal edge of a bench scraper across the bottom. Several pans had perfectly flat bottoms with absolutely no gaps or light between the scraper and pan surface. Other pans were slightly raised at the edges, so that the scraper was not in direct contact with the center of the pan.

I measured the space between the center of the pan and scraper and found that the Calphalon and Tramontina pans were the flattest, with less than $1/4$ millimeter difference between the edges and center. The difference between the edges and center of the remaining pans was less than 1 millimeter with two exceptions: The edges of the T-Fal and Cuisinart pans were close to $1 1/2$ millimeters higher than the center.

So what does this mean in the kitchen? I walked the pans down the street to my neighbors' kitchen and repeated my sauté speed tests on their electric stove.

Perfectly flat pans as well as those with only slightly higher edges performed similarly on gas and electric stoves. The T-Fal and Cuisinart pans, with their markedly higher edges, burned the onions around the circumference of the pan where the bottom was actually resting on the burner. Both had done poorly on a gas stove in this test, but the problem seemed slightly exacerbated on my friends' electric stove. My conclusion is that unless a pan has edges that are more than a millimeter higher than the center, performance on gas and electric stoves will be similar.—J.B.

very important. Pans that weigh between two and three pounds are ideal. Pans that weigh less than two pounds, such as the T-Fal, Wearever, and Cuisinart, are prone to scorching. But really heavy pans (more than four pounds), like the Le Creuset and Mauviel, can be difficult to lift when filled.

Finally, whether or not the handles become hot proved to be another crucial difference among the pans. If you are paying $165 for a small saucepan, I think you should be able to boil carrots for five minutes and then carry the pot to the sink, without an oven mitt, in order to drain the contents. The handles on the

Cuisinart, conventional Calphalon, and Mauviel pans became scorching hot when boiling water. Given the alternatives (hollowed-out cast stainless steel handles like that on the All-Clad or even a cheap plastic sheath like that on the Wearever), I think hot handles are unacceptable.

RATING SAUCEPANS

Fourteen saucepans, each with a capacity of two to three quarts, were tested and evaluated based on the following criteria. The saucepans are listed in order of preference within nonstick and conventional categories.

Materials: The materials for each pan (in some cases the exterior and interior are different) are listed as well as for the lid and handle. Note that stainless steel pans are made with a core layer of conductive metal, usually aluminum. If this layer goes all the way up the sides of the pan, the note below says "complete aluminum core." The phrase "aluminum sandwich in bottom" means this layer does not go up the sides of the pan.

Price: Refers to prices from mail-order sources listed in Sources and Resources, page 32, and does not include shipping. Note that cookware is often heavily discounted, and you may see very different prices in your local stores. We tried to find the lowest prices possible.

Size: For this article we tested two-quart saucepans. For companies that don't make a two-quart size, we chose the next higher size rather than a smaller pan. The first measurement is the diameter of the pan measured across the top from inside edge to inside edge; the second is the actual volume in quarts when filled to the brim. Some European pans are larger than the volume indicated on the box because of the difference in liters and quarts. (Also, some companies must not measure the full volume of pans.) Note that pans with a smaller diameter will retain heat slightly better.

Weight: Pans of medium weight, between two and three pounds, were preferred. Pans over four pounds can be difficult to lift when filled, and light pans under two pounds can scorch during sautéing. The figures below do not include the lid.

Handle: Handles that remained cool when water was boiled for several minutes were preferred. Pans with handles that became hot were severely downgraded.

Sauté Speed: One tablespoon of butter and one-quarter cup of minced onion were placed in each pan and set over medium heat. The onion was sautéed for six minutes. Slow pans that took extra time to heat up and then produced barely translucent onions were downgraded slightly. Fast pans that burned the onions at medium heat were severely downgraded. Medium-speed pans that cooked the onion evenly to a rich golden color without burning or smoking were preferred. This factor was especially important in the overall ratings.

Rice: One cup of long-grain rice was prepared according to the recipe that ran in the May/June 1996 issue. If the rice burned or stuck to the bottom, the pan received a poor rating. If the rice stuck a bit but did not burn, the pan received a fair rating. Pans able to turn out fluffy rice without any grains stuck to the bottom received a good rating. Only nonstick pans took the top rating here.

Pastry Cream: We scalded milk in each pan and then cooked pastry cream over medium heat until it registered 180 degrees on an instant-read thermometer. Pans able to turn out perfect pastry cream without scorching or sticking received top marks. Pans that made good pastry cream but required scrubbing with a scouring pad received a fair rating. Any burning, usually around the edges of the pan, translated into a poor rating.

Nonstick Saucepans

BEST NONSTICK SAUCEPAN

All-Clad Nonstick—Our favorite saucepan has superior conductivity, beautiful design, and proper heft. But $108, ouch!

BEST BUY:
Look—Design cannot match All-Clad or Calphalon, but performance is similar and price is hard to beat at just $57.

Calphalon Nonstick—Slower than other nonsticks to heat up, but otherwise a good choice, although pricey at $97.

Berndes—A nice pan with good conduction, but lighter than top choices. Also, rice cooked up a bit crunchy on three separate tests.

Scanpan—Nonstick surface can tolerate metal utensils but does not clean up as well as other nonsticks. Cool plastic handle.

T-Fal—Extremely light pan overheats quickly and burns onions. Bottom is not very flat. No bargain at $27.

Gormé—Endorsed by Eydie Gormé and Steve Lawrence, this featherweight pan burns onions but is good with rice and pastry cream.

BEST CONVENTIONAL SAUCEPAN

All-Clad Stainless—Perfect conductivity because of complete aluminum core. Proper sauté speed and heft.

BEST BUY:
Tramontina—This Brazilian pan sautés a tad faster than All-Clad, but otherwise pans are comparable. A real bargain.

Le Creuset—Stay-cool wooden handle and easy-to-clean enamel finish are admirable, but pan will be too heavy for many cooks.

Paderno—This pan sautés too quickly, and pastry cream scorched a bit around the edges. A lightweight contender at only 2 pounds.

Calphalon—Pan is slowest to heat up. Even more troublesome, handle becomes hot when boiling water. Fair overall performance.

Mauviel—Five-pound pan can double in weight-training exercises. For $165, handle should at least stay cool.

Cuisinart—Lightweight pan overheats quickly and scorches food. Handle gets hot, and uneven bottom is ill suited to electric burners.

	Brand	Materials	Price	Size	Weight	Handle	Sauté Speed	Rice	Pastry Cream
NONSTICK SAUCEPANS	All-Clad Stainless Nonstick 5202NS	stainless exterior, complete aluminum core, and nonstick interior; stainless lid and handle	$108	5⅞" 2 qt	2 lb,3 oz	Cool	Medium	Good	Good
	Look Cookware Original Cast Aluminum 418	cast aluminum with nonstick exterior and interior; glass lid and plastic handle	$57	7⅛" 2.5 qt	2 lb,4 oz	Cool	Medium-Slow	Good	Good
	Calphalon Professional Nonstick N8702½	anodized aluminum with nonstick exterior and interior; glass lid and stainless handle	$97	6⅞" 2.5 qt	2 lb,13 oz	Cool	Slow	Good	Good
	Berndes 75022	cast aluminum with nonstick interior; glass lid and wood handle	$60	7¾" 2.5 qt	1 lb, 13 oz	Cool	Medium	Fair	Good
	Scanpan 2001+ 7801/90	cast aluminum with nonstick exterior and interior; glass lid and plastic handle	$75	7" 2.2 qt	1 lb, 15 oz	Cool	Medium-Slow	Good	Fair
	T-Fal Resistal Excellence 8412362	cast aluminum with enamel exterior and nonstick interior; stainless lid and plastic handle	$27	7" 2.3 qt	1 lb, 4 oz	Cool	Fast	Good	Good
	Gormé Limited Edition Collection by Wearever	aluminum with nonstick interior; glass lid and stainless handle with removable plastic sheath	$40	6⅞" 2 qt	1 lb, 7 oz	Warm	Very Fast	Good	Good
CONVENTIONAL SAUCEPANS	All-Clad Stainless 5202	stainless exterior and interior with complete aluminum core; stainless lid and handle	$75	5⅞" 2 qt	2 lb, 3 oz	Cool	Medium	Fair	Fair
	Tramontina Sterling II Pro 18/10 Stainless Steel Cookware 6501/20	stainless exterior and interior with aluminum sandwich in bottom; stainless lid and handle	$48	8" 3 qt	2 lb, 10 oz	Cool	Medium-Fast	Fair	Fair
	Le Creuset Traditional with Wood Handle 2539-20	enameled cast-iron pan and lid; wood handle	$70	7⅜" 2.1 qt	4 lb, 3 oz	Cool	Medium	Fair	Fair
	Paderno Grand Gourmet Series 1100 Inox 18/10 1106-16	stainless exterior and interior with aluminum sandwich in raised bottom heat conductor; stainless lid and handle	$85	6⅛" 2.3 qt	2 lb	Cool	Fast	Fair	Fair
	Calphalon G8702½ HCB	anodized aluminum pan and lid; nickel-plated cast iron handle	$85	6⅞" 2.5 qt	3 lb	Hot	Slow	Fair	Fair
	Mauviel Cuprinox 6501-18	copper exterior with stainless interior; copper lid and brass handle	$165	6⅞" 2.6 qt	4 lb, 11 oz	Hot	Fast	Fair	Fair
	Cuisinart Everyday Collection 919-16	stainless exterior and interior with copper sandwich in bottom; stainless lid and handle	$72	6¼" 2 qt	1 lb, 11 oz	Hot	Very, Very Fast	Fair	Poor

Frozen OJ Concentrates Score Well

Fresh-squeezed orange juices come out on top, but old-fashioned, inexpensive frozen concentrates hold their own against all other chilled juices.

by Jack Bishop

The invention of frozen concentrate in the 1940s assured a cheap, year-round supply of orange juice to all Americans. Until the 1970s, though, frozen concentrate and juice fresh-squeezed at home were the only options.

These days, many supermarkets squeeze their own juice, and there are also a whole range of ready-to-serve chilled juices in the dairy case. Chilled juices from concentrate now have the biggest market share (about 45 percent) while chilled juices not-from-concentrate are growing fast and hold about 33 percent of the market. Frozen concentrate commands just 20 percent of the market.

To make sense of the many choices, we decided to conduct a tasting. We evaluated eleven brands that represent all five types of orange juice (*see* "OJ Smorgasbord," below).

Our panelists rated each juice according to thirteen sensory characteristics, including aroma, color, flavor, freshness, sweetness, tartness, peel flavor, texture, and aftertaste. They also assigned each sample an "overall liking" score.

Not surprisingly, flavor was the greatest predictor of overall liking. Aftertaste was the second most important criterion for judging the juices. From the testers' comments, it was clear that many juices left a lingering foul taste in the mouth and were severely downgraded. Fresh-squeezed flavor and aroma were also good predictors of overall liking.

Good texture, too, was important. Tasters rewarded juices that were a tad thick but downgraded juices that were thin and watery or overly viscous. Likewise, our panelists liked a medium amount of pulp.

Surprisingly, sweetness and tartness were only weak indicators of overall liking. For an explanation, we turned to David Fishken, president of Sensory Resources, a consumer-oriented product development firm in Newton, Massachusetts, and author of the evaluation sheets we use in our tastings. He ran a number of statistical analyses of our data and found that the ratio of sweetness to tartness correlated with overall liking while the two individual traits did not. In other words, our panel liked juices where these two traits were in balance.

The Results

As expected, fresh-squeezed juices took first and second places in our tasting. We held our tasting early last December, at the beginning of the orange season when most fruit is still fairly tart. The juice we squeezed one hour before the tasting was delicious but very tart and took a strong second place.

Our top juice had been squeezed the day before at a local supermarket. It had a strong, fresh aroma (most of the other juices had almost no "nose") and excellent balance of sweetness and tartness. The produce manager at the store where we bought the juice told us that the store blends oranges in order to produce good-tasting juice. His blend changes depending on what varieties of oranges are available.

Our testing showed that buying fresh-squeezed juice from a store that blends orange juices can be better than squeezing one kind of orange at home. Any loss in freshness is often offset by the more complex and balanced flavor in a blended juice.

This trait is also shared by all commercial juices. Whichever variety you buy, it will be a judicious blend of various juices. In fact, blending is the biggest advantage of buying juice rather than squeezing it yourself. Manufacturers juice oranges almost year-round and hold them at subzero temperatures for weeks or months. Various lots are then blended and put into either cartons or cans to ensure a consistent taste year-round.

Frozen Concentrates Shine

Although no one was surprised at the top finish of the fresh-squeezed juices, the strong showing of the major brands of frozen concentrate (fourth, fifth, and sixth places) was a shock. Frozen concentrate has a dowdy, old-fashioned reputation. Most consumers assume chilled not-from-concentrate juices are superior. Our results show that just isn't so. In addition, our testing showed that the category of juices that holds the largest market share—chilled juices from concentrate—are also generally inferior to frozen concentrates.

We talked to a number of citrus experts who all told us they were not surprised by the strong showing of frozen concentrates in our tasting. Heat is the biggest enemy of orange juice. Frozen concentrates and chilled juices not-from-concentrate are both pasteurized once at around 195 degrees to eliminate microorganisms and neutralize enzymes that will shorten shelf life. However, chilled juices from concentrate are pasteurized twice, once when the concentrate is made and again when the juice is reconstituted and packaged. This accounts for the lack of fresh-squeezed flavor in the chilled juices from concentrate that we tested.

Another important factor is freshness. Frozen concentrates offer the flavor of the oranges at their peak. In fact, they contain more nutrients than chilled juices, which were probably once frozen as well and then defrosted many days or several weeks before you purchase them.

For superior taste, mix frozen concentrate with ice-cold bottled water. Our tap water was fine, but orange juice made with Poland Spring water tasted better.

OJ Smorgasbord

The average American supermarket stocks dozens of brands of orange juice. There are five types, all of which we tested.

Fresh-squeezed: If kept between 32 and 36 degrees, fresh-squeezed juice has a shelf life of seventeen days although the flavor will start to deteriorate immediately and after several days there is a noticeable drop in quality.

Frozen fresh: Fresh-squeezed unpasteurized juice can be frozen at the plant and then shipped to supermarkets. Some stores defrost the juice and sell it in the produce aisle as "fresh." Can be kept frozen for several months. Once defrosted, this juice is best used within a week.

Frozen concentrate: Juice is concentrated and pasteurized under vacuum and then reinforced with a little fresh pasteurized juice before freezing. If kept at 0 degrees, frozen concentrate has a shelf life of one year.

Chilled, not-from-concentrate: This juice may be made in either of two ways. Some companies freeze fresh-squeezed juice for many months. When juice is needed, they defrost several samples and then blend and pasteurize them. Other companies blend and pasteurize fresh-squeezed juice and then store it in special aseptic tanks just above freezing for as many as six or eight months. Both methods allow companies to maintain a year-round supply even though oranges are seasonal. Once the juice is packaged, it has a shelf life of about eight weeks.

Chilled, from concentrate: Sold in the dairy case, this juice is made from frozen concentrate that is reconstituted by the manufacturer. The juice is pasteurized twice and has a supermarket shelf life of eight weeks.

RATING ORANGE JUICES

Thirty-four nonexpert panelists rated eleven samples of orange juice on a variety of characteristics. Frozen concentrates were mixed with chilled bottled water. All samples were served well chilled. Panelists had access to bottled water and plain crackers during the tasting. The locations below refer to the manufacturing plant or corporate headquarters listed on package labels. Samples were purchased in Boston area supermarkets, and prices indicate actual retail cost. When shopping, we selected chilled juice samples with expiration dates that were many weeks away.

HIGHLY RECOMMENDED JUICES

Bread & Circus Fresh-Squeezed Orange Juice (Cambridge, MA), $4.98 for sixty-four-ounce carton. This fresh-squeezed from a top gourmet supermarket chain in Boston was described as "sweet" and "fresh-tasting" by one panelist. Overall, it received high marks for flavor and freshness and beat out the juice we squeezed ourselves by being considerably sweeter. "Tastes like the real thing," wrote one panelist.

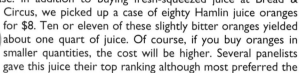

Fresh-Squeezed, about $1 per quart when oranges are bought by the case. In addition to buying fresh-squeezed juice at Bread & Circus, we picked up a case of eighty Hamlin juice oranges for $8. Ten or eleven of these slightly bitter oranges yielded about one quart of juice. Of course, if you buy oranges in smaller quantities, the cost will be higher. Several panelists gave this juice their top ranking although most preferred the sweeter juice purchased at Bread & Circus. "Tastes authentic, but too tart for me," was a typical comment, as was "a bit bitter but natural-tasting."

RECOMMENDED JUICES

Tropicana Pure Premium Not-From-Concentrate Grovestand Fresh Squeezed Taste Florida Orange Juice (Bradenton, FL), $2.49 for sixty-four-ounce carton. This "pulpy" juice doesn't have the aroma of fresh-squeezed but is still a good product. "Slight tang of peel and fairly fresh flavor" was the general consensus though a few dissenters felt the flavor was "phony."

Minute Maid Premium Frozen Concentrated Orange Juice Country Style (Houston, TX), $1.29 for twelve-ounce can. Second highest pulp rating with decent if not overwhelming scores for flavor although noticeably less fresh than top choices. "Texture is odd with pulp all floating on top," wrote one panelist. Another thought there was "a slight cooked flavor."

President's Choice Florida Valencia Frozen Concentrated Orange Juice (West Seneca, NY), $1.29 for twelve-ounce can. All Florida oranges are used to make this concentrate, available in some supermarkets as a house brand. "Not bad for canned juice," wrote one astute taster. Others were slightly more generous: "Clean, strong orange flavor with nice balance of tartness and sweetness."

Tropicana Season's Best Frozen Concentrate Homestyle Orange Juice (Bradenton, FL), $.99 for twelve-ounce can. Many tasters had strong reservations about this sample. "Sharp and metallic" or "odd aftertaste." Others were more enthusiastic with comments like "balanced" and "not bad for a juice that's not fresh-squeezed."

Just Pik't Florida Frozen Orange Juice Fresh Squeezed (Great Neck, NY), $2.19 for 1-liter carton. This juice is squeezed and then frozen as is without pasteurization. It's generally sold in the frozen food aisle, and you defrost it at home. Our panel thought this was the sweetest juice in the tasting. The juice has little pulp and received surprisingly low ratings for freshness. "Not terrible but very far from fresh-squeezed."

Florida's Natural Brand Premium Not-From-Concentrate Florida Pasteurized Orange Juice Home Squeezed Style (Lake Wales, FL), $2.49 for sixty-four-ounce carton. This juice received only marginally positive scores and comments. Most tasters thought it was "too bitter," and many detected an "odd aftertaste." As one wrote, "barely acceptable."

NOT RECOMMENDED JUICES

Minute Maid Premium Orange Juice From Concentrate Country Style (Houston, TX), $1.69 for sixty-four-ounce carton. The general consensus here was too tart, not sweet enough, and not nearly enough pulp. "No real character and no hint of freshness," wrote one panelist. Other comments ranged from "flat and cardboard-tasting" to "pathetic."

Tropicana Season's Best Orange Juice From Concentrate Homestyle (Bradenton, FL), $1.99 for sixty-four-ounce carton. This chilled juice was judged to be "overly bitter" and "lacking in freshness." As one taster wrote, "very sour with hints of grapefruit and lime but little orange flavor."

Cascadian Farm Organic Orange Juice Frozen Concentrate (Rockport, WA), $2.89 for twelve-ounce can. This natural foods store staple racked up some truly awful scores. Absolutely no fresh flavor with plenty of "syrupy sweetness." One taster thought there was "so little pulp, can it be real?"

Tasting Italian Whites

*Italian white wines offer reasonable price and clean flavor, but little complexity;
we found several drinkable wines, but only one wine of note.*

by Mark Bittman

Our last wine tasting focused on ABC (Anything But Chardonnay) wines from the United States. This time around, we judged ABC wines from Italy, which, like California, features a reliable climate that allows it to produce large quantities of better-than-decent wines at reasonable prices. In fact, Italy produces more wine than any other country.

Italian whites have changed greatly since the advent of refrigerated fermentation. Up until twenty or even ten years ago, the wines were made at ambient temperatures, which, in the southern European autumn, means hot. Furthermore, the crushed grapes were often left mixed with their skins during fermentation. This combination produced fairly dark wines, heavy in alcohol and usually far from refreshing. On the other hand, they had loads of character.

Now the wines are made as they are made almost everywhere else in the world: at controlled temperatures and without the skins. Going into the tasting, I was of the mind that inexpensive Italian whites are, generally speaking, clean and crisp. But more often than not, I felt, their varietal character is minimal, and the wines are virtually neutral—great for quaffing on warm days, but unremarkable. A few have personality, but these are rare; you have to move up to the $20 price range to see those regularly.

The tasting verified my beliefs. The wines, which all cost less than $20, did little to distinguish themselves. Most were eminently drinkable, but only one drew oohs and aahs. Other than that first-place wine, made with the distinctive but little-used greco grape, this is a mixed bag of decent, reasonably priced whites, usually made with grapes that few people have heard of.

In fact, the wines, which are regional, only sometimes indicate which grapes are used (of course, if you lived in the region, you'd know). Here, then, is a list of the types of wines we tasted, along with a brief description of each:

Arneis: A Piedmontese wine named after its own grape. Can be complex and interesting or extremely vague; most are the latter.

Frascati: A blend of grapes from the countryside around Rome. Made for quaffing; if it were as cheap here as it is in Rome, it might be equally popular.

Gavi: Made in the Piedmont from the cortese grape. Sometimes pleasantly fruity, rarely superior.

Greco di Tufo: The greco grape is, as its name indicates, of Greek origin. Used in southern Italy, especially around the village of Tufo, in Campania. Distinctive and usually worth trying.

Orvieto: The Umbrian wine from the town by the same name, made with trebbiano and other grapes. Nutty and complex at its best, which is, unfortunately, rare.

Pinot Grigio: Grown from north to central Italy. At its best, it has some intensity of flavor; more usually it is watery and uninteresting.

Soave: The standard white wine of the Veneto, in northern Italy. Dominated by the often harsh garganega grape, but may be tamed by the addition of trebbiano, chardonnay, pinot blanc, or other classier grapes.

Verdicchio: A grape from central Italy that made strong, flavorful wine until new techniques were adapted. Now generally undistinguished.

Vermentino: A grape found traditionally in Sardinia and Corsica, it is now gaining more attention on the mainland. Can make interesting wine.

Vernaccia: A name given to several different grapes. The wine made from it that we see most often is Vernaccia di San Gimignano, the towered hilltop town of Tuscany. Capable of producing good wine in the right hands.

Rating the Wines

The wines in our tasting, held at Mt. Carmel Wine and Spirits in Hamden, Connecticut, were judged by a panel made up of both wine professionals and amateur wine lovers. In the judging, seven points were awarded for each first-place vote, six for second, five for third, and so on. The wines were all purchased in the Northeast; prices will vary considerably throughout the country.

Within each category, wines are listed based on the number of points scored. In this tasting, the Highly Recommended wine received what amounted to rave reviews. Recommended wines had predominantly positive comments. The wines in the Recommended with Reservations category had an approximately equal number of positive and negative comments. The Not Recommended wines had few or no positive comments.

Highly Recommended

1995 *Feudi di San Gregorio Greco di Tufo,* $16. Seven of ten tasters ranked this wine first, a clear signal of quality. Most found it on the "sweet" side, but this was not seen as a problem. Rather, the wine was described as "unusual," "nutty," and "interesting" in addition to "well balanced and long in the finish."

Recommended

1994 *Anselmi Soave,* $11. "Nice nose, with fruit, character, and weight," wrote a professional. But an amateur found it "uninteresting," and another "almost cloyingly sweet." At this price, worth trying.

1994 *Argiolas Vermentino di Sardegna,* $11. A pro found this "bright and dry, with good balance," and another said it "has character." Both pros and amateurs, however, detected a "medicinal" nose that turned them off.

1994 *Curpese Verdicchio Classico,* $10. "Full, fruity, and very drinkable," said one amateur, who ranked it first. Most tasters liked this wine, but a few detected an "off" flavor.

Recommended with Reservations

1995 *Ceretto Arneis "Blange,"* $15. "Zippy" wine with some effervescence. No raves.

1995 *Regaleali Tasca d'Almerita,* $10. "Fruity and clean," with "decent body." Many found it "uninspiringly neutral."

1994 *Santa Margherita Pinot Grigio,* $18. As one pro said, "the wine is intense, but you may not like the taste." Some did, some did not. Worth a try.

1994 *Bolla Soave Classico,* $9. Experienced pro found it "rich, strong, and good." Although quantitative score didn't indicate it, comments showed that most tasters liked this wine.

1995 *Luna di Luna Pinot Grigio/Chardonnay,* $10. Distinctive blue bottle contains wine that "looks like water and tastes like water...eminently quaffable." You could do better.

1993 *Principessa Gavi,* $13. "Light," "pleasant," "crisp"...and "watery."

Not Recommended

1995 *MezzaCorona Pinot Grigio,* $8.50.
1994 *S. Quirico Vernaccia di San Gimignano,* $9.
1995 *Fontana Candida Frascati,* $8.
1994 *Bigi Orvieto Classico,* $6.

Book Reviews

Baking with Julia
Dorie Greenspan
William Morrow, $40

Julia Child has always been a hands-on teacher. Hands thrust gamely into a twenty-pound turkey or whacking away at a cold piece of pâte brisée with a Paul Bunyan–sized rolling pin, she forged an immediate bond with her audience. In her books, too, Julia was both authoritative and intensely personal because she spoke from a rich mother lode of experience. She helped introduce modern American cooks to the virtues

of professionalism. In fact, more than any other cook of this century, Julia laid the foundation for the resurgence of the culinary arts in America.

Baking with Julia, however, is, on the face of it, a different animal. Based on the public television series of the same name, the book is a collection of recipes from thirty-nine professional bakers who appeared on the show. As usual with such efforts, my initial question was whether this would be a serious cookbook in its own right or just a companion book to the television series. My second question was whether Julia's keen eye for detail and "at-your-elbow" instruction survived the collaborative process. Lastly, I wondered how *Baking with Julia* would successfully translate baker's recipes calling for ten pounds of flour into practical instruction for the home cook.

The first impression, when one opens this oversized and weighty tome, is that someone at William Morrow, Julia's publisher, knows a great deal about cookbook publishing. It is the most visually impressive cookbook I have seen in years, from the type and recipe layouts to the inspiring, energetic color photography, which captures the sensual immediacy of fresh-baked breads and desserts. I was also struck by the detailed professionalism of the recipe instructions. Well-written recipes provide plenty of visual clues about what to expect and what to do if things go wrong.

Our test kitchen offered mixed but generally encouraging results. I made the Brioche Tart with White Secret Sauce for Christmas Eve dinner, and it was superb, a heavenly mixture of crust, ethereal bread, a thin hint of custard, and a pool of chilled sabayon sauce. It was pretty much an all-day affair—the recipe runs six pages (three for the brioche dough and three for the recipe itself) without a hint of

compromise or shortcut for the home cook. It must be noted, though, that the extraordinary wordiness of the recipes does have its advantages. In the brioche recipe, there is a terrific note to the effect that "This is the point at which you'll think you've made a huge mistake, because the dough that you worked so hard to make smooth will fall apart—carry on." A more parsimonious recipe would have left the home cook awash in fears of ruined dough. An apple tart made with a base of home-made applesauce was fine, but, to my taste, not as good as a quick and easy old-fashioned apple pie. I also made the pie dough, which was very good, with excellent instructions, and a country bread that I liked, very similar to a recipe run in this magazine two years ago.

Other *Cook's Illustrated* editors, who together tested a total of sixteen recipes, had good but mixed results as well. We liked the lemon loaf cake, for example, the challah was outstanding, the bagels were great, and the cornmeal biscotti were top-notch. Other recipes had minor problems.

What struck us most of all during the recipe testing, however, was that Julia's voice and attention to detail is alive and well. We assume that a good measure of credit must be given to author Dorie Greenspan and to the book's editor, Ann Bramson. Although some recipes are better than others—an unavoidable problem with such a wide-ranging collaboration—most of the recipes worked as promised and the translation from the professional to the home kitchen was, for the most part, a success. Many of these recipes could be streamlined, though, and peppered with practical shortcuts for the time-starved home cook.

On the whole, then, *Baking with Julia* is an outstanding achievement not only for Julia but for everyone else who contributed to this project. Best of all, Julia has rekindled my love of baking. It has been years since I spent an entire Saturday in the kitchen, kneading dough, whipping egg whites, and making sugar syrup. With Julia's clear, resonant voice rising clearly from the pages, it seemed just like old times.
—*Christopher Kimball*

Jacques Pépin's Table
Jacques Pépin
KQED Publishing, $35

As our culture worships at the altar of whatever is new and exciting, it is no wonder that our tastes have become increasingly childlike. We prefer soft, sweet foods (yogurt, ice cream, soft cookies) or savory foods with no chew. A boneless tenderloin, for example, is an American steak lover's ideal, whereas a French or Italian diner might prefer an entrecôte or bistecca taken from the chewier but more flavorful front section of the ribs. So, how does Jacques Pépin,

a seasoned culinary veteran and, I say this with nothing but admiration, a confirmed grown-up, make himself appealing to cookbook buyers for whom his very name probably calls to mind thoroughly adult culinary activities, making demi-glace or, say, skinning rabbits? The answer, as it turns out, is to write *Jacques Pépin's Table*.

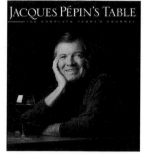

Like Julia's book, his book is based on a television series, *Today's Gourmet*, and also like *Baking with Julia*, the book stands successfully on its own.

Unlike some of Pépin's earlier work, the recipes are relatively short and appear slimmed down from the admitted excesses of haute cuisine; the food is current and appealing. Jacques even includes the dreaded nutritional breakdowns, something that I can live without but that was telling nonetheless; there was a conscious effort to appeal to the American home cook. But the revelation came in the recipe testing.

I started with a tart of halved apples—it was delicious and brilliantly simple. A red snapper sautéed in a crust of thinly sliced potatoes appeared fussy at first, and did take more cooking time than indicated, but was delicious and quite manageable on a Tuesday night. Braised Endive in Lemon Juice was too slimmed down for me; the thin, tannic taste of endive needs a silky, more luxurious sauce. A dozen other recipes, however, from Christmas Oysters to Crab Ravioli, received straight As. We had quibbles with a few recipes, but the percentage of fresh, interesting recipes we would make again was extremely high, and the instructions were clear and professional.

Jacques Pépin's Table and *Baking with Julia* are refreshing and welcome because they are projects directed by immensely likable pros who, as Julia herself is wont to say, know how food is supposed to taste. The really good news is that Jacques has successfully made the transition to American home cooking and that Julia has managed to bring together a variety of cooks and recipes into a cohesive whole that speaks with one thoroughly professional voice. The depth and maturity of these two books remind me that there will come a point at which I will tire of the notion of yet another newfangled recipe. I will shoo the overnight celebrities out the door, call up Jacques and Julia, and pray that they accept my invitation for a quiet dinner. The deal is simple. They'll do the cooking, and I'll leave the kids upstairs. This dinner will be for adults only.
—*Christopher Kimball*

Sources and Resources

Most ingredients and materials necessary for the recipes in this issue are available at your local supermarket, gourmet store, or kitchen supply shop. The following are mail-order sources for particular items. Prices listed were current at press time and do not include shipping or handling unless so indicated. We suggest you contact companies directly to confirm current prices and availability.

Saucepans

When testing two-quart saucepans (*see* page 25), we found that nonstick saucepans, although expensive, were our favorite for overall performance and easy cleanup. Among the nonstick varieties, we liked best the All-Clad Stainless Nonstick saucepan, which is available for $108 from Williams-Sonoma (Mail Order Department, P.O. Box 7456, San Francisco, CA 94120-7456; 800-541-2233). For a more affordable not-too-distant runner-up in the nonstick category, try the heavy, cast aluminum saucepan by Look. It can be ordered by mail for $57 through A Cook's Wares; so can the All-Clad Conventional for $75 (211 37th Street, Beaver Falls, PA 15010-2103; 412-846-9490). Tramontina's two-and-three-quarters-quart saucepan is a bargain but lacks the cleanup ease of nonstick. It is available for $47.50 from The Gooseberry (Route 7A, Manchester Center, VT 05255; 802-362-3263).

Muir Glen Diced Tomatoes

In the 20-minute tomato sauce story on page 10, we found that Muir Glen Diced Tomatoes offered the best balance of sweet and sour. While Muir Glen organic tomato products are available in most natural foods stores, they are not yet readily available in all supermarkets. In the meantime, Muir Glen Diced Tomatoes can be ordered through the mail from Walnut Acres Organic Farms catalog (Penns Creek, PA 17862; 800-433-3998) in lots of three 14.5-ounce tins for $4.99 or twelve tins for $18.95.

Lobster

Although Atlantic lobster is harvested all along the northeastern U.S. coast, Maine is the largest lobster-producing state, harvesting thirty-eight million pounds in 1995. The Maine Lobster Promotion Council offers a brochure listing more than sixty-five Maine companies that will ship live lobsters overnight to your home. Because lobsters can live out of water for twenty-four to forty-eight hours provided they are kept cold with gills moist, they are typically wrapped in seaweed or in wet newspaper and placed in a Styrofoam cooler for overnight shipping. Market prices for lobster vary daily, and shipping rates vary with distance. For the listing of Maine companies that ship live lobsters, write or call the Maine Lobster Promotion Council (382 Harlow Street, Bangor, ME 04401; 207-947-2966).

Nonstick Baking Sheet Liners

While the lace cookies on page 20 are simple and quick to prepare, the challenge lies in removing the delicate wafers from the baking sheet without their crumbling. We discovered that using a bakeware liner was a no-nonsense solution to this problem. Our test kitchen found that the Silpat food-safe, silicone-coated liner was quick to release both warm and cooled lace cookies. This liner did not shift on the cookie sheet, and it rendered the thinnest, roundest lace cookies of all the liners tested. The eleven-and-seven-eighths-by-sixteen-and-one-half-inch sheets sell for $16 and can be used up to two thousand times. To locate a distributor near you, contact Demarle Inc. (2666-B Route 130 North, Cranbury, NJ 08512; 609-395-0219).

Griddles

Editor and publisher Christopher Kimball has been using his Vitantonio Gourmet Griddle three times a week for two years to make French toast and pancakes for his children. And the sleek, black nonstick electric griddle still looks practically brand new. In the testing for the French toast article on page 22, our test kitchen preferred this model over other electric griddles for its even heat and solid construction, including a tidy, removable grease drawer. It is available by mail in black or white for the price of $88.15 through Vitantonio Products (A Division of Kadee Products, Ltd., 6225 Cochran Road, Cleveland, OH 44139; 800-837-1661). If you're content with cooking just four slices of French toast at a time, we found that a stovetop cast-iron griddle makes the kind of crisp crust we like. As noted in the March/April 1997 Sources and Resources, Lehman's Non-Electric Catalog carries a variety of cast-iron cookware, including a nineteen-and-three-quarters-by-nine-inch griddle for $29.50 and a twenty-and-three-quarters-by-ten-and-one-half-inch griddle for $42. The griddles weigh ten and fourteen pounds, respectively.

Splatter Screen

In the panfried steak article on page 8, we found that the secret to attaining a thorough sear is preheating the pan for about ten minutes. But transferring a raw steak onto any hot surface means splatter. Fortunately, there's a simple and inexpensive remedy for that: a splatter screen, which tames the spit of grease without steaming the meat. For $3.25, Lehman's Non-Electric Catalog (One Lehman Circle, P.O. Box 41, Kidron, OH 44636; 330-857-5757) carries an eleven-and-one-half-inch, round, heavy-gauged mesh splatter screen with a long, black plastic handle.

Biscuit Cutters

The strawberry shortcake recipe on page 18 recommends using a biscuit cutter with a two-and-three-quarters-inch diameter. The Wooden Spoon (P.O. Box 931, Clinton, CT; 800-431-2207) carries a biscuit cutter this size as the largest among a four-piece biscuit cutter set. These stainless steel cutters have high sides and handles and nest just like measuring cups for easy storage. The smallest measures one and one-half inches, which would work well for making cocktail-sized crab cakes as Forbes Maner suggests in Notes from Readers on page 2. The set costs $7.95.

Focaccia Pans

Among the many baking pans in our test kitchen are several commercial-style half-sheet pans measuring eleven and one-half by sixteen and one-half inches with short, one-inch sides. These pans were ideal for making the freeform rounds of focaccia on page 7, as well as for using with a nonstick baking sheet liner to make the lace cookies on page 20. The commercial-style baking sheets are heavier than those you find in most stores, so they tend to cook more evenly. We've liked using them for roasting as well as baking. Williams-Sonoma (Mail Order Department, P.O. Box 7456, San Francisco, CA 94120-7456; 800-541-2233) recently began carrying professional-weight bakeware, including a thirteen-by-eighteen-inch baking sheet for $15. The baking sheet is made of aluminum-coated steel that won't rust or warp.

Sheet Gelatin

While powdered gelatin is readily available, the sheet, or leaf, gelatin described in Notes from Readers, page 3, is difficult to find at all on the retail level; not one of our local supermarkets carried it. We were able to locate a mail-order source, however. The Sweet Celebrations Inc. Maid of Scandinavia catalog (P.O. Box 39426, Edina, MN 55439-0426; 800-328-6722), which specializes in baking and candy-making supplies, sells packages containing twenty 2³⁄₄-by-9-inch sheets for $3.95. It is also sold at Sweet Celebrations' retail store in Minneapolis, Minnesota, where a representative told us that the vast majority of the sheet gelatin they sell is used not for cooking, but rather for windows in gingerbread houses.

Panfried Steak with Roquefort Butter *page 9*

RECIPE INDEX

Lace Cookie Bowl with Ice Cream *page 21*

Strawberry Shortcake *page 19*

**Sugar Snap Peas
with Hazelnut Butter and Sage** (front),
with Ham and Mint (left),
**with Lemon, Garlic,
and Basil** (right) *page 12*

**Focaccia with Black Olives
and Thyme** (bottom),
Rosemary Focaccia (top) *page 7*

**Escarole Salad with Bacon and
Poached Egg** *page 24*

PHOTOGRAPHS BY CARL TREMBLAY/FOOD STYLING BY EVA KATZ

Watercress, Endive, and Radicchio Salad
with Smoked Salmon and Mustard-Horseradish Vinaigrette

Mix 2 tablespoons grainy mustard with 1½ tablespoons prepared horseradish in medium bowl. Add 6 tablespoons olive oil in slow, steady stream, whisking constantly to incorporate. Whisk in 2 tablespoons juice from 1 small lemon, 1½ teaspoons sugar, 2 tablespoons coarsely chopped fresh parsley leaves, 1 tablespoon drained capers, 2 tablespoons minced red onion, and salt and ground black pepper to taste. In large bowl, mix 3 cups (about 1 bunch) cleaned and trimmed watercress, 3 cups julienned inner leaves from 1 head radicchio, and 2 cups sliced inner leaves from 1 head Belgian endive. Moisten greens with about half the dressing, toss to coat, and divide among six salad plates. Top each with 4 very thin slices smoked salmon and a drizzle of remaining dressing. Serve immediately. *Serves 6.*

Adapted from

Lettuce in Your Kitchen

(Morrow, 1996)

by Chris Schlesinger

and John Willoughby

COOK'S
ILLUSTRATED

Rating Kitchen Thermometers
Digital Models Win Top Honors

Authentic Pulled Pork BBQ at Home
Special Method Delivers Real Fall-Apart Texture

Best Hot Fudge Sauce
Thick, Rich, and Creamy

How to Grill Chicken Breasts
Brine, Use a Two-Level Fire, and Cover with a Pan

Perfecting Upside-Down Cake
One Recipe, Many Cakes

AMERICAN ALES WIN TASTING

A BETTER SHRIMP COCKTAIL

HOW TO GRILL SALMON

FOOLPROOF MAYONNAISE

$4.00 U.S./$4.95 CANADA

Contents

About *Cook's Illustrated*

Cook's Illustrated *is published every other month (6 issues per year) and accepts no advertising. A one-year subscription is $24.95, two years is $45, and three years is $65. Add $6 per year for Canadian subscriptions and $12 per year for all other countries. Gift subscriptions may be ordered for $19.95 each. You will receive a Cook's Illustrated gift card for each subscription which can be used to announce your gifts. The editors of Cook's Illustrated also publish an annual hardbound edition of the magazine which includes an annual index. These are available for $24.95 each plus shipping and handling. Discounts are available if more than one year is ordered at a time.*

Cook's Illustrated *also publishes single topic books,* How To Make A Pie, How To Make An American Layer Cake, How To Stir Fry *and* How to Make Ice Cream. *All are available for $14.95 each. The* Cook's Bible, *authored by our editor and published by Little Brown, is also available for $24.95. Back issues are available for $5 each. We also accept submissions for both Quick Tips and Notes From Readers. See page 5 for more information.*

All queries about subscriptions or change of address notices should be addressed to Cook's Illustrated, P.O. Box 7445, Red Oak, IA 51591-0445. A free trial issue of our sister publication, Handcraft Illustrated, may be requested by calling 800-526-8447.

To order either subscriptions or books use the cards bound into this issue or, for faster service, call 800-526-8442 for subscriptions and 800-611-0759 for books and annuals.

"WATERMELON"

by Brent Watkinson

"RASPBERRY SPRITZER"

by Rene Milot

COOK'S
ILLUSTRATED

Publisher and Editor	Christopher Kimball
Executive Editor	Pam Anderson
Senior Editor	John Willoughby
Senior Writer	Jack Bishop
Associate Editor	Adam Ried
Contributing Editors	Mark Bittman Stephanie Lyness
Test Kitchen Director	Eva Katz
Test Cooks	Dawn Yanagihara Melissa Hamilton
Assistant Editor	Maryellen Driscoll
Test Kitchen Intern	Marnie M. Casavant

Art Director	Cathy Copeland
Special Projects Manager	Amy Klee

Managing Editor	Keith Powers
Editorial Prod. Manager	Sheila Datz
Copy Editor	Gary Pfitzer

Marketing Director	Adrienne Kimball
Circulation Manager	David Mack
Fulfillment Manager	Larisa Greiner
Newsstand Manager	Jonathan Venier
Marketing Assistant	Connie Forbes
Circulation Assistant	Steven Browall

Vice President Production and Technology	James McCormack
Systems Administrator	Paul Mulvaney
Production Artist	Kevin Moeller
Editorial Production Assistants	Robert Parsons Daniel Frey

Controller	Lisa A. Carullo
Accounting Assistant	Mandy Shito
Office Manager	Tonya Estey
Special Projects	Fern Berman

Cook's Illustrated (ISSN 1068-2821) is published bimonthly by Boston Common Press Limited Partnership, 17 Station Street, Brookline, MA 02146. Copyright 1997 Boston Common Press Limited Partnership. Periodical postage paid at Boston, MA, and additional mailing offices, USPS #012487. For list rental information, please contact List Services Corporation, 6 Trowbridge Drive, P.O. Box 516, Bethel, CT 06801; (203) 743-2600, FAX (203) 743-0589. Editorial office: 17 Station Street, P.O. Box 470589, Brookline, MA 02146; (617) 232-1000, FAX (617) 232-1572. Editorial contributions should be sent to: Editor, *Cook's Illustrated*. We cannot assume responsibility for manuscripts submitted to us. Submissions will be returned only if accompanied by a large self-addressed stamped envelope. Subscription rates: $24.95 for one year; $45 for two years; $65 for three years. (Canada: add $6 per year; all other countries: add $12 per year.) Postmaster: Send all new orders, subscription inquiries, and change of address notices to *Cook's Illustrated*, P.O. Box 7446, Red Oak, IA 51591-0446. Single copies: $4 in U.S., $4.95 in Canada and other countries. Back issues available for $5 each. PRINTED IN THE U.S.A.

EDITORIAL

Wild Things

CHRISTOPHER KIMBALL

In our travels, my wife and I have always tried to seek out wild places, exploring Mayan ruins in Guatemala or camping out in a fishing village in a Caribbean backwater. But now that we have three children, we decided to stay at a family-friendly resort in the British West Indies replete with poolside cabanas, acres of fresh towels, and possibly the most insipid food imaginable, beautifully presented but bland and domesticated.

Striking out on our own, we dined exclusively at local eateries, some at the end of potholed dirt roads, others nestled in town by an old wharf littered with rusting lorries and backhoes. We cleaned our plates of parrot fish stewed in sweet curry sauce, freshly grilled mahimahi, mounds of rice and peas, roasted plantains, toasted coconut slices served with rum punch made with fresh-squeezed lime juice, soursop ice cream ("soursop" is the local name for chayote, a white-fleshed fruit), and a sandwich of flying fish served on thick slabs of homemade bread with fresh whisked mayonnaise and a large bowl of icy chocolate ice cream for dessert.

Although these eateries were visually unappealing—cinder block construction painted white, sagging rows of brightly colored Christmas tree lights lining the front walkway, Formica tabletops, and the blare of CNN—they were alive with good home cooking, the soft gurgle of Carib beer being poured into glasses, the wild clatter of pans in the kitchen, and the cheerful presence of the proprietors.

Back at the resort one evening, our family walked the perfectly groomed, well-lit walkways with an islander who recounted the legend of the jumbees. It was believed that these evil spirits crouched beside footpaths, waiting to kidnap unsuspecting children. But amidst this transient paradise, the spirits were no more than legend, having left long ago in search of wilder places. Also gone were the serendipity of adventure, the great meal found in a local haunt, the chance meeting with strangers who change your life.

On our last full day, we struck out in search of a local church service and found ourselves in a district called Fig Tree, high up on the side of a dormant volcano, in a small Anglican church called St. George's. It was Palm Sunday, the fronds noisily whipped about by the white and blue electric fans set high on the columns. The church had no windows, just arched openings facing out onto an unkempt graveyard, overgrown slabs of stone set flat on the ground. Thin, long, fluorescent lights lit the nave, and the sound of the glassed-in organ pipes and the ripe scent of incense swirled about the pews, mixing with a faint sea breeze and the sweet perfume of unfamiliar blossoms.

The minister served three churches on the island and was blessed with a booming voice that carried a tune—and the sermon— far out through the arches, where it spread over the parched valley and then floated down onto the small, whitewashed houses. After a few minutes, our family set out with the rest of the congregation, singing hymns in a procession along a mountain road with the altar boys in front and the minister in back, the notes from the organ fading as we descended. Here was a place truly wild with anticipation, I thought, as I marched along with strangers, lungs filled with unfamiliar hymns, traffic stopped. A place perhaps still haunted by jumbees, late at night, after the lights of the town had been swallowed by darkness.

Back in Vermont, it was mud season, in between the crisp, biting days of winter and the budding pale greens of springtime. I set out on a short walk through a recently cleared field, water bubbling through the drainage ditches, weaving in and out of crisscrossed piles of recently cut locust, black birch, ash, and pine, the breeze alternately warm with a hint of wood smoke and boiling sap, and then chilling, as if I had just stepped into a dark, frozen hollow. And then bits of Anglican hymns came to me, the faded notes from the old organ still hanging in the air, and I was walking once again in a sacred place. I headed back, the tops of the ridges bathed in a fading rusted orange glow, to our small farmhouse and a simple dinner in a place wild with the shadowy hoots of bear, the barking of coyotes, and long-buried old-timers who snatched at our memories like jumbees along a deserted forest path.

Notes *from* Readers

OATMEAL COOKIE WOES

Several readers let us know that the oatmeal cookies they were making from our recipe in the January/February 1997 issue seemed overcooked even when baked exactly according to our directions. We decided to check them yet again.

Tracking with our belief that large cookies tend to be moister and chewier than smaller ones, we had designed this recipe to yield large cookies, anywhere from three to four inches across. And to get a large cookie, you need to start with a large ball of dough. The recipe directions state that you should form two-inch balls of dough, which turn out to be the size of small limes. Even to us, these seem huge in the hands, in fact, way too large, thus causing the urge to reduce their size. Resist that instinct, though, because if the dough balls are made smaller, the twenty-two-minute-to-twenty-five-minute cooking time will surely produce hard, overbaked cookies. Incidentally, the same holds true for our January/February 1996 chocolate chip cookie recipe.

Another consideration is the type of baking sheet you use. Thin cookie sheets do not conduct heat as evenly as the heavy professional-style half-sheet pans we use in the test kitchen (*see* Sources and Resources, May/June 1997, for information on ordering half-sheet pans). Batches of the oatmeal cookies baked side by side on a cheap cookie sheet and a professional half-sheet pan demonstrated the difference. After twenty-five minutes in the oven, some of the cookies baked on thin sheets were very light on the bottom while others were very dark, though not unpleasantly so. By contrast, the bottoms of the cookies baked on the heavy sheet pans were uniformly light golden brown.

Two other pointers might also help. Rather than waiting for the full twenty-two minutes of baking time, start checking the cookies after fifteen minutes, no matter what kind of sheet you're using. Second, be sure to remove the cookies from the oven when they *just start* to brown around the edges. They will appear undercooked and, in fact, will be undercooked when they come out of the oven, but resist the temptation to bake them any longer. After the thirty-minute cooling time (or, preferably, even longer), they will set and become more cooked.

UNDILUTED ICED DRINKS

Instead of discarding extra coffee that nobody drank, pour it into an ice cube tray, freeze it, and use it for iced coffee instead of regular ice cubes. This way, your iced coffee won't dilute as the cubes melt.

ELLEN BREITMAN
IRVINE, CA

We tested your idea, and it works well. We suggest dedicating an ice cube tray just for this purpose, though, as we caught a distinct coffee odor and flavor in regular ice cubes frozen in the same tray after freezing the coffee cubes. Incidentally, another reader, Ellen Oliviera from West Hollywood, California, submitted the identical idea for freezing tea to cool glasses of iced tea. We tested that with equal success, but we offer the same caveat: Dedicate a tray for making tea cubes.

FLOUR FLAVOR

In response to your article on Irish soda bread in the March/April 1997 issue, I agree with the author (Marie Piraino) on many points. We disagree, however, on how to achieve a flour (using what is available in this country) that most closely resembles a true Irish flour.

Marie suggested a ratio of one cup of cake flour to three cups of bleached all-purpose flour. American cake flour is the lowest protein flour available (about 8 percent), and it is heavily bleached with both a powder (benzoyl peroxide) and a gas (chlorine). This treatment alters the nature of the starch in the flour so it gelatinizes at lower temperatures and can thus contain and "hold up" a very large percentage of sugar and fat, resulting in cakes that are very light. But these bleaches also leave a residue (benzoic acid and hydrochloric acid) in the flour that is detectable to a sensitive palate. This is less of a flavor issue in cakes that contain ingredients whose flavors will mask these additives than in a product whose major ingredient is flour.

Instead of your mix of cake and bleached all-purpose flour, our first choice would be a pastry flour that is free of bleaching agents. Pastry flour is slightly higher in protein than cake flour, about 9.2 percent, but lower than a bleached all-purpose flour, which is about 10.5 percent protein.

BRINNA SANDS
KING ARTHUR FLOUR
NORWICH, VT

You raise an interesting point about the flavors of bleached versus unbleached flours. After consulting several flour and baking experts at your own King Arthur Flour, we learned that the off flavor you ascribe to bleached flour translates to a slight bitterness, and also that only about 10 percent of the population have palates sensitive enough to detect it.

While developing the master soda bread recipe, the author made more than fifty loaves using various flour combinations. Neither she nor her tasters ever caught any strange flavors in the bleached flour versions. The same held true for *Cook's Illustrated* staffers who tasted numerous loaves we produced while testing the recipe prior to publication and also while retesting side-by-side loaves made with unbleached pastry flour, as you suggest, and our master recipe ratio of one part cake flour to three parts bleached all-purpose flour. We did notice a slight texture difference, though, and we preferred the denser, more tender crumb of our master recipe. The pastry flour version, while certainly acceptable, seemed a little doughy, or cakey, by comparison.

So we fall into the 90 percent who cannot detect the flavor difference between bleached and unbleached flour. If readers with extra sensitive palates want to try the experiment for themselves, they can order five-pound bags of unbleached, white pastry flour (called Round Table Pastry Flour) from the King Arthur Flour Baker's Catalogue (P.O. Box 876, Norwich, VT 05055-0876; 800-827-6836) for $3.50 a bag. None of the seven local supermarkets we checked carried it.

CREAM OF TARTAR

Please explain the role of cream of tartar in the Irish soda bread recipe (March/April 1997). Can baking powder be substituted?

S. HALE
NANTUCKET, MA

Baking powder could be substituted, but not for the cream of tartar alone. You would have to reduce the quantity of baking soda as well.

Cream of tartar is a natural acidic compound that mixes with alkaline baking soda and liquid in a batter to produce carbon dioxide bubbles that leaven baked goods. Baking powder, however, is both alkaline and acid rolled into one. It is composed of one part baking soda (the alkaline), two parts acid (which react with the soda at room and oven temperatures), and one part cornstarch. Generally, baking powder is used in batters that do not contain acidic ingredients.

Irish soda bread requires powerful chemical leavening to provide enough lift for the heavy dough and the desired crumb texture, and the author concluded that one and one-half teaspoons of baking soda was right for the job. The one and one-half cups of buttermilk in the recipe was both an essential flavor component and an acidic ingredient. It takes one-half teaspoon of baking soda to neutralize one cup of buttermilk, thus the total quantity of buttermilk is neutralized by three-quarters teaspoon of baking soda. That leaves behind three-quarters teaspoon of baking soda in need of an acidic partner. Enter the acidic cream of tartar. Because it takes two parts cream of tartar to balance one part baking soda, the recipe calls for one and one-half teaspoons.

One tablespoon of baking powder could be substituted for that three-quarters teaspoon of baking soda and the full one and one-half teaspoons of cream of tartar, but the author preferred (marginally) the performance and the authenticity (it is called soda bread, after all) of the baking soda and cream of tartar combination.

CAKE YEAST
A couple of Sundays ago, I was baking the slow-rise version of the No-Knead Sandwich Bread in the Cook's Illustrated *May/June 1996 issue. I got to reading the bit of the article about yeast ("Best Yeast for American Sandwich Bread?") that said cake yeast scored well in the tasting. But there wasn't much more information. How is this stuff different from dry yeast and how much of it should I use in place of the dry?*

CALEB GERHARD
CAMBRIDGE, MA

Cake yeast, also known as "fresh-active," is less-processed than yeast in powdered form. According to Pam Smith, manager of the Fleischmann's Bake Lab, all yeast begins as a small, cultured, purified sample that feeds and multiplies continuously in a liquid medium until it reaches the desired volume and stage of development. This liquid yeast, also known as "cream yeast," is sold by the tankerful to huge-scale manufacturers, who pump it from vats into their doughs. When some of the moisture is removed from liquid yeast, the resulting product is "crumbled yeast," which is packaged in fifty-pound bags and sold to bakeries. The next processing step extrudes the crumbled yeast to make a product that remains fully hydrated, yet fine enough to press into the small cakes you see for sale on supermarket shelves. Further processing yields dried, powdered yeast in its various forms.

To substitute fresh yeast for active dry powder, use a ratio of roughly 2:1. Fleischmann's makes it easy to trade the two forms of yeast by packaging them in units of the correct weight to exchange one for one. For instance, a recipe calling for one envelope of active dry yeast (which weighs one-quarter ounce, or a scant tablespoon by volume) would require one small cake (which weighs 0.6 ounce) of compressed fresh yeast. Because fresh yeast is already hydrated, it can be crumbled directly into the dough without soaking it in water first (the same is now true of active dry yeast too; the old practice of soaking it is no longer necessary). We retested fresh and active dry yeast by making loaves of bread with each in the test kitchen. Sure enough, we once again preferred both the flavor and the aroma of bread made with the fresh yeast.

We should mention two additional points regarding fresh yeast. It is also sold in two-ounce, household-sized cakes, which, we're told by the Fleischmann's marketing people, are much less common than the smaller 0.6-ounce size. Last, fresh cake yeast is highly perishable and has a shorter shelf life than the powdered varieties. Cake yeast must be refrigerated at all times, and you should try to use it as far in advance of its expiration date as possible.

KEEPING COUNT
When you are preparing a recipe that requires multiple small measurements of a single ingredient, such as beating eggs into a batter one at a time, count out loud as you add each one. The sound of your voice will reinforce your memory, which will make it easier to remember where you left off when you resume after the inevitable interruption.

GINNY MONTBLANC
ROGERS, AR

This trick may sound funny, but it's also a habit of one of our editors, who swears by it.

GRILLING STEAKS
Thank you for Stephanie Lyness' article on grilling steaks in the May/June 1996 issue. I achieve a seared crust with a juicy interior by using a cast-iron grill grate. The cast iron absorbs enough heat to both properly sear the meat, and leave a wonderful pattern on the steak.

TIMOTHY GRANZEAU
SPRINGFIELD, IL

We experimented with a cast-iron grate, which did indeed leave dark, distinctive grill marks on our steaks. The cast iron absorbed much more heat than the steel wires of a regular grate, so it did an excellent job of searing the meat with which it had direct contact. By comparison, the areas of the meat's surface between the grates seemed pale, giving the steak an attractive, striped appearance.

Regardless of appearance, steaks grilled according to our method on both cast-iron and steel grates had excellent, well-developed flavor. So it boils down to choice. If attractive grill marks are important to you, a cast-iron grate is very effective and worth the added expense. Cast iron is not necessary, however, to grill a delicious, well-seared steak.

SALAD WITHOUT THE BOWL
To prepare and dress a salad without having to clean a bowl afterward, I place washed and dried greens in a large plastic bag, like those from the supermarket produce section. Then I prepare the dressing separately in a jar. At serving time, I pour the dressing onto the greens in the bag, twist it shut at the top, and shake. The dressing coats the greens evenly, you can pour them directly onto serving plates, and then discard the oily bag. No cleanup necessary.

ELLEN LORD
MIAMI BEACH, FL

We tried your method and found it just as easy as you do. Though there are times when we prefer to toss the salad in a large bowl at the table, we'd certainly use your method for picnics, at sparsely equipped vacation cottages, or whenever no large bowl is available.

ERRATA
The photographs of the "best buy" Tramontina saucepan and the Paderno saucepan were transposed in our May/June 1997 testing on page 27.

WHAT IS IT?
Recently, while cleaning out my mother's kitchen, I came across this implement. I haven't a clue what it is used for, do you?

PAM GROSSMAN
BERKELEY, CA

Most often called a V-shaped melon cutter, what you have is a common garnishing tool, also referred to as a garnish knife, wedge knife, food decorator, or decorator tool. Regardless of what you call it, you use this tool primarily to create uniform zigzag edges on both halves when splitting firm fruits and vegetables (particularly melon, but also tomatoes and winter squash) along their equator. Insert the tool repeatedly in a line around the middle of the melon, making sure that each new cut connects to the last, then pull the halves apart.

You can get a melon cutter by mail order, for $3.95 plus shipping and handling, from Utilities, Inc.(393 Commercial Street, Provincetown, MA 02657; 508-487-6800).

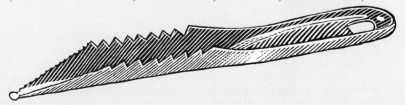

EASY DUSTING TECHNIQUE

To achieve a light, even dusting of confectioners' sugar or cocoa on cakes, truffles, or cappuccinos, Brendan Zahner of Forest Hills, New York, employs a small sieve.

1. Spoon a small amount of confectioners' sugar or cocoa powder into a fine mesh strainer.

2. Pass the strainer over the items to be dusted while tapping it gently with your hand or a spoon to help the powder fall through the wires. Any leftover powder can be dumped easily back into its container.

Quick

The editors of *Cook's Illustrated* would like to thank all of our readers who have sent us their quick tips. We have enjoyed reading every one of them and have learned a lot. Keep them coming. We will provide a one-year complimentary subscription for each quick tip that we print. Send a description of your special technique to *Cook's Illustrated*, 17 Station St., Brookline, MA 02146. Please write "Attention:

MAKING ROOM IN MUSHROOMS

Isabelle Wolters of Scituate, Massachusetts, has come up with this method of preparing stuffed mushrooms that will accommodate more stuffing.

1. Invert the cleaned mushroom and pull off the stem.

2. Use the small end of a sharp melon baller to scoop excess mushroom flesh from the underside of the cap. The flesh that is removed can be chopped and added to the stuffing mixture.

CRACKING PEPPERCORNS NEATLY

Cracking peppercorns on a cutting board or counter can be a nuisance when they fly all over the place. Joanne Leonard of Rockville, Maryland, has come up with a solution. She places the peppercorns in a cast-iron skillet and uses a smaller pot to grind the pepper with a downward, rotating motion.

DISPOSING OF BACON FAT

Carolyn Adams of Hilton Head Island, South Carolina, has come up with a good method for disposing of small quantities of bacon fat.

1. Line a coffee mug with tinfoil, then pour in the rendered fat from the bacon pan.

2. When the fat has hardened, pick the foil out of the mug and throw it away, or reserve for future use.

QUICK CAKE DECORATIONS

GingerLee Kams of Kohler, Wisconsin, has developed this way of creating make-ahead chocolate decorations that harden into shape so they can be stood up vertically on a frosted cake.

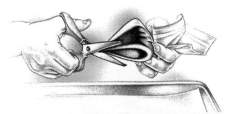

1. Place chocolate in a heat-safe zipper-lock bag, seal it tight, and immerse it in simmering water until the chocolate melts. When the chocolate has melted, snip off the tip of one corner of the bag with scissors or poke it with a toothpick to make a small opening.

2. Using single or double strokes, pipe chocolate designs such as stars, hearts, spirals, letters, numbers, and so forth onto a parchment paper– or plastic wrap–covered baking sheet. Refrigerate or freeze until firm.

3. Carefully remove the decorations from the sheet and stand them up on the cake, anchoring them with a dollop of whipped cream or icing if need be.

Tips

Quick Tips" on the envelope and include your name, address, and daytime phone number. Unfortunately, we can only acknowledge receipt of tips that will be printed in the magazine. In case the same tip is received from two readers, the one postmarked first will be selected. Also, be sure to let us know what particular cooking problems you would like us to investigate in upcoming issues.

SPLATTER-FREE MIXING

A May/June 1994 Quick Tip showed how to avoid splatters by fitting the beaters of your electric mixer through a paper plate, which then covers the mixing bowl. Kacy Richardson of Berkeley, California, came up with this idea for those times when there are no paper plates available.

1. On a piece of waxed paper cut larger than the size of your workbowl, make two holes, spaced as far apart as the beater openings on your electric mixer. Insert the beater stems through the holes and into the beater base.

2. While you're mixing, the waxed paper will hang over the edges of the bowl, preventing the contents from splattering out.

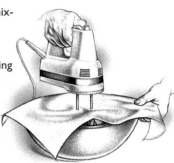

LIGHTENING BATTERS WITHOUT WASTE

When preparing a dish like a soufflé, in which a bit of whipped egg white is added to an egg yolk base to lighten it before the bulk of the whites are blended in, Joanne Leonard of Rockville, Maryland, simply swirls the whisk, with the beaten white still clinging to it, into the yolk mixture.

GETTING THE MOST MUSTARD

Rather than throwing away an almost empty jar of mustard, Kristen Mills of San Francisco, California, uses the jar to mix up a salad dressing or marinade.

1. Pour the other dressing ingredients directly into the mustard jar.

2. Replace the lid and shake the jar vigorously. The liquids will pick up the mustard that's clinging to the sides of the jar.

ADAPTING YOUR CARVING BOARD

If, like Lisa Keys of Middlebury, Connecticut, your meat carving board does not have a reservoir to collect juices as they run off the meat, try her solution.

1. Place the board in a lipped cookie sheet or a sheet pan and carve the meat on the board as usual.

2. Transfer the meat to a serving platter, remove the board, and pour the collected juices from the pan.

ELEGANT DIPPED STRAWBERRIES

Agnes Overby of Shawnee, Kansas, was always bothered by the flat spot that develops when chocolate-coated strawberries are placed on a flat surface for the coating to harden. She came up with this technique to avoid the problem.

1. Stick strong toothpicks into the stem end of the berries, then proceed to coat the berries with chocolate, shaking off any excess.

2. Turn the dipped berries upside down and stick the toothpicks into a block of Styrofoam packaging. The berries are held upright until the coating sets, so the finished berries have an elegant coating with no flat spots.

KEEPING CAN TOPS AFLOAT

To prevent severed can tops from sinking down into the contents of the can, John Adamson of Medfield, Massachusetts, slips a small butter knife under a partially opened top before he finishes removing it. The knife holds the separated top.

How to Grill Salmon

*For salmon that is beautifully seared outside and moist inside,
cook over direct heat and forget the cover.*

by Stephanie Lyness

Salmon is my favorite fish to grill. Not only does it taste great but it's firm enough to hold together better than many other fish. An additional salmon advantage lies in the fact that modern fish-farming technology all but guarantees that I can buy excellent-quality salmon any day of the year. Even at my local supermarket, where other fish is often not up to my admittedly exacting standards, salmon steaks and fillets come in so fresh and sell out so fast that I have yet to be dissatisfied.

That said, salmon grilling has its pitfalls. Many is the time I've put perfect, gleaming fillets on a too cool grill only to have them stick and tear when I tried to turn them so that the presentation side of the fish ended up looking like something the cat dragged in. Too hot and the flesh blackened while the charcoal flamed, ruining the delicate flavor of the fish.

I wanted to find a technique for grilling the fish that I could depend on. I wanted the well-browned crust, crisp skin, firm, succulent flesh, and light woody flavor that high-heat grilling accomplishes so beautifully, without the heavy, smoky flavor that sometimes overpowers grilled food. I wondered how to gauge when the salmon was cooked, what heat was correct, and whether this was a time to use the grill cover to promote gentle, even cooking. I was also interested to find out whether farmed salmon grilled any differently than wild. And what about those baskets they advertise for grilling fish?

Grilled Fillets: No Bones, No Oil, No Lid

I started my testing with boneless, individual-portion farmed salmon fillets with skin, weighing six to eight ounces each. I used my twenty-two-and-one-half-inch kettle grill and various charcoals (*see* "Fuels," page 16). Whenever possible, I bought fillets cut from the center of the fillet, because center-cut fillets from farmed salmon are often almost exactly one and one-half inches thick and cook consistently. Cuts from the tail are thinner, thus easier to overcook, while cuts from the head end are thicker and tend to take too long to cook through.

My first test was to determine the proper heat. Several tests proved that a medium-high heat (I could hold my hand five inches above the grill for about four seconds) browned without burning and, more importantly, created the necessary crust so that I could turn the salmon fairly easily after some initial prodding with long-handled tongs or a spatula.

Next, I tested a fillet brushed with vegetable oil against one that was unoiled. I was surprised (and pleased) to find that the untreated fillet detached as easily as the one that had been oiled; not only did I lose a messy step here, but any added fat surely must encourage flaming. I did, however, find it useful to steal a suggestion from Evan Kleiman's *Cucina del Mare* (William Morrow, 1993): I rubbed the heated grill grate itself with a wad of paper towels dipped lightly in vegetable oil, held by long-handled tongs. No, the paper doesn't catch fire. This extra step not only lubricated the grate but cleaned off lingering residue as well, important given the delicate flavor and light color of a salmon fillet.

Finally, I tested fillets grilled entirely over direct heat, grilled one side over direct and the second over indirect (that is, not directly over the coals), and covered over both direct and indirect heat. There was no difference in taste or texture between the fillets grilled entirely over direct heat and those finished over indirect. Because direct heat cooks faster, I opted for that. That said, I found the direct-indirect method to be an excellent way to cook the thin tail pieces; by the time the flesh has seared enough to turn, the fish is almost cooked through and needs just a minute or so of gentle heat to finish it without overcooking.

As concerns the tests with the cover, the fillet that was cooked covered over indirect heat looked baked and slightly smoked rather than grilled. If this is your goal, go to it (skin side down so the flesh doesn't stick), but I'm looking for real grilling. The fillet grilled covered over direct heat looked great and felt carefree (like having someone else babysit the grill), but the cover infused the flesh with a smoky, fatty flavor that got in the way of the really fresh, direct taste I wanted. So I nixed, with regrets, the cover.

As I grilled the salmon, I remained alert for clues to tell when it was properly cooked. I like salmon medium-rare in the center, or still slightly translucent. Mostly I found that by the time my one-and-one-half-inch-thick fillets were well-browned on both sides, the center was perfect, that is, slightly undercooked but close enough to finish cooking the last little bit on the plate. I also developed a tactile test: As the salmon cooks, I pull it off the grill every now and then and squeeze the sides of the fillet gently between my fingertips. Raw salmon feels squishy; medium-rare salmon is firm, but not hard. If you're stumped and want to really be sure, cut into the fillet with a paring knife and look.

Now that I had a dependable technique, I figured it would be an easy matter to plug in salmon steaks. As I proceeded to test steaks of different thicknesses, though, I found a hitch. Not only do one-and-one-half-inch-thick steaks take longer to cook than fillets of the same thickness, but the outside of the steak gets overcooked before the inside has a chance to cook. Clearly I would need to modify my technique and cook steaks of this thickness at least partially over indirect heat. Steaks that were one inch thick grilled fine with my technique, but because I think one of the charms of a steak is that it be thick (and perhaps boned and tied as well), I leave the issue of salmon steaks to another article.

The Grill Basket

My final test was to compare fillets grilled in a grill basket against fillets cooked straight on the grill. A grill basket is a long-handled wire contraption that's shaped something like a sandwich press: The two rectangular halves

REMOVING PIN BONES FROM SALMON

1. Using the tips of your fingers, gently rub the surface of the salmon fillet to locate any remaining pin bones.

2. To remove the bones once you have found them, grasp them with a pair of needle nose pliers and pull them out.

(each half is a wire grid) sandwich the food between them. The food (in this case salmon) is cooked in the basket on top of the grill grate. Because the grate of my kettle grill sits one to two inches below the lip of the grill itself, I was concerned that the basket wouldn't lie flat on the grate (so the cooking would be uneven). As it turned out, the grate was large enough to accommodate the handle. Since I'd only built a fire in half of the grill, the handle didn't even get particularly hot. My first attempt was a bust; the fillets browned well but stuck to the basket. So I oiled the basket for the next test, and then this method worked beautifully.

A basket takes all the guesswork out of manipulating the fish on a grill. There's no chance it will stick to the grill grate, and it won't fall apart while you turn it or take it off. One word of caution: Remove the fish immediately from the basket once cooked. The skin, particularly, will stick to the wire as it cools.

Wild Salmon Modifies Technique
I knew there was a big difference in flavor and texture between farmed and wild salmon and wondered whether that difference would extend to grilling technique. (Wild salmon has a more complex, less homogenous flavor than the farmed and a meaty texture.)

Unfortunately, because I was doing my testing during the winter months, I was only able to find frozen, thawed wild king salmon: One fish had been frozen on the boat very shortly after harvest while the other had been frozen on shore, theoretically within twenty-four hours of harvest. Both arrived in good shape although with predictable softening of the flesh and moisture loss; the shore-frozen fish had a slight odor.

I grilled both fish using my master technique and found, not too surprisingly, that both salmon were a little drier than they should have been and had distinctly less fat than the farmed variety. Mark Bittman, author of *Fish: The Complete Guide to Buying and Cooking* (Macmillan, 1994), confirmed that, even fresh, wild salmon are slightly less fatty and therefore drier than the farmed variety.

So, after consulting with the authors of "How to Grill Bone-In Chicken Breast"(*see* page 14), I amended my master technique for those occasions when wild salmon is the fish of the day. When cooking wild salmon, brown it for two minutes over direct heat, then pull the salmon off the coals, cover it with an aluminum turkey roasting pan, and finish cooking over indirect heat for four to five more minutes.

SIMPLE GRILLED SALMON
Serves 4
Whether hot from the grill, at room temperature, or chilled, I usually serve grilled salmon very simply, with a drizzle of lemon juice, salt and pepper, one of the glazes below, or a homemade mayonnaise (*see* page 9). If your fillets are less than one and one-half inches thick, decrease the grilling time by roughly thirty seconds per side. If using a gas grill, heat it for ten minutes and then grill the salmon over direct heat for four to five minutes per side. To test fillets for doneness, either peek into the salmon with the tip of a small knife as described below or remove the salmon from the grill and squeeze both sides of the fillet gently with your fingertips (raw salmon is squishy; medium-rare salmon is firm, but not hard).

Vegetable oil for grill grate
4 center-cut salmon fillets, each 6 to 7 ounces and 1½ inches thick
Salt and ground black pepper

1. Ignite enough charcoal briquettes or hardwood charcoal to fill slightly less than two shoeboxes, and burn until completely covered with thin coating light gray ash, 20 to 30 minutes. Spread coals in single layer to make medium-hot fire (judge by holding outstretched hand 5 inches above coals for 4 seconds; if you cannot make it the full 4 seconds, fire is too hot). Position grill grate over fire and rub cooking area of grate with oil-dipped paper towel wad (*see* illustration, page 17).
2. Generously sprinkle each side of fillets with salt and pepper. Place fillets in an oiled grill basket, if you like. Place fillets skin side down on grill grate; grill until skin shrinks and separates from flesh and turns black, 2 to 3 minutes. Flip fillets gently with long-handled tongs or spatula; grill until fillets are opaque throughout, yet translucent at very center when checked with point of paring knife, 3 to 4 minutes (*see* above for an additional doneness test). Transfer to serving platter and serve.

GRILLED SALMON WITH INDIAN FLAVORS AND FRESH MANGO CHUTNEY
Serves 4
For marinade, mix 2 tablespoons vegetable oil, 2 tablespoons peeled, grated fresh gingerroot, 1½ teaspoons each ground cumin, ground coriander, and salt, and ¼ teaspoon cayenne pepper together in shallow bowl; set aside. For chutney, mix 1 ripe mango cut into ½-inch dice, 3 tablespoons juice from 1 small lemon, and 1 tablespoon chopped fresh cilantro in small bowl; set aside. Follow recipe for Simple Grilled Salmon, marinating fish while coals are heating and omitting salt on fish. Serve cooked salmon with mango chutney.

QUILTED GIRAFFE'S GRILLED SALMON WITH MUSTARD GLAZE
Serves 4
Mix 2 tablespoons each dry mustard and sugar and 2 teaspoons water to make thick paste. Follow recipe for Simple Grilled Salmon, spreading mustard mixture over flesh side of fillets before grilling. Drizzle cooked salmon with extra-virgin olive oil.

Supreme Chicken Salads

*Roasted chicken breasts and hand-shredding
deliver superb salad.*

by Pam Anderson with Karen Tack

To me, classic chicken salad consists of tender breast meat, pulled apart by hand rather than cubed with a knife, and bound loosely with mayonnaise. There's a little celery for texture, some parsley or tarragon for flavor, and a squeeze of lemon juice for freshness. I often make this salad from leftover roast or poached chicken, and I put it together by taste and sight.

So what didn't I know about chicken salad? After a little thought, I had only one question. When making the classic version from scratch, and not from leftover meat, how should I cook the chicken?

Although there were many choices, they basically fell into two camps, wet cooking and dry cooking. The wet cooking methods included poaching (my usual method), steaming, roasting in foil, and a method new to me, dropping the chicken into simmering aromatic water and then removing it from heat and letting it cool to room temperature.

Unfortunately, chicken cooked by each of these methods had a bland, unmistakably boiled flavor. Chicken cooked in the microwave also had that wet-cooked taste.

Roast chicken, which is cooked with dry heat, was a very different matter. Even after the skin and bones were removed, the meat tasted roasted and the resulting chicken salad was superb.

SIMPLE ROAST CHICKEN BREASTS

2 large whole bone-in, skin-on chicken breasts (at least 1½ pounds each)
1 tablespoon vegetable oil
   Salt

Adjust oven rack to middle position and heat oven to 400 degrees. Set breasts on small, foil-lined jelly roll pan. Brush with oil and sprinkle generously with salt. Roast until meat thermometer inserted into thickest part of breast registers 160 degrees, 35 to 40 minutes. Cool to room temperature, remove skin, and continue with one of salad recipes that follow. (Can be wrapped in plastic and refrigerated for 2 days.)

CLASSIC CREAMY CHICKEN SALAD
Serves 6
In addition to the parsley leaves, you can flavor the salad with two tablespoons of minced fresh tarragon or basil leaves.

1 recipe Simple Roast Chicken Breasts, skinned and boned, meat shredded into bite-sized pieces (about 5 cups)
2 medium celery ribs, cut into small dice
2 medium scallions, white and green parts, minced
¾–1 cup mayonnaise
1½–2 tablespoons juice from 1 small lemon
2 tablespoons minced fresh parsley leaves
   Salt and ground black pepper

Mix all salad ingredients together in large bowl, including salt and pepper to taste. Serve. (Can be covered and refrigerated overnight.)

CHICKEN SALAD WITH HOISIN DRESSING
Serves 6
Try serving this Asian-style salad on a bed of young spinach leaves with sliced cucumber and radishes or rolled in a flour tortilla with shredded iceberg lettuce or watercress.

Hoisin Dressing
⅓ cup rice wine vinegar
1½ tablespoons soy sauce
3 tablespoons hoisin sauce
1 tablespoon minced fresh gingerroot
1 tablespoon Asian sesame oil
3 tablespoons vegetable oil

1 recipe Simple Roast Chicken Breasts, skinned and boned, meat shredded into bite-sized pieces (about 5 cups)
2 medium celery ribs, cut into small dice
2 medium scallions, white and green parts, minced
2 tablespoons minced fresh cilantro or parsley leaves

1. For the dressing, whisk vinegar, soy, hoisin, and ginger together in small bowl; whisk in both oils and set aside.

2. Mix remaining salad ingredients in large bowl. Add dressing; toss to coat. Serve. (Can be covered and refrigerated overnight.)

WALDORF CHICKEN SALAD
Serves 6
Follow recipe for Classic Creamy Chicken Salad, adding 1 large crisp apple, cored and cut into medium dice, and 6 tablespoons chopped toasted walnuts.

CURRIED CHICKEN SALAD WITH RAISINS AND HONEY
Serves 6

1 recipe Simple Roast Chicken Breasts, skinned and boned, meat shredded into bite-sized pieces (about 5 cups)
2 medium celery ribs, cut into small dice
2 medium scallions, white and green parts, minced
2 tablespoons minced fresh cilantro or parsley leaves
¾–1 cup mayonnaise
1½–2 tablespoons juice from 1 small lemon
6 tablespoons golden raisins
2 teaspoons curry powder
1 tablespoon honey
   Salt and ground black pepper

Mix all salad ingredients together in large bowl, including salt and pepper to taste. Serve. (Can be covered and refrigerated overnight.)

PREPARING THE CHICKEN

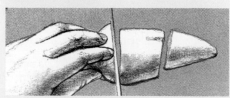

To prepare the chicken, first pull the whole breast away from the bone (see left). Cut the breast into thirds and then shred by hand into small pieces.

ILLUSTRATIONS BY NENAD JAKESEVIC

Making Sense of Mayonnaise

*Use a mild-flavored oil, fresh lemon juice, and a bit of patience,
and this incredible emulsion sauce will work every time.*

by Mark Zanger with Dawn Yanagihara

When I was a starving teenager, I liked mayonnaise a lot. One of my favorite snacks was a whole head of iceberg lettuce, cut up, with gobs of mayonnaise right out of the jar. I put mayonnaise on baked potatoes in preference to butter or sour cream and spread it thickly between slices of bread for a sandwich.

As a grown-up, though, I gradually lost my taste for commercial mayonnaise. It seemed to taste of cooked egg, with a tartness more mustardlike than lemony, and a slightly stale aftertaste. I thought, "I can do better than this with fresh ingredients."

And I could—but it took a while to reach my goal. I was looking for a fresh-tasting mayo with a delicate egg flavor, a slightly lemony tang, and a texture that was thick and creamy but not stiff. I'm strictly a home cook, so I also wanted a quick and easy method. I wasn't too concerned about making a mayo that would keep for weeks in the refrigerator either; I just wanted a simple version to serve as a sauce, spread, or dip in small quantities for family dinners or maybe a few guests.

The Nature of the Beast

My first task was to learn about mayonnaise, which is actually a very strange substance. It is semisolid despite the fact that its primary components are three relatively thin liquids—vegetable oil, lemon juice, and egg yolk—and it neither feels nor tastes oily despite the fact that it is mostly comprised of oil. These unusual characteristics, and some of the mysteries involved in making mayonnaise, are explained by the fact that it is an emulsion.

An emulsion is a mixture of two things that don't ordinarily mix, such as oil and water. The only way to mix them is to stir or whisk so strenuously that the two ingredients break down into tiny droplets. Many of these droplets will continue to "find" each other and recoalesce into pure fluid. But eventually one of the fluids, usually the less plentiful one, will break entirely into droplets so tiny that they remain separated by the opposite fluid. Imagine a swimming pool filled with water that is chock full of floating marbles, none of which are quite touching each other, and you will have the idea of an emulsion.

The liquid in droplet form (the marbles, in our example) is called the "dispersed phase" because the droplets are dispersed throughout the emulsion. The liquid that surrounds the droplets (the water in our example) is called the "continuous phase" because it is all joined together, however thinly, around the droplets. Because the continuous phase forms the surface of the emulsion, that's what your mouth and tongue first feel and first taste. So because the lemon juice is part of the continuous phase of mayonnaise, this sauce is not greasy to the touch and does not taste oily at first.

Mayonnaise is one of the most remarkable emulsions because so much oil—more than a cup in some recipes—can be emulsified into so little water-based fluid—perhaps one and one-half tablespoons from the egg yolk and another teaspoon or two of lemon juice and vinegar. It works because the egg yolk is such a good emulsifier and stabilizer (*see* "What Makes Mayo Thick?" page 10).

Once I understood the nature of mayonnaise, I began to test the individual ingredients as well as methods of forcing them into an emulsion. I found myself with three primary tasks: to make sure the emulsion did not "break," to get the proper consistency, and to achieve just the right flavor.

You may not notice the difference in tuna salad, but fresh mayonnaise is vastly superior to commercial when used on fish, on raw or steamed vegetables, as a sandwich spread, or as a dip.

Breaking Up Is Easy to Do

The main problem to avoid when making mayonnaise is the "breaking" of the emulsion, a process in which the mixture suddenly goes limp and liquid as the emulsion "inverts" back to its original components. In the case of mayonnaise, a broken mixture looks like scrambled eggs floating in oil.

Most of the cookbooks I researched described mayonnaise as an emulsion of oil in egg yolk. This is inexact. In fact, an egg yolk is about half water and one-third fatty substances, so the initial whisking of the yolk makes the yolk itself into an emulsion. As you whisk, you can see the yolk getting more opaque and thicker, two signs that it has become an emulsion. To make the emulsion even thicker, you add the oil and emulsifying agents—a name given to any substance that helps prevent the individual components of an emulsion from regrouping back into their original forms, in this case, mustard and salt.

However, the oil must be added slowly. Most of my sauces that failed did so early on, with only an ounce or less of oil in the mix, well short of even the half-cup limit suggested by the most conservative authors. My sauces were breaking up because I was adding more oil than I could whisk quickly enough into droplets. The big batch of oil was gathering all those previously emulsified droplets into a big pool of oil. I would be stirring a thickening bowl of mayonnaise, add too much oil, whisk frantically, and find myself whipping a suddenly thin bowl of oil with granular-looking droplets of water and egg yolk. My emulsion had reversed.

As I gained experience, I realized that my first mayonnaise of the day always worked, and when I was hurrying to finish, I had a high percentage of failures. Stress and impatience were causing me to rush the oil, and panic was also a problem. As I realized that a big pour of oil doesn't quickly mix with mayonnaise, I began to work in only a safe, small amount of the oil at a time instead of frantically whisking in loose oil.

Adjusting Flavor and Consistency

Because oil is by far the major constituent of the mayonnaise emulsion,

DRIZZLING THE OIL

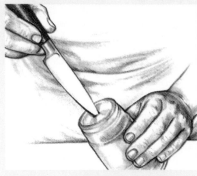

An easy way to drizzle oil into mayonnaise slowly and evenly is to punch a small hole in the bottom of a paper cup, pour the oil into the cup while holding your finger over the hole, then hold the cup above the bowl and remove your finger.

it is also the most important flavor component. Because mayonnaise was developed in the olive oil regions of France, Spain, and Italy, I invested in three-quarters of a cup of good-quality extra-virgin olive oil from Italy—and made a mayonnaise that tasted harsh and throat-burning.

After getting the same results with several other extra-virgin oils, I went on to pure olive oil. It did not have the bitter flavor, but it was somewhat heavy and awkward. My favorite oil for mayonnaise ended up being 100 percent corn oil, which makes a rich, eggy-tasting mayonnaise with plenty of body, followed by canola oil, which is lighter and more lemony.

Because I was aiming for a lemon flavor, I worked primarily with fresh lemon juice. A national brand of lemon juice from concentrate wasn't bad, but it wasn't fresh lemon juice and lacked the bright flavor of the real thing. Lime juice, however, worked almost as well as lemon.

I then moved on to getting just the right consistency for my mayonnaise. This factor is dependent upon the ratio of oil to liquid ingredients. Contrary to what would seem like common sense, adding more oil makes a stiffer mayonnaise. If a mayonnaise is too

stiff, but you don't want to alter flavoring, you can simply whisk in a bit of water.

When I made a recipe with half a cup of oil, the mayonnaise was very thin, too salty, and too acidic; there was not enough oil to counteract the salt and lemon juice. Adding a full cup of oil, though, resulted in a mayo that was stiff and almost rubbery, with too strong an oil flavor. With three-quarters of a cup of oil, I got just what I wanted: a smooth but not stiff consistency, and a flavor in which the egg and lemon were distinct but not overwhelming.

MASTER RECIPE FOR HOMEMADE MAYONNAISE
Makes 3/4 cup

Each time you add oil, make sure to whisk until it's thoroughly incorporated, but it is fine to stop for a rest or to measure the next addition of oil. Mayonnaise should have a smooth, uniform consistency. If it appears grainy or beaded after the last oil addition, as if it has broken, continue to whisk and it should emulsify. To keep the bowl stable while whisking, set it on a wet dishcloth.

1	large egg yolk
1 1/2	teaspoons salt
1/4	teaspoon Dijon-style mustard
1 1/2	teaspoons juice from 1 small lemon
1	teaspoon white wine vinegar
3/4	cup corn oil

Whisk egg yolk vigorously in medium bowl for 15 seconds. Add all remaining ingredients except oil and whisk until yolk thickens and color brightens, about 30 seconds. Adding 1/4 cup oil in slow, steady stream, continue to whisk vigorously until oil is incorporated completely and mixture thickens, about 1 minute. Add another 1/4 cup oil in same manner, whisking until incorporated completely, about 30 seconds more. Add last 1/4 cup oil all at once and whisk until incorporated completely, about 30 seconds more. Serve. (Can be refrigerated in airtight container up to 7 to 10 days.)

LEMON MAYONNAISE
Follow Master Recipe for Homemade Mayonnaise, adding 1 1/2 teaspoons grated lemon zest along with the lemon juice.

DIJON MAYONNAISE
Follow Master Recipe for Homemade Mayonnaise, whisking 2 tablespoons Dijon-style mustard into completed mayonnaise.

TARTAR SAUCE
Follow Master Recipe for Homemade Mayonnaise, mixing 1 1/2 tablespoons minced cornichons (about 3 large), 1 teaspoon cornichon juice, and 1 tablespoon each minced scallion, minced red onion, and drained minced capers into completed mayonnaise.

TARRAGON MAYONNAISE
Follow Master Recipe for Homemade

WHAT MAKES MAYO THICK?

The capacity of mayonnaise to hold so much oil in so little water-based fluid—and to end up being so stiff in the process—depends most upon the remarkable chemical properties of the egg yolk. In his book *The Curious Cook* (North Point Press, 1990), Harold McGee explains that a full 28 percent of an egg yolk is made up of phospholipid molecules. These potent emulsifiers have long hydrocarbon tails, as do fats and oils, but they also have electrically charged "heads." In mayonnaise, the tails get embedded in the droplets of oil while the heads stick out from the droplets. Because the heads carry an electrical charge, they repel each other and thus prevent the droplets from joining together.

Phospholipid molecules become embedded in the oil droplets, keeping the oil suspended and preventing the drops from coalescing.

Mayonnaise, mixing 1 tablespoon minced fresh tarragon leaves into completed mayonnaise.

ROASTED GARLIC MAYONNAISE
Follow Master Recipe for Homemade Mayonnaise, adding puree from 1 medium head (about 3 tablespoons) roasted garlic (*see* "Roasting Garlic," September/October 1993) to initial ingredients and substituting 1/4 cup pure olive oil for 1/4 cup corn oil.

FOOD PROCESSOR MAYONNAISE
Makes 1 1/2 cups

Follow Master Recipe for Homemade Mayonnaise, adding 1 whole large egg and doubling quantities of other ingredients. Pulse all ingredients except oil in workbowl of food processor fitted with metal blade three or four times to combine. With machine running, add oil in thin steady stream through open feed tube until incorporated completely.

Mark Zanger is a freelance writer living in Boston, Massachusetts.

Crunchy Cucumber Salads

No matter how you dress them, salting and draining sliced cucumbers maximizes crunchy texture.

by Adam Ried

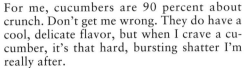

For me, cucumbers are 90 percent about crunch. Don't get me wrong. They do have a cool, delicate flavor, but when I crave a cucumber, it's that hard, bursting shatter I'm really after.

More often than not, though, by the time you eat a cucumber salad, the cucumbers have gone soft and watery, losing their appealing texture and diluting the dressing to near tastelessness. This made the primary goal of my testing simple: Maximize the crunch.

The standing recommendation for ridding watery vegetables such as cucumbers, zucchini, and eggplant of unwanted moisture is to salt them. The salt creates a higher ion concentration at the surface of the vegetable than exists deep within its cells. To equalize the concentration levels, the water within the cells is drawn out through permeable cell walls. In the case of cucumbers, this leaves them wilted, yet very crunchy. Of course, some culinary questions remain: How much salt should be used? Should the cucumber slices be weighted, or pressed, to squeeze out liquid? How long should they drain?

To find out if pressing salted cucumbers really squeezes out more liquid, I trimmed and seeded six cucumbers to eight ounces each, sliced them on the bias, and tossed each batch with one teaspoon of salt in its own colander set over a bowl. Three of them had zipper-lock freezer bags filled with one quart of water placed on top of them; no additional weight was added to the other three. Then I left them all to drain, measuring the liquid each had released after one-half, one, two, three, and twelve hours. At each time point, the weighted cucumbers had released about one tablespoon more liquid than the unweighted cucumbers; three versus two after thirty minutes, four versus three after one hour, and so on. Interestingly, the weighted cukes gave off no more liquid after twelve hours than they had after three (seven tablespoons at both points). So weighting the cucumbers is worthwhile, but forget about draining the cucumbers overnight; it's not necessary.

At the one-hour mark, my tasters and I could not detect an appreciable difference in flavor or texture between weighted and unweighted cukes. But I wanted to see how they would perform in salads with different types of dressings. I mixed one batch each of the weighted and unweighted cucumbers with three types of sauces—creamy, oil-based, and water-based—and allowed each to sit at room temperature for one hour. This is where the true value of better-drained cucumbers became obvious; every single taster preferred the salads made with pressed cucumbers for their superior crunch and less diluted dressings.

As for the amount of salt, some cooks recommend simply using the quantity with which you would normally season the cucumber while others say you should use more, up to two tablespoons per cucumber, and then rinse off the excess before further use. I tried a few cucumbers, prepared exactly as those described above, except with two tablespoons of salt. The cucumbers with two tablespoons did give up about one more tablespoon of liquid within the first hour than those drained with one teaspoon had, but they also required rinsing and blotting dry with paper towels. And despite this extra hassle, they still tasted much too salty in the salads. I would advise forgoing the extra salt.

HOW TO SALT AND DRAIN CUCUMBERS

Peel, halve lengthwise, and scoop seeds from 3 medium cucumbers (about 8 ounces each). Stack halves flat side down; slice diagonally 1/4 inch thick. Toss with 1 tablespoon salt in strainer or colander set over bowl; weight with water-filled, one-gallon-sized zipper-lock freezer bag, sealed tight. (*See* Quick Tips, January/February 1995, page 5.) Drain for at least 1 hour, and up to 3 hours. Transfer to medium bowl; reserve for further use.

SESAME LEMON CUCUMBER SALAD
Serves 4 as a side dish

This salad, with its Asian flavor, is a takeoff on one found in Annie Somerville's cookbook *Fields of Greens* (Bantam, 1993).

- 1/4 cup rice vinegar
- 1 tablespoon juice from 1 small lemon
- 2 tablespoons Asian sesame oil
- 2 teaspoons sugar
- 1/8 teaspoon dried red pepper flakes plus more to taste
- 1 tablespoon sesame seeds, toasted in a pan over medium heat until fragrant and golden, 4 to 5 minutes
- 3 medium cucumbers, sliced, salted and drained (*see* directions above)

Whisk all ingredients except cucumbers in medium bowl. Add cucumbers; toss to coat. Serve chilled or at room temperature.

SWEET-AND-TART CUCUMBER SALAD
Serves 4 as a side dish

Based on a common Thai relish served with saté, this salad is also great with grilled salmon (*see* "How to Grill Salmon," page 6) or grilled chicken breasts (*see* "Grilled Chicken Breasts," page 14).

- 1/2 cup rice vinegar
- 2 1/2 tablespoons sugar
- 3 medium cucumbers, sliced, salted and drained (*see* directions above)
- 1/2 medium red onion, sliced very thin
- 2 small jalapeño chiles, seeded and minced (or more, to taste)

1. Bring 2/3 cup water and vinegar to boil in small nonreactive saucepan over medium heat. Stir in sugar to dissolve; reduce heat and simmer 15 minutes. Cool to room temperature.

2. Meanwhile, mix cucumbers, onions, and jalapeños in medium bowl. Pour dressing over cucumber mixture; toss to coat. Serve chilled.

YOGURT MINT CUCUMBER SALAD
Serves 4 as a side dish

- 1 cup plain low-fat yogurt
- 2 tablespoons extra-virgin olive oil
- 1/4 cup minced fresh mint leaves
- 2 small garlic cloves, minced
- 1/2 teaspoon ground cumin
  Salt and ground black pepper
- 3 medium cucumbers, sliced, salted and drained (*see* directions above)

Whisk first five ingredients, and salt and pepper to taste, in medium bowl. Add cucumbers; toss to coat. Serve chilled, adjusting seasonings if necessary.

CREAMY DILL CUCUMBER SALAD
Serves 4 as a side dish

Salting and draining the onion along with the cucumbers in this recipe removes the sharp sting of raw onion.

- 1 cup sour cream
- 3 tablespoons cider vinegar
- 1 teaspoon sugar
- 1/4 cup minced fresh dill
  Salt and ground black pepper
- 3 medium cucumbers, sliced, salted and drained (*see* directions above)
- 1/2 medium red onion, sliced very thin, salted and drained with cucumbers

Whisk first four ingredients, and salt and pepper to taste, in medium bowl. Add cucumbers and onion; toss to coat. Serve chilled, adjusting seasonings if necessary.

Building A Better Shrimp Cocktail

Yes, you can make a better shrimp cocktail;
all it takes is making a few easy adjustments.

by Mark Bittman

❧

Nothing is more basic than shrimp cocktail, and given its simplicity, few dishes are more difficult to improve. Yet I set out to do just that this past winter and believe I succeeded.

Shrimp cocktail, as everyone must know, is "boiled" shrimp served cold with "cocktail" sauce, typically a blend of bottled ketchup or chili sauce spiked with horseradish. It's easy enough to change the basic pattern in order to produce a more contemporary cold shrimp dish; you could, for example, grill shrimp and serve them with a fresh tomato salsa (and many people have done just that). But there is something refreshing and utterly classic about traditional shrimp cocktail, and sometimes it fits the occasion better than anything else.

I saw three ways to challenge the traditional method of preparing shrimp cocktail in order to produce the best-tasting but recognizable version of this dish. One, work on the flavor of the shrimp; two, work on the cooking method for the shrimp; three, produce a great cocktail sauce.

Flavoring the Shrimp

The shrimp in shrimp cocktail can be ice-cold strings of protein, chewy or mushy, or they can be tender, flavorful morsels that barely need sauce. To achieve the latter, you need to start with the best shrimp you can find (*see* "A Shrimp-Buying Guide," page 13) and give them as much flavor as they can handle without overwhelming them.

If you start with good shrimp and follow a typical shrimp cocktail recipe—that is, simmer the shrimp in salted water until pink—the shrimp will have decent but rarely intense flavor. The easiest way to intensify the flavor of shrimp is to cook them in their shells. But, as I found out, this has its drawbacks. First of all, it's far easier to peel shrimp when they are raw than once they are cooked. More importantly, however, the full flavor of the shells is not extracted during the relatively short time required for the shrimp to cook through. It takes a good twenty minutes to transfer the flavor of the shells to the cooking water, far too long to keep shrimp in a pot.

It's better, then, to make shrimp stock, a simple enough process that takes only twenty minutes using just the shrimp shells, and a process that can be vastly improved if you make it

gradually. To do so, every time you use shrimp for any purpose, place the peels in a pot with water to cover, then simmer them for twenty minutes. Cool, strain, and freeze the resultant stock. Use this stock as the cooking liquid for your next batch of shrimp peels. Naturally, this stock will become more and more intense each time you add to it. Even after one batch of peels, however, it's infinitely better than plain water for cooking shrimp.

Next, I thought, it would be best to see what other flavors would complement the shrimp without overpowering it. My first attempt was to use beer and a spicy commercial seasoning, but this was a near disaster; the shrimp for cocktail should not taste like a New Orleans crab boil. Next I tried a court bouillon, the traditional herb-scented stock for poaching fish, but quickly discovered that the game wasn't worth the candle; I wanted a few quick additions to my shrimp stock that would add complexity without making a simple process complicated.

After trying about twenty different combinations, involving wine, vinegar, lemon juice, and a near ludicrous number of herbs and spices, I settled on the mixture given in the recipe here. It contains about 25 percent white wine, a dash of lemon juice, and a more-or-less

After poaching shrimp in a simple shrimp stock, strain the stock and reserve it for next time—the poaching gives it a very good flavor.

traditional herb combination. Variations are certainly possible, but I would caution you against adding more wine or lemon juice; both were good up to a point, but after that their pungency became overwhelming.

Cooking the Shrimp

Although I was pleased at this point with the quality of the shrimp's flavor, I still thought it could be more intense. I quickly learned, however, that the answer to this problem was not to keep pouring flavorings into the cooking liquid; that was self-defeating because I eventually lost the flavor of the shrimp. I decided to try to keep the shrimp in contact with the flavorings for a longer period of time.

I tried several methods to achieve this, including starting the shrimp in cold water with the seasonings and using a longer cooking time at a lower temperature. But shrimp cooks so quickly—this is part of its appeal, of course—that these methods only served to toughen the meat. What worked best, I found, was to bring the cooking liquid to a boil, turn it off, and add the shrimp. Depending on their size, I could leave them in contact with the liquid for up to ten minutes (even a little longer for jumbo shrimp), during which time they would cook through without toughening, while taking on near perfect flavor.

The Cocktail Sauce

Here I felt I was treading a fine line. I wanted to make a better sauce, but I still wanted it to be recognizable as cocktail sauce. Starting with fresh or canned tomatoes, I discovered, just didn't work: The result was often terrific (some might say preferable), but it was not cocktail sauce. It was as if I had decided to make a better version of liver and onions by substituting foie gras for veal liver—it might be "better," but it would no longer be liver and onions.

I went so far as to make American-style ketchup from scratch, an interesting project but not especially profitable, in that the effect was to duplicate something sold in near-perfect form in the supermarket. Again, there are more interesting tomato-based sauces than ketchup, but they're not ketchup.

So I decided the best thing I could do was to find the bottled ketchup or chili sauce I liked best and season it myself. First I had to determine which made the better base, ketchup or chili sauce. The answer to this question was surprising but straightforward: ketchup. Bottled chili sauce is little more than vinegary ketchup with a host of seasonings added. The less expensive chili sauces have the acrid, bitter taste of garlic powder, monosodium glutamate, or other dried seasonings. The more expensive ones have more honest flavors but still did not compare to the cocktail sauce I whipped up in three minutes using basic store-bought ketchup. In addition, chili sauce can be four to eight times as expensive as ketchup.

My preference in cocktail sauce has always been to emphasize the horseradish. But ketchup and horseradish, I knew, were not enough. Cocktail sauce benefits from a variety of heat sources, none of which overpower the other, and the sum of which still allows the flavor of the shrimp to come through. I liked the addition of chili powder. I also liked a bit of bite from cayenne, but only a pinch. Black pepper plays a favorable role as well (as does salt, even though ketchup is already salty). Finally, after trying high-quality wine vinegar, balsamic vinegar, rice vinegar, sherry vinegar, and distilled vinegar, I went back to lemon, which is the gentlest and most fragrant acidic seasoning. In sum, the keys to good cocktail sauce include: ordinary ketchup, fresh lemon juice, horseradish (fresh is best—even month-old bottled horseradish is pathetic compared to a just-opened bottle), and fresh chili powder. Proportions can be varied to taste.

HERB-POACHED SHRIMP
Serves 4
Note: When using larger or smaller shrimp, increase or decrease cooking times for shrimp by one to two minutes, respectively.

- 1 pound large (16 to 20 count) shrimp, peeled, deveined, and rinsed, shells reserved (*see* "A Shrimp-Buying Guide")
- 1 teaspoon salt
- 1 cup dry white wine
- 4 peppercorns
- 5 coriander seeds
- 1/2 bay leaf
- 5 sprigs fresh parsley
- 1 sprig fresh tarragon
- 1 teaspoon juice from 1 small lemon

1. Bring reserved shells, 3 cups water, and salt to boil in medium saucepan over medium-high heat; reduce heat to low, cover, and simmer until fragrant, about 20 minutes. Strain stock through sieve, pressing on shells to extract all liquid.

2. Bring stock and remaining ingredients except shrimp to boil in 3- or 4-quart saucepan over high heat; boil 2 minutes. Turn off heat and stir in shrimp; cover and let stand until firm and pink, about 8–10 minutes. Drain shrimp, reserving stock for another use. Plunge shrimp into ice water to stop cooking, then drain again. Serve shrimp chilled with cocktail sauce.

A SHRIMP-BUYING GUIDE

It's safe to say that any shrimp you buy have been frozen (and usually thawed by the retailer), but not all shrimp are the same—far from it. The Gulf of Mexico supplies about two hundred million pounds of shrimp annually to the rest of the country, but three times that amount is imported, mostly from Asia and Central and South America.

Frozen boxed shrimp is the best bet for flavor and texture.

After tasting all of the commonly available varieties of shrimp several times, I have little trouble declaring two winners: Mexican whites (*Panaeus vannamei*), from the Pacific coast, are usually the best. A close second, and often just as good, is Gulf whites (*P. setiferus*). Either of these may be wild or farm-raised. Unfortunately these are rarely the shrimp you're offered in supermarkets. The shrimp most commonly found in supermarkets is Black Tiger, a farmed shrimp from Asia whose quality is inconsistent but which can be quite flavorful and firm. And even if you go into a fishmonger's and ask for white shrimp, you may get farm-raised shrimp from China—a less expensive but decidedly inferior species (*P. chinensis*). (There are more than three hundred species of shrimp in the world and not nearly as many common names.)

All you can do is try to buy the best shrimp available, and buy it right. Beyond choosing the best species you can find, here are some of the other factors affecting quality:

- Buy still-frozen shrimp rather than those that have been thawed. Because almost all shrimp are frozen after the catch, **White Shrimp** and thawed shrimp start losing their flavor in just a couple of days, buying thawed shrimp gives you neither the flavor of fresh nor the flexibility of frozen. I found that shrimp stored in the freezer retain peak quality for several weeks, deteriorating very slowly after that until about the three-month point, at which I detected a noticeable difference in quality.

- Avoid prepeeled and deveined shrimp; cleaning before freezing unquestionably deprives shrimp of some of their flavor and texture; everyone I asked to sample precleaned shrimp found them to be nearly tasteless. In addition, precleaned shrimp may have added tripolyphosphate, a chemical which aids in water retention.

Tiger Shrimp

- Shrimp should have no black spots, or melanosis, on their shells, which indicate that a breakdown of the meat has begun. Be equally suspicious of shrimp with yellowing shells, or those that feel gritty, either of which may indicate the overuse of sodium bisulfite, a bleaching agent sometimes used to retard melanosis.

- If you buy thawed shrimp, they should smell of salt water and little else, and be firm and fully fill their shells.

- If your palate is sensitive to iodine—mine isn't, but my wife's is—you might also want to steer clear of Gulf brown shrimp (*P. aztecus*), especially large ones, which are most likely to taste of this naturally occurring element. The iodine is found in a type of plankton that makes up a large part of the diet of brown shrimp.

- Despite the popularity of shrimp, there are no standards for size. Small, medium, large, extra large, jumbo, and other size classifications are subjective and relative. Small shrimp of seventy or so to the pound are frequently labeled "medium," as are those twice that size and even larger. It pays, then, to judge shrimp size by the number it takes to make a pound, as retailers do. Shrimp labeled "16/20," for example, require sixteen to twenty (usually closer to twenty) individual specimens to make a pound. Those labeled "U-20" require fewer (under) twenty to make a pound. Shrimp of fifteen or twenty to about thirty per pound usually yield the best combination of flavor, ease (peeling tiny shrimp is a nuisance), and value (really big shrimp usually cost more than $10 per pound).

Most frozen shrimp are sold in blocks of five pounds (or two kilos, slightly less than that), and should be defrosted in the refrigerator or in cold water. Partial defrosting to cut off a piece of the block, while not ideal, has also worked well in my kitchen. Refreeze the remainder for later use.—M.B.

COCKTAIL SAUCE
Makes 1 cup, serving 4
Use horseradish from a fresh bottle and mild chili powder for the best flavor.

- 1 cup ketchup
- 2 1/2 teaspoons prepared horseradish
- 1/4 teaspoon salt
- 1/4 teaspoon ground black pepper
- 1 teaspoon ancho or other mild chili powder
- Pinch cayenne pepper
- 1 tablespoon juice from 1 small lemon

Stir all ingredients together in small bowl; adjust seasonings as necessary.

How to Grill Bone-in Chicken Breasts

*Brine if you have the time, then cook over a two-level fire and cover the breasts
for most of the cooking time—but not with the grill cover.*

by John Willoughby and Chris Schlesinger

❦

To use an expression from our grandparents' time, grilling bone-in chicken breast is a real bear. A chicken breast is thick, it's got a bone to contend with, and it needs to be thoroughly cooked all the way through while the skin gets nice and crisp but doesn't burn. Achieving all of this is a feat of grilling legerdemain, with a higher level of difficulty than other seemingly more impressive feats such as grilling a whole fish. In fact, our usual practice has been simply to choose the boneless option when grilling chicken breasts, or substitute more forgiving chicken thighs or legs.

But when properly grilled, bone-in breasts can be particularly tasty, with a kind of meatiness often lacking in boneless breasts. So we set out on a quest for the perfect grilled bone-in chicken breast, one with a juicy, tender, evenly cooked interior, a nicely seared, crispy skin, and a robust grilled flavor.

Just as we did a year ago when grilling chicken legs and thighs (see "Grilling Chicken Legs and Thighs," July/August 1996), we decided to check out every backyard myth, rumor, and crackpot idea about how best to grill this popular chicken part. After all, sometimes the strangest ideas prove to be the best.

Having surveyed the field, we found that the various approaches could be divided into three distinct groups, each designed to address the problem of cooking the chicken all the way through without burning the outside. Some cooks rely on partially cooking the chicken before it goes on the grill; others reverse the strategy, starting the chicken out over the coals and then finishing it off the grill. Yet others favor completely cooking the chicken on the grill, either moving or covering it at some point during the process to slow the cooking of the exterior.

Grill Second, Grill First
For our first set of tests, we partially cooked the breast by successively poaching, microwaving, and roasting it before placing it on the grill for final cooking. The poached version looked good on the outside, but the interior was dry, chewy, almost stringy, with little of the smoky flavor we look for in grilled food. The microwaved breast also had beautifully golden skin by the time it came off the grill, but again

To get crisp, nicely seared skin and a breast that is evenly cooked all the way through, you need a combination of high heat, low heat, and an improvised cover.

the interior was dry, with a rubbery texture even worse than the poached version. The roasted version had good grilled flavor and a better texture, but was still dry.

We quickly moved on to those methods that involved starting the breasts on the grill to give them flavor and a good sear, then using other cooking methods to finish cooking.

The microwave once again produced a dry, rubbery breast, while roasting in a 350-degree oven after searing resulted in a breast that was juicy and tender, but unevenly cooked and with little grilled flavor. Increasing the oven heat to 450, though, brought us very close to our goal: tender, very juicy, evenly cooked all the way through, with a crisp, golden skin and good grill flavor. Of all the combination cooking methods, this one was definitely the best, but it still wasn't ideal.

The Grill Alone
Next we went on to the real challenge, the unassisted grill. We were hopeful of finding a winning strategy here, thus avoiding the cumbersome necessity of firing up both the grill and the oven to cook a single dish. We were pretty sure that it would involve using a two-level fire (see illustrations 1 and 2, page 16) with a hot area for searing and a cooler area for slower cooking, but we were unsure about how the cover would come into play.

We figured that it might be possible to grill the breasts without covering them at all, providing a low enough level of heat was used. So we tried starting over a low fire and then moving them to the area with no coals to finish cooking by indirect heat. Unfortunately, the results would best be described as "erratic." The skin was unevenly seared, brown in some spots and black in others, and although the interior appeared evenly cooked, most portions were dry and slightly chewy while a few were inexplicably moist.

After this fiasco, we went back to starting with a medium-hot fire. This time we seared the breasts directly over the coals, then moved them to the low portion of the fire. The skin was nicely seared this time, with good grill flavor, and the meat was more evenly cooked than in the previous attempt, but it was still dry and chewy.

Next we tried the method most often recommended by the manufacturers of covered grills (the type of grill we favor because of its versatility), searing and then covering to finish cooking (over the medium-hot coals). When these breasts came off the grill they looked great, with beautiful dark golden brown skin and flesh that was a uniform off-white throughout.

When we tasted them, though, we experienced the same phenomenon we had come across during last summer's experiments with chicken legs and thighs. The chicken had a slight but noticeable unpleasant taste, a kind of stale smokiness, slightly ashy and a bit metallic. This taste, which is very different from the pleasant smokiness we look for in grilled food, results whenever food is cooked on a covered grill for a relatively short period of time. If the food stays on the grill for forty-five minutes or more, the smoke flavor becomes strong enough to predominate—but less than that, and the result is chicken with that "covered" flavor.

PHOTOGRAPH BY CARL TREMBLAY

So what were we to do? Without the cover the chicken was dry; with the cover it had a flavor we didn't like. We decided to try a version of an old restaurant trick, covering the chicken with a pie plate, a maneuver that creates somewhat of an oven effect but also allows air to circulate around the cooking food. Because we wanted to cook several breasts at the same time and figured few home cooks would have a collection of metal pie plates to use as covers, we substituted a disposable aluminum roasting pan. After five minutes over the coals to acquire a good sear, the breasts were moved to the cooler part of the fire, covered with the pan, and cooked for fifteen minutes.

At last we had success, with breasts that hit on all cylinders. The skin was nicely seared and crisp, the flesh was tender, evenly cooked, and juicy throughout, and a bite revealed that great, smoky grill flavor with no stale taste at all. This was great chicken breast.

Brining

We had found our method, but there was one refinement we wanted to try. Following in the footsteps of executive editor Pam Anderson, who had found that brining a turkey before roasting it improved both flavor and texture (see "The Holiday Turkey Perfected," November/December 1993), we had found in last year's tests that a long dunk in brine also improved chicken legs and thighs. We suspected it would be the same for breasts.

We did discover one problem with the sugar/salt brine, which was that the skin tended to burn rather quickly during the searing process. In an attempt to remedy this, we brined some breasts in a salt-only solution. This made it easier to sear without burning, and the chicken was still moist and juicy, with that same robust grilled flavor and crispy skin. However, the flesh had a saltier taste than the breasts brined with sugar solution, so in the end we came down on the side of the combined brine. It just means that, during those first few minutes of cooking, you need to keep a close

MAINTAINING TEMPERATURE

Covering with a disposable roasting pan creates an oven-like effect, but still allows air to circulate.

eye on the grill, which is not a bad idea whenever you're cooking something directly over the coals, anyway.

MASTER RECIPE FOR GRILLED BONE-IN CHICKEN BREASTS
Serves 4

Flavorings can be added to these chicken breasts before or during cooking: Rub them with a spice rub before they go on the grill or brush them with barbecue sauce during the final two minutes of cooking. Although they won't be quite as plump or deeply flavored, the breasts can also be grilled without brining them first. To do so, simply omit step 1 in the recipe below and sprinkle the breasts generously with salt and pepper before placing them on the grill. Also, if the fire flares because of dripping fat or a gust of wind, move the chicken to the area without coals until the flames die down.

- 3/4 cup kosher salt (or 6 tablespoons table salt)
- 3/4 cup sugar
- 4 split chicken breasts (bone-in, skin-on), 10 to 12 ounces each
  Ground black pepper

1. In gallon-size zipper-lock plastic bag, dissolve salt and sugar in 1 quart water. Add chicken, then seal bag, pressing out as much air as possible; refrigerate until fully seasoned, about 1½ hours. Remove from brine, rinse well, dry thoroughly with paper towel, and season with pepper to taste or spice rub (see recipe, below).

2. Meanwhile, ignite enough charcoal briquettes or hardwood charcoal to fill slightly less than two shoeboxes and burn until completely covered with thin coating of light gray ash, 20 to 30 minutes. When coals are medium-hot (you can hold your hand 5 inches above the grill surface for 4 seconds), spread coals out over half of grill bottom, leaving other half with no coals (see illustration 1, page 16); position grill rack over fire.

3. Place chicken, skin side down, on rack directly over coals; grill until well-browned, 2 to 3 minutes per side. Move chicken to area with no fire and cover with disposable aluminum roasting pan; continue to cook, skin side up, 10 minutes. Turn and cook 5 minutes more. To test for doneness, either peek into thickest part of chicken with tip of small knife (you should see no redness near bone) or check internal temperature at thickest part with instant-read thermometer, which should register 160 degrees. Transfer to serving platter; serve warm or at room temperature.

SPICE-RUBBED GRILLED BONE-IN CHICKEN BREASTS

If brining chicken, proceed with step 1 of Master Recipe for Grilled Bone-In Chicken Breasts. Mix 2 tablespoons each ground cumin, curry powder, and chili powder, 1 tablespoon each allspice and ground black pep-

per, and 1 teaspoon cinnamon in small bowl. Rub prepared chicken generously with mixture; proceed with Master Recipe, starting at step 2.

GRILLED BONE-IN CHICKEN BREASTS WITH BARBECUE SAUCE

Follow Master Recipe for Grilled Bone-in Chicken Breasts. During last 2 minutes of cooking, remove roasting pan, brush breasts generously with barbecue sauce of choice (see recipes, below), cook about 1 minute, turn over, brush again, and cook 1 minute more. Transfer to serving platter, brush with additional barbecue sauce to taste, and serve.

BASIC BARBECUE SAUCE
Makes 3 cups

- 2 tablespoons vegetable oil
- 1 medium onion, minced
- 1 can (8 ounces) tomato sauce
- 1 can (28 ounces) whole tomatoes with juice
- 3/4 cup distilled white vinegar
- 1/4 cup packed dark brown sugar
- 2 tablespoons molasses
- 1 tablespoon each paprika and chili powder
- 2 teaspoons liquid smoke (optional)
- 1 teaspoon salt
- 2 teaspoons ground black pepper
- 1/4 cup juice from 1 medium orange

1. Heat oil in large, heavy-bottomed saucepan over medium heat until hot and shimmering (but not smoking). Add onion; sauté until golden brown, 7 to 10 minutes, stirring frequently. Add remaining ingredients. Bring to boil, then reduce heat to lowest possible setting and simmer, uncovered, until thickened, 2 to 2½ hours.

2. Puree sauce, in batches if necessary, in blender or workbowl of food processor. Transfer to bowl or cover in airtight container. (Can be refrigerated for up to 2 weeks.)

BARBECUE SAUCE WITH MEXICAN FLAVORS

Follow recipe for Basic Barbecue Sauce to completion, adding 1½ teaspoons ground cumin, 1½ teaspoons chili powder, 6 tablespoons juice from 2 limes, and 3 tablespoons chopped fresh cilantro leaves to room temperature sauce.

BARBECUE SAUCE WITH ASIAN FLAVORS

Follow recipe for Basic Barbecue Sauce to completion, adding 1 tablespoon peeled, minced gingerroot, 6 tablespoons soy sauce, 6 tablespoons wine vinegar, 3 tablespoons sugar, and 1½ tablespoons Asian sesame oil to room temperature sauce.

Chris Schlesinger, chef-owner of the East Coast Grill in Cambridge, Massachusetts, is coauthor with **John Willoughby** of five cookbooks, including *License to Grill* (Morrow, 1997).

GRILLING FUELS, TOOLS, AND RULES

Whether you're grilling chicken breasts (see page 14), salmon (page 6), or using your covered grill to approximate Southern barbecue (page 18), these recommendations for the best fuels and the right tools, along with some tips for making the process work more smoothly, should come in handy.

FUELS

Commonly available fuels include (clockwise, from top right) charcoal briquettes, lump hardwood charcoal, wood chips, and hardwood logs. We recommend hardwood charcoal if you can get hold of it. If you want to add some smokiness, we recommend hardwood logs or wood chunks. If using wood chips for smoke flavor, wrap them in aluminum foil, poke some holes in the foil, and put them directly on the coals.

STARTING THE FIRE

Our favorite way to start a charcoal fire is to use a flue starter, also known as a chimney starter. To use this simple device, fill the bottom section with crumpled newspaper, set the flue on the grill grate, and fill the top with charcoal. When you light the newspaper, flames will shoot up through the charcoal, igniting it. When the coals are well lit, dump them out onto the grate and add the rest of the charcoal.

BASIC TOOLS

Many grill manufacturers produce long-handled tools for use with the grill, such as those pictured at left. These tools are perfectly fine, but you can usually get less expensive, sturdier tools by buying them individually at a hardware store.

A long-handled fork, paintbrush, spring-loaded tongs, dogleg spatula, and wire brush for cleaning the grill, all pictured at left, are among the handiest tools to have.

ARRANGING THE FIRE

It is important to build a fire with two levels of heat, which can be done in one of two ways:

1. Place the coals all on one side of the grill. This is the most useful configuration when you will be cooking at least part of the time directly over the coals.

2. Place the coals on either side of the grill. This is a useful configuration for indirect cooking because food placed in the center of the grill will get indirect heat from two sides.

OTHER HANDY GRILLING ACCOUTREMENTS

For smoke-roasting or barbecuing, an oven thermometer wedged and then taped into the vent hole will keep track of the temperature inside the grill.

Rib racks make it possible to cook a large number of ribs simultaneously.

Half-moon-shaped baskets can be used to keep coals neatly along the edges of the grill.

Some manufacturers now sell grill grids with hinged sections, which makes it much easier to add charcoal to the fire during grilling.

Another option for this task is a wire "fence" that hooks to the grill grate.

ILLUSTRATIONS BY ANATOLY

GRILLING TIPS

When grilling a lobster, take a cue from Jasper White, author of the forthcoming *Lobster at Home* (Scribner's) and place it on the grill underside up; the hard shell will protect the meat from burning, and the juices will stay in the shell rather than dripping into the coals.

To help prevent sticking, oil vegetables and lean-fleshed fish lightly before placing them on the grill. Toss vegetables in a bowl with oil, salt, and pepper; brush fish very lightly, using a brush or your hand.

To check the gas level in your propane tank, do the following:

1. Pour a cup of boiling water over the tank.

2. Feel the metal with your hand. Where the water has succeeded in warming the tank, it is empty; where it remains cool to the touch, there is still propane inside.

You can use an indirect fire to cook many items simultaneously. Here, steak grills directly over the coals, vegetables cook around the periphery of the fire where the heat is medium, and bread toasts along the edges of the grill.

Before you begin grilling, assemble all of your tools and place them on a table set right next to the grill.

Just before placing fish on the grill grid, you might want to dip a large wad of paper towels into vegetable oil, grab it with tongs, and wipe the grid thoroughly to lubricate it. This will also clean any remaining residue off the grid.

When threading meat onto skewers, push the pieces closely together if you want the meat to cook less, and space them slightly apart if you want the meat more thoroughly cooked.

If small pieces of charcoal tend to fall through the lower grill grate, place a small cooling rack on the grate at a 90-degree angle, making a smaller grid.

Onions that are cut into quarters with some of the root end left intact will hold together on the grill.

To prevent round items like cherry tomatoes and mushroom caps from rolling around when you turn over the skewers (resulting in the same side once again facing down), thread them onto double skewers.

Home-Style Pulled Pork Barbecue

For the most tender, succulent home version of this Southern classic,
you need two unusual elements: plastic wrap and a paper sack.

by A. Cort Sinnes

When you go chasing after barbecue, it's like being turned on your head, spun around a few times, and then turned loose on a crooked road on a foggy night. To make matters worse, it's not only a crooked road, but there are thousands of side streets and detours along the way. I know—I have been on the road to barbecue before.

When I decided to write an article on a very specific type of barbecue, namely, pulled pork, I thought my previous experiences would stand me in good stead and I'd be able to head straight toward my destination.

Not so.

To give you an idea of just how convoluted this particular dish is, there's not even agreement as to its name. If you say "pulled pork" in parts of central South Carolina, you'll get a blank stare and a "Say what?" in response. After explaining what it is, people will say, "Oh, you mean barbecue...." For the sake of this article—no matter if you call it pulled pork, pulled pig, or just plain barbecue—here's what we're talking about: slow-cooked pork roast, shredded and seasoned, served on the most basic of hamburger buns (or sliced white bread), with just enough of your favorite barbecue sauce, a couple of dill pickle chips, and a topping of coleslaw. This is classic summertime party food, designed to please on a primal level of pleasure.

My goal was to devise a procedure for cooking this classic Southern dish that was at once both doable and delicious, one that would not require any special equipment (such as a smoker) nor an inordinate time commitment on the part of the cook (many barbecue procedures demand the regular attention of the cook for eight hours or longer!).

So once again I set out on the barbecue road. From pit masters in barbecue joints, attendees and lecturers at barbecue conventions, and a fair number of outstanding backyard barbecue chefs, I slowly began to piece together the few parts of the pulled pork puzzle that fit together neatly. Mike McGonigle of McGonigle's Meat Market in Kansas City (a mecca for barbecuers) showed me the differences between the various pork roasts and explained which had the best ratio of fat to meat so it wouldn't dry out during the long cooking process. From a very talented and savvy home cook, I learned the secret of long "marinating" with a dry rub, while an amateur barbecue contestant let me in on his technique of "wrap and rest."

As far as the actual recipes for seasoning the meat—with both a dry rub prior to cooking and a sauce for the meat after cooking—it was open season for me, with literally countless variations from one city to the next.

Flavored with smoke, spice rub, and sauce, pulled pork should be served on plain white bread with coleslaw.

What I finally ended up with is a recipe that is an amalgamation and distillation of many different procedures, practices, and opinions. So while my pulled pork may not resemble any one procedure for barbecuing that you're familiar with, it does, indeed, work, and work well. It requires that you pay attention to the three primary components of the dish: the meat, the rub, and the sauce.

The Meat

There are two pork roasts commonly associated with pulled pork sandwiches: the shoulder roast and the fresh ham (*see* diagram, page 19). In their whole state, both are massive roasts, anywhere from fourteen to twenty pounds. Because they are so large, most butchers and supermarket meat departments cut both the front and the back leg roasts into more manageable sizes: The part of the front leg containing the shoulder blade is usually sold as either a "pork shoulder roast" or a "Boston butt"

roast and runs from six to eight pounds. The meat from the upper portion of the front leg is marketed as a "picnic" roast and runs about the same size. The meat from the rear leg is often segmented into three or four separate boneless roasts, each usually called a "fresh ham" or a "boneless fresh ham roast."

For barbecue, it's always best to choose a cut of meat with a fair degree of fat, which helps keep the meat moist and succulent during long cooking and adds considerably to the flavor. For this reason, I found that the pork shoulder roast (or Boston butt, as it may be called in your market) is the best roast for pulled pork. But picnics and fresh hams will also produce excellent results.

Having decided on the particular cut to use, I went on to test various options for cooking it. To serve as a benchmark for quality, I first tried cooking the pork roast in the traditional low-and-slow barbecue method. Using a standard twenty-two-inch covered kettle grill, I lit approximately thirty-five coals and cooked the roast using the indirect method (with the roast not directly over the coals). Using this approach, and adding a few additional coals every thirty minutes or so, it took seven hours to cook a seven-pound roast. While the results were delicious, let's face it: Seven hours is fine for "high ceremonial cooking" as my barbecuing friends would say, but not practical for most people's schedules.

Next I tried modifying a technique I use with whole turkeys, namely, starting out with much more charcoal (approximately five pounds) and arranging it on either side of the coal grate. After the coals were ready, I placed the pork in a small pan to collect the juices, then positioned it in the center of the cooking grate and covered the grill, top and bottom vents all the way open. The trick to this more intense method is not to remove the lid for any reason until the fire is out (approximately three hours) with the obvious benefit of not having to add extra coals at regular intervals because you put in so many at the beginning. While this procedure works perfectly for large turkeys, the initial heat was too high for the pork roast, resulting in a overly charred exterior and meat that was not as "fork-tender."

Finally, I tried a combination approach: a moderate amount of charcoal (more than the low-and-slow method, but less than the no-peek procedure), cooking the pork roast for three hours on the grill (adding additional coal only four times), and finishing the roast in a 325-degree oven for two hours. This method produced almost the same results as the traditional barbecue, but in considerably less time and with much less effort.

But there was one more important component to the cooking technique, a step that many barbecue enthusiasts include in their instructions almost as an afterthought or simply as a matter of convenience even though it is actually crucial to good home barbecue. As soon as the roast comes out of the oven, you place it inside a paper grocery sack, and let it rest for a full hour. This resting time allows flavorful juices to be reabsorbed by the meat. In addition, it produces a steaming effect that helps break down any remaining tough collagen. The result is a much more savory and succulent roast.

The Dry Rub

Dry rubs are a fantastic way of flavoring any food destined for the grill or smoker. Once you get the hang of them, you may find that you marinate food less and use dry rubs a lot more. If you are new to dry rubs, they are nothing more than a combination of dry seasonings meant to be rubbed into food (primarily meat) prior to cooking.

As with any other aspect of barbecuing, there is considerable controversy over not only what is the best combination of spices, but how to combine them, and even how to apply them. There are some who say the spices should be ground together with a mortar and pestle, others who resort to the convenience of grinding them in an electric coffee grinder or spice mill, and finally those who simply buy the individual spices off the shelf, mix them in a bowl, and call it done. It's your call, but most longtime barbecuers favor the last method; while home-ground spices have more pungent flavors, they are, to put it simply, also a lot more work. For an even simpler method, you can follow the example of those who simply layer one spice over another directly onto the meat.

From repeated experiments, I found that the pork roast absorbs the most flavor from the dry rub if you apply the rub twenty-four hours in advance of cooking it. You can get by with as little as three hours, but the flavor of the dry rub will not permeate the roast like it does with a longer "marinating" time. This is because the salt in the rub, which is slowly absorbed into the meat, carries some of the other spices with it. You should not let the meat sit with the spice rub on it too longer, however; I found that after seventy-two hours the spice flavors overpowered the meat flavor.

The Sauce

Almost all traditional pulled pork recipes involve tossing the shredded meat in a sauce—and that's precisely where the agreement ends. Once again we're in contentious territory where anything stated is sure to offend someone, somewhere. In the Carolinas, where pulled pork is a regional specialty, you might expect there to be some difference of opinion between North and South, but noooooo, they don't even agree about what constitutes a sauce within the boundaries of the state lines. In eastern South Carolina, people like a tangy combination of vinegar and pepper; in the middle section of the state, they favor a mustard-based concoction; and in the western parts, you see the introduction of tomatoes or ketchup. As for North Carolina, the eastern part of the state favors a vinegar and red pepper combo while the Piedmont region adds a little ketchup to vinegar and red pepper sauce—and go west and you'll have a sweeter experience with the addition of tomatoes and brown sugar.

Recognizing the many possibilities, I have given three recipes as a jumping-off point for any and all personal modifications.

MASTER RECIPE FOR PULLED PORK
Serves 8

Preparing pulled pork requires little effort, but lots of time. Plan on nine hours from start to finish: three hours with the spice rub, three hours on the grill, two hours in the oven, and one hour to rest. To give the meat its characteristic smoky flavor, use either hickory chips that you've wrapped in foil pouches or add one medium to large chunk of hickory. We prefer the chunk, even though it has to be soaked in water for at least one hour, whereas the chips do not require soaking. If you go with the chip pouches, the number will determine how strong a smoky flavor you get: One pouch is detectable, two noticeable, and three assertive. Serve the pulled pork on plain white bread or warmed buns with the classic accompaniments of dill pickle chips and coleslaw.

1   recipe Spicy Chili Rub (*see* page 20)
1   bone-in pork roast, 6 to 8 pounds

(preferably shoulder or Boston butt roast, *see* illustration, below)
1   recipe Carolina-Style Barbecue Sauce (*see* sauce options, page 20)

1. If using a fresh ham, remove skin (*see* illustration 1). Massage dry rub into meat (*see* illustration 2). Wrap tightly in double layer of plastic wrap (*see* illustration 3); refrigerate for at least 3, but no longer than 72, hours.

2. At 1 hour prior to cooking, remove roast from refrigerator to stand at room temperature. Soak hickory chunk or assemble hickory chip pouches by wrapping a large handful of wood chips in each of one to three 12-inch squares of tin foil (*see* note above). Prick each foil pack with fork tines to allow smoke to escape. Meanwhile, ignite enough charcoal briquettes or hardwood charcoal to fill slightly less than two shoeboxes, and burn until completely covered with thin coating light gray ash, 20 to 30 minutes.

3. Open bottom grill vents and arrange hot coals into two equal piles on opposite sides of grill, place chunk or pouch(es) directly on one pile of coal, and set grill rack in place. Set unwrapped roast in disposable pan (illustration 4) and place on rack between two piles of coal. Open grill lid vents three-quarters of the way and cover, turning lid so that vents are opposite chunk or pouch(es) to draw smoke through and around roast. Cook, adding fifteen to twenty briquettes every 30 to 40 minutes or seven to ten pieces lump charcoal every 15 to 20 minutes, along with additional pouches (if using), until smoke flavor has fully permeated meat, about 3 hours.

4. Adjust oven rack to middle position and preheat oven to 325 degrees. Place roast in pan and wrap with foil to cover completely. Place pan in oven and bake until meat is fork-tender, about 2 hours.

5. Put foil-wrapped roast in pan into doubled grocery bag (illustration 5). Crimp top

CUTS OF PORK FOR BARBECUE

BOSTON BUTT

PICNIC

FRESH HAM

Although all three of these cuts make good barbecue, Boston butt is the first choice because it has enough fat to stay moist and succulent during the long cooking process.

shut; rest roast 1 hour. Transfer roast to cutting board and unwrap. When cool enough to handle, "pull" pork by separating roast into muscle sections (illustration 6), removing fat if desired, and tearing meat into thin shreds with fingers. Place shredded meat in large bowl (illustration 7); toss with 1 cup barbecue sauce, adding more to taste. Serve with remaining sauce passed separately.

SPICY CHILI RUB
Makes 1 cup

- 1 tablespoon ground black pepper
- 2 teaspoons cayenne pepper
- 2 tablespoons chili powder
- 2 tablespoons ground cumin
- 2 tablespoons dark brown sugar
- 1 tablespoon ground oregano
- 4 tablespoons paprika
- 2 tablespoons salt
- 1 tablespoon granulated sugar
- 1 tablespoon ground white pepper

Mix all ingredients in small bowl.

EASTERN NORTH CAROLINA–STYLE BARBECUE SAUCE
Makes 2 cups

Adapted from a recipe in Chris Schlesinger and John Willoughby's *The Thrill of the Grill* (Morrow, 1990), this is a classic pepper-spiked vinegar sauce.

- 1 cup distilled white vinegar
- 1 cup cider vinegar
- 1 tablespoon sugar
- 1 tablespoon crushed red pepper flakes
- 1 tablespoon hot red pepper sauce
  Salt and ground black pepper

Mix all ingredients, including salt and pepper to taste, in medium bowl.

MID–SOUTH CAROLINA MUSTARD SAUCE
Makes 2½ cups

The pulled pork tossed in this mustard sauce was the hands-down favorite at a recent party. Though we prefer the flavor of Dijon mustard in this sauce, feel free to substitute other mustards to suit your taste.

- 1 cup cider vinegar
- 6 tablespoons Dijon mustard
- 2 tablespoons maple syrup or honey
- 4 teaspoons Worcestershire sauce
- 1 teaspoon hot red pepper sauce
- 1 cup vegetable oil
- 2 teaspoons salt
  Ground black pepper

Mix all ingredients, including pepper to taste, in medium bowl.

WESTERN SOUTH CAROLINA–STYLE BARBECUE SAUCE
Makes 2 cups

Served originally at Mama Rosa's, a long-time barbecue pit restaurant in North Philadelphia, this recipe is adapted from Jim Tarantino's outstanding book *Marinades* (Crossing Press, 1992).

- 1 tablespoon vegetable oil
- ½ medium onion, minced
- 2 medium garlic cloves, minced
- ½ cup cider vinegar
- ½ cup Worcestershire sauce
- 1 tablespoon dry mustard
- 1 tablespoon dark brown sugar
- 1 tablespoon paprika
- 1 teaspoon salt
- 1 teaspoon cayenne pepper
- 1 cup ketchup

Heat oil in 2-quart saucepan over medium heat. Add onion and garlic; sauté until softened, 4 to 5 minutes. Stir in all the remaining ingredients except ketchup; bring to boil. Reduce heat to low, then add ketchup. Cook, stirring occasionally, until thickened, about 15 minutes.

A. Cort Sinnes' most recent book is *The Gas Grill Gourmet* (Harvard Common Press, 1996).

ESSENTIAL STEPS TO HOMEMADE PORK BARBECUE

1. If using a fresh ham or picnic roast, cut through the skin with the tip of a chef's knife. Slide the knife blade just under the skin and work around to loosen the skin while pulling it off with your other hand.

2. Cover the pork generously with the spice rub, pressing gently to make sure it adheres.

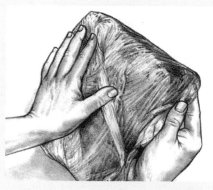

3. Wrap the meat tightly in plastic wrap and refrigerate for a minimum of 3 and a maximum of 72 hours.

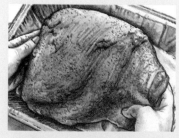

4. While the coals are heating, unwrap the meat and set it into a small, disposable aluminum roasting pan, barely larger than the meat itself.

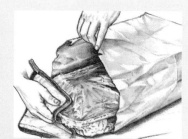

5. When the foil-covered meat has finished its time in the oven, transfer to a brown paper shopping bag, then crimp the bag shut and allow the meat to rest for 1 hour.

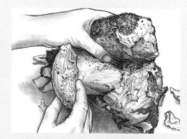

6. As soon as the meat is cool enough to handle, remove meat from bones and separate the major muscle sections with your fingers.

7. Remove as much fat as you want and tear the meat into thin strips.

ILLUSTRATIONS BY JUDY LOVE

Great Hot Fudge Sauce

*For a smooth, rich, silky sauce that turns chewy on ice cream, use
two types of chocolate and be careful about when you add them to the sauce.*

by Stephanie D. Zonis

Chocolate sauces come in innumerable types. They may be thin or viscous, sweet or bittersweet. Many are very simple, made only from chocolate, a liquid, and few other components. But as the queen of chocolate sauces, hot fudge sauce should be lush and complex. Commercial hot fudge sauces, while readily available, are overly sweet, lack chocolate flavor, and contain stabilizers or preservatives. I wanted to develop a master recipe for a smooth, rich sauce, with an intense chocolate impact. The sauce had to be thick and turn chewy over ice cream. And, because ice cream is relatively sweet, the sauce itself needed to be minimally so. I also wished to try a number of cooking techniques I had seen in various recipes.

Although I had tried out a number of hot fudge sauces over the years, I kept coming back to the same one. This sauce used one-half cup of heavy cream, three tablespoons of unsalted butter, one-third cup each of granulated and firmly packed dark brown sugar, a pinch of salt, and one-half cup of sifted Dutch process cocoa powder. To make it, the cream and butter were combined and brought to a boil over low heat. Both sugars were then added and dissolved, and just before the sauce was removed from the heat, salt and cocoa powder were whisked in.

I was pleased with the simplicity of this recipe. I enjoyed the richness contributed by the cream and butter, I liked the high gloss of the sauce, which turned nicely chewy over ice cream, and I appreciated the deep flavor and color of Dutch process cocoa. The use of a small quantity of salt heightened the chocolate flavor without giving a salty taste.

On the down side, however, I found the sauce too sweet. And, while it was definitely chocolaty, there was no complexity in the taste. Finally, I often found it impossible to dissolve the cocoa in the sauce as directed. Of the several batches I tried when preparing this article, all were lumpy. All the same, I felt that this was a sauce I could build upon.

The Right Ingredients

To fashion a sauce of my own, I first had to choose ingredients. Some were identical to those in my "building block" sauce, but now I added just enough water to regulate the consistency of the sauce, along with a little light corn syrup, which I discovered improved body and chewiness. Finally, I decided to add vanilla extract to increase aroma and flavor depth.

And because Dutch process cocoa alone did not provide the serious chocolate impact I sought, I decided to try adding semisweet chocolate to broaden the spectrum of chocolate flavor. I chose semisweet rather than unsweetened chocolate because experimentation had shown me that unsweetened chocolate, even when used along with Dutch process cocoa, resulted in a sauce with a dulled chocolate flavor.

Refining the Technique

Technique proved to be as important as the ingredients in getting the chocolate sauce I was looking for. Initially, I began by melting the chocolate, then I add the other components to the same pot, thus helping to maintain the I simplicity I admired. But the price of simplicity was too high. When the sauce was made this way, the sugar didn't always dissolve completely, even with near constant stirring and boiling of the sauce.

Taking a tip from candy making, I covered the boiling sauce for three minutes to allow accumulated steam to dissolve any sugar granules. This did aid in reducing graininess, but the chocolate stuck to the pot bottom and burned. I also noticed that all of the sauces I made using this technique ended up tasting cooked, which I figured was a consequence of overexposing the chocolate to heat (I wasn't as concerned about the cocoa). I concluded that it would be best to melt the chocolate first, but not to incorporate it into the sauce until the end of cooking time.

I revised my recipe so that the sugar, cocoa, and salt were thoroughly dissolved in the liquids. If there was no graininess before the sauce was boiled, I reasoned, there would be much less chance of any in the finished product. I then added the melted chocolate after cooking. The sauce was much smoother this way, but it still tasted cooked; evidently, the cocoa was more heat-sensitive than I'd realized. Long ago, I'd determined that a good way to dissolve Dutch process cocoa without cooking was to whisk it well into a previously melted chocolate. Thereafter, I employed this technique, dissolving the powder into the melted chocolate, and adding these two chocolate flavor sources to the sauce after it was cooked.

The Proper Chocolate

During the evolution of my sauce, I also had a lesson in the great differences between better-quality and lesser-quality chocolates. It may seem unnecessary to state that chocolate is a key ingredient in a hot fudge sauce, but its importance cannot be overemphasized. Always use the best ingredients you can find, but remember that chocolate is crucial here; the quality of what you use will tell in the end product.

So here it is: thick and smooth, rich beyond belief, and ultrachocolate. Once made, the sauce will keep for at least ten days tightly covered and refrigerated, but it must be served warm. When reheating, be sure to reheat only as much sauce as you need because repeated heating and chilling may make the sauce grainy. Scrape the sauce into a heat-proof bowl and set it over simmering water on low heat. Stir often, heating the sauce just until it is warm. Alternatively, you can reheat the sauce in the microwave at medium (50 percent) power for short intervals, stirring often, just until the sauce is warm.

HOT FUDGE SAUCE
Makes 2 cups

If you wish, melt the chocolate in the microwave at 50 percent power for three minutes, whisking the cocoa powder into the chocolate once it is melted.

- 10 ounces semisweet chocolate, chopped
- 1/3 cup sifted Dutch process cocoa powder
- 1/3 cup sugar
- 3/4 cup light corn syrup
- 1/3 cup heavy cream
- Pinch salt
- 1 teaspoon vanilla extract
- 3 tablespoons unsalted butter, cut into pieces

1. Melt chocolate in small heat-proof bowl set over pan of almost simmering water until smooth, stirring once or twice. Turn off heat and whisk in cocoa until dissolved; set aside.

2. Warm sugar, corn syrup, cream, salt, and 1/3 cup water in medium, heavy-bottomed, nonreactive saucepan over low heat without stirring until sugar dissolves. Increase heat to medium-high; simmer mixture, stirring frequently, about 4 minutes.

3. Turn off heat and whisk in vanilla and butter. Cool mixture slightly, about 2 minutes; whisk in melted chocolate. Serve warm. (Can be refrigerated in an airtight container at least 10 days before serving; reheat over simmering water or in microwave for 1 to 1 1/2 minutes, stirring several times, until sauce is shiny and completely smooth.)

Stephanie D. Zonis is a freelance writer living in New Jersey.

Semifreddo

*A cooked meringue is the secret to a light, airy, mousse-like version
of this classic Italian chilled dessert.*

by Michele Scicolone

❦

When I order semifreddo for dessert in a restaurant in Italy, I brace myself for a surprise. Since all kinds of chilled and frozen desserts come under this heading, which translates as "half cold," I might get anything from tiramisu to ice cream cake.

I do know what I hope for, though: something that resembles the version served at Diana, a bustling trattoria in Bologna, the unofficial semifreddo capital of Italy. Diana's semifreddo is a light vanilla mousse speckled with crushed amaretti cookies and nuts and frozen in a loaf-shaped mold, served in thick slices with a pot of bittersweet chocolate sauce for drizzling. Touched by the warm sauce, the semifreddo immediately begins to melt, blurring the line between cool, airy cream and smooth, rich chocolate.

With that semifreddo in mind, I began my quest for the perfect recipe. Not only did I want to be able to make the semifreddo that I remembered from the restaurant, I also wanted to develop a formula that could be adapted to a broad range of flavors, some typically Italian and some not.

I began by researching various Italian cookbooks and cooking magazines. Though I found several recipes, none seemed quite right. In a couple of cases, semifreddo was described as a type of ice cream, but I suspected that a standard ice cream formula would be too heavy because of the egg yolks. I also knew that if I froze a custard mixture without first churning it in an ice cream freezer, it would become icy and hard, and if I churned the mixture then molded it, it would be just a layered ice cream dessert.

As I remembered it, Diana's semifreddo seemed to be made with just whipped egg whites and cream. Both, I knew, would have to be whipped to incorporate air and make them light and fluffy. All of that air, I suspected, would prevent the semifreddo from turning icy as it froze and give it the easy meltability that I was seeking.

I decided to begin experimenting with a flavor combination that I am fond of: cappuccino and biscotti. I made a standard uncooked meringue by whipping egg whites with sugar until they formed soft peaks when the beaters were lifted. Next I whipped some heavy cream and flavored it with dissolved instant espresso. I folded the beaten whites and cream together along with the biscotti crumbs and froze the mixture in a chilled loaf pan.

The resulting dessert was not bad, with a very good flavor. But the volume was too low. The egg whites had collapsed somewhat from the weight of the biscotti, reducing their volume. The frozen semifreddo was too soft and barely held its shape while the biscotti crumbs absorbed the moisture from the coffee and sank to the bottom of the mold where they formed an icy crust. To remove the dessert from the mold, I had to dip the pan in warm water, which melted the surface and made it look messy.

The next time around, I lined the empty loaf pan with plastic wrap and put it in the

Semifreddo is a great dessert for a dinner party because it can be made several days ahead without damage to its flavor or texture.

freezer while I prepared the semifreddo. I reasoned that lining the pan would make it easier to remove the semifreddo and chilling the pan would jump-start the freezing and thus help prevent the egg whites from losing volume. I also reduced the amount of cookie crumbs so they would be less weighty.

All of my adjustments worked—but too well. This time the mixture was too airy and the volume too great for the pan. The flavor was still good, though, and the plastic wrap lining made removal much easier.

The time had come to reconsider my recipe. Because the biggest problem was the egg whites, which were either too airy or not airy enough, I decided to try a different method of making the meringue the next time around. In a standard uncooked, or Swiss, meringue, such as I had been making, egg whites are beaten just until frothy and sugar is then gradually added until the egg whites form soft peaks. The meringue is delicate, and care must be taken not to overbeat the whites or the cell structure of the foam will break down and the meringue will collapse.

A cooked meringue, which is sometimes called an Italian meringue, seemed to be the better alternative. In this method, a hot sugar syrup is poured onto the egg whites as they are beaten. Because the syrup cooks the whites, this is a more stable, sturdier meringue, which I thought might better support the whipped cream and bits of cookies in my semifreddo. Another advantage is that any concerns about eating uncooked whites are eliminated. I decided to try only a cooked meringue.

When it was done, the cooked meringue looked very promising; it had a high volume and a thick, glossy, marshmallow-like texture. Folding in the whipped cream was a bit difficult because the meringue was so stiff, but I succeeded with very little loss of volume by first adding about one-third of the whipped cream to the meringue then folding in the rest.

I added the coffee flavoring and biscotti as before and spread the mixture in the prepared pan. The volume was just right for a standard six-cup loaf pan, and after freezing, the semifreddo was perfect. The texture was smooth and creamy, and the biscotti crumbs remained suspended in the thick foam. What's more, the semifreddo held its shape well when unmolded. Even though this method required an extra step in making the syrup, it was not at all difficult and well worth the extra effort it required.

Satisfied that I had found the best method, I tried a number of flavor variations next. To keep the technique as similar as possible throughout, I avoided watery fruits like fresh berries, which I suspected would become icy if frozen this way. On several occasions, I experimented with adding liqueurs and spirits to the mixtures but decided to eliminate them because the flavor was fresher and clearer without them.

Semifreddo can be frozen in individual molds or cups—a boon whenever the dessert's appearance is particularly important. It is equally good served plain or with a hot or cold fruit or chocolate sauce.

MASTER RECIPE FOR CAPPUCCINO SEMIFREDDO WITH ALMOND BISCOTTI
Serves 8

When whipping cream during warm weather, you'll get the best results if you chill the bowl and beaters in the freezer for at least twenty minutes first. In this recipe, try to coordinate the sugar syrup reaching 238 degrees and the egg whites reaching soft peaks stage. But don't despair if they are out of sync. Beating the whites can be interrupted just before they reach soft peaks, and resumed at any point. If the syrup heats beyond 238 degrees, you can cool it by adding a small amount of cold water; one tablespoon should cool the syrup about 7 degrees, and you can add as many as four tablespoons if need be.

- 3 large egg whites, at room temperature
- 1 cup heavy whipping cream
- 1/2 cup plus 2 tablespoons sugar
- 2 tablespoons instant espresso dissolved in 1 tablespoon warm water
- 1 teaspoon vanilla extract
- 1/2 cup almond or hazelnut biscotti, crushed into split-pea–sized bits

1. Line 6-cup loaf pan with plastic wrap with a 3-inch overhang all around; place in freezer. Place egg whites in bowl of electric mixer fitted with whisk attachment; set aside. Whip cream to soft peaks at medium speed; cover and refrigerate.

2. Mix 1/4 cup water and 1/2 cup sugar in 1-quart saucepan. Warm mixture over low heat without stirring until sugar dissolves, about 4 minutes. Increase heat to medium-high, simmer mixture toward its final temperature of 238 degrees. When sugar syrup reaches 210 degrees, begin beating egg whites on medium speed until frothy, about 40 seconds. Add 1 teaspoon of remaining sugar and increase speed to high; beat until soft peaks form, about 2 minutes. Gradually beat in remaining 5 teaspoons sugar. Decrease speed to medium-high; pour 238-degree syrup into whites in thin, steady stream (avoid hitting rotating beater and sides of bowl); continue beating until mixture is glossy, doubled in volume, and cooled to room temperature, 4 to 5 minutes. Beat in coffee mixture and vanilla.

3. Gently stir one-third of whipped cream into egg white mixture with rubber spatula; fold in remaining whipped cream and 6 tablespoons biscotti bits. Scrape mixture to prepared pan, spreading evenly with rubber spatula. Fold overhanging plastic wrap over mixture and press gently onto surface; freeze until firm, at least 8 hours (can be frozen up to 1 month).

4. To unmold, remove plastic wrap from surface and invert loaf pan onto serving plate, then remove plastic wrap; smooth surface with spatula if desired. Sprinkle with remaining biscotti bits; slice and serve immediately.

VANILLA SEMIFREDDO WITH ALMONDS AND AMARETTI

Follow Master Recipe for Cappuccino Semifreddo with Almond Biscotti, omitting coffee mixture and substituting 6 tablespoons toasted, chopped almonds and 1/3 cup amaretti cookie crumbs (about 6 cookies, crushed) for biscotti. Fold 4 tablespoons almonds and all crumbs into mixture in step 3; sprinkle remaining almonds on unmolded semifreddo before serving. Serve plain or with Warm Bittersweet Chocolate Sauce.

CHOCOLATE ORANGE SEMIFREDDO

Follow Master Recipe for Cappuccino Semifreddo with Almond Biscotti, substituting 1 tablespoon grated orange zest for coffee mixture and 1/2 cup crushed chocolate wafer cookies (about 15 cookies) for biscotti. Fold 6 tablespoons cookie crumbs into mixture in step 3; sprinkle remaining crumbs on unmolded semifreddo before serving.

WARM BITTERSWEET CHOCOLATE SAUCE
Serves 8

- 6 ounces bitter- or semisweet chocolate, chopped
- 3/4 cup heavy cream

Melt chocolate and cream together, stirring occasionally, in small heat-proof bowl set over pan of almost-simmering water until warm.

Michele Scicolone's most recent cookbook is *A Fresh Taste of Italy* (Broadway Books, 1997).

AVOID STICKY BEATERS

When pouring the hot sugar syrup into the egg whites, make sure the syrup does not touch the beater or the sides of the bowl. Contact with the metal might cause the syrup to solidify into small, hard pieces that won't mix with the whites.

ILLUSTRATION BY ESTHER KATZ

WHAT IS SEMIFREDDO?

Individual interpretation is characteristic of Italian cooking in general, and semifreddi are no exception. Some Italian cooks consider all chilled desserts to be semifreddi. Italian cookbooks, however, exclude desserts like tiramisu or Bavarian creams from the category, restricting it to dishes that resemble ice cream, such as frozen mousses, zabagliones, or custards, all of which share certain ingredients such as eggs, sugar, and cream.

Despite their great variety, I did eventually manage to sort out three distinct categories of semifreddi: those that use uncooked egg yolks and large quantities of whipped cream; custard-like versions using cooked egg yolks and a smaller amount of whipped cream; and those that use egg whites cooked by a hot sugar syrup. To determine the characteristics of each type, we made several versions of each—because within these categories there is still a wide variation in proportions, flavorings, and techniques—and held a tasting.

The recipes that used relatively large quantities of whipped cream folded into small amounts of uncooked, ribboned yolks mixed with sugar tended to be hard and icy, somewhat like unchurned ice cream. We tasted two recipes of this variety, one with and one without egg whites. Both had a predominantly milky flavor, a hard consistency, and a lackluster taste for which additional flavorings could not compensate. That said, we preferred the one with the whites because, unlike cream, egg whites do not freeze and remelt and therefore do not become icy.

On the other side of the spectrum are custard semifreddi made with cooked egg yolks and smaller amounts of whipped cream. This gives them a very rich and luxurious texture, similar to soft-serve ice cream. The ratio of egg yolks to cream and flavorings can run the gamut, and often alcohol plays an important role. A typical variation of such a semifreddo is a frozen zabaglione. Basically, a zabaglione is a wine custard: egg yolks ribboned with sugar into which marsala and other spirits are beaten over simmering water until frothy. For a semifreddo, whipped cream is folded into the mixture, which is then frozen. Our custard semifreddo had a very delicate, silky texture.

Finally, we tested the semifreddo featured here, unique because the egg whites are cooked by adding a hot sugar syrup. In this particular recipe, which contains no yolks, a cup of cream is folded into the cooked egg whites. This lack of yolks gives the semifreddo a delicate and light but not overwhelmingly rich consistency. When tasting all the variations side by side, we noted that this recipe had a decidedly pleasant unfrozen feel almost as if it was not frozen at all. It refreshed the palate without the chilly harshness of some of the other versions.—Eva Katz

Fruit Upside-Down Cake

*The right combination of a lightly caramelized topping, fresh fruit,
and a sturdy but tender butter cake is the key to success.*

by Dede Wilson

To my mind, the ideal fruit upside-down cake has a glistening, caramelized, deep amber topping encasing plump fruit on top of a flavorful, tender butter cake. The proportions and textures must also marry well, providing the perfect balance of topping, fruit, and cake in each bite.

Unfortunately, when I tested the standard recipes, I was left with pale, blonde, anemic-looking desserts consisting of fruit and topping that just sat upon the cake component, without melding with it at all.

These shortcomings told me that there was room for improvement, so I set out to determine what proportions of brown sugar topping, fruit, and batter and what techniques worked most harmoniously. I also wanted to see if a master recipe could be developed that would support a variety of fresh fruits, including pineapple, plums, and peaches, in place of the more common canned pineapple.

Getting Topping and Fruit Right
Most recipes for this cake, including the original and the current one from Dole's test kitchen (where the recipe was first developed in 1925), combine brown sugar and butter for the topping by melting the butter, adding the brown sugar, and immediately proceeding to the fruit. This is why these cakes turn out very blonde and light in taste. I knew I wanted a darker, richer, caramelized topping, so I opted to try the technique used in recipes that follow the method of tarte Tatin, in which the sugar and butter combination is lightly caramelized on top of the stove before the fruit is added.

I tested butter combined with granulated sugar, light brown sugar, and a combination of white and brown. The traditional brown sugar won out, since it added an extra complexity to the final taste. As far as proportions were concerned, the original recipe I was using called for two tablespoons of butter to one cup of brown sugar, which was too sweet and not unctuous enough. After trying several options, I honed in on one-quarter cup of butter to three-quarters cup of brown sugar. The proportions were right, and by simmering and stirring for a few minutes to really meld the butter and sugar and produce a slightly reduced caramel, I hit the mark.

Coincidentally, this very important step of caramelizing and thickening the caramel affected unmolding as well. If the butter and sugar for the topping was simply stirred together, the cake, after being turned out of the pan, had a greasy top, with fruit that tended to alternately stick or fall off to the sides. By cooking the topping first, I discovered that the unmolded cakes consistently yielded beautiful-looking tops with fruit that stayed put and never stuck.

I assumed initially that using fresh pineapple would be a problem and that I might end up preferring the ease of canned fruit. To my surprise, the fresh pineapple worked wonderfully with little preparation.

Fresh peaches and plums were also excellent, and easy to prepare; I simply pitted and sliced them into thin half-inch wedges—no peeling was necessary. Mangoes required a bit more work because they had to be peeled as well as pitted and sliced, but were wonderfully delicious. For all fruits, the slices were placed in concentric circles, filling up the pan in the same way as the pineapple slices.

Batter Up
Having arrived at the proper topping and the right approach to each fruit, I turned to the question of the cake batter. My aim was to make a cake that not only tasted good in its own right but would also physically support the fruit and caramelized topping yet not distract from it. The proportions of cake to topping also had to be just right, and the cake had to meld with the topping and fruit to present a unified whole.

I thought a classic butter-type cake would work best, but I also had a notion that a light, low-fat sponge cake might balance well with the rich topping. I theorized that the syrupy caramel and fruit juices would be soaked up by the intentionally dryish sponge. I was pretty sure that a rich pound cake would be too heavy, but I decided to try both of these extremes first to establish whether or not they were even in the running.

I began with the sponge, and the results were poor. Its excessive dryness in juxtaposition to the unctuous topping did not make a happy pairing texturally. The pound cake similarly placed poorly in tastings; its heaviness prevented it from melding with the topping, and its extra butteriness competed with the caramel. I knew the ideal lay somewhere in between, so my next tests would be with butter cakes.

I began by using all-purpose flour, whole eggs, and milk. Most cooks have this type of flour and milk readily available, so it seemed a logical place to start. The cake texture was a bit coarse, so I went on to try cake flour and separating of the eggs in both separate and combined tests. I found that the differences between flours in this cake were negligible but that the separated eggs improved the texture dramatically. When the whites were whipped separately and folded in, the resulting cake was extremely tender, with a crumb so fine that it was almost too velvety. The combination of all-purpose flour and separated eggs was a winner, though, so to give the cake a slightly coarser crumb and help balance the rich topping, I added three tablespoons of cornmeal.

The milk helped to produce a smooth, moist cake and batter, but I wanted to detour and try buttermilk because it often works so well in butter cake recipes. I thought the sharp flavor might also offset the sweetness of the topping. I reduced the amount of baking powder and added baking soda to offset the acidic

FRUIT FOR UPSIDE-DOWN CAKE
Our favorite fruits for upside-down cakes are peaches, nectarines, and plums (all of which are stone fruits), mangoes, and, of course, pineapple. Below are instructions to prepare enough of each fruit for one upside-down cake.

FRUIT	QUANTITY	HOW TO PREPARE
Peaches or Nectarines	4 medium	Halve fruits pole to pole; remove stone. Cut each half into slices 1/2-inch thick.
Plums	5 medium	Halve fruits pole to pole; remove stone (cutting halves in half again, if needed). Cut into slices 1/2-inch thick.
Mangoes	2 medium	Peel and pit. Cut flesh into slices 1/4-inch thick.
Pineapple	1 small	Stem, peel, quarter, and core. Cut each quarter into pieces 3/8-inch thick.

nature of the buttermilk. The cakes baked well and looked fine, but a more open crumb, a by-product of the baking soda, was not well-received by tasters, including myself.

At this point I had the basic formula figured out but still wanted to try a variation or two. Up until now, I had been creaming the butter with the sugar, a very standard technique, and the results were fine, but I wanted also to try a technique called the two-stage method. Some bakers prefer this technique, which consists of adding sugar to the dry ingredients, then cutting in the butter and proceeding with the wet ingredients. Although the original recipe from 1925 creamed butter and sugar, the current Dole recipe suggests the two-stage method, which I found interesting. Because I had made a good cake with the creaming method, I could now apply the developed recipe to this technique and compare results. But with this technique, I soon realized, the fact that all of the moist ingredients ended up being added after the dry ones posed a problem. In order to incorporate the wet ingredients thoroughly, I found myself consistently overworking the batter, which yielded a tougher cake.

As far as flavorings were concerned, I had always thought vanilla should be included, and it did add a rounder, fuller flavor to the butter cake. I experimented with cinnamon and ginger, which were interesting, and lemon rind added a nice zesty flavor, but all of these additions veered away from what I thought a very basic pineapple upside-down cake should taste like. Vanilla was necessary, but no other flavoring was required.

To sum up, the creaming technique, along with separated eggs and whole milk, gave me the result I was after: a cake with a clean, buttery taste that harmonized with the sweet, caramelized topping and moist fruit.

While I had discovered early on the value of the caramelized topping to easier unmolding, I also came to understand that the length of cooling period is crucial. In short, the best procedure is to remove the cake from the oven when done, let it sit for two minutes on a rack, then flip it over onto a plate. This minimal cooling time allows the caramelized top to solidify just a bit so that it does not flow down off of the top after unmolding, yet the time is not long enough for the caramelized sugar to set, which would lead to unmolding problems. If any fruit does stick, it is easy enough to remove manually and place it properly on the cake top.

MASTER RECIPE FOR FRUIT UPSIDE-DOWN CAKE
Serves 8 to 10

Using a nine-inch-by-three-inch round pan to bake the cake gives it straight sides. If you prefer slightly flared sides on your cake instead, bake it in a ten-inch cast-iron skillet, which streamlines the process in three ways. First, the skillet need not be buttered; second, the caramel topping can be prepared in it directly; and third, the total baking time is cut

to fifty minutes, which is ten to fifteen minutes faster than the cake pan.

Topping
4 tablespoons unsalted butter, plus more for cake pan
¾ cup light brown sugar
Prepared fruit (*see* "Fruit for Upside-Down Cake," page 24)

Cake
1½ cups all-purpose flour
1½ teaspoons baking powder
3 tablespoons cornmeal
½ teaspoon salt
8 tablespoons unsalted butter, room temperature
1 cup granulated sugar, plus 2 tablespoons for egg whites
4 large eggs, separated
1½ teaspoons vanilla extract
⅔ cup whole milk

1. *For the topping*: Butter bottom and sides of 9-inch-by-3-inch round cake pan. Melt 4 tablespoons butter in medium saucepan over medium heat; add brown sugar and cook, stirring occasionally, until mixture is foamy and pale, 3 to 4 minutes. Pour mixture into prepared cake pan (*see* illustration 1); swirl pan to distribute evenly. Arrange fruit slices in concentric circles over topping (*see* illustration 2); set aside.

2. *For the cake*: Adjust oven rack to lower-middle position; heat oven to 350 degrees. Whisk flour, baking powder, cornmeal, and salt together in medium bowl; set aside. Cream butter in large bowl with electric mixer at medium speed. Gradually add 1 cup sugar; continue beating until light and fluffy, about 2 minutes. Beat in yolks and vanilla (scraping sides of bowl with rubber spatula if necessary); reduce speed to low and add dry mixture and milk, alternately in three or four batches, beginning and ending with dry ingredients, until batter is just smooth.

3. Beat egg whites in large bowl at low speed until frothy. Increase speed to medium-high; beat to soft peaks. Gradually add 2 tablespoons sugar; continue to beat to stiff peaks. Fold one-quarter of beaten whites into batter with large rubber spatula to lighten. Fold in remaining whites until no white streaks remain. Gently pour batter into pan and spread evenly on top of fruit, being careful not to disperse fruit. Bake until top is golden and toothpick inserted into cake center (not fruit, which remains gooey) comes out clean, 60 to 65 minutes.

4. Rest cake on rack for 2 minutes. Following illustrations 3 and 4, remove cake from pan to serving plate. If any fruit sticks to pan bottom, remove and position on top of cake.

Dede Wilson, a freelance author living in western Massachusetts, is working on a book about wedding cakes.

DOING UPSIDE-DOWN RIGHT

1. After cooking the butter-sugar mixture, pour it into a buttered cake pan and swirl to distribute evenly over the pan bottom.

2. Arrange fruit slices over the butter-sugar mixture in concentric circles on the pan bottom.

3. After baking, slide a paring knife around the edge of the cake to loosen it, then place a serving platter over the pan and hold tightly. Invert the cake onto the platter.

4. Carefully remove cake pan. If any fruit clings to the pan, simply remove and place on the cake.

Homemade Salsa Is Worth the Effort

*A blind tasting reveals that bottled salsas
range from boring to disgusting. Our advice? Make your own.*

by Jack Bishop

In 1991, salsa surpassed ketchup to become America's leading condiment, and sales have ballooned to $600 million a year. What started out as a Mexican table condiment has become mainstream American food with giants like Pillsbury, Campbell's Soup, Pepsico, and Nestlé dominating the market.

We wanted to taste as many brands as we could to see which ones are worth buying. We also wanted to compare bottled salsas to the real thing, made with fresh tomatoes, onions, chiles, garlic, cilantro, and lime juice.

We pretasted dozens of brands of salsa in order to narrow the field down to twelve. We decided to include the brands that dominate the category (Old El Paso, Pace, Tostitos, Ortega, and Chi-Chi's) along with some smaller brands that had shown well in our informal tasting.

We also pretasted four refrigerated salsas. Unlike bottled salsas, these products, which are sold in plastic tubs, have a shelf life of a month or two. (Bottled salsas will stay "fresh" for a year or more.) Manufacturers add preservatives to keep refrigerated salsas from becoming moldy, but there is little they can do to prevent the mushy texture and slimy mouth feel. The refrigerated salsas that we tasted ranged from possibly edible after many margaritas to inedible under any circumstances. Most refrigerated salsas are also regional brands, so we decided to omit this category from our final tasting.

Supermarket brands of bottled salsa come in three different styles: mild, medium, and hot. Mild salsas are generally quite bland (some would say insipid) with little or no heat. Hot salsas can be difficult to taste, especially one after another, so we settled on medium salsas for this article.

It was not a big surprise that our homemade salsa won the tasting. However, the margin of victory, especially considering that we made this salsa with mediocre winter tomatoes, was a shock. Our panel gave each salsa an overall score from 0 to 100, with 0 indicating "dislike extremely" and 100 indicating "like extremely." Our homemade salsa received an average score of 68 from our panel of culinary students and *Cook's Illustrated* staff. There was a tie for second place among Green Mountain Gringo, Tostitos, and Old El Paso, but this wasn't much of an honor given that all three received a score of 46. In fact, all of the salsas in the "acceptable" category in the chart below earned similar scores.

The results of this tasting are fairly easy to interpret: Make your own salsa, even if the tomatoes don't look that good. Some of the products we tested were made with fresh tomatoes (as opposed to tomato puree) and fresh onions and garlic (as opposed to dehydrated), but our panel could not tell the difference. Jarred salsas are cooked in order to kill off any bacteria and to keep them from going bad on the shelf, a process that evidently renders any differences in initial ingredients hard to taste.

RATING SALSAS

Thirty-three panelists rated thirteen salsas on a variety of characteristics. All samples were served in plastic cups with spoons. Panelists had access to bottled water and bread during the tasting. The locations below refer to the manufacturing plant or corporate headquarters listed on package labels. Samples were purchased in supermarkets in New York and Massachusetts, and prices indicate actual retail cost.

HIGHLY RECOMMENDED
Homemade salsa was the clear winner.

Homemade Salsa, about $7 for 40 ounces. "100% better than all the others. I will never buy commercial salsa again."

ACCEPTABLE
Scores were slightly better for brands at the top of the category, but differences were slight.

Green Mountain Gringo Medium Salsa (Chester, Vermont), $4.79 for 16-ounce jar. "Much too sweet," but "thankfully mild on the salt." Most tasters wanted more heat in this expensive "gourmet" salsa.

Tostitos Restaurant Style Medium Salsa (Dallas, Texas), $2.49 for 16-ounce jar. "A small step above others" was the general consensus.

Old El Paso Thick 'n Chunky Medium Salsa (Anthony, Texas), $2.69 for 20-ounce jar. Tasters could only muster faint praise. "Not great but not wretched."

Pace Thick & Chunky Medium Salsa (San Antonio, Texas), $2.89 for 16-ounce jar. Spiciest salsa in tasting. Some cynics thought heat "might be masking some flaws."

Newman's Own Medium Salsa (Westport, Connecticut), $1.69 for 11-ounce jar. Least salt among jarred samples, but "too much sugar" and "mushy, disgusting texture."

Guiltless Gourmet Medium Salsa (Austin, Texas), $2.89 for 11.5-ounce jar. "Low sweetness quotient," but "brown color" and "old, musty flavor" were severely downgraded.

Chi-Chi's Chunky Restaurante Medium Salsa (Austin, Minnesota), $2.49 for 16-ounce jar. Tasters found that "mushy texture" was the most serious flaw.

Fred Imus Hot Stuff Southwest Medium Salsa (Santa Fe, New Mexico), $3.99 for 16-ounce jar. Good heat, but "soggy vegetables" and "thick, ketchuplike texture."

Wise Bravos Thick and Chunky Medium Salsa (Columbus, Ohio), $1.99 for 11.5-ounce jar. Very mild, but with "strong cooked tomato flavor."

Muir Glen Organic Medium Salsa (Sacramento, California), $2.69 for 11-ounce jar. Most panelists found this quite mild and excessively sweet. "More like tomato sauce with oregano than salsa."

Ortega Thick & Chunky Medium Salsa (Glendale, California), $1.99 for 16-ounce jar. The saltiest, most acidic sample. "Too much like tomato sauce."

NOT RECOMMENDED
This brand scored considerably behind the rest of the pack.

La Victoria Medium Salsa Suprema (City of Industry, California), $1.99 for 12-ounce jar. "Where are the vegetables?" in this smooth, watery sauce "masquerading as salsa."

Digitals Top Instant-Read Thermometer Testing

*You can spend almost $60 on a digital thermometer,
but even less expensive models are accurate and easy to read.*

by Adam Ried with Eva Katz and Dawn Yanagihara

Sight, touch, and instinct are age-old ways to gauge when food is done, but for consistent results, none is as reliable as taking the food's internal temperature.

There are many types of specialty thermometers on the market, designed specifically for everything from meat to cappuccino. Yet for home cooks the most useful model is the least specialized of them all, the instant-read thermometer. This device can be inserted into almost any kind of food to display a reading of its internal temperature within seconds. Unlike traditional meat thermometers, these quick-reading units are not designed to be left in the oven. Prolonged exposure of the whole unit to heat will destroy an instant-read thermometer.

Assembling and Evaluating the Field

For our testing, we purchased nine instant-read thermometers in various sizes, shapes, and configurations. Three were dial face types while six had digital displays. The most unique among them was the Polder Cooking Thermometer/Timer, a high-tech contraption with a dual purpose that was also included in our previous testing of kitchen timers (*see* "Multifeatured Electronic Timers Win Testing," September/October 1996).

Our basic testing was threefold. First we used each thermometer to measure the internal temperature of baking bread and roasting meat, both of which depend on proper internal temperature for consistent results. We evaluated each thermometer with regard to readability, response time, accuracy, and length of stem (which dictates the ability of the thermometer to reach to the center of a large roast or bread loaf). Readability and response time were particularly important to us; if these two characteristics are up to snuff, you'll be able to get in and out of any temperature-taking operation quickly, perhaps even *instantly*, which is the aim.

We also looked at less obvious concerns raised by other *Cook's Illustrated* editors based on many accumulated years of thermometer use. Issues such as temperature range or performance in shallow liquid and thin foods may not be obvious at buying time, but their significance becomes clear with continued use. To evaluate these factors, we tested each thermometer in four cooking situations: heating a shallow depth of sugar syrup, which performs differently in recipes depending on the stage to which it is heated; melting and tempering chocolate, which requires precise temperatures between

80 and 100 degrees; sautéing thin, boneless chicken breasts; and monitoring the freezing temperature of sorbet and ice cream.

Last, and basically just for fun, we asked ourselves whether any of our instant-read units could perform cross duty as a candy/jelly/deep-fry thermometer. Many true candy/jelly/deep-fry thermometers are made of glass and therefore both cheap to buy and easy to break. In our experience, they're also very difficult to read. If any of our instant-reads could pinch-hit, we thought, perhaps there would be no need to own two types of thermometers. To find out if this was the case, we used each of our instant-read thermometers to measure the temperature of oil to be used for deep-fat frying.

A Key Difference

One of the primary design differences among instant-read thermometers was the type of display—dial face or digital. Though pocket-sized dial face thermometers are less expensive than digital models, they are much less legible, and most have narrower effective temperature ranges than the digitals. Both digital and dial thermometers are mechanically capable of covering wide temperature ranges, but dial thermometers cannot offer the same readability over wide ranges because their faces become too compressed graphically to read small changes. As a result, while digital displays show the numbers clearly and display the temperature to the degree (or in some cases, even tenths of a degree), most dial faces are marked with faint lines every two degrees, leaving you squinting and unsure of whether your loaf of bread is at exactly 195 degrees.

Another important difference between digital and dial models is the location of the temperature sensors (*see* "Digital vs. Dial: How They Work," right). On dial face thermometers, the sensors are located roughly one and one-half inches up from the tip of the stem. The sensors on digital thermometers, on the other hand, are located at the very tip of the stem. In our testing, this difference mattered most when measuring the temperature of shallow liquids. Our top digital thermometers could produce an accurate temperature reading in liquids of one inch deep or even less whereas the dial models needed at least one and one-half inches.

On the other hand, some cooks prefer dial face thermometers because many of these models can be recalibrated manually by adjusting a nut at the base of the dial whereas

DIAL VS. DIGITAL: HOW THEY WORK

As we learned from the engineers at Taylor Environmental Instruments, dial thermometers work on the principle that different metals expand and contract at different rates when subjected to increases or decreases in temperature.

The embodiment of this principle in a dial thermometer is a coil sensor that is made of two different types of metal bonded together (see illustration). The coil is connected to the pointer on the dial face. The two metals in the coil have different expansion characteristics, and because they are bonded, they work in unison to dictate the coil's change in length as the temperature changes. This in turn causes the pointer on the dial face to rotate to indicate the temperature.

Most digital thermometers, as you might guess, are more high-tech. Again according to Taylor engineers, digital instant-read thermometers generally use a thermistor sensor, which is a metal oxide semiconductor that acts as a temperature-sensitive resistor. The sensor's resistance decreases rapidly as the temperature increases, and the change in resistance is used by a microprocessor to compute a temperature, which it displays as a number on a liquid crystal display.

Our favorite thermometer, the Thermapen, uses yet a different type of sensor called a thermocouple. According to Randy Owen, president of Owen Instruments, thermocouple sensors are made from two different metal alloy wires that are welded at one end to form a "thermal junction." As the temperature changes, the wires produce a very small change in voltage that is measured, converted by a microprocessor to a temperature, and displayed as a number on the display, just as it is in other digital models. Thermocouple sensors can operate over a very wide temperature range, often making thermocouple units the thermometer of choice in food service settings—A.R.

coil

digitals cannot be recalibrated. However, we tested the calibrations of all our units in boiling water, which should read 212 degrees, and in a slurry of ice and water, which should read 32 degrees, at both the beginning and the end of our six-week testing period. All of their calibrations held from beginning to end, which led us to believe that the digitals' lack of ability to recalibrate is not the disadvantage it might seem at first.

Given these factors, we found that we generally preferred digital thermometers over those with dial faces.

The Results

Quick response times of ten seconds and clear digital displays made the Owen Instruments Thermapen and the Taylor Digital Pocket Thermometer our top two choices. The broad, flat surfaces of the hefty Thermapen made it a breeze to clean, and it also stored easily because the stem folds back into the body. These benefits don't come cheap, however; at $59, this thermometer is more than twice the price of all the other units.

Despite the fact that it was calibrated two degrees high, the Taylor Digital Model 9840 edged out the Polder for Best Buy (see "Honorable Mention," page 29) because it was quick-reading and simpler to use. The Cooper Digital might have taken Best Buy honors for its wide temperature range and its smart automatic shutoff feature, but these virtues were overshadowed by one major Achilles heel: the "update" button. This unit updates its temperature reading automati-

cally every ten seconds, but you must press a tiny, awkwardly placed "update" button for more frequent readings. On many occasions, we found that losing track of the ten-second increments or forgetting to press the button resulted in inaccurate temperature readings.

Digitals are electronic and do require batteries. This might be annoying when you reach for a thermometer and find that the battery has died unexpectedly, as the Polder's did once during our testing period. Among our group, only the Cooper Digital offered an automatic shutoff feature, though we were told by representatives of Owen Instruments that a new version of the Thermapen shuts off automatically when the stem is folded back for storage. By contrast, neither the Polder nor the Maverick Redi-Chek could be turned off at all. The worst feature of our winning Thermapen was its need for an odd-sized (12-volt) battery, which we found only in large, especially well-stocked hardware stores and electronics stores such as Radio Shack. Because battery life can be extended by shutting the thermometer off when it is not in use, we think it's best for digital thermometers to have an automatic shutoff, or at least an on/off switch.

When you buy a thermometer, you expect accuracy, and not all of ours delivered. In fact, our Best Buy Taylor Digital was two degrees high, but this flaw was more easily forgiven than we had imagined. Because we established that it was two degrees inaccurate from the outset, we simply compensated for

that fact by adding the two degrees to its readings. We never felt put out by having to do so. Likewise, we'd recommend testing your own thermometer when you buy it. If its calibration is off, you'll know right away so you can compensate when you use it.

No Pinch Hitters

The Owen Instruments Thermapen, the Polder, the Cooper Digital, and the Taylor Bi-Therm Dial model all offered high enough temperature ranges to use for deep frying or sugar syrup. However, none really made it as high-quality pinch hitters in this department. The Taylor Bi-Therm did have a clip by which it could be attached to a pan wall so the stem could remain in the hot oil or sugar syrup, but its face was as difficult to read as many true candy/jelly/deep-fry thermometers. The other three candidates offered clearer readouts than most of the true candy/jelly/deep-fry thermometers we've used, but only the Polder had a design that allowed the probe to be left hands-free in the boiling syrup and hot oil. However, the instruction booklet for the Polder warned against subjecting the probe to temperatures greater than 392 degrees, lest its wires become damaged. So, while it is capable of measuring 375-degree oil for deep frying, you have only a 17-degree temperature margin before you risk damaging your thermometer. Because we always monitored the Polder attentively in these situations, we never encountered any trouble, but it did require extra care.

TESTERS' COMMENTS

BEST THERMOMETER

Owen Instruments Thermapen 5 (Digital): Quick response time and very easy to read, store, and clean. Test kitchen favorite. Odd-sized batteries can be difficult to find.

BEST BUY

Taylor Digital Pocket Thermometer, Model 9840: Easy to use and to read and registers quickly, but unfortunately has a limited high temperature range and is 2 degrees inaccurate.

Polder Cooking Thermometer/Timer (Digital): Feature-laden and versatile, this combination unit is also bulky and prone to premature battery death due to no on/off switch.

Cooper Digital Test Thermometer, Model DFP450: Light, compact model tested well in every respect, but we hated the update button.

Taylor Bi-Therm Dial Thermometer, Model 60848: Extra long stem and a clip for deep frying or sugar syrups, but insufficiently low temperature range and dial face is hard to read. This one is no bargain for the price.

Taylor Instant Read Meat Thermometer, Model 5989 (Dial): Bolder graphics and easier to read than the Cooper dial, but still impossible to get very specific readings. Inaccurate from the very first reading and hard to adjust.

Cooper Commercial Grade Test Thermometer, Model 1236-32 (Dial): Inaccurate when purchased, poor high temperature range, and dial face difficult to read.

Component Design Digital Pocket Thermometer, Model DT300: Very short stem and 1 degree inaccurate. Gimmicky and unimportant "data hold" feature locks in last temperature reading but is of little use.

Maverick Redi-Chek Electronic Food Probe Thermometer, Model ET-3 (Digital): Poorly designed, wide, flared stem leaves large holes in food and still won't reach center of a loaf of bread. It does beep when final temperature is reached.

PHOTOGRAPHS BY JACK CERVEIRA

RATING INSTANT-READ THERMOMETERS

Nine instant-read thermometers were tested and evaluated according to the following criteria. They are listed in order of preference.

Price: Retail price paid in stores and from mail-order catalogs.

Readability: Thermometers were rated on how clearly we could see and read the numbers.

Response Time: Simply put, the faster, the better. When tested in boiling water, times of ten to twenty seconds to achieve a readout of 212 degrees were rated excellent, twenty to thirty seconds were rated fair, and times above thirty seconds were rated poor.

Accuracy: Thermometers should register exactly 212 degrees in boiling water and exactly 32 degrees in a slurry of crushed ice and water. If these readings were off, the thermometer was downgraded.

Design/Features: This category encompasses disparate factors that can make the thermometer a breeze or a real pain to use, such as the length of the stem; the ease of cleaning of screens or dials; on/off switches or automatic shutoff to save batteries; battery availability; and accurate readings in shallow liquids. See Testers' Comments, page 28, for any particular notes on these issues.

Temperature Range: More often than not, instant-read thermometers are used within the relatively narrow temperature range necessary to monitor the internal temperature of meat, poultry, or bread. Occasionally, though, you may wish to know the temperature of a freezing sorbet or ice cream, or double-check the temperature of hot oil prior to frying in it. Therefore, thermometers capable of taking very low (0 degrees and below) through very high (375 degrees and above) were upgraded.

◉◉◉ = excellent   ◉◉ = fair   ◉ = poor

Brand	Price	Readability	Response Time	Accuracy	Features	Temperature Range
BEST THERMOMETER Owen Instruments Thermapen 5 (Digital)	$59	◉◉◉	◉◉◉ 10 seconds	◉◉◉	◉◉◉ 4½-inch stem	◉◉◉ -50° to 550°
BEST BUY Taylor Digital Pocket Thermometer, Model 9840	$15	◉◉◉	◉◉◉ 10 seconds	◉ 2° high	◉◉◉ 4¾-inch stem	◉◉ -58° to 302°
Polder Cooking Thermometer/Timer (Digital)	$29.95	◉◉◉	◉◉ 30 seconds	◉◉◉	◉◉◉ 5¾-inch stem	◉ 32° to 392°
Cooper Digital Test Thermometer, Model DFP450	$24.50	◉◉◉	◉◉◉ 17 seconds	◉◉◉	◉ 4⅝-inch stem	◉◉◉ -40° to 450°
Taylor Bi-Therm Dial Thermometer, Model 60848	$32.50	◉◉ 5° increments	◉◉ 30 seconds	◉◉◉	◉◉◉ 8-inch stem	◉◉◉ 50° to 550°
Taylor Instant Read Meat Thermometer, Model 5989 (Dial)	$14.95	◉ 2° increments	◉◉ 25 seconds	◉ 2° high	◉◉ 5-inch stem	◉◉ 0° to 220°
Cooper Commercial Grade Test Thermometer, Model 1236-32 (Dial)	$8.50	◉ 2° increments	◉ 35 seconds	◉ 2° high	◉◉ 4¾-inch stem	◉◉ 0° to 220°
Component Design Digital Pocket Thermometer, Model DT300	$32.50	◉◉◉	◉◉ 30 seconds	◉◉ 1° high	◉ 2¾-inch stem	◉◉ -40° to 300°
Maverick Redi-Chek Electronic Food Probe Thermometer, Model ET-3 (Digital)	$29.99	◉◉◉	◉◉ 25 seconds	◉◉◉	◉ ⅛-inch tip with wide plastic 3⅛-inch body	◉◉ 32° to 239°

Honorable Mention

Strictly speaking, the Polder Cooking Thermometer/Timer is not meant to be used as an instant-read thermometer, though it can be. When used as such, the response time was slow, and some testers thought its unusual design a nuisance. We had to learn how to handle the forty-five-inch wire that connects the probe to the base unit without tangling it in burner grates or stove knobs. Also, because the bare metal probe is not really designed to be held by hand in hot food, it gets mighty hot itself.

Despite these drawbacks, we almost named it our Best Buy because of its many clever features. It is the only thermometer in our group whose probe is designed to be left in a roast as it cooks. The long wire mentioned above connects the probe (which is lodged in the food, in the oven) to the base unit, which is either sitting on a nearby counter or attached to the outside of the oven door via a magnet. This setup allows you to monitor the internal temperature of the food you're cooking without having to open the oven door. Even better, you can preset a target temperature using the alarm feature, and the Polder will beep loudly when that temperature has been reached. Also, the Polder's probe can, if you keep a keen eye on it, be left in pots of hot oil or sugar syrup, providing a precise temperature readout to its base unit, sitting a safe distance away. In addition, it has Fahrenheit and centigrade readouts, outstanding readability, and a reasonable price.

In light of all it does have, we're baffled by what it does not have: a simple on/off switch. Because of this, its weakling AAA batteries wear out all the sooner.—A.R.

The Best Ales? American!

*To the surprise of everyone, English classics are beaten out
by American upstarts in our first tasting of high-quality, full-flavored ales.*

by Mark Bittman

There are almost as many categories of beer as there are of wine, so it took some negotiating to organize our first *Cook's* "beer" tasting. Since we wanted to zero in on flavorful brews, we quickly eliminated the American standards such as Budweiser and its competition. We also disposed of the "premium" beers, most of which are indistinguishable from Bud.

We wanted to judge only nationally available products; this eliminated microbreweries, many of which are producing fine beers and ales, but few of which ship outside of their state or region. So we settled on super-premiums (a marketing term that means "expensive and targeted at a well-heeled crowd"), and finally narrowed the category down to super-premium light ales, which are increasing in popularity and number at a faster rate than super-premium "beers," more correctly called "lagers."

All premium beers, whether ales or lagers, share a dependence on just four ingredients: good water, which generally brings some flavor of its own; barley malt, which lends sweetness and body; yeast, which is the agent of fermentation but adds its own character; and hops, an herb that delivers complexity and bitterness. Although there are production differences between lagers and ales, the real differences are stylistic. Ales generally have a fuller body and a more complex, bitter flavor than lagers. Both the sweet, syrupy character of malt and the wild, aromatic, bitter nature of hops are more powerful and up front in ales. In great ales, they combine to form a brew that is as complex as good wine.

In England, ale sold in pubs, from a barrel, is generally called "bitter." When ale is bottled, it becomes "pale," or "light" ale, with a higher degree of carbonation and, sometimes, a stronger flavor of malt. Not all of the ales in our tasting were labeled "pale," but our extensive pre-tasting resulted in sixteen ales, all from the United States, the United Kingdom, and Canada, that were either classic examples of pale ale (such as Samuel Smith or Bass), established North American versions of the same (such as Molson or Ballantine), or newer entries that seemed well-crafted enough to stand up to those that were grandfathered in.

The results of the tasting were nothing short of astonishing. Despite the presence of six English imports, top place went to Sierra Nevada Pale Ale which, ironically, was among the top finishers in a tasting of micro-brews (the brewery was smaller then) I held for *Cook's Magazine* back in 1990. In fact, it wasn't until third place that a British brew, Samuel Smith's, made an appearance; second place went to an-

other American product, Pete's Wicked Ale.

Equally surprising was the poor finish of Bass Ale, considered a standard in the category by many in both England and the U.S., but whose wonderful appearance was followed by disappointing flavor. It is conceivable that all the English beers suffered some from their longer shipping times (English beer arrives here by boat; American and Canadian by truck), but it's just as conceivable that the export "formula" is milder or—in the case of Bass Ale—that production has been stretched beyond reasonable limits and the beer just isn't as good as it used to be.

RATING THE BEERS

The beers in our tasting—held at Mt. Carmel Wine and Spirits, in Hamden, Connecticut—were judged by a panel made up of beer professionals and amateur beer lovers. Seven points were awarded for each first-place vote; six for second; and so on. The beers were all purchased in the Northeast; prices (which are per six-pack) will vary throughout the country.

Within each category, beers are listed based on number of points scored. Highly Recommended beers received what amounted to rave reviews. Recommended beers had predominantly positive comments. Beers "Recommended with Reservations" had an approximately equal number of positive and negative comments. "Not Recommended" beers had few or no positive comments.

HIGHLY RECOMMENDED

Sierra Nevada Pale Ale, $8 (California): Placed in top five by all tasters. "Huge head," "good flavor," "round and bitter," "strong body." Flavor is "not only pleasing but exotic."

Pete's Wicked Pale Ale, $7 (Minnesota): Close second. "This had the best balance of all," wrote one of those who ranked it first.

Samuel Smith's Old Brewery Pale Ale, 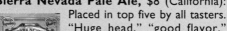 $13 (England): Close third, but note price. "Very, very good," but "perhaps not as complex as [Sierra Nevada]," wrote one. "Beautiful head and very smooth."

RECOMMENDED

Morland Old Speckled Hen English Fine Ale, $8 (England): "Dark and creamy," with "great body" and a "good bitter flavor," which some found to be "too much."

Whitbread Traditional Pale Ale, $7.50 (England): Much closer to a stout, so out of place in this tasting. Yet widely admired:

"Smoky and rich," and "very, very, smooth."
Samuel Adams Boston Ale, $7 (Massachusetts): "Head faded" on this "rather sweet," "malty" brew.
Red Hook Ballard Bitter India Pale Ale, $6.75 (Washington): "Not strong but full-bodied and good-tasting," was the dominant view. Two tasters detected "off-flavors."
Ballantine India Pale Ale, $6.45 (Indiana): An American classic, still worth drinking; essentially a toned-down version of the winners; comments ranged from "some bitterness, nicely rounded," to "too neutral for me."

RECOMMENDED WITH RESERVATIONS

Latrobe American Pale Ale, $5.49 (Pennsylvania): "Lovely sweet and bitter flavor" went over well with most tasters. Not high rankings, but generally enjoyed; good price.
Eldridge Pope Royal Oak Pale Ale, $12. (England): "Fruity and bitter at once; very nice." Some found it "too bitter," with a "harsh finish."
Double Diamond Original Burton Ale, $8. (England): Some found this "bitter and complex," but others thought it "rather bland," especially given its "lovely appearance."
12 Horse Celebrated Ale, (New York) $4.69: Just squeaked into this category. Despite its "lame yellow" appearance, an ale that drew a few decent comments: "Malty, fairly creamy, and not at all bad." Worth a shot at this price.

NOT RECOMMENDED

Bass Ale, $8 (England): "Disappointing." Ranked only by taster who recognized it immediately, and called it "steady and reliable." But most others thought it had "nice color and good head" but "little" or "no" flavor.
Anchor Liberty Ale, $8.59 (California): "Fruity to a fault." One taster found it "too bitter" but rich. All tasters appeared confused by its flavors.
Labatt 50 Canadian Ale, $5.75 (Canada): "Might as well be Budweiser."
Molson Export Ale, $5.69 (Canada): "Has the cheapness of commercial beer."

Book Reviews......................................

On a recent visit to a local bookstore, I was surprised to find that the section devoted to vegetarian cookbooks had more running feet of books than any other single category. At the same time, because I am also the publisher of *Natural Health* magazine, I know from surveys that very few readers of that publication are true vegetarians; more than 90 percent of them eat chicken or fish while 50 percent eat a standard American diet. I suspect, therefore, that most home cooks turn to vegetarian cookbooks not for all of their meals but for a good source of recipes for grains, pasta, vegetables, and fruits. With that premise in mind, we thought that a survey of the field was in order.

Given the proliferation of titles that can be classified as vegetarian, I must admit at the outset to a certain lack of rigor in our cookbook selection. We could not possibly review hundreds of titles and therefore started out, after much research and consultation, with a list of a dozen or so of the most promising books. Through recipe testing, we pared this list down to a more modest list of five titles. Our apologies to those cookbook authors whose worthy volumes missed our selection process.

Just published this spring, **Vegetarian Planet** (The Harvard Common Press, $29.95) by Didi Emmons shows plenty of

fresh talent from the chef at The Delux Cafe, a hole-in-the-wall eatery in Boston's South End. We tested eighteen recipes from Planet. Why so many? Well, we started out with a long list because the recipes sounded fabulous, then tested even more because we soon discovered that the instructions and ingredient listings were often problematic. Ingredients were left out of ingredient lists in two recipes, for example, and in several other recipes either the cooking times were off or we found ourselves having to improvise to overcome directions that were either incomplete or incorrect. (To be fair to the publisher, we were testing from galleys, not the final book. Many of the errors were corrected in later versions.) We also felt that many recipes were underseasoned and found the author to be no stranger to relatively hard-to-find ingredients such as daikon, cracked spelt, and wasabi powder.

That being said (and assuming that the final book has dealt with the more obvious shortcomings), we found many of the recipes in this collection to be exceptional—interesting, fresh, and innovative without being silly. Jicama Slaw, Carrot Dumplings in Lemongrass Broth, Baba Ghanoush, Fruit and Nut Tabouli, and Tuscan White-Bean Soup were all top-notch. Harry's Famous Home Fries were, in the words of one editor, "most excellent." Falafel Burgers, Golden Rice Cakes with Sweet Potato–Ginger Sauce, and Baked Rigatoni with Broccoli and Gorgonzola, on the other hand, were a bit dull.

On balance, though, *Vegetarian Planet* is a fresh, important addition to the field from an original, well-traveled cook who skates perilously close to her outer limits, picks herself up after the occasional fall, and then turns in a flawless triple axel. With a bit more experience, Emmons will be a world-class contender.

We decided to include **Moosewood Restaurant Low-Fat Favorites** (Clarkson

Potter, $22) because the previous entries in the Moosewood line of cookbooks have been so influential and highly successful. I must admit, however, to a primal fear of any cookbook with "low-fat" in its title. This usually implies taking recipes that are "high-fat" and fixing them, an exercise that is almost always ill-advised.

As it turns out, we were pleasantly surprised by the recipes. Gingered Fennel with Garlic, Dried Mushroom Soup with Barley, Thai Fish Cakes, and Dark Chocolate Pudding were all worth making again, although Five-Spice Rice was dry and uninteresting. The criticism of this book lies in the title. Because there are only a handful of baked goods (a few muffins and cookies), the bulk of the recipes are simply vegetarian, which, by default, tend to be low-fat. The authors admit as much in the introduction, thankfully disowning low-fat cheesecake and other silly substitutions. In the final analysis, although *Vegetarian Planet* has more intriguing recipes and the voice of the author rings loud and clear (*Moosewood* is written by a collective, which reduces the prose to the level of a corporate report), *Moosewood Low-Fat* nevertheless has solid, well-tested recipes that are well worth the price.

Darra Goldstein's **The Vegetarian Hearth** (HarperCollins, $26) is a culinary poem to the joys of cold weather vegetarianism, snug by the fireside with a rough-hewn plate full of roasted root vegetables. I give her high marks for finding a refreshing approach to this field without

bending to the whims of the market as Moosewood did. Like a cold winter night, the book is subdued, a collection of quiet, reserved offerings. The recipes themselves are also quiet; Baked Millet with Winter Squash, a Sweet Potato and Clementine Pudding, and Brandied Onions were no walk on the wild side, sounding more exciting than they tasted. But Goldstein is a professional, and the recipes are generally solid. If you love winter vegetables, this book belongs on your shelf even if it doesn't contain "dazzling crystal...of rare Aladdin's wondrous cave" as promised in the introduction.

Viana La Place's **Unplugged Kitchen** (Morrow, $25) is so cutely packaged and written that it reminds me of a $3,000 Armani suit: stylish, well-made, but jeez, it's just a cookbook. The writing also runs frequently amok, referring to the "sparkling aquamarine sea" or stating that "I can taste this sandwich in my

mind." I have to admit, however, that this is an exceptional book, full of carefully crafted and interesting recipes. La Place's sense of taste is impeccable, and to her enduring credit, the ingredient lists are short and to the point. This is no intergalactic hodgepodge of ingredients, designed to impress and awe. This is the real thing. Recipes such as Orange and Leek Salad, Ginger Carrot Salad, Cauliflower with Fresh Coriander, and Rustic Mushroom and Bread Skewers were all first-class. The food is simple, approachable, interesting, and refreshing.

Although Deborah Madison's **The Savory Way** (Bantam, $24.50) was published in 1990, we felt obliged to include it in this review given that her first book, **The Greens Cookbook** (Bantam, 1987), is one of the classics of the genre. Clearly written by a seasoned professional, the recipes work, and there were no surprises. We tested recipes for hummus from four different books, for example, and Madison's

version was the clear winner with just the right flavor and texture. Other recipes from *Savory Way* were also good. Capellini with Lemon and Basil was simple and refreshing if a bit too lemony, and a vegetable hash recipe received great acclaim when served as a main course to a group of carnivores. We also tested Cumin Rice with Eggplant and Peppers, Red Bean and Rice "Soup," and a Summer Squash and Spinach Gratin with Ricotta Custard, which ranged from very good to acceptable but not worth the effort. We also have to say that we did begin to pine for the simplicity of *Unplugged* with its fewer ingredients to prepare—one recipe calls for turnips, rutabagas, broccoli stalks, and carrots. At the time it was published, *The Savory Way* was on the cutting edge of this burgeoning field. Today, however, newer entries have inevitably taken this sort of cooking to greater heights both in terms of imagination and ease of preparation. (Madison herself has a new book coming out shortly.) Yet *Savory Way* remains a solid, well-tested classic, a good addition to any cookbook shelf.

—*Christopher Kimball*

Sources and Resources

Most ingredients and materials necessary for the recipes in this issue are available at your local supermarket, gourmet store, or kitchen supply shop. The following are mail-order sources for particular items. Prices listed below were current at press time and do not include shipping or handling unless otherwise indicated. We suggest you contact companies directly to confirm current prices and availability.

Instant-Read Thermometers

When it comes to readability, quick response time, accuracy, and ease, the Owen Instruments Thermapen 5 came out on top in our instant-read thermometer testing on page 27. This top-performing thermometer, however, is also top price among the instant-read thermometers tested. The Thermapen 5 can be purchased for $59 through King Arthur Flour's mail-order service (The Baker's Catalogue, P.O. Box 876, Norwich, VT 05055-0876; 800-827-6836), though it is not pictured in the catalog. The Taylor Digital Pocket Thermometer, Model 9840, proved the runner-up in our thermometer tests. While it could not compete with the Thermapen's high performance in accuracy, we found it was easy to use and read, quick to register, and affordable. The Taylor Digital Pocket Thermometer is available for $15 in the Williams-Sonoma catalog (Mail Order Department, P.O. Box 7456, San Francisco, CA 94120-7456; 800-541-2233). The third-place Polder Cooking Thermometer/Timer with its distinguishing high-tech features, (*see* "Honorable Mention," page 29, for more details), can be purchased for $29.95 through the King Arthur Flour Baker's Catalogue and includes a one-year warranty.

Tongs for Grilling

Spring-loaded tongs are a must-have when it comes to grilling (see "Grilling Fuels, Tools, and Rules," page 16). We especially prefer sixteen-inch tongs because the added length protects your hands from the heat whether you are using the tongs to add coals to the fire, turn food, or transfer food to and from the grill. If you cannot find these in a local store, you can order a pair of twelve-inch and sixteen-inch tongs by mail from The Chef's Catalog (3215 Commercial Avenue, Northbrook, IL 60062-1900; 800-338-3232) for $9.99. These stainless steel tongs have blunt scalloped edges to prevent food from tearing.

Chimney Starter

We also highly recommend using a chimney starter to ignite coals. Chimney starters are an ecologically sound method of lighting charcoal without lighter fluid, they are simple, and they work every time. Most hardware stores carry some sort of chimney starter. Look for one with a heat-resistant handle and a separate chamber on the bottom in which to place pieces of crumpled newspaper. Weber manufactures a chimney starter with a stay-cool thermoplastic handle plus a wire foldout handle for added leverage to safely pour out the hot coals or briquettes. A cone-shaped interior grate supports the coals and accelerates ignition by exposing more of the coals' edges to the flame. Weber's coated steel chimney starter, which is seven and one-half inches in diameter and twelve inches high, sells for $15 through the company's catalog service (250 South Hicks Road, Palatine, IL 60067; 800-999-3237).

Charcoal Baskets or Rails

When grilling with indirect heat (see "Grilling Fuels, Tools, and Rules," page 16), either charcoal baskets or charcoal rails are useful for holding piles of charcoal along the sides of the grill. Two half-moon-shaped charcoal baskets made of coated steel are available for $10 through the Weber catalog service (*see* chimney starter listing, above). These fit in twenty-two-and-one-half-inch-diameter kettle grills only. Weber's charcoal rails act like a fence by holding charcoal against the sides of the kettle; they fit all kettle grills that are eighteen and one-half inches in diameter or larger. A set of two rails is $7 through Weber's mail-order service.

Griddle Update

The Vitantonio Gourmet Griddle listed in the May/June 1997 Sources and Resources has since been picked up by a number of cookware catalogs for a $20 savings over ordering directly through the manufacturer. In the testing of the French toast article in the May/June 1997 issue, we found the Vitantonio model preferable to other electric griddles for its even heat and solid construction. It is available by mail order for $59.95 through Kitchen & Home catalog (New Oxford, PA 17350-0129; 800-414-5544). In the May/June 1997 issue, the manufacturer's price of $88.15 included shipping costs.

Smoke and Fire

In "How to Grill Salmon" (page 6) and "Pulled Pork" (page 18) we found that hickory and mesquite wood chunks flavor slightly more than chips. Peoples Smoke'n Grill Shop (75 Mill Street, Cumberland, RI 02864; 800-729-5800) sells a twenty-pound bag of wood chunks for $11.95. The chunks are approximately three inches by six inches and come in the following varieties: hickory, ash, apple, cherry, sugar maple, and mesquite. Peoples also sells hardwood charcoal, which has none of the additives and chemicals used in briquettes. Lump hardwood charcoal also burns hotter and cleaner without imparting undesirable flavors or odors to the grilled food. Peoples hardwood charcoal can be ordered in 8 kg (17.6-pound) lots for $8.90 each or $7.90 each for two lots or more.

Grilling Hot Line

For the fourth consecutive year, the people at Weber are offering a toll-free hot line devoted to answering questions about outdoor grilling. Calls are fielded by a team of home economists, who are available Monday through Friday, 8 A.M. to 6 P.M., CST, through Labor Day. Dial 800-474-5568.

Upside-Down Cake Pan

Many upside-down cake recipes call for baking the cake in a cast-iron skillet. We found that cast iron works well, but it's heavy and therefore makes inverting a cake quite difficult. Our test kitchen tried a number of different pans and found that a professional-quality, straight-edged cake pan created an attractively shaped cake that was easy to flip. Kitchen Krafts carries such a pan. It is nine inches in diameter and has three-inch straight sides that make for the kind of deep upside-down cake we liked. The U.S.-made, heavy-gauge aluminum pan can be purchased for $7.25 by mail from the Kitchen Krafts catalog (P.O. Box 442, Waukon, IA 52172; 800-776-0575). The cake pan also comes in nine other sizes for making tiered cakes.

Amaretti Cookies

Sometimes referred to as Italian macaroons, amaretti are round cookies—crisp on the outside, crisp on the inside—with a faint bitterness derived from their almond base. While these cookies are tasty by themselves, they are also commonly crumbled and incorporated into a variety of Italian desserts, such as in the semifreddo recipe on page 23. Balducci's of New York, sells tins of individually wrapped amaretti cookies through its mail-order service (P.O. Box 10373, Newark, NJ 07193-0373; 800-225-3822). A 4.4-ounce tin sells for $7.50 and a 32-ounce tin sells for $32. Balducci's amaretti cookies are made in Italy.

Plum Upside-Down Cake
page 25

RECIPE INDEX

Grilled Salmon
with Indian Flavors and Fresh Mango
Chutney *page 7*

Chocolate Orange Semifreddo
with Bittersweet Chocolate Sauce
page 23

Pulled Pork Sandwich
with Western North Carolina–Style
Barbecue Sauce *page 19*

Grilled Chicken Breast *page 15*
with Sesame Lemon Cucumber Salad
page 8

Waldorf Chicken Salad
page 8

PHOTOGRAPHS BY CARL TREMBLAY/ STYLING BY EVA KATZ

Raspberry Spritzer

Puree 2 ¾ cups fresh or thawed frozen raspberries (one 12-ounce bag, frozen) with 2 tablespoons sugar in blender or food processor fitted with metal blade. Strain mixture through sieve, pressing on solids to release juice (should yield about 1 cup). Combine puree, ⅓ cup sugar, 1 tablespoon fresh lemon juice, and a dash salt in medium bowl; mix to dissolve sugar. Mix ¼ cup raspberry mixture with 1 cup seltzer in each of four tall pilsner-style glasses. Garnish with 1 scoop vanilla ice cream and a few fresh raspberries; serve immediately. Serves 4.

Adapted from Four Star Desserts (HarperCollins, 1996) by Emily Luchetti

COOK'S
ILLUSTRATED

Prebaking Pie Shells
Chill Two Ways for
Foolproof Results

Rating Food
Processors
Which Full-Size Models
Are Worth the Money?

How To Roast
Cornish Hens
Brine and Roast in a Hot
Oven for Moist, Tender Meat

Fast Vegetable
Lasagne
No-Boil Noodles Really Work

Rich, Foolproof
Rugelach
The Best Way to Make
this Tender Cookie-Pastry

HOMEMADE BAGELS

QUICK BROCCOLI SIDE DISHES

TASTING INEXPENSIVE
BORDEAUX

PAN SAUTÉED PORK TENDERLOIN

CAESAR SALAD REDISCOVERED

$4.00 U.S./$4.95 CANADA

Contents

About *Cook's Illustrated*

Cook's Illustrated *is published every other month (6 issues per year) and accepts no advertising. A one year subscription is $24.95, two years is $45, and three years is $65. Add $6 per year for Canadian subscriptions and $12 per year for all other countries. Gift subscriptions may be ordered for $19.95 each. You will receive a* Cook's Illustrated *gift card for each subscription which can be used to announce your gifts. The editors of* Cook's Illustrated *also publish an annual hardbound edition of the magazine which includes an annual index. These are available for $21.95 each plus shipping and handling. Discounts are available if more than one year is ordered at a time.*

Cook's Illustrated also publishes single topic books, How To Make A Pie, How To Make An American Layer Cake, How To Make Ice Cream, How To Stir Fry *and* How To Make Pizza. *All are available for $14.95 each. The* Cook's Bible, *authored by our editor and published by Little Brown, is also available for $24.95. Back issues are available for $5 each. We also accept submissions for both Quick Tips and Notes From Readers. See page 5 for more information.*

All queries about subscriptions or change of address notices should be addressed to Cook's Illustrated, P.O. Box 7445, Red Oak, IA 51591-0445. A free trial issue of our sister publication, Handcraft Illustrated, *may be requested by calling 800-526-8447.*

To order either subscriptions or books use the cards bound into this issue or, for faster service, call 800-526-8442 for subscriptions and 800-611-0759 for books and annuals.

"TOMATOES"

by Brent Watkinson

"PEACH BRUSCHETTA"

by Rene Milot

COOK'S
ILLUSTRATED

Publisher and Editor	Christopher Kimball
Executive Editor	Pam Anderson
Senior Editor	John Willoughby
Senior Writer	Jack Bishop
Associate Editor	Adam Ried
Contributing Editors	Mark Bittman Stephanie Lyness
Test Kitchen Director	Eva Katz
Test Cooks	Dawn Yanagihara Melissa Hamilton
Assistant Editor	Maryellen Driscoll
Test Kitchen Intern	Marnie M. Casavant
Art Director	Cathy Copeland
Special Projects Manager	Amy Klee
Managing Editor	Keith Powers
Editorial Prod. Manager	Sheila Datz
Copy Editor	Amy Finch
Marketing Director	Adrienne Kimball
Circulation Manager	David Mack
Fulfillment Manager	Larisa Greiner
Newsstand Manager	Jonathan Venier
Marketing Assistant	Connie Forbes
Circulation Assistant	Steven Browall
Vice President Production and Technology	James McCormack
Systems Administrator	Paul Mulvaney
Production Artist	Kevin Moeller
Editorial Production Assistants	Robert Parsons Daniel Frey
Controller	Lisa A. Carullo
Accounting Assistant	Mandy Shito
Office Manager	Livia McRee
Special Projects	Fern Berman

Cook's Illustrated (ISSN 1068-2821) is published bimonthly by Boston Common Press Limited Partnership, 17 Station Street, P.O. Box 569, Brookline, MA 02147-0569. Copyright 1997 Boston Common Press Limited Partnership. Periodical postage paid at Boston, MA, and additional mailing offices, USPS #012487. For list rental information, please contact List Services Corporation, 6 Trowbridge Drive, P.O. Box 516, Bethel, CT 06801; (203) 743-2600, FAX (203) 743-0589. Editorial office: 17 Station Street, P.O. Box 470589, Brookline, MA 02146; (617) 232-1000, FAX (617) 232-1572. Editorial contributions should be sent to: Editor, *Cook's Illustrated*. We cannot assume responsibility for manuscripts submitted to us. Submissions will be returned only if accompanied by a large self-addressed stamped envelope. Subscription rates: $24.95 for one year; $45 for two years; $65 for three years. (Canada: add $6 per year; all other countries: add $12 per year.) Postmaster: Send all new orders, subscription inquiries, and change of address notices to *Cook's Illustrated*, P.O. Box 7446, Red Oak, IA 51591-0446. Single copies: $4 in U.S., $4.95 in Canada and other countries. Back issues available for $5 each. PRINTED IN THE U.S.A.

EDITORIAL

Dear Charlie

You're my first son, your two older sisters having exhibited a startling disregard for gender-neutral behavior, quickly abandoning the train set and Tonka toys (presents from Dad) in favor of bright-pink Lisa Frank diaries and endless rolls of glow-in-the-dark stickers (presents from Mom). I didn't know I wanted a son until you came along one January afternoon, the plumbing merely a passing detail at the time. But today as I sat on the half-rusted International, ploughing up the lower corn field, you sat on my lap, lulled by the warm spring sun and the churning of the tiller, until your small body went soft, eyes half-closed, rocking gently in my arms. The roar of the tractor's engine is always a call to action, sending your short legs into a frenzy of motion, racing down the driveway as you call after your dad on the big red machine. It is honest work we do together, the two of us, watching the swallows swoop over the just-ploughed fields, your dad trying frantically not to let the moments fade.

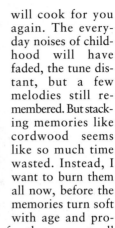

CHARLES KIMBALL

But for now, I take comfort that my life is filled with a great inventory of moments yet to be lived: our first fishing expedition, watching the sun burn through the thick, early morning mist on the Battenkill; splitting and stacking oak and chestnut on a chilly November afternoon, the two of us working as one; our first hunt together, flushing a grouse or woodcock, the great beating of wings sending our hearts racing at the same instant. As a father of older children, I know that the innocence fades over time and the special moments are of a different sort, no less magical, but painted in more subtle, often darker hues. They come not in great waves of joy but in single, unexpected moments; a parent's ear must be well-tuned not to miss them. But you are still young and a boy, all bluff and swagger, without the skill or need to hide what you are really thinking. Your deepest desires are etched plainly in your smile.

Yet during these postcard summers, I am constantly reminded that the time will come when the farmhouse will be still, abandoned by small voices. I see your mother and I, standing by the stove, troubled, not knowing when we will cook for you again. The everyday noises of childhood will have faded, the tune distant, but a few melodies still remembered. But stacking memories like cordwood seems like so much time wasted. Instead, I want to burn them all now, before the memories turn soft with age and produce little heat. Living for the moment, all the bright, crisp New England days will collapse together as one, the two of us driving the old Ford in circles in the lower meadow, laughing, banging the horn, getting stuck in mud up to the axles and not caring. We'll set aside the camera and notebook and explore old hay lofts, finding great treasures: a dusty bottle of number two colic drops or an old issue of *Hoard's Dairyman*. We'll be a right pair, you and I, going everywhere, doing everything, the neighbors expecting to see your small, round face peering through the steering wheel each time I drive by. And when our summers together are over, and time enough has passed to cloud memories of frog hunts and muddy boots, bowls of homemade peach ice cream, old yellow casseroles filled with silky custard, and the crashing of thunder as we sit snug on the front porch, I will drive the old pickup down the same dirt road we travelled many summers before. On that day, you will have long said goodbye to this small town, but our neighbors will see your face in mine as I pass; happy, expectant, full, I hope, of the joy of a two-year-old, eyes keen with the excitement of a new world just around the next bend.

And on another day, you will come back home to show us your trophies and scars, having struck, I hope, a few shrewd blows in favor of civilization. I will search your face for a hint of your dad: The way I squint into the bright sun or the way your eyes reflect a passing memory, a small wisp of smoke from that blazing fire we started so many years ago. But if I look hard and see nothing of myself, that will be no disappointment. I'll know that each time I start up the old tractor, you will be there for me, asleep in my arms as we plough together the fields of your childhood.

Notes *from* Readers

Nonstick Cookware Abuse

Recently, I set about two cups of water to boil over high heat in a Berndes nonstick two-quart sauce pot, promptly forgot all about it, and took my dog out for a walk. When I returned home, the water had boiled off completely and the pan was burning away, filling the kitchen with dense, awful-smelling smoke. Actually, calling this smoke awful does not do it justice—acrid, choking, and chemical describe it better. Once the disaster cleared, I was surprised to find that the pan appeared to be just fine. Can I continue to use it or should it be thrown out?

SHERMAN M.A. RAOUF
WESTPORT, MA

We checked with representatives from both Berndes and DuPont, maker of Teflon™ (a DuPont trademark) nonstick finishes for cookware lines such as Berndes, Farberware, Revere Spectrum, and Circulon. Both sources agreed that your pot is safe for continued use, although its nonstick performance may be compromised.

Nonstick coatings are made from a base of fluorocarbon resin that is bonded to the pans through a series of applications. One of the drawbacks of these materials, as you found out, is that they will begin to burn and give off noxious gas at roughly 500 degrees, a temperature achieved on a home stovetop if a pan is left empty and unattended. For this reason, DuPont recommends cooking with nonstick pans at low or medium heat. At the 500-degree volatilization point, deterioration of the coating begins, resulting in smoke and fumes. At about 660 degrees, there is significant decomposition.

The fumes and dense smoke you've described indicate such a deterioration of your pot's nonstick coating. Christa Kaiser, communications manager for DuPont's Teflon™ Finishes said that reusing the pot does not pose a health risk, and the United States Food and Drug Administration (FDA) agrees. According to the FDA, if there were flaking of the Teflon™ coating, which can occur if a metal utensil scrapes against it, the human body would not absorb any ingested particles, which are nontoxic and inert. In a poorly ventilated area, fumes from an overheated nonstick are unpleasant and have, in rare instances, caused mild and temporary flu-like symptoms, but they are not notably toxic.

Irene Muzio, a representative for Berndes, told us that regardless of incidents of dramatic overheating, the nonstick coatings on cookware will deteriorate gradually with use. Though overheating will accelerate the process, one incident should not ruin the pan. Repeated overheating may discolor the pan and eventually result in flaking.

Kaiser did suggest, however, that you replace the pot if the nonstick coating is visibly ruined—or if flaking begins—because the nonstick surface will no longer be effective.

Another Kind of Pomi Tomatoes

I was very surprised to find in your article on canned crushed tomatoes (March/April 1997) that our Pomi tomatoes came in last place compared to other products. I must say, however, that I was relieved to find out what you were comparing. You see, all the products mentioned were crushed, with the exception of our strained tomatoes. I think that Pomi chopped tomatoes, not our strained product, should have been included in the article. I am sure that if the comparison was made with this product, the results would be quite different.

PATRIZIO SPAGNOLETTO
PARMALAT USA
TEANECK, NJ

Unfortunately, we were unaware of Pomi chopped tomatoes when assembling the field for our tasting. Therefore, we decided to hold a second blind tasting with the two top finishers from the original tasting (Progresso and Muir Glen) and Pomi chopped tomatoes. Our tasters (from the editorial and kitchen staffs of the magazine) clearly preferred Muir Glen and Progresso to the Pomi chopped tomatoes.

Like our favorite canned crushed tomatoes, Pomi chopped tomatoes have plenty of seeds and tomato chunks. However, like the low-rated Pomi strained tomatoes, our tasters found the flavor of Pomi chopped tomatoes to be bland and watery. Both the chopped and strained Pomi tomatoes lack the sweet, ripe tomato flavor we prefer in any canned (or aseptically packaged) tomato product.

Cheesecake Slicing

In the November/December 1996 issue, you suggested using dental floss to cut cheesecake. I've found that lightweight monofilament fishing line works better because no loose particles from the floss end up in the cake.

GUSTAV BAHRUTH
FORT MYERS, FL

We cut a dense cheesecake with both dental floss and fishing line, which does indeed make nice clean slices. Not all households will have fishing line on hand, though, whereas most probably do have dental floss. Because we did not experience shredding of the floss in the cake, we'd use either, whichever you happen to have around.

Real Key Lime Pie

Is it possible to make a sweet potato pie with pumpkin? Can you make buttermilk biscuits with sweet milk? Can you make pecan pie with pistachios? No more can you make a Key Lime pie with "supermarket" Persian limes! Your "supermarket" Persian lime pie is delicious... but KEY LIME PIE IT AIN'T!

I fear that you missed the point of Key Lime pie. The operative word is KEY, not lime. Regardless of the other ingredients used, a Key Lime pie must contain Key Lime juice, which is responsible for the pie's characteristic pale yellow color and tart, biting flavor.

WILLIAM E. PATTERSON
MIAMI, FL

Your letter was one of many we received that contested our use of the name "Key Lime pie" for our pie recipe based on Persian limes, published in the March/April 1997 issue. Susan Dollinger, of Islamorada, FL, for example, pointed out, "There is a very real difference between the two pies in both color and taste.... Both pies are good, but they are different pies."

Now that our eyes have been opened to this concern by so many readers, we concur. In a side-by-side tasting of pies, one flavored with fresh-squeezed juice from Key Limes and the other with Persian lime juice, our tasters agreed that there is a discernible difference. The pie with Key Lime juice tasted sharp and intense. The pie with Persian lime juice was milder by comparison. The color was another noticeable difference. Key Lime juice, and the pie made with it, was a pale, milky yellow, not the light green that we achieved by tinting the filling of the other pie with the lime zest. Our apologies to Key Lime fans.

The Water in Bread

My friend and I were discussing your article on whole wheat bread (January/February 1997) in which you said that most tasters preferred bread made with bottled water, instead of water from the tap. Since bottles of water are heavy to lug around and are an added grocery expense, I wondered about using plain tap water that has been boiled instead?

JILL STARKEY
RACINE, WI

We checked out your question by conducting a blind tasting of three loaves of the whole wheat bread, one made with tap water, a second with bottled water, and a third with tap water that had been boiled and cooled to room temperature. While the taste differences between the three were relatively minor, the loaf made with the boiled and cooled water was the unanimous last choice of all five tasters, garnering comments such as "harsh," "off," and "metallic tasting." Consistent with the tests we ran while developing the recipe, everyone chose the loaf made with bottled water for its sweeter, fuller flavor. The tap water loaf, which had a somewhat saltier, though not "off" flavor, fell between the two.

We consulted six leading food scientists about what could have happened to the boiled water, and no two of them agreed. One of the few points on which they did agree, however, is that tap water varies widely from place to place, containing different combinations and concentrations of solids such as minerals, salts, chemicals, and organic matter. For this reason, municipalities usually subject the water to a chemical treatment. We spoke with a manager at Monadnock Mountain Spring Water, the company that supplies our office, who posited that the bottled water probably tasted best because it travels through pipes made exclusively of stainless steel, is treated without chemicals, and is filtered extensively.

...and in Pastry Dough, Too
Most pie crust recipes call for ice water, but because I do not usually have ice on hand, I pour the water into a metal bowl and place it in the freezer. The metal conducts the cold quickly, so the water rapidly becomes ice cold.

SYLVIA LIM
DURHAM, NC

If ice were unavailable, we'd use your system, too. We put one-half cup cold tap water (at 68 degrees) in a small stainless steel bowl and placed it in the freezer. After five minutes, it had chilled to 48 degrees; at ten minutes it was 40 degrees; and after fifteen minutes it was 36 degrees, with ice just beginning to form around the edges. Use this water just out of the freezer, though, because it had warmed up to 42 degrees after sitting on the counter for five minutes.

Keeping Whipped Cream
Recent articles such as "Classic Cream Pies" (March/April 1996) and "Real Strawberry Shortcake" (May/June 1997) resulted in numerous reader inquiries and suggestions about the best way to keep whipped cream for a day or two without a loss of volume. Ideas fell into two categories. One group of ideas recommended adding various common pantry ingredients (exclusive of stabilizers available to professional pastry chefs) to the cream as you're whipping it, to stabilize the finished product. Suggested additions, each to one cup of cream, included one teaspoon of light corn syrup, one tablespoon of dry milk powder, one teaspoon cornstarch heated in one-fourth cup of the cream, and one teaspoon of melted, unflavored gelatin. The second category of suggestions concerned different methods of storing the finished whipped cream. Holding methods included keeping the whipped cream in a paper filter-lined coffee filter holder set over a mug, in a pastry bag fitted with a metal tip and set upright in a tall glass or container, and in a strainer set over a bowl, as we directed in the strawberry shortcake piece.

In the category of cream whipped with added ingredients, the dry milk powder was the most successful. After 48 hours in the refrigerator the cream was still full and moist, as if freshly whipped. There was no pool of excess liquid collected at the bottom of the bowl because the powdered milk had absorbed it, and we were not able to detect any change in the flavor. When piped into rosettes, however, none of these whipped creams, including that made with the powdered milk, remained firm enough to give sharp definition.

The three storage methods yielded very similar results. All the creams had been drained of excess moisture, which created a somewhat dry, though not unpleasant, consistency. The drained creams produced sharp, well-defined rosettes when piped, but after 48 hours, none were as close in consistency to freshly whipped as the powdered-milk whipped cream.

So, if you must whip cream far in advance of using it, choose the method best suited to your needs. Powdered milk is a fine addition if you'll be serving the whipped cream in dollops, but if you plan to pipe it for decoration, we recommend a storage method that allows it to drain.

Dégorger
I enjoyed your July/August 1997 article about preparing cucumber salads, and those I've tried were delicious. The recipes are based on a technique of salting sliced cucumbers and weighting them down to help eliminate some of the water in the vegetable. I am convinced that there is a one-word name for this culinary process, but I can't remember the word to save my life. I've asked friends and consulted culinary dictionaries, but still haven't come up with the answer.

SHIRLEY JACOB LANTZ
BRIDGEPORT, CT

The word you've been looking for is dégorger (pronounced day-gor-jay). It is a French term, the literal translation of which is "to overflow" or "to flow out." According to the latest American edition of the classic French culinary encyclopedia, *Larousse Gastronomique* (Crown Publishers, 1988), dégorger means to soak fish, poultry, meat, or variety meats in a cold water and vinegar solution, or often just cold water, to draw out blood and impurities prior to cooking. The process is used especially when the food will be made into a 'white' dish, with a light colored sauce. The term also encompasses the salting of watery vegetables, such as cucumbers and cabbage, and of snails, to eliminate excess liquid.

What Is It?
I just moved away from home, and into my first apartment. My mom packed up a few of her old kitchen utensils—stuff she no longer uses—for me to take. Along with the potholders and spatulas and colanders was this thing. I'm not totally inept in the kitchen, but I don't have a clue what this is.

TY HOLLAND
BLOOMINGTON, IN

Your mother gave you a pasta portioner. A common, inexpensive item often found among the kitchen gadgets in supermarkets and hardware stores, it is supposed to eliminate the guesswork when determining average portions of spaghetti to cook. Made from either wood or plastic,  pasta portioners, which are known also as spaghetti measures, have from three to six holes that progress in size from small to large. The amount of dry spaghetti or linguine that fits within the diameter of a particular hole should equal average portions, once cooked, for the number of people that corresponds to the size of that hole. Sometimes, the holes are labeled with numbers to indicate portions.

ILLUSTRATION BY DAN KROVATIN

TESTING INGREDIENT ADDITIONS

If you cook on the fly like Bambi Vincent of Las Vegas, Nevada, but aren't always sure of your improvisations, try her method of sampling a new ingredient before adding it to the entire pot. This way, you don't risk ruining the whole dish with a flavor that doesn't work out well.

1. Dip a ladle into your pot and raise a small amount of the food up and out. Add a drop of the ingredient you are considering.

2. Taste, and if you dislike the result, discard or stir the ladleful back into the pot and move on to the next ingredient choice.

Quick

The editors of *Cook's Illustrated* would like to thank all of our readers who have sent us their quick tips. We have enjoyed reading every one of them and have learned a lot. Keep them coming. We will provide a one-year complimentary subscription for each quick tip that we print. Send a description of your special technique to *Cook's Illustrated*, P.O. Box 569, Brookline Village, MA 02146-0569. Please write

EASY BACON BITS

Rather than frying bacon slices whole and then crumbling them to make bits, Carole Barenys of Brentwood, Tennessee, streamlines the operation by slicing across a whole package of bacon at $1/8$-inch intervals and cooking the presliced bacon, breaking it up as it fries.

SAFE BAGEL SLICING

Cook's Illustrated senior writer Jack Bishop recommends that, when slicing a bagel, you wear a thick oven mitt to protect your hand.

EASY RICE HANDLING AND STORAGE

If you buy rice or popcorn kernels in bulk, try this method that Don Chu Mun of Jackson Heights, New York, devised to solve the problems of storing and pouring from large, cumbersome sacks.

1. Position a funnel in the mouth of a clean half-gallon plastic jug and fill it to the top with rice or popcorn kernels. Screw the cap on for sealed, protected storage.

2. With its handle and narrow pouring spout, the jug makes it easy to dispense a small amount of its contents needed for a single recipe.

CONTROLLING YOUR TONGS

If you own spring-loaded tongs that do not lock in the closed position, follow this tip from Verna Brown of Missoula, Montana, to make them easier to store. Just slip a simple key ring over the hinged end of the tongs and down the shaft; this will keep the tongs closed so they'll fit neatly in a drawer.

QUICK SHAKER JAR

When your shaker jars and strainers are otherwise occupied and you need a very fine dusting of flour, confectioners' sugar, cornmeal, or the like, make a homemade version of a shaker using this method submitted by Theresa Gallagher of Wilmington, Delaware.

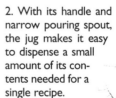

1. Place the ingredient in a glass jar and cover the mouth with a single layer of cheesecloth, secured with a rubber band.

2. Now go ahead and shake out the contents. This is especially useful when a very lightly floured surface is necessary.

3. Screw on the lid with the cheesecloth still in place to keep the jar airtight for storage.

Tips

"Attention: Quick Tips" on the envelope and include your name, address, and daytime phone number. Unfortunately, we can only acknowledge receipt of tips that will be printed in the magazine. In case the same tip is received from two readers, the one postmarked first will be selected. Also, be sure to let us know what particular cooking problems you would like us to investigate in upcoming issues.

ALWAYS READY TO DIP AND SWEEP

Sometimes you forget to grab a knife on the way to the flour canister to level your cup measurements. If so, do what Mary Johnson of Topeka, Kansas, does.

1. Keep a wooden tongue depressor right in the canister with the flour.

2. That way, you will always be ready to level your measurement.

BLANCHING SALTED NUTS

When a recipe calls for unsalted nuts but all you have on hand are salted, do not despair. Follow the tip of our test kitchen director Eva Katz and immerse the nuts in boiling water for 1 minute, then remove them with a slotted spoon onto a baking sheet and roast them at 350 degrees until dry to the touch.

LISTING NEW PROPORTIONS

Rather than converting ingredient proportions every time you halve or double a favorite recipe, try this tip suggested by Sandy Lewis of Malibu, California. Calculate the new measurements just once and list them in the same order as the ingredients in the recipe on a narrow slip of paper or a Post-it note. Clip or stick the paper with the new measurements next to the original measurement column in the recipe. No more strained memory or guesswork.

STACKING NONSTICK PANS

Because the nonstick surface on pans can be fragile and scratch easily if scraped against another metal, Frances Katsuleas of Oak Brook, Illinois, places the plastic covers from coffee cans between pans when she stacks them for storage.

IMPROMPTU STEAMER

For those times when you find yourself without a true steamer basket, try this setup suggested by Kenneth Wong of South St. Paul, Minnesota. Place the food to be steamed in a metal colander, then place the colander over a pot of water and cover the pot.

PREFLAVORING FROZEN CHICKEN BREASTS

Sharon Meadows of Radford, Virginia, often cooks with boneless chicken breasts that she has frozen and then thawed. She devised this way to give the chicken an extra flavor boost.

Place the chicken breasts in a labeled zipper-lock freezer bag, then add your favorite marinade, seal the bag, and place it in the freezer. When thawed, the chicken will be flavored with the marinade.

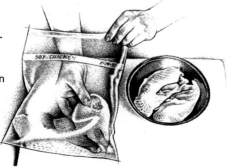

INSTANT COOLING RACK

Brenda Theodore of Montreal, Quebec, has found a good use for emptied 28-ounce tin cans. Clean the cans inside and out, then open both ends with a can opener. Rest hot-out-of-the-oven cake pans, cookie sheets, casseroles, or roasting pans on two, three, or four cans, depending on the size of the pan.

Quick Vegetable Lasagne

Precooking the vegetables drives off moisture and boosts flavor. No-boil noodles,
which simplify preparation, soften properly when used with plenty of sauce.

by Jack Bishop

A lasagne with no-boil noodles needs about forty minutes in the oven, as compared to twenty to twenty-five minutes for a conventional recipe, but less time is spent on the dish overall.

Vegetable lasagne sounds wonderful, but the reality is often quite disappointing. Too often, the dish is bland and watery, nothing like the rich, hearty version with meat. (For information on classic lasagne with tomato sauce and meatballs, *see* "Classic Lasagne Made Easy," November/December 1994.) But I also know that vegetable lasagne can be full-flavored and delicious. I wrote a book on the subject and have developed some good recipes in the past. For this article, I wanted to test every possibility and figure out definitively what works and what doesn't.

I knew from past experience that precooking the vegetables not only drives off excess liquid but gives the cook a chance to boost their flavor, either by caramelizing their natural sugars or by adding ingredients such as olive oil, garlic, hot red pepper flakes, or herbs. The moisture content of the vegetable determines which cooking technique should be used. For example, high-moisture mushrooms are best sautéed or roasted, but low-moisture broccoli must be chopped, blanched, and then sautéed. (For information on how to cook specific vegetables, *see* "Preparing Vegetables for Lasagne," page 7.) While it is possible to combine two (or more) vegetables in one lasagne, choose vegetables that can be cooked in the same fashion to keep prep time to a minimum.

No-Boil Noodles Save Time

At this point in my testing, several colleagues suggested that I attempt to develop a master recipe with no-boil noodles. I was skeptical but thought the potential time savings warranted some effort.

The first no-boil lasagne noodles appeared on supermarket shelves several years ago just as I was finishing up my book on lasagne. I tried them in my favorite lasagne recipe with tomato sauce, tiny meatballs, and mozzarella cheese and was unimpressed. The noodles sucked all the moisture out of the sauce, leaving tiny bits of dried-out tomato pulp on them. As for the noodles, they were way too stiff, almost crunchy in places. The label on one brand suggested pouring stock over the lasagne just before it went into the oven. The result was a watery mess. I thought no-boil noodles would be a passing fad and did not use them in my book.

Fast-forward several years. No-boil lasagne noodles are now standard items in most supermarkets. I figured someone must be using these noodles successfully. Or maybe the noodles themselves (there are now American as well as Italian brands) had improved.

Some recipes I ran across in my research for this story suggested soaking the noodles in either cold or hot tap water before layering them with the sauce and cheese. I found that this step made the pasta too soft after baking.

As I had observed several years ago, just layering the noodles and sauce into the pan and then baking is not acceptable. The sauce dries out, and the noodles are too crispy. In an attempt to keep the sauce from drying out, I wrapped the lasagne pan with foil and then baked it. This step was clearly an improvement. The noodles were tender, not crunchy, and the sauce was not overly reduced.

It also helped to use more sauce than I ordinarily use with boiled noodles. I found that leaving my tomato sauce fairly watery (I simmered it for just five minutes and then added a little water) was a benefit. The no-boil noodles soaked up some of the excess liquid, and

the sauce reduced to the proper consistency. (If you want to use conventional noodles in the vegetable lasagne recipes that follow, simmer the tomato sauce until fairly thick, about fifteen minutes, and do not add the water.)

Covering the lasagne with foil as it bakes does present a couple of problems. First, the foil tends to stick to the top layer of cheese. Spraying the foil with vegetable oil is an easy solution. The other issue is browning the top layer of cheese. When you bake a conventional lasagne uncovered in the oven, the top layer of cheese becomes golden and chewy in spots. I found that by removing the foil during the last fifteen minutes of baking, I was able to achieve the color and texture I wanted.

In addition, I found that tomato sauce works much better than béchamel as a binder when using no-boil noodles. The béchamel (a white sauce made with milk, butter, and flour) cooks down and becomes gluey. More important, béchamel, even when made with extra milk, has less available moisture (the starches in the flour hold on to any extra liquid) than tomato sauce and does not rehydrate no-boil noodles, especially those on the top layer, as well.

Five years after my first failed attempts at using no-boil noodles in vegetable lasagne, I have finally succeeded. The secrets: precook the vegetables, use plenty of liquidy tomato sauce, and cover the pan during the first part of the baking time.

MASTER RECIPE FOR VEGETABLE LASAGNE WITH TOMATO SAUCE
Serves 6 to 8

Smoked mozzarella, Gruyère, or Fontina can be substituted for the mozzarella and Pecorino Romano for the Parmesan. Also, three and one-half cups of your favorite prepared tomato sauce can be substituted for the sauce in this recipe. Because no-boil noodles come twelve to sixteen in a box, we suggest buying two boxes to ensure that you'll have the fifteen required for this lasagne.

- 2   tablespoons olive oil
- 2   medium garlic cloves, minced
- 1   28-ounce can crushed tomatoes
- 2   tablespoons chopped fresh basil or parsley leaves
    Salt and ground black pepper
- 15 dried 7-by-3½-inch no-boil lasagne noodles
- 3   cups cooked and seasoned vegetables (*see* "Preparing Vegetables for Lasagne," page 7, or recipes that follow)

1 pound mozzarella cheese, shredded (about 4 cups)
5 ounces Parmesan cheese, grated (about ⅔ cup)
Cooking spray for foil

1. Heat oil and garlic in 10-inch skillet over medium heat until fragrant but not brown, about 2 minutes. Stir in tomatoes; simmer until thickened slightly, about 10 minutes. Stir in basil or parsley and salt and pepper to taste. Pour into large measuring cup. Add enough water to make 3½ cups.

2. Spread ½ cup sauce evenly over bottom of greased 13-by-9-inch lasagne pan. Lay three noodles crosswise over sauce, making sure they do not touch each other or sides of pan. Spread ¾ cup prepared vegetables evenly over noodles, ½ cup sauce evenly over vegetables, and ¾ cup mozzarella and 2 generous tablespoons Parmesan evenly over sauce. Repeat layering of noodles, vegetables, sauce, and cheeses three more times. For fifth and final layer, lay final three noodles crosswise over previous layer and top with remaining 1 cup tomato sauce, 1 cup mozzarella, and 2 tablespoons Parmesan. (Can be wrapped with plastic and refrigerated overnight or wrapped in plastic and aluminum foil and frozen for up to 1 month. If frozen, defrost in refrigerator.)

3. Adjust oven rack to middle position and heat oven to 375 degrees. Cover pan with large sheet foil greased with cooking spray. Bake 25 minutes (30 minutes if chilled); remove foil and continue baking until top turns golden brown in spots, about 15 minutes. Remove pan from oven and let lasagne rest 5 minutes. Cut and serve immediately.

ROASTED ZUCCHINI AND EGGPLANT LASAGNE

Adjust oven racks to upper- and lower-middle positions and heat oven to 400 degrees. Toss 1 pound each zucchini (about 2 medium) and eggplant (about 2 small), cut into ½-inch dice, with 3 tablespoons olive oil, 4 minced garlic cloves, and salt and pepper to taste. Spread out vegetables on two greased baking sheets; roast, turning occasionally, until golden brown, about 35 minutes. Set vegetables aside. Follow Master Recipe for Vegetable Lasagne with Tomato Sauce.

SPINACH AND MUSHROOM LASAGNE

Cremini mushrooms are particularly good in this dish, but any fresh mushroom is fine.

Heat 2 tablespoons olive oil over medium heat in soup kettle. Add 1 minced medium onion; sauté until translucent, about 5 minutes. Add 1 pound mushrooms, trimmed and sliced; sauté until golden, about 8 minutes. Season with salt and pepper to taste. Remove mushrooms; set aside. In same pan, heat 1 tablespoon olive oil over medium heat; add 10 ounces (12 cups) washed, stemmed, and chopped spinach leaves.

Cook, stirring often, until wilted, about 5 minutes. Season with salt and pepper to taste. Set vegetables aside. Follow Master Recipe for Vegetable Lasagne with Tomato Sauce, Mozzarella, and Parmesan.

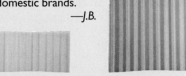

PREPARING VEGETABLES FOR LASAGNE

Use the following vegetables, either singly or in combination, in the master recipe. You need a total of three cups of cooked and seasoned vegetables. Toss the vegetables with enough olive oil to coat them lightly before roasting or sauté them in a few tablespoons of olive oil. Season the vegetables with salt and pepper as well as fresh herbs, garlic, or hot red pepper flakes, if desired.

Vegetable	Preparation and Cooking Method
Asparagus	Trim tough ends, slice in half lengthwise, and cut into ½-inch pieces; blanch until crisp-tender, about 1 minute, drain well, and sauté until tender, about 3 minutes.
Broccoli/ Cauliflower	Cut into florets; blanch until crisp-tender, about 2 minutes, drain well, chop into ¼-inch pieces, and sauté until tender, about 4 minutes.
Eggplant	Cut into ½-inch dice; roast until tender, about 35 minutes at 400 degrees.
Fennel	Cut bulb into very thin strips; sauté or roast until tender, about 15 minutes for sautéing or 30 minutes at 400 degrees for roasting.
Mushrooms	Trim and slice or dice; sauté or roast until golden, 8 minutes for sautéing or 20 minutes at 400 degrees for roasting.
Onions	Peel and cut into thin slices; sauté or roast until soft and golden, 5 to 7 minutes for sautéing or 20 minutes at 400 degrees for roasting.
Spinach/ Swiss Chard	Wash, stem, and chop; sauté until wilted, about 5 minutes.
Zucchini	Cut into ½-inch dice; sauté or roast until tender, about 7 minutes for sautéing or 35 minutes at 400 degrees for roasting.

Quick Broccoli Side Dishes

*Tossing broccoli with a potent dressing or sauce delivers
maximum impact with minimum effort.*

by Jack Bishop

As vegetables for side dishes go, broccoli is certainly appealing. It's available in good quantity year-round and generally holds up well both in supermarkets and at home in the refrigerator.

The challenge for many cooks, though, is figuring out how to flavor broccoli.

For instant flavor without fuss, uncooked dressings and sauces can be tossed with steamed broccoli. Like all brassicas (think cabbage and brussels sprouts), broccoli has a strong flavor, so equally strong dressings, flavored with chiles, ginger, garlic, citrus juices, and spices, are best. The four recipes that follow offer some good examples.

MASTER RECIPE FOR
STEAMED BROCCOLI
Serves 4

If you prefer, follow the illustrations at right for rapidly trimming the broccoli and proceed directly to steaming. While the broccoli cooks, prepare one of the sauces below.

1½ pounds broccoli (about 1 medium
      bunch), rinsed
½ teaspoon salt

1. Separate florets from stalks at points where floret stems meet stalks. Cut off woody bottoms of stalks; trim away ⅛ inch of outer peel. Cut stalk in half lengthwise and then into bite-sized pieces. If desired, separate florets into smaller sections and peel stems; arrange in steamer insert or basket.

2. Bring about 1 inch water to boil in deep, wide pot. Lower insert or basket with broccoli into pot so it rests above water; cover and simmer until just tender, 4½ to 5 minutes. Remove broccoli; continue with one of the following recipes.

BROCCOLI WITH SPICY BALSAMIC
DRESSING AND BLACK OLIVES
Serves 4

2 teaspoons balsamic vinegar
2 teaspoons red wine vinegar
1 medium garlic clove, minced
½ teaspoon hot red pepper flakes, or to
      taste
¼ teaspoon salt
¼ cup extra-virgin olive oil
1 recipe Steamed Broccoli
12 large black olives, such as Kalamata
      or Gaeta, pitted and quartered

1. Whisk first five ingredients in small bowl;
whisk in oil until dressing is smooth.

2. Gently toss steamed broccoli with dressing and olives. Adjust seasonings; serve hot or at room temperature.

BROCCOLI WITH ORANGE-GINGER
DRESSING AND WALNUTS
Serves 4

1 tablespoon peanut oil
1 tablespoon soy sauce
1 tablespoon honey
1 tablespoon grated zest and 3 table-
      spoons juice from 1 large orange
1 medium garlic clove, peeled
1 piece (about 1 inch) fresh gingerroot,
      peeled
¼ teaspoon salt

QUICK BROCCOLI PREP
This quick, easy method works well on heads of broccoli with widely separated branches.

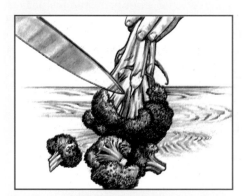

1. Place the head of broccoli upside down on a work surface. Use a large, sharp knife to quickly trim off the florets very close to their heads.

2. To trim the stalks, stand them up on the cutting board and square them off with a large, sharp knife.

1 recipe Steamed Broccoli
2 medium scallions, white and green
      parts, sliced thin
⅔ cup walnuts, toasted and chopped
      coarse

1. Process first seven ingredients in workbowl of food processor or blender, scraping down sides as needed, until dressing is smooth.

2. Gently toss steamed broccoli with dressing, scallions, and walnuts. Adjust seasonings; serve hot or at room temperature.

BROCCOLI WITH
LIME-CUMIN DRESSING
Serves 4

Caribbean flavors characterize this easy dressing, and residual heat from the broccoli tames the raw red onion.

1 teaspoon grated zest and 1 tablespoon
      juice from 1 large lime
½ teaspoon ground cumin
½ teaspoon salt
      Hot red pepper sauce
3 tablespoons extra-virgin olive oil
¼ cup minced red onion
1 recipe Steamed Broccoli

1. Whisk first four ingredients (pepper sauce to taste) in small bowl. Whisk in oil until dressing is smooth; stir in onion.

2. Gently toss steamed broccoli with dressing. Adjust seasonings; serve hot or at room temperature.

BROCCOLI WITH SPANISH GREEN
HERB SAUCE
Serves 4

The fresh herbs in this sauce will be pureed, so leaving a few small stems is fine.

2 medium garlic cloves, peeled
½ cup tightly packed fresh cilantro
      leaves
½ cup tightly packed fresh parsley leaves
3 tablespoons extra-virgin olive oil
1 tablespoon juice from 1 small lemon
½ teaspoon salt
1 recipe Steamed Broccoli

1. Process first six ingredients in workbowl of food processor or blender, scraping down sides of bowl as needed, until sauce is smooth.

2. Gently toss steamed broccoli with sauce. Adjust seasonings; serve hot or at room temperature.

The Secrets of Prebaking Pie Shells

Unless you both refrigerate and freeze pie pastry before prebaking, it will shrink and puff in the oven. After four months and over fifty baked shells, we share a dozen secrets to foolproof prebaking.

by Eva Katz

A smooth, perfectly browned pre-baked pie shell depends on dual chilling, but does not require docking.

Baking an unfilled pie pastry, commonly called blind baking, can turn out to be the ultimate culinary nightmare. Without the weight of a filling, a pastry shell set into a hot oven can shrink dramatically, fill with air pockets, and puff up like a linoleum floor after a flood. The result? A shrunken, uneven shell that can hold only part of the filling it should. But there is hope. Months of testing and a bit of luck have revealed the secrets of prebaking, and a foolproof recipe.

I started out with one strong advantage: a pie crust recipe that I really liked, developed for "Pie Pastry Revisited" (September/October 1996). This pastry dough holds its shape when baked but is still flaky, tender, and full of flavor.

I also started with the knowledge that dough needs to rest once it is rolled out and placed into a pie dish. What was less clear to me was whether the dough should do its resting in the refrigerator or the freezer. In my experience, freezing has offered some advantages over refrigerating: It is faster, and because it produces a firmer dough, it allows you to press foil securely into the corners of the pastry without inadvertently damaging the fluted edges. However, I was uncertain as to whether freezing would have equally positive effects on the crust while in the oven. I wondered whether it would result in more or less shrinkage during baking, for example, and whether it would have an adverse effect on texture.

My first side-by-side testing of freezing versus refrigeration showed few noticeable differences in texture, flavor, or shrinkage. However, I still wondered if this was in some way the result of the fact that I work with crusts and pastry on a daily basis. It occurred to me that perhaps a less experienced cook, who might be apt to work the dough a bit harder during rolling and fitting, might have different results. I found just such a cook and asked her to prepare and prebake three separate pie shells. The first shell she neither rested nor chilled, the second she refrigerated before baking, and the third she froze.

This time the differences among the pie shells were dramatic. The unrested, unchilled pastry drooped, shrank in many spots, and lost much definition. It was easy to identify spots where the dough had been pulled and stretched into place. The bottom of the shell had undesirable holes and cracks where the cook had attempted to seal tears that she had made while working. Pinching and squeezing these cracks back together before baking only caused them to spring open when baked. The refrigerated shell, on the other hand, maintained most of its edging and had no cracks.

The most profound difference between the refrigerated and unchilled pastries, though, was textural. The unchilled shell was compressed, sandy, and completely lacking in flaky layers. In contrast, the dough that had been refrigerated was quite tender, with visible layers of flaky pastry. To my surprise, the shell that had rested in the freezer produced a finished pastry that had shrunk, lost much of its edging, and cracked on the bottom. On the other hand, it was still very flaky—even flakier, in fact, than the refrigerated version.

Because both methods had advantages— less shrinking when refrigerated and a flakier texture when frozen—I decided that perhaps an initial rest in the refrigerator with a final chill in the freezer would produce a superior pastry to either method alone. This hunch proved correct. One last round of testing showed that a forty-minute rest in the refrigerator followed by twenty minutes in the freezer produced a shell that not only kept its original shape and definition but also achieved optimal flakiness.

To explain this phenomenon, I called food scientist Shirley Corriher. She agreed that there are two issues at hand: shrinkage and flakiness. Pastry shrinkage is caused by gluten. Simply put, when you add water to the proteins in flour, elastic strands of gluten are formed. The strands of gluten in the dough get stretched during the rolling process, and if they are not allowed to relax after rolling, the pastry will snap back like a rubber band when baked, resulting in a shrunken, misshapen shell. Resting allows the tension in the taut strands of dough to ease so that they remain stretched and do not shrink back when heated. This does not happen, however, when the dough is immediately placed in the freezer during its postrolling resting period. When frozen, the water in the crust solidifies, freezing the gluten in place so it is not free to relax. When you bake the dough, therefore, the tense, stretched strands of gluten snap back, producing shrinking.

It seemed, therefore, that refrigerating was part of the answer—at least to the problem of shrinkage, but not to attaining the desired degree of flakiness that freezing had seemed to produce. More investigation uncovered another fact. Pastry is made up of layers of dough (protein and starch from the flour combined with water) and fat. Dough and fat have different heat capacities. When you place the pastry in the oven after freezing it (rather than just refrigerating it), the dough heats up and starts to set relatively quickly in comparison to the time it takes for the butter to melt and then vaporize, since butter has a much higher proportion of water than the dough. As a result, by the time the water in the butter starts to turn to steam, the dough is well into its setting phase. The air spaces occupied by the frozen butter, now that it has largely turned to steam, hold their shape because the dough is far along in the baking process. Dough that you have refrigerated, on the other hand, is not as well set by the time the butter vaporizes; hence the air pockets disappear, the soft dough simply sinking into the spaces left by the butter. So the conclusion was simple: First refrigerate the pie shell to relax the gluten, thus solving the problem of shrinkage during baking, then pop the dough in the freezer to improve flakiness.

This bit of science led to one other fascinating discovery. It is common knowledge that lard or vegetable shortening such as Crisco produces very flaky doughs. In fact, we use a combination of butter and shortening in our recipe because of the improvement in texture over an all-butter crust. The explanation for this phenomenon is simple. Lard and Crisco don't melt as quickly as butter when heated. Therefore, they retain their shape as the dough sets up, keeping the layers of pastry separated.

Keeping a Stiff Lip
When you bake an unfilled pastry shell, the sides of the shell have a strong tendency to fall, reducing the amount of filling that can be held in the pie. The traditional remedy for this is to place small weights in the shell on top of a lining before the shell goes into the oven.

The first question I had about this procedure was what sort of weights work best. Personally, I have always used whatever I have had on hand, usually dry rice or beans,

and therefore have had little experience with commercial pie weights. When tested, however, pie weights did a better job than the rice or beans. They are heavier and therefore more effective at preventing the pastry from puffing. Because they are metal, they are also better heat conductors, which promotes more thorough browning of the pastry. I also tested ceramic weights, which worked equally well. Rice and beans tested poorly because they are light and do not conduct heat. The sides slipped away, and the bottom of the shell was gooey, producing an even worse crust than one with no weights.

For the lining on which to place the weights, I tried aluminum foil versus parchment paper and waxed paper. The foil tested best: It is flexible, so you can sculpt it into the corners of the pastry, and it securely covers the pie edge. Parchment paper and waxed paper are too stiff, so it is difficult to tuck them into the corners of the pie and cover the edges. Furthermore, neither conduct heat, so they hinder browning. I also tested the foil shiny side up versus shiny side down. Shiny side down browns the crust better because the dull side that is facing up does not reflect the heat away.

No Need to Dock
Ballooning occurs when air pockets form beneath the surface of the crust. I had been taught, and every source I researched confirmed, that the solution to this problem is to "dock," or prick, the raw dough with fork tines, which allows air to escape during baking. Yet, when I tested baking pastry dough without this step, making sure I had properly lined and weighted the dough, little or no ballooning occurred. I thought it strange enough that so many recipes take this precaution that I decided to cross-check the method using other pastry dough recipes. Through testing, I discovered that doughs for which docking is essential are those that contain eggs. (*See* "Egg Doughs Lift Off," page 11.)

Two Levels of Doneness
Finally, I tested various oven temperatures, baking times, and baking positions in the oven. I got the most consistent results and even browning by baking in the middle rack at a constant 375 degrees. At higher temperatures the pastry was prone to overbrowning and burned spots while lower temperatures caused the edges to brown well before the bottom. More important than temperature and placement, though, was cooking time. There are two stages to prebaking. In the first stage, the dough is baked with a lining and weights. This stage usually takes about seventeen minutes; the objective is to cook the dough until it sets, at which point it can hold its shape without assistance. For the second stage, the foil and weights are removed, and the baking continues. At this point, if you are going to fill the pie shell with an uncooked filling such as pumpkin or pecan and then bake it again, you should bake it until it is just lightly browned, about nine minutes. Pie shells destined for fillings that require no further cooking, such as cream pies or fruit tarts, should be baked for about fifteen minutes.

The Last Word on Prebaking
If you are not skilled with pastry dough, you are likely to work the dough too hard, developing gluten that is apt to shrink back when baked. This is why expert bakers don't understand all of the fuss about blind baking. They handle the dough gently and experience few problems. So if you are an amateur pie maker, here are the three most important tips to remember. First, it is better to add a bit too much water to the dough than too little. A dry dough is impossible to roll out. Second, the more time the dough rests in the refrigerator (up to two days), the better. Resting makes up for a heavy and inexperienced hand with the rolling pin. Finally, the point at which the aluminum foil is removed is crucial. Carefully touch the hot sides of the pie shell to make sure that they are firm and set before removing the foil. A little extra time with the foil in place is better than removing it too soon.

FITTING PASTRY INTO PIE DISHES
For Standard Pie Pan

1. Lift the edge of the pie dough with one hand and ease the pastry along the bottom into the corners with the other hand; repeat around the circumference of the pan. Do not stretch the dough.

2. Use kitchen scissors to trim the dough to within 1/2 inch of the lip all the way around. Tuck the overhanging dough back under itself so the folded edge extends 1/4 inch beyond the pan lip. Press it to seal.

3. Flute the edges all around; an exaggerated fluted edge is helpful for obtaining maximum holding capacity.

For Quiche or Tart Pans

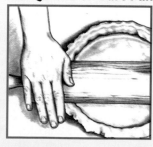

4. Lift the edge of the dough to ease it into the dish, allowing the extra dough to flop over the sides.

5. Run the rolling pin over the top of the pan to remove excess dough.

6. Using your forefinger and thumb, press the dough evenly up the sides from the bottom to increase the height of the rim.

ILLUSTRATIONS BY JUDY LOVE

MASTER RECIPE FOR PREBAKED PIE SHELL

For an 8- to 9-inch single pie shell

Once the pan is in the oven, leave the foil lining and weights in place until the dough loses its wet look, turns an off-white from its original pale yellow, and the edges just start to take on a very light brown color. Carefully (the dough is hot) touch the side of the shell to make sure that the crust is set: firm and able to hold itself up. If you remove the weights too soon, the dough sides will slip down, ruining the pie shell. Bake the shell partially (another nine minutes)—until just golden brown—if the pie is to be baked again with an uncooked filling such as pumpkin or pecan pie or quiches. Bake the shell fully (another fifteen minutes from the point the foil is removed)—to a deep, golden brown—when no additional baking is required as with fruit tarts and cream, chiffon, or lemon meringue pies.

1¼   cups all-purpose flour, plus extra for dusting
½   teaspoon salt
1   tablespoon sugar
4   tablespoons chilled unsalted butter, cut into ¼-inch pieces
3   tablespoons chilled all-vegetable shortening
4–5 tablespoons ice water

1. Pulse flour, salt, and sugar in food processor workbowl fitted with steel blade. Scatter butter pieces over flour mixture, tossing to coat with flour. Cut butter into flour with five 1-second pulses. Add shortening and continue cutting in until flour is pale yellow and resembles coarse cornmeal, with butter bits no larger than small peas, about four more 1-second pulses. Turn mixture into medium bowl.

2. Sprinkle 4 tablespoons ice water over mixture. With blade of rubber spatula, using folding motion to mix. Press down on mixture with broad side of spatula until dough sticks together, adding up to 1 tablespoon more ice water if it will not come together.

Shape dough into ball, squeezing two or three times with hands until cohesive, then flatten into 4-inch-wide disk. Dust lightly with flour, wrap in plastic, and refrigerate at least 30 minutes, or up to 2 days, before rolling.

3. Remove dough from refrigerator; let stand at room temperature to soften slightly, about 10 minutes if dough has chilled for 30 minutes or 20 minutes if it has chilled overnight. (The dough should be pliable. Use your hands to squeeze the dough; if you can squeeze it without applying too much pressure, it is ready to roll.) Roll dough on lightly floured work surface or between two sheets plastic wrap to a 12-inch disk about ⅛ inch thick. Fold dough in quarters, then place dough point in center of pie pan. Unfold dough. Alternatively, roll dough in 2-gallon zipper-lock bag to a 12-inch disk about ⅛-inch thick. Cut away top of bag. Grasping bottom, flip dough into pie pan and peel off bag bottom.

4. Working around circumference of pan, press dough carefully into pan corners by gently lifting dough edges with one hand while pressing around pan bottom with other hand (*see* illustration 1, page 10). Trim edge to ½ inch beyond pan lip. Tuck this rim of dough underneath itself so that folded edge is about ¼ inch beyond pan lip (illustration 2); flute dough in your own fashion (illustration 3). For quiche or tart pans, follow illustrations 4-6, page 10. Refrigerate pie shell for 40 minutes and then freeze for 20 minutes.

5. Meanwhile, adjust oven rack to middle position and heat oven to 375 degrees. Press doubled 12-inch square of aluminum foil inside dough shell; evenly distribute 1 cup or 12 ounces ceramic or metal pie weights over foil. Bake, leaving foil and weights in place, until dough dries out, about 17 minutes. Carefully remove foil and weights by gathering sides of foil and pulling up and out. For partially baked crust, continue baking until lightly golden brown, about 9 minutes more; for fully baked crust, continue baking until deep golden brown, about 15 minutes more. Transfer to wire rack to cool.

BLIND-BAKING DIFFERENT DOUGHS

The dough we used for blind baking is at once flavorful, tender, and sturdy because of its ratio of butter and shortening to flour. It is a standard all-purpose American pie crust suitable for both sweet and savory applications. There are, however, numerous other types of crusts, each having a specific application.

The two doughs closest to an American pie pastry are both French: a pâte sucrée and pâte sablée. The former is a basic pie dough but with extra sugar. This pastry blind-baked beautifully, with minimal shrinkage, a perfectly flat bottom, and great edge definition. Expect doughs like this one with larger amounts of sugar to be crumblier in texture and brown more readily, so take care not to overcook them, reducing the baking time slightly once you have removed the pie weights. Pâte sablée, a cousin of pâte sucrée, begins with the creaming of butter and sugar, much like a cookie dough, and bakes up similarly with a sandy texture akin to shortbread.

Pâte sablée
The dense texture of this sweet dough makes for perfect blind baking.

This pastry exemplified perfection when blind-baked: It was a rich golden brown, did not shrink nor slip, and held its fluted edge perfectly. Because of its dense texture, pâte sablée is best suited to the likes of fresh fruit tarts, for which a sturdy container is a pleasant counterpoint to the pastry cream and fruit filling. On the other hand, pâte sablée is too dense a crust for apple pies or savory dishes.

A nut crust, in which you replace a portion of the flour with ground nuts, is the choice for the classic linzertorte. It baked to a sturdy and flavorful conclusion, experiencing only minor shrinkage, holding its edge well, and browning evenly all around.

Cream cheese crusts are doughier, less delicate, and more biscuitlike than standard doughs. In my testing, they took slightly longer to set before the weights could be removed (about twenty to twenty-four minutes, depending on the dough). They also tended to lose their edge, shrink, slip, and balloon severely. In general, cream cheese crusts don't lend themselves to blind baking, and I didn't care for the flavor or texture. If you're looking for a faint acidic bite in your crust but don't want the difficulties of prebaking a cream cheese crust, try a sour cream pastry.

—Dawn Yanagihara

Quiche Worth Eating

*By using the proper combination of heavy cream, milk, whole eggs, and egg yolks,
you can produce a custard that makes quiche worth eating once again.*

by Susan G. Purdy

❧

There is no dispute about the characteristics of an ideal quiche: It must have a tender, buttery pastry case embracing a velvety smooth custard that is silken on the tongue and neither too rich nor too lean.

Because other authors were investigating the issues involved in blind baking a pastry crust (*see* "The Secrets of Prebaking Pie Shells," page 9), I devoted myself to searching out the ideal quiche filling formula. In my quest, I tried every probable and improbable custard combination, from whole eggs and whole milk to whole eggs with half-and-half to whole eggs with half milk and half heavy cream to eggs with several added yolks and all heavy cream.

The leanest of these mixtures tasted so, and I rejected it as boring, with no creamy mouth feel. The one with half-and-half was not as rich as one would think because the liquid contains just 11.7 percent butterfat; it was okay but not great. The mixture containing half whole milk and half heavy cream was significantly richer because heavy cream contains three times the butterfat (an average of 36 percent) added to the approximately 3.7 percent fat of the whole milk. Whole eggs, extra yolks, and all heavy cream produced a custard that was just too much of a good thing: overpoweringly rich, too creamy even for me.

The best mixture, a medium-rich custard with good mouth feel, fine taste, and a good set, combined two whole eggs with two yolks, one cup of milk and one cup of heavy cream. Baked in our favorite crust, it was just what we were looking for: a custard that was creamy but not cloyingly rich, with excellent mouth feel and perfect set, its tender skin a luscious golden brown hue. It puffed slightly while baking, settled neatly as it cooled. Impossible to eat just one bite. Sexy and irresistible.

Of course, baking temperature is also an important factor regulating custard texture. High heat toughens egg proteins and shrinks the albumen, separating, or curdling, the mixture and

The best quiche holds together well but is still soft and velvety.

squeezing out the water instead of keeping the egg in perfect suspension. Moderate heat proves best.

I tested my different quiche formulas at temperatures ranging from 325 degrees to 400 degrees. Some chefs prefer to start baking at 400 degrees for fifteen minutes, then reduce the heat to 350 degrees for the remaining time. I found 350 degrees slightly slow; by the time the custard set, the top, which remained a pallid yellow hue, had developed into a slightly rubbery, chewy skin. On the theory that warming the liquid in the custard would shorten baking time and keep the custard smoother, I tried heating the milk to 100 degrees before whisking in the eggs. Indeed, this custard set a few minutes faster, but it was otherwise unremarkable and still had a pallid color on top. I found that baking at 375 degrees was exactly right, setting the custard gently enough to maintain its creamy consistency, yet hot enough to brown the top before it dried out and became rubbery.

As a test for doneness, I advise watching the oven, not the clock, looking for a light golden brown coloring on the quiche surface, which may puff up slightly as it bakes. A knife blade inserted about one inch from the edge should come out clean; the center may still be slightly liquid, but internal heat will finish the baking and it will solidify when cool. If your test blade comes out clean in the center, the quiche may already be slightly overbaked and should be removed from the oven at once. Be sure to set the baked quiche on a wire rack to cool, so air circulates all around it, preventing condensation on the bottom. Allowing the quiche to cool until it is either warm or at room temperature also lets the custard settle before serving. The cooler the quiche, the more neatly it will slice.

MASTER RECIPE FOR QUICHE LORRAINE
Serves 8

The center of the quiche will be surprisingly soft when it comes out of the oven, but the filling will continue to set (and sink somewhat) as it cools. If the pie shell has been previously baked and cooled, place it in the preheating oven for about five minutes to warm it, taking care that it does not burn. Because ingredients in the variations that follow are bulkier, the amount of custard mixture has been reduced to prevent overflowing the crust.

1   9-inch partially baked pie shell, warm
8   ounces bacon, cut into 1/2-inch pieces (about 8 slices)
2   large eggs, plus 2 large yolks
1   cup whole milk
1   cup heavy cream
1/2   teaspoon salt
1/2   teaspoon white pepper
    Pinch grated nutmeg
4   ounces Gruyère cheese, grated (1/2 cup)

1. Adjust oven rack to center position and heat oven to 375 degrees. Fry bacon in skillet over medium heat until crisp and brown, about 5 minutes. Transfer with slotted spoon to paper towel–lined plate. Meanwhile, whisk all remaining ingredients except cheese in medium bowl.

2. Spread cheese and bacon evenly over bottom of warm pie shell and set shell on oven rack. Pour in custard mixture to 1/2 inch below crust rim. Bake until lightly golden brown and a knife blade inserted about one inch from the edge comes out clean, and center feels set but soft like gelatin, 32 to 35 minutes. Transfer quiche to rack to cool. Serve warm or at room temperature.

CRABMEAT QUICHE
Follow Master Recipe for Quiche Lorraine, reducing quantities of milk and cream to 3/4 cup each. Add 2 tablespoons dry sherry and a pinch cayenne pepper to custard mixture. Substitute 8 ounces (1 cup) cooked crabmeat tossed with 2 tablespoons chopped fresh chives for bacon and cheese.

LEEK AND GOAT CHEESE QUICHE
Sauté white part of 2 medium leeks, washed thoroughly and cut into 1/2-inch dice (about 2 cups), in 2 tablespoons unsalted butter over medium heat until soft, 5–7 minutes. Follow Master Recipe for Quiche Lorraine, reducing quantities of milk and cream to 3/4 cup each. Omit bacon; substitute 4 ounces mild goat cheese, broken into 1/2-inch pieces, for Gruyère. Add leeks with cheese.

HAM AND ASPARAGUS QUICHE
Blanch 8 asparagus cut on the bias into 1/2-inch pieces (about 1 cup) in 1 quart salted boiling water until crisp-tender, about 2 minutes. Follow Master Recipe for Quiche Lorraine, reducing quantities of milk and cream to 3/4 cup each. Replace bacon and cheese with asparagus and 4 ounces deli baked ham, cut into 1/4-inch dice.

Susan G. Purdy is a Connecticut-based food writer, baking instructor, and cookbook author. Her newest book is *Let Them Eat Cake* (Morrow, 1997).

Better than Store-Bought Bagels

*When you can't buy chewy, first-rate bagels, you can make them at home
in just 45 minutes after chilling the dough in the refrigerator overnight.*

by Todd Butcher

❁

My favorite way to eat a bagel is plain and unadorned, still warm from the oven. I linger on the details: the complex, yeasty aroma; the golden crust, stubbled with the crispy fermentation bubbles that bakers call "fish eyes"; the tenaciously chewy interior. I can say without reservation that I am a bagel fanatic.

So I knew I was in trouble when I moved to a town without a decent bagel shop. What was needed, I decided, was a simple process for baking delicious, attractive, authentic bagels at home.

I started out with great confidence. Looking at all the home recipes I could get my hands on, I developed a fairly typical recipe using bread flour, salt, sugar, yeast, and water, reasoning that the bread flour would give my bagels the chewy texture I was looking for. Following the procedure outlined in all the recipes, I kneaded the dough and then allowed it to rise for about an hour. Next I shaped it into rings, then proofed, boiled, and finally baked the bagels.

Rather than plump, smooth, golden brown bagels, I ended up with small, dense hockey pucks, with crusts that were dull, wrinkled, and mottled brown. The flavor was bland and unappealing, and the internal crumb structure was very dense. Although they were somewhat chewy, these bagels lacked the crisp crust and springy interior texture I associate with well-made bagels. I had my work cut out for me.

The Well-Shaped Bagel

I decided that the first issue I needed to address was appearance. One problem I had encountered in forming the bagels was that after the first rise, the dough was somewhat grainy and loose. Instead of stretching easily, it was more inclined to tear. Forming bagels at this stage, as all recipes I came across advocated, tended to result in a lumpy, uneven crust. To overcome this difficulty, I tried forming the bagels immediately after I kneaded the dough, letting the rings rise until puffy, then boiling and baking as before.

This approach turned out to be an improvement in terms of handling the dough, and also in the appearance of my bagels. However, they were still small and tough.

I began to question my choice of flour. I

Malt syrup, the sweetener traditionally used in bagels, delivers an authentic bagel flavor that is impossible to match with honey or sugar.

figured that bread flour, with about 13 percent protein content, was probably an improvement over all-purpose flour, with about 12 percent protein content. I knew that the higher protein level would lead to the formation of more gluten, that network of elastic protein strands that traps the carbon dioxide released by the activity of the yeast, allowing bread to rise. It stood to reason, then, that a higher-protein flour would rise better, thus yielding a bagel that was plumper and had a finer, chewier texture.

The next flour up the scale in terms of protein content is high-gluten, a flour produced by the milling of high-protein wheat. High-gluten flour has the highest protein content of any flour, usually around 14 percent, and is the flour of choice at most professional bagel bakeries and pizza parlors. I made my next batch of bagels using high-gluten flour and saw a difference the moment I removed the dough from the mixer. This dough was satiny smooth and much more elastic than the dough made with bread flour. And the bagels made with high-gluten flour were larger and rose higher. In addition, the crust was smoother and more at-

tractive. The interior structure of these bagels was also better; they were lighter and chewier than previous attempts.

I was getting close now, but my bagels were still a bit flat on the bottom. A little fiddling around with the water-to-flour ratio quickly solved that problem. Initially, I was treating the bagel dough like any other bread dough, trying to achieve a smooth, slightly tacky consistency. A few test batches using less water in relation to flour revealed that a stiff, drier dough produces a firmer-textured, even chewier bagel. "Dry," however, may not be the most appropriate word to use in describing the correct consistency. A dough with the right consistency will be smooth and elastic, though somewhat firm. After the dough has come together in the first five minutes of mixing, it should not stick to your finger when pressed. And when you have completely kneaded the dough, a piece formed into a golf ball–sized ball should hold its shape and should not sag.

With the shape and texture of my bagels very much improved, I turned to the issue of flavor.

Retarding, the Professional's Secret

Traditionally, bagels are placed in a specially designed refrigerator, called a retarder, for several hours or overnight after being formed. This practice allows for a slower, more natural fermentation. It is during this retarding process that bagels develop most of their flavor. I wanted to test the impact of retarding for myself, so after mixing and forming a batch of bagels, I placed them in the refrigerator overnight. The results were both dramatic and surprising.

The most obvious change in my bagels was in their size. What had gone into the refrigerator as tight, shapely rings of dough came out as flaccid blobs. The yeast fermentation had continued unabated, and my bagels had overproofed. I finished the boiling and baking process anyway.

In spite of being overlarge and flat-bottomed, the result of overproofing, these bagels were a vast improvement over my previous attempts. When I sliced one open, I was greeted by a heavenly aroma. This was more than just flour, salt, and yeast! The long, slow fermentation process the bagels had undergone had yielded the complex flavor and aroma I was seeking. So retarding really was crucial for great bagel flavor. I was even more surprised by the other effects of retarding; the crust of the retarded bagels had taken on a dark, reddish sheen and the surface was covered in crispy fish eyes.

For an explanation of what was actually happening to my bagels in the retarder, I called Wulf Doerry, retired Director of Cereal Technology at the American Institute of Baking in Manhattan, Kansas. According to Doerry, the primary mechanism involved in the retarding process is bacterial fermentation. At the lower temperatures of the retarder, the yeast fermentation is suppressed and the lactobacilli bacteria naturally present in the flour and the yeast begin to produce a variety of organic acids, primarily lactic acid and acetic acid. These organic acids, the same acids present in a healthy sourdough culture, give the dough a more complex flavor.

But what about those fish eyes? Doerry explains that this same bacterial reaction breaks down some of the gluten in the dough. The weakened gluten structure on the surface of the bagels allows the formation of fermentation bubbles.

I also noticed that the retarded bagels have a richer, reddish brown crust color, the result of what Doerry calls the Maillard, or browning, reaction. He explains that during the retarding process, enzymes produced by the bacteria convert wheat starch into simple sugars and protein into peptides and amino acids. As the product loses moisture during baking, the reaction between these sugars and the amino acids—the Maillard reaction—produces a rich brown crust color.

In subsequent tests, I lowered the yeast level in my recipe by a full half. I also lowered the temperature of the water I used in the dough to control the activity of the yeast. Initially, I had been proofing the active dry yeast in 110-degree water as recommended on the package. The procedure I settled on was to not dissolve the yeast before adding it to the flour, and to use 80-degree water.

Experimenting with different retarding times, I eventually concluded that a period of between twelve and eighteen hours is best for a balance between flavor and crust development. Less time and the flavor did not develop as fully, although a short retarding time is better than none. More than eighteen hours and I began to notice some adverse effects on the bagels, such as an excessive darkening of the crust, the formation of large bubbles inside the bagels, and the development of too many fermentation bubbles on the surface.

A Quick Boil Is Best
Boiling the dough, which is the most unique step in the bagel-making process, is also responsible for the bagel's most unique characteristics, the shiny crust and chewy tex-

ture. Boiling the bagels before baking them serves three purposes. Most importantly, it sets the shape of the bagel by cooking the surface and killing off some of the yeast in the outer layer of dough. This helps to limit the expansion of the bagel when it is baked. A bagel that is not boiled, I discovered, will expand into a round ball in the heat of the oven. The second function of the boiling process is to give the bagel its characteristic shine. When you boil the bagel, starches on the surface become gelatinized. These starches then cook to a crispy, shiny coating in the oven. The third purpose of boiling is to activate the yeast in the inner layers of dough, which has been made sluggish by the retarding process.

All of the home recipes I reviewed recommended boiling the bagels for a period of from one to four minutes. I tried the whole range of suggested times and found, surprisingly, that a shorter boil of about thirty seconds yielded the best results. Bagels boiled for four minutes had noticeably less shine and were not as plump as those boiled for thirty seconds. I surmised that the bagels boiled for four minutes had developed such a thick crust that they were unable to expand fully in the oven.

MASTER RECIPE FOR PLAIN BAGELS
Makes 8 bagels
Because bagel dough is much drier and stiffer than bread dough, it takes longer for the ingredients to cohere during mixing. For this

---

THE BEST WAY TO SLICE A BAGEL

Ever since the '90s boom of bagel shops and franchises, there's been a pilgrimage of bagel lovers to hospital emergency rooms, according to doctors. The round shape of bagels makes them awkward to grip, and their tough exterior is difficult to slice through. An accidental slip doesn't take much.

It was inevitable, then, that bagel slicing contraptions would begin popping up in cookware stores and catalogs—as they did. We decided to try out a few and compare them with manual methods to determine the safest and easiest technique.

The bagel guillotine ($30) raised the most curiosity. This gizmo has a V-shaped blade that pierces and slices through the bagel, which is cradled in a base. We liked the plastic shield around the blade because it makes it nearly impossible to slice your fingers. Safety aside, however, we had trouble slicing all the way through our homemade bagels. The guillotine did slice through tougher store-bought bagels fairly easily, but another problem emerged with these bagels. Because they were not as thick as the one-and-three-quarter-inch guillotine cradle, the bagels tilted and sliced unevenly.

Thickness presented just the opposite problem for the two wooden cradle bagel slicers ($7) we tested. Both were under one and one-half inches wide, and neither store-bought nor our homemade bagels would fit.

Fit was not an issue with the Bagel Trap ($20). This device has a plastic slotted cradle with a spring arm that allows for flexibility in width and securely holds the bagel in place. For both these reasons, we liked it. Unfortunately, it holds too well, tending to squish softer bagels and mar them with the waffle grid of its back holding plate.

Between the costs and inconvenience of the bagel-slicing gadgets, we found that slicing by hand is still the best way to go. To do so safely, however, you must use a bread knife. The teeth of a bread knife are essential to sawing through the crust of any bread. Smooth-bladed knives, such as a chef's knife, tend to slip.

We recommend two methods for slicing bagels with a bread knife. One of our writers prefers to put on a clean oven mitt to cradle the bagel in his hand and slice. The knife just won't puncture through all that fabric and padding (see Quick Tips, page 4). Another editor prefers to simply rest a thick towel folded over in her hand.

Personally, I like making a horizontal cut halfway through the bagel, then propping the bagel on its side to finish the cut. (For a similar technique using a Chinese chef's knife, see page 16.) Be sure to prop the bagel on a cutting board with the sliced side up. Hold it steady at the top where the knife has already passed.

Any of these techniques should render you evenly halved bagels, safely—without the gimmicks.

—*Maryellen Driscoll*

BAGEL GUILLOTINE
Failed to slice homemade bagels, and sliced store bought versions unevenly.

WOODEN CRADLE SLICERS
Not wide enough for homemade or most store-bought bagels to fit into.

BAGEL TRAP
Holds bagels so tight that it squishes softer ones and mars all with waffle marks.

PHOTOGRAPHS BY JACK CERVEIRA

same reason, we recommend that you neither double the recipe nor try to knead the dough by hand. Most good natural foods stores carry barley malt syrup. High-gluten flour might be more difficult to find. You can order both the syrup and the flour from the King Arthur Flour Baker's Catalogue (*see* Sources and Resources, page 32).

- 4   cups high-gluten flour
- 2   teaspoons salt
- 1   tablespoon barley malt syrup or powder
- 1½   teaspoons active dry yeast
- 1¼   cups lukewarm water (80 degrees)
- 3   tablespoons cornmeal, for dusting baking sheet

1. Mix flour, salt, and malt in bowl of standing mixer fitted with dough hook. Add yeast and water; mix at lowest speed until dough looks scrappy, like shreds just beginning to come together, about 4 minutes. Increase to speed 2; continue mixing until dough is cohesive, smooth, and stiff, 8 to 10 minutes.

2. Turn dough on to work surface; divide into eight portions, about 4 ounces each. Roll pieces into smooth balls and cover with towel or plastic wrap to rest for 5 minutes (see illustration 1, right).

3. Form dough balls into dough rings (illustrations 2 through 4), place on cornmeal-dusted baking sheet, cover tightly with plastic wrap, and refrigerate overnight (12 to 18 hours).

4. About 20 minutes before baking, remove dough rings from refrigerator. Adjust oven rack to center position and heat oven to 450 degrees. Fill large soup kettle with 3-inch depth of water; bring to rapid boil. To test the proofing of the dough rings, fill large bowl with cool water. Drop dough ring into bowl; it should float immediately to surface (if not, retest every 5 minutes).

5. Working four at a time, drop dough rings into boiling water, stirring and submerging loops with Chinese skimmer or slotted spoon (illustration 5), until very slightly puffed, 30 to 35 seconds. Remove rings from water; transfer to wire rack, bottom side down, to drain.

6. Transfer boiled rings, rough side down, to parchment paper–lined baking sheet or baking stone. Bake until deep golden brown and crisp, about 14 minutes. Use tongs to transfer to wire rack to cool. Serve warm or at room temperature.

TOPPED BAGELS
Topping ingredients stick to the bagels best when applied to the dough rings just as they come out of the boiling water, while still wet and sticky.

- ½   cup single topping ingredient of choice, such as raw sesame seeds, poppy or caraway seeds, dehydrated onion or garlic flakes, or sea or kosher salt or:

FORMING AND COOKING

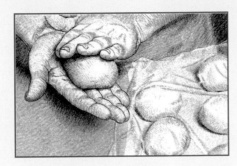

1. Divide the dough into eight even-sized pieces. Roll each piece into a smooth ball and cover the balls with a towel or a piece of plastic wrap for 5 minutes to rest them.

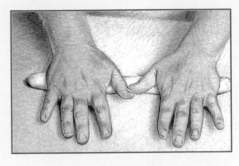

2. Form each dough ball into a rope 11 inches long by rolling it under your outstretched palms. Do not taper the ends of the rope.

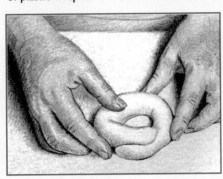

3. Overlap the ends of the rope about 1 1/2 inches and pinch the entire overlapped area firmly together. If the ends of the rope do not want to stick together, you can dampen them slightly.

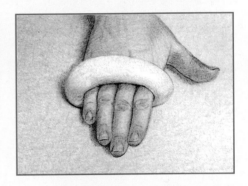

4. Place the loop of dough around the base of your fingers and, with the overlap under your palm, roll the rope several times, applying firm pressure to seal the seam. The bagel should be roughly the same thickness all the way around.

5. While boiling the bagels, press them down with the back of a slotted spoon or Chinese skimmer to keep them submerged.

6. To top the bagels, dunk them into a small bowl of the desired topping.

- ½   cup combination of topping ingredients, including 2 tablespoons each of sesame and poppy seeds and 1 tablespoon each of caraway seeds, sea or kosher salt, dehydrated onion flakes, and dehydrated garlic flakes

Follow Master Recipe for Plain Bagels, dunking bagel into topping ingredient(s) (illustration 6) while still wet and sticky.

CINNAMON RAISIN BAGELS
Follow Master Recipe for Plain Bagels, mixing 1 teaspoon vanilla extract, 1 tablespoon ground cinnamon, and ½ cup raisins into flour, salt, and malt in step 1.

Todd Butcher is a baker and food writer in Wilmington, North Carolina.

HOW TO USE CHINESE CLEAVERS

by Maryellen Driscoll

A Chinese cleaver can seem like a frighteningly large and treacherous knife. But with practice and proper technique, you'll find it as safe as and even more versatile than the chef's knife. A cleaver chops, slices, and minces. It also smashes, mashes, scrapes, and scoops.

There are two basic Chinese cleavers: the heavyweight meat cleaver and the delicate vegetable cleaver (also known as a Chinese chef's knife).

The meat cleaver is a rugged, blunt knife meant solely for hacking through bones—though not all bones. It works great on chicken and fish. We found that making a clean cut through large bones, such as beef bones, is best left to a hacksaw or your butcher.

Unlike the meat cleaver, the vegetable cleaver has a delicate, sharp edge, like a chef's knife. It is used to cut vegetables and boneless meats; we found it also juliennes more finely than the chef's knife.

The best cleavers are made of high-carbon stainless steel because they will not corrode and can hold an edge well. Never run a cleaver through the dishwasher or soak it in water, particularly if it has a wooden handle. Immediately clean and wipe it dry after each use.

THE TWO CLEAVERS

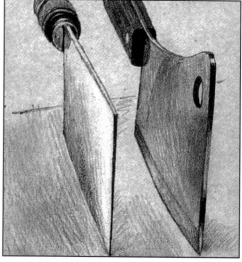

The top edge of both vegetable and meat cleavers measures about 3 millimeters thick. However, the blade of the vegetable cleaver (left) tapers gently to a slender cutting edge while the meat cleaver is more like a wedge, tapering within the last 2 centimeters. The hole at the top corner is for hanging.

CHOPPING THROUGH BONE WITH A MEAT CLEAVER

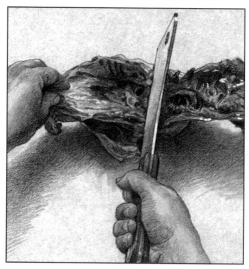

To hack through bone, place your hand near the far end of the meat cleaver's handle, curling your fingers securely around like a fist. Handle the meat cleaver like you would a hammer, with the motion in the arm rather than the wrist, and the weight of the blade's front tip leading the force of the chop. If you cannot chop the bone in one strike, place the cleaver in the groove of the first chop, then strike the blade's blunt edge with a rubber mallet.

SLICING WITH A VEGETABLE CLEAVER

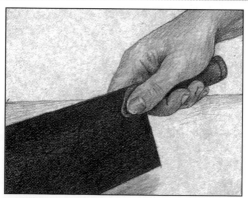

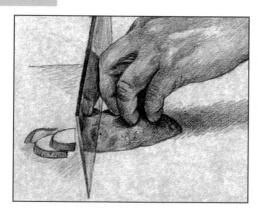

To hold the vegetable cleaver for slicing, lay your palm on the handle near the blade so that you can rest your thumb and your index finger on opposite sides of the blade. Slightly curl your index finger. Curl your remaining three fingers around the handle. The thumb and index finger allow for better control of the knife. The wrist should barely move when slicing.

With your other hand curl your fingertips like a claw to anchor the food. This serves as a guide for the blade. Never lift the blade's edge higher than your knuckles when slicing.

MINCING WITH A VEGETABLE CLEAVER

To "rock-mince" firmer foods, hold the cleaver as you would for slicing but press the palm of your free hand across the far end of the blade's blunt edge. Lift the blade, keeping its tip in constant contact with the cutting board, then mince continuously from one side to the next, pivoting from the tip.

To mince soft foods, curl your index finger around the neck of the vegetable cleaver's blade, place your thumb on top of the blunt edge of the blade, and curl your remaining fingers around the handle. Flick the cleaver up with your wrist and let the weight of the knife drive the fall.

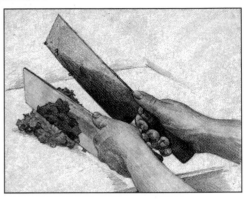

To mince with two vegetable cleavers, grip one knife in each hand, alternating the lift-and-fall rhythm of the knives. Frequently scoop up minced ingredients and flip them back into the pile to ensure even mincing.

CLEAVER QUICK TIPS

To julienne vegetables, slice them diagonally into thin oblong coins. Stack the coins and finely slice them lengthwise at a diagonal.

Use the front blunt edge of either the vegetable or meat cleaver as a dough scraper.

You can use the blunt edge of the cleaver blade to pound both sides of meat in a crosshatch pattern in order to tenderize it.

Use the broad side of the cleaver to loosen garlic cloves from a head, loosen skin on garlic, or pound meat to uniform thickness.

Roll-cutting coarse cylindrical vegetables creates a crude triangular cut that maximizes the exposed surface area to speed up cooking. Place a peeled carrot on a cutting board. Beginning at the carrot's tip, slice diagonally at about 45 degrees. Roll the carrot toward you with a quarter turn. Slice again. Repeat.

The large flat surface of the cleaver blade acts as a quick, mess-free scooper for carrying piles of chopped food from the cutting board to a pan or plate. Use your hand to anchor food against the cleaver as you lift and carry it.

To butterfly a steak, pork chop, or boneless chicken breast (shown here), place the food by the edge of the cutting board, then place the palm of your free hand on top with your fingers slightly flexed. Hold your vegetable cleaver parallel to the cutting board and butterfly the food with a gentle sawing motion.

To mash ginger, herbs, peppercorns, or a small bowl of beans, place the food in a small bowl, then grind it with the butt of the cleaver handle.

Pan-Sautéed Pork Tenderloin

Instead of roasting, we found that it was faster and more flavorful to slice, sauté, and then finish with a quick pan sauce.

by Adam Ried with Eva Katz

❧

Pork tenderloin has many charms. The tenderloin is exceptionally lean and tender, and because it usually weighs between twelve and twenty-four ounces, it cooks very quickly—perfect for weeknight dinners.

The tenderloin is a small, boneless, torpedo-do-shaped muscle nestled against the rib bones in the loin section, which is roughly equivalent to a position deep inside the mid-back on a human. The cut is notable for its remarkable lack of marbling, the ribbons of intramuscular fat that run through meat. While this is a virtue in terms of fat intake, it also presents a pitfall in that the tenderloin is particularly vulnerable to overcooking, which can lead to dry meat. To protect the tenderloin's characteristic tenderness, we prefer that it be cooked medium-well, so it is slightly rosy inside. This translates to between 145 degrees and 150 degrees internal temperature. If you prefer to cook pork well-done and gray-white throughout, this may not be the cut for you. We also realized from the outset that the tenderloin's lack of fat leaves it in need of a flavor boost, perhaps in the form of a dry spice rub or paste, or a sauce.

After perusing many recipes, we saw that we had three basic options in terms of cooking technique: broiling, grilling, and roasting. Broiling practically turned the pan drippings to carbon and gave the meat an overly chewy texture. Grilling the tenderloin smeared with a spice paste or rub produced a fabulous seared crust cloaking potently flavored, tender, juicy meat within. This method did require some finesse, however, and because grilling is not practical year-round for us Northerners, we decided to reserve that method for a future summer issue and press on to determine the best indoor cooking method.

The Quest for Crust

We knew from our success on the grill that the tenderloin required searing to optimize its own flavor. Roasting presented us with three choices for achieving a good sear in a short time. We could pan-sear the tenderloin on the stovetop and finish cooking it in the oven; sear it in the oven at a high temperature and then lower the temperature to finish the cooking; or start the meat at a low temperature, cranking the temperature up to sear near the end of the cooking time.

Searing in a preheated pan on the stovetop before placing the meat in the oven shrank the meat excessively and sacrificed too much tenderness. So we tried using the oven for the entire cooking time, experimenting with different temperatures, as well as different combinations of both low and high heat to see if we could oven-sear at either the beginning or the end of the cooking time. Of these, starting the meat at 325 degrees in a preheated pan, cooking it to an internal temperature of 110 degrees, and then increasing the oven to 450 degrees to sear seemed most promising. Usually, we got a reasonable crust, tender meat, and nicely caramelized pan drippings from which to make a sauce.

But not a hundred percent of the time. Catching the meat at 110 degrees meant frequent checks in the oven with an instant-read thermometer. More often than not, the meat reached 120 or 130 by mistake, which robbed it of valuable high-temperature searing time on its way to a final internal temperature of 145 to 150 degrees. Once the temperature had been increased, we had to go back into the oven several times to turn the meat so it would sear on all sides. Worst of all, these hurried trips into and out of the oven took our cooking process

We prefer a heavy-bottomed, stainless steel–lined pan, but tenderloins will also brown well in a thinner, less expensive pan. Avoid nonstick pans, which brown poorly because the hot oil does not distribute evenly.

from simple to complicated and finicky.

The Final Cut

It was at this point that we realized we hadn't yet tried slicing the tenderloin and sautéing it on the stovetop, avoiding the oven altogether. So we cut the tenderloin into one-inch slices and pounded them down to three-quarters inch with the flat side of a chef's knife (to increase the surface area for searing), then sautéed them in a bit of sizzling oil for about one minute per side. At the end, every single slice was seared beautifully on both sides, pan drippings were perfectly caramelized and ready to deglaze for a flavorful, simple sauce, and we had shaved about ten minutes off the cooking process. The whole operation, from refrigerator to table, took only fifteen minutes. Beneath the seared crust on each slice was juicy, succulent meat that met all our expectations for this supertender cut.

While testing and retesting our chosen method, we came up with a few pointers to help ensure successful sautéing. First, trim the pearlescent membrane, called the silver skin, from the tenderloin before cutting the medallions (*see* illustration, page 19). If left on, the silver skin shrinks in the heat of the pan, pulling the meat up and out of the hot fat, thereby inhibiting browning. Second, do not overcook the meat. There should be just a tinge of pink when you peek into a piece with the tip of a paring knife. The meat will not be completely cooked at the end of the searing time, but that is fine because you later return it to the pan to reheat and meld with the sauce. Finally, if you are preparing more than one tenderloin, sauté in two pans simultaneously instead of more than two successive batches in the same pan. This will protect the pan drippings from burning.

MASTER RECIPE FOR SAUTÉED PORK TENDERLOIN MEDALLIONS

Serves 3 (3 or 4 slices per person)
Serve these pork tenderloin medallions with one of the pan sauces, page 19. To promote even cooking, cut your slices to a uniform thickness. If it helps, lay a ruler in front of the loin and slice at the one-inch marks. If you've got one, cover the pan with a splatter screen to prevent spattering (*see* Sources and Resources, May/June 1997).

1 teaspoon salt
¹/₂ teaspoon ground black pepper
1 pork tenderloin (about 1 pound), silver skin removed, cut into 1-inch slices, each pounded to ³/₄ inch with flat side of chef's knife blade
2 tablespoons olive oil

Sprinkle salt and pepper over both sides of pork slices. Heat oil until shimmering in heavy-bottomed pan, at least 10 inches across bottom, over medium-high heat, swirling pan to distribute oil. Working in batches of no more than six slices to avoid overcrowding, sear medallions without moving them until brown on one side, about 80 seconds (oil should sizzle, but not smoke). Turn medallions with tongs to avoid scraping off the sear; sear until meat is mostly opaque at sides, firm to the touch, and well browned, about 80 seconds. Transfer pork to plate; continue with pan sauce recipe using drippings in pan.

PORT PAN SAUCE WITH DRIED CHERRIES AND ROSEMARY
Serves 3 (saucing one tenderloin)
Dried cranberries or chopped dried apricots can substitute for the cherries.

¹/₂ cup dried sweet cherries
¹/₃ cup port
²/₃ cup chicken stock or low-salt canned broth
2 teaspoons minced fresh rosemary leaves
Salt and ground black pepper

1. Set pan in which pork was cooked over medium-high heat; add port and cherries. Boil, scraping pan bottom with wooden spatula to loosen browned bits, until liquid reduces to about 2 tablespoons, 2 to 3 minutes. Increase heat to high; add stock or broth, rosemary, any accumulated pork juices; boil until liquid reaches consistency of maple syrup, about 2 minutes. Add salt and pepper to taste.

2. Reduce heat to medium; return pork to pan, turning meat to coat. Simmer to heat pork through and blend flavors, about 3 minutes. Adjust seasonings, adding salt and pepper to taste. Transfer pork to serving plate and spoon sauce over meat. Serve immediately.

CREAM PAN SAUCE WITH APPLES AND SAGE
Serves 3 (saucing one tenderloin)

1 tablespoon unsalted butter
1 Granny Smith or other firm apple, peeled, cored, and cut into 12 slices
¹/₂ medium onion, sliced thin (about ¹/₂ cup)
¹/₃ cup apple cider
3 tablespoons applejack or brandy
¹/₂ cup chicken stock or low-salt canned broth
2 tablespoons minced fresh sage leaves

¹/₄ cup heavy cream
Salt and ground black pepper

1. Melt butter in pan in which pork was cooked over medium-high heat, swirling to distribute. Add apple and onion; sauté until apple starts to brown, about 4 minutes. Add cider and applejack or brandy; boil, scraping pan bottom with wooden spatula to loosen browned bits, until liquid reduces to a glaze, about 2¹/₂ minutes. Increase heat to high; add stock or broth, sage, and any accumulated pork juices; boil until liquid reaches consistency of maple syrup, about 3 minutes. Add cream; boil until reduced by half, about 2 minutes.

2. Reduce heat to medium; return pork to pan, turning meat to coat. Simmer to heat pork thoroughly and blend flavors, about 3 minutes. Adjust seasonings, adding salt and pepper to taste. Transfer pork to serving plate and spoon sauce over meat. Serve immediately.

WINE VINEGAR PAN SAUCE WITH WARM SPICES AND RAISINS
Serves 3 (saucing one tenderloin)

¹/₂ teaspoon ground cinnamon
¹/₄ teaspoon ground cloves
¹/₈ teaspoon ground cayenne pepper
2 teaspoons sugar
1 tablespoon olive oil
1 medium onion, sliced thin (about 1 cup)
¹/₄ cup dry sherry
¹/₄ cup red wine vinegar
¹/₂ cup chicken stock or low-salt canned broth
¹/₄ cup raisins
Salt

1. Mix first four ingredients in small bowl; set aside. Heat oil in pan in which pork was cooked over medium heat, swirling to distribute. Add onion; sauté until softened and starting to color, about 2 minutes. Add spice mixture, sherry, and vinegar; boil, scraping pan bottom with wooden spatula to loosen browned bits, until liquid reduces to a glaze, about 2¹/₂ minutes. Increase heat to high and add stock or broth, raisins, and any accumulated pork juices; boil until liquid reaches consistency of maple syrup, about 3 minutes.

2. Reduce heat to medium; return pork to pan, turning meat to coat. Simmer to heat pork thoroughly and blend flavors, about 3 minutes. Adjust seasonings, adding salt to taste. Transfer pork to serving plate and spoon sauce over meat. Serve immediately.

ORANGE PAN SAUCE WITH FENNEL AND GREEN OLIVES
Serves 3 (saucing one tenderloin)

1 tablespoon olive oil
¹/₂ medium fennel bulb, sliced thin (about 1 cup)
2 medium garlic cloves, minced (about 1 tablespoon)

PREPARING THE TENDERLOIN

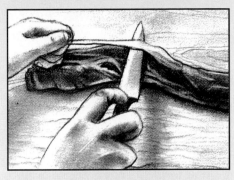

To remove the silver skin, slip a paring knife between the silver skin and the muscle fibers. Angle the knife slightly upward and use a gentle back-and-forth sawing action.

One or two smacks with the flat side of a chef's knife should flatten the slices to about three-quarters of an inch thickness.

¹/₃ cup juice and 1 teaspoon zest from 1 large orange
²/₃ cup chicken stock or low-salt canned broth
¹/₄ cup pitted green olives, sliced
2 tablespoons chopped fresh parsley leaves
Salt and ground black pepper

1. Heat oil in pan in which pork was cooked over medium heat, swirling to distribute. Add fennel; sauté until softened and starting to color, about 2 minutes. Add garlic; sauté 1 minute more. Add juice; boil, scraping pan bottom with wooden spatula to loosen browned bits, until liquid reduces to a glaze, about 2¹/₂ minutes. Increase heat to high and add stock or broth and any accumulated pork juices; boil until liquid reaches consistency of maple syrup, about 3 minutes.

2. Reduce heat to medium; return pork to pan with zest, olives, and parsley, turning meat to coat. Simmer to heat pork thoroughly and blend flavors, about 3 minutes. Adjust seasonings, adding salt and pepper to taste. Transfer pork to serving plate and spoon sauce over meat. Serve immediately.

How to Roast Cornish Hens

Brine these little birds to deepen their flavor, then roast them at relatively high heat and brush them with a glaze to ensure good color.

by Pam Anderson with Melissa Hamilton

⁂

Having spent weeks roasting turkeys for previous *Cook's Illustrated* articles, I thought roasting a little one-and-a-half-pound-pound Cornish game hen would be an afternoon project. But a week of testing made me wise: These little birds are every bit the challenge of the big ones.

Even though Cornish hens are cheap enough (two for five bucks in my grocery store) and cook quickly enough for a weeknight supper (less than thirty minutes unstuffed), most people think of them as festive fare. And for good reason. They make a stunning presentation, they stuff beautifully, and they appeal to a wide range of tastes.

Cooking a large number of Cornish hens to perfection, however, is not an easy task. As with all poultry, if the hen is roasted breast side up, the breast will surely overcook before the legs and thighs get done. Getting the birds to brown properly with such a short stay in the oven is difficult too, especially with six in a pan. If you think a 500-degree oven is the answer, think again. Six little birds dripping fat onto an overheated roasting pan automatically sets off the smoke alarms. Roasting these birds at high temperatures also causes their skin to bubble and blister.

Stuffing them presents problems as well. Because the cavity is the last spot to heat up, getting the stuffing to reach a safe internal temperature of 160 degrees means overcooking the meat.

One final problem: After roasting a few batches, we realized that these birds didn't taste superb. Because most Cornish hens are mass-produced and not premium-quality, we were faced with the added challenge of trying to deepen their flavor.

We had our mission: to stuff and roast at least six grocery store–quality Cornish hens in a way that they looked good, tasted great, and weren't overcooked, all without smoking up the kitchen.

Get 'Em Up, Roast 'Em High

You may as well steam Cornish hens as roast six of them in a high-sided roasting pan. The pan sides shield the birds from oven heat, and their snug fit in the pan further prevents browning. So our first move was to get the birds up out of the roasting pan and onto a wire rack set over the pan. Our second step in the right direction was to space the birds as far apart as possible. Just as chops won't brown if overcrowded in the frying pan, Cornish hens won't brown if arranged too close together on the rack.

From initial testing, we determined that rotating the birds was crucial for moist and juicy breast meat. In a side-by-side taste test of hens roasted breast side up and those turned during roasting, the turned birds won easily. Though browner in color, the breast meat of the unturned birds was indeed drier and coarser-textured than those that were rotated. But because Cornish hens are in the oven for such a relatively short time, and because there are so many of them, multiple turns are out of the question. One turn, from breast side down to breast side up, was our limit.

After roasting Cornish hens at temperatures ranging from 350 degrees to 500 degrees, as well as roasting high and finishing low and roasting low and finishing high, we found that all oven temperatures had their problems. We finally settled on 400 degrees, cranking up the oven to 450 degrees during the last few minutes of roasting. This roasting temperature was high enough to encourage browning while low enough to keep the oven from smoking dramatically. Adding water to the roasting pan once the chicken fat starts to render and the juices start to flow further ensures a smokeless kitchen at both the 400- and 450-degree temperatures. Another perk: The pan is automatically deglazed in the oven. Once the birds are roasted, you can pour the pan juices into a saucepan without having to deglaze the roasting pan over two burners.

Even roasted at a relatively high 400 degrees with a 450-degree finish, our birds still lacked that gorgeous mahogany turkey skin color. We quickly realized that these expectations were unrealistic. Unlike turkeys, Cornish hens must brown in forty-five minutes (and about half that time, with our method, is breast side down). As we stared at these blond birds we thought of Kitchen bouquet, a standard food-styling remedy for pale poultry and gravy. Though we were both opposed to using this product outside a photographer's studio, the idea got us thinking in the right direction. We began to consider glazes.

To test this idea, we roasted six birds, brushing two with soy, two with balsamic, and two with jam thinned with a little soy right before they were turned, and once after the oven was increased to 450 degrees. All the birds colored more beautifully than any of our unglazed birds had, because the high oven heat caramelized the sugar in these glazes. But the balsamic glaze finished as our favorite, giving the hens a pleasant spotty brown, barbecued look.

Brining and Stuffing

I don't think there is a bird or piece of chicken out there that doesn't benefit from a few hours in a saltwater brine. Cornish hens are no exception. Having roasted the first few birds without brining, I wondered if they tasted good enough for me to even bother writing about. Although I can buy premium-quality poussins (baby chickens) at my grocery store, I can only buy mass-produced Cornish hens. Just two hours in a saltwater bath, however, transformed these mediocre-tasting birds into something I would proudly serve to guests. Much like koshering, brining draws out the blood, giving the bird a clean, fresh flavor. The salt water permeates the birds, making each bite, rather than just the skin, taste seasoned. Regardless of how you roast your Cornish hens, brining improves them immensely.

Our final challenge was how to roast these birds, stuffed, without overcooking them. From previous poultry testing, I knew that bringing a stuffed cavity to a salmonella-safe temperature of 160 degrees meant keeping the bird in the oven longer than it needed to stay. Although

Roasting Cornish hens on a rack and placing them as far apart as possible helps brown them, but for a really attractive, dark brown skin, use a flavorful glaze.

IMPORTANT STEPS IN ROASTING HENS

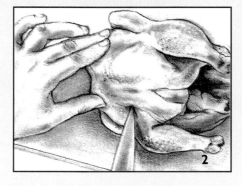

1. Brine hens breast side down, to ensure full, even flavoring.
2. To prevent the skin from "ballooning" when juices build up, carefully prick the skin (but not the meat) on the breast and legs with the tip of a knife before roasting.
3. Spoon about ½ cup of hot stuffing into the cavity of each hen.
4. Tie the legs of the hen together with a 6-inch piece of kitchen twine.
5. After 25 minutes, remove the hens from the oven, brush with glaze, turn them breast side up, and brush them with glaze again.

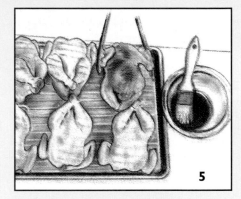

I'm certain that slightly overcooking a stuffed bird is inevitable, two things help. Starting the birds breast side down keeps the breast meat from drastically overcooking. And heating the stuffing before spooning it into the birds' cavities—a trick I picked up from cooking colleague Stephen Schmidt—also reduces oven time. By stuffing the birds with microwave-hot stuffing, we were able to roast birds that registered 172 to 174 degrees in the breast and 176 to 178 degrees in the leg/thigh by the time the stuffing reached 160 degrees. Even though I thought breast meat at this temperature might be borderline dry (160 to 165 is ideal to me), I found this petite breast tender and juicy. Of course, the leg/thigh meat, which always tastes best at a higher temperature, was perfect.

Although we were aware that trussing would slow down the roasting of the hens' legs and thighs (*see* "Roasting Chicken 14 Ways," January/February 1996), we knew we had to do something. With their more fragile, loose frame, Cornish hens are unsightly with their dangling legs. Stuffing the bird further increases the need to close the cavity. We quickly discovered that simply tying the hens' legs together was all that was needed to improve their looks and secure the stuffing without impeding the roasting.

ROAST STUFFED CORNISH HENS
Serves 6
Brining the birds breast side down ensures that the meatiest portions are fully submerged. Pouring a little water into the roasting pan at the 25 minute mark, once the birds have been turned, both prevents them from smoking during cooking and makes instant "jus," eliminating the need to deglaze the pan over two burners. To enrich the flavor of the jus to use as a sauce, pour it into a small saucepan, spoon off the fat that collects on the surface, and simmer it with a little vermouth or white wine.

2 cups kosher or 1 cup table salt
6 Cornish hens, (each less than 1½ pounds if possible), trimmed of extra fat, giblets removed, rinsed well
1 recipe stuffing (*see* below), heated until very hot
6 tablespoons balsamic vinegar
3 tablespoons olive oil
¼ cup dry vermouth or white wine

1. Dissolve salt in 5 quarts cold water in small clean bucket or large bowl. Add hens breast side down; refrigerate 2 to 3 hours. Remove, rinse thoroughly, pat dry, and prick skin all over breast and legs with point of a paring knife.

2. Adjust oven rack to middle position and heat oven to 400 degrees. Whisk balsamic vinegar and oil in small bowl; set aside. Spoon ½ cup hot stuffing into cavity of each hen; tie its legs together with 6-inch piece of kitchen twine. Leaving as much space as possible between each bird, arrange them breast side down and wings facing out, on large (at least 19-by-13–inch) wire rack, set over equally large roasting or jelly-roll pan. Roast until backs are golden brown, about 25 minutes. Remove pan from oven, brush bird backs with vinegar and oil glaze (re-blending before each bird), turn hens breast side up and wings facing out, and brush breast and leg area with additional glaze. Returned pan to oven, add 1 cup water, roast until meat thermometer inserted into the stuffed cavity registers about 150 degrees, about 15 to 20 minutes longer. Remove pan from oven again, brush birds with re-blended glaze, return pan to oven, add another ½ cup water to pan and increase oven temperature to 450 degrees. Roast until birds are spotty brown and cavity registers 160 degrees, 5 to 10 minutes longer, depending on bird size. Remove birds from oven, brush with remaining glaze, and rest for 10 minutes.

3. Meanwhile, pour hen "jus" from roasting pan into small saucepan, spoon off excess fat, add vermouth or wine, and simmer over medium-high heat until flavors blend, 2 to 3 minutes. Drizzle about ¼ cup sauce over each hen and serve, passing remaining sauce separately.

COUSCOUS STUFFING WITH CURRANTS, APRICOTS, AND PISTACHIOS
Makes about 3 cups, enough to stuff 6 Cornish hens
Toasted slivered almonds can be substituted for the pistachio nuts.

2 tablespoons butter
1 small onion, minced (½ cup)
2 medium garlic cloves, minced
¼ teaspoon ground cinnamon

HENS FOR TWO

Removing the back and flattening a Cornish hen before roasting solves many of the cooking problems of roasting a whole one. Of course, you can't stuff the flattened birds, and the presentation is not nearly as nice, so this approach is not really the best for a company meal. But for a weeknight dinner, it is ideal. Removing the back also reduces cooking time (twenty-five minutes compared to forty-five minutes for whole, stuffed birds).

SIMPLE ROAST BUTTERFLIED CORNISH HENS
Serves 2 to 4

Birds weighing more than one and one-half pounds can serve two people for weeknight dining. During the week, there's probably no time to brine, but it's easy to lift the skin of these butterflied birds and season the meat directly with salt, pepper, and herbs. You can roast up to four hens at a time if using a nineteen-by-thirteen-inch rack set over a large roasting or jelly roll pan.

2   Cornish hens (1½ to 1¾ pounds), backbones removed with kitchen shears, birds flattened, breast side up, with palm of hand
    Salt and ground black pepper
    Dried herbs, such as thyme, basil, or tarragon, for sprinkling
2   teaspoons butter, softened

1. Adjust oven rack to lower-middle position; heat oven to 400 degrees. Loosen skin around legs/thighs of hens and along breastbone to expose meat. Generously sprinkle exposed meat with salt, pepper, and herb of choice; return skin to place. Pierce skin in four or five places to prevent bubbling (see illustration page 21). Rub skin side of each hen with softened butter. Place hens on large (at least 19-by-13-inch) wire rack set over an equally large roasting or jelly roll pan.

2. Roast hens 20 to 25 minutes until golden brown and juices run clear. Turn oven from bake to broil; broil until nicely browned, about 5 minutes. Remove from pan, split each hen down the breastbone with chef's knife or kitchen shears if hens are to be split between two people. Drizzle pan juices over each portion and serve.

Split hens with poultry shears to simplify cooking without stuffing, perfect for a quick, mid-week meal.

¹⁄₈   teaspoon ground ginger
¹⁄₈   teaspoon ground turmeric
1   cup plain couscous
1¹⁄₃   cup chicken stock or low-sodium canned chicken broth
¼   cup dried apricots (8 to 9 whole), chopped fine
3   tablespoons currants
¼   cup shelled, toasted pistachio nuts, chopped
2   tablespoons minced fresh parsley leaves
1   teaspoon juice from one small lemon
     Salt and ground black pepper

Heat butter over medium heat in a medium saucepan. Add onions, garlic, cinnamon, ginger, and turmeric; sauté until onions soften, 3 to 4 minutes. Add couscous; stir until well coated, 1 to 2 minutes. Add chicken stock, bring to simmer, remove from heat, cover, and let stand until couscous has fully rehydrated, about 5 minutes. Fluff couscous with fork; stir in dried fruit, nuts, and parsley and lemon juice. Season to taste with salt and pepper. Transfer mixture to microwave-safe bowl; set aside.

WILD RICE STUFFING WITH CARROTS, MUSHROOMS, AND THYME
Makes about 3 cups, enough to stuff 6 Cornish hens

The wild rice blend in this stuffing holds together when pressed with a fork. You can use wild rice, but the cooked grains will remain separate.

1   ounce dried porcini mushrooms, rehydrated in 1 cup hot water
1¼   cups chicken stock or low-sodium chicken broth, or more if necessary
1   cup wild rice blend
2   tablespoons butter
1   small onion, minced (½ cup)
1   small carrot, minced (¼ cup)
½   small celery stalk, minced (¼ cup)
4   ounces fresh shiitake mushrooms, stemmed and sliced thin
2   teaspoons minced fresh thyme leaves
2   tablespoons minced fresh parsley leaves
     Salt and ground black pepper

1. Lift rehydrated porcini from liquid, squeeze dry, and chop coarse. Strain rehydrating liquid through sieve lined with paper towel and reserve (should be approximately ³⁄₄ cup).

2. Add enough chicken stock to mushroom liquid to equal 2 cups. Bring liquid to boil in medium saucepan, add rice blend, and return to boil. Reduce heat to low, cover, and simmer until rice is fully cooked, 40 to 45 minutes. Turn rice into a medium microwave-safe bowl; fluff with fork.

3. Meanwhile, heat butter in medium skillet over medium heat. Add onions, carrots, and celery; sauté until softened, 3 to 4 minutes. Add shiitake mushrooms; sauté until tender and liquid evaporates. Add porcini mushrooms and thyme; cook, stirring until well coated and blended with other ingredients, 1 to 2 minutes longer. Add this mixture to rice; toss to combine. Add parsley and season to taste with salt and ground black pepper.

WILD RICE STUFFING WITH CRANBERRIES AND TOASTED PECANS
Makes about 3 cups, enough to stuff 6 Cornish hens

2   cups chicken stock or low-sodium canned chicken broth
1   cup wild rice blend
2   tablespoons butter
1   small onion, chopped fine (½ cup)
½   small celery stalk, diced fine (¼ cup)
¼   cup toasted pecans, chopped coarse
¼   cup dried cranberries
2   tablespoons minced fresh parsley leaves
2   teaspoons minced fresh thyme leaves

1. Bring chicken stock to boil in medium saucepan. Add rice blend; return to boil. Reduce heat to low, cover, and simmer until rice is fully cooked, 40 to 45 minutes. Turn rice into medium microwave-safe bowl; fluff with fork.

2. Meanwhile, heat butter in medium skillet over medium heat. Add onions and celery; sauté until softened, 3 to 4 minutes. Add this mixture, as well as pecans, cranberries, and parsley and thyme, to rice; toss to coat.

BIG BIRD

These days, it is becoming more and more difficult to find small Cornish hens. Not long ago, these dwarfed birds hovered at around a pound, but for economic reasons, producers have started growing them bigger. Now the consumer is lucky to find one under one and one-half pounds.

This larger size is perfect for two people (each one-and-one-half-pound hen yields about twelve ounces of cooked meat and skin), but for individual presentation, seek out the smaller hens or look for poussins. Though a little more expensive, these baby chickens usually weigh about a pound and are perfect for one person.

Chickens (left) usually weigh 3½ to 4 pounds, while Cornish hens (middle) hover at about 1½ to 2 pounds. Poussins (right) weigh about a pound—perfect for individual servings.

PHOTOGRAPH BY JACK CERVEIRA

Caesar Salad Rediscovered

A coddled egg gives the dressing its distinctive smooth texture – or, if you prefer,
soft tofu and a food processor can create a thick dressing without the egg.

by Jack Bishop

✻

As originally conceived by Caesar Cardini, a restaurant owner in Tijuana, Mexico, Caesar salad was a tableside creation. A waiter would first place leaves of romaine lettuce in a large bowl, then lightly dress them with olive oil. Salt, pepper, more oil, lemon juice, and Worcestershire sauce were added along with two eggs that had been boiled for one minute and then cracked right into the bowl. In went the cheese and garlicky croutons and after much mixing and showmanship, the salad was transferred to a chilled plate and eaten immediately.

This recipe became a restaurant sensation in the 1920s, and unlike other classics of that era, Caesar salad has grown in popularity ever since. My goal for this piece was to re-capture the flavors of the original recipe while simplifying the technique. I often serve Caesar salad but, as opposed to the original tableside concept, I want to have the dressing in the re-frigerator when my guests arrive.

I first focused on the lettuce and croutons. I was intrigued by the packaged romaine hearts now sold widely in supermarkets. My tasters could not tell the difference between bagged romaine hearts and leaves taken from the hearts of whole heads of romaine, so feel free to choose either one. Just make sure that you end up with ten cups of torn lettuce leaves, which should be enough for four to six first-course servings.

The croutons were also fairly straightfor-ward. I found that bread cut into half-inch cubes was the right size for this salad and that two cups of cubed bread made plenty of crou-tons. After trying six basic methods for mak-ing croutons, I ended up preferring those that were tossed with garlic oil and then baked in a 350-degree oven.

With the croutons and lettuce issues re-solved, I turned to the dressing. Using a sim-ple version of the original recipe with extra-virgin olive oil, lemon juice, Worcestershire sauce, salt, and pepper, I set out to explore the role of the egg, which I consider the central question of this singular dressing.

I tried one and two raw eggs as well as one egg coddled for forty-five seconds, one minute, and two minutes. Two eggs caused the dressing to separate; one was enough for this recipe. I liked the effect coddling has on the egg. The heat unleashes the thickening powers of the egg and results in a smoother, creamier dressing. However, coddling for more than forty-five seconds can present some problems. As the egg continues to cook, the white will solidify and start sticking to the

shell. When you go to crack an egg that has been coddled for two minutes, the shell shat-ters and can end up in the dressing. I prefer to coddle the egg for just forty-five seconds. The shell still cracks neatly and although a little of the white is opaque, most of the egg slides right into the bowl with the dressing.

I also decided to explore various options for those who do not wish to use a raw or cod-dled egg in their dressing because of fear of sal-monella. I had seen several recipes for "mod-ern" Caesar dressing made with a hard-boiled egg. Although the egg does an excellent job of thickening the dressing, it leaves behind that unmistakable sulfur smell of cooked eggs. I also detected a little grittiness even when I made this dressing in the food processor.

Finally, I tried replacing the egg with a lit-tle soft tofu. I had seen this suggestion in sev-eral health foods cookbooks and was skepti-cal. However, tofu is the perfect thickener for this dressing because it is bland and smooth. There's no grittiness, and the flavors are basi-cally the same as in my original recipe. I found it best to use the food processor because it completely incorporates the tofu into the dressing. My "modern" Caesar dressing has a lighter color and slightly thicker texture than the traditional recipe.

My final tests revolved around seasonings. Although I wanted to remain faithful to the classic recipe, I was missing the garlic and an-chovy hit I associate with Caesar salad. Without these ingredients, the dressing tastes more lemony, but also a bit flat, at least to me. I found that adding a little garlic (one small clove put through a press) and four minced anchovies adds sufficient zing without be-coming overpowering.

BEST CAESAR SALAD
Serves 4 to 6 as a first course

If you don't own a garlic press, chop the gar-lic for both the croutons and dressing by hand; sprinkle it with the salt and then continue mincing it until it is almost pureed. The garlic and anchovies in the dressing are optional but strongly recommended. Without them, the salad is a bit bland. For Grilled Chicken Caesar Salad, add two grilled boneless, skin-less chicken breasts, sliced crosswise into half-inch strips, to the salad along with the cheese.

Garlic Croutons
2   large garlic cloves, peeled and pressed
        through a garlic press
1/4   teaspoon salt
3   tablespoons extra-virgin olive oil

2   cups 1/2-inch white bread cubes (from
        a baguette or country loaf)

Caesar Salad
1   large egg
3   tablespoons juice from 1 medium lemon
1   teaspoon Worcestershire sauce
1/4   teaspoon salt
8   grindings fresh black pepper
1   small garlic clove, pressed (1/4 teaspoon)
1 1/2   teaspoons anchovy paste (or 4 flat
        anchovy fillets, minced)
1/3   cup extra-virgin olive oil

2   medium heads romaine lettuce (large
        outer leaves removed) or 2 large
        romaine hearts; washed, dried, and
        torn into 1 1/2-inch pieces (about 10
        cups, lightly packed)
1/3   cup grated Parmesan cheese

1. *For the croutons*: Adjust oven rack to cen-ter position and heat oven to 350 degrees. Mix garlic, salt, and oil in small bowl; set aside for 20 minutes. Spread bread cubes out over small baking sheet. Drizzle oil through fine-mesh strainer evenly onto bread; toss to coat. Bake until golden, about 12 minutes. Cool on bak-ing sheet to room temperature. (Croutons can be stored in airtight container for up to 1 day.)

2. *For the dressing*: Bring water to boil in small saucepan over high heat. Carefully lower whole egg into water; cook 45 seconds. Remove with slotted spoon. When cool enough to handle, crack egg into small bowl with all other dressing ingredients except oil; whisk un-til smooth. Add oil in slow, steady stream, whisking constantly until smooth. Adjust sea-sonings. (Dressing may be refrigerated in airtight container for 1 day; shake before using.)

3. Place lettuce in large bowl; drizzle with half of dressing, then toss to coat lightly. Sprinkle with cheese, remaining dressing, and croutons; toss to coat well. Divide among in-dividual plates; serve immediately.

CAESAR SALAD WITH TOFU DRESSING
This eggless dressing will keep for a week in an airtight container in the refrigerator.

Follow recipe for Best Caesar Salad, sub-stituting 2 ounces soft tofu, drained and crumbled (about 1/3 cup), for egg. Process dressing ingredients except oil in food proces-sor workbowl fitted with steel blade, scraping down sides as needed, until tofu is incorpo-rated fully and mixture is smooth, about 1 minute. With motor running, add oil in slow, steady stream until smooth.

Homemade Rugelach

*Tender, flaky pastry dough that holds its shape–and holds in the filling–
is the key to these traditional but easy-to-make cookie-pastries.*

By Lisa Yockelson

It was my mother who introduced me to rugelach, a traditional Jewish pastry snack. In her hands, rugelach were seasoned with a sweep of apricot preserves and cinnamon sugar and laced with raisins and walnuts. Remembering the rugelach of my childhood has prompted endless musing about this fabulous sweet, which, to my mind, is part cookie, part pastry, and just a little bit like a sweetmeat.

My exploration of rugelach has led me to rethink and refine this cookie-pastry. Along the way, I've created a "wish list" for making memorable rugelach. First, it should be made out of a meltingly tender, delicate dough with a slightly acidic tang. Second, the dough should bake to a stable (but not rigid) conclusion. And finally, the filling should be a bounteous combination of preserves, fruit, and nuts, plus a spice-spiked sugar. As a baker, these have become my personal criteria.

To achieve these goals, I needed to address a number of interrelated issues. I began with the most crucial element, the dough.

I used my mother's dough recipe as the launching point but quickly found that it was much too sticky. As I attempted to fill and roll the cookies, the fully chilled dough adhered to the bottom sheet of waxed paper. I placed the rounds in the freezer and, thirty minutes later, worked with the frozen rounds of dough. Eventually, I could fill and roll the rugelach, but at that point my exchange with the dough seemed endless, and I got cranky. Then the rugelach collapsed as they baked.

Eventually, through many trials and errors, I found that by increasing the amount of flour, adding one egg yolk and two tablespoons of sour cream, then freezing the circles of rolled-out dough before applying the filling, I could create a dough with a silky, flaky quality and light, creamy "crumb." The addition of one and one-half tablespoons of granulated sugar gave it depth and helped in the final color. This was a dreamy, supple dough, and the best of them all.

Next came the issue of assembling the filling and dealing with its tendency to leak out as the cookies baked. After several more batches of rugelach, I found two techniques that helped control excessive amounts of leaking. First, I chopped the nuts very fine and added them to the filling last, so they

would block seepage. Secondly, I processed the preserves briefly in the food processor to break up larger pieces of fruit, which tend to spill out during baking. A little of the preserves still puddle around the baked rugelach, though, so I resigned myself to the fact that my rugelach would also always have a bit of that quirky charm of my mother's. The preserves will settle around the edges of the rugelach and darken slightly during baking, so it's important to remove cookies from the pans as soon as they are baked. If you leave them a little longer, the preserves will form a lacy edge on the cookies; simply cut away the border with a small paring knife.

Once I had filled and rolled the rugelach (*see* "Filling and Forming Rugelach," page 25), I placed them on heavy rimmed baking pans lined with parchment paper. If you don't have any of these rimmed pans, use the heaviest baking sheets you have in order to avoid scorching and possibly over-caramelizing the bottoms of the rugelach as they bake. Alternately, you can double up lightweight baking sheets by stacking one directly on top of the next.

To test oven temperatures, I baked some rugelach at 375 degrees and others at 350 degrees. At the higher temperature, the rugelach held their shape better and baked more evenly.

These rugelach are indeed worth discovering—and baking—again and again.

MASTER RECIPE FOR CRESCENT-SHAPED RUGELACH WITH RAISIN-WALNUT FILLING
Makes 32 cookies

If the dough gathers into a cohesive mass around the blade in the food processor workbowl, you have overprocessed it. Make sure to stop processing at the point where the mixture is separate and pebbly. If at any point during the cutting and rolling of the crescents the sheet of dough softens and becomes impossible to roll, slide it onto a baking pan and freeze it until it is firm enough to handle. Once the crescents are baking in the oven, start checking them for doneness at eighteen or nineteen minutes,

especially those on the top-level rack. Feel free to substitute an equal quantity of chopped pitted prunes, chopped dried apricots, dried currants, dried cherries, or dried cranberries for the raisins in the filling.

Cream Cheese and Sour Cream Dough
- 2¼ cups all-purpose flour
- 1½ tablespoons sugar
- ¼ teaspoon salt
- ½ pound unsalted butter (2 sticks), chilled and cut into ¼-inch pieces
- 8 ounces cream cheese, chilled and cut into ½-inch chunks
- 2 tablespoons sour cream

Fruit Filling
- 1 cup sugar
- 1 tablespoon ground cinnamon
- ⅔ cup apricot preserves, processed briefly in food processor to break up large chunks
- 1 cup raisins, preferably golden
- 2¼ cup walnuts, chopped fine (about 2 cups)

Egg-Yolk-and-Milk Glaze
- 2 large egg yolks
- 2 tablespoons milk

1. *For the dough*: Pulse flour, sugar, and salt to combine in food processor fitted with steel

PHOTOGRAPHS BY JACK CERVEIRA

blade. Add butter and cream cheese pieces and sour cream; pulse until dough comes together in small, uneven pebbles the size of cottage cheese curds, about sixteen 1-second pulses. Turn mixture onto work surface, press into 9-inch-by-6-inch log, divide log into four equal portions (*see* illustration 1), and press each into 4½-by-¾-inch disk. Place each disk between two sheets plastic wrap; roll out to form 8½-inch circle (illustration 2). Stack dough circles on plate; freeze 30 minutes (or up to 1 month if stored in zipper-lock freezer bag). Meanwhile, mix sugar and cinnamon in small bowl; set aside with other filling ingredients.

2. Working with one dough round, remove from freezer and spread 2½ tablespoons preserves, ¼ cup raisins, 2 tablespoons cinnamon sugar, and ½ cup walnuts, in that order, over dough; pat down gently with fingers (illustration 3). Cut dough round into eight wedges.

Roll each wedge into crescent shape and place at 2-inch intervals on parchment paper–lined heavy rimmed baking pans (illustration 4). Freeze crescents at least 15 minutes. (Frozen crescents, if well-wrapped, can be frozen in a zipper-lock bag up to 6 weeks.) Repeat with remaining dough rounds.

3. Adjust oven racks to upper- and lower-middle positions and heat oven to 375 degrees. Whisk egg yolks and milk in small bowl until smooth. Brush top and sides of frozen crescents with egg-milk mixture. Bake crescents, turning baking pans from front to back and top to bottom halfway through baking time, until pale gold and slightly puffy, 21 to 23 minutes. Immediately sprinkle each cookie with scant teaspoon cinnamon sugar; carefully transfer hot, fragile cookies to cooling rack using thin-bladed spatula. (Can be stored in an airtight container up to 4 days.)

ROULADE-SHAPED RUGELACH

Follow Master Recipe for Crescent-Shaped Rugelach with Raisin-Walnut Filling, rolling dough to an 11-inch by 7-inch rectangle. Follow illustrations 5 and 6 to roll dough and form roulades.

RUGELACH WITH CHOCOLATE-WALNUT FILLING

Chocolate-and-walnut rugelach are excellent without preserves altogether or with seedless raspberry preserves in place of the apricot.

Follow recipe for either Crescent- or Roulade-Shaped Rugelach with Raisin-Walnut Filling, omitting apricot preserves (or substituting raspberry) and substituting 1 cup semisweet chocolate minichips for raisins.

Lisa Yockelson is a food journalist and author of Layer Cakes and Sheet Cakes *(HarperCollins, 1996).*

FILLING AND FORMING RUGELACH

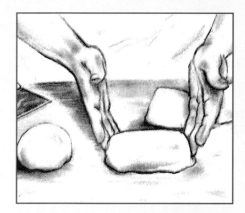

1. Cut the dough into even quarters. Press each quarter into a round, flat disk about 4½ inches in diameter for crescents; or an 8-inch by 4-inch rectangle for roulades.

2. Place each disk between two pieces of plastic wrap and roll it into an 8½-inch disk, or an 11-inch by 7-inch rectangle. Leave in the plastic wrap and stack on top of each other on a large plate.

3. Remove the dough from the freezer, place it on a work surface, peel off the top layer of plastic wrap, and cover the dough with preserves, raisins, cinnamon sugar, and walnuts.

For Crescents

4. For crescents, cut the dough into eight pie-shaped wedges. Starting with the wide side opposite the point, roll up the wedges to form crescents. Freeze them for 15 minutes, then bake as directed.

For Roulades

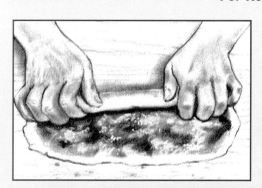

5. For roulades, starting from the long side, roll the dough tightly into a cylinder, taking care not to squeeze any filling out the sides as you roll.

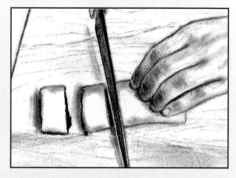

6. Cut off a ¼-inch section from each end of the cylinder and discard it. Cut the roll into 1-inch pieces. Place them seam side down on parchment paper–lined baking pans or cookie sheets. Freeze them for 15 minutes, then bake as directed.

Organic Beans Run Out of Gas

*Supermarket brands take top honors as panelists value
creaminess and saltiness over firmness.*

by Jack Bishop

I should confess up front that until recently I never liked canned beans. I thought most brands were too soft and too salty—fine in a pinch for a white bean puree or hummus, but never good enough for soups or stews. But a year or two ago, I discovered several brands of organic beans that were dramatically less salty (I'd rather add my own, thank you) and considerably firmer than supermarket standards. When organizing this tasting, I felt sure the organic brands would come out on top.

Well, it seems I'm a bit of an odd bean. Although I gave high marks to the organic beans in our blind tasting (I had no trouble picking them out), almost no one else liked them. Most tasters found them to be overly bland and too firm and chalky. Creamier, moister beans took top honors.

Assembling the Field

As in all of our tastings, we started with products that are very widely available. Pillsbury owns Green Giant, a top national brand of canned beans, as well as Progresso, a regional brand that dominates the market in the Northeast. Because beans are used in many Latin dishes, it's no surprise that Goya is also a leading national brand. The last major player is S&W, a California brand with wide distribution on the West Coast and some spotty presence in the East. In addition to these four brands, we added the two leading brands in natural foods stores, Eden and Westbrae, sometimes sold in supermarkets.

To give each brand a fair chance, we sampled two different kinds from each company. We chose dark red kidneys, the most popular bean (people use them in chili), and white beans, a leading bean that is notoriously mushy. (Black beans and chickpeas are the two other best-selling types of beans.) Although all six companies sell dark red kidneys, each offers a different kind of white bean, including cannellini (also called white kidney) and smaller navy or Great Northern beans.

Although dark red kidney beans received slightly higher scores than the white beans (our panel thought the red kidneys had more flavor), the rankings within each type of bean were remarkably similar. Green Giant was the favorite among both whites and red kidneys while Goya was the second favorite for both types of beans and S & W was the third choice for both.

Tasters easily detected the stark differences that I had also noticed among brands when researching this story. Organic white beans from Eden and Westbrae were deemed firmer and dramatically less salty than the competition. Among the red kidneys, tasters also detected far less salt in these two brands. (Tasters found most brands of red kidneys to be quite firm.)

While I happen to prize less salt and more firmness, most of our tasters did not. They felt the organic beans had a much weaker bean flavor. Quite frankly, I thought these beans tasted more like beans because there were fewer distractions. However, our panel was quite strong in its preferences. More salt (and in the case of the red kidneys, more sugar) meant more flavor and a higher rating. In fact, while Green Giant red kidneys received an average overall score of 73 (on a scale from 0 to 100), poor Eden red kidney beans managed only an 18 (*see* "Rating Canned Beans," page 27, for detailed results).

Upon reflection, I found the salt issue to be fairly easy to understand; firmness took longer.

HOW DO THEY COOK UP?

We wondered if the differences our panel detected when tasting beans straight from the can would hold up under real-life kitchen conditions. So we used the white beans to make a simple bean and vegetable soup and added the red kidneys to a tomato-based chili with ground beef.

The results of this second tasting were basically the same as when the beans were tasted straight from the can. The organic beans were strongly downgraded in terms of flavor. They tasted "bland and lifeless" when compared to saltier brands like Green Giant and Goya, which were the favorites in both the soup and the chili.

Interestingly, some of the dryness and crumbly texture that tasters complained about when tasting the organic beans straight from the can was gone. Cooking the beans in liquid (either soup or the chili) made them moister, and it was harder to detect the chalkiness that bothered panelists in the original tasting.

Tasters did notice that the organic beans were considerably firmer in the soup and chili than the top choices. While panelists rejected the "extremely mushy" Progresso white beans, they clearly preferred the "creamy but not too soft" texture of the Green Giant white beans to the firmer organic beans.

When tasting beans straight from the can, I had to agree that the lower-salt organic brands did seem bland. (Tasters had the same reaction to lower-salt organic beans when sampling dishes made with them. For more information, *see* "How Do They Cook Up?" above.)

As for firmness, I would rather buy firm beans than beans that are already soft. However, our tasters felt there was a downside to all that firmness. The organic brands were drier and much more crumbly, even chalky. The top brands in our tasting were far creamier and smoother with a moister, softer interior. After flavor, texture was the most important factor in determining tasters' overall response to a specific sample. And they were happy to trade a little firmness for more creaminess.

The Sweetness Issue

When reviewing labels, I was surprised to see that many canned kidney beans contain sugar and/or high-fructose corn syrup. Evidently, manufacturers add sweeteners to play up the natural sweetness of the beans. It seems to be working. The four brands of kidney beans with sugar beat out the two organic brands made

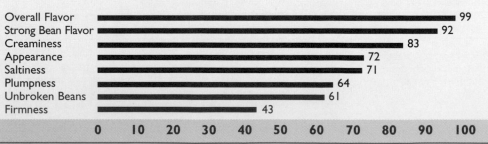

WHAT MAKES GOOD BEANS?

A statistical analysis of the responses given by our panelists to various questions about flavor, texture, and appearance revealed some interesting information about what people look for in canned beans. Numbers close to 100 indicate a high correlation between a specific trait and overall liking; numbers below 50 indicate little or no correlation. As the chart shows, a salty, strong bean flavor was preferred, as was a creamy (not firm) texture.

Trait	Score
Overall Flavor	99
Strong Bean Flavor	92
Creaminess	83
Appearance	72
Saltiness	71
Plumpness	64
Unbroken Beans	61
Firmness	43

0   10   20   30   40   50   60   70   80   90   100

without any sweetener.

I talked to several industry experts, and they said that any sweetener (or salt) in the bean brine has a tremendous effect on the flavor because of the way canned beans are processed. I had assumed that dried beans were cleaned, soaked, cooked, and seasoned, and then canned in fresh liquid.

This is not the case, however. Linda Kamps, a spokesperson for Pillsbury, explains that beans are actually cooked in their sealed cans. After cleaning and soaking, the plumped-up beans are put into cans with a seasoned brine (as simple as water and salt or as elaborate as water, salt, sugar, corn syrup, calcium chloride to help retain firmness, and disodium EDTA, a preservative). The cans are then sealed and thermal-processed in order to cook and sterilize the beans at the same time. The bean-packing liquid is so thick and viscous because it has cooked down as the beans were rehydrating. Because the beans are not drained after cooking, they continue to absorb any seasonings in the brine as the cans sit on supermarket shelves.

RATING CANNED BEANS

Twenty-one nonexpert panelists rated beans from six companies. In general, red kidney beans scored slightly higher than white beans. Beans are listed in order of overall finish in the tasting. All samples were drained and rinsed. Panelists tasted beans as is and had access to water and bread. Locations refer to the manufacturing plant or corporate headquarters listed on can labels. Samples were purchased in New York supermarkets, and prices indicate actual retail cost. Ingredients are listed exactly as written on labels.

Red Kidney Beans

RECOMMENDED

Green Giant Dark Red Kidney Beans (Minneapolis, Minnesota), $.59 for 15.5-ounce can. "Very nice-looking beans" with "great, smooth" texture and "good flavor." Contains soaked dark red kidney beans, water, sugar, corn syrup, salt, calcium chloride, disodium EDTA.

Goya Dark Red Kidney Beans (Secaucus, New Jersey), $.59 for 15.5-ounce can. "Beautiful red plump beans" with "very sweet, strong bean flavor." Contains kidney beans, water, high-fructose corn syrup, sugar, salt, calcium chloride added as a firming agent, disodium EDTA added for color retention.

S&W Dark Red Kidney Beans (San Ramon, California), $1.09 for 15-ounce can. These beans were described as "very dark" and "very big." As one panelist summed up, "good flavor with nice amount of salt" and "nicely creamy." Contains prepared dark red kidney beans, water, sugar, salt, calcium chloride.

NOT RECOMMENDED

Progresso Dark Red Kidney Beans (Vineland, New Jersey), $.89 for 19-ounce can. Much softer (and, in fact, too mushy) for most tasters. Contains soaked red kidney beans, water, sugar, corn syrup, salt, calcium chloride, disodium EDTA (preservative).

Westbrae Natural Organic Kidney Beans (Carson, California), $1.59 for 15-ounce can. As one taster wrote, "bland, bland, bland." Too chalky as well. Contains organic kidney beans (soaked in water), water, sea salt.

Eden Organic Kidney Beans (Clinton, Michigan), $1.99 for 15-ounce can. "No flavor" and "too crumbly" were two biggest faults with this low finisher. Contains organic kidney beans, water, kombu (seaweed).

White Beans

RECOMMENDED

Green Giant Great Northern Beans (Minneapolis, Minnesota), $.59 for 15.5-ounce can. A tad less salty than other top white beans. Contains soaked Great Northern beans, water, salt.

Goya White Kidney Beans (Secaucus, New Jersey), $.59 for 15.5-ounce can. These very plump beans are larger than other white beans in the tasting. "Not quite as creamy" as top white beans. Contains beans, water, salt.

S&W White Beans (San Ramon, California), $1.29 for 15-ounce can. A notch down in quality from top white beans. Contains prepared small white beans, water, salt, sugar, dehydrated onion, calcium chloride.

NOT RECOMMENDED

Westbrae Natural Organic Great Northern Beans (Carson, California), $1.59 for 15-ounce can. "A bit chalky" and "way too bland" was the general consensus. Contains Great Northern beans (soaked in water), water, sea salt.

Progresso Cannellini Beans (Vineland, New Jersey), $.89 for 19-ounce can. "Extremely soft" with "overcooked, old flavor." Contains soaked white kidney beans, water, salt, disodium EDTA (to retain color), calcium chloride (to retain texture).

Eden Organic Navy Beans (Clinton, Michigan), $1.99 for 15-ounce can. "Very bland and fairly firm" with "odd, little green flecks" (probably seaweed) that displeased many tasters. Contains organic navy beans, water, kombu (seaweed).

Testing Full-Size Food Processors

*Useful attachments and good, solid bases give
KitchenAid and Cuisinart a tie for first.*

by Adam Ried with Dawn Yanagihara

The day my compact food processor died, I rejoiced. Finally I could justify purchasing a full-size food processor, with a large bowl and enough "oomph" to make bread dough.

When I went to make my purchase, however, confusion took over. There were numerous brands, sizes, and features from which to choose, and prices were all over the place, from less than $100 to almost $400. Which features were the most important, I wondered, and were price and quality directly related? We decided to hash this out.

To do so, we first identified the major players in the field. We then evaluated each machine's overall performance in sixteen tests divided among five general categories: chopping and grinding, slicing, grating, pureeing, and kneading.

We wanted to look at machines that could slice enough potatoes to make a gratin for six, or handle a double batch of pesto. After some consideration, we settled on eleven cups as our maximum size and seven cups as the minimum. Within this range, we went for the largest model available from each manufacturer (*see* chart below for details).

Even for those of us who don't mind doing plenty of chopping and dicing with a chef's knife, there are several jobs for which the food processor is the perfect tool. Among them is chopping large quantities of ingredients such as onions or parsley, to be used in several dishes; slicing lots of potatoes and other vegetables for gratins; making creamy dressings and purees, such as pesto; grinding crumbs from

stale bread; grating cheese (so you can save your knuckles from the box grater); and cutting fat into flour to make pastry dough. These tests were our most important because all involve chopping, grinding, and slicing, the raisons d'être for food processors.

Other tests, which carried somewhat less weight in our ratings, involved tasks that may be best performed by other kitchen tools, but which a food processor should be able to do in a pinch, such as pureeing soup or kneading bread dough.

Test Results

To test the machines' chopping and mincing prowess, we chopped onions and minced fresh parsley leaves. The Waring, Cuisinart, and Braun models chopped onions best; Waring

and Braun also took top parsley-chopping honors.

We then moved on to grinding, which is essentially mincing carried further. We ground Parmesan cheese, graham crackers, and stale baguette slices for bread crumbs. Surprisingly, none of the units did a top-notch job at this task. All the machines produced pebbly Parmesan, and even after extensive processing, the Cuisinart, the Waring, the KitchenAid, and the Black & Decker all left large pieces of graham cracker behind. KitchenAid and Black & Decker, however, did make quick work of the bread crumbs.

Next we sliced soft zucchini, then tried slicing hard items such as potato, carrot, and pepperoni. Here we were looking for even, clean, round slices that fell into the bowl in a neat stack. The

RATING FULL-SIZE FOOD PROCESSORS

We tested and evaluated eight full-size food processors (including the prototype Black & Decker) according to the following criteria. The food processors are listed in order of preference. An asterisk indicates a tie with the one above.

Price: Manufacturer's suggested retail promotional price.

Bowl Capacity and Base Weight: Larger bowls were upgraded, as were heavier bases.

Design/Features: Includes disparate factors that influence ease of use. Also encompasses any special features.

Chopping/Grinding: Machines that chopped and ground most evenly, with good, clean cuts, were rated good.

Slicing: We sliced carrots, potatoes, pepperoni, and zucchini. Thin, round, stacked slices of even thickness were rated good.

Grating: Machines that produced mozzarella shreds of consistent width and length rated good.

Pureeing: The smoothest puree and the most cups of liquid processed without leaking were rated good.

Kneading: We made pie dough and bread dough. The best-incorporated doughs and most stable machines were rated good.

= good = fair = poor

Brand/Model	Price	Bowl Capacity/ Base Weight	Design/ Features	Chopping/ Grinding	Slicing	Grating	Pureeing	Kneading
KitchenAid Ultra Power KFP 600	249.95	11 cups/ 12 lb, 6 oz	good	fair	good	poor	good	good
*Cuisinart Pro Custom 11, DLC-8S	199.00	11 cups/ 10 lb, 13 oz	good	fair	good	good	poor	good
Braun 5-in-1 Food Prep Center, K1000	289.99	11 cups/ 5 lb, 8 oz	fair	good	fair	fair	good	good
Waring Pro Food Processor, PFP 15	335.00	7 cups/ 13 lb, 5 1/2 oz	fair	good	poor	fair	fair	fair
Regal Food Processor, K7755	59.99	9 cups/ 4 lb, 14 1/2 oz	poor	fair	fair	good	fair	fair
Krups Master Pro Deluxe, 706	100.00	7 cups/ 7 lb	good	fair	fair	fair	fair	fair
Hamilton Beach Chef Prep, 70700	49.99	7 cups w/o chute/ 4 lb, 14 oz	fair	fair	poor	fair	fair	fair

Black & Decker and the Cuisinart performed well, in part because they each offer a dual feed tube, the smaller branch of which can hold a single carrot or thin zucchini for neat, round slices. (The Krups also offers a dual feed tube, but it did not salvage generally poor slicing performance.) The Cuisinart had the additional advantage of an extra large feed tube, which could accommodate a whole potato.

Though not perfect, the Cuisinart won the grating test, producing the greatest percentage of even mozzarella shreds. Once again, the Cuisinart's large feed tube proved itself to be a real convenience because we didn't have to trim the mozzarella block to make it fit.

Next we pureed three-cup batches of pesto, parsley butter, and carrots and onions cooked until tender in stock. All of the machines except the Krups whizzed through the pesto-pureeing test, producing smooth, emulsified sauces with no bunching of the basil beneath the blades. The Krups left large pieces of basil and nuts and also bruised the basil. The KitchenAid earned top honors for the parsley butter, making a smooth, homogenous butter with no chunks left. With the exception of the KitchenAid and the Black & Decker, which both produced almost blender-quality soups, most of the machines did a lousy pureeing job, leaving tiny grains of solid floating in separate liquid.

We also wanted to know which machines would hold the most pureed liquid before leaking. The Braun held an amazing nine cups before it began to leak, while the Black & Decker and the KitchenAid held seven and six cups, respectively. In contrast, none of the other models held more than four cups without leaking.

We tested pastry dough by pulsing fat into flour, a job handled easily by the Cuisinart, KitchenAid, Braun, Waring, and Black & Decker. The Regal, Hamilton Beach, and Krups required more pulses, and therefore time, attention, and effort, to break up the fat into tiny, even pieces. We also tested bread dough because many cooks who do not have standing mixers

make bread dough in a food processor. The processor won't really knead it fully, but the dry and wet ingredients come together beautifully to form the dough. Success in this arena was linked directly to large bowl size as well as to the weight of the base. The eleven-cup machines were best because they provided ample space for the ball of dough to move around. A heavy base provided stability, and the nods went to KitchenAid and Cuisinart, with their substantial, ten-pound-plus bases.

Features from Functional to Freaky

These machines have a wide range of features, some of which actually turned out to be very useful. The KitchenAid and the Black & Decker, for example, were equipped with useful mini-bowls that could be mounted inside the larger bowls. We also appreciated the pinholes in the feed tubes of the Cuisinart, Krups, and Black & Decker, which create a slow, steady stream of oil flowing into the bowl for making mayonnaise and salad dressing.

On the other hand, some machines had unusual features that turned out to be worthless. Worst of all was the Hamilton Beach's food chute, which sprays the user with crumbs and juices of the item passing through the chute.

Some Conclusions

All the machines costing $100 or less were generally poor performers, so we would not advise wasting your money on them. Yet even among the more expensive models, none excelled in all the tests. KitchenAid and Cuisinart performed best overall, but each had its weak points.

So our advice is this: Assess the type of jobs you'll ask of your food processor and buy either the KitchenAid or the Cuisinart based on how their particular strengths and features meet your needs. If you have neither a minichopper nor a blender, consider the KitchenAid for its minibowl and superior pureeing ability. But if an extra large and small dual feed tube, with a pinhole for dribbling oil into the workbowl are important, opt for the less expensive Cuisinart.

TESTERS COMMENTS

RECOMMENDED

KitchenAid Ultra Power, KFP 600 Has a heavy, well-designed, easy-to-clean base, a mini-bowl, and superior pureeing ability.

Cuisinart Pro Custom 11, DLC-8S Performance in all areas except pureeing on par with KitchenAid. Dual feed tube is extra large but has a difficult-to-clean design.

NOT RECOMMENDED

Braun 5-in-1 Preparation Center, K1000 Blade is a menace; two out of three testers cut themselves cleaning it. Bowl and blade are difficult to clean because they have many ridges and odd angles. It was, however, the most quiet in operation.

Waring Professional Food Processor, PFP 15 For that kind of money? Not in a million years. Controls feel shoddy and are hard to operate. It did, however, chop and grind well.

Krups Master Pro Deluxe, 706 Must really bare down hard on food in feed tube to push it through. Mangled parsley without ever chopping it sufficiently.

Regal Food Processor, K7755 Slicing blade bent during testing. Blades were difficult to position on machine. Poor fit between bowl and base. Peanut-grinding test damaged the bowl stem.

Hamilton Beach Chef Prep, 70700 Sounds like a chain saw. Food chute gate leaks when in position, so user is showered with fragments or juices from the food being processed.

Preproduction Black & Decker

The Black & Decker Kitchentools food processor is a brand new model that, at the time we were testing, had not yet been released to the public. Thus, we conducted our tests on a preproduction prototype rather than an off-the-shelf unit as is our custom. Because we did not work with a standard production unit, we felt obligated to separate this machine from the rest of the pack. That said, though, the preproduction unit was a winner and certainly would have placed right up there with the KitchenAid and Cuisinart in terms of performance, features, and price. If Black & Decker can maintain the same quality in production, the Kitchentools food processor is certainly worthy of consideration.—A.R.

Tasting Bordeaux Under $20

*For the same price as a good California wine, you can still find
high-quality Bordeaux filled with character.*

by Mark Bittman

With the prices of the highest-ranked reds from Bordeaux going through the roof (a single bottle of 1995 Château Margaux will set you back $150, and the wine has yet to be bottled!), it seems more important than ever to find affordable specimens that represent the region's distinctive style. This style has not been duplicated anywhere else in the world, but it is expressed in a simpler, less dramatic form in many of the relatively inexpensive wines of the region.

There are many reasons why Bordeaux—the wines, not the region—remain unique: climate, soil, technique, and of chief importance, the skill with which the Bordelaise meld the two major grape varieties, cabernet sauvignon and merlot, with a number of lesser varieties, such as cabernet franc, malbec, and others. Beginning in the late '60s, top California winemakers hailed cabernet sauvignon as the premier red grape and concentrated their efforts on "varietal," that is, unblended, wines made from it. In more recent years, they have focused on the softer, more accessible merlot. But only a handful of Californians have experimented with making Bordeaux-style blended wines. And although some of these have been wonderfully successful (*see our tasting of Meritage wines in the January/February 1995 issue*), there is still no comparison between California and Bordeaux when it comes to either breadth or depth of the selection.

Nevertheless, looking for winners among the lesser-known (and less expensive) Bordeaux is always an adventure. The top fifty or so wines from Bordeaux, whose names are familiar to every wine lover, do not change much from year to year and have become sound investments more often than dinner accompaniments. Lesser wines—those made from grapes grown outside of the absolutely prime growing areas, or on the wrong end of the vineyard, or at too high a yield—do not vary so much as a group, but individually. A top château may decide to put some very good but imperfect grapes into a "second label" wine and sell it for a quarter of the price of its more familiar product. A great winemaker may turn a formerly unremarkable vineyard around, to the point where its wines are superior to those of its neighbors. Or a well-known wine may have such an off vintage that it lowers its price to the point at which the wine is selling for the same price as that of its unknown neighbors.

Almost all of the wines were enjoyed by almost all of the tasters. It's worth noting, though, that our choice of wines was limited by our desire to find wines that would be available in most major markets in the United States. It's not only conceivable but likely that industrious importers in your area have found small batches of well-made Bordeaux wines that would have done brilliantly in our tasting but that, because of our national audience, would have caused too much frustration were they included here.

RATING THE WINES

The wines in our tasting, held at Mt. Carmel Wine and Spirits, in Hamden, Connecticut, were judged by a panel made up of both wine professionals and amateur wine lovers. In the judging, seven points were awarded for each first-place vote, six for second, five for third, and so on. The wines were all purchased in the Northeast; prices will vary considerably throughout the country.

Within each category, the wines are listed based on the number of points scored. In this tasting, the Very Highly Recommended wines received rave reviews. Highly Recommended wines had predominantly positive comments, and Recommended wines had a majority of positive comments. Wines in the Recommended with Reservations category had low quantitative scores and a number of negative comments but were still enjoyed by several tasters.

Very Highly Recommended

1993 Château Meyney, Ste. Estephe, $20. This wine is almost always a good buy. "Real wine," wrote one taster. Should show nicely for a few years.

1994 Château Jonqueyres, Bordeaux Supérieur $10. High merlot content (80 percent) produced a real crowd pleaser: "Tastes like a French-California hybrid, with advantages of both." A wine for current drinking.

Highly Recommended

1994 Château Greysac, Haut-Médoc, $12. Popular wine, as it should be—note the favorable price. Like Meyney, above, cited as "real wine" by several tasters. "Mushroomy" nose and "thin" body were noted by some.
1994 Château Rochebrune, St. Emilion, $12. Another favorable price for a very good wine. "Soft, open, and approachable," but "a wine built to last." Some thought the nose "vegetal" and the fruit "unripe."
1994 Château Le Sartre, Pessac-Leognan (Graves), $13. No one raved about this wine, but almost everyone ranked it fairly high. "Balanced nose," but "pestering tannic finish."

Recommended

1992 Château Clerc Milon, Pauillac, $20. Proof that there are good wines in bad vintages; most '92s aren't worth drinking, but this one showed nicely. "Tremendous character," wrote its most ardent admirer. Others found the nose "overwhelmingly stinky."
1994 Mondot, St. Emilion, $20. The second label of Troplong-Mondot, one of the hottest properties in St. Emilion. "Has depth, complexity, and class," said one, but others disagreed.
1993 Château Potensac, Médoc, $15. "Lush bouquet," "deep color," full" flavor.
1994 Château d'Angludet, Margaux, $20. A wine of good reputation, but one that blew no one away. "Ripe and sweet." Might be worth trying, but not a wine for cellaring.
1993 Clos Beauregard, Pomerol, $19. "Light and pleasant" but not an earthshaker. Some found it "boring" and "soft."
1994 Château Larose Trintaudon, Haut-Médoc, $15. Very tannic, young-tasting wine that showed some promise. Deserves to be revisited in a year or two.

Recommended with Reservations

Vintage Château Fourcas Hosten, Listrac Médoc, $18. Usually reliable wine that got mixed reviews: "Nice and mellow on the palate" but "pungent and unyielding."
1994 St. Paul de Dominique, St. Emilion, $19. "Ripe fruit but tannic to a fault."
1994 Ste. Estephe (Cos d'Estournel), $18. "Nice nose," but "more tannin than fruit."
1994 Château Martinet, St. Emilion, $18. The winner of our tasting of a couple of years ago disappointed all but a couple tasters. Most found it "short on fruit."
1994 Merlot, Christian Moueix, $10. "Okay, but not great."

Book Reviews

Every reviewer has prejudices, many of which swim dangerously just below the surface, unseen but leaving a telltale wake. Others are more openly threatening, the rigid dorsal fin in full view of the desperate author, who flails madly toward shore. Because the mandate of *Cook's Illustrated* is to investigate how to prepare food and to communicate that information clearly to anyone who might wander into the kitchen, I am keenly biased on the topic of how to teach cooking properly. In my view, a truly first-class introductory cookbook needs to start out with a clear sense of organization and purpose, followed by a careful selection of basic recipes from which a beginner can learn. One also hopes that the author consistently treats the material in depth, rather than going into brilliant detail on page 36 only to gloss over techniques and terms when you turn the page. Finally, the recipes ought to be worth printing, with sufficient testing to convey why a particular technique or ingredient is included. I don't demand a tome on the science of cooking (although that is my personal bias), but I do want the author to explain clearly what is really important about sautéing, stir-frying, or roasting and then to demonstrate the theory through well-constructed recipes.

Cooking for Dummies Bryan Miller and Marie Rama, IDG Books, $19.99. There are reasons to like this book. The cookware section is particularly lucid, the illustrations are clear and most often useful, and the book is a good once-over review. In the recipes, the authors nail many important cooking facts, pointing out, for example, that marinades don't tenderize meat, a roast chicken needs to be turned in the oven for even cooking, knives require professional sharpening or the purchase of a good electric sharpener, and pie pastry is best made with a combination of butter and vegetable shortening. And, to be fair, most of the recipes were clear, concise, and tasted just fine, from a delicious vanilla sauce to an excellent, workhorse recipe for sautéed chicken breasts made with tomatoes and thyme. However, the recipe directions were not always thorough, not clearly explaining why a certain technique is called for or how things are supposed to look as you go along. And the tone? Well, humor is best left to experts. For instance, after a useful and straightforward description of a chinois, the authors point out that "A chinois also looks funny when you put it on your head and chase the kids around the house with a rolling pin." This grating change of tone, in a practical cookbook, would be like watching Calvin Coolidge jump down from the podium to do the funky chicken.

That said (authors, head for shore), I wonder what they and their publisher were thinking. Like a cheap Hollywood set, *Cooking for Dummies* does not bear close examination. The chapter on boiling, poaching, and steaming has four recipes for rice, two for stock, and one each for mashed potatoes, poached salmon, and steamed broccoli. If you wanted to boil, poach, or steam anything else, you are out of luck. One might also query whether beginners are wont to make stock, especially a chicken stock that calls for three to four chicken carcasses and takes two hours. Kitchen dummies (and many experts) are more likely to buy canned stock, but the authors might, if truly tuned in to the needs of culinary novices, offer a quick one-hour stock using a whole chicken, an ingredient that is often on hand.

There are plenty of other disconnects. The authors wax poetic about a $200 French copper sauteuse evasée (a saucepan with flared sides—hardly essential for the beginning cook) and suggest buying a stockpot for $75 to $150, even though a $20 model works fine for most applications. We are reminded of the virtues of lemongrass, but the basic information on meat is sadly lacking. We are also told to cook pork to 160 degrees (at which point it is overcooked), are given a recipe for salad dressing that starts out with a whopping two tablespoons of mustard, and are advised to grill half-inch-thick hamburgers over hot coals for twenty minutes (hockey pucks, anyone?). A "quick" recipe for Broiled Porgies in Rosemary Oil requires that the cook prepare homemade rosemary-infused oil that must steep all day. The book includes a recipe for roast duck but virtually no desserts, offering only an apple pie, two soufflés, and a berry salad.

In sum, *Cooking for Dummies* is clever, much too clever for its own good and the good of the novice home cook. Although there is much useful material here and plenty of straightforward recipes, it is poorly organized and the authors exhibit an erratic depth of culinary knowledge.

The Complete Idiots Guide to Cooking Basics Ronnie Fein, alpha books, $18.95. Any fledgling cook who was given this cookbook would throw up his or her hands in despair, turn the kitchen into a family room, and order takeout. Ronnie Fein makes the authors of *Cooking for Dummies* look good. To begin with, the book starts out with 155 pages of generic (and therefore not very useful) information about ingredients, cookware, and shopping lists before it even gets to the subject of cooking. Here we are, eager to make an omelet or sauté a boneless chicken cutlet, and first we have to wade through pages of unnec-

essary advice about how important it is to follow a recipe precisely the first time out. It's like buying a new sports car and having the salesman give you a two-hour lecture about the design, philosophy, and function of the air bag. Gimme the keys!

But the real clincher, what makes this a clunker of a cookbook, is that it does nothing to organize cooking methods clearly or help explain what is and what is not important in basic cookery. All the recipes, which are a mixed bag from lamb shanks braised in an unpleasant, mouth-puckering mixture of lemon juice and stock to some real winners such as fried rice and a spiced coffee shake, are simply thrown together at the back of the book with no explanation and no reference to the generic information earlier on. And the general information scattered throughout the book is pitiful in its brevity and lack of knowledge. The baking section, for instance, is about a third of a page, maybe two hundred words in total. Does the author elucidate the reason behind creaming butter? Explain how to know when a cake is done? Of course not. The four tips are to preheat the oven (as the author points out, "This is especially important for cakes, pies, pastries, and cookies"), bake on the center shelf, not open the oven door, and keep your oven clean.

Okay, let's say that I've bought a chicken and I want to roast it. I look up chicken and get a page of information about the different types. At the back of the book I find a recipe for roast chicken that isn't half bad, but it suggests roasting until the bird is 180 degrees in the thigh (at which point the breast will be overcooked), and there are no detailed instructions about how to take the temperature reading, a detail that *Cooking for Dummies* did manage to include. In fact, there is no place to go to at all to learn about cooking chickens, from the safety issues to cooking just the breast to dealing with boneless chickens, and so on. It's like trying to deliver a baby at home and using a medical textbook that is so poorly organized that the author conveniently omits any discussion of the actual birth; all you can find, as your firstborn rapidly emerges into the world, are endless lists of things to have on hand for delivery. "Be sure to have plenty of clean towels and boiling water!" Thanks.

Do yourself or a beloved kitchen novice a favor. Buy a cookbook by an author who really knows his or her subject. Learn from the likes of Julia Child, Marcella Hazan, Marion Cunningham, Jacques Pépin, Richard Sax, or so many others who have spent a lifetime in the kitchen and really know their stuff. Anyone who buys either of these books expecting to acquire a well-researched, thoughtful guide for kitchen beginners is the real dummy.

—*Christopher Kimball*

Sources and Resources

Most of the ingredients and materials necessary for the recipes in this issue are available at your local supermarket, gourmet store, or kitchen supply shop. The following are mail-order sources for particular items. Prices listed below were current at press time and do not include shipping or handling unless otherwise indicated. We suggest that you contact companies directly to confirm current prices and availability.

Food Processors

In our tests of food processors on page 28 two models stood out among the others: KitchenAid and Cuisinart. Both performed well in our slicing and kneading tests, but differed in their strengths and weaknesses at other tasks (*see* chart, page 28). If you use your food processor for pureeing and also need a mini-bowl, we recommend the KitchenAid Ultra Power Food Processor, Model KFP 600. While the manufacturer's list price is $249.95, it can be purchased for $199.99 through The Chef's Catalog (3215 Commercial Avenue, Northbrook, IL 60062-1900; 800-338-3232). For grating and chopping we recommend the Cuisinart Pro Custom 11, Model DLC-8S model. We also liked its extra-large and small dual-feed tube, with a pinhole for dribbling oil into the work bowl. It can be purchased for $199 from A Cook's Wares (211 37th Street, Beaver Falls, PA 15010-2103; 800-915-9788).

Meat Cleavers

We spent an afternoon in our test kitchen hacking through boned meats with an assortment of meat cleavers, from bargains to high-end models. A $25 meat cleaver made by Lamson turned out to be the favorite. Though at 17 ounces it was more hefty than many others, it was comfortable to hold. It also made the cleanest cuts. Lamson's meat cleaver has a blade seven-and-one-quarter-inches long and four-and-one-quarter-inches at its widest. We found the size offered a better feel for the knife's falling motion and made it easier to control than the smaller meat cleavers (about six inches long by three inches wide). Manufactured in Massachusetts, the Lamson cleaver is made of stamped high-carbon stainless steel with a triple riveted rosewood handle. It can be purchased by mail order through Stoddard's (50 Temple Place, Boston, MA 02111; 617-426-4187), which has specialized in cutlery since 1800.

Vegetable Cleaver

We are fans of Dexter's vegetable cleaver, also known as a Chinese chef's knife. Made in Massachusetts, this cleaver is an elegant knife with a round, grooved hardwood handle, a brass ferrule and a fine, slightly rounded high-carbon stainless steel blade. It can be purchased for $36 at Kitchen Arts (161 Newbury Street, Boston, MA 02116; 617-266-8701) or at Stoddard's (50 Temple Place, Boston, MA 02111; 617-426-4187).

Blade Guards

If you don't have a safe place to store your cleaver, or any knife for that matter, you can purchase inexpensive plastic edge guards to keep your knives sharp and to protect against cuts. Kitchen Arts (161 Newbury Street, Boston, MA 02116; 617-266-8701) sells them in various sizes. The eight-inch guard designed for chef's knives comfortably fits the Dexter vegetable cleaver. The edge guards come in various sizes and range in price from $1.95 to $3.50.

Pie Weights

In our blind baking testing we found that ceramic or metal pie weights not only hold down a crust best and prevent crust shrinkage, but also conduct heat to aid in browning the pastry. Sur La Table (1765 Sixth Avenue South, Seattle, WA 98134-1608; 800-243-0852) sells both the ceramic and aluminum reusable pie weights, which are about the size of large pebbles. The ceramic weights cost $6.95 per package. Aluminum weights cost $7.95 per package. One package of weights is enough for one pie.

High-Gluten Flour

Most supermarkets and health foods stores do not carry the high gluten flour that makes our bagels (*see* page 13) light and chewy. In our test kitchen we used Sir Lancelot High-Gluten Flour from The King Arthur Flour Baker's Catalogue (P.O. Box 876, Norwich, VT 05055-0876; 800-827-6836). Milled in the northern Great Plains from hard red spring wheat, the flour's protein content is so high that it is difficult to develop the gluten. For this reason King Arthur does not recommend this flour for kneading by hand. A five-pound bag of Sir Lancelot High-Gluten Flour costs $3.95.

Malt Syrup

Our bagel recipe calls for barley malt syrup, which is a natural sweetener that can be found in many natural foods stores. More nutritious than white sugar, malt syrup is derived from roasted barley kernels. The King Arthur Flour Baker's Catalogue sells one-and-three-quarter pound jars of malt syrup for $5.50.

Dark-Finished Tart Pans

During our extensive testings for blind baking pie crusts (*see* page 9) we experimented with various pans. For tart shells we found that the darker color of the blue steel tart pan absorbs and distributes the heat instead of reflecting it (as tinned steel tart pans can do). This creates a nicely browned pastry. Ten-inch blue steel tart pans made in Belgium can be ordered for $12.60 through A Cook's Wares (211 37th Street, Beaver Falls, PA 15010-2103; 800-915-9788).

Porcelain Quiche Dishes

We also tested fluted, one-inch, straight-sided quiche dishes made of earthenware and of porcelain. Unlike the earthenware, the porcelain dish rendered an evenly browned crust. We also liked the extra bit of depth the pan had—about one-and-a-half-inches deep. A Cook's Wares (211 37th Street, Beaver Falls, PA 15010-2103; 800-915-9788) sells a ten-and-one-half-inch porcelain quiche dish for $32.90. This white pan can go from freezer to oven and can also be placed directly under the broiler.

Larousse Gastronomique

Larousse Gastronomique (Crown Publishers, 1988) is the Brittanica of food and cooking. This culinary encyclopedia begins on page one with abaisse, ends 1,168 pages later with zuppa inglese, and in between details, among other things, 295 ways to prepare eggs. Originally published in French in 1938, *Larousse Gastronomique* was translated to English for American cooks in 1988. Many bookstores carry this tome in their cookbook sections. It can also be ordered for $60 from Jessica's Biscuit (The Cookbook People, Box 301, Newtonville, MA 02160; 800-878-4264) or Kitchen Arts and Letters (1435 Lexington Ave., New York, NY 10128; 212-876-5550). Kitchen Arts and Letters also carries a 1996 revised edition but currently it is only published in French.

Dried Sweet Cherries

We used dried Bing cherries in the Port pan sauce that accompanies our pork tenderloin recipe (*see* page 19). Dried Bing cherries are dark and sweet with a slight tang. A six ounce bag of these cherries can be ordered for $6.95 from Chukar Cherries (P.O. Box 510, 320 Wine Country Road, Prosser, WA 99350-0510; 800-624-9544). A one pound bag costs $13.95. Chukar's dried cherries are grown and dried in the Pacific Northwest without the use of sulfites or preservatives. They have a shelf life of about 18 months. Do not refrigerate. Seal and store in a cool, dry place or in the freezer.

Broccoli
with Orange-Ginger Dressing and Walnuts
page 8

Spinach and Mushroom Lasagne
page 7

Caesar Salad
page 23

RECIPE INDEX

Cornish Hen with Couscous,
Currants, Apricots, and Raisin Stuffing
page 21

Crabmeat Quiche
page 12

Rugelach
page 24

PHOTOGRAPHS BY CARL TREMBLAY/ STYLING BY EVA KATZ

Baked Peach Bruschetta

Adjust oven rack to center position and heat oven to 425 degrees. Immerse 2 ripe peaches or nectarines in boiling water with slotted spoon for 10 seconds. When cool enough to handle, remove skin, halve, pit, and cut into ¾-inch slices. Spread 4 day-old or oven-dried 1-inch-thick slices of crusty country loaf bread, preferably about 5 inches across, with 1 teaspoon unsalted butter each, and sprinkle each with 1 teaspoon sugar. Arrange fruit slices over bread and sprinkle another 1 teaspoon sugar over fruit on each slice. Place slices on baking sheet and bake until fruit softens, bread edges are toasted, and sugar caramelizes to light golden brown, 20 to 25 minutes. Serve immediately. Serves 4.

Adapted from *Panini, Bruschetta, Crostini Sandwiches, Italian Style* (Hearst Books, 1994) by Viana La Place

Number Twenty-Nine

November / December 1997

COOK'S
ILLUSTRATED

All-Season Apple Pie
Combine Two Common Apples
for Best Flavor and Texture

Perfect Stuffed Turkey
Three Secrets for a Safe,
Juicy Bird

Chocolate Truffles
No Gimmicks, Just Deep,
Pure Chocolate Flavor

Holiday Pork Roast
How to Cook Today's
Low-Fat Pork

Corkscrew Kitchen Test
Long-wormed models
get top ratings

ALPINE GINGERBREAD
COTTAGE

HOW TO ROAST AN ONION

QUICK WINTER RELISHES

CRISPY, CREAMY POTATO
PANCAKES

RATING DESSERT WINES

$4.00 U.S./$4.95 CANADA

Contents

About *Cook's Illustrated*

Cook's Illustrated *is published every other month (6 issues per year) and accepts no advertising. A one year subscription is $24.95, two years is $45, and three years is $65. Add $6 per year for Canadian subscriptions and $12 per year for all other foreign countries. Gift subscriptions may be ordered for $19.95 each. You will receive a Cook's Illustrated gift card for each subscription which can be used to announce your gifts. The editors of Cook's Illustrated also publish an annual hardbound edition of the magazine which includes an annual index. These are available for $21.95 each plus shipping and handling. Discounts are available if more than one year is ordered at a time.*

Cook's Illustrated also publishes single topic books, How To Make A Pie, How To Make An American Layer Cake, How To Make Ice Cream, How To Stir Fry, How To Make Pizza, *and* How to Make Holiday Desserts. *All are available for $14.95 each. The Cook's Bible, authored by our editor and published by Little Brown, is also available for $24.95. Back issues are available for $5 each. We also accept submissions for both Quick Tips and Notes From Readers. See page 5 for more information.*

All queries about subscriptions or change of address notices should be addressed to Cook's Illustrated, *P.O. Box 7446, Red Oak, IA 51591-0446. A free trial issue of our sister publication,* Handcraft Illustrated, *may be requested by calling 800-526-8447.*

To order either subscriptions or books use the cards bound into this issue or, for faster service, call 800-526-8442 for subscriptions and 800-611-0759 for books and annuals.

"CLEMENTINES"

by Brent Watkinson

"GINGERBREAD HOUSE"

by Rene Milot

COOK'S
ILLUSTRATED

Publisher and Editor	Christopher Kimball
Executive Editor	Pam Anderson
Senior Editor	John Willoughby
Senior Writer	Jack Bishop
Associate Editor	Adam Ried
Contributing Editors	Mark Bittman Stephanie Lyness
Test Kitchen Director	Eva Katz
Test Cooks	Dawn Yanagihara Melissa Hamilton
Assistant Editor	Maryellen Driscoll
Test Kitchen Intern	Marnie M. Casavant

Art Director	Cathy Copeland
Special Projects Manager	Amy Klee

Managing Editor	Keith Powers
Editorial Prod. Manager	Sheila Datz
Copy Editor	Amy Finch

Marketing Director	Adrienne Kimball
Circulation Director	David Mack
Fulfillment Manager	Larisa Greiner
Newsstand Manager	Jonathan Venier
Marketing Assistant	Connie Forbes
Circulation Assistant	Steven Browall

Vice President Production and Technology	James McCormack
Systems Administrator	James Burke
Desktop Publishing Manager	Kevin Moeller
Production Artist	Robert Parsons
Editorial Prod. Assistant	Daniel Frey

Controller	Lisa A. Carullo
Senior Accountant	Mandy Shito
Staff Accountant	William Baggs
Office Manager	Livia McRee
Special Projects	Fern Berman

Cook's Illustrated (ISSN 1068-2821) is published bimonthly by Boston Common Press Limited Partnership, 17 Station Street, P.O. Box 569, Brookline, MA 02147-0569. Copyright 1997 Boston Common Press Limited Partnership. Periodical postage paid at Boston, MA, and additional mailing offices, USPS #012487. For list rental information, please contact List Services Corporation, 6 Trowbridge Drive, P.O. Box 516, Bethel, CT 06801; (203) 743-2600, FAX (203) 743-0589. Editorial office: 17 Station Street, P.O. Box 470589, Brookline, MA 02146; (617) 232-1000, FAX (617) 232-1572. Editorial contributions should be sent to: Editor, Cook's Illustrated. We cannot assume responsibility for manuscripts submitted to us. Submissions will be returned only if accompanied by a large self-addressed stamped envelope. Subscription rates: $24.95 for one year; $45 for two years; $65 for three years. (Canada: add $6 per year; all other countries: add $12 per year.) Postmaster: Send all new orders, subscription inquiries, and change of address notices to Cook's Illustrated, P.O. Box 7446, Red Oak, IA 51591-0446. Single copies: $4 in U.S., $4.95 in Canada and other countries. Back issues available for $5 each. PRINTED IN THE U.S.A.

EDITORIAL

Ox Roast

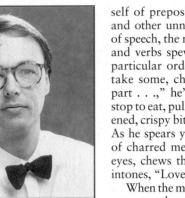

CHRISTOPHER KIMBALL

In mid-August, our small town puts on a huge potluck supper called the "Ox Roast," which is attended by almost all of the 300 residents. The night before, we start a bonfire in the roasting pit, collapsible lounge chairs pulled up, thermoses of coffee and boxes of donuts at the ready. Early in the morning, about 6 a.m., two of the quarters of a young heifer are skewered with metal rods used for reinforcing concrete and then wired to the makeshift rotisserie, using sheep fencing and metal bed-springs. The motor is plugged into a series of bright orange extension cords from the house. All day, the meat lurches up and down, round and about, the motor clicking and whirring.

During the afternoon, picnic tables are dropped off and table lamps are duct-taped to the crotches of apple trees and to the top posts of the run-down tennis court. A long stretch of hay bales serves as a groaning board for the potluck salads and casseroles. Last summer the salad section alone included four fruit salads, all served in watermelons; four potato salads, macaroni salad, three pasta salads, two coleslaws, two marinated cucumber salads, rice and tomato salad, three bean salad, nacho salad, baked rice salad, and pink cottage cheese and Jello salad. For dessert, there was carrot cake squares, blondies, peach pie, apple pie, snickerdoodles, molasses cookies, two blueberry cobblers, brownies, banana nut bread, date nut bread, yellow sheet cake with peaches and raspberries and whipped topping, chocolate cake, blueberry grunt, orange jello, lemon cucumber pickles, a pumpkin pie baked with no crust, and orange cake. This was all washed down with gallons of sweet iced tea held in a huge metal urn and plenty of Mountain Dew. A few guests brought their own coolers of beer, sitting off to the side, drinking quietly so as not to disturb the unstated rule about no alcohol.

When the meat is ready to be taken off, we unhook one quarter, slide one end of the metal rod out of the rotisserie, and then carry it over to the carving table, a piece of old plywood rescued from the barn just behind us. And there I hack away at the huge steamship round of heifer. Every year, one of my favorite locals works his way over to the carving table equipped with his own pocketful of plastic forks, a good steak knife, and a few napkins. He speaks in a series of half-connected thoughts, ridding himself of prepositions, adverbs, and other unnecessary articles of speech, the remaining nouns and verbs spewed forth in no particular order. "Nice meat, take some, charred bits, best part . . .," he'll say, and then stop to eat, pulling at the blackened, crispy bits on the outside. As he spears yet another piece of charred meat he closes his eyes, chews thoughtfully, and intones, "Lovely, lovely . . . ."

When the meat is carved, it is set out on huge carving boards and ironstone platters. The crowd moves pretty quickly at this point, forming a queue in seconds, hoping to get to a particular dish spied earlier before it's all gone. Metal grates are set over the still-red-hot fire for the soaked field corn, which has been delivered in large, sturdy grain sacks. The kids finish up eating quickly, and then run around in threes and fours, hiding behind the berry patch or running up behind the old henhouse with the metal roof.

When the food is gone, the last cakey bits of grunt scraped from the corners of the dish and the second-string salads finally eaten, we walk down to the tennis court, where the makeshift band is tuning up and sorting equipment. Groups of eight dancers form in circles and then the old fiddle tunes start up. We shuck the oyster and dig the clam. We swing our partners and do the do-si-do. We go back the other way and then on the same way. As the couples become more experienced, the fiddler speeds up the calling, trying to mix us up, like a musical version of red light. Many of the old-timers pull up lawn chairs and watch; others get right into the thick of it, changing partners with city visitors and young kids, swirling in a mix of workboots and sandals, dark green farmer's pants and light blue summer dresses.

As the moon rises over the sharp peak behind us, the crisp night air rolls down into the small hollow. The vast stretch of stars and sky explodes upward from the tennis court, and I walk away from the dancing, up into the pasture. The mountains thrust upwards, dwarfing the bonfire, and the fiddle playing, and our small house set amidst the orchard and the overgrown briars. It is not now or a hundred years ago or anytime or place. We are all floating in time, moorings cut, out over the valley with its cornfields and rivers, free from everything that is heavy and limiting. The country has moments like this, when I am torn from my earthly tether, lifted up and away from all that I know is possible.

Notes *from* Readers

Cooking in Copper

In your September/October 1996 issue, you answered a letter regarding cookware reactivity. Your comment that unlined copper must never come into contact with food seemed odd. Copper bowls have been the preferred, if expensive, choice for beating egg whites for a long time and copper saucepans are preferred by confectioners. Without question, copper that comes into contact with these foods must be scrupulously cleaned, because verdigris, which may form on the copper, is poisonous. Please comment.

PETER ALLEN
THREE RIVERS, CA

Your point is well taken. Our September/October 1996 Notes from Readers piece on cookware reactivity did fail to account for the traditions of beating egg whites and boiling sugar syrups in unlined copper vessels. In fact, unlined copper was also the traditional choice for making fruit preserves and jams, as well as for the frothy, sweetened, wine-flavored egg custard sauce called either *sabayon*, in French, or *zabaglione*, in Italian.

Your observation begs a two-part question, concerning both safety and cooking science. First, why have culinary authorities considered it okay—in fact, preferable—for egg whites, sugar syrups, preserves, and *zabaglione* to touch copper, when in most circumstances copper-lined pans are covered with another metal to prevent contact with food? And second, what is it about copper that is beneficial for these specific preparations?

We spent hours of research time, consulted numerous books and called more than fifty experts in the fields of cookware, confectionery, jams and preserves, food chemistry, nutrition, copper manufacturing, and metallurgy, in order to address the first part of the question. Amid the many different theories put forth by our sources, the agreement was that unlined copper cookware should be carefully and thoroughly cleaned before every use in order to rid it of verdigris. Beyond that, many sources offered a similar perspective on the situation, which was that health threats arise from ingesting really excessive amounts of copper, and, more than likely, the amount of copper provided by these particular foods in question would be minuscule. Dr. Herbert Scheinberg of the National Center for the Study of Wilson's Disease (a rare genetic disorder that is the only significant cause of copper toxicity in humans), stressed that copper, along with several other minerals, is a necessary human nutrient. Yet Dr. Joyce Nettleton, a nutritionist and Director of Science Communications for the Institute of Food Technologists, pointed out that the body does a poor job of absorbing most minerals, including copper. Therefore, only a small percentage of the copper to which we are exposed would actually be absorbed.

In its Recommended Dietary Allowances (National Academy Press, Washington, D.C., 1989), the National Academy of Science's U.S. Food and Nutrition Board supports this notion, stating that: "Usual diets in the United States rarely supply more than 5 milligrams per day, and an occasional intake of up to 10 milligrams per day is probably safe for adults. Although storing or processing acidic foods or fluids in copper vessels can add to the daily intake, overt toxicity from dietary sources is extremely rare in the U.S. population."

Concerning the egg whites in the second part of the question, food scientist Harold McGee, in *On Food and Cooking* (Collier, 1984), explains that whites beaten in copper bowls are thought to form more stable foams, which resist overbeating. This is because one of the egg white proteins, conalbumin, picks up copper ions from the surface of the bowl and binds them to itself, resulting in molecules that resist denaturing, or unwinding. This strengthens the walls of the air bubbles that compose the foam, thereby stabilizing it.

The assertions about egg whites proved true in our kitchen tests. We whipped two batches of whites, one in a copper bowl that had been cleaned with lemon and salt, rinsed, and dried, and the second in a perfectly clean stainless steel bowl. The copper-whipped whites did, in fact, appear to make a denser, tighter foam than the other, which had larger visible bubbles and a looser consistency. Also, try though we did, we were not able to overwhip the whites in the copper bowl. Instead of turning grainy and blocky, they remained smooth. Then we let each batch sit at room temperature to see if the foams broke down. Both foams suffered some degradation after one and one-half hours, but the copper-whipped foam was in much better shape than the other, from which a large pool of liquid had leached.

Finally, we whipped two more batches of whites in the same manner, and used them to make two angel food cakes. Somewhat surprisingly, both cakes rose at the same rate. So, as long as you are careful not to overwhip your whites, we consider the copper egg white bowl non-essential.

With regard to sugar syrups, confectionery and cookware industry experts agreed that copper's outstanding heat conductivity and quick reaction to temperature changes offers precise control over the different stages of sugar syrup, caramel, and chocolate preparation. Copper's speedy distribution of heat is also considered an advantage when making jam and preserves be-

What Is It?

I bought this strange, bumpy rolling pin at a garage sale for $1.00. The sellers could tell me neither where it came from nor what it's used for, but I took it anyhow because it was intriguing. I have used it, with the lightest possible touch, on pie and cookie doughs, which it ravages. Do you know what it is really meant for?

LESLIE TAKAO
HYDE PARK, MA

The notched pin you've got is known as a hardtack rolling pin, used to mark Scandinavian flatbreads and crackers such as the Swedish crackers called knäckebröds, also known simply as Swedish hardtack. When the dough, often flavored with rye or oatmeal, has been rolled flat with a regular rolling pin, a light once-over with a hardtack embosses it with 3/8-inch indentations that restrict oven rise and give the crackers a rough texture and a scored, easy-to-break finish. If no hardtack pin is available, baker Beatrice Ojakangas, in her recipe for Swedish Oatmeal Hardtack in Dorie Greenspan's *Baking with Julia* (Morrow, 1996), suggests simulating the pocks made with a hardtack pin by pricking the dough at quarter-inch intervals with the tines of a fork.

Anyone who wants to experiment with the real thing, however, can purchase a hardtack rolling pin by mail order from the King Arthur Flour Baker's Catalogue. The cost is $26.95, plus shipping and handling.

ILLUSTRATION BY DAN KROVATIN

cause the fruit and sugar reach the desired consistency quickly, before the fruit looses its natural color and fresh flavor.

Despite all of this, with the exceptions of egg whites, sugar syrups, jams and preserves, and *zabaglione*, the general recommendation not to cook in unlined copper stands.

More Lobster Lore

In the "Lobster Lore" section of your May/June 1997 article about lobsters, you missed an idea that I heard years ago. It was suggested to me that sliding the lobster into a bucket of cheap white wine for a brief Bacchanalian swim before plunging it into the cooking pot would be the most humane method of relaxing the beast to produce a tender result. However, I've never been inclined to part with enough wine to put this notion to the test.

PAMELA BLITTERSDORF
COLLEGEVILLE, PA

Like you, we had to think twice about letting go of so much wine, but because several other readers wrote with the same idea, we forged ahead in the name of testing. In our opinion, the result was not worth the wine.

We used this method with four 1¼-pound lobsters, two at a time in a tall, narrow bucket filled with two bottles' worth of wine. Pam Anderson, our executive editor and author of the lobster piece, observed the lobsters and commented that the exercise felt "...like a horrible way to go," just as cruel as microwaving or inserting a chopstick up the live lobster's tail. All four lobsters lost control of their bodily functions, excreting from both ends into the wine, and finally died after five to eight minutes. She then steamed two of the lobsters in water and the other two in the wine, noting no benefit to either flavor or tenderness, and only the slightest wine flavor in the wine-steamed lobsters. Our advice, then, is that your wine is better drunk by you, not your lobsters.

Espresso Spick-and-Span

Jack Bishop made a funny comment in a sidebar to your November/December 1996 rating of espresso machines, about his wife's aggravation over the mess involved in making cappuccino or espresso. There is no denying the mess, but I have a very simple and inexpensive solution. Simply spread a few sheets of heavy-duty paper towel near the coffee grinder and espresso machine and empty the grinder bin, fill the machine basket, and tamp the grounds over the towel. When you're done, shake the towel out over the sink or trash basket, fold it, and tuck it under the machine for the next use. The tow-

els last a long time and the procedure is neat, fast, cheap, and works with any machine on the market.

So, Jack, you can have fine coffee and preserve marital bliss, without spending a fortune on Nespresso pods.

R.J. PELUSO
PITTSBURGH, PA

Jack and his wife both appreciate your suggestion. They expanded on your idea, using several sheets of paper towel or a cloth kitchen towel, which spreads out to cover more area on the counter than a single sheet of paper towel. Simply wash the kitchen towel when it gets grimy, and then re-use it.

Salsa Tasting Recipe

The bottled salsas we rated in the July/August 1997 tasting article "Homemade Salsa Is Worth The Effort" paled in comparison to the homemade salsa our test kitchen turned out, even using less-than-perfect winter tomatoes. A flood of reader inquiries ensued about the salsa recipe we used for the tasting, thus we offer it here. This salsa is a slight variation on the Classic Red Table Salsa recipe we ran in the July/August 1996 article "Easy Summer Salsas," from John Willoughby and Chris Schlesinger. We substituted fresh jalapeño chile pepper for the smoky chipotles in the original.

3	large, very ripe tomatoes (about 2 pounds), diced small
½	cup tomato juice
1	medium jalapeño chile pepper, cored, seeded, and minced
1	medium red onion, diced small
1	medium garlic clove, minced
½	cup chopped fresh cilantro leaves
½	cup juice from 4 medium limes Salt

Mix all ingredients, including salt to taste, in medium bowl. Cover and refrigerate to blend flavors, at least 1 hour or up to 5 days.

Grilling Salmon Fillets Another Way

Your July/August 1997 article "How to Grill Salmon" brought to mind a simple and brilliant trick for preparing salmon fillets taught to me years ago by the venerable chef Greg Martin at Cafe Annie in Houston, Texas. Lay a 3-inch–wide center-cut fillet skin side down and cut lengthwise down the middle of the fillet, as if you were dividing the 3-inch piece into two one-and-one-half-inch pieces. Cut slowly and carefully and stop just above the skin. With the skin holding the almost separated sides together, fold them outward so

that the skin folds back on itself. Voila! You have a uniform, symmetrically grained one-and-one-half-inch thick fillet that resembles a steak and cooks up evenly and beautifully, with no thin edges or burnt skin to worry about.

TODD THOMPSON
PRANGINS, SWITZERLAND

We had a difficult time visualizing this popular trick, sent in by several other readers as well, until we tried it. Essentially, you are butterflying the fillet by cutting through the flesh from the top of the fish to the bottom, but leaving the skin intact to connect two flesh portions. The skin acts as a hinge, folding back-to-back on itself. The result looks like a salmon steak, with the skin running down the middle.

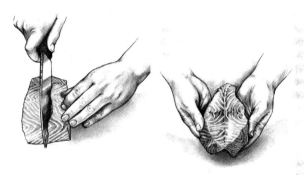

Cut through the fillet lengthwise down to, but not through, the skin (left). Fold the two flesh pieces out with the skin acting as a hinge (right).

The method works beautifully for a couple of reasons. As you note, the piece of fish is a uniform thickness from top to bottom, and you can determine that thickness for yourself. We started with a 3-inch wide fillet, which became a one-and-one-half inch "steak" when folded in half (so we were cooking two single portions at once). The medium-hot fire and cooking times from our original recipe were ideal for the "steak." The second advantage is that you can sear both sides of the steak, whereas in our original method, the skin protects one side from searing. Last, the "steak" is boneless, as it is formed from a fillet. Sticking was not a problem with the "steaks," though it hadn't been with our original method either.

The only drawback we encountered was for skin lovers. The skin crisps nicely in our original method, becoming quite a treat for those who care for it. In the "steak" method, however, the skin never crisps because it is protected from the grill. If the skin is unimportant to you, you'll probably like this method as much as we did.

FILLING SALT AND PEPPER SHAKERS

The spice funnel tip in our March/April 1997 issue moved Patricia Miller of Bellingham, Washington, to share her method for avoiding spills when filling a shaker with salt or a grinder with peppercorns.

1. Snip off the very corner of a standard envelope with a scissors, making sure that the resulting hole is smaller than the mouth of the vessel you want to fill.

2. The envelope now functions as a small, efficient funnel.

Quick

The editors of *Cook's Illustrated* would like to thank all of our readers who have sent us their quick tips. We have enjoyed reading every one of them and have learned a lot. Keep them coming. We will provide a one-year complimentary subscription for each quick tip that we print. Send a description of your special technique to *Cook's Illustrated*, P.O. Box 569, Brookline Village, MA 02146-0569. Please write

FREE DECORATING BOTTLES

Instead of purchasing special squeeze bottles, Fran Goldberg of Boston, Massachusetts, uses empty mustard or ketchup bottles for decorating desserts, soups, or other dishes with a contrasting colored liquid or sauce.

STAIN-FREE PLASTIC CONTAINERS

Diane Sandoval of Issaquah, Washington, found that her reusable plastic containers stained red when used to store tomato-based sauces. Then she discovered this trick.

1. Coat the container lightly with cooking spray.

2. Fill it with sauce worry-free; the cooking spray keeps the plastic from staining.

GINGERBREAD COIFFURE

Kim Lampe of Englewood, New Jersey, has discovered a new use for her garlic press—it's ideal for making gingerbread hair for her gingerbread people. To make the "hair," simply press a tiny ball of gingerbread dough through the press, then affix to a gingerbread figure.

INDENTING COOKIES FOR FILLING

Some holiday cookies require a shallow indent on top to fill with jam or chocolate or the like. Anne Blumenfeld of San Diego, California, has found that the rounded end of a honey dipper is ideal for the task.

NO-STICK LASAGNA NOODLES

To avoid the common problem of boiled lasagna noodles sticking together as they cool in the colander, Claire Huismann of Madison, Wisconsin, keeps the cooked and drained noodles separate by draping them over the rim of the pot.

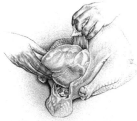

HOMEMADE STUFFING BAG

We liked using the canvas turkey stuffing bag (*see* Sources and Resources, page 32) when making the stuffed roast turkey (page 9). You can also make your own bag out of cheesecloth.

1. Cut a double layer of cheesecloth about 15" square and place the stuffing in the center of the cheesecloth.

2. Fold the cheesecloth over, gather it together at the two top corners, and tie it at both corners.

3. Slip the stuffing into the turkey and cook as instructed on page 10. When the turkey is removed from the oven, simply remove the cheesecloth bag from the turkey, cut it open, and remove the stuffing, which will be imbued with the juices of the turkey.

Tips

"Attention: Quick Tips" on the envelope and include your name, address, and daytime phone number. Unfortunately, we can only acknowledge receipt of tips that will be printed in the magazine. In case the same tip is received from two readers, the one postmarked first will be selected. Also, be sure to let us know what particular cooking problems you would like us to investigate in upcoming issues.

MAKING EXTRA COUNTER SPACE

Anyone with a tiny apartment kitchen knows the challenges of cooking with very limited counter space. Mary Jo Morris of Orinda, California, alleviates this problem by bringing out her ironing board, which is easily moveable, adjustable for height, and provides four extra feet of space for cooling baked goods or placing bowls and utensils as you work.

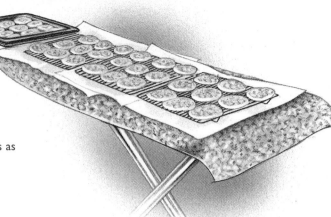

TAMING TOASTED SEEDS

Toasting in a dry skillet brings out the flavor of dry spices. When mustard or coriander seeds are toasted, however, they tend to pop—often right out of the pan. Philip Sugerman of Jamaica Plain, Massachusetts, solves this problem by covering the pan with a splatter screen to stop airborne seeds.

SUBMERGING REHYDRATING MUSHROOMS

When you are rehydrating dried mushrooms or tomatoes, sometimes the pieces near the surface of the bowl bob up, and therefore rehydrate slower than those fully submerged in the liquid. Dale Chao of Concord, California, combats this problem by filling the bowl with hot water to about an inch below the rim, adding the food to be rehydrated, then laying a piece of plastic wrap right on the surface of the liquid and attaching the wrap to the inner rim of the bowl. This system keep all of the pieces below the surface of the liquid so that they rehydrate evenly.

LOOSENING SMALL JAR TOPS

Especially for those with arthritis or other disability in their hands, it can be difficult to loosen the tops of very small jars, such as bottles of extract or hot pepper sauce. Edna Brown of Tinley Park, Illinois, has found the perfect solution to this problem in her old fashioned nutcracker, with teeth along both interior sides.

LOOSENING A STICKY MIXER BOWL

Alice Gordenker of Arlington, Virginia, used to sometimes have difficulty removing the bowl from the base of her KitchenAid mixer. She has since discovered that wearing rubber kitchen gloves, like those used for washing dishes, provides enough extra grip to unscrew the bowl from the base with no trouble.

EXTENDING SPATULA LIFE

Over time, the edges of rubber spatulas can get stained, brittle, cracked, and cut. Mary Hooten of Richmond, Virginia, simply snips off the damaged outer edge of rubber, creating a fresh, sharp edge. You can usually do this twice before having to discard the spatula.

FREEZING PIE PASTRY

Linda Sebesta of Rochester, Minnesota, suggests this way to streamline the process of baking pies. Prepare several batches of dough at once, roll them out between sheets of plastic wrap, then stack the resulting discs in a pizza box and keep the box in the freezer. Next time you're making pie, simply pull out the required crusts and concentrate on the filling.

LEAVING VISUAL CUES WHEN BAKING

If you are easily distracted or frequently interrupted while you bake, follow this advice from Jo Ann Noonan of Los Angeles, California. Once the flour is in the mixing bowl and you begin to add other dry ingredients, dump each teaspoon of baking powder, baking soda, or salt in a different spot in the flour. If you are interrupted before you've had a chance to add the total number, this provides a quick visual reference to the number of teaspoons already added.

MESS-FREE PIPING

When you use a pastry bag, food left in the top portion of the bag is always wasted, and often oozes out over your hand when you squeeze the bag. To avoid this, test cook Dawn Yanagihara recommends using a plastic spatula to efficiently push all of the food down to the bottom of the bag.

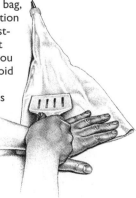

Traditional Potato Latkes

A two-step potato grating technique yields latkes that are crispy around the edges but still creamy in the center, with serious potato flavor.

By Lisa Weiss

For many years, beginning as newlyweds, my husband and I attended the family Passover Seder at his grandmother Rose's house. Often she would serve latkes as a side dish to the roast turkey or braised brisket. Rose would grate the potatoes coarsely by hand, put them through the meat grinder with the onions, add eggs and matzo, then cook and serve them immediately from the frying pan.

Like Grandma Rose's, the latkes of my dreams are somewhat thick, golden, very crisp on the outside, with a creamy potato center. To figure out how to make these ideal latkes, I had to find the best potato, the best grating method, and the best frying technique.

I began with the potatoes, which can be classified into three categories, according to their starch content. I tested russets, which are high starch; Yukon Golds, which have a medium starch content; and red potatoes, which are low starch. The russet potato pancakes had a pleasantly pronounced potato flavor and a dry texture. The red potatoes were at the other end of the spectrum: very creamy, almost gluey on the inside. The Yukon Golds were the biggest surprise; the pancakes made with these potatoes were an attractive deep yellow-gold color, tasted somewhat sweet and mild, and were creamy in texture, but not gluey or sticky. Everyone who tried the Yukon Gold latkes judged them superior in taste.

Some people feel that latkes made with potatoes grated by hand on a box grater are superior to those made with potatoes grated in a food processor. I tried both methods and found a negligible difference in texture between the two. I did, however, discover a very useful two-step grating procedure.

For the first step, I put the peeled potatoes through the feed tube of the food processor, using the coarse shredding blade. I then removed about half to two-thirds of the shreds and placed them in a separate mixing bowl. Next, I inserted the metal blade, added chunks of onion to the shreds left in the processor bowl, and processed the mixture in spurts until I had a very coarse puree, each piece being no larger than 1/8-inch. Then I combined the pureed potatoes and onions with the shredded potatoes.

This two-step procedure gave me latkes that had some larger shreds that cooked up quite crisp along the outside perimeters while the inside center portion was thicker and chewier, like a traditional pancake. This, I discovered,

was the best of both latke worlds: crispy and lacy along the edges but still thick and chewy in the middle.

A similar result can be obtained without a food processor. First, grate the potatoes on the largest holes of a box grater and place half of them in a sieve set over a bowl. Then, using a chef's knife, chop the other half of the grated potatoes and all of the onions into a fine 1/8-inch dice. Mix this with the larger shreds and proceed with the recipe.

After I pressed the potatoes in a fine sieve to remove their moisture, I set them aside. I allowed the mixing bowl with the potato water to sit for a minute and then very slowly poured off the potato water that had accumulated. At the bottom of the bowl there was a layer of thick, white potato starch. In all of my tests that were successful, this starch proved helpful in binding the latkes, whether or not flour or matzo meal was added.

The Big Question: Frying

Now I began to test the most crucial part of the whole process–frying. First I tested three different frying mediums: a combination of chicken fat (schmaltz) and vegetable oil; solid vegetable shortening (Crisco); and good-quality liquid vegetable oil.

The chicken fat and vegetable combination

was impractical; chicken fat is just not readily available and there are health concerns with its concentration of fatty acids. I thought solid vegetable shortening might work well because Grandma Rose swore by it. But it reached its smoking point much more quickly than the liquid vegetable oil and was difficult to add more solid shortening to the frying pan to maintain a consistent depth as several batches of latkes were cooking. Fresh, high quality liquid vegetable oil, such as corn, peanut, safflower or a combination, proved to be the perfect oil for frying latkes.

I tried cooking my latkes in several depths of oil, from 1/2-inch to only 1/16-inch, and I found that more oil does not necessarily result in oilier pancakes, if the oil is at the right temperature. It is much easier to regulate the temperature of the oil if you have at least 1/8-inch of oil in the pan, and that was the minimum amount for very thin pancakes. Also, if the oil is deep enough from the start you don't have to add oil in between batches as frequently.

The temperature of the oil is crucial to frying the perfect latke. However, this is the one category that defies absolute analysis, because it is really difficult to accurately measure the temperature of oil that is only one-quarter inch deep. The key is to have the oil really hot, but not smoking, when the latkes go in. The temperature of the oil will reduce with the addition of more batter, but should be kept at a constant lively bubble throughout the cooking of all the pancakes. When the oil is hot enough to start frying, it begins to shimmer on the surface and appears kind of wavy. If it is smoking, it's too hot and the heat should be turned down. I tested the oil initially by dropping in about a teaspoon of batter and observing how quickly it cooked. If it browned in under a minute, the oil was too hot. Two minutes was just about right.

Hold and Freeze? Yes!

With every batch of latkes I made, I held some in a 200-degree oven and tried a bite every five to ten minutes. With every bite after the first one, the latkes tasted progressively more old and chewy. I concluded that you cannot hold latkes for more than ten minutes at the most. They may still be hot, but the taste diminishes and the texture deteriorates so much that after all the trouble you have gone to preparing them, you might as well have chosen something else to cook.

I did discover, however, that latkes

Yukon Gold potatoes (rear) make the very best latkes, but old reliable russets (front) are fine if Yukons are not available.

PREPARING THE POTATOES

1. The potatoes are first shredded using the shredding blade, then half of the mixture is removed.
2. Fit steel blade, add onion pieces to remaining potatoes, and pulse to a very fine dice.
3. Alternatively, shred potatoes on box grater.
4. Using a chef's knife, chop remaining half of the potatoes with the onions to a $1/8$-inch dice.
5. Once the potatoes have exuded their liquid, pour the potato water out of the bowl, leaving behind the starch on the bottom.

that have been left to cool at room temperature for a few hours and then reheated in a 375-degree oven for about five minutes are the next best thing to freshly fried.

I also reserved some of my good latke batches for the freezer. I placed them on a parchment-lined baking sheet and allowed them to freeze for about fifteen minutes before I placed them in ziplock freezer bags. When I was ready to serve the latkes, I reheated them on a baking sheet in the middle of a 375-degree oven for about eight minutes per side. All my taste-testers agreed that there was only a slight difference in quality compared to the freshly fried.

THICK AND CREAMY POTATO LATKES
Makes approximately 14 3-inch pancakes
Matzo meal is a traditional binder, though we found that the pancake's texture does not suffer without it. Applesauce and sour cream are classic accompaniments for potato latkes.

    2   pounds Yukon Gold or russet
            potatoes, peeled
    1   medium yellow onion, peeled and
            cut into eighths
    1   large egg
    4   medium scallions, white and
            green parts, minced
    3   tablespoons minced fresh
            parsley leaves
    2   tablespoons matzo meal (optional)
 1½   teaspoons salt
        Ground black pepper
    1   cup vegetable oil for frying

1. Grate potatoes in food processor fitted with coarse shredding blade. Place half the potatoes in fine mesh sieve set over medium bowl and reserve (illustration 1). Fit food processor with steel blade, add onions, and pulse with remaining potatoes until all pieces measure roughly $1/8$ inch and look coarsely chopped, 5 to 6 one-second pulses (illustration 2). Mix with reserved potato shreds in sieve and press against sieve to drain as much liquid as possible into bowl below. Let potato liquid stand until starch settles to bottom, about one minute. Pour off liquid, leaving starch in bowl. Beat egg, then potato mixture and remaining ingredients (except oil), into starch.

2. Meanwhile, heat $1/4$-inch depth of oil in 12-inch skillet or sauté pan over medium-high heat until shimmering but not smoking. Working one at a time, place $1/4$ cup potato mixture, squeezed of excess liquid and pressed into $1/2$-inch thick disc, in oil. Press gently with non-stick spatula; repeat until five latkes are in pan.

3. Maintaining heat so fat bubbles around latke edges, fry until golden brown on bottom and edges, about three minutes. Turn with spatula and continue frying until golden brown all over, about three minutes more. Drain on a triple thickness of paper towels set on wire rack over a jelly roll pan. Repeat with remaining potato mixture, returning oil to temperature between each batch and replacing oil after every second batch. (Cooled latkes can be covered loosely with plastic wrap, held at room temperature for 4 hours, transferred to a heated cookie sheet and baked in a 375-degree oven, until crisp and hot, about 5 minutes per side. Or, they can be frozen on cookie sheet, transferred to zipper-lock freezer bag, frozen, and reheated in a 375-degree oven until crisp and hot, about 8 minutes per side). Season with salt and pepper to taste and serve immediately.

Lisa Weiss is a food writer living in the San Francisco Bay area.

ONIONS' SULFUR PREVENTS BROWNING

Traditional cooks have always sworn that alternating the grating of potatoes with onions helped to prevent the potatoes from darkening. This was one theory that proved true: Potatoes grated alone darkened much more quickly than those grated with onions. According to Dr. Alfred Bushway, a food science professor at the University of Maine, browning occurs because, as potato cells are exposed to air after slicing, certain enzymes add oxygen to phenol compounds found in the potato cells. This process creates an unsightly but harmless brown pigment known as melanin.

There are a number of ways to retard this browning, including cooking, coating the cut surfaces with acid such as lemon juice, or covering the cut food with an airtight coating of plastic wrap. Commercial processing plants often use certain sulfur compounds to prevent browning, says Dr. Ralph R. Price, associate professor of nutrition at the University of Arizona in Tucson, because these compounds inhibit the action of the enzymes that cause browning. Onions, as it turns out, contain several of these sulfur compounds, which not only lend onions their distinct odor, but also act to prevent browning of any cut fruits or vegetables that the onions come into contact with.
—*Maryellen Driscoll*

How to Perfectly Roast a Stuffed Turkey

Stuffing the turkey can lead to overcooked white meat and potential safety problems.
The solution? Preheat the stuffing, brine the bird, and use dual oven temperatures.

By Dawn Yanagihara with Eva Katz

For a less hectic holiday, bread can be dried several days in advance and the turkey brined and the stuffing assembled the night before you actually stuff and roast your turkey.

There is something undeniably festive about a stuffed roasted turkey, and for many people the holidays just aren't the holidays without one. Every year, though, we are warned that for health and safety reasons, turkeys are best roasted unstuffed. Despite these warnings, many cooks (some of us included) continue to stuff their holiday bird. For the sake of flavorful, moist, turkey-infused stuffing, these cooks sacrifice perfectly cooked breast meat and risk food-borne illness from underdone stuffing.

But we refused to settle. There must be a way, we thought, to safely and successfully roast a stuffed turkey, keeping the breast meat succulent and ensuring that the stuffing is fully cooked. Before we began, we decided to limit our turkey to a maximum of fifteen pounds, because it is just too difficult to safely stuff and roast larger birds.

Our objectives were clear. For health reasons, we wanted to find a means of minimizing the amount of time our stuffing would spend in the danger zone of 40 to 140 degrees, in which bacteria grows most quickly. (See "The Real Lowdown on Turkey Safety," page 10, for more information.) In addition, we sought to coordinate the cooking of the breast and the thigh. We knew that the breast meat cooks faster than the thigh by about ten degrees, and because the breast is done at 160 degrees and the thigh at 170, this usually results in choke-

quality white meat. Introducing stuffing into this equation, we thought, was just asking for trouble; testing for our previous articles had demonstrated that stuffing the turkey slows interior cooking significantly, requiring longer cooking times and producing even drier surface meat.

Let the Roasting Begin

After a few introductory tests, it became clear that this was exactly the problem we would face. Using high heat or low, the stuffing lagged behind the meat, remaining five degrees shy of the 165 we were aiming for, even when both breast and thigh were about fifteen degrees higher than we wanted them.

In desperation, we toyed with the idea of sticking hot skewers or a ball of foil into the stuffing in the cavity to help conduct some heat. Suddenly, it occurred to us that if we heated the stuffing for a few minutes in the microwave before filling the cavity, we might give it a head start on cooking. This technique worked for roasting Cornish hens (*see* September/October 1997), so why wouldn't it work for a turkey?

We tested the pre-warmed stuffing hypothesis on a turkey that we roasted at a constant 325 degrees. We heated the stuffing in the microwave to about 120 degrees before stuffing the bird. We opted to roast the bird one hour breast down, one hour on each side, then finish with the breast up. As we monitored the temperature of the stuffing, the outlook seemed grim. The stuffing temperature dropped and bottomed out in the first hour at 89 degrees. Gradually it climbed back up and hit 140 degrees, also free of the danger zone, in two and one-quarter hours, the best time yet. Most impressively, this time we were waiting for thigh to finish cooking, not the stuffing! The breast was long gone at 178 degrees, but we knew we were on to something. This was an enormous improvement over the three and one-half hours it had taken for the cold stuffing used in previous tests to dawdle its way to 165, while the breast and thigh meat invariably overcooked.

We pursued the pre-warming technique and in further tests found that the stuffing hits its lowest temperature in the bird usually at the one hour mark, dropping approximately

20 degrees. In the microwave we were able to heat it to 130 degrees; starting at such a high temperature helps it get out of the danger zone in two and one-quarter to two and three-quarters hours. We checked with food scientists to see if this half an hour differential in times presents a bacterial growth problem. We were told no, since very little occurs above 110 degrees. No longer did we have to wait for the stuffing to finish cooking while the breast and thigh overcooked.

Flip and Flop?

With the stuffing issue resolved, we focused on the best way to roast the turkey. It had become clear to us that high heat and even constant moderate heat wreak havoc on the turkey, resulting in parched breast meat. The low and slow method is, well, too low and slow, and not a safe method for a stuffed turkey. A combination of low heat with high or moderate heat seemed like it would be the answer.

We also determined that, regardless of temperature, roasting the bird breast down for only one hour was not sufficient. In this position, the breast is shielded and its cooking slowed while the thighs are exposed to the heat needed to speed their cooking. If we rotated the breast up after one or even two hours, the breast was guaranteed to overcook in the remaining time. We abandoned roasting leg side up because it was awkward and ineffective.

We then roasted two turkeys, both started breast down. One cooked at a low 250 degrees for three hours, was rotated breast up, cooked for an additional 15 minutes, and then the temperature was then increased to 400 degrees. The breast overcooked as the thigh creeped to 180 degrees. The other turkey we roasted at 400 degrees for one hour, reduced oven temperature to 250 degrees, flipped breast up after a total of three hours, then turned the heat back up to 400 degrees and roasted until done. This bird finished as close to perfection as possible: 163 degrees in the breast, 180 degrees in the thigh and 165 degrees in the stuffing. Clearly, the thigh meat benefited from the initial blast of heat. The only disappointment was the spotty browning of the skin. A few minor adjustments to time spent breast up and we arrived at a safe, perfectly roasted stuffed turkey, one that was flavorful and moist.

The Holy Brine

Our previous turkey articles found that brining made a significant improvement in the overall flavor and texture of the meat. We were concerned that if we stuffed a brined bird, the stuffing might emerge over-salted. Much to our joy, however, we found that this was not the case.

In fact, the benefits of brining are manyfold. First, brining provides a cushion for the breast meat, so even if it overcooks by ten degrees or so, it remains moist. Secondly, the meat of a brined bird tastes pleasantly seasoned, which eliminates the need to season before and after roasting. Because the turkey sits overnight in a tub of salted water, brining also ensures that all parts of the turkey are at the same temperature. This is especially good insurance if you're roasting a previously frozen bird. Yet another benefit is that the turkey meat absorbs water during the brining process. Water is a heat conductor and therefore expedites cooking. We tested this theory and found that indeed, a brined bird cooks faster than an unbrined one by about thirty minutes. Lastly, brining may help inhibit growth of certain types of bacteria. So while it may seem like added work, dunking the bird in the brine is worth it for a whole host of reasons.

STUFFED ROAST TURKEY
Serves 10-12

Roast Turkey:
2   cups kosher or 1 cup table salt
1   turkey (12 to 15 pounds gross
        weight) rinsed thoroughly,
        giblets, neck, and tail piece removed
2   tablespoons butter, melted

Stuffing:
1   recipe (12 cups) prepared stuffing
        (*see* recipes next page)
1   tablespoon butter, plus extra to
        grease casserole dish and foil
1/4 cup turkey or chicken stock or low-
        sodium canned chicken broth

1. *To brine the turkey:* Dissolve salt in 2 gallons cold water in large stock pot or clean bucket. Add turkey and refrigerate or set in very cool (40 degrees or less) spot for 8 to 12 hours.

2. *To prepare stuffing:* Prepare selected stuffing following one of the recipes below, keeping dry and wet ingredients separate until ready to stuff the bird. Refrigerate until ready to use.

3. *To stuff and roast the turkey:* Remove turkey from salt water and rinse both cavity and skin under cool water for several minutes until all traces of salt are gone. Pat dry inside and out with paper towels; set aside. Adjust oven rack to lowest position and heat oven to 400 degrees. Set heavy-duty V-rack, adjusted to widest setting, in pan.

4. Place half of mixed stuffing in buttered medium casserole dish, dot surface with butter, cover with buttered foil, and refrigerate until ready to use. Microwave remaining stuffing on full power, stirring two or three times, until very hot (120 to 130 degrees), 6 to 8 minutes

STUFFING AND ROASTING THE BIG BIRD

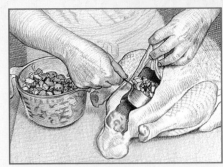

1. Placing the preheated stuffing in the cavity of the bird. Since it's hot, a measuring cup or spoon is needed to handle the stuffing.

2. Alternatively, fill a canvas bag with 4–5 cups stuffing, microwave until 120–130 degrees, and insert into turkey cavity (see Sources and Resources, page 32).

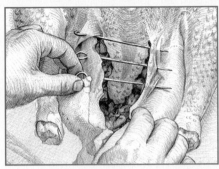

3. To keep the stuffing in the cavity use metal skewers (or cut bamboo skewers) and thread them through the skin on either side of the cavity.

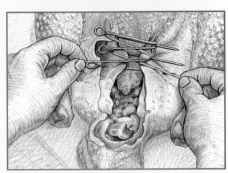

4. Use a piece of kitchen twine to lace up the cavity, as if you were lacing up boots.

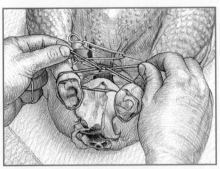

5. Loosely tie the legs together with kitchen twine.

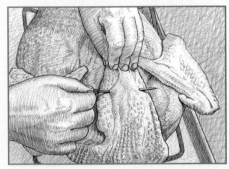

6. Flip bird over onto its breast and place in roasting rack. Stuff neck cavity loosely with approximately one cup of stuffing. Pull skin flap over and use a skewer to pin flap to turkey.

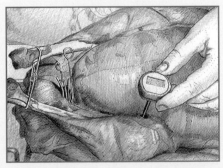

7. Be sure that you measure the temperature of bird at the thickest part of the thigh.

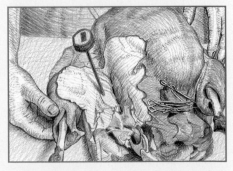

8. This cutaway shows the actual point to which the tip of the thermometer should penetrate.

6 medium, firm, tart apples such as Granny Smith, peeled and diced
4 medium onions, chopped coarse
4 celery stalks, chopped coarse
1/2 cup dry white wine
2 tablespoons minced fresh thyme leaves
2 tablespoons fresh sage leaves
1 1/4 pounds French, country, or Pepperidge Farm white bread, cut into 1/2-inch cubes, dried (about 12 cups dried)
1 3/4 cups turkey or chicken stock or low sodium canned chicken broth
2 eggs, beaten
1/2 cup chopped fresh parsley leaves
Salt and ground black pepper

Fry bacon in 12-inch skillet over medium-high heat until crisp and brown, about 5 minutes. Transfer bacon with slotted spoon to paper towel–lined plate; pour off all but 3 tablespoons fat from pan. Add apples, onions and celery; sauté until softened, 14 to 15 minutes. Add wine, thyme and sage; simmer until wine is almost evaporated, 1 to 2 minutes. Mix with reserved bacon and remaining ingredients, including the salt and ground black pepper to taste, in large, microwave-safe bowl.

CORNBREAD STUFFING WITH SAUSAGE AND PECANS
Makes about 12 cups

Heat 1 tablespoon olive oil over medium-high heat in 12-inch skillet, fry 1 pound crumbled sweet sausage until meat loses its raw color, 5 to 7 minutes; remove with slotted spoon to small bowl. If necessary, add enough butter to rendered sausage fat to equal 3 tablespoons. Follow Master Recipe for Bacon and Apple Stuffing, substituting sausage fat for bacon fat, bourbon for wine, cubed cornbread for white bread, and omitting bacon and apples. Continue with master recipe, mixing reserved sausage and one cup chopped pecans with remaining ingredients.

(if you can handle stuffing with hands, it is not hot enough). Spoon 4 to 5 cups stuffing into turkey cavity until very loosely packed (*see* illustration one). Secure skin flap over cavity opening with turkey lacers or skewers (*see* illustrations 3 and 4, page 9). Loosely tie the legs together with kitchen twine (*see* illustration 5). Tuck wings behind back, brush entire breast side with half the melted butter, then place turkey breast side down on V-rack. Fill neck cavity with remaining 1 to 2 cups heated stuffing and secure skin flap over opening as above. Brush back with remaining butter.

5. Roast 1 hour, then reduce temperature to 250 degrees and roast 1 3/4 hours longer. Remove pan from oven (close oven door) and with wad of paper towel or turkey lifter (*see* illustration at right) in each hand, turn breast side up and baste (temperature of breast should be 145 to 150 degrees). Increase oven temperature to 400 degrees; continue roasting until breast registers 160 degrees, thigh registers 175 to 180 degrees and stuffing registers 165 degrees on instant-read thermometer, 45

minutes to 1 1/4 hours longer.

6. *For remaining stuffing:* When turkey comes out of oven, add the 1/4 cup stock to dish of reserved stuffing, replace foil, and bake until hot throughout, about 20 minutes. Remove foil; continue to bake until stuffing forms golden brown crust, about 15 minutes longer.

7. Remove stuffing from turkey and carve. Serve, passing stuffing separately.

MASTER RECIPE FOR BACON AND APPLE STUFFING
Makes about 12 cups

Trim the bread or not, as you prefer, before cutting it into 1/2-inch cubes. Spread the cubes in a single layer over several baking sheets and dry at room temperature for 2 to 3 days, or in a 225-degree oven for 25 to 40 minutes. The dry and wet elements of the recipe can be made separately up to 24 hours ahead of time, but do not combine them until the last minute.

1/2 pound sliced bacon, cut into 1/2-inch pieces

A COOL TOOL

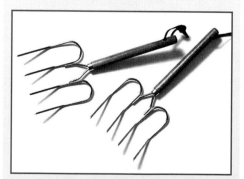

We tested lots of turkey-related gadgets, and the best were these "Roast/Turkey Lifters." Built like small pitchforks, these devices make rotating and lifting the bird a breeze—important when you're shifting a hot turkey.

PHOTOGRAPH BY JACK CERVIERA

Quick Winter Relishes

Cranberries, dried fruit, sweet potatoes, and other winter produce can quickly be transformed into relishes that bring bright, sharp tastes to the table.

By Chris Schlesinger and John Willoughby

Unlike our grandparents, we have little need to pickle and otherwise preserve fresh fruits and vegetables. But these fresh relishes, which will keep for several days in the refrigerator, have the same purpose as our grandmother's pickles—to bring bright, refreshing flavors to the winter table.

CRANBERRY-GREEN GRAPE RELISH
Makes about 4 cups
Ideal with turkey, this relish also complements other roasted poultry and game birds.

- $1/2$ cup white wine
- $1/4$ cup sugar
- $2/3$ cup fresh cranberries
- $1/4$ cup juice from 1 large orange
- 1 teaspoon minced fresh ginger
- 1 pound seedless green grapes, halved
- 2 tablespoons juice from 1 lime
- Salt and ground black pepper

1. Bring wine, sugar, and half the cranberries to boil in small, non-reactive saucepan over medium-high heat, stirring to dissolve sugar. Add orange juice, ginger, remaining cranberries, and half the grapes, return to boil, reduce heat to low, and simmer until about half the cranberries pop and liquid thickens slightly, about 5 minutes.

2. Off heat, mix in remaining grapes and lime juice. Cool to room temperature, then season with salt and pepper to taste (can be stored in airtight container and refrigerated up to 3 days).

GREEN APPLE CHUTNEY WITH APRICOTS AND GINGER
Makes about 5 cups
Try serving this spicy chutney with ham or other roasted pork.

- 2 tablespoons vegetable oil
- 1 medium onion, sliced thin
- 1 medium tomato, cut into $1/4$-inch dice
- 2 green apples such as Granny Smith, cored and cut into $1/4$-inch dice
- $1/2$ cup dried apricots, cut into $1/4$-inch dice
- 1 tablespoon minced fresh ginger
- 2 medium garlic cloves, minced
- $1/2$ small jalapeño chile pepper, cored, seeded, and minced
- $3/4$ cup distilled white vinegar
- $1/2$ cup packed brown sugar
- $1/2$ cup juice from 2 large oranges
- Salt and ground black pepper

Heat oil in large, non-reactive sauté pan over medium heat until shimmering but not smoking. Add onion and cook, stirring occasionally, until softened, 5 to 7 minutes. Add tomato through chile pepper; cook, stirring until fragrant, about 2 minutes longer. Add vinegar, sugar, and orange juice; simmer, stirring occasionally, until juices thicken, about 5 minutes. Cool to room temperature, then season with salt and ground black pepper to taste (can be stored in airtight container and refrigerated up to 2 weeks).

CUMIN-SPIKED ORANGE-RED ONION RELISH
Makes about $4 1/2$ cups
This relish is a good match for firm-fleshed fish such as salmon, tuna, or swordfish.

- 4 medium oranges, peel and pith removed, sectioned, and seeded
- 1 medium red onion, minced
- $1/2$ red bell pepper, cut into $1/4$-inch dice
- 1 medium garlic clove, minced
- 2 teaspoons cumin seeds
- 1 medium jalapeño or other small chile pepper, cored, seeded, and minced
- 2 tablespoons minced fresh oregano leaves
- 1 tablespoon honey
- $1/3$ cup juice from 2 medium lemons
- Salt and ground black pepper

Mix all ingredients, including salt and ground black pepper to taste, in medium non-reactive bowl (can be stored in airtight container and refrigerated up to 4 days).

FENNEL-TANGERINE SLAW
Makes about 4 cups
The small, seedless tangerines called clementines are particularly good in this slaw.

- 2 medium fennel bulbs, trimmed and chopped coarse
- 2 tangerines or clementines, peeled, segmented, seeds removed, and segments halved crosswise
- $1/4$ cup chopped fresh parsley leaves
- 2 tablespoons juice from 1 large lemon
- 2 tablespoons grainy mustard
- 1 medium garlic clove, minced
- $1/2$ cup olive oil
- Salt and ground black pepper

Mix fennel, tangerines, and parsley in large bowl. Whisk lemon juice, mustard, and garlic in small bowl; whisk in oil until dressing is smooth. Toss with fennel mixture and season to taste with salt and ground black pepper (can be stored in airtight container and refrigerated up to 2 days).

CURRIED SWEET POTATO CHUTNEY
Makes about 4 cups
Be careful not to overcook the sweet potatoes when you are blanching them, because you want them to maintain their shape when mixed with the other ingredients.

- 2 medium sweet potatoes, peeled and cut into $1/2$-inch dice
- Salt
- 2 tablespoons vegetable oil
- 1 medium red bell pepper, cored, seeded, and cut into $1/2$-inch medium dice
- $1/2$ medium red onion, peeled and cut into medium dice
- 2 tablespoons minced fresh ginger
- 1 small clove garlic, minced
- 1 medium jalapeño chile pepper, cored, seeded, and minced
- $1/2$ medium fresh pineapple, peeled, cored, and cut into $1/2$-inch cubes (about 2 cups)
- $1/4$ cup raisins
- $3/4$ cup distilled white vinegar
- $1/4$ cup pineapple juice
- $1/2$ cup brown sugar
- $1 1/2$ tablespoons curry powder
- Ground black pepper

1. Bring 3 quarts water to boil in 4-quart non-reactive saucepan. Add sweet potatoes and 1 teaspoon salt and cook until potatoes are tender but still offer considerable resistance when pierced with fork, about 8 minutes. Drain, rinse with cold water, drain again, and set aside.

2. Heat oil in now-empty saucepan over medium-high heat until shimmering but not smoking. Add bell pepper and onion; sauté, stirring frequently, until onion softens, 3 to 4 minutes. Add ginger, garlic, and jalapeño; sauté until fragrant, about 1 minute longer. Add reserved sweet potatoes and pineapple through curry powder; bring to boil. Reduce heat to low and simmer, stirring occasionally, until liquid thickens slightly, about 10 minutes. Cool to room temperature and season with salt and ground black pepper to taste (can be stored in airtight container and refrigerated up to 2 weeks).

Chris Schlesinger is the co-author, with **John Willoughby**, of five cookbooks, including *Thrill of the Grill* (Morrow, 1994).

Holiday Pork Roast

For best results with today's lower-fat (and therefore lower-flavor) pork, use the slightly fattier rib end of the loin and either age the meat for five days in the refrigerator or inject it with a last-minute marinade.

By Pam Anderson

This story was supposed to have been about crown roast of pork. That large, crowd-pleaser of a cut consists of two center cut pork loins trussed together to form a ring. The "frenched" rib bones around the perimeter and stuffing in the shallow cavity make this roast a truly coronal comestible. Already salivating, I laid my plans.

But after cooking eight crown roasts at a range of oven temperatures (200 to 400 degrees) and to varying internal temperatures (145 to 160 degrees), I finally concluded I didn't like this roast enough to serve it for weeknight supper, much less a memorable dinner party. Devoid of fat, the center loin was tasteless and unsatisfying. Even roasted to a low 145 degrees, this lean cut was at once watery and dry, much like white tuna packed in water.

The problem was compounded by the roast's shape. Because the ribs formed the outside of the crown, only the bones browned, while the loin itself steamed rather than roasted.

The night after my disappointing pork loin meal, I was invited to a friend's house for dinner. The main course was grilled beef tenderloin, the large, long muscle attached to the loin. Rather than the usual trim, lean muscle, this roast was rugged and covered with big pockets of fat. I offered to trim the roast a bit for them, but my friend said the butcher had ordered him not to touch it—no trimming, no salt, no pepper, no oil. Just throw it on the grill, he said. The difference between these two dining experiences was dramatic. Eating the super-lean pork loin the night before had made me grumpy, while this well-lubricated, flavorful beef roast made me all smiles. I already knew that lack of fat caused my pork loin's problems, but as I savored my second piece of beef, I finally tasted the difference fat makes. After eating that beef roast, I realized my pork roast needed fat and flavor to make it taste as good as it had looked.

Lean and Mean

Before wasting more time and money on additional roasts, I decided to interview those who know pork best—the producers, the processors, the professors, and the promoters—to see if they could offer me any advice. As I described the crown roast's deficiencies, I expected an in-

For a dramatic presentation and easy carving, have a butcher remove the tip of the chine bone and cut it between each rib, then french the bones.

dustry sales pitch: "Yes, isn't our ultra-lean pork wonderful." But almost without exception, each person readily acknowledged all the problems with today's lean pork.

Up until World War II, hogs were raised as much for their fat as for their meat—a pig with four to five inches of exterior fat (equivalent to about sixty pounds of lard) at slaughter was the norm. After the war, vegetable sources of fat (oil, shortening, margarine) became the fats of choice, and lard was no longer an asset. Coupled with the health trends of the past two decades, this forced the industry to "lean up" its pork, largely through genetic engineering. Today, many processors penalize producers for pigs with more than a mere $4/5$-inch layer (or less than eight pounds) of exterior fat.

Industry's success at eliminating the pig's surface fat, however, has resulted in the loss of its inter-muscular fat as well. Known as marbling, this fat traps and retains juices during cooking and gives the meat flavor and body.

Because of this flavor loss, producers have started to go the other direction, attempting to breed modest amounts of inter-muscular fat back into the pig. In the meantime, processors often "marinate" the loin at the plant to correct this fat/flavor problem, either with injection needles or tumbling machines.

Rack Supplants Crown

Armed with my newfound knowledge of today's pork, I set out to give this cut all the flavor I possibly could. I headed back to the kitchen with a detour at my local butcher, who suggested I switch from a crown roast to a "rack of pork." In this approach, two pork loins are roasted separately, then presented at table with frenched ribs crossed.

This cooking arrangement allowed the loins to roast independent of one another, ensuring that they browned on all sides. Cutting roasts from the rib end, rather than the center or loin end of the whole loin (*see* illustration 1, page 13) also made a big improvement. Located close to the more flavorful shoulder, this part of the loin is multi-muscular, with much-needed fat separating the muscles.

Bones also add flavor to meat. In order to make the loins bend into a crown roast, the chine bone (the backbone) had to be removed, thus further robbing the meat of much-needed flavor. A rack of pork, however, does not require complete removal of the chine bone, so the loin can roast on the bone.

To further improve the roast's flavor, I decided to mimic the pork industry's meat-marinating technique. Using a gadget I found at my local cooking shop, I injected each of three roasts with a different flavor. Dying each mixture blue so that I could track them in the meat, I made one of salt and water; one of salt, sugar, and water; and one of salt, water, and oil. I roasted these three roasts, along with a surface-seasoned only roast.

The results were quite amazing. The injected flavorings permeated the roasts, gravitating to the center and making the loin muscle much more flavorful and juicy than the surface-seasoned roast. This instant marinating step takes about ten minutes, and, to me, the results are worth the effort.

But I had one more test up my sleeve. From my previous work with prime rib and corned beef, I knew that the flavor of beef could be improved with dry curing, the process of salting and aging. It seemed to me that pork might react in the same way. So I bought a second roast, coated each rack with two tablespoons kosher salt, and put them on a wire rack over a paper towel-lined plate set in the refrigerator for one week. After thoroughly brushing off all the remaining salt and removing thin slices of dried-

PREPARING THE ROAST

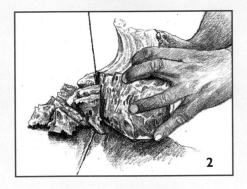

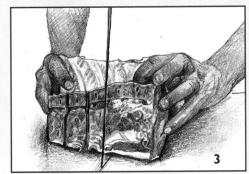

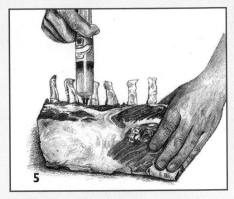

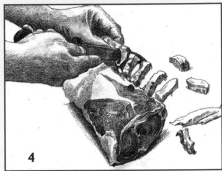

1. Select a roast from the rib end of the pork. Located close to the shoulder, it is more flavorful. Its multi-muscular structure offers bits of fat between the separate muscles.

2. So that frenched bones will cross at presentation, have the butcher remove the tip of chine.

3. So that chops can easily be carved from the roast, have the butcher cut the chine bone between each rib.

4. For festive presentation, remove meat from between each rib.

5. If marinating the roast, inject flavorings all over, particularly at each loin end and between each rib bone.

---

out pork from each end of the roast, I roasted this rack. The flavor and texture of this roast was even better than the injected one. Even though it was a little too salty for my taste, this roast tasted like real pork, with a smooth, buttery texture. Reducing the salt the second time around gave me even better results.

For those who buy their rack of pork the afternoon before they want to serve it, I recommend the injection method. For those who think even three or four days ahead, salting and refrigerating the roast is the ticket. Personally, I look forward to the day when producers figure out how to marble pork again, without the surface fat. Until then, I'm sticking close to the shoulder, hoarding the bones, infusing the meat with a little fat and flavor, and roasting it slow and low.

ROAST CURED RACK OF PORK
Serves 6 to 8

Dry curing requires only that you make space in the refrigerator and purchase the meat three to five days prior to serving it. If you don't have that kind of time, try the optional marinade below. Or, if you're in a real rush, skip both, knowing that choosing the right roast and cooking it according to the suggested method will deliver better-than-average results.

  2 pork loin roasts (5 to 6 ribs each) from the rib end of the loin, tip of chine bone removed, remaining chine cut between each rib (*see* illustrations 1-3), and "frenched"

  2 tablespoons kosher or 1 tablespoon

table salt

For the marinade

  3 medium garlic cloves, minced

  2 teaspoons ground black pepper

  2 tablespoons minced fresh thyme, sage, or rosemary leaves

  2 tablespoons olive oil, plus extra for tossing vegetables

  1 small carrot, cut into 1-inch chunks

  1 small onion, chopped coarse

  3 tablespoons Madeira

1. Scrape rib bones with paring knife to remove any scraps of meat or fat butcher might have missed, until bones are absolutely clean. Rinse roasts and pat dry with paper towels.

2. Rub 1 tablespoon kosher or 1½ teaspoons table salt evenly over each roast. Place on wire rack set over paper towel–lined baking or roasting pan and refrigerate, uncovered, for five days.

3. Adjust oven rack to lower middle position and heat oven to 250 degrees. Shave off very thin exterior layer of hardened, dehydrated meat on roasts. Mix garlic, pepper, herbs, and olive oil in small bowl to make thick paste, and rub half evenly over each roast. Scatter vegetables in roasting pan, place loins on large roasting rack, and set in pan over vegetables. Roast until loins register internal temperature of 120 to 130 degrees on instant-read thermometer, 1¼ to 1½ hours. Increase oven temperature to 425 degrees. When drippings turn brown and just start to smoke, 8 to 10 minutes, add one cup water to roasting pan. Continue roasting until meat registers 145 de-

grees, about 20 minutes longer.

4. Transfer loins to serving platter, arranging so that ribs cross (*see* photograph, page 12). Cover loosely with foil. To make sauce, strain pan drippings into measuring cup, pressing on vegetables to release liquid, and spoon off excess fat. Add additional water, if necessary, to equal 1 cup. Transfer to small saucepan, add Madeira, and simmer to blend flavors, about 5 minutes. Carve roast, cutting between each rib and serve sauce passed separately.

ROAST MARINATED RACK OF PORK
Serves 6 to 8

After curing, the next best (and at just 10 minutes, significantly speedier) way to improve the flavor and mouth feel of the meat is to inject it with this simple marinade. The injector looks like a large doctor's syringe, somewhat shocking in appearance but very effective (*see* Sources and Resources, page 32, for availability). For a hint of sweetness in the meat, dissolve 1 tablespoon brown sugar along with the salt in the marinade.

Follow recipe for Roast Cured Rack of Pork, omitting step 2 and instead dissolving 2 teaspoons salt in ⅓ cup lukewarm water in lidded container. Add ¼ cup flavorless oil, such as canola or corn; shake to emulsify. Fill syringe and, following illustration 5, inject each loin, shaking injector occasionally to ensure that oil and water do not separate (oil alone is difficult to inject). Rub ½ teaspoon salt, then garlic-herb paste, evenly over each rack. Continue with roasting instructions for Roast Cured Rack of Pork.

Pasta with Clam Sauce

*Start with small littlenecks or cockles, cook them separately,
and use the natural clam juices as the basis for a quick sauce.*

By Mark Bittman

Like many Americans, I grew up eating spaghetti with clam sauce that was a soggy mess of canned clams tossed with some overcooked pasta. In my first go-round with the recipe, a number of years ago, I substituted fresh clams for canned, used extra-virgin olive oil, and added just a touch of white wine. I was pretty satisfied with these improvements until recently, when I traveled to Rome, where, as in most of coastal Italy, the technique has been perfected. When I got home last fall I determined to see if I could do better.

First I decided to identify the best clams, and to figure out the best way to cook them. I knew that the tiny clams of

Quahogs (left) can flavor broth, littlenecks (right) provide the meat.

the Adriatic and other small seas adjacent to the Mediterranean were better than the littlenecks I'd been using, but I couldn't find those clams unless I begged them from chefs. So I began by buying the tiniest littlenecks I could find. This helped somewhat, but with clams selling for about $5 a dozen regardless of size, a simple pasta dish for four quickly became an extravaganza.

At that point, I detoured to see whether I could make a credible dish using canned clams. In recent years, tiny canned clams have appeared on the supermarket shelves, and, at about $1.50 a can, they seemed worth a try. Although using these tiny clams improved on the canned clam sauce of my childhood, it didn't measure up to even the worst pasta sauce with fresh clams I'd ever produced.

So I went back to finding a substitute for expensive littlenecks. First I tried the larger cherrystones and even giant quahogs (they're each the same species, just increasingly bigger specimens), lightly steamed and chopped into pieces. But no matter how long or short I cooked them, they were tough, and they lacked the distinctive, fresh brininess of littlenecks. However, I did learn something: Large, less palatable, and far less expensive clams gave me the same kind of delicious clam juice—the backbone of this dish—as small clams.

Then I found some cockles, baby clams that are almost as small as the kind you find in Italy. Because they're sold by the pound, not the dozen, and because they're small, these were less expensive, and quite delicious. Unfortunately, they're not nearly as widely available as littlenecks. The alternative is littlenecks, the littler the better, and at least eight (preferably a dozen or more) per person.

Recipe Repairs

Because I still favored using all littlenecks or cockles, my dish remained quite expensive. So I resolved that if I was going to pay a small fortune for the dish, I would make sure that it would be uniformly wonderful each time I cooked it. There were three problems with my original recipe, I thought. One was that the clam meat tended to become overcooked in the time it took to finish the sauce; the other was that there was often not enough clam juice; finally, I thought that the sauce itself could use another dimension of flavor.

Solving the first problem was easy: I cooked the clams first, just until they gave up their juices. Then I recombined the clams with the sauce at the last minute, just enough to reheat them.

Next I turned to the occasional dearth of clam juice. When I was too cheap to buy enough littlenecks, or couldn't find cockles, I combined a couple of dozen littlenecks with about six large quahogs, which I could often buy for just a couple of dollars. Because it's the juice I'm after—not the clam meat—this worked out fine; I simply discarded the quahog meat after cooking it.

I liked the flavor of white wine mixed with clam juice, but I did not like using more than a one-half cup or so, because its distinctive flavor was somewhat overwhelming. Cutting back on the wine, though, robbed the dish of needed acidity. I experimented with lemon juice, but felt that the flavor was too strong. Vinegar, of course, was even worse. Finally, I added just a little bit of diced plum tomato, barely enough to color the sauce. The benefits were immediate: Not only was the flavor balanced, but another welcome texture was added to the dish.

Satisfied at last, I pronounced myself done. With the final recipe, you can steam the clams open while bringing the pasta water to a boil and preparing the other ingredients. Once the clams are done, begin browning the garlic; five minutes later, put in the pasta and finish the sauce. The timing is perfect, and perfectly easy.

PASTA WITH FRESH CLAM SAUCE
Serves 4

You can save a little money by substituting 6 large, inexpensive quahogs, which provide plenty of liquid for a briny, brothy dish, for about half the price of littlenecks or cockles. Because quahogs are so cheap, discard the steamed meat without guilt and dine on the sweet, tender littlenecks or cockles with the pasta. Don't worry if some of the clams never open, as often happens with littlenecks and cockles; just open them at the table with a paring or similar small knife.

40	littleneck clams (the smaller the better), or 3 pounds cockles, *or* 24 littleneck clams and 6 quahogs (the larger the better), all scrubbed thoroughly
$1/2$	cup dry white wine
	Pinch cayenne
$1/4$	cup extra-virgin olive oil
2	medium garlic cloves, minced
1	large or 2 small plum tomatoes, peeled, seeded, and minced
	Salt
1	pound spaghetti, linguine, or other long-strand pasta
$3/4$	cup chopped fresh parsley leaves

1. Bring one gallon water to boil in large soup kettle. Bring clams, wine, and cayenne to boil in deep, 10 to 12-inch, covered skillet over high heat. Boil, shaking pan occasionally, until littlenecks or cockles begin to open, 3 to 5 minutes. Transfer littlenecks or cockles with slotted spoon to medium bowl; set aside. (If using quahogs, recover pan and continue cooking until their liquid is released, about 5 minutes longer. Discard quahogs; strain liquid in pan through paper towel-lined sieve into large measuring cup. Add enough water to make 1 cup; set aside.)

2. Heat oil and garlic in cleaned skillet over medium-low heat until garlic turns pale gold, about 5 minutes. Add tomatoes, raise heat to high and sauté until tomatoes soften, about 2 minutes longer. Add littlenecks or cockles and cover; cook until all clams open, 1 to 2 minutes longer.

3. Meanwhile, add 1 tablespoon salt and pasta to boiling water; cook until al dente, 7 to 9 minutes. Drain pasta; transfer to skillet and toss. Add reserved clam liquid and cook until flavors meld, about 30 seconds. Stir in parsley, adjust seasonings, and serve immediately.

How to Make a Gingerbread Alpine Cottage

Here's how to make a professional-looking gingerbread house using construction and decorating tips we gleaned from two weeks of our own Alpine cottage homebuilding.

By Michio Ryan

Making a gingerbread house can be easy. Making a good-looking one, however, often is not. The following recipes, techniques, tips, and step-by-step illustrations ensure a sturdy, beautiful house whose decorations will stay put.

CONSTRUCTION GINGERBREAD
Enough for a 9x10x12½-inch house

Make this sticky dough in two batches to avoid the stress that a large single batch would place on your mixer.

- 8½ cups all-purpose flour
- 2½ teaspoons baking soda
- ¾ teaspoon salt
- 2 teaspoons ground ginger
- 2½ sticks unsalted butter, softened
- 1¼ cups loosely packed dark brown sugar
- 1¼ cups unsulphured molasses
- ⅔ cup water

1. Whisk one-half of dry ingredients together; set aside. Beat one-half of butter and sugar in bowl of standing mixer until light and fluffy, about 4 minutes; beat in one-half of molasses. Add flour mixture, a little at a time, alternating with one-half of water, to form a stiff dough. Gather dough into a ball with lightly floured hands, knead slightly to make sure flour is incorporated. Quarter, then shape each portion into flat square. Wrap in plastic and refrigerate until firm, at least 1 hour.

2. Repeat step 1 with remaining one-half of ingredients.

3. Enlarge and cut out templates (page 17), using X-Acto knife to cut out windows and door.

4. Adjust oven rack to lower and upper middle positions and heat oven to 325 degrees. Roll out each portion of dough between parchment paper to ³⁄₁₆-inch thick. Remove top layer of parchment. Place template over dough and, with a ruler as a guide, use knife or pizza cutter to cut 2 sides, 2 ends, 2 roof halves, 4 chimney pieces, and door; re-roll dough scraps for reuse as necessary. Slide cut dough onto heavy gauge cookie sheet.

5. Bake until puffed, slightly brown around edges, and firm to the touch, 15 to 17 minutes. Remove from oven and cool on baking sheet until crisp, about 20 minutes. If dough is still pliable, bake 5 minutes longer and cool again.

MULTI-PURPOSE ROYAL ICING
Enough to assemble and ice a 9x10x12½-inch house

This recipe is made in two batches; two-thirds of the ingredients are used to make a thin icing for coating walls and roof and attaching candies, and the remaining one-third to make a thick construction icing.

- 9 large egg whites, at room temperature
- 3 pounds confectioners' sugar
- 1½ teaspoons cream of tartar
- 1–2 drops food coloring, color of choice

1. Beat 6 egg whites, 2 pounds sugar, and 1 teaspoon cream of tartar at high speed until thick, sticky, and slightly looser than marshmallow fluff, 3 to 4 minutes, to make thin icing for decorating walls and roof and adhering candies; cover with plastic wrap directly on icing and set aside.

2. Beat remaining 3 egg whites, 1 pound sugar and ½ teaspoon cream of tartar in same fashion to stiff peaks, 4 to 5 minutes, to make thick construction icing. Cover with plastic wrap directly on icing surface and set aside.

3. When ready to use, spoon thicker construction icing into pastry bag fitted with ⅛-inch plain tip. Divide decorating icing into thirds, spooning ⅓ into pastry bag fitted with ¹⁄₁₆-inch plain tip, tinting second ⅓ with food coloring for cottage walls, and setting aside final ⅓ for coating roof.

CONSTRUCTION MATERIALS

Select a large (at least 15x18 inches), sturdy base for your gingerbread house. A meat carving board, large platter, piece of plywood or two-ply chipboard are all good choices.

Make sure to let sides and roof halves of the house set completely before assembly, at least thirty minutes but preferably overnight.

- 1 Recipe Construction Gingerbread, cut and baked according to instructions (*see above*)
- 6 hard candies (preferably yellow orange, and red), crushed in their wrappers with a rolling pin or meat pounder, then unwrapped and set aside
- 1 Recipe Multi-Purpose Royal Icing (*see above*)
- 1 package (12 ounces) Sunshine Sugar Wafers, each split with serrated knife through filling, 4 halves trimmed to window length for shutters
- 1 chocolate twizzler, halved lengthwise and cut into four 1-inch pieces for window
- 8 ounces small jelly beans (preferably red, green, and white)
- ½ cup jimmies (preferably multi-colored)
- 3 ounces granular sugar (1 jar)
- 16 3-inch cinnamon sticks
- 1 8¼ x 9¾ inch sturdy cardboard for gingerbread floor
- 8 ounces pastel mint lentils
- 1 pound speckled candies, such as filled pebbles and jelly beans, or an assortment of colored Jordan almonds (or a combination)

Michio Ryan is the Senior Editor of *Handcraft Illustrated.*

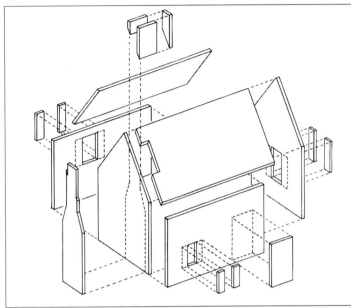

The cottage is made from six large sheets of gingerbread (four walls and two roof sections) plus small pieces for the front door and the chimney.

CONSTRUCTING AND DECORATING A GINGERBREAD

1. Place windowed cottage pieces one by one on a greased parchment-lined baking sheet. Drop a generous teaspoon of cracked hard candies into openings. Use your fingers to distribute the candies evenly. Bake in a 250-degree oven until candies melt, ten to fifteen minutes. Cool for five minutes. Invert walls; peel off parchment.

2. Attach door to the front wall with construction icing. Pipe decorator icing around the inside parameters of the door panes. Pipe a thin line of decorator icing around panes to frame windows; pipe thin crosshatch designs on windows. Set two side sections aside.

3. With an off-set frosting spatula, thickly cover remaining surface of front wall with tinted decorator icing.

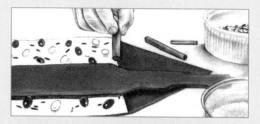

5. Set jelly beans horizontally over wall, arranging them about one inch apart. Sprinkle colored jimmies, then coarse sugar around jelly beans.

6. For the wall that holds the chimney, cover bottom section with decorating icing, align and place chimney, then decorate wall as in step 5. Repeat steps 3, 4, and 5 with remaining two walls, leaving the triangular peak of the remaining end wall undecorated.

7. Separate peak from walls on each of the two end pieces with cinnamon sticks. Set all walls aside.

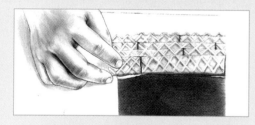

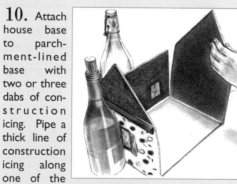

9. Repeat with remaining nine rows of tiles, overlapping them about 1/8-inch along the top of the previous row and making sure that the center of each wafer is in line with the 1/8-inch space between wafers in previous row. Set aside to dry. Note: in the area of the chimney the tiles should be flush with the outside edge of the roof so there is room to place the chimney.

10. Attach house base to parchment-lined base with two or three dabs of construction icing. Pipe a thick line of construction icing along one of the ten-inch sides of the floor base. Set front wall into this icing. Prop with bottle for support. Attach the two peaked sides of house by piping construction icing along each side of the side wall and along the two sides of the floor base. Support with bottles as well. Attach back wall by piping construction icing along final side of the floor base and along sides of each peaked wall. Let dry for thirty minutes; remove supports. Note: extra construction icing should be piped inside at the seams for reinforcement.

11. Pipe construction icing along each wall corner. Decorate wall corners with pastel mints.

13. Thin remaining third of decorator icing with one and one-half tablespoons of water to a consistency of latex paint. Brush this thinned icing over roof tiles.

15. Assemble chimney by piping construction icing onto side and bottom of rectangular chimney piece and attaching to roof and edge of front of chimney. Pipe construction icing onto the angled piece and adhere to roof and rectangular chimney piece. Pipe construction icing onto remaining chimney piece and adhere. Let dry for fifteen minutes.

14. To finish the roof, pipe a line of construction icing on roof peak and adhere cinnamon sticks. Pipe construction icing onto additional cinnamon sticks and adhere at intersections of roof and eaves.

ILLUSTRATIONS BY ESTHER KATZ

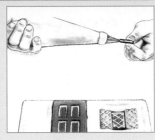

4. Adhere trimmed sugar wafers to each side of the window and twizzler pieces to the top and bottom of the window with construction icing.

8. Working one roof side at a time, pipe a heavy line of construction icing along bottom edge of the roof so that first row of roof tiles will be slightly raised. Pipe construction icing to underside of wafers, arrange them, pressing lightly, 1/8-inch apart, leaving 1/2-inch overhang. Trim sides with scissors if necessary.

12. Pipe construction icing along back wall and the back side of each peak; set one roof section in place. Repeat with second roof section, using bottles as support. Let dry for thirty minutes.

16. Cover chimney with a combination of rock candies and speckled jelly beans working with six pieces at a time. Pipe a generous amount of decorating icing onto candies so once pressed into place,  the icing will squish out and resemble mortar. Once adhered, let them dry for five minutes before proceeding. See back cover for landscaping details.

Templates
enlarge by 400%

Roof

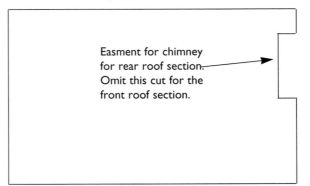

Easment for chimney for rear roof section. Omit this cut for the front roof section.

The roof consists of two rectangular sections 12" x 7 1/4". Follow the solid line for the back panel, leaving room for the chimney. The front panel is a perfect rectangle.
Where the two roof sections meet, the edge of the rear section overlaps the front section.

Front and Rear Walls

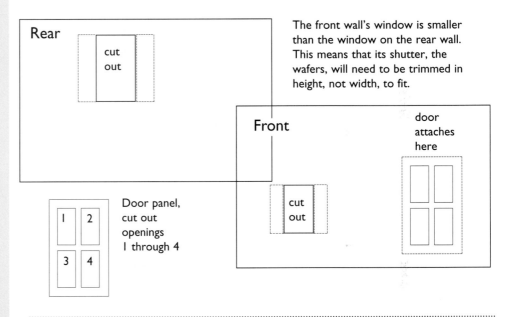

Rear

cut out

The front wall's window is smaller than the window on the rear wall. This means that its shutter, the wafers, will need to be trimmed in height, not width, to fit.

Front

door attaches here

cut out

Door panel, cut out openings 1 through 4

| 1 | 2 |
| 3 | 4 |

Side Walls and Chimney

Chimney pieces

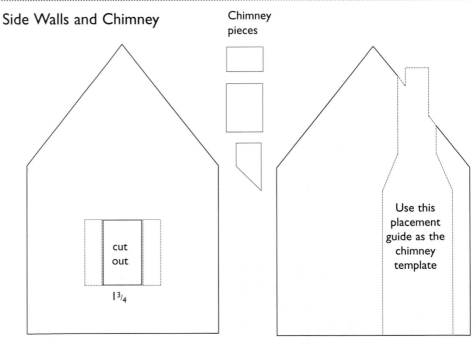

cut out

1 3/4

Use this placement guide as the chimney template

The Best Roasted Onions

*With almost no oil and limited preparation, everyday
yellow onions can be transformed into a special side dish.*

by Adam Ried

❧

I always seem to have a bag of yellow storage onions hanging around, even when the vegetable bin in my refrigerator is bare. The happy result is that some manner of cooked onions is often the side dish of choice at my house.

Though sautéed onions are wildly popular in restaurant and home cooking, to my palate, roasting produces cleaner, purer tasting onions because it requires considerably less fat than sautéing.

Roasting instructions, however, vary widely with regard to cutting and peeling the onions, oven temperature and timing, and the use of fats and liquids. By testing all the variables, I wanted to come up with roasted onions that met three criteria. First, the interior should be tender and moist throughout all the layers, rather than mushy on the inside and leathery toward the outside. Second, for a pleasing presentation I wanted to serve them reasonably intact, perhaps halved or whole, like a baked potato. Finally, I wanted caramelization on at least some of the surfaces.

I started by trying to determine whether onions for roasting should be cut, and if so, how. Roasting onions whole, whether peeled or not, worked poorly because they became caramelized only at the small points where they touched the baking pan. I tried rolling them around from time to time during the cooking to increase the contact area between onion and pan, but repeatedly opening the oven door to do so was a nuisance. Quartered onions caramelized better because they had more surface area to touch the pan, but the presentation fell short: Even with the root end intact, the quarters disintegrated into their separate sections, many of which turned mushy or dry during cooking.

Then I tried a straightforward method described by Jacques Pepin in his latest book, *Cooking with Claudine* (KQED Books, 1996), in which he halved unpeeled onions crosswise (which helps keep them from falling apart) and roasted them cut side down on a pan rubbed with a small amount of oil. These were the best of the bunch by far. All the layers were fully tender, neither mushy nor dry, and the caramelization of the cut surface was impressive. With good results and final preparation limited to a quick chop, this method clearly showed promise.

Moving forward with the halved onions, I set out to determine the optimum oven temperature and whether to cover the onions with foil during cooking.

With a dozen two-pound bags of yellow

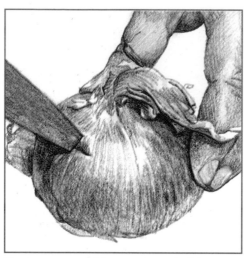

Cutting two small X's near the end of the onion allows moisture to escape during cooking. This helps keep the rings level as they cook.

onions at my side, I went to town, trying 15-minute time intervals between 15 and 60 minutes; 25-degree temperature intervals between 350 and 500 degrees; pans both uncovered and covered with foil for the full cooking time and half the cooking time; and different oven rack adjustments, including directly on the oven floor. Among all those variations, the onions cooked for 30 minutes, at 400 degrees, uncovered, with the rack positioned just off the floor, turned out best, and quite beautifully at that. The layers were perfectly and evenly tender, and cut surfaces were caramelized to a dark brown, though the outside rings of the onions were lighter than the inside rings because they had popped up off the pan surface during cooking.

With the basic questions answered, I went after the other variables. My research turned up variations that called for peeling the onions, soaking them in water, rubbing them all over with fat, roasting in butter rather than oil, and roasting with various liquids, from water to vermouth to stock to vinegar, in the pan. Though none of these experiments improved the onions, I did discover a minor beneficial change. During cooking, the outer rings of onion rose off the pan, so they caramelized less than the inner rings. The remedy I devised was to cut two small X's at the top of each onion half, near the root and stem, with the tip of the knife. This provided a means for evaporated moisture to escape during cooking, which helped limit the elevation of the outer rings. I never found a way to keep them com-

pletely level on the pan, but I did note that a five-minute rest before removing the onions from the pan allowed the outer rings to settle back into position for an improved presentation.

EASY ROASTED ONIONS
Serves 6

Roasted onions make a fine side dish, alone or with a glaze made from the onion pan drippings and 1/3 cup balsamic vinegar, boiled until reduced by almost half. They can be peeled and cut into salads, mixed with white beans, used as a bruschetta topping sprinkled with minced fresh parsley or oregano leaves and shaved Parmesan, or served with other small bites as part of an antipasto.

> 6 medium yellow onions, halved
>   crosswise, root and stem
>   ends X'd twice (*see* illustration)
> 1 tablespoon olive oil
>   Salt and ground black pepper

Adjust oven rack to lowest position and heat oven to 400 degrees. Line a baking sheet or jelly roll pan with aluminum foil; rub foil with oil. Place onions cut side down on baking sheet. Roast until dark brown around bottom edge and tender when pierced with thin skewer or knife tip, about 30 minutes. Transfer pan to rack; let onions rest for 5 minutes before lifting off pan with metal spatula. Peel if desired, season with salt and pepper to taste, and serve.

ROASTED ONION AND BACON DIP
Makes 3 cups

With its fresh ingredients, this dip tastes like an uptown version of the old standby made with powdered onion soup mix. Serve with chips or crudités.

> 1 recipe Easy Roasted Onions (*see*
>   above), cooled and peeled,
>   and chopped fine
> 6-8 slices bacon, cooked crisp and
>   drained, crumbled
> 2 cups sour cream
> 2 1/4 teaspoons Worcestershire sauce
> 1 teaspoon Dijon mustard
> 1/2 teaspoon celery seed
> 3 tablespoons snipped fresh chives
> 1/2 teaspoon salt
>   Ground black pepper

Mix all ingredients in medium bowl. Serve immediately or chill.

ILLUSTRATION BY ANATOLY

All-Season Apple Pie

Here's a recipe that works not only with the best fall apples but with a combination of Granny Smith and McIntosh, which are available everywhere, anytime.

By Christopher Kimball

I am sitting at a neighbor's kitchen table in Vermont on a raw Sunday in early May. A good run of windows gives me a sweeping view of our farm across the way, the pale yellow farmhouse squatting in an old cornfield, a row of dancing white birches holding back the oaks, maples, and hickory, protecting our open upper fields from the encroaching forest. Just a few trees have sprouted leaves, a pale yellowish-lime color on the poplars; deep maroon buds and a hint of pink on the wild cherries.

As I walk home, I stop in our apple orchard, the whips of Macoun and Northern Spy mature now, with trunks as thick as my forearm. A hint of wood smoke still lingers from an early morning fire, the wind is from the west, gusting through the valley. And then the sun breaks out between running clouds, a farmhouse down the road lights ups, pale greens and muddy browns surrounding a blaze of country white. And I know when October comes, and I sink my teeth into the flesh of a fresh-picked Macoun, I will be able to taste this raw day in May, the tart bite of wind, the sweet scent of fresh earth. Each apple contains its own personal history, taste-memories of each day of the growing season, the brisk New England weather building strength of character into every mouthful.

This essence of apple, the crisp texture and the tang of fruit flavor is what must be honored and preserved in a good apple pie. With many apple varieties, these sensations are fleeting and lose their balance very quickly— a Macoun going soft in the late fall, a McIntosh losing its bite in storage. Cooks who slather the apple with cinnamon, sugar, and a starchy thickener do themselves and the apple disservice, so we set out to make a pie in which the apples shine through. We started last fall, when apple varieties were fresh and plentiful, by holding a series of blind tastings, to determine which varieties of apples are best suited to a pie. We baked seventeen different varieties in ramekins, tossed with sugar, spices and lemon juice, and found a few favorites (*see* "Climbing The Apple Family Tree," page 21). But we quickly de-

In the fall, when local apple varieties are in good supply, we recommend searching out your favorite for this pie. At other times of year, combine McIntosh and Granny Smith apples to get the best flavor and texture.

termined that this approach had drawbacks. The first problem was that as the testing passed from fall to winter, the range of apple varieties became narrower. This led to the decision to create a master apple pie recipe that used varieties available all year in all regions of the country. Second, we discovered that an apple variety is no guarantee of consistency. One week a Granny Smith apple pie was topnotch, with plenty of juice and flavor; the next week it was bland and dry. Unlike a store-bought pickle or a canned tomato, a particular variety of apple can change radically in taste and cooking properties by virtue of the weather, the growing conditions at the orchard, the storage facilities, and the length of time spent in your local supermarket. (Apples are stored in a 31-degree, low oxygen environment that retards respiration and, in the words of an industry expert, "puts the apples to sleep.") Finally, we also found that pie filling does not exist in limbo, it is married to a crust. Tasting apples baked on their own or in a commercial crust was misleading. All testing had to be performed using the homemade pie pastry recipe that I had developed two years ago. Its rich, buttery flavor and flaky texture demands, as a counterpoint, a tart, lively apple.

Of those apple varieties that are ubiquitous, we tested the top nine sellers. We determined that Granny Smith and McIntosh both had excellent qualities; the former was tart with good texture and the latter had excellent flavor. But each of them also had drawbacks—a pie made with just Grannies was too sour and a bit dull in flavor, while an all-McIntosh pie was too soft, more like applesauce than apple pie. A pie made with both varieties, however, was outstanding. The Grannies hold up well during cooking, the Macs add flavor, and the mushy texture of the Macs becomes a virtue in this setting, providing a nice base for the harder Grannies and soaking up some of the

DO-AHEAD FRESH-BAKED APPLE PIE

I have been asked many times about whether an unbaked pie could be frozen and then baked off days or weeks later. We tried this overnight and then also tried it after two weeks and six weeks. The two-week pie was flatter than the freshly baked version, the flavor was a bit muted, and the apples were slightly on the spongy side. Nevertheless, we all felt that the results were good, a reasonable sacrifice in the name of convenience. However, the pie frozen for six weeks was a disaster, resulting in foamy, soft apples and a lackluster, greasy crust.

For best results, freeze the pie for two to three hours, then cover it with a double layer of plastic wrap, and return it to the freezer for no more than two weeks. To bake, remove the pie from the freezer, brush it with the egg wash, sprinkle with sugar, and place directly into a preheated oven. After baking it for the usual fifty-five minutes, reduce the oven to 325 degrees, cover the pie with foil so as not to overcook the crust, and bake for an additional twenty to twenty-five minutes.

—C.P.K.

SEALING THE PIE IN THE PASTRY

1. Make sure to use enough apples to mound the filling so a large space does not develop between crust and filling during baking.

2. Using kitchen scissors to trim the overhanging edges of the top and bottom crusts to approximately one-half inch.

3. For a neat edge that stays sealed, tuck this rim of dough underneath itself so the folded edge is flush with the pan lip.

4. Finish the formation of the double crust by pressing the edges with a fork or fluting them (as shown) to seal them well.

juice. Finally, we had a good year-round combination.

Other Ingredients

I have always used butter in my pies. In fact, I used to use up to six tablespoons in a deep dish pie, cutting this back to a more modest two tablespoons over the years. But when we taste-tested pies with and without butter, the leaner pies won hands down. Butter simply dulls the fresh taste of apples. Lemon juice, however, is absolutely crucial to a good pie. By properly balancing the sweet with tart, a good apple pie tastes like a crisp October morning rather than a muggy August afternoon. In the end, we settled on one-and-one-half tablespoons of juice and one teaspoon of zest. (However, one cannot take an overly sweet apple and balance it successfully with lemon juice. The citric acids in lemon juice have a different flavor than the malic acids in apples. It would be like substituting vinegar for lemon juice. The same is true of a tart apple; white granulated sugar is entirely different from the sucrose found in an apple.)

Finding just the right combination of spices took more work. In order to give the apples the upper hand, we used only small amounts, one-quarter teaspoon or less, of cinnamon, nutmeg, and allspice, the latter adding unexpected balance to the lemon juice. Vanilla was voted down by all tasters as a meddlesome addition. The choice of sugar was clear cut: Plain white sugar didn't overpower the fruit, whereas light or dark brown sugar did.

Even a cursory review of apple pie recipes reveals a wide range of preferences for thickeners, with flour, tapioca, and cornstarch being the most common. We did try flour and tapioca and found that they over-thickened the pie. A bit of tart, thin juice gives the pie a breath of the orchard,

whereas a thick, syrupy texture is dull.

Testing Cooking Techniques

Many cookbooks claim that letting apples sit in a bowl with the sugar, lemon juice, and spices, otherwise known as macerating, is key in developing flavors and juice. We found, however, that this simply caused the apples to dry out, making them rubbery and unpleasant. In addition, the apples themselves lose flavor, having exuded all fruitiness into the juice. So macerating, a frequent step in apple pie making, was clearly out.

We ran across this same texture issue once again when investigating the thickness of the apple slices. At first we thought that we could control texture by varying the thickness of slices, but this was not the case. A half-inch slice cooked no more slowly than a quarter-inch slice. It turned out that baking time was the more crucial issue. We had been baking the pies for twenty minutes at 425 degrees and then twenty minutes at 375, and found that the apples were undercooked, and often rubbery. By increasing baking time to fifty-five minutes (twenty-five minutes at 425 and thirty minutes at 375), the juices bubbled, the crust turned a rich brown, and the apple slices were cooked through.

Although we had already done our homework on crust in past issues (*see* September/October 1994 and 1996), there were a few loose ends to tidy up. One of our editors was concerned about pies in which the top crust sets up quickly, leaving an air space between it and the apples, which reduce in volume as they cook down. With our crust recipe, however, this is not an issue. There is sufficient shortening cut into the flour that the crust sinks down onto the apples as they cook. We did notice, however, that this high ratio of shortening produces a very flakey

TASTING THE PERFECT APPLE

Apples have six basic characteristics: sweetness, tartness, fruitiness, texture, color, and shape. According to Dr. Susan Brown, a specialist in apple breeding at Cornell University, the ratio between sweetness and tartness is a key measure of apple desirability. A good tasting apple should be well balanced in this regard. In addition, it is important to have enough sweetness and acidity present, regardless of the ratio. In storage, sweetness will increase and acidity will decrease, some varieties holding better than others. Braeburn keeps well, for example, but Jonagold and Gala have short storage lifespans. Fruitiness or "apple flavor" is more complicated. Scientists have developed a technique called "charm" analysis using a combination of the human nose and a gas chromatograph. A trained researcher with a highly developed sense of smell can identify different flavors or characteristics that are then measured by machine. This eventually leads to a blueprint,

sort of a DNA profile, of the different volatiles or aspects of apple flavor. This can then be used to measure the potential desirability of a new breed of apple. Texture is also key. A Fuji, for example, holds well up to a week when sitting in a basket on a kitchen counter, whereas a Macoun would start to get soft. Unfortunately, color and shape are still the overriding factors. To make matters worse, consumers and supermarket managers insist on bright, primary colors for apples. Ever wondered why a Granny Smith often tastes acerbic, almost unripe? Because they are usually picked too early, when they are bright green, a color that consumers and store managers prefer. The best Grannies are light green, indicating a riper, more mature apple. This insistence on bright colors is one reason apple production has moved west. In a desert climate, the more intense light coupled with warm days and cold nights produces more overall red in an apple.

ILLUSTRATIONS BY JUDY LOVE

crust, one that is not easily cut into perfect slices. In addition, there is still a fair amount of juice, which we find essential for good flavor, and the filling may spread slightly once cut into individual slices.

Second, we wondered if we could solve the problem of the soggy bottom crust. Partial prebaking of the crust is the obvious but impractical solution for a two-crust pie; in my opinion, it is not worth the effort. We tried coating the bottom of the crust with egg whites and, in a separate test, sprinkling a layer of breadcrumbs on the crust, but neither helped. We tested four different types of pans—glass, ceramic, metal with holes, and metal without holes—and it didn't make much difference although glass is cheap, cleans up easily, and does a slightly better job of browning the crust. We did find that overall cooking time was a factor, the longer fifty-five minute baking period being substantially better. With longer baking times in a glass pie plate, we did have some success. The outside of the crust was crisp and, although the inside was still a little bit moist, none of the tasters found this objectionable.

Finally, we wondered what sort of wash might be applied to the top of the pie to give it color. Whole eggs, with or without milk, turned the pie an unpleasant yellow. Egg yolks only yielded dark yellow splotches and when paired with cream, created a top surface that was shiny and reminiscent of store-bought apple pies sold at third-rate diners. We did like, however, a simple mixture of egg whites and sugar. The pies had a pretty, frosted appearance, maintaining a natural, lighter color.

To finish up the testing, we tried baking a pie with no air vents and it turned out just fine. Our pastry recipe is so flaky that steam found its own way through small cracks in the top crust. Vents are attractive, however, and probably make sense with tougher doughs, ones that use less shortening.

So, after six months of testing, we had arrived at a recipe that is frugal in its use of spices, independent of flavor-dulling thickeners, and simple in construction. Stripped down to its essence, this is one apple pie that has memories of morning frosts and the bright, pale sun of late October. Picture perfect slices? Maybe not, but each bite is true to its roots.

MASTER RECIPE FOR CLASSIC APPLE PIE
Serves 8

If you are making this pie during the fall apple season, when many local varieties may be available, follow the recipe below using one of the varieties recommended in the "Climbing The Apple Family Tree," at right. These are well-balanced apples, unlike Granny Smith, and work well on their own without thickeners or the addition of McIntosh. Placing the pie on a baking sheet in the oven inhibits cooking, so cover the bot-

CLIMBING THE APPLE FAMILY TREE

We baked seventeen different apple varieties for this article, including Jonagold, Braeburn, Macoun, Fuji, McIntosh, Empire, Crispin, Golden Delicious, Granny Smith, Royal Gala, Spencer, Rome, Red Delicious, Cortland, Winesap, Rhode Island Greening, and Jonathan. The winners were Macoun, Royal Gala, Empire, Winesap, Rhode Island Greening, and Cortland. We discovered a wide range of flavors, sweetness, acidity, shape, color, and texture and were curious about how different varieties are developed.

Until the advent of genetic engineering, most new apple varieties were created by cross-pollinating trees, taking the pollen from one tree and using it to pollinate the flowers of another. (For example, an Empire is a cross between a Red Delicious and a McIntosh.) Today, however, genetic engineering has taken over. Desirable DNA characteristics are identified and then tranferred to bits of leaves using an organism called agrobacterium. This mixture then takes root and generates a new tree. (A good analogy is the African Violet. Pick off one of its leaves and stick it directly into a pot of soil. It will take root and grow a new plant.)

A call to Eugene Kopferman, a horticulturist at Washington State University, revealed that many popular apples such as Braeburn, Golden Delicious, and Red Delicious are the result of "chance seedlings." Each seed within an apple contains slightly different genetic material, much like sisters and brothers from the same family. So, if one were to plant two separate trees using two different seeds from, say, a Golden Delicious, the resulting fruit and the size of the tree itself could be quite different. (Another reason for this difference is that in uncontrolled circumstances, the pollen carried by a bee could come from any variety of apple tree that happened to be nearby. It would be like children who share the same mother but have different fathers.) So a variety resulting from a "chance seedling" is just that—a seed was planted and resulted in an unexpected new variety.

I was most interested in finding out why so many terrific varieties, so popular in the early part of the century, are now hard to find. Jim Cranney at the U.S. Apple Association told me that since the advent of national distribution after the Second World War, production has been shifting from small to large growers and from the east to the west coast, especially in the arid regions of Washington State, where the combination of climate and irrigation increased production per tree. (In 1996, Washington State produced 131 million bushels, or 5$^{1/2}$ billion pounds of apples; New York State produced only 1 billion pounds.) Smaller growers, those farmers who often produce better tasting, older varieties, can't compete on price or marketing muscle, so your local supermarket is unlikely to stock a Northern Spy, a Macoun, or a Rhode Island Greening. (The top-five selling apples in the United States, among one hundred varieties that are grown commercially, are, in order of popularity, Red Delicious, Golden Delicious, Granny Smith, Rome, and Fuji. Rhode Island Greening and Northern Spy make the list, but only securing 14th and 15th place, respectively.) Specialty food stores and farmstands, both of which are supplied by smaller growers with local varieties, continue to buck the consolidation trend. This may account for the more than forty-eight different varieties currently grown in New York State alone. —C.P.K.

tom of the oven with a sheet of aluminum foil to catch a dripping juices. The pie is best eaten when cooled almost to room temperature, or even the next day.

Pie Dough

2$^{1/2}$ cups all-purpose flour, plus extra for dusting
1 teaspoon salt
2 tablespoons sugar
12 tablespoons chilled unsalted butter, cut into $^{1/4}$-inch pieces
8 tablespoons chilled all-vegetable shortening
6-8 tablespoons ice water

Apple Filling

2 pounds Granny Smith (4 medium) and 2 pounds McIntosh (4 medium) apples (about 8 cups sliced)
$^{3/4}$ cup plus 1 tablespoon sugar
1$^{1/2}$ tablespoons juice and 1 teaspoon zest from one medium lemon
$^{1/4}$ teaspoon salt
$^{1/4}$ teaspoon ground nutmeg
$^{1/4}$ teaspoon ground cinnamon
$^{1/8}$ teaspoon ground allspice
1 egg white, beaten lightly

1. Pulse flour, salt, and sugar in a food processor workbowl fitted with the steel blade. Add butter and pulse to mix in five 1-second bursts. Add shortening and continue pulsing until flour is pale yellow and resembles coarse cornmeal, four or five more 1-sec-

ond pulses. Turn mixture into medium bowl. (To do this by hand, freeze the butter and shortening, grate it into the flour using the large holes of a box grater, and rub the flour-coated pieces between your fingers for a minute until the flour turns pale yellow and coarse.)

2. Sprinkle 6 tablespoons ice water over mixture. Press mixture together with broad side of rubber spatula, adding up to 2 tablespoons more ice water if dough will not hold together. Squeeze dough gently until cohesive and divide into two equal balls. Flatten each into a 4-inch-wide disk. Dust lightly with flour, wrap separately in plastic, and refrigerate at least 30 minutes, or up to 2 days, before rolling.

3. Remove dough from refrigerator. If stiff and very cold, let stand until dough is cool but malleable. Adjust oven rack to center position and heat oven to 425 degrees.

4. Roll one dough disk on a lightly floured surface into a 12-inch circle. Fold dough in quarters, then place dough point in center of 9-inch Pyrex regular or deep dish pie pan. Unfold dough.

5. Gently press dough into sides of pan leaving portion that overhangs lip of pie plate in place. Refrigerate while preparing fruit.

6. Peel, core, and cut apples into $1/2$-to-$3/4$-inch slices and toss with $3/4$ cup sugar and lemon juice and zest through allspice. Turn fruit mixture, including juices, into chilled pie shell and mound slightly in center (*see* illustration 1, page 20). Roll out other dough round and place over filling. Following illustration 2, page 20, trim top and bottom edges to $1/2$ inch beyond pan lip. Tuck this rim of dough underneath itself so that folded edge is flush with pan lip (illustration 3). Flute edging or press with fork tines to seal (illustration 4). Cut four slits at right angles on dough top. Brush egg white onto top of crust and sprinkle evenly with remaining 1 tablespoon sugar.

7. Bake until top crust is golden, about 25 minutes. Reduce oven temperature to 375 degrees; continue baking until juices bubble and crust is deep golden brown, 30 to 35 minutes longer. Transfer pie to wire rack; cool to almost room temperature, at least 4 hours.

APPLE PIE WITH CRYSTALLIZED GINGER
Follow master recipe for Classic Apple Pie, adding 3 tablespoons chopped crystallized ginger to apple mixture.

APPLE PIE WITH DRIED FRUIT
Macerate 1 cup raisins, dried sweet cherries, or dried cranberries in the lemon juice and 1 tablespoon Apple Jack, brandy, or cognac. Follow master recipe for Classic Apple Pie, adding macerated dried fruit and liquid to apple mixture.

APPLE PIE WITH FRESH CRANBERRIES
Follow master recipe for Classic Apple Pie, increasing sugar to 1 cup and adding 1 cup fresh or frozen cranberries to apple mixture.

THE BEST WAY TO PEEL, CORE, AND SLICE APPLES

As we sliced our way through more than one hundred pounds of apples en route to these apple pie recipes, the easiest way to peel, core, and slice apples became a hotly debated subject. We began to wonder about all those kitchen gadgets designed to help with some or all phases of apple preparation. Glancing through catalogues, we came across apple corers, corer/slicers, and a fancy, crank-operated gizmo that peels, cores, and slices in a single motion. In addition, we found that some knife manufacturers make small paring knives with special curved blades, called bird's beak knives, specifically designed for peeling round fruits. We decided to give them all a try.

None of us were fans of the apple corer, which handles only one step of the peeling, coring, and slicing process and does not even perform that task well. Most corers have a diameter between three-quarters and seven-eighths inch (ours was three-quarters), which is too small to consistently remove all of the seeds and seed cavity. Consequently, pieces of the seed cavity were left behind in the flesh and had to be removed later with a paring knife. We also found the corer difficult to aim straight down the center of the apple, which increased the chance of missing some of the seed cavity. Given the fact that you still have to peel and slice the apple, this device saved no time or effort at all.

The next machine we tried was the corer/slicer, which is designed to accomplish two steps of the apple prep process. After peeling the apple, you plung the corer/slicer down through the fruit to core and slice it. However, we had the same problem with bits of seed cavity being left in the flesh, and we were stuck with thicker slices than we wanted.

Several companies market crank-operated apple paring machines that handle all three parts of the job. We tried the Apple Potato Master, a $32 contraption from Back To Basics Products, Inc. After the machine is attached to a table or counter, you spear an apple on a three pronged fork which is attached to a rod that you turn with the crank. As the handle is turned, the apple moves forward, coming into contact with a peeling blade mounted on a spring-loaded arm. This allows the blade to adjust to the contours of the apple as it moves past. The apple then passes by a second blade that both cores and slices.

While it was somewhat of an improvement, this machine didn't wow us. The suction grip worked well on a smooth countertop, but was much less effective on a wooden tabletop because of the slightly uneven, textured surface.

The Apple Potato Master looks like a great idea, but has a number of mechanical limitations.

(Other paring machines use a clamp to mount to a work surface, which can be a problem because the clamps often open to only one inch, and many table and countertops are thicker than that.) In addition, the slicing blade cuts the apple into very thin, horizontal slices instead of the thick wedges we wanted for our recipe.

There was yet another limitation to this piece of equipment. Apple Potato Master's instructions warned, and our experience confirmed, that it works best with very hard, fresh fruit. Some of our Macs were less than perfectly firm, and the peeling blade slid right over the skin, failing to do its job. When the peeling blade did work well on a firm Granny Smith, it showered us with apple juice as it peeled.

These objections aside, we still wanted to see if the paring machine was really faster and easier than hand work, so we ran a friendly competition. We pitted the machine against a paring knife to peel (only, not core or slice) eight apples. The person using the machine got through all eight in four minutes forty-seven seconds, including the time necessary to clean up the poorly peeled Macs with a paring knife. The person using the paring knife took six minutes nine seconds to get through eight apples. The upshot? If we had to bake a bunch of pies (say, four or more), we'd consider the Apple Potato Master, but for one or two pies, stick to the paring knife.

Since none of us liked peeling the apples with a vegetable peeler, we agreed on the paring knife as the do-it-all tool of choice. We tested the straight edged paring knife against the curved blade bird's beak model, but none of the testers found the bird's beak significantly easier to use or more effective.

Yet the debate was still not settled. Those of us on staff who were trained in formal cooking programs all learned to quarter the apple first, peel each quarter separately, core, and then slice them. Others among us peel the apple intact, spiraling down from top to bottom, then quarter, core, and slice. After some practice with the spiral peeling method, though, even the trained cooks among us converted, finding it easier and quicker to peel the apple whole, then proceed.

—Adam Ried

ILLUSTRATION BY JUDY LOVE

Holiday Eggnog

*A custard base provides well-rounded, creamy flavor, and combining
the milk and eggs in several stages yields ultra-smooth texture.*

By Anne Tuomey and Ann Flanigan

❧

Traditional eggnog has a little something for everyone in the 90's to criticize. Heavy cream, raw eggs, and alcohol, the building blocks of eggnog recipes for centuries, are not on the A-list of many cooks today. But just as creamed onions, prime rib, and pecan pie are reserved for a once- or twice-a-year event, so is eggnog, and it should be enjoyed in moderation without fear of the food police. The rich, deep, creamy flavor of a really fine eggnog is just too good to pass up.

The eggnog recipes we gathered fell into two categories, uncooked and cooked. Making an uncooked eggnog generally involves beating whole eggs or yolks with sugar, adding alcohol and dairy (milk, cream, or a combination of the two), and finally, folding in beaten egg whites to create a frothy texture. The cooked versions use a custard base of beaten whole eggs or yolks that are heated with milk and sugar and then combined with alcohol and heavy cream (either whipped or not) to create a thicker, creamier texture.

We really had no bias toward one or the other when we began testing, and were prepared to deal with the raw egg issue if we liked the uncooked eggnog better. However, we ended up preferring the custardy flavor and creaminess of the cooked versions.

Smooth and Thick, Eggy but Sweet

Starting with a standard custard recipe (six eggs to four cups of milk to one-half cup of sugar), we tinkered around to find improvements. We finally settled on adding two extra egg yolks to our original recipe to improve the custard flavor and richness—a small but noticeable change—and added another two tablespoons of sugar as well as a dash of salt to enhance the flavor.

Although we felt we had the right custard proportions, we still had a problem refining the smooth texture. Many, but not all recipes, specified adding the milk gradually to the beaten eggs. We had taken this for granted in our usual desire to hurry up the final product but now we found that the smoothness of the custard really did depend on how well the milk blended with the beaten eggs. If the eggs were not beaten in completely, we ran the risk of finding little bits of egg in our final nog. By adding the milk in smaller amounts, we were forced to make sure the mixture was blending well before we added more. Finally, if a few pieces of egg did make their way into our mix, we decided to strain it as insurance.

Making It Creamy

We wanted a rich eggnog with a relatively thick, creamy texture. The custard base alone was quite flavorful and thick, but it was not quite eggnog. Most recipes we had seen used heavy cream to enhance the custard, and we tended to agree. We tried adding all kinds of other dairy products to the custard, including light cream, half and half, whole milk, 2% milk, non-fat milk, and evaporated milk. But we found that none gave us the consistency or color or flavor provided by whipped heavy cream.

The amount of heavy cream we used seemed to depend on how much alcohol we added. The alcohol thinned out the custard while the cream replaced some of this lost heft. You can decrease the cream slightly if you eliminate the brandy or increase it proportionally if you enjoy a stiffer eggnog. Lesser amounts of cream and unwhipped cream failed to adequately thicken the eggnog, while too much cream drowned out the custard and alcohol flavor, and separated from the custard too easily. Softly whipped cream blended in very smoothly with the custard, while cream beaten to stiff peaks was somewhat difficult to fold in completely, creating globules of whipped cream that were hard to blend. Half a cup of whipped cream worked well with the amount of alcohol we were using.

Last, but not least, were the flavorings. We tested recipes that used everything from blades of mace and split vanilla beans to whole cloves and cinnamon sticks. Call us traditionalists, but in the end we felt you just cannot beat vanilla extract and nutmeg for true holiday eggnog flavor.

HOLIDAY EGGNOG
Serves 12-16

Adding the milk to the eggs in small increments and blending thoroughly after each one helps ensure a smooth custard. To prevent curdling, do not heat custard beyond 160 degrees. If it does begin to curdle, remove from heat immediately and pour into a bowl set over a larger bowl of ice water to stop the cooking, and proceed with recipe. You can omit the brandy to make a non-alcoholic eggnog, but you should also decrease the cream to 1/4 cup in order to keep the right consistency. For the same reason, increase the cream to 3/4 cup if you choose to add another 1/2-cup alcohol for a high-test nog.

- 6 large eggs plus 2 yolks
- 1/2 cup plus 2 tablespoons sugar
- 1/4 teaspoon salt
- 4 cups whole milk
- 1/2 cup brandy, bourbon, or dark rum
- 1 tablespoon vanilla extract
- 1/2 teaspoon grated nutmeg, plus extra for garnish
- 1/2 cup heavy cream, whipped to soft peaks

1. Off heat, whisk eggs, yolks, sugar, and salt in heavy 3- or 4-quart saucepan. Stir in milk, one-half cup at a time, blending well after each addition. Heat slowly over lowest possible flame, stirring constantly, until custard registers 160 degrees on instant read thermometer, thickens, and coats the back of a spoon, 25 to 30 minutes. Pour custard through sieve into large bowl; stir in liquor, vanilla and grated nutmeg. Cover with plastic wrap and refrigerate until well chilled, at least three hours and up to three days.

2. Just before serving, whip cream in medium bowl to very soft peaks and gently fold into custard mixture until incorporated. Serve in chilled punch bowl or cups, garnishing with optional grated nutmeg.

Anne Tuomey and **Ann Flanigan** live and write in Wellesley, Massachusetts.

A judicious balance of eggs, milk, and sugar creates a smooth, thick nog with just the right egginess and sweetness.

A Simple Chocolate Truffle

These days, chocolate truffles have been tarted up with most every ingredient in the baker's pantry. Here's how to make it simple, showcasing the deep, pure flavor of chocolate.

By Nick Malgieri

The best rule of thumb for choosing a chocolate for truffles: The chocolate should taste good—good enough to eat by itself in large quantities. If it satisfies this criterion, it will make excellent truffles.

The perfect chocolate truffle is easy to define: It is a balanced amalgam of texture and flavor that results in perhaps the ultimate chocolate experience. The flavor should be chocolate—not liquor, nuts, butter, or eggs. The texture should be sensuously creamy and light for the richness it packs—a truffle should feel as good as it tastes. The chocolate coating on the outside should be thin and delicate—just enough to keep the creamy center mixture from losing its shape. Truffles should be luscious little morsels—an inch in diameter at the largest— small enough so that you shouldn't think twice before indulging in a second or third.

Though the ingredients in a perfect truffle are simple, problems may arise at several key points along the way: in mixing the center mixture, in whipping it after cooling, or in shaping and coating the truffles. The methods outlined below take the risks and guesswork out of making the perfect truffle so you won't wind up with a separated center mixture or one that refuses to whip up properly. These truffles are easy to shape—either with a bag and tube to pipe them or a small scoop to spoon them out. And the coating process, for finishing the truffle, is the simplest of all; it allows you to coat the truffles and finish the outside with cocoa all in one easy step.

The Ganache

Truffle center mixture, or ganache, is one of the foundation preparations of all pastry and confectionery work. Basically a mixture of chocolate and cream, ganache may be used for filling cakes, glazing cakes and pastries, or as the center for chocolate candies. For all ganache, hot cream is combined with cut-up chocolate so that the chocolate melts. The ganache is then mixed smooth and allowed to cool. Finally, according to its purpose, it is either used as is or whipped (moussed) to lighten both color and texture, basically making it into an extremely rich chocolate whipped cream.

The key difference among the various types of ganache is the proportion of chocolate to cream. Thin, glazing, or "ordinary" ganache is made from equal weights of chocolate and cream. Rich or spreading ganache, used for cake fillings, is made from one-and-one-half parts chocolate to one part cream. Finally, classic truffle ganache, the richest of all, uses two parts chocolate to one part cream. Simple, no? No!

Mixing the ingredients together poses the first challenge. In most recipes, the cream is brought to a boil and poured over the chopped chocolate. If the chocolate is very finely chopped, it melts easily. Sometimes, however, a granule or two of chocolate remains unmelted, resulting in a lump in a glaze, or grainy texture in a whipped ganache. After many experiments, I realized that the best way to combine chocolate and cream for ganache—especially for the heaviest of all ganaches used for truffles—was to melt the chocolate first and then combine warm cream with it. The temperatures are fairly low, precluding separation, and the chocolate is already melted and smooth, eliminating all possibilities of lumps.

Other Ingredients

Though there are confectioners who make truffles simply by mixing chocolate and cream, this won't result in an extremely complex flavor.

Early on I had learned that a bit of butter added to the ganache helps both flavor and texture. Butter gives the heavy, chocolate-rich ganache a fresher, lighter flavor without masking any of the intrinsic chocolate flavor. Because butter has a lower melting temperature than chocolate, the "mouth feel" of truffles that contain butter is a little more delicate. The amount was small—only an ounce of butter to a pound of chocolate. After a few experiments, I concluded that a little more butter would be fine—in combination with the rest of the ingredients and flavorings, up to two ounces of butter for a pound of chocolate neither obscured the chocolate flavor nor made the ganache difficult to handle.

Though corn syrup is sometimes used to promote smoothness in glazing and spreading ganache, I had never tried using it in truffles. Fortunately, I hit on the right combination early in my experiments; two tablespoons added to a pound of chocolate made the ganache smooth and creamy, but not too soft. More corn syrup makes an elastic, rubbery-textured ganache and less was undetectable.

I tried the recipe with several types of cream. No difference was detectable between ultra-pasteurized and pasteurized heavy whipping cream. I even sought out and tried an extra-rich cream with 40% butterfat (as compared to the typical 35 or 36%) and it presented a slight difference—the ganache seemed a little fluffier and inclined to whip up and lighten more quickly; but after the truffles were formed and coated, the difference in the texture of the centers was undetectable.

Liquor is the easiest and most common flavoring used for truffles. No more than an ounce or two of liquor need be added to a pound of chocolate to convey a delicate flavor. Long ago, I learned from my own teacher, Albert Kumin, to add an extra ounce of chocolate for every ounce of liquor added to the ganache to counteract the diluting effects of the liquor. Classically, the liquor is added during the whipping, though I have come to prefer adding it directly to that ganache with the other ingredients—it makes the ganache less likely to separate during the whipping. Liquors I have tried successully include Cognac, dark rum, light rum, orange, raspberry eau de vie (Framboise), Kirsch, creme de cassis. Remember—just a subtle liquor flavor— truffles are not Jello-shots.

You must use something to roll the chocolate-covered truffles in. Because the chocolate is not fully tempered, it will not set to a smooth sheen, and makes the truffles an unappetizing gray color. If cocoa is your choice for the coating, I recommend alkalized (Dutch process) cocoa, which is a little less bitter than plain, non-alkalized cocoa. Finely ground, toasted nuts or grated chocolate (grated on the food processor grating blade or on the coarse holes of a hand grater) also make good choices for the outside of truffles.

MASTER RECIPE FOR PERFECT CHOCOLATE TRUFFLES
Makes 2 dozen 1-inch truffles

These truffles are meant to look like the real thing—small, irregular mounds instead of perfectly spherical balls. If you decide to omit the liquor flavoring, reduce chocolate from 9 to 8 ounces. For microwave-oriented cooks, you can melt the chocolate at 50% power for about 3 minutes. The ganache mixture is quite forgiving. If it cools too much in step 1, place the bowl in a larger pan of warm water and stir the mixture until it has softened and warmed up. If this overwarms the mixture, cool it again as directed. The same flexibility applies if you overwhip the ganache by mistake. Simply warm it over the hot water, cool it, and whip it again.

One person alone can dip and coat the truffles, but the process is simpler with a second person to roll coated truffles in cocoa and lift them onto a clean pan.

Ganache
- 9 ounces semisweet or bittersweet chocolate, chopped coarse
- 1/2 cup heavy whipping cream
- 2 tablespoons unsalted butter
- 1 tablespoon light corn syrup
- 2 tablespoons of one of the following: Cognac, dark rum, Grand Marnier, Framboise, Kirsch, Frangelico, Amaretto, Kahlua, or port

Chocolate and Cocoa Coating
- 8 ounces semisweet or bittersweet chocolate
- 2 cups sifted Dutch process cocoa powder

1. *For the ganache:* Melt chocolate in medium heatproof bowl set over pan of almost simmering water, stirring once or twice,

until smooth. Set bowl aside. Bring cream, butter, and corn syrup to strong simmer (about 160 degrees) in non-reactive pan over low heat. Remove pan from heat, cool for 5 minutes, then whisk into chocolate. Whisk in liquor. Refrigerate mixture until it cools to 80 degrees, 15 to 20 minutes.

2. Either in bowl of electric mixer fitted with whisk attachment or with handheld electric mixer, whip mixture at medium speed until slightly lightened and thickened to a texture like store-bought canned chocolate frosting, 25 to 30 seconds. Spoon ganache into large pastry bag fitted with 1/2-inch plain tube. Following illustration 1, hold bag perpendicular to pan and with tip about 3/4 inch above work surface, and pipe 3/4-inch mounds (pulling tube away to the side to avoid leaving points) onto parchment or wax paper-covered baking sheet. Alternatively, scoop mounds with tiny (less than 1 tablespoon) ice cream scoop or melon baller. Refrigerate mounds until hardened, at least an hour.

3. *For coating:* Following directions in step 1, melt coating chocolate, then cool to 90 degrees, making certain that no water comes into contact with chocolate. Arrange chilled truffle mounds, bowl of melted chocolate, and cocoa-filled high-sided roasting pan on work surface. Working one mound at a time, dip palm of one hand about 1/4-inch deep into melted chocolate, pass one truffle mound with other hand to chocolate-covered hand and close hand around mound to coat, re-dipping hand into chocolate every third or fourth mound (*see* illustration 3). Drop coated truffle into cocoa; roll to coat using fork held in now empty clean hand, leaving truffles in cocoa until chocolate coating has set, about 1 minute. Repeat process until all mounds are in pan of cocoa. Following illustration 4, gently roll 5 to 6 truffles at a time in medium strainer to remove excess cocoa, then transfer to serving plate or tightly covered container. (Can be refrigerated for up to one week.)

CHOCOLATE NUT TRUFFLES
Makes 2 dozen 1-inch truffles

Pulse 1 cup unsalted pistachio nuts or toasted hazelnuts, almonds, pecans, or walnuts with 1 tablespoon sugar to a fine powder (about the texture of coarse sand) in food processor workbowl fitted with steel blade. Follow Master Recipe for Perfect Chocolate Truffles, substituting ground nuts for cocoa powder.

CHOCOLATE COCONUT TRUFFLES
Makes 2 dozen 1-inch truffles

Adjust oven rack to middle position and heat oven to 350 degrees. Spread 1 cup grated, sweetened coconut in thin layer on dry cookie sheet; toast until golden brown, about 8 minutes, stirring every 2 minutes. Follow the master recipe for Perfect Chocolate Truffles, substituting toasted coconut for cocoa powder.

Nick Malgieri is the author of *How To Bake* (HarperCollins, 1995).

THE PERFECT CHOCOLATE TRUFFLE

1. Forming truffles: Using a pastry bag fitted with 1/2-inch plain tube, pipe 3/4-inch spheres onto a pan covered with parchment or wax paper. They do not form perfect balls and will droop slightly.

2. Use mini ice cream scooper/cookie scooper to form truffles.

3. Use one hand to coat the truffles in the chocolate glaze. Drop the coated truffles into a roasting pan filled with cocoa. Toss in the cocoa mix with hands or with fork.

4. Gently toss finished truffles in strainer (in batches) to remove excess cocoa.

Tasting White Chocolates

After tasting a dozen varieties, most tasters agreed that although white chocolate has limited application, some brands were "nutty" and "buttery" while others were almost inedible.

By Maryellen Driscoll

❦

White chocolate is the troubled child in the family of chocolates. It can be fussy to cook with and unpredictable in flavor and consistency. Even so, it can sweeten a dessert unlike any other chocolate.

Much of the confusion that surrounds this confection springs from the fact that it is not really chocolate at all. In order to be called "chocolate"—at least according to the U.S. Food and Drug Administration (FDA)—a product must contain chocolate liquor, which lends the bitter, intense chocolate flavor (as well as brown color) to dark and milk chocolates. Traditionally, white chocolate contains milk, sugar, flavorings, and cocoa butter, which is the fat from cacao beans, but no chocolate liquor. Of the twelve brands we tasted, only one (Baker's) labels itself "white chocolate." It can do so only because it has a federal temporary marketing permit. This identity crisis should be resolved by January 1998, when an FDA standard is scheduled to go into effect. It will require that any product calling itself "white chocolate" must contain at least 20 percent cocoa butter. (Chocolate liquor will not be required.)

Cocoa butter, the world's most expensive edible natural fat, is renowned for its "mouthfeel" and the fact that its melting point—95 degrees Fahrenheit—is just below body temperature, so that it melts slowly and evenly in the mouth. This smooth, creamy texture is one of the qualities that confectioners like about white chocolate.

But cocoa butter has little effect on the flavor of most white chocolates, according to Mel Warnecke, a technical consultant to the confectionary industry from Chattanooga, Tennessee. Unadulterated cocoa butter does carry a mild chocolate flavor and, like wine, also has many residual flavors and odors that result from soil conditions, climate, and maturity at harvest. But nearly all chocolate manufacturers deodorize their cocoa butter, a process that strips any "off" flavors, but also leaves the cocoa butter tasting bland, according to Warnecke. This is done because manufacturers buy cacao beans from all over the world, and they would have competing (and not necessarily complementary) odors and flavors if not deodorized.

Going with the Pros
We began our white chocolate taste test with a panel of thirty-five nonprofes-

sionals who sampled a dozen white chocolates plain. Unfortunately, the test results were sketchy, and our questionnaires showed that tasters were starting from zero, with very little idea as to what white chocolate should taste like.

This led us to suspect that white chocolate is one of those rare ingredients that you have to know well in order to evaluate. To test our suspicion, we decided to conduct a second tasting, this time with an expert panel consisting of nine pastry chefs who work with white chocolate regularly. The chefs listed mousses, ganaches, buttercreams, cheesecakes, and sauces as recipes in which they commonly use white chocolate.

Our expert panel clearly knew what flavors and textures they wanted in a white chocolate. They agreed that their ideal white chocolate would be rich, mellow, not too sweet, and free of artificial vanilla flavors. "In my baking, white chocolate is used as an undertone, a background flavor, one that supports the main flavors of a dessert," said David Broderick, of Icarus Restaurant in Boston.

Using these criteria, the chefs chose Barry Callebaut White Superior as their favorite, followed by Lindt Swiss White. Pastry chefs were also definite fans of El Rey, but several explained after the tasting that they felt it was too complex to support the flavors and desserts with which they typically pair white chocolate.

Because white chocolate is more commonly used in desserts than eaten plain, we decid-

ed to conduct one final taste test, this time with a sauce of white chocolate melted in heavy cream. The tasters, a panel of ten nonprofessionals separate from the first nonprofessional group, also expressed an indifference to the products, except for one, El Rey ICOA. This finished first, while, ironically, it had ranked last among the first nonprofessional panel.

To try to understand this anomaly, we called Rand Turner, president of Chocolates El Rey, Inc. Turner explained that, unlike all the other manufacturers in this testing, El Rey does not deodorize its cocoa butter because all of its cacao beans come from a single, concentrated region in Venezuela. So instead of being stripped of flavor the cocoa butter carries unusual, complex flavors (tasters noted hints of nut, coffee, and butter).

So our conclusion is that El Rey white chocolate is best saved for those occasions when a distinctive flavor is appropriate. When you are looking for creaminess and a subtle flavor, Barry Callebaut White Superior is the best bet.

Tasting White Chocolates
For our tastings, we selected a dozen plain white chocolates or confections found in Boston-area supermarkets and specialty food stores and nationwide mail-order outlets. Our first panel of thirty-five nonprofessionals tasted the products chopped up plain. A panel of nine Boston-area pastry chefs also tasted the products plain. Lastly, a panel of ten nonprofessionals tasted the products melted in heavy cream as a sauce. The products were rated for aroma, flavor, texture, and overall liking. Total overall scores for the three tastings were averaged. Products are ordered by ranking on page 27.

The location following each product name refers to the manufacturing plant or corporate headquarters listed on the package label. Prices indicate actual retail cost.

The following pastry chefs from Boston and Cambridge, Massachusetts, participated in our tasting: Roger Bencivenga of Club Cafe, David Broderick of Icarus Restaurant, Maria Cavaleri of Harvest Restaurant, Lee Napoli of Maison Robert, David Ogonowski of Chez Henri, Suzy Parks of Wedding Angels, Paige Retus and Maria Wharton of Olives, and Jennifer Zachariah of Upstairs at the Pudding.

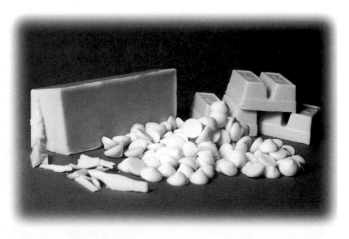

White chocolate comes in block, chip, and bar form; as of January 1, when the new FDA standards go into effect, some will be unable to be labelled white chocolate because they contain too little cocoa butter.

PHOTOGRAPHS BY JACK CERVEIRA

RATING WHITE CHOCOLATE

RECOMMENDED

Barry Callebaut White Superior (Belgium), solid chunk for $9 per pound. This white chocolate ranked the highest overall when tasted plain by pastry chefs and nonprofessionals but lost much of its popularity when served as a sauce. Experts gave it tops for creaminess, rapid melting in the mouth, and its "nice middle-of-the-road flavors—not too bold." Contains 30 percent cocoa butter. Available by mail from New York Cake & Baking Distributors (56 West 22nd Street, New York, NY 10010; 800-942-2539) or A Cook's Wares (211 37th Street, Beaver Falls, PA 15010-2103; 800-915-9788).

Lindt Swiss White (Switzerland), 13-ounce bar for $5.99. This white bar held second place in all of the tastings. Many were taken by its "sweet and pleasant" qualities. As a sauce tasters found it to be more like a "pudding" or "custard" but not so thick that it was disliked. Strong (artificial) vanilla flavors were noted. Contains 30 to 35 percent cocoa butter. Available in gourmet stores and by mail from Dairy Fresh Candies (57 Salem Street, Boston, MA 02113; 800-336-5536).

Peter's Snowcap (Glendale, California), solid chunk for $3.99 per pound. This was one of few white chocolates that carried a detectable pleasant aroma and a slight chocolate flavor. Among pastry chefs it finished fourth overall. Nonprofessionals gave it an overall third ranking. As a sauce it fell to fifth place. Don't confuse this with Peter's Icecap, a sister "white chocolate" that does not contain cocoa butter. Contains 38 percent cocoa butter. Available by mail from Dairy Fresh Candies (57 Salem Street, Boston, MA 02113; 800-336-5536).

NOTEWORTHY

El Rey ICOA (Venezuela), $10.70 for two-pound solid chunk. The new kid on the block as well as the oddball of the pack, El Rey ICOA crowned the sauce tasting but ranked at the bottom when tasted plain by nonprofessionals. Among pastry chefs it landed solidly in third. This is the only white chocolate with cocoa butter that is not deodorized and thus it carries complex, distinct flavors native to its Venezuelan origin. Tasters described it as "nutty," "earthy," and "buttery," with hints of "coffee" and "cocoa." None of the tasters found it to be especially creamy in texture. Contains 34 percent cocoa butter. Available in some gourmet stores and by mail from Simpson & Vail, Inc. (3 Quarry Road, P.O. Box 765, Brookfield, CT 06804; 800-282-8327).

NOT RECOMMENDED

Nestle Toll House Premier White Morsels (Glendale, California), 12-ounce bag of chips for $2.39. Tasters either loved or hated this sugary confection. Its strong vanilla flavor won over some, but others deemed it "artificial" and suspect. More than one taster likened its flavor to vanilla frosting in a can or to sweetened condensed milk with vanilla. Quite smooth and creamy, it melted rapidly and had the strongest aftertaste when tasted plain. Pastry chefs could detect the absence of cocoa butter flavor. Contains palm kernel oil and artificial and natural vanilla flavors. Available in supermarkets nationwide.

Perugina Classic White (Saddle Brook, NJ), three-ounce bar for $1.59. A little on the sweet side and a little bit gritty too, this product received lukewarm reactions. As a sauce, tasters found it "thin" and "watery" and generally unappealing. Pastry chefs found it creamier than most but "a bit too sweet." Contains no less than 20 percent cocoa butter. Available in gourmet stores and by mail from Dairy Fresh Candies (57 Salem Street, Boston, MA 02113; 800-336-5536).

Ghirardelli White Confection (San Leandro, California), four-ounce bar for $2.29. This bar fell into the middle ranks in all three tastings. As a sauce it was the sweetest. Eaten plain it carried a strong aftertaste and lacked a creamy quality. Both of these qualities improved in the sauce. Non-professionals and pastry chefs suspected artificial vanilla flavors although its packaging lists natural vanilla as an ingredient. Contains 36 percent cocoa butter. Available in supermarkets nationwide.

Merckens Ivory (Mansfield, Massachusetts), solid chunk for $4.50 per pound. This chocolate was one of the top scorers for smoothness and creaminess among pastry chefs as well as nonprofessionals. It was also a top scorer for liking of flavor and strength of flavor among nonprofessionals. As a sauce, though, it took a dive to last place in terms of overall liking. Contains between 30 and 40 percent cocoa butter. Available by mail from A Cook's Wares (211 37th Street, Beaver Falls, PA 15010-2103; 800-915-9788).

Baker's Premium White Chocolate (White Plains, New York), six-ounce box of solid squares for $2.19. The only "white chocolate" with a federal marketing permit to call itself so. It scored unremarkably in all three taste tests except for its runner-up ranking to Nestle for being extremely sweet. Tasters noted artificial and excessive vanilla flavors as well as a slight grittiness. "The only good thing going here is a batch of good childhood Easter memories," said one pastry chef. Baker's declined to disclose the product's cocoa butter content. Contains artificial and natural vanilla flavors. Available in supermarkets nationwide.

Valrhona Ivory (France), solid chunk for $10.21 per pound. One pastry chef summed up this upscale white chocolate saying, "Good, creamy feel and melt but zippo in the flavor department." Ratings in all three tastings were similar to its flavor—unremarkable. Contains 35 percent cocoa butter. Available in gourmet stores and by mail from New York Cake & Baking Distributors (56 West 22nd Street, New York, NY 10010; 800-942-2539).

Van Leer Van Gogh (Jersey City, New Jersey), solid chunk sells for $5 per pound. Despite the high content of cocoa butter, tasters found this product eaten plain to be a bit gritty, gummy, and not especially pleasant in flavor. Many described an "off" taste. Served as a sauce it was sweet but not too sweet and gained major strides in texture. Even so, sauce tasters felt the flavor was slightly lacking. Contains 39 percent cocoa butter. Available in gourmet stores and by mail from New York Cake & Baking Distributors (56 West 22nd Street, New York, NY 10010; 800-942-2539).

Barry Callebaut Ultimate Line 1000 (Belgium), One pound of white chips for $3.80. These white chips, until recently made by Van Houten, didn't fare well in any of our three tests. Many tasters described unpleasant perfume and soapy flavors. Others were a little more forthright, with comments such as "bogus" and "nasty." It upped its standing amongst the other brands as a sauce but was still not popular. Contains 24 percent cocoa butter. Available by mail from A Cook's Wares (211 37th Street, Beaver Falls, PA 15010-2103; 800-915-9788).

Building a Better Corkscrew

Corkscrews that work by continuous turning (torque) easily outperform those that combine turning with levering.

By Adam Ried with Dawn Yanagihara

Corkscrews may be small and relatively inexpensive, but they often get far more use than more substantial kitchen tools. A bad corkscrew makes this oft-repeated task of uncorking a bottle a pain, whereas the right one elevates it to a pleasure.

In this investigation we were looking for the corkscrew that would minimize the force required for the job, thus making uncorking an easy, reliable process for an average home user. Because cork loses strength and elasticity with age, we also wanted to see which corkscrews would successfully liberate a dry or fragile cork from an older bottle, doing so gently enough to limit the amount of cork crumbs left floating in the wine.

In consultation with several wine retailers and sommeliers, we gathered common examples of each corkscrew type, then spent several successive Friday afternoons (followed by particularly jolly weekends) opening the bottles in case after case of wine, carefully noting our observations as we went. In one of our cases, the corks were especially dry and brittle, and prone to disintegrating around the corkscrew, which was a great test of a corkscrew's ability to uncork older bottles. Several other cases were of the opposite extreme: a very recent vintage, with fresh, tight-fitting corks.

The Best

Even in a device this small and seemingly simple, we found that engineering makes a big difference. The heart of most corkscrews is the spiraling metal shaft called the worm. Corkscrews with worms fall into two major categories—those that employ some kind of lever to help raise the cork from the bottle, and those that rely on continued turning action (also called torque) after the worm has already gone all the way through the cork.

The two best corkscrews of the bunch, the Screwpull and the Zyliss Self-Puller, have three factors in common. First and most importantly, they are the only two of the group that operate by continually turning after the worm fully penetrates the cork. This is possible because the worms in both corkscrews are four to five inches long, as opposed to the standard length of one-and-one-half to two inches, which is the same length as most of the corks we measured. The extra length gives the cork someplace to go so that as you continue turning the handle, the cork rides up the worm and out of the bottle, with no yanking or pulling. Second, the worms on these corkscrews are non-stick coated, which reduces resistance so they pierce and glide through the cork easily. Last, the worms in both models were encased in frames which slip over the bottle neck, helping to guide the worm straight into the cork.

With the exception of the Screwpull Lever LX, which was fabulous but priced itself out of the running (see "The Ultimate Corkscrew," page 29), the best of the five Screwpull models we tried was the Table Model. It combined a slightly less bulky design than its Screwpull siblings (except for the Pocket model) with a T-type handle that operated especially smoothly and easily. In addition, only a small amount of pressure was required to start the worm in the cork, and it was uniformly effective yet gentle with corks from old and dry to new. No cork crumbs were left floating in any of the bottles uncorked with the Screwpull, and the corks were all in perfect condition. We did note, however, that removing the liberated cork from the Screwpull could be tricky.

By comparison, the Zyliss Self-Puller was slightly harder on the cork, though it left no crumbs behind in the wine. Though the Zyliss does offer a built-in foil cutting blade that worked well, this model has a significant drawback in that it will not open the new wide-rim, flanged bottles because the housing is too small to slip over the wider rim. Zyliss representatives said that design modifications to correct this shortcoming are in the works.

The Rest

None of the other models worked as smoothly and consistently as the Screwpull or Zyliss. The familiar Waiter's Friend corkscrew operates via leverage provided by a hinged arm that swings out to brace against the rim of the bottle. Admittedly, it takes both strength and experience to get the hang of this design, but once you've got it this corkscrew works just

RATING CORKSCREWS

We tested a total of eighteen corkscrews. Of some types, however, there were more than one example, so only the model we liked best appears in the chart. They are listed in order of preference, with manufacturer's name in parenthesis.
Price: Retail price paid in stores or from mail-order catalogs.
Design: The means by which the corkscrew works.
Operation: Level of effort required to uncork a bottle.
Flanged Bottles: Will it open the new flanged, or wide rimmed, bottles?

Type	Price	Design	Operation	Flanged Bottles
Screwpull Table Model (Le Creuset)	$22.99	Continuous Turning	Easy	Yes
Self-Puller (Zyliss)	$20.00	Continuous Turning	Easy	No
Waiter's Friend (Franmara)	$5.99	Leverage	Moderate	Yes
Corkette Cork Extractor (Norpro)	$17.95	Air Pump	Moderate	Yes
Wing Corkscrew (Pedrini)	$4.99	Leverage	Moderate	Yes (but just barely)
Lazy Fish (La Cafetiere)	$39.99	Leverage	Moderate	Yes
Ah-So (Monopol)	$12.50	Prongs	Difficult	Yes
T-Type (No Specific Brand)	$1.99	Brute Force	Very Difficult	Yes

fine. We noted initially that the cork required a stout final tug to wrest it from the bottle, but found also that we could get around that by pulling the cork halfway out, then giving the worm another half-to-full turn. That extra turn gave the arm just enough extra leverage to pull the cork all the way out, sans tug. Several of the dry, brittle corks we tried with the Waiter's Friend cracked, but not badly enough to leave particles in the wine, and the built-in foil cutter worked well.

The two wormless corkscrews we tested did not fare well. The Ah-So, also called the Butler's Friend, has two prongs of uneven length. The user is supposed to insert the longer prong first, wiggle both prongs between the cork and the glass, and use a twisting motion to pull the cork up. For one of our testers, this process invariably pushed the cork into the bottle. Though we did manage to remove many corks with the Ah-So, the procedure seemed unsure at best, requiring finesse developed with experience.

The Corkette Air Pump has a syringe-type needle that pierces the cork and allows the user to pump air into the bottle, pushing the cork up and out with a pop. Though not re-ally difficult to use, this device felt as odd opening the last bottle as it did the first. It required a fair amount of strength to pierce the cork with the needle, followed by an average of sixteen pumps per bottle to remove the corks, much more work than the winning corkscrews. Several additional disadvantages of the Corkette appear right on its packaging, which warns that the device should not be used on bottles of any shape other than cylindrical, or on bottles that are partially empty or "damaged or faulty." So you're out of luck if you want to open the occasional corked bottle of cognac or eau de vie. Also, the built-in foil cutter ripped, rather than cut, the foil.

The other model to which we never fully adjusted was the Lazy Fish. Actually styled to resemble a fish and much heavier than the others, the Lazy Fish felt bulky and poorly balanced while screwing the worm into the cork. As a result, the worm had a tendency to tip and enter the cork crooked, causing it to crack on the way out of the bottle. Extracting the cork was easier, though, by virtue of the Fish's elaborate extension mechanism. Pulling on the tail made the whole body of the fish extend like an accordion, pulling the cork up and eas-ily out of the bottle, with nary a crumb left in the wine. While some may consider the Fish's design elegant, we did not.

Neither the Wing nor the real dog of the group, the T-Type, offered a foil cutter, and both ravaged the drier corks, leaving a slew of crumbs floating in the wine.

WORM STYLES

Many experts touted the advantages of worms with an open, hollow helix (left) over auger-like helixes with solid center shafts and sharp edges (right). In side-by-side tests, the solid-core worm did gouge the cork more than the hollow type. However, the hollow type was not without its own difficulties. Some testers found the angled point difficult to center, driving it down the side rather than the middle of the cork.

TESTERS' COMMENTS

THE ULTIMATE CORKSCREW

The portable **Le Creuset Screwpull Lever LX** dazzled us with its smoothness and ease of use—simply clamp the handles around the neck of the bottle and move the top lever down and back up. The downward stroke drives a nonstick coated worm into the cork, and the upward stroke pulls it up and out, all in less than two seconds. Every time we used it, the cork emerged in perfect condition; sometimes it was difficult to see that it had even been punctured. Of course, such flawless performance doesn't come cheap. We saw retail prices for the Lever LX between $100 (on sale) and $150. See Sources and Resources, page 32, for availability information.

THE BEST CORKSCREW

Screwpull Table Model
A breeze to use, though it can be difficult to remove the cork once it is out of the bottle.

Self-Puller
Easy to use on most bottles, but won't fit over the rim of flanged bottles. Built-in foil cutter.

Waiter's Friend
A classic that takes some finesse to use smoothly, but with experience it works well. Has a built-in foil cutter and is eminently compact and portable.

Corkette Cork Extractor
It works, but it feels odd even after opening many bottles, and the manufacturer's list of ominous caveats is off-putting. Built-in foil cutter shreds the foil.

Wing Corkscrew
Will not remove the cork fully by the end of the lever's travel, leaving you to give it a swift yank. Cheap and portable, though.

Lazy Fish
Bulky to store, unwieldy to use, and silly looking, but it sure will start a conversation. No foil cutter and a solid-core worm that was less than gentle.

Ah-So
Very mixed results: some testers found it workable, and others found it impossible. Definitely requires a knack developed with experience.

T-Type
A bear to use for every tester. No small degree of strength required.

American Dessert Wines Arrive

*Too-hot weather producing too-ripe fruit is often a problem in California,
but it works to the region's advantage when it comes to producing sweet wines.*

By Mark Bittman

Intensely sweet dessert wines comprise less than one percent of the total wine market. But making dessert wine is so challenging that a great one bestows prestige on its makers. So many wineries seem to figure, "let's give it a shot." And some, in California at least, actually succeed.

Although there are several kinds of sweet wines, many of the best-known—such as Port, Madeira, and sweet Sherry—are fortified wines, in which fermentation is stopped by the addition of spirits when plenty of sugar remains in the juice. Here, however, we consider unfortified sweet wines, the paragon of which is Chateau d'Yquem, which comes from Sauternes in Bordeaux and is consistently rated the best sweet wine in the world.

Germany also produces great sweet white wines, and until recently only those two—plus a sprinkling of others from Italy and France, and the Tokaji wines of Hungary—were considered in discussions of great sweet whites. But in recent years, California, especially Napa Valley, has shown that its blazing sun is just the thing for bringing out all the sugar a grape is capable of producing. This is not always an advantage: Extreme sugar levels translate to high-alcohol wines—yeasts convert sugar to alcohol—and high-alcohol wines are difficult to balance.

There are three ways to make wine sweet without fortifying it or adding sugar. The first, and most common, is to start with such sugar-laden fruit that some sugar remains when the alcohol kills the yeast and effectively stops fermentation. Usually, such grapes must be hand-picked at just the right moment, always late in the harvest. The timing and method of picking explains the high price of most sweet wines and the "late-harvest" designation on many labels. The second is to stop the fermentation by the addition of sulphur dioxide, a method less popular in America (where the first method is often possible) than in Germany (where ultra-high levels of sugar are rare). Finally, the fermentation may be stopped by using what amounts to rotten grapes—but very special rotten grapes.

At certain vineyards in Sauternes and elsewhere—including California—ripe, healthy grapes are sometimes attacked by botrytis, or noble rot (these days, botrytis can also be injected into grape vines). The effect is to dry out the grapes, leaving the sugar levels intact. At this point, grapes must be hand-picked in an even more labor-intensive process than usual (resulting in even higher prices than usual), and the quantities are minuscule—it's usually estimated that d'Yquem realizes about a glass of wine per grapevine. Not only does the botrytis lend the wine an unusual and desirable aroma and flavor (of tropical fruit, if you ask me), it gives off an antibiotic that stops fermentation at just the right moment, when the wine has reached about fourteen percent alcohol and twelve percent sugar—a perfect balance.

There are not a lot of intensely sweet, non-fortified wines produced on the West Coast (we pretty much covered the bases), but our tasters found most of them enjoyable. A couple of recommendations emerged from our tasting, however. One, most of these wines are as intensely priced as they are sweet; see if you can find the Beringer, our Best Buy, or be prepared to shell out as much as you would for a bottle of vintage Champagne. (That said, the wines are favorably price compared to similar Sauternes.) Two, even a half-bottle of dessert wine goes a long way, because this is really wine for sipping—alone, or with a piece of ripe blue-veined cheese and a pear, or a sweet dessert.

Finally, you'll note that the entries from the Northwest did not do as well as those from California. As I said at the beginning, making a credible sweet wine is a prestigious achievement, so it's understandable why many wineries try it; but not all can pull it off.

RATING THE WINES

The wines in our tasting, held at Mt. Carmel Wine and Spirits, in Hamden, Connecticut, were judged by a panel made up of both wine professionals and amateur wine lovers.

Within each category, wines are listed in order of the number of points scored.

Note that most prices are per half-bottle.

HIGHLY RECOMMENDED

Silverado Late Harvest Limited Reserve, $45. No vintage, no grapes listed, and "no way to know it's from California." This wine has more botrytis than most, and would be considered great even if it were from Sauternes—a real winner.

1994 Phelps Late Harvest Semillon, Napa Valley, $36 per half bottle. "Nicely botrycized," but also tastes very much like fruit. "Clean, not at all cloying." Not quite the power of the Silverado, but "very, very nice."

1993 Beringer Special Select Late Harvest, Johannesburg Riesling, $12 per half bottle. Easily our Best Buy: Deep golden, "high quality" wine "with little acidity but so sweet that you won't care." "Imperfect, but as intense a dessert wine as you could ask for."

RECOMMENDED

1992 Steele Select Late Harvest Chardonnay, $27 per half bottle. "Sauternes-like" wine with plenty of botrytis. Finish was "slightly hot," but wine was generally enjoyed.

1993 Dolce Late Harvest Table Wine, $54 per half bottle. First off, note the price, which is more than a little over the top. Other than that, "really rich;" "you finish it and you want more."

1994 Phelps Late Harvest Johannesburg Riesling, $20 per half bottle. A good buy. "Great balance," "absolutely delicious." "Some vegetal flavors" were detected, but the wine was considered "admirable."

1995 Phelps Eisrébe, $39 per half bottle. An ice wine made from the scheurbbe grape, a hybrid of Johannesburg riesling and sylvaner. "Very complex," with "loads of fruit," yet "quite light on its feet." Aromas of pineapple are "enchanting."

RECOMMENDED WITH RESERVATIONS

Callaway "Sweet Nancy" Late Harvest Chenin Blanc, $23 per half bottle. "Great texture," but "cloyingly sweet."

1995 Chateau Ste. Michelle Late Harvest White Riesling, Columbia Valley (Washington), $17 per half bottle. "Lovely, botrytis-laced nose," "good texture," and "very refreshing," but almost everyone found "off-flavors" or "something icky" in the finish.

1995 Columbia Crest White Riesling Ice Wine, Columbia Valley (Washington), $26 per half bottle. "Rosemary-scented(!), a good combination of sweetness and acidity," "although neither is intense."

NOT RECOMMENDED

1995 Chateau Ste. Michelle White Riesling Ice Wine, Columbia Valley (Washington), $30 per half bottle.

1995 Columbia Crest Late Harvest Semillon, Columbia Valley (Washington), $22 per half bottle.

Book Reviews *Cookbooks with Passion*

A great cookbook, like any work of art, is not just about recipes. It is also about seeing the world afresh, the author taking us on a journey where we meet unlikely friends who become part of our life, part of how we cook. These books are rare because the author must speak from a vast amount of personal experience, and from a deep affection for and knowledge of the foods and cooks that are the stuff and fodder of the work in question.

Even the most promising cookbook author can fall by the wayside, presenting an historical work with no currency in modern times, a collection of recipes so personal that it cannot speak beyond one kitchen, or (the worst offense of all) recipes simply packaged for marketing, without passion and commitment.

The worth of *In Nonna's Kitchen* was obvious from the very beginning. Cookbook

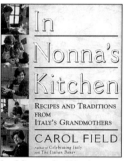

In Nonna's Kitchen
Carol Field
HarperCollins, $30

introductions are usually drowsy bits of prose, but this one made me sit up and read every word. I learned that pot roast is called *arrosto morto* or "dead roast" because the nonnas (the grandmothers) were accustomed to roasting meat on a rotating spit and, by contrast, meat cooked on the stove was immobilized in a pan and therefore lifeless. I also found out that in the old days nursing mothers stayed in bed for eight days consuming only pigeon broth, and that the frugal nonnas believe that when someone dies they are sent to Purgatory, where every crumb of bread he or she has wasted during a lifetime is counted. The penitent then has to pick up an equivalent number, using only their eyelashes as tools.

Of course, an introduction does not make a book, much less a cookbook, but it is indicative of both the affection that Ms. Field has for her cooks and her total immersion in the topic. She takes us on a journey beneath the over-marketed, high-gloss image of Italian cooking, bringing us into the simple, well-scrubbed working class kitchens of her nonnas, showing us around with a reporter's eye. She is not afraid to display the poverty, the occasional poor ingredients, and the make-do necessities of country cooking.

All of this, of course, is merely context for what any good cookbook must give us—the gift of well-constructed recipes that not only bring the voices and customs from one people to another, but that translate admirably in a modern kitchen. On this score, *In Nonna's Kitchen* succeeds as well. Of the

nine recipes we tested, seven were not only great tasting but also straightforward. The Lemon Flavored Ricotta Cake was easy, light, creamy with a nice overtone of lemon; Grilled White Fish with Garlic and Parsley was outstanding and quintessentially Italian (simple and flavorful); Cake Covered with Cherries was consumed in a matter of minutes. A couple of recipes were more complicated. Filled Artichoke Pie lacked useful artichoke preparation instructions and was labor-intensive, but well worth the effort for a party. Stuffed Cabbage Leaves, like most recipes of this genre, took lots of preparation, but it was by far the best version I have ever tasted, the filling made with a creamy blend of bread, milk, meat, parsley, and garlic.

After spending much time with the nonnas of Carol Field's acquaintance, I felt as I had come to know them and agree with the comment of one Italian immigrant at the end of the introduction: "The stones in the street will cry when we are gone."

Unlike the broad scope of *In Nonna's Kitchen*, which featured cooks from all over Italy, the vantage point of Marcella Hazan's new book is limited to both Hazan and Venice.

As the author notes in the introduction, an Italian would translate the title as Marcella Cooks, which is an excellent description of not only the content but the tone and point of view. This narrower, more personal approach has both advantages and drawbacks. On the

Marcella Cucina
Marcella Hazan
HarperCollins, $35

one hand, thoughtful, experienced writers can take us into their world, sit us down at their kitchen table, and speak to us casually as they prepare lunch. This approach falls short if the cook is only a tolerable conversationalist or if the cooking is so personal that it is difficult to translate to our kitchens when we get home.

After the extraordinary introduction in Carol Field's work, Hazan's seems rather perfunctory, a discussion of taste, flavors, and cooking that feels like a lecture. However, she does come to life when taking the reader on a tour of the local food markets, discussing the "castration" (castraure) of the tiny bud at the top of an artichoke plant, the blushing crimson flesh of small sharks, and tubs of sinuous eel "ceaselessly doing their snake dance." She also addresses more basic ingredients available to Americans, such as olive oil, Parmigiano-Reggiano, salt, and tomatoes, rising to the

occasion with specific buying instructions that are both useful and informed.

We made a total of thirteen recipes from *Marcella Cucina* and found them to be a mixed bag. That does not mean that this is a lackluster group of recipes, however. Marcella is particularly good at exporting the full, well-balanced flavors of Italy whether in a simple potato salad with anchovies and Greek olives, or a pasta sauce of sage and rosemary, or chicken with bay leaves, or a yogurt and sambuca cake. This is her great strength—teaching American cooks the virtues of balance and restraint and how to use the strong, country flavors of Italian cooking to full advantage without muddying them through carelessness or a gourmand's wonton disregard for subtlety.

I sense, though, that Hazan is impatient with American cooks, unwilling to stand beside them in the kitchen in an effort to understand their customs and deficiencies. As a result, a surprising number of recipes I tried lacked accurate or detailed directions. The most common problem was a lack of accurate cooking times. A recipe for poached tuna, for example, resulted in overcooked fish when the directions and timing were followed precisely. Some visual guidance about when the fish is properly cooked would have been helpful. A dish of sautéed tuna left this home cook wondering how to sauté twenty-five tuna cubes on all sides in a twelve-inch skillet without overcooking them. In addition, they were not seasoned before cooking and were therefore bland. Two pasta sauces turned out too dry: we had to add one-third cup of white wine to one, and the other was fine when cooked less than the suggested twenty minutes. I made three different fricassees of chicken, one excellent, one good, and one rather disappointing—although I suspect if I had made these recipes with ingredients purchased in Venice, they all would have been top-notch. A fritatta had no cooking times for the onions and eggs, and the time listed for the potatoes was off.

Hazan's passion for her hometown, for her food, and for her cooking needs no defending. But passion for one's own cooking and for one's own life is best paired with a passion for how others live, for those who might pick up and read your book. The nonnas of Carol Field's acquaintance always cooked for others, preparing riso in bianco for the sick, or standing by your elbow, encouraging you to eat more of the gnocchi. Their food was a gift, their way of bringing people together around a long wooden table. In *Marcella Cucina*, however, the kitchen feels quieter, the author cooking more for herself than for others. This leaves the reader with just the recipes, not the passion—a banquet of honest Italian fare spread out on a table set for one.

—Christopher Kimball

Sources and Resources

Most of the ingredients and materials necessary for the recipes in this issue are available at your local supermarket, gourmet store, or kitchen supply shop. The following are mail-order sources for particular items. Prices listed below were current at press time and do not include shipping or handling unless otherwise indicated. We suggest that you contact companies directly to confirm up-to-date prices and availability.

Corkscrews

Among the more affordable corkscrews that we tested, the handy Screwpull Table Model by Le Creuset was rated the highest. The Table Model was easy to operate, and its non-stick coated worm consistently glided through even the driest corks. The Screwpull Table Model is available by mail for $22.99 the Chef's Catalog (3215 Comercial Avenue, Northbrook, IL 60062-1900; 800-338-3232). The Table Model is sold in black and includes a foil cutter and storage case. Another Le Creuset corkscrew, the Screwpull Lever LX, performed head and shoulders above all of the tested corkscrews in efficiency and smoothness. With two easy motions—down and up—the cork is removed. The Lever LX, however, also outshined the other corkscrews in cost at $139. The Lever LX can be purchased through Williams-Sonoma catalog (Mail Order Department, P.O. Box 7456, San Francisco, CA 94120-7456; 800-541-2233).

Stuffing Bag

Scooping pre-heated stuffing into a turkey with a measuring cup can be sloppy and time-consuming. A clever alternative is to pre-heat the stuffing in a canvas Turkey Stuffing Bag. Place cold stuffing into the bag, pull the draw strings, and heat in microwave. The hot stuffing bag is inserted directly into the bird, the legs tied loosely, and roasting begins. Simply pull out the bag when cooking is completed and empty the stuffing into a serving dish. The Turkey Stuffing Bag from Clipper Mills is about 14 inches long and 8 inches wide, so it easily holds the four to five cups of stuffing we recommend in our recipe. It costs $2.50 and can be ordered by mail through Kitchen Etc. catalog services (Department TM, 32 Industrial Drive, Exeter, NH, 03833; 800-232-4070).

Poultry Lacers

Without the stuffing bag (see above), keeping the stuffing from falling out of the turkey can be a problem. We tested three products (the Turkey Clip Set, Turkey Taks, and Poultry Lacers) specifically designed to secure stuffing inside birds during roasting. The lacers—a set of six 5-inch metal skewers that have a sharp tip on one end and loop on the other—proved the best. Four or five skewers are used, depending on the size of the bird. Each skewer is alternately passed through the skin on one side of the opening, across the opening, and through the skin on the other side. Butchers' twine is criss-crossed around the ends of the skewers, as if lacing up a boot. Pulling the twine tightens the sides and closes the cavity. This method is great for containing the stuffing and the skewers are a breeze to use. These reusable skewers, manufactured by Hoan's, cost just $1.25. To order by mail, contact Kitchen Etc. catalog services (Department TM, 32 Industrial Drive, Exeter, NH 03833; 800-232-4070).

Turkey Lifters

Of all the turkey gadgets we tested, the best were the "Roast/Turkey Lifters."

Built like small pitchforks, the tines of these handy tools pierce into the sides of the bird and make rotating and lifting the bird simpler and safer than gripping with wads of paper towel. The lifters have six-inch long wooden handles and four stainless-steel tines, each of which are about four inches long. You can order Norpro's turkey lifters by mail for $3.95 from Kitchen Arts (161 Newbury St., Boston, MA 02116; 617-266-8701).

Wine Tasting Wheels

Wine drinkers interested in learning to better identify the aromas and flavors of wine might enjoy using wine tasting wheels by Beringer Vineyards. The set includes two colorful cardboard wheels—one for white wines and one for red wines—each of which lists forty terms often used to describe the aromas, tastes, flavors, and mouthfeel of wine. The wheels are modeled after the original wine aroma wheel created for experts by Professor Ann C. Noble of the University of California at Davis. Beringer's wheels are intended for nonprofessional and even beginning wine drinkers. To order, send $3.00 (cash or check) to Beringer Vineyards' Fulfillment Center (615 Airpark Road, Napa, CA 94558). One dollar of your payment will be donated to the sensory research department at U.C. Davis.

Mini Ice Cream Scoop

To make uniformly sized chocolate truffles (see page 24) we found that we liked using a mini ice cream scoop rather than a pastry bag; cleanup was easier and there was less waste. This one-ounce scoop, known as a "half-sphere" or "trigger" scoop, has a metal strip at the bottom of the spoon's bowl. When the handle is squeezed, the strip slides from one side to the other, easily releasing the chocolate. This stainless steel mini ice cream scoop can also double as a melon baller. It costs $9.99 and can be ordered by mail from the Chef's Catalog (3215 Commercial Avenue, Northbrook, IL 60062-1900; 800-338-3232).

Gingerbread House Candies

For our gingerbread house we created the authentic look of a fieldstone chimney with Koppers filled pebble candies. The candies have the look and shape of granite and limestone rocks but are the size of medium-to-large gumballs. Under the marbled candy shell is a layer of milk chocolate, and inside that is one of several assorted sweet fillings. For our gingerbread house we used two half-pound bags to cover the chimney. A half-pound bag costs $2.99 and can be ordered from Dairy Fresh Candies (57 Salem St., Boston, MA 02113; 800-336-5536).

Flavor Injector

To boost flavor and juices, our pork roast recipe on page 13 calls for salt-curing the roast for three to five days before serving it, or, if you haven't planned that far in advance, injecting the roast with salted water and oil. To follow the latter method you need a flavor injector. This looks like a syringe from a toy doctor kit. Its dull tip can puncture a roast but is unlikely to break through human skin (if child safety is a concern). The Zap Flavor Injector can hold two tablespoons of liquid and costs $5.95. Order by mail from Kitchen Arts (161 Newbury St., Boston, MA 02116; 617-266-8701).

Universal Pan Cover

Occasionally we need a skillet lid to sweat foods or to keep foods warm after being cooked. But most skillets are not sold with lids. A flexible solution to this problem is the Universal Pan Cover, a lid that can fit three different sized pans. This stainless steel pan cover has grooved rings at eight inches, ten inches, and twelve inches in diameter to fit a variety of standard sized pans. It is dishwasher safe with a heat-resistant knob handle and two small retractable vents. The Universal Pan Cover costs $12.99 and can be ordered by mail from Chef's Catalog (3215 Commercial Avenue, Northbrook, IL 60062-1900; 800-338-3232).

Potato Latkes
page 6

RECIPE INDEX

Stuffed Roast Turkey
page 8

Classic Apple Pie
page 20

Pasta with Fresh Clam Sauce
page 14

Eggnog *page 23*
and Assorted Truffles *page 24*

Cured Roast Rack of Pork *page 12*
and Easy Roasted Onions *page 18*

PHOTOGRAPHS BY CARL TREMBLAY/ STYLING BY EVA KATZ

Gingerbread House Landscaping

Spread very thin layer decorating icing, like glaze on a cake, over entire board around house. Dab bottoms of taffy bull's-eyes, halved horizontally, with construction glue and position on board leading from edge to front door to resemble front walkway. Sprinkle about two cups shredded coconut over surface of board and around walkway to resemble snow. Pipe half-inch dabs of construction icing in front of windows and around house as desired; position two or three one-inch rosemary sprigs in each dab to resemble bushes. Scatter small filled pebble candies or jelly beans (as used on chimney) around house and bushes to resemble stones. Stack sixteen halved cinnamon sticks in pile on chimney side of house to resemble log pile. Dust bushes, stones, and wood pile with confectioner's sugar to resemble frost, if desired.